PELICAN BOOKS
THE COMMITTEE

Walter Goodman was born in New York City and
received his B.A. degree in Economics from Syracuse
University and his M.A. in Philosophy from Reading
University in England. His reviews and articles have
appeared in numerous periodicals, including *The New
York Times Magazine, Life, The New Republic,
Commentary, Redbook,* and *The American Scholar.*
He is the author of two earlier books about
contemporary American life: *The Clowns of
Commerce,* a report on the world of advertising,
and *All Honorable Men,* a study of ethics in big
business, politics, and the mass media.

Mr. Goodman lives with his wife and two sons in
Greenburgh, New York.

The Committee

*The extraordinary career
of the House Committee on
Un-American Activities*

by Walter Goodman

FOREWORD BY RICHARD H. ROVERE

PENGUIN BOOKS, INC.
Baltimore, Maryland

Penguin Books, Inc.

7110 Ambassador Road, Baltimore, Maryland 21207

This edition first published 1969 by arrangement with Farrar, Straus and Giroux

Printed by Kingsport Press, Inc., Kingsport, Tennessee

For my sons, Hal and Bennet

Foreword

Walter Goodman's accomplishment is a large and salutary one—very much *pro bono publico*, very much what the age demands, or at least requires. It is the work of a man who knows and loves this country and has a deep understanding of its political processes, the noble ones as well as those that are ugly and despicable. The prose is elegant, often eloquent; the mood, as befits the matter, ironic and at times comic.

My tribute, I feel, should be taken not merely at face value but at somewhat more than face value, for I must explain that I approached this book with about as much resistance as sympathy. To read it was, of course, a professional responsibility, even an act of civic virtue. But virtue, as all the virtuous know, cannot buy happiness. I could not approach a volume of formidable bulk on this particular subject without a certain amount of self-pity. It so happens that the House Committee on Un-American Activities and I are, in professional terms, exactly of an age. We both set up shop just thirty years ago. The Committee has had its ups and downs, as have I. By and large, though, my legitimate grievances have been few in number and of no great magnitude. But a recurring chore that I have found odious in the extreme has been keeping abreast of the doings of this preposterous and often vicious product of American democracy. I would hate to see an accounting of the number of hours I have spent, or misspent, attending its open hearings, reading its zany reports, and writing about the people who have served on it or been victimized by it. The rewards of diligence have been meager, for, with few exceptions, the investigators and the investigated have seemed richly to deserve each other—though, of course, poetic justice is never to be equated with that of the blindfolded goddess with the true scales. In any case, I have always found the Committee a disagreeable subject to write about, and I could not help feeling somewhat put upon as I faced the prospect of reading a long book about it. Others, I thought, might benefit from a study of what the Committee had been up to for thirty long years, and it might be a good thing for me to commend such an exercise to them and explain wherein the profit might lie. But for me a recitation of this history could only be coals to Newcastle all the way—a journey of whose squalor I already knew too much.

Mr. Goodman did not allow me to feel dutiful or self-pitying for more than a few moments. I was almost immediately swept up by the freshness of his narrative, impressed by the display of intellectual toughness, delighted by his instinct for the sardonic. More than that, I learned, almost at the outset, a lesson I hope not to forget about the frailty of memory and the need for humility. I had thought that Mr. Goodman could not tell me anything about the Committee that I did not already know. This was arrogance of a sort, and I have, I hope, been purged of it. Mr. Goodman has told me a great deal I either never knew or had forgotten. (The distinction is trivial; if a fact has fled my mind, I am as ignorant as if I had never known it.) At all odds, the pathetic role of the anti-Nazi Samuel Dickstein in fathering the Committee was news to me—and a valuable addition to my collection of boomerang effects in politics. I was also, until I read this book, unaware of the extent to which the Committee, in its early days, was as racist as it was anti-Communist and anti-New Deal. In all probability, I was aware of this a quarter of a century ago—I put in more time covering the Committee in its earlier years than in its middle and later ones —but it was an aspect of its being that, in retrospect, was not part of my knowledge. I think I understand why. In the years since 1948, the cold war has dominated the thinking of everyone—liberal journalists and heresy-hunters not excluded. (Some liberal journalists, alas, became heresy-hunters.) Also, in this period, we have seen the death of anti-Semitism as an important motivating force in American politics. In the early years of the Committee's existence, overt anti-Semitism among Con-

gressmen was no more disreputable than overt anti-Negro sentiment is in certain Southern legislatures today. There are no
doubt anti-Semites in Congress at present, but any open expression of the bias today would be so widely regarded as "un-
American" as to make it politically dangerous. The day of anti-
Semitism's respectability is far enough in the past that some of
us have difficulty in recalling it. I like to think that this kind
of history will repeat itself—that bigotry in every form will become politically disreputable.

The Committee is far more than a history of the Committee.
It is a work that contributes greatly to our understanding of the
American Left in the mid-twentieth century and also, to a
slightly lesser extent, of the American Right. Mr. Goodman
deals sharply with both these movements—or, better perhaps,
tendencies, since neither was ever any more than a cluster
of factions—and I suspect that some of his younger readers
will be impatient with him for the even-handedness of his contempt for the Stalinist Left and the yahoo Right. The fashion
now, in many intellectual circles, is to be intolerant of those
who are not indiscriminately tolerant of radical "dissent." This
modishness has no appeal for Mr. Goodman. Though plainly
more Left than Right in his own sympathies, he does not accept
the view that the Communists whom the Committee harassed—
along, of course, with many non-Communists—were undeserv-
ing of any form of investigation or political censure. The excesses of the cold war, particularly in the years of McCarthyism
rampant, and the increasing impotence of orthodox Communists have led many to think that no one ever had a legitimate
cause for apprehension over the political power of the Communist Party of the United States. Mr. Goodman thinks otherwise and so, emphatically, do I. It is, to be sure, easy to
exaggerate the influence of Communists in America—J. Edgar
Hoover has been doing this for going on half a century—but
underestimation is equally easy and equally fatuous. If one
wishes to understand the weakness and fragmentation of the
Left in the 1960's, one must know something of the strength
and character of the Left in the 1930's. There was, as I see it,
then a chance for an indigenous radical movement of sufficient

force and integrity to have endured into the present and to
have played a part in strengthening American democracy. It is
often said that the New Deal stole all the thunder of the Left
and institutionalized it inside the Democratic Party. This is
partly true—the New Deal gave some scope to radical theorists
and even to radical activists. But the New Deal cannot be
blamed for the political disarray and intellectual shoddiness of
the American Left today. Nor can the Communists be held
altogether responsible. But a great deal of damage was done by
Communist bureaucrats who feigned a concern for the future
of American society when what in fact concerned them above
all other things was the national interest and foreign policy of
the U.S.S.R. Discovering what the Communist Party had really
been up to was, for many American radicals, far more traumatic
and destructive than the later discovery of some that they had
served the interests of the Central Intelligence Agency. Though
individual Communists may have been men of a rather simple-
minded integrity, the Party was a totalitarian wrecker. Mr.
Goodman has a solid appreciation of this basic truth, and this
lends added force to his indictment of the Committee. He is
no less anti-Communist than Martin Dies or any of Dies's successors. To some, such a statement may seem not faint praise
but downright condemnation. I will stand by it. What distin-
guishes Mr. Goodman from most of those he writes about on
both sides of the hearing-room table is his own liberal and
humanistic intelligence, his commitment to democratic values
—a commitment shared neither by the Committee nor by most
of its victims.

The Committee goes on—it may survive the century, if America survives the century, and outlast most of us now alive. It
has never been quite the same since Joe McCarthy muscled in
on the territory eighteen years ago, but it nevertheless survived
McCarthy and the specific virus we called McCarthyism. It is
something of an anachronism, rather like the heraldry units
that are rumored still to be found in Robert McNamara's Pentagon. Yet there are authentic historical reasons for its survival.
Once more running counter to the conventional wisdom of today's liberalism, Mr. Goodman writes that "there is nothing

un-American about the Un-American Activities Committee."
In liberal and intellectual circles, it has long been the custom
to mock the very notion that such ungainly words as "Americanism" and "un-Americanism" could have any real meaning
or content. Behind the mocking, there was a romantic idealism
—a picture of this country as so diverse, so committed to
Thomas Jefferson's dream of the open marketplace of ideas that
no specific dogma and no specific heresy could be labeled
"American" or "un-American." But this, as Mr. Goodman says,
is nonsense. Ours "is not the land exclusively of Lincoln and
Jefferson." Martin Dies, Joe Pool, Joe McCarthy, Barry Goldwater, George Wallace are every bit as American as Jefferson,
and it is for their America that the Committee has spoken and
will continue to speak. It is not an attractive thought, but it is
an inescapable conclusion and one we shall have to live with
and adjust to. Those of us who want Jefferson's America to
survive and perhaps in time prevail will find guidance and a
fortifying good humor in this admirable book.

Richard H. Rovere

NEW YORK CITY
NOVEMBER, 1967

Preface

IF the House Committee on Un-American Activities had not been invented, there would be no good reason for it to exist. But exist it does, and this chronicle is designed neither as polemic nor, emphatically, as apologetics. That is not to suggest that I am lacking in opinions about the Committee and all that it has represented for three decades; the reader will have to go no great distance before he can clear me of that crime at least. But while I would be dismayed at a charge of indifference, it was never my principal intention to produce a document for service in the fitful campaign for abolition. Such documents have been produced, on both sides of the case, and whatever their individual merits, all are hobbled by constraints endemic to the form.

Still, a reader approaching a book on so controversial a subject is entitled to know something of the author's stance. As a liberal—I confess it, though I fear to think what the word may convey to any given reader—I find myself fraternally troubled by the dilemma which the Committee has from the first constituted for liberals in this country. The Communists, despising us, have exploited our good names for their own interests. The hunters of Communists, despising us, have offended our dearest beliefs and attacked our cherished causes. We can, it seems to me, do nothing but bear up—continue to oppose the Committee, continue to champion the political freedoms of persons who, we know, mock us for soft-headedness, and make clear that we are doing so not out of misplaced affection for totalitarians of the left but out of reverence for liberty.

How liberals have reacted to the Committee's recurrent challenges is one theme of this book, but not *the* theme. That is not so readily summarized. I began my research in the belief that the Committee's activities have a good deal to tell us about the nation that has endured them for thirty years, the system that has sustained them, and the times to which they have lent inimitable color. I complete the writing with the hope that some of this may be found in these pages.

W. G.

GREENBURGH, NEW YORK
NOVEMBER, 1967

Contents

Illustrations

All photographs from Wide World Photos

FOLLOWING PAGE 204

FOLLOWING PAGE 428

THE United States, to my eye, is incomparably the greatest show on earth. It is a show which avoids diligently all the kinds of clowning which tire me most quickly—for example, royal ceremonials, the tedious hocus-pocus of haute politique, the taking of politics seriously—and lays chief stress upon the kinds which delight me unceasingly—for example, the ribald combats of demagogues, the exquisitely ingenious operations of master rogues, the pursuit of witches and heretics, the desperate struggles of inferior men to claw their way into Heaven.

H. L. MENCKEN

The Committee

1

★ ★ ★ ★ ★

Dickstein's Monster

IN THE RANKS of those public men, from Pyrrhus forward, who have striven and striven and at last succeeded, only to have their triumph turn shortly to gall, a place must be set aside for Samuel Dickstein. He served in the House of Representatives for twenty-two years, from 1923 to 1944, and during that whole time no cause took more of his energies or his passions than the creation of a committee to investigate subversive activities. Assigning political paternity is a speculative game, but if any man deserves the title of Father of the Committee, it is Representative Dickstein. He earned the distinction by relentless trying from 1933 to 1938 and had the rest of his life to regret it.

There was nothing unnatural in Sam Dickstein's growing passionate over what he, with many others, viewed as seditious behavior in the nineteen-thirties. Germany was on the march in Europe, and at home Nazi sympathizers were openly rallying, goose-stepping, and reviling Jews. Congressman Dickstein's New York City district, running along the East River from Chatham Square to East Houston Street, was the home of immigrants from Eastern Europe. Like his own parents, who had carried him to America at the age of three, these thousands and tens of thousands had run away from the pogroms of the Old World only to find that the New World was not able to repeal their history. In their East Side ghetto, their beards were pulled, their wives insulted, their sons beaten. That much was

[3]

acceptable, but now in Germany torment of the Jew had become not just an entertainment but an expression of political faith, and all that the East Side immigrants had ever learned told them that their adopted home was not immune to the madness.

Sam Dickstein, who started his career as a special deputy attorney general in New York State and would end it, in the tradition of loyal city-machine Democrats, as a state Supreme Court justice, sought to strike at the danger not with the legislative arm of the Congress but with its investigative arm. It was difficult in a free country to pass laws against individuals joining together in Teutonic fellowship to drink beer and rail at Jews, but nothing in the Constitution prohibited investigating them. In demanding an investigation of the German-American Bund, the New Yorker was merely availing himself of a weapon which the national legislature had used, with notable effect, since its beginnings. The exigencies of ordinary politics often led legislators to peep into odd corners of the executive establishment and elsewhere, and there was no requirement that they produce a law to justify the time and money they spent; the public enlightenment that presumably attended their revelations together with the *possibility* that a law might actually emerge at some future time or other was justification enough. Unrestricted, for practical purposes, as to the subject matter of their inquiries or the manner in which these were conducted, uncommitted to tangible results, each committee chairman might allow his inclinations generous sway.

Congressional investigations were particularly in vogue after World War I, as indeed they always are after a war, when our political parties shake off an enforced unity and return to their natural life of mutual recrimination. In the nineteen-twenties and thirties, there were investigations into the conduct of the war, into the Teapot Dome scandal, into banks, lobbies, railroads, the munitions industry, strike breakers, the stock exchange. The nation's moneyed interests were the defendants in nearly all these inquests, and so the hearings were attacked by conservatives as Star Chamber proceedings and defended by liberals as legitimate expressions of the people's right to know. In the same year that Andrew W. Mellon protested to President Coolidge that "government by investigation is not government," Felix Frankfurter told the readers of *The New Republic*: "The procedure of Congressional investigations should remain as it is. No limitations should be imposed by Congressional legislation or standing rules. The power of investigation should be left untrammeled." Professor Frankfurter did, however, add the caution that it depends on the Congress itself, on the press, and on the good sense of the people to keep this large power from degenerating into partisan advantage. Nearly thirty years later, when Senator McCarthy was abroad in the land, Mr. Justice Frankfurter would raise his voice in concern over the use of the power he had once championed.

As for subversive doctrines and activities, they had occupied the attention of Congressional investigators, off and on, since the Armistice. In February 1919, the Senate, unnerved by the Bolshevik ascendance in Russia, took the occasion of two pro-Soviet rallies in Washington as the starting point for an investigation of "any efforts being made to propagate in this country the principles of any party exercising or claiming to exercise authority in Russia . . . [and] any effort to incite the overthrow of the Government of this country, or all governments, by force or by the destruction of life or property or the general cessation of industry." Hearings were held by a committee originally set up to look into "the brewing industry and German propaganda" and a report was issued. In March 1919 the New York legislature established a joint committee, under Senator Clayton R. Lusk, to investigate seditious activities. The Lusk Committee would be a beacon to Communist-hounders still unweaned, but it was not yet the time of the investigator in the land. Even the great Red Scare of 1919–1920, complete with strikes, bombings, Attorney General Palmer's raids on radicals, and the expulsion from these shores of 246 men and three women aboard the S.S. *Buford*, popularly known as the Soviet Ark, passed smoothly into the euphoria of the Harding-Coolidge decade.

It was not until after the stock-market crash that the House

of Representatives decided that the domestic menace of Bolshevism was worthy of formal study by a proper committee of
the House. Their decision followed hard upon a revelation in
May 1930 by Grover Whalen, lately of Wanamaker's Department Store and at that moment New York City's police commissioner,[1] that he had seven documents which connected the
Soviet Amtorg Trading Corporation with the dissemination
of Communist propaganda in this country. Commissioner
Whalen's charges would never be proved; indeed, as Fiorello
La Guardia demonstrated in one of his last acts as a U. S. Congressman, the documents were forgeries—the commissioner
had been put upon. But this was not yet certain when the Committee on Rules acted. It reported a resolution that it had
killed two months earlier which provided for an investigation
not only of Communist propaganda, the Communist Party and
all affiliated organizations, the Communist International, the
Amtorg Trading Corporation and the *Daily Worker*—but of
"all entities, groups or individuals who are alleged to advise,
teach or advocate the overthrow by force or violence of the
Government of the United States, or attempt to undermine our
republican form of government by inciting riots, sabotage or
revolutionary disorders."[2] Hamilton Fish of New York, original
sponsor of the ambitious proposal, explained to his colleagues:
"It is not the purpose of this resolution to interfere with any
group except the Communists in the United States, and we
propose to deport all alien Communists." In response to Representative Ramseyer of Iowa, who suggested that Congress
ought to be doing something about unemployment, Fish
pointed out that after deporting "every single alien Communist", one could "give those jobs to honest, loyal American

[1] Those who lived in New York during the thirties will remember the robustly
elegant Mr. Whalen not as police commissioner, a title he held for only seventeen months, but as the town's official greeter, splendidly mustached, a smile
on his heavy face, a flower in his buttonhole, a big hand at the ready for
shaking; it was a position that satisfied his particular gifts better than detective
work.
[2] When in the course of the House debate on the resolution, Representative
Huddleston of Alabama brought up the question of investigating fascism,
Representative Snell, chairman of the Rules Committee, replied that he didn't
know what that was, but he guessed the resolution covered it "if it is something
wrong."

citizens who are unemployed." Thus counseled, the House established the Committee by a vote of 210 to 18, the first in a not yet ended series of lopsided votes in favor of such investigative bodies, and Fish was named chairman.

In the demonology of the liberal press of the time, Ham Fish was a throwback to the Salem witch hunters (who could resist a joke about the Fish-ing expedition?), but with the advantage of three inquisitorial decades behind us, we can see now that the New York aristocrat, though no less of a Communist-hater than the chairmen who would follow him, was more of a gentleman. Edmund Wilson, then entering his brief Communist phase,[3] reported that Fish looked like "a Hannibal turned tailor's dummy or a blank-eyed vacuous Bashan bull," and, considering the fellow's size, was the more impressed with his manners. But although Fish may not have been as rude as some, he equaled any man in the House in his ignorance of the subject he was investigating. (Except, possibly, his fellows on the Committee, who had difficulty with unfamiliar words such as "bourgeoisie" and "liquidate.") The prevailing ignorance in Congress about Communism reflected that of the national electorate, and the hearings served as a display case for all sorts of foolishness. "What?" exclaimed Fish to Peter A. Bogdanov, chairman of the board of Amtorg. "You were a prisoner under the Czar and you don't know how many political prisoners there were in Siberia?" Mr. Bogdanov chuckled and his interpreter replied, "He says that the Czar didn't send him to Siberia to count the number of prisoners." Nor did it

[3] The Un-American Activities Committee would for many years be much involved with persons who were drawn to radical movements by the same dismal vision of America that troubled Wilson at the start of the thirties: "There are today in the United States, according to the census director, something like nine million men out of work; our cities are scenes of privation and misery on a scale which sickens the imagination; our agricultural life is bankrupt; our industry, in shifting to the South, has reverted almost to the horrible conditions, before the Factory Acts, of the England of a hundred years ago, and the fight of the unions there for recognition is all to begin again; so many banks are failing that the newspapers do not dare to print the truth about them. And when we look to South America or to the European countries west of Russia, we see only the same economic chaos, the same lack of capacity or will to deal with it, and the same resultant suffering. May we not well fear that what has broken down, in the course of one catastrophic year, is not simply the machinery of representative government but the capitalist system itself?"

help the Committee's reputation for seriousness when it discovered a case of vegetables in a Baltimore warehouse where it had expected to find a case of bombs.

In his exchanges with Communist Party leaders, like William Z. Foster, Chairman Fish was operating under a joint disability. Not only didn't he know much about matters that Foster, though far from an intellectual, had taken pains to absorb,[4] but he was so steeped in his own old-American, upper-class, private-school values—values that would ultimately bring him to leadership of the most perverse element of the America First movement—that he could not credit these people with really believing what they said they believed. William Foster may have drawn his strength from a sense of history moving implacably toward the destruction of Hamilton Fish and all his sisters and his cousins and his aunts, but Hamilton Fish had a no less powerful sense of history as name, family, and Harvard. It was narrow but powerful, and there was no place in it for the eccentricities of the unwashed. In the committee room, Fish was like a schoolmaster faced with a class from Hell's Kitchen who were doing their nasty darndest to put one over on him. His strategy was to trip the witnesses up, make them admit that really, at bottom, they did too believe in God and capitalism just as all the Fishes had down the years.

The hearings, carried on in fairly haphazard style, took six months, from July to December of 1930, at the end of which time the Committee produced a report. It credited the Communist Party with a dues-paying membership of about 12,000 and little noticeable influence despite an estimated half-million sympathizers. It attacked the Civil Liberties Union for its defense of Communists and noted that Grover Whalen's charges against Amtorg had not been supported by the evidence. Out of these mild ingredients, the Committee managed to distill thirteen hearty recommendations, which included declaring the Communist Party illegal, deporting alien Communists, enacting federal laws to prevent Communists from

---

[4] Foster put his lifetime ideology in a nutshell in 1925: "I am for the Comintern from start to finish . . . and if the Comintern finds itself criss-cross with my opinions, there is only one thing to do and that is to change my opinion to fit the policy of the Comintern."

spreading false rumors that might cause runs on banks, and considering an embargo on all articles imported from Russia. Its most intoxicating proposal called on the Department of State to get permission for Treasury agents to go to Russia— the government of which we had yet to recognize—and study the use of forced labor in the timber industry to determine whether we should stop importing Red timber. The want of diplomatic relations between America and the U.S.S.R. also interfered with Fish's dream of sending all the Reds back where they came from.

Doctors who recommend major surgery for a case of heart-burn leave themselves open to the suspicion that they simply like to cut, and the Fish Committee's recommendations were taken in this spirit. In a calm minority report, Representative John E. Nelson of Maine pointed out that Communists did exist, unfortunately, but even granting that their intentions were frankly subversive, the problems they presented were related to the country's larger economic and social problems and these did not lend themselves to solution by criminal statute. Of the numerous bills put forward in 1931 and 1932 to deport alien Communists—and most C.P. members at the time were aliens, with East European Jews particularly noticeable among them—only one, introduced by the young representative from Orange County, Texas, Martin Dies, managed to get through the House, and it was never called to a vote in the Senate.

Although Samuel Dickstein did not take a starring role in these events, he was a featured player. In 1930 he joined Hamilton Fish in condemning religious persecution in Russia. In 1932 he brought Martin Dies's anti-Communist bill to the floor of the House. In 1933, after the assassination attempt on President-elect Roosevelt, he called for a Congressional investigation of anarchists. A few months later, as chairman of the House Immigration Committee, he conducted his own unofficial inquiry into Nazi propaganda, featuring secret letters, smuggled papers, and a witness named Mr. X, who wore spats. He predicted, in words that soon became a refrain, that his revelations would "shock the country."

It was not his revelations that did most to forward his plans, however, but the rise of Adolf Hitler. On the return of Congress to Washington in January 1934, Dickstein offered a resolution to investigate Nazi activities in the United States, and other forms of subversive propaganda. It was supported by Hamilton Fish and after a lively debate, in which a Congressman from Nebraska suggested that the whole thing was a scheme by Jews to offend German-Americans like those in his state who admired the Führer, the Dickstein resolution was authorized by 168 to 31; appointed to the chairmanship of the Committee was John McCormack of Massachusetts, destined to grow old as Speaker of the House. Samuel Dickstein made it known that he had been passed over in deference to his own feeling that a non-Jew should conduct this particular inquiry. Perhaps that was only a rationalization, but he accepted the position of vice chairman along with the gratification of hearing people speak for years thereafter of the "Dickstein Committee."

The McCormack-Dickstein or Dickstein-McCormack hearings began in the summer of 1934 and continued off and on into the fall. For the most part they were based on competent investigation and were fairly respectful of witnesses. The majority of the hearings were held in executive session, and the few public sessions, at which witnesses were permitted counsel, were conducted in a relatively orderly way—when Chairman McCormack was present. When the more emotional Dickstein was on his own in two days of hearings he conducted in New York as a subcommittee of one, he kept getting into arguments with the editor of *Healey's Irish Weekly,* who insisted on making cracks about the "radical Jewish minority influence in Washington." "Don't give me that junk," the Congressman told the anti-Semite. "Don't let you and I get into an argument, because I am not looking for any unless you want some. I am prepared for you." He left little doubt of that. In a thesis on investigating committees written in 1937, a Ph.D. candidate at Syracuse University observed:

Much of the investigation into Nazi propaganda activities may be classified into two parts: first, the counsel usually questions the witnesses upon the facts of his activities ("What have you done?") and presents exhibits accordingly and, second, one of the committee, nearly always Mr. Dickstein, then proceeds to explore the witness' opinions ("Why did you do it?" "Is it right?" "Is it American?") and to bait him further if it can be found that he has not taken out his second citizenship papers or if he has allowed the first ones to lapse. A large number of the Nazi sympathizers were found to be between the receipt of their first and second papers and this gave Mr. Dickstein an opportunity to explore the witness' opinion upon what was right and proper for an American citizen or a prospective American.

It was one of Sam Dickstein's boasts that at the beginning of his career he defended, without compensation, 30,000 New York City tenants against landlords, and one can readily imagine him going after landlords or anarchists or Nazis in the same hot temper. Chairman McCormack's coolness as an inquisitor could only have exasperated Vice Chairman Dickstein (asked at the conclusion of the hearings whether the Nazis were a threat, McCormack replied, "The movement is nowhere near as strong as it was"), but the New Yorker found means of drawing attention to his case. He emerged from a closed one-man session on the establishment, by the Friends of New Germany, of a *Wille und Macht* children's camp in New Jersey, to tell reporters: "I would not keep a dog there. The camp is full of poison ivy, and there are unsanitary conditions. They goose-step all day." A few days later, the camp leader sent the children home. At the final hearings of the Committee, held in the New York City Bar Association building, several hundred German-Americans helped satisfy Mr. Dickstein's taste for excitement and publicity by packing the hearing room, cutting radio wires, chanting "Down with Dickstein," and bringing the meeting to a disorderly climax with Nazi salutes and shouts of "Heil Hitler!"

In the Committee's report, submitted in February 1935, we hear the voice of McCormack. It cited examples of pro-German propaganda paid for by German diplomats, and reported that the youth camps were pro-Hitler. It noted the existence of other anti-Semitic organizations such as William Dudley Pel-

ley's Silver Shirts, and concurred in the Fish Committee's
conclusion that the Communist Party was a branch of the
Third International. Two of McCormack's recommendations,
a far more moderate assortment than that of Ham Fish, were
actually destined to become law—the compulsory registration
of foreign agents distributing propaganda in the United States,
and an extension of subpoena powers to Congressional investigating committees holding hearings outside of the District
of Columbia.

It is tempting, from a distance of three decades, to be patron-
izing about the political nightmares of the thirties, but in fact
there were fascists in America and there were Communists,
both groups at their peaks of strength and both possessed by
dreams that could not thrive in our frustrating democracy. One
might sneer away the Red-baiting of the Hearst press and shrug
off the ceaseless cries of "Fascist!" from the left, and yet be
uneasy about the future. As Arthur Schlesinger, Jr., was to comment twenty years later, "For a moment in 1935, intelligent
observers could almost believe that the traditional structure of
American politics was on the verge of dissolution."

Whether a Congressional committee was equipped to shore
up the structure, however, was another matter. One of the
earliest and still popular charges against Congressional investigations in general, and those into subversion in particular, is
that they are not motivated by any real legislative intent and
produce few laws worth mentioning. Years after the Fish
Committee concluded its work, critics were still pointing out
that it took testimony from 225 witnesses in fourteen cities,
produced a voluminous report, and passed at once into obscurity. Yet a lack of legislative progeny by itself is not sufficient
to prove a committee of Congress sterile. Before the turn of
the century, Woodrow Wilson wrote what would stand among
his most quotable lines in the twenties and thirties—"the informing function of Congress should be even preferred to its
legislative function"—and whatever their shortcomings of intelligence, organization, and good intentions, both the Fish
and McCormack committees undoubtedly carried out an in-

forming function. But it was early recognized that in the course of publicizing Communist and fascist techniques, committee members might yield to a craving for personal publicity, might make careless charges or engage in common politicking. Neither Representative Fish nor Representative Dickstein was able to resist temptation altogether. Thoughtful defenders of Congressional investigations like the young Felix Frankfurter and thoughtful critics like the young Walter Lippmann came to much the same conclusion about them. In Lippmann's words: "Essentially, the case is one in which good precedents must be made by the legislative bodies themselves . . ." And Frankfurter wrote: "The safeguards against abuse and folly are to be looked for in the forces of responsibility which are operating from within Congress . . ."

In practice, as the contrast between the methods of the irascible Dickstein and the reserved McCormack demonstrated, the conduct of a Congressional investigation generally proceeds from the temperament and objectives of the committee chairman—unless he is an unusually weak figure, in which case a more forceful member can be counted on to fill the breach. The chairman's prerogatives are a cherished part of our Congressional tradition. Within wide limits, he sets his own rules of procedure, and his personality as much as his conscious intention determines how witnesses will be treated. The rules of the courtroom do not here prevail. They neither restrain the prosecutor nor shield the defendant. A forceful exercise of the chairman's power was a disturbing feature of Senator Thad Caraway's 1930 investigation of lobbyists as well as of Ham Fish's 1930 investigation of Communists and would remain an acute source of trouble during the innumerable hearings into subversion that lay ahead.

The word "subversion" itself, particularly as understood by men like Fish, Dickstein, and Dies, could only compound the difficulty of holding an orderly inquiry. In January 1937, Dickstein, whose inquisitorial passions had been choked rather than slaked by the McCormack hearings, introduced a resolution in language that opened up spectacular new investigative vistas. In the previous year he had asked, unsuccessfully, to be allowed to investigate the Black Legion, an insignificant anti-Semitic gang. Now he wanted to probe all organizations "found operating in the United States for the purpose of diffusing within the United States of slanderous or libelous un-American propaganda of religious, racial or subversive political prejudices which tends to incite the use of force and violence or which tends to incite libelous attacks upon the President of the United States or other officers of the Federal Government, whether such propaganda appears to be of foreign or domestic origin." Dickstein promised that his resolution—with its evocative term, "un-American," destined for so long and famous a life—would permit the investigation not merely of Nazis, but of "Everybody!"

When the resolution came to the floor of the House in April, it found almost no support. Representative Johnson of Minnesota asked a question—"What is meant by un-American activities?"—which was to echo down the decades without ever receiving a much better answer than it received that day, when it was ignored. Civil libertarians opposed the resolution as a witch hunt, and Maury Maverick of Texas cautioned Dickstein that it could "start a wave of anti-Semitic propaganda all over this country." The pro-German contingent was opposed because the gentleman from New York had made it abundantly clear that what he meant by "un-American activities" were pro-German activities. Even so confirmed a subversive-hunter as Hamilton Fish—perhaps taking personally the reference to libels on the President—came out against Dickstein, warning in the very language of his enemies: "This bill sets up an un-American check-up, nothing more or less, and restores the Alien and Sedition laws." J. Parnell Thomas of New Jersey, a freshman already winning a reputation for being able to spot Communist subversion in the fall of any sparrow, mocked the Dickstein resolution as inviting the investigation of soldiers parading in kilts and playing bagpipes.

Sam Dickstein must be forgiven if he suspected that it was not so much the language of his resolution that offended men like Fish and Thomas, as its sponsor. He, Sam Dickstein, was the main obstacle to his own ambitions. The entire House understood whom Representative Lindsay C. Warren of North Carolina had in mind when he observed that "investigations of this nature, and the membership of the House knows it, are generally for the self-glorification and advertisement of those who conduct them and who have an itch and flair for publicity and advertisement in the papers of the nation rather than in the sober forum of the committee rooms." In truth, Dickstein had asked for it. In a few years he had succeeded in making a national reputation for himself with his campaign, in and out of Congress, against pro-Nazi groups. He spoke incessantly of fascist plots, of "Nazi rats, spies and agents . . . recruiting and drilling uniformed and armed groups . . . I will name you one hundred spies . . ." He proclaimed that there were 50,000 fascists in Connecticut alone, and held aloft pictures of goose-stepping youths in New Jersey. He brought the name of Fritz Kuhn, leader of the native Nazi movement, to the attention of the country, and began an extended exchange of epithets with the recently naturalized Ford Motor Company chemist over which of them was a better type of citizen. (Kuhn said that Dickstein was a spy for Soviet Russia.) It was in vain that the New Yorker now assured the House that he had no itch for personal glory, and did not even want to be appointed chairman of his proposed committee. No pretense of rationality could conceal his obsession. Despite the calm support of Representative McCormack, the resolution was tabled by a vote of 184 to 38. Only two Republicans supported Dickstein, and most members of his own party refrained from declaring themselves. "It is a vote," he told the House, with his accustomed flourishes, "which gave aid and comfort to all the enemies of America and all subversive organizations plotting to destroy our form of government."

The House voted down another resolution that day—this one the child of Martin Dies, for an investigation of sit-down strikes, an epidemic of which, he reported, "is sweeping the nation and threatening the very foundations of orderly government." One among several investigations unavailingly proposed by the young Texan in 1937, it was frankly designed to counteract the Senate's Civil Liberties Committee, headed by Robert M. La Follette, which, with the blessing of F.D.R. and the C.I.O., was effectively exposing labor espionage and violent union-busting tactics in the steel and automobile industries. Dies, who had recently helped lead the opposition to the wages and hours bill, identified himself as a friend of labor, which caused some merriment in the chamber, and after a noisy debate, supporters of the Administration turned him back. But three months later, Martin Dies, with the encouragement of Vice President Garner, Speaker Bankhead, and Majority Leader Rayburn, and with the assured support of the Southern bloc, put forward a new version of the Dickstein resolution—and the two men, the small, dressy unpopular New York New Dealer and the big, rowdy popular Texan who had already made an imposing place for himself among the restive conservatives of both parties, joined in the cause of a committee to investigate "subversive and un-American propaganda."[5] The fact that a victory for the Dies resolution could only be taken as a personal rebuff to himself could not have been lost upon Sam Dickstein, yet he became its most fervent advocate. Whereas Dies had modestly requested merely a special committee, Dickstein declared: "There should be a standing committee of this House known as the Committee on Un-American Activities, which should watch every subversive group in this country." He would live to see his dream realized by a Jew-hater from Mississippi.

In the months leading up to the House debate on the Dies resolution, Dickstein's campaign of exposure was abetted by Germany's heightening pressures on its European neighbors and by the behavior of those thousands of Germans in this country who were caught up in the old country's madness. They held larger rallies, flew greater numbers of swastikas,

[5] The resolution, as passed, read as follows: "Resolved, that the Speaker of the House of Representatives be, and he is hereby, authorized to appoint a special committee to be composed of seven members for the purpose of conducting an investigation of (1) the extent, character, and object of un-American propaganda activities in the United States, (2) the diffusion within the United States of subversive and un-American propaganda that is instigated from foreign countries or of a domestic origin and attacks the principle of the form of government as guaranteed by the Constitution, and (3) all other questions in relation thereto that would aid Congress in any necessary remedial legislation."

made more arrogant speeches, and took to behaving like the advance contingent of an already triumphant faith. Herr Kuhn called on his fellows to form a bloc "to deepen the German-conscious attitude" in the United States. A Stuttgart newspaper had the poor judgment to extoll the German-American camps as places where boys and girls could "learn to harmonize their duties as American citizens and their national and racial mission as Germans.". White Russians, Italian fascists, and members of organizations with names like the American Gentile League came to drink beer with their Teutonic brothers. Dickstein made the most of their celebrations. In Detroit, he reported, "many thousands of little tots, ranging from four to six years of age" were "parading around in the Youth Movement uniforms crying 'Heil Hitler' and swearing by the Nazi Government." He told of 25,000 men and women in Nassau County "going crazy, dressed in uniforms and goose-stepping their way for miles at all hours of the night . . . disturbing the peace of the community and defying the police . . ." Even the neighborhood of Westchester was contaminated. So advanced among its adherents was the illusion of Nazi power that when American Legion posts, aroused by Dickstein, began to growl threateningly, the head of Camp Nordland in Andover, New Jersey, warned that if any Legionnaires trespassed upon his property, "they would not get out alive."

When six Bundists from Camp Yaphank on Long Island went on trial for failing to register as members of an oath-bound organization as required by a 1923 anti-Klu Klux Klan law, the courtroom was filled with uniformed veterans and Bund members in regalia, all hoping for trouble.[6] In April 1938, the ill will between Legionnaires and Bundsmen burst into riot at a meeting at the Yorkville Casino of 3,500 admirers of Adolf Hitler on the occasion of his forty-ninth birthday. When a speaker commended the German seizure of Austria as a "birthday gift by Chancellor Hitler" to Greater Germany, a man in the audience rose to inquire, "Is this an American or a

---

[6] At a Yorkville rally to protest the convictions of the Bundists, a speaker from Ohio asked the five hundred German-Americans before him whether they wanted a government by Hitler in the United States. "Yes!" they chorused back with lusty good will. "You should have said 'No,'" chided the speaker.

German meeting?" As uniformed storm troopers converged on him, several dozen Legionnaires also rose and donned their blue overseas caps. They were, unhappily, no match for the *Ordnungsdienst,* who were equipped with blackjacks and heavy-buckled belts. However, an unfriendly crowd soon gathered outside the casino, and police reserves had to be called to protect the Germans as they made their way home.

So successful were the native Nazis in provoking distaste for themselves that the F.B.I. opened an investigation of the Bund camps and the American Civil Liberties Union joined with the nonlibertarian Hamilton Fish in proposing a ban on private military groups. The weeks before the Dies resolution came up in Congress were troubled by the Sudeten crisis in Europe and a German spy trial in New York. Dickstein capitalized untiringly on every incident and every fear. "You can find almost 200,000 men of the Bund ready to put on uniforms and to use a gun," he warned. "There are 200,000 people in this country who should have their citizenship papers canceled because they are a burden and a threat to the country." He told of millions of dollars being taken out of the United States by the "secret Nazi police" and of millions more being sent in for subversive purposes. He reported that Bundists were setting up their camps suspiciously close to arms factories, and forecast bloody battles on the streets of America as aroused patriots took action.

As part of his campaign, Dickstein began inserting into the Congressional Record the names of suspect firms, organizations, and individuals—"expert spies," "smugglers," "Nazi aides," and "agitators." Most of the names came from the files of the McCormack Committee, which, out of regard for ordinary rules of evidence, had been sealed to the public. On being asked for documentation to back up his charges, Dickstein explained that putting all his mass of evidence into the Record would be a frightful drain on the Government Printing Office but that any colleague who wished to pay a visit to his office might have a look at it. When Representative Cochran of Missouri produced affidavits from six of eighteen persons in St. Louis named by Dickstein, swearing they had never been Nazis, the

New Yorker declined even to place their denials in the Record. He had no apologies to make: ". . . if out of these hundreds of names that I have buttonholed as fascists and Nazis or whatever I have called them, only six filed a protest, I think I have done a pretty good job."

In this aggressive defense, made in December 1937, and in the reply of Maury Maverick we find ourselves at the center of an enduring debate. Maverick argued that when the names of individuals "whose honor and patriotism are questioned" are put in the Record, "it should only be after an investigation, with the witnesses under oath. I do not think people should be libeled through the country by mere rumor. It is unfair." Dickstein was unmoved, just as later investigators would be unmoved by the remonstrances of those whom Joe McCarthy called the "bleeding hearts." There was a threat abroad; there was a threat at home. Was this an hour for legalistic niceties?

No man worked harder or more effectively than Samuel Dickstein to rally support for the Dies resolution. And it was support of a kind that the Texan could not attract on his own. The veterans' organizations were primed to back any investigation of practically anybody, Communist, fascist, or osteopath. The perfervid anti-Communists were of course with Martin Dies. But the affections of single-minded anti-fascists would never go out to the swaggering Congressman from Orange County. To them, Dickstein's voice and intentions were comforting. Among the organizations that came through with an endorsement of an investigation which they believed would be directed primarily at Bundists were the Federal Council of Churches, the Non-Sectarian Anti-Nazi League, the New Jersey C.I.O., and the American League for Peace and Democracy. All would have reason to rue the day.

For the coalition of Republicans and Southern Democrats in the House, who had perforce been growing closer since Roosevelt's 1936 sweep, Martin Dies was a David come to judgment on the New Deal. John Rankin of Mississippi opposed the creation of an un-American activities committee until he was assured that it would be headed by the Texan, Dies, and not by the Jew, Dickstein. The country was still deep in depression, and disturbing currents were running through the land. Radicals of many varieties, some taking inspiration from the Soviet experiment, roamed freely among the discontented, making up in vehemence and foolhardiness what they lacked in numbers. Major sections of American industry were in turmoil as industrial workers organized and struck and fought their bloody battles. To heirs of an older America, where economic and political power resided in the propertied man, the owner of a business, the farmer, the shopkeeper, it was as though some subterranean monster were breaking through the shell of the earth and overturning all the dear landmarks. To them, Samuel Dickstein, the rabbi's son from Russia via the Lower East Side, was irredeemably alien. As Representative Shannon of Missouri explained with nice delicacy, "Many members of Congress felt that an investigation of this kind should not be headed by a foreign-born citizen." But Martin Dies was one of their own. His father, Congressman from Texas from 1909 to 1919, mistrusted immigrants, despised Bolsheviks, and broke with President Wilson over the League of Nations. Big, boyish Martin, an impetuous lock of hair complementing his smooth boyish features, often included a proud reference to Dad in his juicy back-country speeches. With the patronage of Vice President Garner, the young man had found a place on the House Rules Committee, where he was able to assist in holding up the Administration's wages and hours bill, which the South viewed as a discriminatory measure. As representative of the hill people of east Texas, more than ninety percent of them of undiluted Anglo-Saxon stock, he epitomized an entrenched, embattled suspicion of big cities, big capital, big labor, and big government as well as of foreigners, big and small, whom he perennially proposed to deport, and foreign ideologies. His first bill, introduced the day after he took his seat in Congress in 1931, would have suspended immigration to the United States for five years. America's unemployment problem, he agreed with Ham Fish, had been caused by the flooding of the land by foreigners, and would not be solved until they were sent back home. Here was a man who could be trusted with

an investigation of "the extent, character and object of un-
American propaganda activities in the United States."

And Martin Dies wanted very much to lead an investigation
—practically any investigation. Impressed with the success of
Senate committee chairmen like Nye and La Follette in getting
their names in the papers, he proposed looking into, among
other things, Administration restrictions on freedom of press
and radio, the resignation of government officials to take
lucrative jobs in private industry, charges that America was
controlled by sixty families, and the sugar lobby. Finally, on
the verge of success, young Martin the Populist appeared
before the House for the calling up of his resolution on May
26, 1938, like the rehabilitated slum boy at the end of the
B-movie, combed, scrubbed, and ready for prep school. "I
am not inclined to look under every bed for a Communist,"
he assured his listeners. He was concerned over the photographs he had seen of Bundists saluting the swastika, and over
the danger that President Roosevelt might be assassinated by
one of the 480,000 Nazis in the United States. He was aware
of the peril to "fundamental rights far more important than the
objective we seek," in any legislative attempt to prohibit un-
American activities. He acknowledged that a committee composed of publicity seekers could do more harm than good:
"I believe all depends on the way the committee is handled."
He did not favor a lavish expenditure of money on such investigations, and he did favor free speech. When Representative
Warren said that seven months was "long enough to investigate
any subject on earth," Dies agreed and at once accepted an
amendment that the Committee conclude its business and issue
its report by the end of that very session of Congress.

It was left to supporters of the investigation, like Taylor of
Tennessee, to go to work on the Communists. Taylor, who had
favored an investigation of the sit-down strikes because most
of the Detroit agitators did not have American names and who
took public pride in having helped to write the first restrictive
immigration law ever placed on the statute books, told the
House that "Communist radicals recently for the second time
had the unmitigated audacity and depravity to desecrate that

hallowed shrine to every red-blooded American—Plymouth Rock—by enveloping it in red paint. The miserable wretches who committed this dastardly deed ought to be hunted down, like rattlesnakes, and kicked out of the country." He was applauded. Robison of Kentucky asked: "Now why should we permit a lot of Communists from Russia or elsewhere who hate religion, who hate this government, and desire to see it overthrown and a Communist dictatorship established to organize on American soil, march under the red flag of Communism and engage in subversive propaganda and activities for the purpose of destroying our government?"

The opposition, led by Maury Maverick, warned that the resolution gave "blanket powers to investigate, humiliate, meddle with anything and everything . . . from the German Saengerfest to B'nai B'rith . . ." When Patrick of Alabama asked yet again, like the chorus in an Edward Lear rhyme, "But what is un-Americanism?" Maverick could barely hold himself in: "Un-American! Un-American is simply something that somebody else does not agree to." Representative Boileau of Wisconsin predicted that Dies would be investigating the wages and hours bill and Thomas would be investigating the whole New Deal before they were through, and several Congressmen made the point that the nation's real problem was its millions of unemployed. "Whenever a parliamentary body in any country of the world has found itself unable to deal with the economic problems that face the people," said O'Malley of Wisconsin, "they go on a witch hunt."

But the Dies-Dickstein strategy had been well conceived. There was anxiety in the country over the parading Nazis and the incendiary radicals, and an investigation that promised to expose subversives on the left as well as on the right was bound to command popular support. As Representative Cochran observed, the resolution had gone too far to be turned down now. And he added in words that many Congressmen have repeated, though not so openly, since that momentous day: "I do not want to be accused of refusing to vote for legislation to investigate un-American activities."

The Dies resolution was approved by a vote of 191 to 41, and when the freshly victorious Representative Dickstein rose to request permission to speak for three minutes, he was unceremoniously turned down. A week and a half later, the Chair appointed the members of the new Committee. Sam Dickstein, who had labored with all his heart for this day, was not among them.

2

1938: The Dies Committee

THE company from which Representative Dickstein had been excluded was a conservative one. It contained one unflaming New Dealer, John J. Dempsey of New Mexico; one wavering New Dealer, Arthur D. Healey of Massachusetts; two old-school Democrats, Joe Starnes of Alabama and Harold G. Mosier of Ohio; and two Republicans of the distant right wing, Noah M. Mason of Illinois and J. Parnell Thomas. Thomas, born Feeney, of Allendale, New Jersey! The pudgy, belligerent bond salesman and insurance broker made a home with the Committee. Here his disposition could find expression, his animosities find scope, his politics find fellowship. Alone of the six, he would stay with his chairman until the end—and after, until the day of his due reward. When J. B. Matthews, soon to be established as chief Committee investigator, wrote his autobiography, *Odyssey of a Fellow Traveler,* he dedicated it to but five of the Congressmen—"Three Democrats, Two Republicans: Five Americans"—pointedly leaving out the unfraternal Dempsey and Healey. The Committee on Un-American Activities would suffer the usual goings and comings over the next thirty years of political wars, but it would hold its conservative cast. Liberals who joined it with intimations of reform invariably gave up after a while, missionaries turning from a fatally damned congregation to more hopeful work.

The Committee on Accounts allotted Chairman Dies $25,000 instead of the $100,000 he had requested. Although the sum was more than the Fish Committee spent and only $5,000 less than that given to the McCormack Committee, it was a painfully small allocation, considering the expansive language of the resolution. This led in the following months to an intragovernmental charade that hinted at a rupture to come. Dies asked for the loan of investigators from the Departments of Justice and of Labor, a favor to which he was entitled by the terms of the resolution ("The head of each executive department is hereby requested to detail to said committee such number of legal and expert assistants as said committee may from time to time deem necessary"), and which he knew that his arch nemesis, the La Follette Civil Liberties Committee, had received. The executive departments turned him down. "Ho-hum," commented the President on being informed of Dies's complaints. When the La Follette Committee, as a sort of practical joke, offered the loan of two of its investigators, Dies questioned the men, convinced himself that "they were either Communists or Communist sympathizers," and declined. As several staff members of the Civil Liberties Committee were later pronounced Communists by Senator La Follette himself, Dies's suspicion may have been sound. In any case, the limited funds available to the Committee obliged it to make do with two stenographers, four investigators, three of whom would quickly be dismissed, and a youthful clerk named, haply, Robert E. Stripling, whom Dies had brought to the capital from Texas to be assistant sergeant of arms of the House and who would stay on with the Committee for a long time. The shortage of staff reinforced the chairman's predilection for witnesses from groups such as the American Legion's Americanism Committee. Their voluntary testimony would become a characteristic of the Committee's first months of operation and a point of dispute for years thereafter.

The opening of hearings in mid-August 1938 was preceded by two fanfares. At the end of July, J. Parnell Thomas demanded a sweeping investigation of the W.P.A.'s Federal Theatre and Writers Project. On the basis of "startling evidence" in his possession, he concluded that the project was "a hotbed for Communists," "infested with radicals from top to bottom," and "one more link in the vast and unparalleled New

Deal propaganda machine." Observers acquainted with the language and learning of Parnell Thomas would find nothing out of the ordinary in this announcement, but it was the beginning of the end for the government's first and only venture into subsidized theater.

In August, Dies himself swept on to the stage where he would star for many seasons to come. He announced to the press that he had issued a subpoena to the pro-German propagandist, George Sylvester Viereck, upon learning that Viereck was about to pay a call on Adolf Hitler. Viereck explained that he was indeed going to Europe—but it was to see his old friend the Kaiser and other prominent persons, and not Hitler, whom he doubted would have time for him. Nevertheless, he canceled his passage. Having thus found his way on to page 1 —DIES OPENS WAR ON PROPAGANDISTS—the Congressman lost interest in the case, and Viereck sailed for Europe a week later without appearing before the Committee. This apparently unproductive gesture of the new chairman had two useful results, not counting that of inconveniencing the friend of the Kaiser. It alerted newspaper readers to the imminent opening of an investigation into subversion, and prolonged for another hour the hopes of those of Mr. Dickstein's persuasion as to the Committee's intentions. It also showed Martin Dies at his most engaging, when at the press conference called to publicize his pass at Viereck, he expressed his disdain for "the old kind of investigation that would go after somebody only for cheap publicity." The ability to divorce one's mind from one's actions is, enlightened persons recognize today, a symptom of psychological aberration, but it is also a cherished political talent.

In a radio speech three days before the start of hearings, Dies again promised that there would be no three-ring circuses, that he would not "permit any individual or organization to use the Committee as a sounding board to obtain publicity or to injure others." And on August 12, as hearings—from which the public was at first excluded—were about to begin in the air-cooled caucus room on the second floor of the Old House Office Building, he laid aside his cigar and delivered a statement that might have been written by Roger Baldwin:

... this Committee is determined to conduct its investigation upon a dignified plane and to adopt and maintain throughout the course of the hearings a judicial attitude. The Committee has no preconceived views of what the truth is respecting the subject matter of this inquiry ... We shall be fair and impartial at all times and treat every witness with fairness and courtesy ... This Committee will not permit any "character assassination" or any "smearing" of innocent people ... It is the Chair's opinion that the usefulness or value of any investigation is measured by the fairness and impartiality of the committee conducting the investigation. Neither the public nor the Congress will have any confidence in the findings of a committee which adopts a partisan or preconceived attitude ... It is easy to "smear" someone's name or reputation by unsupported charges or an unjustified attack, but it is difficult to repair the damage that has been done ... when any individual or organization is involved in any charge or attack made in the course of the hearings, that individual or organization will be accorded an opportunity to refute such charge or attack.

He concluded by cautioning the assembled reporters and photographers against calling people un-American just because of "an honest difference of opinion with respect to some economic, political or social question."

In the days that followed, observers began to wonder whether the lady of breeding who had made such a dignified entrance into town was in fact setting up a bawdy house. The Dies Committee established itself on the nation's front pages at once and stayed there for most of August. *The New York Times* accorded it more than five hundred column-inches of space in its first month and a half of life, and other newspapers were even more accommodating. This triumph with the press was generally attributed to the chairman's shrewdness in opening hearings in mid-August when the capital is no fit place to be; F.D.R. was away and news was scarce. One pair of analysts suggested that Dies was fortunate in having a name that came to only three and a half characters in the count of headline writers. But there was no need to strain for explanations. The reason that the Dies Committee received such extensive coverage in its first weeks was simply that it provided such good copy.

It all started off fairly quietly with a set of witnesses discussing the activities of the German-American Bund. They were led by John C. Metcalfe, a German-born former reporter for the Chicago *Daily Times* who had been assigned in 1937 to infiltrate the Bund. He joined the Astoria, Queens, chapter under the name of Hellmut Oberwinder, became a storm trooper, and won the confidence of Fritz Kuhn himself. Metcalfe, who had served the McCormack Committee and was now working as a kind of voluntary investigator for Representative Dies, told of the Bund's direction by the German Auslands Bureau in Stuttgart, of its plot to establish "a vast spy network" and a "powerful sabotage machine" among the German minority in America. There were 500,000 Nazis and Nazi sympathizers in this country, he said. His report was not startling to anyone who had been paying attention to Samuel Dickstein for the past several years, and indeed it provided one of the few bits of satisfaction that Dickstein would be able to draw from the Committee's work. At odd moments in the ensuing weeks, Metcalfe would reappear with further news of Nazi plottings, like the comic who pops out between burlesque skits with a broom and sets diligently to sweeping up the stage until he is kicked off so that the show may proceed.

It proceeded on August 13 with John P. Frey, president of the Metal Trades Department of the American Federation of Labor. *The New York Times* gave him a two-column headline on its Sunday front page:

COMMUNISTS RULE THE C.I.O.
FREY OF A.F.L. TESTIFIES;
HE NAMES 284 ORGANIZERS

Just two days before, the La Follette Civil Liberties Committee had held its final hearings on anti-union activity at General Motors. Now it was the turn of the anti-C.I.O. forces. The Administration had feared just such an attack on its political and ideological allies, and had employed Representative McCormack to urge Dies to restrain himself. "From this intramural Congressional struggle," as one historian has observed, "emerged a facsimile in microcosm of the battle between the New Deal and its political enemies."

Frey was a blunt witness. He told the Committee that the Communists had made no progress in the United States until the C.I.O. was organized, but "since then the Communist Party had become a definite factor in the American labor movement." The C.I.O. program of sit-down strikes and mass picketing had the "hearty endorsement of the Communist Party," since it trained Party members "for the day when the signal for revolution is given." Already they were infiltrating the Democratic Party and nudging the Administration to the left. Frey charged that the La Follette Committee, darling of the liberal community,[1] was cooperating with the Communists, and in his three days of testifying, hardly a major industrial union escaped the charge of Communist influence.

One of the many names uttered by Frey was that of Harry Bridges, the Australian-born head of the West Coast longshoremen, a most aggressive and effective union chief with a pronounced affinity for Communist causes. On August 14, while Frey was still testifying, Dies released to the newspapers a report from the Committee's main investigator, Edward F. Sullivan, who had been out surveying the Pacific Coast. He wrote that Harry Bridges was responsible for 60 per cent of the labor strife in that area, and that he was being protected from deportation by "an outstanding official" in the Department of Labor. Sullivan also observed that Communism was rampant in the movie industry—the start of a long-lasting fascination with Hollywood on the part of the Committee—and in the schools. As for Nazi activities, Jewish organizations "were naturally concerned," but this concern was "not shared by any other agency."

On August 16 it was the turn before the Committee of Walter Steele, editor of the fiercely conservative *National Republic,* as well as chairman of the American Coalition Committee on

---

[1] Under a headline, SAVE THE CIVIL LIBERTIES INQUIRY, in November 1939, *The New Republic*'s editors used the language of Congressional inquisitors of all periods: "Nothing holds the forces of darkness in check like a Senatorial searchlight always in readiness to be turned upon their activities."

National Security, an organization that took in 114 other organizations of a patriotic nature. Thus, as Steele conceded, he spoke for some twenty million people. He was an experienced witness, having testified before both the Fish and Dickstein committees, and would perform yet again for the Thomas Committee. In his two days of testimony in August, he named hundreds of infested organizations, from the American League for Peace and Democracy, with which the Committee would wrestle for months to come, to the American Civil Liberties Union to the Camp Fire Girls, who were in danger of being misled by persons who claimed they were interested in forwarding international understanding.

The Frey and Steele hearings established a tone and a mode of operation for the Dies Committee in its first year. Samuel Dickstein promptly denounced his child, but Hamilton Fish, the grandparent, said, "I love the Dies Committee for the enemies it has made." The *Daily Worker,* possessed of a limited stock of invective, called the Committee an "outfit of storm troopers," and the non-Communist liberals running *The Nation* and *The New Republic* thoroughly agreed. Catholic diocesan papers, on the other hand, complimented the Committee for its "distinguished service to the country," and so did the *Chicago Tribune.* Chairman Dies was the "Man of the Week" for Father Coughlin's *Social Justice* in September 1938, and by 1939 the anti-Semitic priest from Royal Oak was promoting the Protestant Fundamentalist from Texas for President. And in between Dies's allies and enemies were many newspapers which were impressed by some of the testimony but disturbed by the rough-and-ready rules of procedure.

For Martin Dies the surge of newspaper attention was one of those crucial events in the life of the young child which, we are told, makes it so difficult to shake off bad habits later. It was not that the reporters were uncritically accepting of all that went on in the caucus room; on the contrary, in a poll taken in October 1938 by a pair of New York *Daily News* columnists, of the eighteen reporters who regularly covered the proceedings—and were the only outsiders who had the privilege of viewing them at first-hand—only two, from conservative newspapers, thought they were fair, while eleven thought they were unfair; the others either straddled or declined to commit themselves. The problem before the newspapermen was that the charges being made day after day were newsworthy in themselves, whereas the observation that the Committee allowed charges to be made without asking for supporting evidence verged on editorial comment. Denials came late and were relegated to back pages and ends of columns.

It was a well-advertised secret that major C.I.O. unions such as the Auto Workers, the Maritime Workers, and the Transport Workers harbored Communists in important positions and that Ben Gold, the head of the Fur Workers, was a genuine, deep-dyed Red. John L. Lewis needed their organizing skills and their physical courage in the mid-thirties, and they reciprocated by using the growing C.I.O. power for their own ends. Zygmund Dobrzynski, a former national director of the U.A.W. organizing drive at Ford who appeared before the Committee in 1938, gave an illuminating and typical instance of Communist tactics:

> During the first organizational days, when the U.A.W. was formed, and the men were beginning to recognize that unionism was the thing they needed, they came in by the hundreds; the automobile industry was made up of men, primarily, who had never been in any union before, and who were completely inexperienced, not knowing even how to make a motion on the floor . . . the members of the Communist Party knew how to speak; some of them had extensive soap-box experience . . . It is very simple for a man who understands public speaking and parliamentary rules to control a meeting of uninitiated people . . . By preparing motions ahead of time, having discussions ahead of time, and then dividing up in various sections of the hall [the Communists] would give the impression that the particular policy they were trying to have the meeting adopt was generally supported throughout the membership.

But did the evidence support Frey's indictment of the C.I.O. as a tool of Moscow? Particularly when the indictment was issued by an old-line craft-union chieftain, a delegate from

the Iron Molders, who looked upon the unorganized unskilled
in much the way a Southern sheriff looked upon the voteless
Negro, and who had led the effort to kick the C.I.O. out of
the A. F. of L. It was his dictum that "Unskilled labor must
become skilled before it can gain its rights." A few weeks after
Frey's appearance, another witness, in the course of testifying
quite convincingly about Communist influence in Mike Quill's
Transport Workers Union, remarked: "I would not have joined
if the A. F. of L. had done its job." It was a critical point for
understanding the Communist intrusion into the C.I.O., but
it was of no interest to the Committee.

After Frey left the stand, newspaper reporters speculated
on his batting average. How many of the hundreds of persons
he had named were actually under Communist Party direction?
How many were dupes? How influential were the C.P. members? Did membership mean the same thing to all of them?
And what did it mean for the labor movement? The reporters
could only wonder. Considering the numbers of persons implicated in the first weeks of testimony, it would have been
impossible within the space of a Congressman's lifetime to give
every one of them an opportunity to defend himself; a study
of the 1938 hearings published by *Public Opinion Quarterly*
noted that "of the hundreds or perhaps thousands of persons
who were accused of being "Communists' or (infrequently)
'Nazis' . . . with a single possible exception not one of the
accused has been called to the stand . . ." Nor did the Committee make any effort at cross-examination. Dies lounged
back and smoked his cigar or chewed his gum and watched
reporters taking notes about the C.I.O., the American Civil
Liberties Union, or the Farmer-Labor Party, about John
Dewey, Paul H. Douglas, or H. L. Mencken. When he or
Starnes or Mason or Thomas broke in, it was usually to spur a
witness on to more stimulating charges: "Do you not think,"
Thomas inquired of one man, "that the many steps taken by
our government in recent years such as the reorganization bill
and the Supreme Court bill constitute a prelude to dictatorship
in this country?" (The Democrats present, in a rare exercise

of loyalty to the Administration, objected and the question was not answered.)

Attempts to get supporting evidence for the deluge of charges were desultory. When, for example, investigator Metcalfe told of a Nazi scheme to plant spies in American munitions plants, shipyards, and airplane factories, Dies asked: "How do you know this?" Metcalfe replied: "We have checked our sources and find them absolutely reliable," and went on as though he had answered the question. Investigator Sullivan's report on Harry Bridges was certified by nothing more than the investigator's remark that it was "based upon the statements of persons in all walks of business, industrial and agricultural life on the West Coast." As an informal preliminary and private report to the Committee, his conclusions about Bridges's affinity for the Communist Party might have been useful and appropriate, but the chairman released them to the press as written and then a day later, after they had been widely circulated, commented that while he thought it was "advisable that the public should have the benefit of the report," the Committee did "not now vouch for its accuracy."

Dies did, however, vouch for the accuracy of Frey. At the close of the A. F. of L. leader's time before the Committee, the chairman said: "I am convinced of the reliability of those sources"—which Frey had said that he could not "openly give." When John Brophy, the most prominent of the dozens of C.I.O. officials named by Frey, took exception to being labeled a Communist consort (and produced two priests to affirm that he was a thoroughgoing Catholic with a son in training for the priesthood, the ultimate defense in cases of this sort), Frey replied: "The Communist connection was not mine. I quoted the official journal of the United Mine Workers Union, and they charged him with being tied up with Communism and endeavoring to sell the Miners Union. It is the testimony of the U.M.W. and not mine. I merely introduced their testimony." He did not add that the U.M.W. charge was based on a statement made by John L. Lewis in the mid-twenties when he was contending against Brophy, who did have Communist support for a time but was never one of their own, for leadership of the union—

or that Brophy might have won had not the Communists deserted him in a typical shift of Moscow-directed policy. A rare instance of the chairman rousing himself to chide one of his volunteer witnesses came during a discussion of education when one of the pieces of evidence cited of John Dewey's radicalism was that he had been attacked by Matthew Woll of the A. F. of L. Dies interjected that "the mere fact that somebody denounced him is no particular proof." It was an unusual nod to courtroom amenities, and it did not stop the witness for very long.

The Committee's decision to welcome volunteer witnesses as the Fish Committee had, made partly because it had not been granted enough money to do its own investigating, was in itself a guarantee that the proceedings would be diverted into irregular byways, by volunteers like the pastor of a Washington Congregational Church who was upset that James Roosevelt's published income tax returns for five years listed no church contributions. The best people do not offer themselves for such work, and the volunteers of 1938 turned out to be a gamy bunch. Walter Steele, the representative of twenty million patriots, was on the advisory board of the Paul Reveres, an active anti-Semitic group of the political fringe. His credentials as an expert on un-Americanism, as he had explained at the Fish hearings, were that he read Communist publications and collected names from them. His magazine, the *National Republic*, was emphatically anti-Communist, but it was also emphatically anti-labor, anti-alien, and pro-Franco. Edward Sullivan, the Committee's preeminent investigator, was dropped from the small staff in September—for financial reasons, the chairman explained—after the La Follette Committee reminded the press that he had been identified in its hearings as a labor spy of standing for the Railway Audit and Inspection Company of Pittsburgh, with a history of Jew-baiting and Catholic-baiting. Sullivan, who had worked and shared an office with James True, inventor of the "Kike Killer," an instrument for bashing in the heads of Jews, found employment after his release from the Committee with the Ukrainian Nationalist Federation, whose mission it was to annex the Ukraine to the Third Reich.

Along with witnesses from the ranks of the ultra-right and a few ordinary criminals came a number of persons with conspicuous axes to grind, like Alice Lee Jemison who accused the Indian Bureau of the Department of the Interior of trying to spread Communism and paganism. "The Jemison dame," as Secretary Ickes ungallantly spoke of her, had been going around for years trying to get the government to pay $3,500 to every Indian from whom she had collected one dollar in dues. Ickes, whose feud with Dies began early and lasted to the end, charged, without offering any more evidence than Miss Jemison did, that Nazi agents had collaborated in her testimony so that they could attack the United States for treating Indians worse than the Germans treated Jews. The lady had never been able to get any publicity for herself, he observed, "until the accommodating Congressman Dies came along intent on smearing the New Deal whenever he could." Later on, the pleasures of 1938 having receded, Dies himself would grant, in one of his periodic nods to critics as appropriation time approached, that his Committee had had some "screwball witnesses" before it and that, unfortunately, some decent American may have been "smeared."

But that was later. In mid-August, the Congressmen were still splashing around like kids in a new swimming hole, with no particular direction and only the vaguest notion of a future that would call them home to supper. It was all quite hit and miss. Then, on August 20, arrived Joseph Brown Matthews. Where the Committee knew nothing about Communism except what it did not like, J. B. Matthews, who had been recommended to Dies by the columnist George Sokolsky, knew everything, and gave freely of his knowledge. Soon he would put much of it into an illuminating book, *The Trojan Horse in America,* published under the by-line of Martin Dies. The Committee would cling to Matthews for years to come, like ladies to the interior decorator who is able to dignify their tastes and bolster their pretensions with the jargon of the expert. "The nation owes him [Matthews] a debt of gratitude which will not be paid or even acknowledged in this generation," wrote Dies in his 1963 autobiography. That is a controversial assessment, but of Martin Dies's own debt there can be no question.

The howlers committed by the members of the Dies Committee were something special even for Congressional committees. Having heard something about the John Reed clubs, Dies asked a witness if a Michigan labor leader named John G. Reid was the fellow who founded them. Starnes had the misfortune to mix up a British Laborite, Tom Mann, with Thomas Mann, the writer—an understandable mistake, as it turned out, since both men were opposed to fascism. And it was Starnes too, class of '21 at Alabama U. and a former schoolteacher in Guntersville, who on hearing a witness mention the name Christopher Marlowe, demanded, "You're quoting from this Marlowe. Is he a Communist?"

J. B. Matthews was above such gaffes. He spent his boyhood in Kentucky, where he was born in 1894, and his young manhood in Malaya as a Methodist missionary and student of exotic languages. On his return to this country in the early nineteen-twenties he became imbued with the social gospel. His gift was for preaching, in the piss-and-vinegar mode of Kentucky Methodism; his two main themes were racial equality and pacifism; for a dozen years he gave himself unstintingly to these and related causes.

> I moved from religious fundamentalism to the social gospel. From the social gospel with its earnest humanitarianism, I went to political reform à la La Follette the Elder. I moved to pacifism. After pacifism came socialism of the Norman Thomas brand. I went, finally, from socialism to communism.

There were a handful of men and women in the thirties, not members of the Communist Party, whose names on a letterhead constituted a kind of imprimatur for the board of a radical organization, the rally of protest, the appeal for justice, the petition for redress of grievances: Reinhold Niebuhr, Harry F. Ward, Roger Baldwin, Robert Morss Lovett—and J. B. Matthews. Such associations, Carlyle discerned, are the "surest symptom of Social Unrest: in such a way, most infallibly of all, does Social Unrest exhibit itself, find solacement and also nutriment." Matthews was abundantly solaced and richly nourished during the nation's parlous time. It was not mere boasting when he wrote of himself: "No other person in the United States had such an impressive united front record." During his years of faith he wrote for, spoke for and lent his name to more than sixty organizations and publications active in the service of peace, race relations, labor solidarity and anti-fascism. He held official positions with fifteen of them, and gave more than a hundred speeches before audiences mass and select. "*What* we join," he wrote, "may be and, indeed, often is un-American, but the *act* of joining is typically American." If that is so—and the excuse was rarely extended by Matthews to unrepentant joiners—no more typical American ever breathed. Matthews covered the spectrum of radical life—Socialist, Stalinist, Lovestoneite, Musteite, Trotskyite, I.W.W., Socialist Labor Party— without favoritism. "The catholicity of my radicalism," he wrote, "is in the record beyond dispute."

The instinctive reaction on the left after his appearance before the Dies Committee was to deny his credentials, which were stunningly authentic (Earl Browder said Matthews was merely secretary of the American League Against War and Fascism for a while, when everyone knew he was its first national chairman); to give the lie to his charges of Communist domination of united front organizations, which were in the main convincing; to argue that non-Communists could work profitably with Communists where the liberal, anti-fascist community was united—a hotly disputed position on the left at that time; and to impugn the motives behind Matthews's startling reformation.

What made his reformation so very startling was that unlike many who had disengaged themselves from the Popular Front dream of the thirties, he had for years been the least questioning of fellow travelers. He wanted, he claimed, symphony not cacophony in the leftist orchestra. It is true that he resigned the chairmanship of the American League Against War and Fascism (later the American League for Peace and Democracy) in 1934, after the Communists broke up a Madison

Square Garden memorial meeting called to honor the Austrian Social Democrats defeated by the Dollfuss regime,[2] but he remained on the organization's board. In 1932, on one of his annual trips to the Soviet Union, he saw the ravages of famine in the Ukraine. Three years later, when the Hearst press ran an accurate series of articles on the famine, he wrote a rebuttal in the *Daily Worker*, condemning as a betrayal of the working class the thought that there could be famine in the Socialist Fatherland. When at a meeting of the Student Congress Against War in 1934 Jane Addams made a speech denouncing all wars, Matthews, although a pacifist of long standing, took issue with her in accord with the Stalinist line of the period and reminded the students that there were differences between imperialistic wars and non-imperialistic wars. The congress, under the skilled control usual at such gatherings, voted its agreement with him. The Socialist Party, already vigilantly anti-Stalinist, suspended Matthews for his attendance on Communist needs, and he was dismissed from his post as executive secretary of the pacifist Fellowship of Reconciliation because he took the position that a pacifist should support the workers in a hypothetical class war.

When it came to fellow traveling, Matthews was a prodigy. But for a man who had spent so much of his life among ideologies, he had only a scant acquaintance with politics or economics. His fervor for pacifism and racial equality was certainly sincere, but they seem to have been fired by a need to be fervent about something—a common enough need, particularly among performing orators—when the heat of rural methodism could no longer warm him. But this fuel would run out too, and he would grow old tending the fires of anti-Communism. In 1935 he was warning that big business, government officials, and blind liberals were opening the way to fascism. Three years later he was warning that labor unions, government officials, and blind liberals were opening the way to Communism. Fi-

[2] This riot caused great indignation on the left. Such names as Edmund Wilson, John Dos Passos, Lionel Trilling, John Chamberlain, and Clifton Fadiman were signed to an open letter denouncing "the culpability and shame of the Communists" for their "disruption of working-class action in support of the Austrian worker."

nally, after an hour of renewed glory with Senator McCarthy's Investigation Subcommittee, he became a private consultant on Communism to Hearst, whom he had denounced to the cheers of his comrades in his earlier incarnations.

Replying, in his post-reformation autobiography, to the Socialists who accused him of having been an agent provocateur, he wrote: "Communists and Socialists have difficulty in understanding the obvious; they incline toward suspicions of conspiracy." Indeed they do, and Matthews was not free from the inclination. Again and again, in his charges of Communist control of this organization or that, he presented as proof positive a Communist boast that it was so controlled: "Nor is it necessary for us red-baiters to formulate accusations of Communist leadership; we need only quote the Communists themselves who had affirmed it over and over again." Because Earl Browder took credit at a Moscow meeting for the formation of the American League Against War and Fascism, which was to become the leading united front group of the thirties, that settled the matter for Matthews: "This could dispose, once and for all, of the question of whether or not the American League was launched by the Communist Party." He quoted Browder incessantly and without a hint of skepticism. "In the center, as the conscious moving and directive force of the united front movements in all its phases, stands the Communist Party," boasted Browder, and for Matthews this was a compelling item of proof.

In Matthews's time of grace, as in his period of sin, the columns of the *Daily Worker* were a prime source of truth, and would remain so for his successors. When he found, however, that the *Worker* had listed his name on a committee he had never heard of, or on a report he had never signed, he commented, "There is nothing extraordinary about Communists using the names of persons without their permission." He demonstrated convincingly how the front organizations inflated their membership figures; then he used the inflated figures as evidence of the national peril. He never appreciated the contradictions in which he was entangled, or the humor of them. He was a man of so little humor that he could allow himself to mention Shirley Temple in his testimony as having unwittingly served the interests of the Communist Party by sending greetings to the French Communist paper *Ce Soir* and then be outraged with Harold Ickes, Frances Perkins, and other antagonists who made fun of him for it.[3]

Not being anything of an ideologist, Matthews made few distinctions between the feuding elements of the radical left when he belonged to it, and forgot even those as soon as he departed. In 1934 he was reprimanded by the Socialists because "I believed wholeheartedly in the united front of all radical groups and accepted their invitations without regard to the bitter enmities which separated them." In 1938 his message was that the philosophy of every group on the left would lead equally and surely to a reaction which would bring on fascism. He accorded each of them, from the biggest front to the tiniest splinter, the same importance that each accorded itself. And just as every group was of immense consequence, so every member was either a conspirator or a dupe.

Despite all of his experience, Matthews had no perspective on the times that produced the fronts and small insight into the motives that drew people to them. If it ever occurred to him that there were differences between Heywood Broun and Reinhold Niebuhr, he never paused over them. As for the fronts he had served so faithfully, his error was not so much that he overestimated the power of the Communists within them, as liberals of the time protested, but that he overestimated the significance of the organizations themselves. They were, as Murray Kempton has observed, "structures of enormous pretension and pathetic foundation." They would not long survive.

In his confessions, *Odyssey of a Fellow Traveler*, Matthews explains that he left the radical cause when the scholarly Dr. Jekyll in his nature won the battle with the Marxist Mr. Hyde.

[3] Liberals, understandably but unjustly, would never let the Shirley Temple incident die. Ickes commented: "They've gone into Hollywood and there discovered a great red plot. They have found dangerous radicals there, led by little Shirley Temple. Imagine the great committee raiding her nursery and seizing her dolls as evidence." Madame Perkins said it was fortunate that Shirley was born an American citizen or Dies would have tried to get her deported.

This occurred in 1935. Some time before that glad triumph, Matthews had become an executive of Consumers Research, an organization dedicated to protecting the citizenry from hazardous, poisonous and shoddy goods foisted upon it by big business abetted by minions in advertising. As with all organizations that he touched during this period, C.R. attracted numbers of Communists, and when, in 1935, the organization's employees went on strike after three of their number had been fired for union activities, Matthews felt that he had observed Communist maneuverings long enough to recognize a play for power when he saw one. What he saw now were such prominent fellow travelers as Vito Marcantonio and Heywood Broun leading the Town Hall rally called to damn him.

Matthews was a vice president and member of the Board of Directors at Consumers Research, the most respectable position he had held in years, and he was even trying to get the Democratic nomination to run for the New Jersey Assembly; he took his stand against the strikers. "I cannot name the precise day on which I became a socialist or the precise day on which I ceased to be one," he wrote, but the second event seems to have occurred precisely at this time. The strike was bitter; Matthews refused arbitration because he was convinced the Communists would rig the results, and he held fast against an N.L.R.B. decision that would have reinstated the fired workers. The employees never returned to Consumers Research—which would soon begin leavening its analysis of merchandise with assessments of the Wagner Act ("the greatest piece of legislative chicane") and the Social Security Act ("the most dishonest piece of legislation ever devised")—but went off to form the rival and more successful Consumers Union. Now J. B. Matthews was no longer a suitable attraction for left-wing rallies. By 1936 he was out of radical politics, and in mid-1938, having studied and found that he was, after all, "a political and economic conservative," he enlisted with the armies of the right and was given a bodyguard by Chairman Dies. Soon he was employing his oratorical powers on behalf of organizations like American Patriots, Inc., and the League for Constitutional

Government, and having his work printed in Father Coughlin's *Social Justice*.

It was J. B. Matthews's curse to be unable to survive except in extravagant company. He looked at America and saw nothing between Earl Browder and Martin Dies. "Seven generations of American ancestry," he confessed, "were not enough despite even their Northern European derivation, to save me from heeding the appeals of a collectivism which is at war with every basic concept that has made America great." Nor were all those North European-derived generations able to give him any sense of the realities of American politics in the nineteen-twenties and -thirties. He knew that the Communists were conspirators—and in denying this many liberals would hurt their own cause. ("A twentieth century American 'liberal,'" Matthews observed only too accurately for the period, "would rather face the charge of slapping his grandmother than to be accused of 'red-baiting.'") But he also believed that the conspiracy was working; he shared the Communists' own severe delusions.

The Dies Committee prized Matthews for his delusions, for his simplifications, and, most especially, for his supply of names. His files, consisting mainly of mailing lists, letterheads —"To me the letterhead of a Communist front is a nugget"— and back copies of radical magazines, were the richest store of names Dies had yet happened on, of particular delight because they included so many individuals associated in one way or another with the Administration. The Dies Committee was from the outset on the track of the New Deal and all its works. That Mr. Roosevelt did not see this is unthinkable—there was only a perfunctory effort at concealment—but it would take a little time before the President correctly estimated the Committee's potential for political damage.

The attack on the W.P.A.'s Federal Theatre and Writers Project, anticipated by J. Parnell Thomas in July, struck the Administration where it was especially vulnerable. Subsidized theater was not a program that the Democrats could count on the nation to support with passion. Its record in some ways was impressive enough—more than a thousand productions in twenty-two states in a few years, most of them given free to school and community groups. The quality varied, but the enthusiasm was remarkably sustained. The W.P.A. shows ranged from hits like *Swing Mikado*, presented in New York at a $1.10 top, and *Run Little Children*, which ran for forty-two weeks in Chicago, to *Twelfth Night* and *Dr. Faustus*, from tawdry comedies to the Negro *Macbeth* to *Murder in the Cathedral*. The greater part of its audience had never seen live theater before; the W.P.A. brought *She Stoops to Conquer* to remote reaches of Florida and invaded the Dakotas. But among the W.P.A. projects, Federal Theatre was always something special, a somehow frivolous enterprise when so many were out of work and hungry. The fact that the performers were paid only $22.73 a week plus $3 a day living expenses on the road could hardly justify, in the popular mind, an endeavor that was so far removed from the urgent concerns of the country. Moreover, the notion of singling out for subsidy several thousand writers and actors strained the generous impulses of many Congressmen. Even if Federal Theatre had been operated in a condition of absolute ideological purity, it could not have held out against the anti-New Deal forces who were regrouping in 1938 and dreamed of destroying the W.P.A. altogether; if they could not have hung Federal Theatre on a charge of radicalism, they would have done it on a charge of using dirty words. But ideological purity was not one of Federal Theatre's strengths.

"Practically every play presented under the auspices of the Project," charged Thomas before any hearings had been held, "is sheer propaganda for Communism or the New Deal." The Project, he said, was dominated by Communists, working through the short-lived Workers Alliance,[4] a sort of labor union for people on relief that was put to such uses as helping Congressman Vito Marcantonio get elected. Although the testi-

---

[4] At one point a major Committee witness, in the course of listing Workers Alliance officials who were Communists, mentioned one "radical socialist" who was related to "an attorney for the Civil Liberties Union, prosecuting the case in Jersey City against Mayor Hague." Thomas thereupon interjected: "In other words, that is the second connection, then, that you have made between the Communists and the Federal Writers Project in New York City and the Jersey City Civil Liberties Union?"

mony before the Committee contained the usual proportion of oddities (There was the slightly anti-Semitic witness, later employed as a Committee investigator, who identified herself as secretary of an organization called the Committee of Relief Status Professional Theatrical Employees of the Federal Theatre Project, to which practically nobody belonged, and there was the small blond actress who disclosed that a colored man named Van Cleve had called her for a date and her superiors had not taken her complaints about it seriously), the plain fact was that Communists were exceedingly active in the W.P.A. Theatre and Writers Project; they did all they could to get their own people into it and to turn the whole enterprise into an agitprop machine.

Ellen S. Woodward, assistant administrator of the W.P.A., and Hallie Flanagan, director of the Theatre Project, were the first aggrieved persons accorded the privilege of testifying before the Dies Committee. They managed to maintain a fair degree of dignity in the face of severe heckling from Committee members, a contrast to the placid acceptance of the testimony of those who had come bearing charges.[5] But their cause was hopeless. Mrs. Flanagan, who had arrived at Federal Theatre after an outstanding career at Vassar, had had the bad luck to have co-authored a play which was described by the *New Masses* as the "best revolutionary play yet produced in America." She said that only ten per cent of the plays presented by Federal Theatre dealt with social and political problems, in the manner of *Triple-A Plowed Under, One Third of a Nation,* and *It Can't Happen Here,* but she must have known that such questions were not susceptible to measurement by percentages. How, after all, was one to measure the inspiration of the Brooklyn W.P.A. Theatre, where *Julius Caesar* was staged "to emphasize the dictator angle and show Brutus as the defender of the rights of freedom"? The revolutionary

[5] MRS. WOODWARD: You know, it seems to me the capitalistic press would certainly say so if we were doing that [spreading Communist propaganda].

THOMAS: What press did you say?
STARNES: She said the capitalistic press.
THOMAS: What do you mean by capitalistic press?
DIES: That is a Communistic term.

dream was the literary catalyst of the time, the great generative impulse of the depression. Little that came out of it would endure, but for young writers of that era, with no stake in a business society, infected still with the excitement of the Soviet experiment, there was small appeal in drawing room comedy or melodrama. They loaded their works with Social Seriousness and passed heavy, sometimes indigestible portions on to their audiences, thereby bringing about what persons with a casual interest in letters, such as Earl Browder, would believe was a renaissance of American drama and literature. The cultural tone they established, as Richard Rovere has observed, was "deplorable because it was metallic and strident. Communist culture was not aristocratic; it was cheap and vulgar and corny." The left-wing writers of the thirties sought their heroes among working stiffs and bloodied Negroes and their plots in ghettos and slums. Those with genuine talent shook off the ailment sooner than the others, who continued to use their social consciousness as a substitute for genius until the movement ran out on them and they settled down in their advertising agencies or Hollywood studios. Their spirit thrived for nearly a decade and naturally flourished in the W.P.A. Theatre, which brought together writers, performers, and directors with the least to lose.

In July 1939, a month after the Federal Theatre's brief existence had been ended by Congress, a critic proposed that a tombstone be put up, with the words KILLED BY THE COMMUNISTS OF NEW YORK. Certainly the Communists participated in the murder—although for men like Thomas, Dies, and Starnes, who judged plays by their titles and were never accused of having actually witnessed any of the productions that outraged them, virtually all theater of the time was subversive.[6] The

---

[6] During the Federal Theatre debate in the House on June 16, 1939, Everett Dirksen, then at the start of his own long histrionic career, entertained his colleagues with a list of plays, none of which he had seen, that the Federal Theatre had presented: "I have one here—*A New Deal for Mary*, which is a grand title. Then there is *The Mayor and the Manicure* and *Mother Goose Goes to Town*. Also, *A New Kind of Love*. I wonder what that can be. It smacks somewhat of the Soviet. Then there is *Up in Mabel's Room*. There is an intriguing title for you . . . Here is another, *Be Sure Your Sex Will Find You Out* . . . Then there is *Cheating Husbands*. That would be well for the front page of some Washington daily. Next we have *Companionate Maggie*, and this

Communists used Federal Theatre as a patronage tool in their little conspiracies as well as a weapon in their endless ideological wars. They were especially arrogant in the New York bastion, where they busied themselves in collecting for China, recruiting for Spain, and stirring things up in any way they could. When it came to art, the Communists were by no means un-American; they cared as little for it as the Committee did, as little as the nation did. With the pressure on after the rebuff of the 1938 elections, the Administration chucked Federal Theatre. Emmet Lavery, its program director, later blamed W.P.A. Administrator Harry Hopkins for not rising to the defense, for trying to prevent Mrs. Flanagan even from testifying before the Dies Committee in his concern over getting his W.P.A. appropriation through a resistant Congress. Corrupted from within, belabored from without, dependent on a public and an Administration with more important things on their minds, Federal Theatre never lived to realize its promise. Its career presents both a caution and an inspiration to those who are enthusiastic about federal subsidies to the arts, but for Thomas and Dies, its death was taken as a personal victory in a continuing vendetta.

Another assault on the Administration began very early in the Dies Committee hearings with the report of investigator Sullivan that "an outstanding official" of the Department of Labor was protecting Harry Bridges. Dies translated "outstanding official" to mean Secretary of Labor Frances Perkins herself, and in a series of public attacks—culminating in a gesture at impeachment instigated by Thomas in January 1939—charged her with refusing to enforce the law and deport the Australian-born unnaturalized Bridges, whom Dies certified to be a Communist.

great rhetorical and intriguing question, *Did Adam Sin?* Another one that they have dished up is *Go Easy, Mabel,* and still another that would strike the fancy of anybody—*Just a Love Nest.* Here is one that is surely adapted to the temple of the modern age, *Lend Me Your Husband.* And then this very happy title, *Love 'Em and Leave 'Em.* Also we have *Mary's Other Husband.* Now, if you want that kind of salacious tripe, very well, vote for it, but if anybody has an interest in decency on the stage, if anyone has an interest in real cultural values, you will not find it in this kind of junk . . ." A few minutes later, an amendment to save Federal Theatre was voted down, 56 to 192.

Many Labor Department employees at the time doubtless had kinder feelings toward Harry Bridges than toward Martin Dies, but even if they had shared the latter's distaste for the former, deportation would still have been something of a problem. There was no question that Bridges, then West Coast regional director of the C.I.O. and president of the International Longshoremen and Warehousemen's Union, was a tough labor leader; he had proved that in the 1934 West Coast maritime strike when he displaced the old waterfront bosses. (As the Dies Committee hearings began he was leading a warehouse strike that was threatening the West Coast with a severe pickle shortage.) Nor was there much question that, like numbers of other C.I.O. officials of the period, he had only the friendliest feelings for Communists; if anything his feelings were friendlier than most. It was a large question, however, whether anyone could prove that he was a member of the Communist Party. Moreover, even if an old Party card of his had been unearthed, the Department of Labor would have faced difficulties in evicting him. As Madame Perkins repeatedly explained through the latter part of 1938, the U.S. Court of Appeals had recently ruled that "Membership in the Communist Party is not ground for deportation." The Labor Department had suspended proceedings in the Bridges affair while this ruling, made in the case of a man named Strecker, was being appealed before the U.S. Supreme Court. Strecker had actually admitted past Party membership, and so the case against him was that much stronger than the one against Bridges. Strecker would finally win his case when the Supreme Court ruled that an individual could not be deported because he had at some time in the past belonged to the Communist Party, but nothing could persuade Dies that there was not a high-level conspiracy afoot to keep Harry Bridges safe and well in this country.

The Bridges case occupied our courts for years. James M. Landis, liberal dean of the Harvard Law School, who was delegated to study the case, ruled in 1939 that on the basis of the evidence against Bridges, he was not a Communist, but J. Edgar Hoover reported that he was, and periodically the controversial union organizer found himself on the verge of being shipped back to Australia by the Justice Department—under continual pressure from Congress—only to be rescued in the nick by a higher power, like the girl in the Saturday serials. Finally, in 1945, the Supreme Court overturned his deportation order for once and all. "Seldom, if ever, in the history of this nation," wrote Justice Murphy in a concurring opinion that owed less perhaps to a judicial mind than to a generous heart, "has there been such a concentrated and relentless crusade to deport an individual because he dared to exercise the freedom that belongs to him as a human being and that is guaranteed to him by the Constitution."

Sorties such as those against Frances Perkins and the W.P.A. were annoying to the Administration but bearable. The elections of 1938, however, gave Dies an opportunity to show that he could be a severe threat to New Deal candidates involved in close races. California, Minnesota, and Michigan were the three states that enjoyed the Committee's attention that fall. No incident in its history demonstrates more clearly the Texan's aims or the methods he was prepared to use to achieve them.

From California in the latter part of October came Harper Knowles, described as chairman of that state's American Legion Radical Research Committee, and Ray E. Nimmo, a Los Angeles attorney, to testify in duet, first, that Frances Perkins was guilty of "gross malfeasance of office" for "coddling" Harry Bridges, and, climactically, that the Democratic candidates for governor, lieutenant governor, and senator (Culbert Olson, Ellis Patterson, and Sheridan Downey, respectively) were in the pockets of the Communist Party. Knowles was at once disowned by the commander of the State Legion Department and was revealed to be on leave as secretary of the Associated Farmers, a West Coast organization dedicated to preventing the spread of unionism and headed by the Republican candidate for the Senate. (Knowles showed his colors when he complained that a wage of three dollars a day for farm workers would bankrupt California's fruit growers and packers. When he appeared before Dean Landis in connection with the investigation of the Bridges case the following year, Landis found him to be "neither candid nor forthright.")

From Minnesota came seven persons, for whom the chairman had cordially supplied invitations in the form of blank subpoenas issued via a former Republican mayor of St. Paul. They reported that the Farmer-Labor Party had been taken over by Communists and that Governor Elmer A. Benson had not repudiated an endorsement by Earl Browder in his election campaign against young Harold Stassen, that he had led a New York City parade of the American League for Peace and Democracy in August 1937, and that he had allowed himself to be photographed standing next to a C.P. official. "Where Communism goes, that's where we will go," proclaimed Dies in defense of his election-time hearings, which he conducted without the participation of most members of his Committee, who were out campaigning. "We're not going to let questions of political expedience stop us from getting at the facts."

And from Michigan, where Governor Frank Murphy was caught up in an exceedingly hard election fight, came a Republican Circuit Court judge, Paul V. Gadola, and a former city manager of Flint, John M. Barringer, to accuse the governor of a "treasonable attitude" in condoning Communist-led sit-down strikes against General Motors in 1937.

The Michigan case was the critical one. Frank Murphy, a particular friend of the President, was campaigning under two serious handicaps: he was a Catholic and his term as governor had been shaken by the most dramatic labor conflict in the country's history. When he came to office in January 1937, C.I.O. organizers in the automobile industry had grown bold enough and desperate enough to begin taking over the plants. From November 1936 to July 1937 there were 147 sit-down strikes in Detroit, and Murphy found himself between union militants, including Communists and their allies like the Reuther brothers, and men of vigilante disposition, such as Barringer and his supporters in the American Legion. If Murphy had been a stronger personality, blood would probably have run in Detroit, and in that sense his weakness was a blessing to the nation. Moreover, he had sympathy for the strikers; when they took over the Fisher body plants in Flint and held them for several weeks, he resisted pressure to send in the

National Guard, which had been assembled in the city to dis-lodge them. In this he had the support of the White House. On being informed that the governor desired an adjournment of hearings on a writ to evacuate the two seized plants, Judge Gadola, no friend of the C.I.O. or the New Deal, replied: "To hell with the governor!" and issued the writ anyway. Where-upon Murphy prevented the sheriff from executing it. These actions won him the support of the Communist Party in his 1938 campaign.

Murphy's plausible defense was that "a civil war was immi-nent in Flint in February of 1937" and that any attempt to eject the workers would have provoked a riot. Less plausible was his claim to have honored the order of the court. But his strongest point was that in the end a quarter of a million men went back to their jobs and "not a single human life had been lost, not a liberty had been suppressed, even though we had passed through the most terrifying industrial strike in history." A few years later, according to Dies, Frank Murphy, then a Supreme Court Justice, apologized to him in private for his behavior as governor and urged Dies to carry on his work and get the Communists out of government. "Mr. Dies," he is sup-posed to have said, "I know you have no reason to like or respect me, but I was under terrific pressure from the President and many of my political friends, and I let them pressure me against my better instincts." Whatever the Justice's remorse in 1940, what his political enemies could not forgive in 1938 was that the peaceful settlement which he hailed signaled the tri-umph of the C.I.O. in the automobile industry.

The attack on Murphy wounded Mr. Roosevelt much more deeply than the attacks on Madame Perkins or Federal Theatre. He had already remonstrated privately with Dies for giving John Frey a platform upon which to campaign against the New Deal's friends in the C.I.O., and now he vented his pain by issuing the first formal criticism of a committee of Congress ever made by a President. In a lengthy statement, he called the hearings "a flagrantly unfair and un-American attempt to in-fluence an election" and warmly defended Murphy. He antici-pated the sensitivities of future administrations by asking that the Committee "abandon the practice of merely providing a forum for those who for political purposes, or otherwise, seek headlines which they could not otherwise attain." And he concluded, somewhat unfortunately, by comparing Murphy's achievement in the Detroit strikes to the recent agreement at Munich: "People may properly differ as to the results of such negotiations but the fact remains that bloodshed was averted." Representatives Healey and Dempsey, themselves busy campaigning in their home districts, wired Dies asking for a recess in the hearings until after the election. The chairman, whose victory in the Texas primaries weeks earlier saved him the bother of campaigning in October, spiritedly rebuked both his colleagues and the President and pledged in words that would serve him as a peroration for years to come that "I wish to make it plain that I shall continue to do my duty undeterred and unafraid."

Frank Murphy's defeat in Michigan in 1938 was accounted by the Administration as the most serious loss in a year of Democratic losses. The Republicans gained eighty seats in the House and eight in the Senate and deposed eleven Democratic governors. For Dies, that amounted to a famous victory. The New Deal won in California but lost in Minnesota; as for Michigan, the results there would stand as one of the Congressman's proudest accomplishments. The memory of the sit-down strike, freshly awakened by the Committee hearings a few weeks before the election, hurt Murphy badly. His plurality in Flint, center of much of the strife, dropped from 13,000 in 1936 to 1,396 in 1938, while the incumbent sheriff, bitterly opposed by the auto workers, led all candidates.

But the election of 1938 represented more than a reaction to the sit-down strikes, frightening as they were. The nation had absorbed many changes, and deep ones, in the foregoing six years, and had given the New Deal its enthusiastic mandate for three elections in a row; now the time had come to take stock. Insofar as there had been a radical temper in America in the first half of the decade, by 1938 it was pretty well spent. The New Deal had not turned the corner to prosperity, but it had brought the Depression under control, and now there was time for native conservatism, particularly in the South and the Midwest, to catch its breath and reassert itself. Arthur Krock could rejoice:

> As the final returns are counted the New Deal has been halted; the Republican Party is large enough for effective opposition; the moderate Democrats in Congress can guide legislation . . . the sit-down strike and the Democratic-C.I.O. alliance have been emphatically rebuked; the country is back on a two-party system . . .

Even if the Dies Committee had never existed, 1938 would have been a dark year for the New Deal, but it was Martin Dies's good luck to be part of, to speak for, a significant national feeling. "When Roosevelt was elected he had no more enthusiastic and sincere advocate than myself," Dies wrote in 1963. That was something of an overstatement, but certainly he was no enemy to the Administration during his first terms in Congress. He took pride in the fact that F.D.R. gave orders to admit him to the Presidential office by a side door. The only reference to the young Texan in the initial volume of Harold Ickes's diaries had to do with his appearance among a group of Congressmen "in full sympathy" with the Public Works Administration. Ickes would find no kinder word for him thereafter than "ass," "moron" and "fascist."

In April 1936—months after F.D.R.'s discernible move to the left—Dies was calling on the country to "keep in the White House that great leader of the plain people, the Jefferson and Jackson of the twentieth century, our present and future president, Franklin D. Roosevelt." A year later, by which time Southerners had become painfully aware that their concept of the Democratic Party was different from that of their nominal allies in Northern cities and in the industrial unions, and the President's courtpacking plan had resulted in a stalemated session of Congress, Dies was still able to josh with F.D.R. at a June "harmony outing" on the shores of Chesapeake Bay. In his self-created role of Supreme Shouter, Dies inducted F.D.R. into the "Demagogue Club" after pledging him never to do anything that would injure his chances of election, to appropriate generously but not to tax and never to be consistent. "I wish to caution you," intoned the Supreme Shouter, "upon penalty of being ejected from the Club, not to embarrass the Congress with any more legislation of a controversial nature." It was great fun, but weak salve for the wound in the Democratic Party. To Martin Dies, even before he became a specialist on Communism, the people who descended upon Washington with the New Deal seemed an alien bunch—all those "idealists, dreamers, politicians, professional 'do-gooders' and just plain job-hunters." In Dies's home district, there were no big cities, not many college graduates and hardly any foreign-born voters. The New Deal harbored big-city types, alumni of Eastern colleges, second-generation Americans, Jews, persons who would support the C.I.O.'s organizing drives of oil refinery workers in Texas and hold unsettling ideas about the condition of the Negro. The South had not turned Democratic for them.

If Dies needed further confirmation that he was on the right track after the November elections, it came in December in the form of a Gallup Poll. Of the three out of five voters who had heard of the Committee, 74 per cent were in favor of continuing the investigations. Republicans were substantially more in favor than Democrats, and the investigations had left the best impression in the Midwest and the South. "He is publicity mad," wrote Harold Ickes, "and the unfortunate Gallup Poll will make him worse than ever." Public support for Dies ranged from the wholehearted embrace of the far right to the friendly but slightly exasperated acceptance of the center. The editors of *Colliers*, in a good example of a popular position, wrote:

> Not that Dies runs a top-notch show, nor is he the ideal man for the job. Obviously he is not impartial. Anything but. Most of the witnesses he has produced to date have been funny-looking phonies whom, we surmise, he dug up under wet stones, and most of their yarns about Fascist and Communist activities in this country have been fantastic. Seemingly, the man has no judgment about such things, no sense of perspective, no instinct for effective showmanship.

Thereupon, *Colliers* asked that he be given more money for the new year. Whatever critics thought of his showmanship,

Dies had produced the outstanding political show of 1938, and he was almost as annoyed by the quibblings of the conservative press as by the outright damnation of the liberals.

The election results and the Gallup Poll, meat for the Dies Committee, was food for thought for New Dealers. Ickes confided to his diary in December that the Cabinet agreed that Dies was becoming "a hair shirt for the Administration . . . because apparently his chief object in life is to smear the Administration, incidental of course to getting publicity for himself"—but the Cabinet was divided over tactics. Ickes, like Madame Perkins and W.P.A. Administrator Harry Hopkins, served Dies as a major target, and so wanted to make an all-out fight of it. When Dies placed him in the company of Browder and Stalin as a "purveyor of class hatred," Ickes retaliated by telling a press conference that Dies was "the outstanding zany in our political history."[7] Shortly before he was due to make a speech to a Washington convention of the American League for Peace and Democracy entitled, "Playing with Loaded Dies," Ickes received a message from Roosevelt, via White House Press Secretary Steve Early, telling him "for God's sake not to do it," lest it antagonize Congress. Across the Cabinet table from the explosive Secretary of the Interior sat Vice President Garner, a patron of Dies, and Postmaster General Farley, the ultimate politician, who proposed that Harry Bridges be deported for the good of the Democratic Party.

The President, informed by Congressmen returning to the capital for the new session that sentiment back home made it impossible to vote against continuance of the Committee, took a middle course. He directed Frank Murphy, his newly appointed Attorney General, to have agents of the Department of Justice investigate all charges of Communist activity raised

[7] In his autobiography written when the Dies Committee was still in flower, Ickes gave free play to his feelings for the chairman as well as to his feeling for invective: "For his unmitigated gall, for his long-winded yammerings that seemingly go 'babbling' on forever, and for the strange power that he appears to have over Congress, I christen him 'Bubble Dancer' Dies who cavorts lumberingly on the Congressional stage with nothing but a toy balloon with which to hide his intellectual nudity. To my mind, the most contemptible human being in public life is the one who will recklessly smear another's character and then wrap himself tightly in his Congressional immunity."

by the Dies Committee. His hope was that some of the Committee's funds and functions might thereby be diverted to the executive branch. When in January, F.D.R. denied reappointment on the National Labor Relations Board to Donald W. Smith, a member who had been criticized by the A.F. of L. and by Dies for giving undue aid and comfort to the C.I.O., it was interpreted as a further gesture of conciliation. But Dies was too far gone in triumph to be responsive to conciliation. The first report of his Committee, issued January 3, 1939, led off with a criticism of the Administration for its lack of co-operation. It attacked the Federal Theatre and Writers Project, the National Labor Relations Board, Frank Murphy's behavior during the sit-down strikes, and the Department of Labor's indulgence of Harry Bridges. Along with the report Dies brought in a resolution asking for $150,000 and a two-year extension. A few weeks later, Thomas offered a motion of impeachment against Secretary Perkins and two other Labor Department officials for failing to rid the land of Bridges. The proposal came to nothing, but it put the Administration on notice that the Committee's most aggressive members were feeling their political muscle. In February the House, responding to mail in support of the Committee, voted 344 to 35 to give Dies $100,000 for his work in 1939—"a complete falling down of the so-called Democratic leadership of the House," complained Ickes somewhat unjustly. The Administration's faithful Sam Rayburn was closer to the mark when he said: "Martin Dies could beat me right now in my own district."

Representative Rayburn and Speaker Bankhead were sent by Roosevelt to bring the light to Dies early in 1939. They explained, in case it had escaped his notice, that his accusations against Cabinet members were hurtful to the Democratic Party. Bankhead did not exercise himself over this mission, but relations between the fellow Texans, Rayburn and Dies, deteriorated from this time. When Dies returned to Washington in 1953 for his second tour of Congressional duty, Rayburn, that "Democrat without any prefixes or suffixes," would barely speak to him. The major result of the January 1939 negotiations was that Jerry Voorhis, a young, well-to-do liberal hope from California, was named to replace Representative Mosier, defeated in the Ohio primaries to the glee of that state's C.I.O. A Yale Phi Beta Kappa, Voorhis had been in Congress since 1936 and was one of the small group who voted against continuation of the Dies Committee in 1939. Rhea Whitley, a thirty-five-year-old former F.B.I. agent who had reputedly helped get John Dillinger, became Committee counsel, and J. B. Matthews was given the job of chief investigator.

Whereas the Administration dealt with the Dies Committee as an unfortunate incident in the political game, a nuisance on the way to becoming a threat, the liberal community was unable to deal with it at all, except through jeremiads. As the nineteen-thirties drew to a close, the nation's liberals were still going through their great crisis of conscience with regard to Communism, and the Dies investigation, with all of the attendant publicity, was aggravating their condition. Revolution in Russia, depression in America, fascism in Italy and Germany, the ruin of the beginnings of democracy in Spain—these events had drawn America's liberals into alliance with the Communists, and it would not be easy for many to disengage themselves despite purges in Moscow and machinations in New York. They saw that the attack by Dies was aimed as much at them as at the Communist Party and they sprang to the barricades. Had they been less committed to the united front, less bemused by the Soviet experiment, or had Dies and Thomas been somewhat less disposed to random attacks, the liberals might have been spared some heartache. As it was, the major organs of our liberal intelligentsia responded to Dies with cries of "Fascist!" and statements of principle that give off a sickly glow in the unsentimental light of history.

"When the Communists come to the aid of what we regard as a worthy cause," wrote the editors of *The New Republic* in June of 1938, "we propose to welcome their help as we would that of anyone else. If they advocate what we consider wrong, we shall attack them as we would anyone else." And a few months after John Frey's testimony they assured their readers and themselves that if John L. Lewis and Sidney Hillman countenanced "a few" Communists, "it is because the persons in question are able and conscientious trade-unionists who do not allow party politics to interfere with their jobs." Paul Y. Anderson, the newspaperman who covered the Dies Committee for *The Nation,* headed his first dispatch: FASCISM HITS WASHINGTON. An editorial in that issue declared:

> It is hardly news that Communists participate, with varying degrees of influence in a host of left organizations, with whose aims their own party politics coincide. Why shouldn't they? And why should the fact of their participation make such movements untouchable for other anti-fascists inside the government or outside?

The most amiable assessment of our domestic Communists was made early in 1939 by a group of prominent lawyers who petitioned the House of Representatives to abolish the Dies Committee. Having examined the Party, the lawyers found no proof of its domination by Moscow. "A reasonable construction of language," they reported, "compels the conclusion that the members of the Communist Party of the U.S.A. have the right, power and authority to make their own decisions precisely as members of any other American organization." Furthermore, there was nothing to show that the Party had failed to work in the "traditions of Jefferson, Paine, Jackson and Lincoln." When a group of liberals, led by John Dewey and Sidney Hook, formed the Committee for Cultural Freedom in 1939, and issued a manifesto calling for the "clearest differentiation from Stalinism together with all its fronts, stooges and innocents," Freda Kirchwey, editor and publisher of *The Nation,* responded:

> To advocate a policy of "clearest differentiation" on the left is a counsel of disruption. With all their faults, the Communists perform necessary functions in the confused struggle of our time. They have helped to build up and to run a string of organizations known as "fronts" by their opponents—which clearly serve the cause not of "totalitarian doctrine" but of a more workable democracy. And the value of these organizations lies largely in the energy and discipline and zeal of their Communist elements.

Martin Dies held no illusions about the possibilities of cooperating with the Communists for any but Communist goals.

But such wisdom came easier to him than to those who shared many of those goals. "In instance after instance," as *The New Republic*'s editors kept reminding themselves, "the Communists have fought and are fighting for civil liberties, for union principles, for social legislation." Representative Dies, whose passions did not include civil liberties, union principles, or social legislation, was above temptation. He detested the Reds not in spite of their devotion to such causes but on account of them. Nineteen thirty-nine, the year of the outbreak of war in Europe and of the Hitler-Stalin pact, was traumatic for the American liberal's attachment to Soviet Communism. Some non-Communists learned early; many learned late; a few will never learn. But in matters of the heart, there is always the question of who calls forth the greater sympathy—those who have been led up blind alleys by their infatuations, or those who never fell in love at all.

3

★ ★ ★ ★ ★

1939: Disarray on the Left

IT WAS a running source of irritation to liberals for the whole life of the Dies Committee that its chairman was more readily aroused by seditionists of the left than by those of the right. While the Nazis marched in Europe, at home Bundists rallied, Christian Fronters conspired, anti-Semites howled on street corners—and Dies was scarcely moved. Every whisper on the left, however, set his blood racing. He was prone to declarations like "We are going to investigate and expose the Nazi and fascist movements in this country as thoroughly as we do the Communist movement." But his heart wasn't in it.

Yet in May 1939 the Dies Committee suddenly announced that it was investigating a plot that involved friends of fascism. It also involved Jews. That much could be gathered from the first announcements, but not much more than that. The announcements were accorded the generous newspaper attention to which Dies was by now accustomed, but in this case the publicity received was a function of the secrecy invested. It was all very secret. Nameless and closely guarded witnesses, hidden one from the other, were led to the Committee room along devious routes. The members of the Committee had pledged themselves to secrecy. It was reported that Dies had requested and received special permission from the Messrs. Rayburn and Bankhead to undertake this special investigation. A letter was made public from George Van Horn Moseley, a retired major general in the U.S. army, to a captain in the army reserve; it contained the stimulating sentences, "If the Jews bump me off, be sure to see that they get the credit for it from coast to coast. It will help our cause." On the basis of the first reports out of Washington, a careful newspaper reader could be sure only that the Committee was about to investigate either a Jewish plot or a plot against the Jews.

It turned out to be a little of both. As Dudley Pierrepont Gilbert, a Manhattan socialite, dilettante anti-Semite, and organizer of American Nationalists, Inc., explained it—a waiter at New York's Harmonie Club, organized by and for well-to-do Jews of the city, had been conveying to him (Gilbert) reports of plottings on which he (the waiter) had eavesdropped. Gilbert forwarded the eavesdroppings to James Erwin Campbell, an army reserve captain in Kentucky, who mimeographed them and distributed them to American Legion posts. It was a Legion official in the South who brought them to the Committee's attention. Most of the reports were never made public by Dies because they were so viciously anti-Semitic, but the gist was that rich Red Jews were planning to take over the government in August. With the help of a force of 150,000 mercenaries from Spain and elsewhere, who were being smuggled into this country through Mexico, they were going to seize eight of the army's eleven arsenals. Simultaneously, with their tentacles among both capitalists and the proletariat, the Jews were going to depress the value of stocks and bonds and foment strikes.

Headline writers tended to play the story nearly straight. New York *Post*: 'RED ARMY PLOT' TO SEIZE GOVERNMENT IS BARED. Baltimore *Sun*: FANTASTIC PLOT TO SEIZE NATION BARED BY DIES. New York *Daily News*: 'RED ARMY PLOT' TO TAKE OVER NATION STIRS U.S. PROBERS. St. Louis *Star Times*: DIES HEARS OF 'M-DAY' PLOT TO SEIZE U.S. An exception was Hearst's New York *Journal-American*, which reported: ANTI-SEMITIC PLOT EXPOSED BY DIES. The *Journal-American*, it developed, had gotten the story right. Two main figures called before the Committee were General Moseley and George E. Deatherage, national commander of the Knights of the White Camelia. Deatherage, who described himself as a construction engineer whereas reporters referred to him as a house painter, had a plan to save the nation from the Jewish plot and had selected General Moseley, who combined an estimable military record with open disgust for the New Deal, to mount the white horse. Lacking the genteel inspiration of a Cliveden, such was the most elegant strategy that America's fascists could work out.

At the first reports that the Jewish plot was being investigated, Deatherage wired Dies "a great big kiss" from "all the boys," but by the time he came before the Committee he had lost his amiability. His appearance, behind a small mustache and dark glasses, befitted his sinister name, and he was truculent from the start. When Dies told him not to volunteer information, he said "I don't know about that"—and stood up. "You sit down," ordered Dies. "You come over here and make me sit down," returned Deatherage. He threatened to "pop" a man in the audience who he believed was "sneering and smiling" at him. As he explained later, he was "of a rather nervous disposition." Most of the Knight's testimony concerned his efforts to mobilize the anti-Semites of the country against the Jewish international bankers and Communists who were conspiring to take things over. Dies was put in the unaccustomed position of defending the President and Mrs. Roosevelt from slanders, as he exhorted Deatherage to mend his ways. "All American citizens have rights," the chairman reminded the witness. "That is right," Deatherage countered, "except I am bigoted enough to believe in white supremacy in the South." "With that exception," Dies allowed, "you agree with the statement?" "Yes," said Deatherage.

General Moseley, who had retired as commander of the army's Fourth Corps in September 1938, after nearly forty years of service in the Philippines, in Mexico, with the A.E.F. in France, and against Depression mobs or what were imagined to be mobs in this country, preceded his appearance before the Committee with a call to the American people "to save our republic now before it is too late." Secretary of the Army Woodring attributed Moseley's politics to pique over not being named army chief of staff, but his anti-Semitism seems to have been in earnest. He liked the idea of sterilizing all refugees disembarking on these shores. A speech he made in Springfield, Illinois, a few weeks before being summoned to Washington gives a fair example of his approach to the Jewish problem:

> The problem of the Jew in America must be studied and solved without further delay. We cannot expect to escape the experience of every other nation in the world which has been faced with the very same problem. Jewish refugees from abroad are entering this country in large numbers, lawfully and unlawfully, from those parts of the world where anti-Semitism is growing. That same feeling is growing rapidly in America from coast to coast. The problem should be recognized before further tragedy overtakes the Jews who live in the United States of America . . . Over two thousand years of recorded history shows very clearly that those traits which have made the Jew unwelcome every place he has been domiciled cannot be bred out.

Moseley was attended in the hearing room by a loyal cadre, including freshman Representative Thorkelson of Montana, who had just been described by William Dudley Pelley, the nation's leading Jew-baiter, as a "new statesman rearing high above the miasma of skulduggery," and by an aide who rushed forward to snatch a cup of drinking water from the general's reach and refill it from the cooler in the corner of the room in order to save him from being poisoned. Voorhis, Healey, and Dempsey enjoyed getting the general to say silly things, and his performance together with that of Deatherage and their associates exposed our native fascists as a ragtag bunch whose delusion it was that if they acted as mad as Adolf Hitler they too might become führers or friends of führers.

After its muddled beginning, the Committee handled the case with surprising efficiency, but there was still dissatisfaction on the left. It was charged that Dies had not followed through on this investigation, though it was difficult to see what could have been gained by giving the clownish head of the White Camelias further opportunity for display. A major proposition of the Popular Front period—the years between 1935 and 1939 when Moscow found it beneficial to cooperate with mere liberals—was that It Could Happen Here—indeed that It Was Happening. Those under its spell belittled any suggestion that the U.S. followers of Stalin were not devoted to democracy, but were insistent on the black menace of fascism. Communists were profligate with the word "fascist"—the Party press would have been in serious trouble for copy without it—and many non-Communists joined them in hurling it at Martin Dies. Yet despite their unbending antagonism, even these critics could find little to complain of in the opening weeks of the Committee hearings, which resumed in mid-August, when Dies returned to Washington after one of the lengthy illnesses that would keep him at home in Texas during a good part of his tenure as Congressman.

First in the witness chair was Fritz Kuhn, another aspiring führer. Under Rhea Whitley's questioning, a good deal of information was brought out on the Bund's structure, its relations with like-minded groups, its ties to Hitler's Germany, and its free and easy financing, for which Kuhn would quite soon be sent to jail. The Bund president had been arrested a few weeks before for drunkenness, profanity, and grand larceny; the temperature in Washington was in the nineties; and he was in an atrocious humor. The high point of his appearance occurred in an exchange with Representative Starnes, who with cotton-patch subtlety, was attempting to refute Kuhn's contention that the Bund was a thoroughly patriotic American institution, with minimal ties to the old country.

STARNES: Is not Mr. Hitler against the Communists?

KUHN: Aren't you against the Communists?

STARNES: Is not Mr. Hitler anti-Semitic?

KUHN: Aren't you anti-Semitic?

STARNES: I am asking you the question. Is not Mr. Hitler anti-Semitic?

KUHN: I suppose so, from what I hear.

STARNES: Has he not driven hundreds of thousands of those unfortunate people out of the country?

KUHN: Have not the Communists driven hundreds of thousands of people out of Russia?

STARNES: I am asking you the question with reference to the treatment of Jews in Germany.

KUHN: That is up to Mr. Hitler, not to me. What do I have to do with Mr. Hitler? Subpoena Mr. Hitler here.

STARNES: You want to establish a party with the same position in this country, do you not?

KUHN (*banging on the table*): That is absolutely a lie!

STARNES: Don't you call me a liar!

Whereupon Representative Starnes leaped up and plunged through a line of photographers toward Kuhn. Two Capitol policemen intervened; the chairman said, "Sit down, Joe"; and the hearings proceeded.

Other witnesses were produced who told of the Bund's pro-Nazi indoctrination courses, and a nineteen-year-old former Bundist maiden provided a peek into the sexual play at Bund camps. When Kuhn was brought back a few weeks later, after the Wehrmacht had overrun Poland, he was free on bail of $50,000, having been indicted for misusing Bund funds; now he was accompanied by two lawyers and was still in bad humor. His career was sinking fast.

The second star witness of mid-summer 1939 was Earl Browder, the Kansas-born secretary of the U.S. Communist Party, who was to enjoy the paeans of his comrades until 1945, when he would be abruptly toppled by order of the Kremlin and made fit subject for vilification, an early fatality of the cold war. But in 1939 he was still the beloved leader.

On August 24 the U.S.S.R. signed its non-aggression pact with Germany. As August Raymond Ogden, that diligent chronicler of the Dies Committee, observes, the pact was a "godsend" to the Committee and would keep it on the front pages despite competition from the outbreak of World War II and a special emergency session of Congress. The summer's hearings had been rambling along with stray anti-Semites, persons of tiny followings and of no consequence in themselves, who had the pleasure of explaining in the hearing of newspapermen why they detested Jews. Now the domestic Communist Party, trying clumsily to get into a different pair of ideological trousers, stood exposed as a total creature of Moscow. Just a few weeks before, Browder had been fiercely condemning the speculation of "reactionaries" that the U.S.S.R. might join hands with Hitler: "There is as much chance of agreement," he told an audience in Charlottesville, Virginia, in July, "as of Earl Browder being elected president of the Chamber of Commerce." He was at the Committee's mercy.

There were satisfactions for everyone at the hearings. Browder's admission that he had traveled on false passports, which would send him to prison from 1940 to 1942, the interval between the end of the Popular Front and the start of the U.S.–Soviet alliance, served Dies as a major accomplishment for the rest of his career. Browder's pioneering refusal to respond to questions about his forgery on the grounds of possible self-incrimination would light the way for Communists yet unsung. Matthews, ever in search not of information but of confirmation and equipped with his endless lists of names, drew from Browder a definition of a Communist "transmission belt" —"a technical term referring to the tactics whereby the Communists establish their relations with the masses of the people"—broad enough to be applied as anyone cared to apply it. Thomas observed that Mrs. Roosevelt and Secretaries Ickes and Wallace had addressed or sent greetings to a number of the organizations that fitted Browder's definition, and concluded: "It seems as though the New Deal was hand in glove with the Communist Party." He took offense when Representative Dempsey called his statement "a cheap political speech." Starnes, too, participated in his manner. "The greatest authorities on the theory of Communism are Marx, Engels, Lenin and Stalin," said Browder. "Who was the second?" interjected Starnes. "I did not get the second name." A few minutes later Starnes found himself arguing that there had been no killing in the American Revolution, unlike in the Russian Revolution.

Despite such passages, this was one of the Committee's better hearings. Whitley's conduct of the examination, except for a moment when he somehow got off on the activities of some of Browder's relatives in Russia, was straightforward and not argumentative. In contrast to Matthews, he was not bent on scoring points. Browder made a pleasant witness. There were the necessary evasions and lies, but he was considerably more responsive than Kuhn. The most revealing parts of his testimony, on his Party's *volte face* after the Nazi-Soviet pact, came in colloquies with Voorhis, assisted by Representative Joseph E. Casey of Massachusetts, a liberal who had recently been named to the Committee to replace Healey. Browder conceded that there had never been a fundamental disagreement between the U.S. Party and the Communist International; he defended the outlawing of political parties in the Soviet Union; he explained to the bewildered Starnes that the Trotskyites, those scoundrels, had no purpose in life other than to wreck the work of virtuous Communists—they are "all bad," he said; he stated with no glint of humor that "The *Daily Worker* is completely free to develop and conduct the paper in any way in which the editorial staff in America desires . . ." And he praised the German-Soviet nonaggression pact as a "very big concession by Hitler" which was entirely in the interests of America because it broke up the Axis, relieved the Japanese pressure on American interests in the Far East, and "dissolved the threat to the Monroe Doctrine" by Spain. The pact, he affirmed, "was an act of friendship between these [German and Russian] peoples and in no way an alliance between governments."

Browder was living proof of all that old-time radicals had been saying about the Stalinists for years. Long before this demonstration, an astute former Communist, J.B.S. Hardman, wrote that the Communist Party went on the rocks in America "because of the inability of its leadership to read developments and trends in American reality and to measure up to the possibilities of the situation." He continued:

> There undoubtedly is room in the United States for a realistically aggressive labor movement, but obviously such a movement will not thrive on a foundation of canonized truths and canned reasoning, and under the tutelage of political puppets manipulated from a distance of seven thousand miles.

The explanations by Party functionaries of their startling twists of policy had been a source of hilarity to ex-Communist radicals like Hardman for years; now a wider audience could enjoy them. The Soviet Union, explained Browder, "in the interest of stopping this whole drifting into war, and this conspiracy of hiding the realities of the situation had to demonstrate before the world that it was not bound by any compact to go to war."

Even those who were most impatient with Chamberlain and Daladier for balking at an agreement with the U.S.S.R. would be struck by the instantaneousness and thoroughness of the American Party's embrace of Stalin's tactics. Alfred Kazin recalls in his autobiography that he followed the *Daily Worker* diligently during this period "with savage joy at its confusion as those who had been eloquent about the Oakies, the unemployed, the victims of fascism now tried to explain the secret contribution that the noble Stalin, the great Stalin, the all-wise and far-seeing Stalin, had made to the cause of world peace." For a Party member to take issue with the Hitler-Stalin pact, explained Browder, "would be a demonstration of a most serious lack of understanding of politics, and a serious disregard of the national interests of America which have been helped by the pact."[1] Soon the Communists and the more adjustable fellow travelers would be charging F.D.R. with using the Dies Committee to whip up war hysteria.

Other Communist officials and former officials were called—notably Benjamin Gitlow, twice the Communist candidate for vice president, who broke in 1929 after his faction was rebuffed by Stalin and was now setting out on the path of professional anti-Communism walked by J. B. Matthews. Gitlow provided interesting information on Party operations and finances in the twenties, filling in some of the gaps left by Browder's selective recollections; Walter G. Krivitsky, a former general in Soviet

[1] One exchange with Voorhis made the C.P.'s position as clear as it would ever be.

VOORHIS: Have you any doubt as to who the aggressor is?
BROWDER: I have no real doubt.
VOORHIS: And, as you expressed previously, you said the Soviet Union was against aggressor nations?
BROWDER: Yes.
VOORHIS: And you think this pact with Germany, an aggressor nation as you determine it, is being against the aggressor?
BROWDER: Yes.
VOORHIS: It is consistent with their being against it, to make a pact of non-aggression?
BROWDER: Absolutely.

military intelligence who had fled the purges in 1937[2] and was to die in New York under mysterious circumstances in 1941, told of the world-wide activities of the O.G.P.U.; but Committee members had their most fun in trying to get current C.P. officials to say whether they would fight for this country in a hypothetical war against Russia.

William Z. Foster, who owed his place as the Party's national chairman to the Moscow decision that rejected Gitlow, testified on September 29, after the U.S.S.R. had marched into Poland. Foster said that the Soviet Union was "one hundred per cent justified in thereby extending its protection over the former Russian people."

"Have you ever settled any question regarding the Party line independent of the Comintern?" asked Dies.

FOSTER: Tens of thousands.

DIES: Independent of the Cominform?

FOSTER: Independent of course; every day; every day, on every question that comes along, we make settlements.

DIES: Every day—can you cite a single instance where any decision of the Communist Party finally taken has conflicted with the decision of the Comintern?

FOSTER: Well, no, I cannot—no major decision.

When Foster was done testifying, spectators cheered Dies's proposal, to be raised innumerable times thereafter, that the Communist Party be disbanded.

It was a difficult period for the C.P., and the Dies Committee must be granted the credit it claimed for making it more difficult. The membership was in turmoil; the Russian-born Jews who were so large a part of the small Party fled from an alliance with Hitler, and even those intellectuals who had been able to reconcile themselves to the amenities of dictatorship had trouble adapting to such a pact. Granville Hicks, the Party's preeminent academic adornment in its united front manifestation, now departed the fold, with more candor and less anguish than many. A few weeks after Browder, a squire speaking of a prize bull, described Hicks as "one of our most distinguished

2 "General Krivitsky, you are Smelka Ginsberg!" announced the *New Masses*.

Communist educators," the writer and critic issued his melancholy farewell in a communication to *The New Republic*. (The *New Masses* had declined to print it.) He wrote:

> If they had only admitted their ignorance, the Communist Party of the United States would be intact today. But instead they insisted that the Soviet-German nonaggression pact was the greatest possible contribution to peace and democracy and offered anything that came into their heads as proof. They rushed into print with apologies completely devoid of clarity and logic. Only one conclusion could be drawn: If the Party leaders could not defend the Soviet Union intelligently, they would defend it stupidly.

The stupidity was what most annoyed Hicks.

> The leaders of the Communist Party have tried to appear omniscient, and they have succeeded in being ridiculous. They have clutched at straws, juggled sophistries, shut their eyes to facts . . . They have shown that they are strong in faith—which the future may or may not justify—and weak in intelligence.

As the U. S. Communist Party made its conversion from collective security to isolationism, front groups found themselves in a barely tenable position. Having become adept at holding to the necessary line by the tips of their fingers, they were now called on to do so by the skin of their teeth. The photograph of that smiling group in the Kremlin—Stalin, Ribbentrop, Molotov—as J. M. Cameron, an English leftist of the period would write, "gave visible substance to the reality that lay behind the fictitious account of Soviet affairs that we took to be a true account in that age of faith." It made things very difficult. For the fellow travelers to continue to be of use to the Party, they had to become isolationists, but that would expose their want of independence to their densest friends, and so terminate their usefulness anyway.

The largest and most important of the front organizations of the period was the American League for Peace and Democracy —though its claim to represent upwards of seven million people was typically generous; the League at no time had more than 20,000 individual members, nearly half of them in New York City. It was formed in 1933, as the American League Against

War and Fascism, an outgrowth of a 1932 Congress Against War, organized in Amsterdam by Henri Barbusse and Romain Rolland, who had been aroused by Japan's conquest of Manchuria. J. B. Matthews was its first national chairman, and from the beginning it was controlled by Stalinists through the various organizations that constituted the bulk of its membership. The only people who took the seven-million membership figure straight were Dies, Matthews, and boosters on the left. In 1934 Dr. Harry F. Ward, a Methodist clergyman and professor of Christian Ethics at Union Theological Seminary, became chairman, and three years later, in an early bow to the power of the positive slogan, the organization became the American League for Peace and Democracy. Its influence grew through 1938. The name of Earl Browder, who had been a vice president at the outset, was scratched from the letterhead—though the C.P. continued to be a major financial contributor—and such prominent New Dealers as Harold Ickes, Elmer Benson, and Robert Jackson sent warm greetings to its congresses. Newspapers treated it with respect; *The New Republic* commissioned its officials to write of its high purposes; and it had advocates in Congress.

Dr. Ward came before the Dies Committee on October 23, 1939, during an unresolved dispute over the behavior of Committee agents while taking records from the League's Washington and Chicago offices. Ward was the model of a model fellow traveler—"a distinguished divine," as the New Deal's Representative Coffee described him, "one of the leading and most learned scholars in America." Under the questioning of his A.L.W.F. predecessor J. B. Matthews, Ward explained that he was neither for nor against Communism. "My position on Communism is that of a critical student, sir." In his five years as chairman of the League, he had never noticed any attempt at domination by the Communist Party. He emphasized that the League had policy differences with the Communists, but his main example—"we never stood for collective security as a broad policy. We stood only for concerted action to prevent aggression, that is, aggression of the fascist powers, by withholding economic aid to them from the democracies"—

was not overpowering. As for the Nazi-Soviet pact, he had lately observed "an increasing recognition . . . that the action of the Soviet Union in regard to Hitler has given him more of a check than it has helped him." From his study of Soviet society Ward had concluded that Soviet workers "have a better opportunity than the unorganized workers in this country and just about the same as effectively organized workers," and he was at pains to point out that "there is a vital difference between Communism and fascism so far as war and dictators are concerned . . . they are not the same kind of dictators." Pressed by Voorhis, he explained that the difference lay between the "collective dictatorship of the Soviet Union" and the "personal dictatorship of Hitler."

It was an exemplary performance. In staging it, Dies did a service for the nation's liberals. But that was not sufficient satisfaction. Now, as throughout his captaincy of the Committee, he needed blood, and organizations do not bleed. Its members do, however, and virtually the entire membership of the League's Washington, D.C., chapter was made up of government employees, including a number of high officials. Here was an opportunity to get at the New Deal and at individual New Dealers. The temptation was, as always, irresistible. The League's Washington list (whether it was the membership list or just a mailing list nobody seemed certain) was made public on October 25, at the insistence of Mason and over the mild objections of Voorhis. It contained the names of 563 federal employees, the great majority in positions paying under $3,000 a year, but a few of greater consequence. The featured names were Oscar Chapman, then Assistant Secretary of the Interior; Louis Block, a member of the Maritime Labor Board; Mordecai Ezekiel, an influential official in the Agricultural Adjustment Administration; Edwin S. Smith, a member of the National Labor Relations Board, whose partiality toward the C.I.O. had already been the subject of Committee testimony; and Nathan Witt, the N.L.R.B.'s executive secretary.[3]

[3] A year later the Communist Witt and the fellow traveler Smith would lose their places in the N.L.R.B. and their power to nudge the American labor movement along Communist lines. We shall come across their names again in this history.

For the League itself, the publicity was only another bump on the road to the graveyard. It was fast expiring, strangled in the twists of Soviet policy. Under pressure to make some statement on the Nazi-Soviet pact and the partition of Poland, its national board announced: "We neither condemn nor approve the actions of the Soviet Union. Our members will have their own opinions on these matters and will express and implement them in their political organizations outside the League."[4] Their members did indeed have their own opinions; they quit by the thousands. Roger N. Baldwin, who had worked closely with Ward at both the League and the American Civil Liberties Union, was one of those who resigned. He denied to the end, however, that the League had been "controlled" by the Communist Party, explaining: "We were, of course, prevented from taking any position in opposition to Communist policy, for they would have withdrawn and thus wrecked the united front. But the area of conflict was comparatively slight. When it became acute, after the Nazi-Soviet Pact, it killed the League." Baldwin said on resigning that he was still willing to collaborate with Communists on domestic matters, but he gave up on them where the interests of the U.S.S.R. were concerned. Thousands of other non-Communists came to a similar or harsher conclusion, and within four months the American League for Peace and Democracy, bereft of members and of money and of reputation, dissolved itself.[5] "There was no middle way, no fence that could be straddled," lamented its ex-director of religious work in an ingenuous post-mortem. "The toleration fundamental to a broad united front has disappeared." The Reverend Dr. Ward, ever strong in

[4] The position is much the same as that adopted nearly twenty years later by the remnant U.S. Communist Party, confronted by the Soviet repression in Hungary: "We do not seek to justify the use of Soviet troops in Hungary's internal crisis on November 4 [1956]. Neither do we join in the condemnation of these actions . . ."

[5] One of its final actions was to urge friends of the League to buy Christmas cards at 5¢ apiece, containing this greeting:

> Peace on earth, good will toward men
> Our wish to you before Congressman Dies decides
> That Peace, good will and Christmas are
> Un-American.

faith, went on to become honorary co-chairman of the Civil Rights Congress.

Criticism of the Committee for making public the Washington A.L.P.D. list swelled beyond the usual dimensions. Representative Dempsey, annoyed that Dies and Mason had refused to wait for him to finish a telephone call and had issued the list in his absence, complained of inaccuracies. The Committee should have taken the time to do some checking, he protested, and cited the case of a Washington schoolteacher who found herself listed as a member of a Communist front with which she had had no connection whatever. In reply, Mason adopted a remarkable line of reasoning: "If there were mistakes of names being on the list that were not members it was not the mistake of the Dies Committee, it was the mistake of the records and the local chapter of the League. Please, therefore, do not blame the Dies Committee if there were names on that list that should not have been on it." Coffee charged that the list's release was "obviously for the purpose of intimidating government employees." Mason preferred to call it the "culmination of a campaign of 'moral suasion.'" He and Dies pointed out that the Committee had listed the League as a Communist front in its first report, early in 1939; hence its members had had plenty of time to see the light and withdraw. If the League were not a Communist front, adherents of the Dies position asked, why should its members be ashamed of being identified with it? If it were, why, having been put on notice, did they continue to belong?

The liberal press was annoyed partly on principle and partly because its editors and writers rather admired the League; they would surely have been little disturbed had the Committee published a membership list of the Silver Shirts. In November, the editor of *The Nation* was still able to write that the League's members "represent a wide variety of points of view" and "if it has been 'controlled' by its Communist members their influence has been singularly moderate." The League itself issued a statement whose rhetoric was sufficient to damn it as a front group without further evidence:

Long after Mr. Dies' name has been forgotten the six hundred names of the members of the American League for Peace and Democracy in Washington will stand as a testimonial to the courage of Americans who refuse to be intimidated by this twentieth century inquisition. No American is safe so long as the Dies Committee is permitted to defy the American Bill of Rights. The American League for Peace and Democracy will continue to expose the enemies of peace and democracy in the United States.

The publication of the list was an outburst of that vigilanteeism that Dies and his man Matthews could never repress for very long. "The real job this Committee has to do," said Voorhis in his civilized way during the debate on the floor, "is not that of questioning individuals or obtaining and publishing lists of individuals but determining as near as it can the facts about organizations." But Matthews, brimming with the passions of the apostate, and Dies, with his flair for page-one copy, would be satisfied with nothing less than public repentance or public retribution. The published list contained many inaccuracies. ("The remedy is simple," observed Congressman Gifford. "Those on the list can explain whether or not they ought to be on it. Their character is not assassinated except for a moment.") Like all membership (or mailing) lists of large organizations, it contained the names of persons who had only the remotest connection with the League and the vaguest idea of what the commotion was about. Some of those listed were Communists; the majority were not; many were merely foolish or careless. To most of them, deeply worried over the continuing triumphs of fascism, it must have seemed, as it seemed to *The New Republic* in 1938, that "the Communists today are not acting as a revolutionary group; they are so committed to the policy of cooperation with all democratic forces that one can hardly tell them from New Deal Democrats." The Communists *were* acting that way—numbers of them quite sincerely—in the late thirties. By its act of mass exposure, the Dies Committee had obliterated all distinctions. It had used its powers to punish, en masse, hundreds of persons innocent of any known crime whose motives for being in the League were diverse and whose actions while in it, never investigated, were by no means *per se* subversive of America's interests. After a few good weeks, the Dies Committee had returned to the bad old ways of 1938.

Mr. Roosevelt, not unattuned to the political reverberations of the list publication, termed it a "sordid procedure." Dies replied, on the C.B.S. network, that he was "grieved and pained" by the comment, but that he was determined to carry on his high task despite all obstacles. Although neither seemed eager to resume their feud of the year before, they could not help rubbing one another the wrong way. When Dies announced that the Administration had asked the Justice Department to begin "purging" 2,850 "known Communists" in key government positions, Roosevelt replied that he was waiting for Dies to let him in on the source of his information. When Thomas attacked Attorney General Murphy as being "strangely indifferent and listless in the case of Browder," shortly before the Communist leader was indicted for passport forgery, Dies unpredictably called his statement "most inappropriate"; then he began badgering Murphy to indict the entire League for Peace and Democracy. The mild Murphy could not find anything to indict the League for, but he expressed his gratitude to the Dies Committee for all its help. (Ickes wrote in his diary that Dies had the Attorney General "buffaloed," and added dryly that fighting back did not seem to fit in with Murphy's disposition.)

In its remaining public hearings of 1939, the Committee entered two other areas which, like the peace groups, gave America's Stalinists vast illusions of success for a time but finally ended in irrelevance and futility. Dies and Matthews saw and made much of Communist influence in the labor movement as represented by Joe Curran's Maritime Workers, and in youth groups such as the American Youth Congress and the American Student Union. Like the Stalinists, they made too much of a limited and short-lived influence. Under Matthews's tutelage, Dies learned to share the Communists' own enchantment with their conspiratorial string-pullings, and long after the strings were frayed to tatters, he would still be sawing away at them.

Joseph Curran, president of the National Maritime Union, owed his ascendancy over the sailors in the thirties to the Communists; it was with their brain and muscle that he built up a powerful union machine. Disaffected N.M.U. members identified him to the Committee as a Communist figurehead, and indeed he was obliging to his various *eminences rouges*. During the Hitler-Stalin pact, his men picketed the White House with signs reading NO CONVOYS!, but once Russia was at war, he became anti-fascist to the point of strike-breaking. Yet, as he would prove, it was an oversimplification to write him off as another stooge of Moscow.

Before being selected for union leadership by the Communists, Curran, the bucko boatswain's mate, was known among the men who sailed with him as "No-Coffee-Time Joe" because he would not give them fifteen minutes off for a cup of coffee. "He was strictly a company man at that time," recalled a former shipmate. In his bellowing appearance before the Committee—"What a circus!" he yelled—Curran gave his own explanation of his relations with the Communists:

> . . . my stomach, when it comes to looking for a pork chop in it and I am out on the picket line, does not know whether a dollar bill is red or green, as long as it buys a pork chop. And our respectable citizens would not give us anything and I did not question the character of each individual which offered me the price of a meal when I was on strike to better my conditions. And it seems to me that those people that fed us at that time were so-called Communists.

His speech, though disingenuous, was not without a portion of truth. In the desperate early thirties the A.F. of L.'s International Seamen's Union was more concerned with taking rake-offs from shipowners than in assisting the sailors. It was destroyed in the bitter seamen's strike of 1936–37 which lasted for ninety-nine days and from which emerged the N.M.U., headed by Joe Curran and his palace guard of Communists. From 1938 to 1945 he was their man, but then in 1945, as the cold war took form and Communist allies were neither an indispensable support nor an unmitigated blessing, he threw them out. In the nineteen-sixties he would be a booster of the war in Vietnam.

Curran was innocent of Marxism-Leninism. He found in the Communist Party a ladder by which he could ascend, and when it had served its purpose, he kicked it over. Neither the Communists nor Matthews could fathom a union leader like Curran—not because he was so deep but because he cared so little for the strange world on which their minds were centered. As Murray Kempton wrote of the case, "Curran was only a sailor. There had been a time when he was hungry, and the Communists had fed him when no one else would. But it had been enough for him, as for most of the other seamen, to be fed and to win for himself a place in the here and now." Curran was too devoted to the here and now to thrive on dreams of the millennium, too self-serving to give himself for long to any outside cause, and too tough to allow any cause to take what he saw no advantage in giving.

At the end of November, the Committee, chaired by Starnes, began taking testimony from the officers of two youth groups which had been repeatedly labeled Communist fronts by volunteer witnesses, beginning with Walter Steele. The three days of rather inconclusive hearings were distinguished by the presence of Mrs. Eleanor Roosevelt, a supremely tolerant patron of the American Youth Congress and good friend of Joseph P. Lash, national secretary of the American Student Union. Declining the invitation of Representative Starnes to take a place at the Committee table, the First Lady showed solidarity with the young folks by sitting beside them in the hearing room, to the delight of press photographers, and taking seven of them back to the White House for lunch each day in official cars.

In 1939, the American Youth Congress, yet another fruit of the Popular Front clime, claimed four and a half million members. These were not individuals, however, but persons who belonged to some sixty affiliated groups, ranging from the Y.W.C.A. to the American League for Peace and Democracy, from the Esperanto Association of North America to the Association of Lithuanian Workers. How many of the four and a half million knew that they were counted on the membership rolls of the congress is moot. Still, numbers of New Dealers, particularly in the National Youth Administration, took the A.Y.C. at its own estimate and listened attentively to the recommendations of its leaders on what should be done to help the nation's young people with employment and education. Their recommendations for federal aid in these areas no longer seems revolutionary. When it came to international affairs, however, the congress was another of those organizations, like the C.P. itself, whose passport for protest was good only up to the borders of the Soviet Union. It was made indignant by events in Mississippi and Mongolia and Madrid, but Moscow was Moscow's business. Although, as Congress leaders repeatedly emphasized, avowed Communists represented but a small minority on its governing body, they were invariably joined by fellow travelers to give the party line certain victory when the occasion demanded. The mechanics of Communist control have been set forth by Irving Howe and Lewis Coser:

> Let us suppose that a local branch of a Methodist youth organization, numbering a thousand, affiliated with the A.Y.C. Generally this would happen after one member—he might be a young Communist who had "colonized" or, better yet, a Methodist with "progressive" leanings—took the floor to propose affiliation to a Congress representing all of American youth. What, after all, could seem more reasonable? And naturally it would be the member who had made the proposal that would probably be sent as delegate to the A.Y.C. Soon most of the other young Methodists turned back to their Methodism and forgot about the A.Y.C. while their delegate continued to "represent" them. Thus, to control the bloc of votes he held, the A.Y.C. leadership needed to deal only with him and, more often than not, could ignore the members of his organization. It was neat.

As the hearings started, the presence of Mrs. Roosevelt and the absence of Mr. Dies seemed to have a calming effect on everyone. Whitley conducted the questioning of the A.Y.C. leaders politely and after being permitted to offer the Committee a petition for its abolition, they responded politely. They denied "absolutely" that they were Communist-dominated, and noted that their last congress had passed a resolution condemning "all forms of dictatorship" whether Communist, fascist or Nazi. They did not add that a resolution condemning Communism more directly had first been rejected, which placed the youngsters in a position of either voting for the second resolution or embarrassing themselves in public. Mrs. Roosevelt, ever largehearted in such matters, told reporters that she had conducted her own investigation long before the Dies Committee and found nothing "to indicate any outside control . . . nothing that was not within the actions which any American citizen could take with propriety." The young folks had simply lied to her, and she had believed them.

By one of those unhappy strokes that kept shaking front groups during these months, the Russians chose to invade Finland bare hours before the Youth Congress leaders proclaimed their independence to the Dies Committee. A few weeks later, more than 4,000 A.Y.C. delegates assembled in Washington for a Citizenship Institute. They sang their songs in a drenching February rain before the South Portico of the White House to the tune of *I Can't Give You Anything But Love, Baby:*

> We've been getting nothing else but love, Franklin.
> That's the thing youth has plenty of, Franklin.
> Dies has said that we're "red"; don't be misled.
> Lies are spread, when instead
> Jobs for Youth is where we're head-in'.

Then they stood silent as the President, who in 1937 had written them that they had "the good will and the best wishes of all who are concerned with the future of American democracy," strongly denounced the U.S.S.R. for its aggression. The only youthful cheers came when F.D.R. referred to a vote by their New York affiliate against a U.S. loan to Finland. At their congress early in 1940, the A.Y.C. refused to take a stand on the Soviet invasion just as the A.L.P.D. had refused to take a stand on the Nazi-Soviet pact, and shouted down a resolution

to bar from their organization all supporters of totalitarian organizations. For the rest of the year, the A.Y.C. denounced
the "war hysteria" in this country, termed the Administration's
defense program an effort to "Hitlerize" America, and opposed
aid to England, the sale of arms to belligerents, compulsory
military training and conscription. They favored strict neutrality in any European war, and picketed the White House where
they had once been guests. "Don't lease or lend our lives!" was
their slogan in early 1941. By now even Mrs. Roosevelt had
given up on them, and refused to speak at their meetings. They
had to settle for Paul Robeson as their guest of honor. Then came
the German invasion of Russia and the peace-loving, sturdy-
lunged representatives of American youth demanded cooperation "with the peoples of the world to protect our national
interests and our security which are menaced by fascism." It
must sometimes have seemed to fellow travelers between 1939
and 1941 that the course of world affairs was directed to no
other end than to embarrass friends of the Soviet Union.

Where the leaders of the A.Y.C. would go down the line
into political eccentricity on the Stalinist train, singing about
Joe Hill, Joseph Lash was a more interesting case. His questioning by Matthews, who had been hastily summoned back from
New York by Starnes for the purpose, made for a less decorous
scene than Whitley's questioning of the lads from the A.Y.C.
Representative Rankin, sitting in on the proceedings, thought
Matthews did fine, but Mrs. Roosevelt disagreed. His "whole
attitude, tone of voice and phraseology," she observed in one
of her *My Day* columns, "made one feel that a prisoner, considered guilty, was being tried at the bar." Lash responded in
song: "If you see an un-American lurking near/ Why, alkalize
with Martin Dies and he will disappear." He was applauded,
and the session broke up amid a flurry of excitement when
Matthews charged abruptly that the previous day's denials of
Communist tendencies by A.Y.C. leaders were "false." "That's
not true!" cried one of them, jumping to his feet. Starnes told
him to sit down, and they all adjourned for lunch.

Lash was a young Socialist who split with his anti-Stalinist mentors in 1937 and succumbed to the dream of the united front. He wrote at the time: "Under the vigorous leadership of the Soviet Union (whom we are quick to berate but slow to praise) the world labor movement is rallying around the concept of collective action against the aggressor." In that year, the Oxford Peace Pledge, a personal renunciation of all wars, sponsored by the American Student Union, was abandoned in favor of a pledge against "imperialist" wars, in accord with the "collective security" line then coming into its own. Lash acknowledged that Communist influence within the A.S.U.— which had been created in 1935 by a merger of Communist and Socialist youth groups and never had more than a few thousand members—was strong. He had opposed the original merger and, when he came before J. B. Matthews, he had taken to heart the lesson of the Nazi-Soviet pact and was close to getting a divorce from his Communist associates—but he could not bring himself to do so under the auspices of the Dies Committee. "I tried not to answer questions," he explained a couple of years later, "because the more I answered questions here the more difficult it made my work in trying to get the Communist influence out of the A.S.U." Instead, he delivered speeches that he seemed to have saved from a junior high school play:

> I know that there are young Communists and I have had a great many disagreements with them, but I say if I am honest and can stand up against others in the light of day that they will have to give way, and that they are sincere and honest people and that it is the job of those of us who believe in democracy to talk with them, to work with them and to show them how democracy works.

Hardly had he finished telling the Committee that he believed that the Russian invasion of Finland should be condemned, then more than one hundred leaders of A.S.U. college chapters in New York City adopted a resolution defending the invasion of "a puppet state created and maintained by imperial powers from abroad." At the A.S.U. annual meeting in Madison, Wisconsin, Lash spoke against "those who are prepared to justify any policy of the Soviet Union," whereupon his comrades rejected a resolution condemning the attack on Finland by 322 to 29. Lash did not seek reelection.

Early in 1942, still under the patronage of Mrs. Roosevelt, Lash was given a second hearing by the Dies Committee, this time behind closed doors. Now he was seeking absolution from Dies so that he might obtain a commission in Naval Intelligence. He apologized for singing his song during his previous visit, and spoke much more frankly about the extent of Communist domination of both the A.S.U. and the A.Y.C. during their green years. Now the thirty-two-year-old Lash, whom Dies enjoyed calling "a perennial student", was general secretary of the International Student Service and was trying to keep his former collaborators out of positions of influence. He refused to become a source of names for the Communist-hunters, however, and instead of giving him clearance for a commission, the majority of the Committee, with Thomas as spokesman, judged that he ought to be drafted right away. Dies, on the other hand, felt that this would imperil U.S. security: "Anyone who has been active in Communist or Nazi movements should not be taken into our armed services." Lash, who had never requested deferment but had been placed in a 1-H classification because he was over twenty-eight, declared, in the language of A.S.U. platforms, that he "would be glad to serve with the millions of other young Americans in this great struggle for human freedom," and he wound up in the army.

The progress of men like Joseph Lash from a flirtation with Stalinism to marriage with the New York *Post* was not rare. The radical movement of the thirties was the training ground for many liberal warriors of the fifties. It nurtured a great deal of foolishness, but at the same time strained out the easy enthusiasms of youth and left the grownups politically more mature, in closer touch with America. But for Dies this was small progress indeed. In 1954 he still thought of Lash as a Communist, or at best a former Communist:

I submit that Mr. Lash's admission before our Committee that he had associated closely with the Communists and was in substan-

tial agreement with the Communists was a confession that he was
a Communist. It was not necessary for Joseph Lash to be a card-
holding member of the Communist Party of the United States to
be a Communist. It has been clearly established that some Communists do not hold a formal membership in the Party for strategic reasons.

Dies had, predictably, missed the whole meaning of Lash's experience. He saved his absolution for the repentant radical who
chose to go the way of J. B. Matthews.

In the weeks preceding the turn of the year, as the time
approached for the Committee's annual reckoning and reestab-
lishment by Congress, Dies's normal hunger for publicity grew
acute. It was now that he could be counted on to announce
that Leon Trotsky and Diego Rivera were coming up from
Mexico to testify and to promise on one of his frequent radio
addresses that, given one more year, his Committee would
see to the "deportation of no less than seven million aliens
employed in American industries while Americans go without
employment." Trotsky did not come (owing to Administration
resistance, Dies charged); the seven million did not go; but
the Committee carried on.

The public hearings of 1939 ended with testimony on Communist tactics by Jay Lovestone, who had been deposed as
U.S. C.P. chieftain by Stalin in 1929, but that did not end the
Committee's work for the year. On Sunday, December 10, in
time to make the lean Monday newspapers, Dies released to
the press a report written by J. B. Matthews on consumer
groups. Matthews charged that all the major national consumer organizations, except for his own alma mater, Consumers Research (where his wife was still employed), were
Communist transmission belts. He charged that many of their
leaders, particularly the renegade founders of Consumers
Union, were Communists in fact or at heart, and that all were
engaged in a plot "to sabotage and destroy advertising, and
through its destruction to undermine and help destroy the
capitalist system of free enterprise." The Communists believed,

he explained, that this was "a revolutionary tactic worthy of a great deal of attention."

That Communists were influential in consumer organizations such as the League of Women Shoppers was a reasonable surmise, but Matthews's report—riddled with inaccuracies, straining after incriminating clues, and relying heavily on mere assumption—was not a persuasive document. In one place he mentioned that an official in the Department of Agriculture had investigated *Good Housekeeping* magazine, and he went on: "While there is no record of the findings of the investigation being used as a basis for action against the magazine, it may be assumed that such was the intention." He quoted Arthur Kallet, one of the founders of Consumers Union, as saying that "cooperation does provide a splendid escape for participants in the day-to-day struggles against the capitalist system . . ." Matthews commented: "The politically informed person will have no difficulty in recognizing the strictly Communist phraseology of the foregoing statement." The exegesis told at least as much about Matthews as about Kallet.

As a preliminary indictment in preparation for an investigation of consumer groups, the Matthews report might have had some utility. But it was made public without benefit of any hearings whatever, and without the participation or even the knowledge of the other members of the Committee. Dies, Matthews, and two staff members held a brief and secret meeting at 6 p.m. on a Sunday evening; security was so tight that two weeks later other Committee members still did not know where the meeting had taken place. Wherever it was, Matthews presented the report and it was immediately released to the press. Voorhis complained that the work was "purely and simply the opinion" of Matthews, and post-publication protests kept it from ever being printed in the Committee record.

The union of Dies and Matthews had never been more productive. The staff director's vendetta against Consumers Union and all its allies mated perfectly with the chairman's quest after support from businessmen for his political ambitions. A few weeks before the issuance of the report, Dies promised the annual convention of the Associated Grocery Manufacturers

of America that he was about to give the consumers movement
the once-over, in appreciation of the fact, as *Business Week*
noted, that "Some businessmen have never been able to look
at the consumer movement without seeing red."

The activities of Matthews and certain friends leading up
to the report were equally unedifying. In August the Federal
Trade Commission had issued a complaint against the Hearst
Corporation's *Good Housekeeping* magazine, charging it with
"misleading and deceptive acts and practices in the issuance
of Guarantys, Seals of Approval and the publication in advertising pages of grossly exaggerated and false claims of products
advertised therein." Richard Berlin, executive vice president
of the Hearst magazines, retorted that subversive elements
such as Consumers Union were out to harm advertising in general. Shortly thereafter, Matthews attended a dinner at the
home of George Sokolsky, the conservative columnist and
sometime employee of the National Association of Manufacturers. Present were representatives of several big manufacturers of consumer goods as well as F. J. Schlink, Matthews's
former partner at Consumers Research. There the strategy was
developed to attack the competing consumer groups as anti-
advertising and Communist. The Dies Committee's report was
released to the New York papers by the Hearst organization,
at which time vice president Berlin, who had seen the report
before most of the members of the Committee, gave it his
personal seal of approval.[6]

The New Dealers on the Committee—Voorhis, Casey, and
Dempsey—whom Dies had efficiently ignored in his release of
both the A.L.P.D. names and the Matthews report, were
aroused yet again by a draft of the Committee's second annual
report. Presumably written by Matthews and destined never
to be made public, it charged that Communists had from the
beginning wielded "the dominant influence" in the C.I.O. and
reiterated the "shameful and alarming" finding that hundreds
of employees of the federal government belonged to the

---

[6] Relations between Matthews and *Good Housekeeping* had improved spec-
tacularly since 1935, when the former was attacking the latter for having
reached "the nethermost depth of vulgarity on the subject of toilet tissue."

A.L.P.D. But now the liberal Democrats had a bargaining point; they threatened to issue a minority report and so emphasize the dissension within the Committee if the Matthews-Dies draft were not rewritten.

Dies gave in and the result, issued early in January 1940 was a sober statement, evenly divided between fascist and Communist activities, which began, unexceptionally:

> Every modern democratic nation is confronted by two pressing problems. The first is the preservation of the constitutional liberties which their people have gained through years of struggle; the second is the problem of adjusting the economic life to the difficulties of the machine age . . .

This was no longer the language of Matthews. Of the C.I.O. it reported mildly that while ten or twelve unions were "more than tinged" with Communism, the leadership had been trying to clean up the situation and "most of its largest organizations are free of Communist control, domination or even serious influences.[7] It listed only eleven organizations as Communist fronts, including the American Student Union but excluding the American Youth Congress, which it merely chided for permitting Communists to affiliate; and it did not mention consumer groups at all. It even warned against loose usage on the right of the epithet "Communist," and went so far as to remind the nation that during its united front phase the C.P. "was deliberately refraining from preaching Communism in any real sense of the term." The Committee's sternest critics had difficulty in faulting a report that *The New York Times* called "an astonishingly able and balanced document." As a further show of repentance, Dies decided not to make public a report of two Committee investigators on Communist activities in Hollywood.

---

[7] Voorhis, Casey, and Mason each expressed his regrets to the House later for the listing in the "more than tinged" category of the United Electrical, Radio and Machine Workers. They explained that James Carey, the union's president, had protested the slur. Some years later Carey would explain to another Congressional committee how he had discovered at just about this time that he was "isolated" in his own union: "It was now easy to spot the Communists because of their flip-flop on the war, and as months passed I discovered that they were in complete control of the national office; they dominated the executive committee, ran the union paper and were strongly entrenched in the locals and districts. All the organizers were Party-liners."

Flushed with this victory, Voorhis drew up a four-point recommendation for the improvement of Committee procedures and presented it to the Rules Committee. He called for a regular executive meeting at least once a week; an end to the issuance of public statements, press releases or reports which had not first been submitted to the entire Committee; efforts to call accused persons as soon as possible after the accusation had been made; and no public utterances by Committee members about ongoing investigations. There were smiles at the Rules Committee at the thought of Martin Dies being bound by such a table of etiquette, and the recommendation was set aside.

The House debate over continuing the Committee followed the previous year's pattern. Although a Gallup Poll, released in mid-December, showed a perceptible decline in support of the Committee following the release of the A.L.P.D. list, still three-quarters of the population appeared to favor its continuance. Some newspaper editorials again lamented the fact that Martin Dies had to be the one doing the job, but the majority agreed it was a job that had to be done. The House again heard Fish, Thomas, and Starnes defend the Committee as the bastion of our way of life and Coffee and New York City's Vito Marcantonio damn it as a corrupter of our liberties. Voorhis and Casey, while supporting continuance of the Committee, offered reasoned criticisms of their chairman's methods of operation. Dies himself, ill in Texas as he had been for much of the year, was not present to stand in his own defense—though he did muster the strength to deliver a radio talk criticizing the apathy of the Department of Justice in going after subversives, attributing his illness to his labors in behalf of America and warning that "Our government cannot survive unless Christianity remains firm in the hearts of our people." Mail in favor of the Committee was heavy, and many of the 344 Congressmen who voted for a third year's continuance (only 21 voted Nay) must have shared the feeling of Representative Eberharter:

The House today is confronted with the choice of two evils. On the one hand, to adopt this resolution is to seemingly approve the un-American procedure of the Special Committee to Investigate Un-American Activities. On the other hand, to defeat the resolution is to seemingly approve of a continuation of subversive activities.

The majority made peace with its doubts by cutting Dies's appropriation back to $75,000 for the new year.

4

1940: Popularity and Power

LIBERALS of all degrees were necessarily troubled by Martin Dies's outbreaks of vigilanteeism and by his unmistakable political intent. Those who had reveled in the Popular Front and still harbored soft feelings for their late allies, the Communists, were especially aroused, and some of them chose to reply to Dies in his own language. As he had labeled them Communists, they labeled him fascist. As he had placed them in the company of Earl Browder, they placed him in the company of Fritz Kuhn. Like Dies, the liberals who took this line were abiding by the Stalinist principle of "objective truth"— *viz.*, if a man's actions forward the cause of fascism (or Communism) then he is, objectively speaking, a fascist (or Communist) even if he is not literally a fascist (or Communist). A perilous form of reasoning which would lure the anti-Dies forces into a humiliating trap.

A leading voice in the long campaign against Dies belonged to *The Nation*, not Communist, never Communist, but displeased by anti-Communists. The burden of its charge, reiterated many times, was that the Texan was collaborating with the "reputable" periphery of the Christian Front and was avoiding an investigation of people such as Father Coughlin and Gerald L. K. Smith who, unlike Communist fronters, really warranted being investigated. There was good basis to the charge; even so thoroughgoing an anti-Communist as Westbrook Pegler commented: "The Dies Committee should have treated Coughlin just as it treated Earl Browder, but tiptoed around him for

fear that he would cry up a holy war." Dies's critics on the left
went much further, however, not hesitating to convict him of
fascist proclivities. Certainly the small-town Texas lawyer felt
more comfortable in the company of Legionnaires than of professors, and the people who cheered him at rallies where he
said things like "God gave us America and the Marxists shall
not take it away" did not represent the intellectual cream of
American life. But if Dies could be convicted because he had
spoken at a luncheon that Fritz Kuhn happened to attend; if
it was proof of his fascism that he was praised by Joseph P.
Kamp of the far-right Constitutional Educational League and
had dealings with Merwin K. Hart of the far-right New York
State Economic Council—both of whom in turn had dealings
with a still shabbier class of patriots—then by a like syllogism
the editors of *The Nation* and of most other liberal organs could
without further ado be hung as Communists. They argued that
Dies must have a warm spot for William Dudley Pelley of
North Carolina, head of the frankly Jew-hating Silver Shirts,
because the Committee hadn't been able to track him down for
questioning. But those whom Sidney Hook has called our
"totalitarian liberals" had for years been far more closely attached to Earl Browder—and Pelley's influence was hardly
impressive beside that of the Communist leader's in his lionized
days. Moreover, although Dies's claim to credit for the arrest
on charges of sedition of seventeen Christian Fronters in New
York[1] was merely humorous, he had spoken much more harshly
about Nazism and fascism than such liberals as *Nation* editor
Freda Kirchwey had spoken about Communism. Even loyal
readers of *The Nation*, who were prepared to believe anything
ill of the Congressman, however weakly grounded, must have
wished that the evidence of a link between Dies and Pelley
was a little more palpable, a little less conjectural . . . and suddenly, for a few days in January 1940, it seemed that their case
was made.

On January 22, during the Rules Committee's perfunctory

[1] The subsequent acquittal of the Christian Fronters was used by champions
of the Committee in Congress to show that Dies had been right not to bother
about them.

hearings on the continuance of the Dies Committee, Congressman Frank E. Hook of Michigan, a ferocious opponent of Dies, announced that he possessed written evidence of an "understanding between Dies and Pelley." When Representative Starnes started to defend his absent chairman, Representative Cox of Georgia remarked, "He doesn't need any defense before this committee." Hook thereupon inserted in the record of the House excerpts from what he maintained were letters between Pelley and David Mayne, the Silver Shirt leader's representative in Washington. *The Nation* had evidently been given access to the evidence at the same time as Hook or even earlier, for its issue dated January 27 carried an article by assistant editor James Wechsler, who had outgrown the American Student Union and the Young Communist League, which contained portions of the alleged Pelley-Mayne correspondence. Written on stationery of "The Silver Shirt Legion of America," one of these letters referred to "the understanding that Dies will not go out of his way to embarrass us—True—Fr. Coughlin —George or the Legion." In another letter, Pelley explained that a booklet he had issued in 1939 attacking the Dies Committee for harassing Gentile patriots instead of finding out "whether there is any Jewish conspiracy against constitutional forms of government" was intended only "to create the general impression that there existed between Dies and myself a personal 'gripe' sufficient to keep us apart from any form of cooperation . . . and was actually intended . . . to offset any rumors —in the event of suspicion—that he and I through mutual contacts had an understanding." Wechsler delighted in the scoop. But within a week these letters were shown to have been part of a hoax; it was a case of the desire to believe sending respectable men headlong into a slough of gullibility.

The innocent strategist behind the anti-Dies plot was Gardner Jackson, legislative representative of Labor's Non-Partisan League, an indefatigable worker for the underdog, whose name had naturally found its way onto many of J. B. Matthews's lists. Jackson was no Communist, and he had earned, by earnest works, a reputation for integrity as well as for courage and good will, but the thought of the Dies Committee clouded his

nobler faculties. He set a young associate named Harold Weisberg on the track of Dies. Assisted by Drew Pearson, Weisberg
made contact with Mayne, who obligingly turned over the
letters—to put Jackson "out on a limb," he later explained.
Weisberg paid Mayne $105 and promised him a job in the
Department of Agriculture.

With this material in hand, Jackson held a dinner party in
mid-January for a few New Deal Congressmen to discuss how
the letters might be used against Dies as the debate over continuing his Committee approached. Most of Gardner's guests
were skeptical of the letters, and advised against using them,
but Hook, a New Dealer whose mind could not keep apace of
his temper, was . . . yes, hooked. As Pelley himself would later
interpret the event to reporters, "I think he was just played for
a sucker, don't you?" Mayne, who had previously been employed by the Committee to try to get Pelley to testify, had set
as a condition of his handing over the letters that he would be
notified before they were used; Weisberg so notified him,
whereupon, according to some reports, Mayne notified the
Committee counsel, Rhea Whitley. The Committee, it was later
suggested by mortified liberals, had actually hired private detectives to sell false documents to Congressmen who craved
them. This was never proven, but whatever the Committee
staff's part in the initial plotting of this comedy-mystery, they
rubbed their hands at the denouement. Mayne unresistingly
admitted his forgery at once to Dies's young friend, Committee
investigator Robert Stripling, who from then on took credit
for breaking the case. Mayne was eventually brought to trial
for his prank; he pleaded guilty and received a suspended
sentence.

Hook's response, as it dawned upon him that he had been
most grievously taken in, was that of the captain who attempts
to sustain his sinking ship by blustering back at the hurricane:

> If there is any question of forgery then the Dies Committee is
> guilty of conspiracy to bribe a person to commit forgery to cover
> up their past nefarious acts. It is typical Dies Committee smear-
> ing to befog the real issue of collaboration with those closely
> connected with the Christian Front . . . There was only one real

effort to overthrow the government of the United States, and that came from below the Mason-Dixon line. It looks as if another effort is coming from that source.

Hook made much of an affidavit from Mayne to the effect that the signatures on the letters were those of Pelley, and he refused to apologize for entering them into the Record—though he relented to the extent of agreeing to withdraw them, a concession that the defenders of Dies, overjoyed at the way the case had developed, would not accept without an accompanying apology. Hook continued to rant, demanding that the Department of Justice investigate the "charges of forgery, collusion and conspiracy."

At an open meeting of the Committee on February 6, where Mayne testified that he had simply traced the signatures, leaving out the second "e" in Pelley on purpose, Hook, according to an eye-witness account, stood over him "trembling with rage" and "roared his questions until he was requested to stand at the other end of the Committee table." Only then did the choleric gentleman from Michigan finally apologize—"If the House feels its integrity impugned or if any member is aggrieved, I do not hesitate to apologize"—and the forgeries were expunged. A year later he would still be exorcising his embarrassment, blaming everything on "investigators who cooperate and collaborate with men to mislead and entrap a Member of Congress for the purpose of smearing him before the public because he had the courage of his convictions . . ." *The Nation* dealt with the unfortunate fate of its scoop by making light of the letters that had seemed so dramatic to its editors a week or two before. The emphasis on the forgeries, they now protested, was designed to obfuscate the evidence of Dies's hobnobbing with Christian Fronters. Martin Dies, still at home in Orange, Texas, recovering from influenza and a ruptured appendix, was all at once, and most strangely, martyr as well as prosecutor and judge.[2]

[2] In his autobiography Dies claims that the incident of the letters was but one of repeated low efforts to destroy his work. These included, he writes, a New Deal conspiracy to slander him as an income tax evader, an attempt to kidnap his son Bobby, and a plot, which he only narrowly escaped, to entrap him with a pretty girl in her room at the Mayflower Hotel.

At the climax of the affair, William Dudley Pelley, whom the Committee had supposedly been seeking for months to no avail in the back alleys of North Carolina, suddenly appeared in Washington. The Committee, lacking the services of Whitley whose resignation had gone unnoticed in the furor over the Mayne letters, hastily called Pelley before it, for the first, and completely unplanned, public hearing of the year. Stripling would claim credit for this accomplishment too, but it did nothing to enhance the Committee's glory. Starnes presided and obtained little from the long-sought witness other than vagueness as to the Silver Shirts's financial arrangements and compliments—"God bless this Committee"—that could only be compromising from such a source. "I'm giving Martin Dies an absolutely clean bill of health," Pelley told reporters outside the hearing room. "I admire the work he's done." He expressed particular fondness while testifying for Representative Thomas, whom he commended fulsomely for demanding the impeachment of Mme Perkins. "I may say I have yet to admire any action of yours," retorted Thomas. "I am sorry," replied Pelley with fine North Carolina grace, "because I think your work is splendid, splendid." Starnes finally dismissed him with a denunciation of his evil principles, and he was afterward arrested for violating the good behavior proviso in a suspended sentence he had received some years before in a stock fraud case.

William Dudley Pelley was one of those slightly cracked, slightly crooked characters who provided handfuls of followers and a much larger number of opponents with a bit of stimulation in the years of fascism's victories. The rabidity of his anti-Semitism was certified by the stream of pamphlets from his publishing operation in Asheville. "I don't hold any hatred toward any Jews in the United States," he told the Committee, and a few minutes later added, "I feel exactly as the Nazi Party in Germany felt in regard to Germany, regarding the Jewish element in our population, yes sir." The menace he inspired he owed mainly to the fears of the times and the desire on the left to locate and put on display un-Americanism elsewhere than in the Communist Party; Pelley took their attention as a tribute to his effectiveness and made as much of it as he could. That was not much, but today, as yesterday, there is no group in the land so trivial or so lunatic that it cannot arouse anxiety among the anxiety-prone and be exposed in press and from podium to its own boundless satisfaction.

As the stir over Pelley subsided, a recuperated Dies returned to Washington and the leadership of his Committee. His sights were set now on the middling Communist Party functionary: "We're going to try to get all the Communist leaders to come before our Committee, and they will be asked to supply the names. If they don't we will institute contempt proceedings against them. The law will permit the government to keep them in jail if they don't talk." In the first spring weeks of 1940, Dies exhibited a rather private understanding of what was permitted the chairman of a Congressional committee by the laws on which he was relying to keep Communists in jail. At his direction, Committee investigators carried out a series of raids on C.P. offices in the East, climaxing with an assault on the Philadelphia headquarters of the Communist Party and the International Workers Order. On April 12, two investigators, assisted by eight Philadelphia detectives and a squad of motorcycle police, broke into the offices, filled a two-ton truck with books, pamphlets, and files, and sped away across the Delaware River Bridge into New Jersey.

When Federal Judge George A. Welsh angrily ordered the arrest of the raiders and asked Dies not to use his captured documents until the court could pass on a C.P. petition to recover them, the chairman replied that it was too late; he had already placed them in the official record. Fourteen years later, in a magazine interview, Dies was still chuckling over this coup:

Once I got a big haul in Philadelphia. I knew there was a federal judge there who was going to give us trouble so I had it timed and grabbed the stuff about four o'clock and rushed it to a secret place. I had a photostat machine set up and we spent all night making copies of this stuff. The next morning the federal judge issued an injunction. He ordered all the records to be returned, arrested two of my investigators, and so I hid out in a blind office until we completed the photostating. Then I came out and announced we were going to honor and obey this injunction.

In May, Judge Welsh ruled the Committee raids illegal, as violations of the Fourth Amendment, and his eleven-page decision was a ringing defense of the civil liberties of unpopular minorities. The Communists, he observed, are "very much in the minority in our country, but their rights which they claim were invaded are rights that are sacred to us all." Dies could not share this view. He replied: "If we can't obtain legally records of a revolutionary group, records that show seditious activities, then there is no way to defend democracy." For all the dash of their abduction, the Philadelphia records never proved of value to anyone, so far as is known, and certainly they revealed nothing in the way of subversive activities. But the case did provide a view into Dies's conception of the Constitution—which he once described as "simply different words for the Sermon on the Mount." He expressed outrage at the court's defense of "agents of foreign dictators who claim constitutional rights and shirk constitutional duties"—and began a campaign—more oratorical than legislative—for laws to set matters straight.

Dies, as always, wanted names, but the C.P. officials he called up in late March and early April refused to provide them. A Pittsburgh man refused to tell the Committee the real name of the member who used the pseudonym "Franklin Delano Roosevelt" in his Party dues book. (A *Daily Worker* editorial, in its usual spirit of fun, declared that any suggestion that the warmonger Roosevelt was a C.P. member was an insult to the Party.) The C.P. secretary for western Pennsylvania yelled: "I will not give you any names of any people because you are trying to build up a blacklist." The secretary for the District of Columbia and Maryland was defiant: "To answer these questions would assist the Committee in the establishment of a general blacklist of Communists which would make it difficult and uncomfortable for those named to hold jobs and only because of their beliefs." The president of the Massachusetts Young Communist League would not give the names of his fellow members at Harvard on the grounds that they would be subjected to economic persecution in violation of the due process amendment of the Constitution. And the executive secretary of the New England C.P., a particularly obstreperous witness, refused flatly to answer any questions until the Committee allowed him to read a statement from "ten thousand citizens of Boston." "Throw him out!" yelled the audience.

These five persons were cited for contempt by the Committee; there was no question of the readiness of the House to approve the citations—indeed, as it turned out, to approve them unanimously. But again, Dies, impatient with the ordinary course of the law in contempt cases, which called for House approval followed by a grand jury hearing, took a shortcut in getting at the two New England Communists. Without placing the matter before the House, he had them jailed in Washington on warrants obtained directly from a U.S. commissioner. They were promptly freed on a writ of habeas corpus, and a few days later a court ruled that their constitutional rights had been violated by the abbreviated procedure.

Four of the five cases hung fire for the duration of the war. (The C.P. secretary for western Pennsylvania pleaded *nolo contendere*, settling for a six-month suspended sentence and a fine of $150.) The Pittsburgh man was finally acquitted because of the use of coercive tactics by the Committee. The indictment against the man with the petition from Boston was dismissed in 1947 on a motion of the government. The Party official from the District of Columbia and the Young Communist League president were found guilty and sentenced, respectively, to a thirty-day suspended sentence and a fine of $250, and a one-to-six-month suspended sentence and a fine of $150.

A few years after these first contempt-of-Committee cases were mildly resolved, there arose a spate of constitutional challenges to the Committee's powers which would define somewhat the rights of recalcitrant witnesses, but in 1940 a readily resistable force had apparently met a temporarily immovable object, and the result was a standoff. Having been rebuffed in his efforts to increase the efficiency of the law and, incidentally, his own powers, Dies was left with the alternative of continuing to call up Communists who would continue to refuse to testify even though they might wind up in jail in due course. This rigmarole was not in the chairman's style. As Ogden notes, "Even the publicity was lacking, as witnesses who refuse to speak do not make good newspaper copy save on the first or second occasion." So impatient was Dies that several Party officials were dismissed without contempt proceedings despite their refusal to name names.

Dies fired off a final salvo for the benefit of page-one scanners when he sent out subpoenas to ninety leaders of Communist and fascist groups to come to Washington and bring their records with them, but, like so many of his announced campaigns, it never went beyond the gesture. He satisfied himself with predicting that the Communists' tactics would bring legislation requiring all political organizations with international affiliations to register with the Secretary of State and to keep their records open. He never did much about this either—the rigors of drawing up laws and of trying to get them passed seemed to weary him—but in June 1940 the Congress did pass an expanded version of the Smith Act which called for the registration and fingerprinting of all aliens over fourteen, the deportation of the criminals and subversives among them (especially, its sponsors hoped, the detested Harry Bridges), and, in the spacious language of the final bill, defined it a crime "to teach and advocate the overthrow of the United States Government by force and violence." (Representative McCormack specially wished it to be remembered that the "teach and advocate" provision was his contribution to the measure.) A version of this bill had already passed the House over the opposition of a small number of liberals in July 1939, as war jitters began to afflict the nation, and although it would have cleared the Senate easily even without benefit of the Dies Committee's spring hearings, these did undoubtedly whet the appetites of alien-eaters around the land. As Representative Celler said when the bill returned to the House from the Senate in June 1940: "Candidly, I am informed that if we do not accept this bill, we will get one far worse. Any bill containing dreadful provisions against the alien would pass this House with no substantial opposition. In common parlance, it would go through 'like a dose of salts.' " And indeed, it went through by a vote of 382 to 4, with only Marcantonio speaking against it.[3]

A child, frustrated in carrying out an adventure in which he has invested an hour's dreams, will often seek comfort in a retreat to the proven pleasures of yesterday. So, in the weeks following his unprofitable encounter with the lesser Communists, Dies went to the Spanish Civil War, to the C.I.O., to Hollywood, in search of the satisfactions he had been denied elsewhere. And although none of these brief hearings carried the punch that he liked, each was in its way instructive.

The testimony on the Abraham Lincoln Brigade from volunteers and their relatives provided a taste of an especially bitter part of the bitter war in Spain: the use by the Stalinists of their control of the international brigade to carry on their own vendetta against anti-Stalinists. It would always be hard for Loyalist sympathizers in America to face up to this aspect of the Spanish tragedy, and the last person in the world they could take instruction from on so sensitive a matter was Martin Dies, who had never been heard to utter an unkind word about Franco. Yet the story of the war in Spain and of the traumas of American liberalism are not complete without a chapter on the brutalities of the commissars behind the Loyalist lines. The Dies Committee, for its part, showed no interest in any of the other chapters.

The union leaders to whom Dies devoted himself in April and May—Harry Bridges, Mervyn Rathborne of the American Communications Association, and Michael J. Quill of the Trans-

[3] Marcantonio, the tough, hard-working demagogue from East Harlem and Washington's exemplary fellow traveler, warned about the Smith Act taking us "with seven-league boots toward establishing in America, in free America, the slavelike institutions of Nazi Germany." But when the "teach and advocate" law was first used against Trotskyites during the war, the *Daily Worker* supported the prosecution, with an argument that might have been quoted from Martin Dies: "The American people can find no objection to the destruction of the Fifth Column in this country. On the contrary, they must insist on it." When, after the war, the C.P. leaders themselves were brought to trial for violating the Smith Act, Communists discovered again that a question of civil liberties was involved and hastened to defend our free institutions.

port Workers Union—had all been charged with Communist affiliations and sympathies innumerable times before, and the latest witnesses, former members of their unions, only added a few more instances of Communists-at-work to an already substantial body of testimony. Rathborne, who had recently been honored by the President with a position on the board of the National Youth Administration, came before the Committee attended by Vito Marcantonio as his counsel, and politely denied everything. Quill put on a much livelier show. He referred to his predecessor as head of the Transport Workers, Thomas Humphrey O'Shea (who told the Committee he was ejected from the leadership by Communists so that Quill could take over) as "your stool pigeon" and when Representative Thomas demanded that the designation be struck from the record, Quill agreed to change it to "lunatic."

Quill, the former subway station agent, was fresh from having been refused the nomination of the American Labor Party for reelection to the New York City Council. The A.L.P., then attempting to cleanse its ranks of Communists, disowned him when he could not bring himself to criticize the Nazi-Soviet pact. "They are digging up some phoney idea about the Soviet-German pact," Quill explained to the Committee. "I don't know what it had to do with building sewers in Bronx County, New York, but they wanted me to take a stand in it and support the war policy of Chamberlain. We don't support that by anybody. We in the labor movement are against war and anybody who causes war." In this latter group he included the Dies Committee. "You are trying to bring about a war hysteria to stampede the American people into war." He made an impossible witness, loud, gross, and about as responsive as an opposing left tackle; he exasperated even the tolerant Voorhis. When the chairman said, "He came here for the purpose of insulting this Committee," no one could challenge the observation. Finally, when Dies was unable to quiet him down and stop him from hollering about "sabotage" on the subways, he was forcibly ejected from the hearing room, crying "Labor will live!" all the way out.

The lumpy leader of the subway and trolley drivers was very

much the professional Irishman, regaling anybody who would
gather round with his purported experiences in the I.R.A. as a
boy, but only the politically color-blind could believe that his
favorite color was green. His Communism never went deep,
however, and as the fashion in political cosmetics changed
around 1948, he was able to kick his comrades out and forego
ideological coloration entirely. Many Communists of the thirties, wrongheaded and brutal though they frequently were,
showed considerable courage when the pressure was on. "Red
Mike" Quill never cared that much. The great achievement of
his thirty-year career as ruler of the T.W.U. was his tenacity
in holding to power with the collusion of New York City's
Democratic Party machine; his Marxism was blarney from the
start, and some months before his death in 1966, the former
radical was demanding that a policeman be installed on every
bus in New York to save his bourgeois drivers from the dep-
redations of the downtrodden.

In July, Dies, sitting as a one-man committee in executive
session, took testimony from a John L. Leech who identified
himself as an ousted member of the Hollywood Communist
Party. Leech was like those Slavonians described by Rousseau
who spent their lives wandering about and submitting to be
baptized where they found it worth their while. In addition to
revealing that Young Communist Leaguers in California were
luring soldiers and sailors to Red socials, he named forty-two
actors, actresses, writers, producers, and directors as C.P. members, sympathizers, or contributors. In an unaccustomed show
of restraint, Dies did not make public their names, but a few
weeks later a Los Angeles grand jury, which for some unac-
countable reason had also taken testimony from Leech, released
a score of them to the press. It turned out to be a mixed bag—
containing both flaming devotees of the Party and persons who
had merely lent their names or their money to some apparently
worthy cause in which the C.P. had a hand. Leech was habit-
uated to making strong charges against well-known individuals
and then backing down when pressed for evidence or confronted by the accused. Most of his testimony dribbled away
like sand. Still the nation was treated to the odd experience of

reading that the great stars in whom it had invested so much of its emotional life, those near-mythical figures, were appearing one by one before a Congressman from Orange, Texas, for absolution. Dies, sitting alone, received, heard, and issued his clearances to James Cagney, Humphrey Bogart, and Fredric March, to Franchot Tone, Luise Rainer, and Francis Lederer. Neither he nor they gave any sign that they recognized some presumption in these proceedings. (Years afterward, Representative John Rankin of Mississippi, annoyed at Fredric March for his participation in the Independent Citizens Committee of the Arts, Sciences and Professions, would remind the House that the actor had been "identified as a member of the Communist Party by a Party member who testified under oath before the Tenney Fact Finding Committee of the State of California." Such are the uses of the Leeches among us.)[4]

The nervousness of the Hollywood community when faced with the kind of attack at which Martin Dies was expert would be exhibited on a wider screen in 1947. But already in 1940, mere liberals among the actors and directors were being outmaneuvered on both right and left. In response to one of Dies's periodic pledges to investigate subversive influences in Hollywood, the town's fellow travelers organized a meeting in Philharmonic Hall. A skit, *When Martin Comes*, written by Donald Ogden Stewart, a scenarist of comedies and pillar of fellow traveldom, was performed by the author and Dorothy Parker, who had mislaid her renowned wit for the occasion. Every line betrayed the sources of its inspiration, and the production helps

---

[4] Witness Leech also brought up the name, in the closed hearings in Beaumont, Texas, of a California Congressman, Franck Havenner. Leech claimed to have met Havenner at gatherings where only Communists were *persona grata*, and although he confessed to a lack of documentation on the matter, he allowed that it was his "understanding" that the Congressman was a member of the Communist Party. Nothing of this was made public until the 1944 campaign, when an anti-Havenner advertisement in the San Francisco *Chronicle*, sponsored by "a group of citizens who believe in good government and the American way of life", carried selected portions of the testimony. None of the members of the Dies Committee, with the exception of the chairman, had been aware of its existence, but the mystery of its release was lifted somewhat when it was learned that before the 1944 campaign James H. Steadman, a Committee investigator who took part in the Leech interview, went to work for Albert C. Mattei, president of the Honolulu Oil Company, a major financial supporter of the Republican cause in northern California and the chief backer of Havenner's opponent in 1944.

us to recall how funny were Hollywood's serious movies of the period. Here is an excerpt from Miss Parker's entirely unsatiric climactic speech:

> . . . The people want democracy—real democracy, Mr. Dies, and they look toward Hollywood to give it to them because they don't get it any more in their newspapers. And that's why you're out here, Mr. Dies—that's why you want to destroy the Hollywood progressive organizations—because you've got to control this medium if you want to bring fascism to this country . . . We're grateful to Hollywood for our jobs and we're grateful for the opportunity it gives us to speak for American democracy . . .

We shall hear again from those Hollywood voices who, in their next encounter with the Un-American Activities Committee, will tell us in equally hapless prose that our choice in America rests between fascism and them.

The Committee was called upon to sit as judge in yet another case at about this time: a dispute between Representative Wright Patman, a relic of populism from Texas, and Carl Byoir, the preeminent public relations man. While serving the Great Atlantic and Pacific Tea Company, Byoir had helped defeat an effort by Patman to restrict the operations of chain stores. Now Patman charged that Byoir was a German agent, retained by Adolf Hitler through George Sylvester Viereck, "to sell Hitlerism to America." As he warmed to his subject, Patman added that Byoir was supposed to set up "the greatest spy organization in the history of the world" and was unfit to wear the uniform of a lieutenant colonel in the U.S. army reserve.

The nature of the public relations craft does not allow of superfluous fastidiousness in the choice of clients and Byoir, as the McCormack-Dickstein hearings had disclosed years before, had indeed served the German Tourist Bureau at a fee of $6,000 a month from 1933 to 1935, but beyond that he seemed to be as clean as the requirements of his profession permitted. Patman came before the Committee with much more indignation than evidence. The F.B.I. had already cleared Byoir; a subcommittee of the Dies Committee had also cleared him; in September the full Committee cleared him; and again, in August of the following year, for once and all, it "fully exonerated" Byoir "of any charges reflecting on his Americanism or loyalty to the government of the United States." Congressman Patman, having made his accusations while wearing the cloak of Congressional immunity, could not be fitted with a libel suit. It was a passing incident for the Committee, an engagement which, for a change, it had not sought, and which it performed with a sense of fairness that it did not always exert in the cases of persons accused of being hirelings of Moscow, but it raised a question that would prove troublesome in years to come: What is an appropriate tribunal for adjudicating public charges against a man's loyalty? The fact that the job could have fallen to a body like the Dies Committee indicated how far we were in 1940 from a sensible answer.

Dies made passes at other national threats that spring and summer—propaganda in textbooks and conspiracies in Mexico, the T.V.A.,[5] and the W.P.A.—but he was an impatient fisherman. His eye was readily caught, his net quickly cast, but if the game did not jump in at once he moved on. And in these latter months of 1940 there was an inviting place for him to move. Suddenly that spring the war in Europe had turned real; the German blitzkrieg swept through the Low Countries; Mussolini joined Hitler; France fell. In this country attention turned to the rush build-up of war industries, and for the quasi-official hunters of subversion this was taken as an opportunity to cry sabotage. Their cause was abetted by the Communist union leaders, still opposed to aiding Britain, who were bent on creating as much industrial turbulence as they could. As Congress debated the problem of what to do about aliens, particularly those in the defense program, Dies won the standing applause of the House with a half-hour speech on the Trojan Horse in our midst. He reported that he was swamped with "new leads,"

[5] The entirely unincriminating T.V.A. hearings would be exhumed in 1947 by Senator McKellar of Tennessee in an attempt to block the nomination of Gordon Clapp as T.V.A. administrator and of David Lilienthal as chairman of the Atomic Energy Commission. Legislators and publicists of all political hues have found that selected excerpts from transcripts can be useful even when the hearing taken in its entirety does not prove what they wish it had proved.

including an unconfirmed one that the Germans were building air bases in Mexico, and he asked for another $100,000 for his Committee.

Soon he was warning that "Foreign governments have placed agents and saboteurs in every key industry, and unless the government acts within thirty days I predict a series of actual sabotage that will cripple the whole national defense program." A chemist told a subcommittee of Starnes, Voorhis, and Mason of three instances of suspected sabotage at his Pennsylvania shipbuilding firm—such as the stuffing of pieces of a sweater into the oil pressure system of a ship, which he attributed to Communists and Nazis in the vicinity. Starnes warned that there were hundreds of Bundsmen, Communists, and aliens employed in defense plants. Dies improved on this, declaring that there were 5,000 in Detroit alone, and he was planning to publish industry-by-industry lists of all workers with Communist, Nazi, or fascist connections. In this group he included not only Bundists and C.P. card holders, but members of suspect unions such as the N.M.U. and the T.W.U. When the Hercules powder plant in New Jersey blew up in September, killing fifty-one persons and threatening to throw an uneasy nation into a proper panic, Dies proclaimed it was the very incident of sabotage that he had predicted the year before, when federal officials had just "laughed at us."

A few weeks after the Hercules explosion, Congress voted an additional $35,000 to carry the Committee through the end of the year. This brought its total appropriation to $235,000—the largest amount ever appropriated for a special investigating committee in the experience of the chairman of the Committee on Accounts—and it pepped up Dies's attack on federal security measures. "Employers say they cannot fire some of these saboteurs because of the National Labor Relations Board," he protested, and delivered a Texas threat—"We may have a showdown on that." He announced that he had been sending material on the activities of foreign counsulates to the State Department, and threatened to make his information public if the government didn't crack down. He kept demanding an "early answer" from Roosevelt and the Republican Presidential candidate Wendell Willkie, both of whom had criticized the Committee's work, to the question he first put to them in August: "Whether or not, you will advocate, favor and support legislation which will outlaw the Communist Party, the German-American Bund, the fascist organizations and, in fact, all political organizations that are shown to be under the control of foreign governments or the agencies of foreign governments." When, on November 12, three powder plants in the east were blown up within one hour of each other, Dies was ready with a warning that "the acts of sabotage in the past twenty-four hours are only a beginning." He promised to ask Congress for four or five million dollars in order to "close in" on subversive elements throughout the country. Thomas took the occasion of the mysterious explosions to demand "a shakeup in our government so that there will be no more coddling of subversive groups or activities. The federal government should cooperate with the employers so that they can get tough about whom they hire and fire." In particular, he wanted them to be tough on aliens in defense work: "If these men want to work in these industries and these plants, why aren't they patriotic enough to become American citizens?"

Dies offered little evidence to support his riot of charges, and did not stay to see if his predictions would come true. (When he spoke of imminent sabotage in West Coast airplane factories, California's Governor Olson humorously asked him for additional details so that preventive measures might be taken.) But events in Europe made his warnings seem far from incredible. The fifth column was a popular dramatic subject, and even F.D.R. conceded that the Dies Committee had provided the government with some information about its doings. The suspicion of aliens which had resulted in the patriotic excesses of World War I was visible again, with anti-alien legislation being much advocated in the Capitol by men like Thomas and a group of Southern representatives, led by Smith of Virginia, Cox of Georgia, and Rankin of Mississippi.[6] It was a frighten-

---

[6] Among the alien-baiting laws proposed in the House during these years (F.D.R. commented in 1940 that they were coming through at the rate of three a minute) were bills to deport aliens considered "inimical to the public

ing time; there was no reason to doubt that potential fifth columnists were at large and everyone was agreed that something ought to be done about them. What is surprising is not that Dies's hazily substantiated charges should have been taken as evidence of anything besides showmanship, but that despite all the tough talk in Congress, the final results were so mild. We did succumb to the Smith Act, but faced with a far greater threat than in 1917, the nation behaved with far more dignity. In part this was due to less provocation—there was not the kind of opposition among radicals to our participation in World War II that there had been to World War I; but, more important, Franklin Roosevelt proved in this test a sturdier bulwark of civil liberties than Woodrow Wilson.

It took much less political shrewdness than F.D.R. possessed to see that the constant assailing of aliens was merely one more way that his Congressional opponents had found of shooting at their favorite targets—the C.I.O. and the National Labor Relations Act and, through them, at the whole New Deal and all its hated progeny. The twelve-day Vultee aircraft strike in November 1940 was for the New Deal's enemies an opportunity to launch a particularly strong attack on the N.L.R.B. which, they charged, was preventing employers from firing the hoards of subversive aliens in defense plants. The Vultee strike was led by U.A.W. organizers who had been called Communists by John Frey at the start of the Dies Committee hearings, and an F.B.I. investigation of the strike confirmed that it was Communist-directed. Within a year, the U.S.S.R. having entered the war, America's Communists would be patriotic to the point of strike-breaking, but in 1940 they were opposed to the U.S. defense effort and were doing what they could to impede it. Vultee was at the time the only firm producing training planes for the army; to the anti-C.I.O. nativists, the strike bore out all their premonitions of Red subversion, and they were not disposed to suffer their anxieties in silence. "We have coddled that bunch of cutthroats long

interest," to deport aliens who did not take out their citizenship papers within three months, to deport all aliens and prohibit all immigration, and, from Representative Howard Smith, to ban aliens from the practice of optometry.

enough!" proclaimed Representative Sumners of Texas, chairman of the House Judiciary Committee, in a debate on the Vultee strike, aliens, and subversives in general:

> They respect just one thing and I am in favor of giving them a double dose of their own medicine. They preach force. The time has come when America has got to subject them to the only sort of argument that they pay any attention to, and that is all there is to it . . . They come over here, a lot of them do, driven from the countries of their nativity, and they do not more than get to this country until they begin to try to tell Americans how to run this government. We have had enough of it.

His remarks, applauded by his audience, were not the most intemperate of the day—Representative Smith proposed punishing sabotage in defense industries with life imprisonment—and Voorhis pardonably dramatized the temper of his colleagues when he said, "I think the House at the present time is in a completely totalitarian state of mind."

Dies was very much a part of the nativist group, but what brought him into open conflict with the Administration was not the treatment of aliens, about whom he and the Department of Justice definitely differed, but the treatment of pro-German propagandists about whom they quite agreed. Dies had promised to hold no public hearings during the 1940 election campaign, and although he abided by the letter of his pledge, his spirit was not subdued. His calls in speeches and news releases for immediate dismissal from defense plants of workers "suspected of subversive activities" never flagged, and his book *The Trojan Horse in America*—in large part a review of J. B. Matthews's testimony on front groups involving New Dealers—came out in time for the campaign. But Attorney General Robert Jackson, whose distaste for Martin Dies was not classified material—did not pick up the gauntlet until late in November. F.D.R. had been awarded his third term, the Democrats were in secure control of Congress, and Dies had, by issuing with great fanfare a White Book on German operations in this country, opened himself to the charge of interfering with the work of our official law-enforcement agencies.

The Committee's White Book, a collation of correspondence gathered in a series of raids by Committee investigators, presented evidence that organizations such as the Transocean News Service, the German Library of Information, and the German Railroad Office[7] were subsidized by German consulates in this country, and in addition to preaching appeasement were trying to fix up useful business arrangements for the Third Reich. A *New York Times* editorial gave a fair assessment of the report, finding it of value but somewhat anticlimactic after the advance build-up. (Dies had announced that the work of Nazis in the United States would be "destroyed" as a result of his exposé, which was "unique in American history.") The *Times* wrote:

> To anyone who knows the structure of the German Reich, there is nothing surprising in the evidence that German consuls have helped to subsidize a Nazi propaganda service, or that German businessmen have been planning trade conquests in the hemisphere. The Dies "White Book" seems to tell chiefly of little schemes and little men, and of techniques as clumsy as Von Papen's in the days of the World War.

Dies's conclusion that he had uncovered an espionage ring was a leap of imagination; the German representatives came through as more human creatures than the journalism of the day gave them credit for being. Particularly touching in the published correspondence were the pleas for money to the German Embassy in Washington of poor Manfred Zapp, who had been sent to this country in 1938 to run the Transocean News Service: "My postage stamp supply is sufficient for four days, thanks to your remittance of August 1 . . . Berlin has just now sent us $934. That is merely a drop in the bucket. From this I was able to pay immediately the rent, telephone and telegraph bills of last month and the wages . . . I already am dunned from every side and keep away from my office as much as possible." To a German minister in South Africa,

---

[7] The German Railroad Office was surely one of the most feckless covers for subversion ever conceived by the Aryan mind. It was ostensibly in the business of encouraging Americans to come visit the romantic castles of Germany while the war was going on.

he wrote steadfastly: "Almost all New York is enraged against the German barbarians. That is the atmosphere in which I must spread Transocean. However, I believe that I will still succeed in handling the local press." His success was not stunning. When a representative of a Cleveland newspaper expressed interest in taking his service, Zapp told him all about what he was offering, only to have the man publish the whole story in the New York *World Telegram*. ". . . We cannot cooperate with people who are so dishonorable," Zapp decided.

Two days after the White Paper was issued, Attorney General Jackson, in a statement to the press, accused Dies of interfering with the work of the F.B.I. The Committee's prime source, one Fassbender, was, Jackson said, "known as a professional and unreliable informer," of no value in court. (Dickstein, who had had occasion to throw Fassbender out of his office, was left with the impression that the man was "hungry and starving. He would have sold his mother for a dollar and a good meal.") The F.B.I. had been investigating the German representatives for many months, noted Jackson, and the Committee paper would make the building of a legal case that much more difficult. Because of its release, the Justice Department was compelled to bring charges against Manfred Zapp before a grand jury at once although its case was not yet complete. Jackson's statement concluded:

> The F.B.I. has gone about its task in an efficient and workmanlike manner without alarmist tactics and without sensationalism. It will continue to supply the proper agencies and government authorities with reliable, thoroughly sifted evidence as to subversive activities in this country. Efforts to arouse public sentiment or emotion, if that is desirable, will have to come from other sources.

By pitting Dies against J. Edgar Hoover instead of against F.D.R. and by choosing Nazis rather than Communists to fight over, the Administration had gotten the best possible odds for itself, and Dies tried at once to shift the grounds of the quarrel back to tried territory. He attacked "Jackson's record of encouraging Communist organizations in America." He reminded the nation once again that Jackson had endorsed the League for Peace and Democracy, which "openly advocated sabotage against the United States in the event of war," and had spoken before the Consumers National Federation and had written for the League of American Writers. In the following days Dies lumped Nazis and Communists together in the kind of broad-spectrum attack on the virus of un-Americanism which he relished:

I sincerely trust that immediate steps will be taken by the government to end Communist instigated strikes. The only effective measure that will prevent the agents of totalitarian powers from stifling our national defense program through strikes and acts of sabotage is to expel from national defense industries all Communists, fascists and Nazis.

He said there were at least six million people in the United States who belonged to organizations controlled by Germany, Italy, and Russia, and he was going to publish all their names. Late in November the Committee issued a 938-page document which it described as a report of Communist plans for sabotaging American industry in the event of war. This Red Book was, in fact, a compilation of the writings of eminent Communists from Karl Marx to Earl Browder, evidently everything Matthews could lay hands on at short notice regarding the violent overthrow of capitalism. It contained no information on any current plans for sabotaging American industry.

At about the same time, Dies sent a telegram to the President, asking him to coordinate activities against fifth columnists and so avoid "misunderstanding and conflict" between the Committee and the Departments of Justice and State. He held out an olive branch—or was it a sword? "There is plenty of work for all of us to do without indulging in unprofitable dispute and childish rivalries." Whether branch or blade, Dies's ambition to sit with the Administration as a co-equal law enforcement body was rebuked by return wire; F.D.R. reiterated Jackson's warning that the Committee's methods might "defeat the ends of justice." Pressing Dies on his vulnerable spot, Roosevelt pointed out that the administration of justice lay with the executive department, whose plans "may be severely handicapped or completely destroyed by premature disclosure of facts or suppositions to the public, or by hasty seizure of evidence which might with a little patience be obtained in a manner to be admissible in court . . ."

However, F.D.R. relented to the extent of inviting the Congressman in for a visit. A meeting was set up, and on November 29 Dies appeared at the White House, where he was obliged to wait in an anteroom while the President chatted with his old friend Gardner Jackson, instigator of the Pelley affair. Dies took this small joke of F.D.R.'s hard; he would complain of the indignity twice on the floor of the House, the waiting time rising from thirty minutes to forty-five minutes as his memory worked on it. Nor were his feelings assuaged when upon being admitted to the President's office after the half or three-quarters of an hour, he found in addition to the Roosevelt charm a stenographer waiting to make a record of the conversation. No transcript was ever released (the President, grumbled Dies, did not live up to his promise to send him a copy), but the report at the time was that Roosevelt spent the greater part of their fifty minutes together giving the Congressman a dressing down. In the recollection of Dies, published years after F.D.R.'s death, the President told him that day that Josef Stalin was a great leader and that some of his (F.D.R.'s) best friends were Communists. He said further, according to Dies, that the Communists were no threat to America and joshed the chairman with seeing a Red under his bed every night.

We have only Martin Dies's word for what passed between them, but it would not have been out of keeping with Roosevelt's attitude toward the anti-Communist investigations to express sentiments like those—or, more exactly, sentiments that sounded like those to Dies. Mr. Roosevelt was not one to brood about the internal Communist menace; indisputably, some of his best political friends had been, until the Nazi-Soviet pact, assiduous fellow travelers; and although he had sharply denounced Russia's invasion of Finland and was now high on the Communist hate list, he would believe until the end of his life that he could somehow handle Uncle Joe. Moreover, it was abundantly clear by the end of 1940 that the Administration could expect no kindness at the hands of Martin Dies, and secure in his recent election victory, F.D.R. could afford to be lighthearted about the Congressman's crusade. Whatever their conversation, Dies emerged from the meeting to take advantage of the fact that there were reporters waiting for him by calling for a two-year extension of his Committee and one million dollars. A few days later he told a radio audience that termination of his investigation "would bring to me a deep sense of personal relief" but that "it would mean an important victory for the fifth column in America" and so, despite opposition, obstruction, and untold tribulations, he had determined not to spare himself.

The entire Dies-Administration interchange took place in the shadow of the extension vote. The Committee's franchise was due to run out early in January, and as in prior years, the question was only how much money Dies would get this time. His popularity throughout the country was higher than ever; only 7 per cent of Dr. Gallup's sample felt that the life of the Committee should not be renewed, and 57 per cent favored giving Dies the million dollars he wanted. His staunchest support came again from patriotic groups; his opposition on the left was less vocal than in other years, partly because of the dissolution of the Popular Front, partly because he had lately been busy raiding the offices of Nazis instead of Communists. Dies was in a strong position, but he recognized that there has never been any political profit to be garnered in picking a fight with J. Edgar Hoover—"I certainly have no intention of interfering in any way with the work of the F.B.I. If a conflict arises between us, and the F.B.I. is watching a possible law violator, we will leave the case to them"—and he assigned Voorhis, a friend of the Administration, to work out some sort of public *quid pro quo* with the Department of Justice. In mid-December, after Jackson had again rebuked Dies for prematurely implying that an agreement had been reached whereby F.B.I. materials would be placed at his disposal, the attorney general set down in a letter to Voorhis—that carefully avoided all reference to the chairman of his Committee—the mutual understanding that the Justice Department would secretly give the Committee information on fifth column activities not fit for prosecution, and the Committee would furnish the department with material on prosecutable activities. It was a paper agreement with little meaning, but a success for Dies; to the general reader it established him as a recognized force in the anti-subversive campaign, an authorized co-worker of J. Edgar Hoover.

A few days after the agreement, Hoover issued a report of his own, which agreed with the findings of the Committee that Harry Bridges was a Communist, but made a point of disagreeing with Dies on the whole question of sabotage which for months had provided the fuel for his anti-alien campaign. Just two weeks earlier Dies had spoken dramatically of "five separate acts of sabotage" committed on "a most important experimental plane," and now Hoover reported that an F.B.I. survey of 1,200 war plants had uncovered no evidence of organized sabotage in American industry. He went so far as to reprimand Dies for his generalized criticisms of the F.B.I. Hoover's report was open to no interpretation other than that the Congressman was careless with the facts he broadcast abroad so persistently—not a novel suggestion and one which Dies was always quick to quarrel with when it came from the mouths of others. But even Martin Dies could not bring himself to call J. Edgar Hoover a tool of the Communist Party. The mass of his Committee's supporters, after all, revered the F.B.I. and Dies prudently allowed this slap to go unacknowledged.

The Committee ended its third year with three reports. On the first day of 1941, Dies released a translation of an "official confidential manual" of the German-American Bund which, according to the Committee, proved that the Bund was "an absolutely militarized organization patterned after the ruthlessly efficient military set-up which characterizes Hitler's machine in Germany." Unexpectedly, the document lived up to the Committee's description. Concerned mainly with the O.D. or Ordnungsdienst, the Bund's police, the manual clearly took as its model the chain of command of the Nazi storm troopers. It extolled the O.D. men as representatives "of the Fuehrership of American Germania"—their mission "to exterminate with all their power the stinking poison of red Jewish infection in America." The manual was obtained from Gerhard Wilhelm Kunze, the jailed Fritz Kuhn's replacement as national leader of the Bund. Kunze, unlike Kuhn, was born in this country, and he took pains in his appearance before a subcommittee to display his facility with the native tongue. Explaining that the Bund's use of the swastika was not to be construed as a tribute to Nazi Germany, he said:

> We recognize that symbol over there and elsewhere in the world as a symbol of Christian nationalism in contradistinction to atheistic internationalism, and we use it because it happens to be that form most generally used by races of the world closely related to us, but it has no connection whatsoever with the political philosophy of national socialism.[8]

A few days after the release of the Bund manual came a report on how the Axis countries were exploiting our international postal agreements to distribute their propaganda in this country by courtesy of the U.S. Post Office.

And in between these reports Dies made public his official report to Congress on his Committee's activities during 1939 and 1940. It was accompanied by one more of the chairman's sensational announcements: the Committee was investigating the transfer of at least $15 million in the past two months from the Central Bank of the U.S.S.R. to Germany and the other Axis powers. This news might have meant anything, or nothing, and it was to be another of those page one flurries that subsided as the ink dried. The official report, in addition to reviewing the Committee's endeavors and characterizing them without excessive modesty—"Our work has been a type of public education whose importance cannot be exaggerated"—for the first time put forward recommendations for legislation. Most of

[8] In August, some weeks before Kunze's appearance, the Bund held a joint rally with the Ku Klux Klan and the Protestant War Veterans of America at Camp Nordland, which prompted the Committee to call up its first witnesses from the K.K.K. One of them, an elderly minister and former Grand Kaliff from New Jersey, put the organization's essential principle as succinctly as it has ever been put: "I say it and I say it again that this is a free country and it gives me the right to attack . . . any group of people or any race, and I still hold that right."

these proposals Dies and his fellows in Congress had already called for many times: the deportation of alien spies and saboteurs as well as of "aliens who advocate any basic change in the form of government," and an end to immigration from countries that refused to accept the return of their undesirables; the outlawing of all organizations under the control of a foreign government and restrictions on totalitarian propaganda; making the statutory period for revocation of citizenship papers at least ten years and extending the statute of limitations on fraudulent passports to seven years. Voorhis took exception to the recommendation that federal financial support be withheld from educational institutions that permitted faculty members to advocate Communism, fascism or Nazism.

The proposals were in their way perfect, true to the spirit of the Committee and to an irrepressible spirit of America itself. The suspicion of the foreigner and nervousness over foreign ideologies, the mistrust of intellectuals, the impulse toward a show of toughness—powerful forces throughout our history—were primed for bursting in the anxious year of 1940, which began with the democracies beleaguered and ended with Britain standing alone. It was a good year for Martin Dies. He had tracked down no spies and he would not follow through on his legislative proposals, but a large part of the nation looked to him as a guardian of some essence of Americanism against all varieties of imported peril. In addition to exposing Nazis in 1940, his Committee had exposed cases of fraud in Communist Party nominating petitions, which resulted in the Party being taken off the ballot in several states.

The Congressional opposition of previous years was routed by his popularity. In the 1940 election Coffee of Washington, one of the earliest and most forceful critics of the Committee, used as a slogan "The Dies Committee endorses John Coffee's reelection," and when it came time for extending the Committee's life in February 1941, Coffee voted aye. "There is hardly a handful of the House today," said Hamilton Fish, leading the easy way to extension, "that will speak or vote against the continuation of the Dies Committee. Some of those who spoke against it only a year ago are not back in the House."

For the opposition, the debate was a catastrophe. Representative Marcantonio, allowed one minute, inveighed, as was his custom, against the coming of fascism. Representative Hook, allowed one minute, asked what the Dies Committee had uncovered that hadn't been known before, which gave Representative Cox an opportunity to reply, to the vast amusement of his colleagues: ". . . the Committee exposed the fact that there was a half-witted fool around town here that was selling forged materials to members of Congress . . ." Representative Dickstein, allowed five minutes, quickly ruined his day by charging "that one hundred and ten fascist organizations in this country had the back key and have now the back key to the back door of the Dies Committee." Whereupon Rankin of Mississippi immediately obtained an hour's time to attack Dickstein for maligning a member of the House, a parliamentary maneuver that silenced the blustering New Yorker. "I do not want any such man to . . . pretend to speak for me or for those old-line Americans that I have the honor to represent," said Rankin, lest anyone forget that Dickstein was born in Russia and was a Jew to boot. Rankin turned most of his time over to Dies, who used it mainly to defend his extra-Congressional activities, the lectures he had been giving around the country and the articles he had been writing, and to tell of the sacrifices he had endured in the line of duty. He was accorded another standing round of applause when he finished on the verge of collapse. Even some liberals could join in, recalling how much of the year had been taken up with German agents and Bundists. A few weeks later, by a vote of 354 to 6, the Special Committee was given an unprecedented fourth year of life, and was granted the sum of $150,000, the largest yet, to carry it along until April 1942.

A triumphant hour—yet its high promise would not be realized. Dies was only midway through his career as Committee chairman; he now had a thirty-man staff and brave battles lay ahead; but in the coming months political rebuffs at home, dramatic changes in the war, and his uncontrollable animus toward the Administration would conspire fatefully against his ambitions.

5

1941-1944: End of the Tether

THE Committee began 1941 with a change of personnel.
Harry P. Beam, an unmemorable Democrat from Illinois,
replaced Representative Dempsey, who did not stand for reelection. It was of small moment. Dies had always gone where
his temper, public attention, and J. B. Matthews directed without waiting upon his colleagues, and they would play a progres-
sively lesser part in his adventures in the years ahead. As the
careful Ogden notes:

> Somewhere between the fall of France and 7 December 1941
> the Committee, as far as the public record indicates, had dis-
> appeared. Its place had been taken by a one-man agency which
> could not properly be called administrative and yet could not be
> called legislative. The information gathered by the investigators
> was utilized by the chairman who, to all intents and purposes,
> had become the Committee.

From the summer of 1940 to the end of the life of the Dies
Committee, Chairman Dies never appeared at a public hearing.

The first affray of the new season was set off by J. B.
Matthews. In a tactic that recalled his 1939 assault on consumer
organizations, the Committee's chief of staff issued a statement
to the press that an investigation was under way into the Institute for Propaganda Analysis. The I.P.A. had been set up a
few years before by a group of educators with the announced
purpose of "assisting the public in detecting and analyzing
propaganda." (As Edward L. Bernays tells the story, the Institute was conceived at the end of a meeting at the Columbia

University Club called by E. A. Filene, the Boston department store owner. It was a dull, unprofitable meeting, and Filene, ever bent on getting people to buy his ideas as well as his merchandise, finally said to Clyde Miller of Teachers College— who would lose his post because of his political proclivities before the decade was done— "You there—here is ten thousand dollars for the first year. I don't care how you spend the money.")

By 1941 I.P.A. teaching guides were being used by a million children in three thousand public and private high schools around the country, and dozens of textbooks made reference to its work—which treated U.S. institutions and slogans with heavy skepticism. The National Association of Manufacturers was moved to hire an assistant professor of banking at Columbia University to make a survey of textbooks; he read six hundred of them and found that a substantial number "tended to criticize our government and hold in derision or contempt the system of private enterprise." The N.A.M.'s scholar objected strenuously to what he regarded as a program of making children critical without giving them a foundation for criticism: "Let's teach the pupils something about the principles of democracy or private enterprise before we start to tell them it is all run by a bunch of crooks and is no good."

The I.P.A. composed a reply which spoke disparagingly of the role of the N.A.M. in education, and Matthews's statement came out on the very February day that it was published. To support his description of the I.P.A. directors as "frankly left wing," Matthews noted that the president, Kirtley Mather of Harvard, had gone on record as criticizing the Dies Committee, had raised objections to throwing the Communist Party off the ballot, and had asked aid for anti-fascist refugees from Spain. Matthews also noted that in January 1940 I.P.A.'s official bulletin had carried an unflattering survey of his own methods of operation. Entitled *Mr. Dies Goes to Town,* it analyzed Matthews's attack on consumer groups and concluded:

It seems evident, after studying Mr. Matthews' report, that his charges against the consumer movement are wholly unfounded. Of course, the Communists in any group can be expected to exert an influence far beyond their numbers; organized minorities always do. Still, to indict an entire movement, involving hundreds of thousands, if not millions of people, just because three or four of the leaders *may* be Communists is hardly justifiable. They may be Communists, but Mr. Matthews cannot be said to have proved it: his evidence is sparse and flimsy, at best. Moreover, suppose they are Communists: what is Communistic about wanting to make your purchases as economically as possible?

Despite its ingenuous air, the I.P.A. study did pinpoint the weaknesses of the report on consumers, and its criticisms of Matthews's techniques on that occasion could be applied to his report on the I.P.A. itself. Its directors, along with most of the nation's educators, had small use for the Dies Committee; they leaned rather to the left than to the right, and as the resignations the following month of Paul H. Douglas of Chicago University and Eduard C. Lindeman of the New York School for Social Work—both interventionists—would reveal, they disagreed among themselves on whether to oppose Administration policies toward the war in Europe. (In October the I.P.A. bulletin would be suspended "for the duration of the international crisis.") But that it was a Communist voice, Matthews did not exert himself to demonstrate. His release, presumably having gratified the N.A.M. as much as his report on consumers had gratified the Hearst Corporation, was the beginning and the end of his battle with I.P.A. In March its directors wrote Dies to ask that he either carry out a real investigation or announce that the entire indictment had been abandoned.

Dies did neither. His attention had been drawn yet again to a subject dear to him—Communists in the C.I.O. His particular target this March was the Steel Workers Organizing Committee; he inserted a charge into the Congressional Record that at least twenty-seven persons, whom he named as having been identified as Communists before his Committee, were involved with S.W.O.C. As Dies undoubtedly anticipated, this drew blood from Philip Murray, the steel union chief who had recently taken over from John L. Lewis as head of the C.I.O. Murray retorted that of the twenty-seven names, eleven

had never been associated with S.W.O.C., fifteen had been
gone for at least three years, and only one remained.

Dies's rejoinder, in a long telegram which he read to the
House, skipped over his apparent errors of fact and asked
Murray what he planned to do about the numerous Communists still leading unions within the C.I.O.: Curran, Quill,
Bridges, Gold, and the others whose names had been popping
up in Committee hearings since 1938. Murray, in his reply,
followed Dies's example. Instead of answering the question,
he accused Dies of labor-baiting. Whereupon the chairman, an
old hand at this kind of brawl, answered it for him: "You
are unwilling or unable to rid your organization of Communist
influences . . ." Whatever the inadequacies of Matthews's researches into S.W.O.C., the estimate of Murray's position was,
for the time, close to the mark. As Dies told the House: "Communists have obtained such a stranglehold on many of the
unions in the C.I.O. that it is now beyond the power of Mr.
Philip Murray or anyone else in the organization's leadership
to do anything about the matter." In 1941 Murray did not
have the strength to confront the Communists around him—
including so intimate an advisor as Lee Pressman, the union's
tough counsel. A struggle against them was already building
up within the C.I.O., but Murray could not admit to an enemy
like Dies that the species even existed. During the war years,
when the Communists cooperated enthusiastically with the
forces of light, there would be no sense in upsetting arms production with an internecine battle. But soon after the war
the Communists in the C.I.O. would be beaten, and thoroughly
—some ousted, some reformed, some merely grown too tired
to fight in a cause which the Soviet Union's aspirations in
Europe was making untenable at home. Martin Dies deserves
some credit for the defeat of labor's Communists in America,
but Josef Stalin deserves more.

From the time when, as a novice Congressman, Dies was
elevated to the House Rules Committee, he was looked upon
as a coming man in Democratic politics. His remarkable number of citations on page one, his busy schedule of appear-

ances around the country (160 speeches between August 1938 and February 1941), his magazine articles (*Liberty* was his favored outlet) and newspaper interviews about menaces internal and external—all these stirred speculation about his future. So, when Senator Morris Sheppard of Texas died in April 1941, Dies was a foremost candidate for the vacant seat, and he devoted himself that spring to campaigning for the Democratic nomination, on the basis of his Committee's performance.

There were twenty-five aspirants for the job, including another young Congressman, Lyndon B. Johnson, who was a friend of F.D.R. and of the New Deal. The representative from Orange later complained, undoubtedly with justice, that "Word was spread in the right quarters that the election of Dies would mean that Texas would expect much less in federal handouts." To counter this appeal, Henry Ford offered Dies financial support from industrialists to wage an all-out patriotic campaign, with brass bands and movie stars, but there were strings attached and the deal was not consummated. Dies's own explanation of why he rejected the money will not satisfy all students of his career: "Somehow I couldn't bring myself to accept the offer. It went against my grain to thus make a spectacle of patriotism."

The Senate seat went to Governor W. Lee O'Daniel, who beat out Lyndon Johnson by 1,311 votes. Dies came in fourth, behind the state's attorney general, and complained that the "C.I.O. and fifth column organizations poured hundreds of thousands of dollars" into the state to defeat him. But there was no particular need to look to sinister elements to explain his defeat. "Pappy" Lee O'Daniel, who went around campaigning with a hillbilly band and a troop of ballad singers, was a great favorite in rural counties, and Johnson, an all-out New Dealer whose slogan was nothing less than "Johnson and Roosevelt," carried the big cities. Liberal commentators who chose to find in Dies's defeat evidence that his game was up were engaged in wishful thinking, yet his political career never did advance. For all his popularity in the polls, he was no match for the likes of Lyndon Johnson in a major campaign. He was vigorous at attack when he was attacking a target that few cared to defend, but sustained effort of a more complicated, not to say constructive, sort seemed to tire him. He had ruined himself with the Administration, with much of labor, and with many regular Democrats, including some of the most important politicians in his own state, and he never again reached out toward any office beyond the honorable one of U.S. Congressman.

As Dies was campaigning in Texas, in Washington a subcommittee of Starnes, Voorhis, and Mason returned to the ever-sustaining wells of Communist frontism. Hazel Huffman, who had told the Committee years before that the Federal Theatre Project was a Red nest, had been assigned to infiltrate the American Peace Mobilization, and now returned to say what everyone knew: that it was Communist-dominated. She made her case, but the hearing was only a shadow of past Committee glories because the A.P.M. was only a shadow of past Communist glories. The organization was set up in September 1940, at an "Emergency Peace Mobilization" held in Chicago Stadium under sponsorship of a body called the Committee to Defend America by Keeping Out of War. The Socialist Party, with its trained nose for such matters, at once branded the event "Communist inspired and controlled from end to end." A Presbyterian minister from Norman, Oklahoma, was rung in to chair the proceedings, but the main haranguers were circuit standards like Joe Curran who shouted that industrialists and bankers were behind the conscription bill; Mike Quill, who shouted that American labor "will fight only on American soil"; and the hard core leaders of the remnant American Youth Congress. Senators Nye and Clark, isolationist spokesmen, took back their acceptances of invitations to the rally upon being informed of its auspices. The A.P.M. did everything in the manual. It staged demonstrations against the draft, opposed lend-lease, and protested against the no-strike bill. There was a lot of folk singing at their meetings, lyrics like:

> I'd rather be at home, even living in a hollow log
> than go to the Army, be treated like a dirty dog.

And:

Wendell Willkie and Franklin D.
seems to me they both agree
they both agree on killin' me.[1]

In April, three hundred A.P.M. members picketed the Pennsylvania Avenue entrance of the White House and sent a statement to the President telling him that "our foreign policy should seek to prevent the spread of war by establishing genuinely friendly relations with the Soviet Union." In May the A.P.M. started a perpetual Peace Vigil in front of the White House in protest against aid to Britain; it lasted for forty days. Its leaders chose June 21 to issue a call for a National Peace Week. This event was rained out when, on June 22, Germany marched into the Soviet Motherland, and shortly thereafter the American Peace Mobilization became the American People's Mobilization, its new slogan "For Victory Over Fascism!", its new platform "U.S. aid to all peoples fighting Hitler!" War, recently horrendous, had regained its virtues.

For those fellow travelers who still had the strength and will to travel, adjustment to the needs of the U.S.S.R. was second nature by now, and the June 1941 adjustment came easier than most since it permitted them to return from outermost political Siberia. For Dies, on the other hand, the violent break between Germany and Russia offered nothing in the way of profit. He predicted that Hitler would be in control of the U.S.S.R. within thirty days and that "All of those gullibles and fellow travelers in America who aided the Communist cause prior to the alliance may be expected to resume their activities in behalf of Moscow." He was nearer the truth about America than about Russia, but the subject of Communist

---

[1] Another A.P.M. favorite was *Washington Break-Down*:

Franklin D., listen to me, you ain't a-gonna send me 'cross the sea; you ain't a-gonna send me 'cross the sea;
You may say it's for defense, it's that kinda talk that I'm against; I'm against, I'm against, that kinda talk ain't got no sense.
Lafayette, we are here, we're gonna stay right over here; we're gonna stay right over here.
Marcantonio is the best, but I wouldn't give a nickel for all the rest; I wouldn't give a nickel for all the rest.

subversion could not very well sustain him as long as the U.S.S.R. remained in the fight. For the next four years fellow traveling would be one of the lesser offenses in our national life; far from seeking to subvert the defense effort or, in a few months, the war effort, the entire left would be lashing us on to ever greater exertions, particularly in relief of the heroic Soviet people. Dies would be driven to cry in open frustration that ". . . our present foreign policy of all-out aid to Russia is one that makes it very easy for Communists and their sympathizers to pose as the most ardent patriots."

But all was not over yet. As the country moved onto a war footing, Dies was presented with new opportunities for attacks on old targets. Among the men being appointed to responsible positions in Washington's burgeoning bureaucratic establishment were quite a number that Matthews had on his lists, as having been in the thrall of one or more front groups during the thirties. Not only were they suspect in themselves, but they were now going to work for agencies whose purposes were a source of deep suspicion to most Republican Congressmen and to many Democrats. It was only in the nature of things, therefore, that when the far-reaching price- and rent-control bills came up for debate in the House in the summer and fall of 1941, Dies took the occasion to assail Leon Henderson, the President's choice to head the Office of Price Administration and Civilian Supply. While Henderson testified before the Banking and Currency Committee, Dies protested to the House that the new administrator had belonged to five Communist-controlled organizations, in particular the Washington Friends of Spanish Democracy: "I wouldn't put him in charge of dog catchers." In a letter to F.D.R. a few weeks later, Dies accused Henderson, four of his principal subordinates, and fifty unnamed lesser employees of his agency of having Communist-front records. Henderson, no man to remain silent before such an assault, said he would pass along all evidence to the Civil Service Commission but refused to take "funny letters to the President as a basis for firing anybody." He also declared himself ready "to eat on the Treasury steps any Communist organization to which I belong."

As the fight against price-control legislation, pressed earnestly by business and agricultural interests, continued into November, Dies returned to the attack. On the eve of a vote in the House, which watered down the bill significantly before passing it, Dies delivered a long address in which he complained that the four high O.P.A. employees he had exposed in August were still O.P.A. employees: ". . . I demand that before any price-fixing bill is passed we have definite assurance that those charged with the administration of this act shall be loyal, patriotic Americans who believe in our system of free enterprise and who will seek to preserve it." His strongest case was against Robert A. Brady, head consultant to Henderson. In a book published in 1937 by the Left Book Club, a principal organ of England's Marxist establishment, Brady described the business enterprise under capitalism as "centralized, autocratic, intolerant . . . the most completely amoral and materialistic single-purpose institution the human mind has yet devised." He foresaw a choice only between "the triumph of reaction and a new lease on life for capitalism, or else a victory for socialism and the extermination of the rich and powerful of bank, factory, bivouac and cloister." This was heady stuff, coming from a government consultant. "Think of that, my colleagues!" exclaimed Dies. "Here is a man who frankly advocates socialism and the destruction of the church!" If that were not enough, Brady had belonged to the American League for Peace and Democracy and the Harry Bridges Defense Committee, and was among the signers of a manifesto issued in August 1939 in praise of the Soviet regime. Even discounting some of Dies's more vivid language, Brady was an unpolitic choice for an agency with the delicate job of controlling prices in an economy where government controls would be strenuously resisted, and soon afterward the Civil Service Commission recommended that he and his wife, also in the O.P.A. service, be discharged.

While the O.P.A. fight was being resolved, Dies opened a second front—the Federal Communications Commission, which had recently hired Goodwin Watson as a broadcast analyst. Without Committee hearings or consultation with his colleagues, Dies wrote a letter to F.C.C. Chairman James L. Fly, designating Watson as a "propagandist for Communism and the Soviet Union." When ten days passed with no answer from Fly, Dies repeated his charge to the House. He read excerpts from a book of Watson's on the "failure of gradualism" among the Austrian Socialists. The material was not nearly so rousing as that of Robert Brady, exterminator of cloisters, and Watson's record, as recited by Dies, indicated that he was merely a run-of-the-mill fellow traveler. A faculty member at Columbia University for sixteen years and a distinguished social psychologist, he had been associated with the Workers Alliance, Consumers Union, and the League of Women Shoppers, had supported the reelection of Vito Marcantonio, had protested the ban on Communists in the Civil Liberties Union, and had publicly opposed William Randolph Hearst and the Dies Committee. In a letter to *The New York Times* Watson contended that he had actually belonged to only one of the thirteen groups cited by the Congressman—Consumers Union—and had written only two articles on the U.S.S.R. in his entire life.

F.C.C. Chairman Fly held his peace officially, but in January a story appeared in *Newsweek* to the effect that Martin Dies was being praised by Axis propagandists. When Chairman Dies asked Fly what it was all about, the latter explained that in August, September, and October, according to the F.C.C.'s monitoring service, the Congressman from Orange, Texas, had been the beneficiary of "as many favorable references in Axis propaganda as any living American public figure." Representative Marcantonio made much of this piece of news, which owed something to J. B. Matthews's technique of sizing people up on the basis of lines of type in the *Daily Worker,* and the House, angered by this affront to one of its own, voted an amendment to the F.C.C. appropriation which deleted Goodwin Watson's salary. It was turned back by the Senate, but two years later, when another appropriation bill came up for passage, Watson would find himself the center of a constitutional *cause célèbre.*

In January Dies stepped again into the well of the House to inform members that Malcolm Cowley, long the book editor for *The New Republic* and recently hired by Archibald Mac-Leish as chief information analyst of the Office of Facts and Figures at a salary of $8,000 a year, was "one of the chief Communist intellectuals of this country." He noted that his Committee's files gave Cowley seventy-two connections with the Communist Party and its fronts, and the Hearst press, to which the report was leaked, publicized the charges with gusto. Cowley's record as literary wheelhorse for the Stalinists throughout the thirties, up until the Hitler-Stalin pact, could not bear extensive scrutiny, and in March he resigned.

When in February the Congress was debating an appropriation for the newly created Office of Civilian Defense, Dies came forward with the news that in this seemingly harmless agency too, Communists were "trying to take things over." Here he found himself up against several old antagonists. The executive director of O.C.D. was James M. Landis, former dean of the Harvard Law School, who after eleven weeks of hearings in 1939 had judged that there was no proof that Harry Bridges, may we be protected from the evil eye, was affiliated with the Communist Party. The assistant director was no other than Mrs. Roosevelt herself, lately the patroness of radical students, and among the friends and protegés whom the largehearted First Lady had brought with her into the agency were the actor Melvyn Douglas, who had an off-screen affinity for left-wing causes, and, ultimate affront, none other than the celebrated leader of youth, Joseph P. Lash. But this skirmish was lost in a larger controversy as the scourge of un-Americans took time out from meeting the threat of the New Deal to meet the threat from Japan.

Just three days after Pearl Harbor, Martin Dies let reporters know that he had had fifty-two witnesses ready to testify in August on the subject of Japanese espionage on the West Coast and the Pacific islands, but the Department of Justice had withheld approval of hearings—presumably out of delicacy for the feelings of the Japanese, with whom negotiations were then in progress. From this kernel quickly sprung up an enormous tree. A few weeks later, while arguing unsuccessfully for an amendment to the foreign agents registration bill to compel the Communist Party, the German-American Bund, and the Kyffhauserbund to furnish the names of their members, Dies told the House he was convinced that if his hearings had gone off according to schedule, "the Pearl Harbor tragedy never would have occurred because we would have made public the plans of the Japanese to seize control of the Pacific."[2] He now predicted that if the government did not become more alert to the activities of subversives, the West Coast was in for "a tragedy that will make Pearl Harbor sink into insignificance." Some days after this speech he charged that 15,000 Japanese nationals were involved in espionage and he promised to issue a Yellow Paper containing "impressive evidence," which had been turned over to the several intelligence departments in the fall of 1941, that the Japanese had planned to attack where indeed they did attack—Pearl Harbor. Following a number of such handbills, the 285-page Yellow Paper—one quarter of it given over to a Justice Department list of Japanese treaty merchants—made its appearance. It told a moderately interesting story of Japanese espionage efforts, but did not live up to the advance promotion. As Voorhis observed, none of the information in the Committee's possession that he had seen "was anywhere near definite enough to show that a Japanese attack would take place in Hawaii on December 7 or to predict when such an attack might be made."

Freshman Representative Thomas Eliot of Massachusetts, then coming into leadership of the sparse anti-Dies forces, pointed out that contrary to what Dies had told the newspapers (or, anyway, what the newspapers had printed, since Dies claimed frequently that he was a victim of the misquote), the Department of Justice had done nothing to prevent the issuance of his Japanese report, though it had relayed the feelings of the Secretary of State and the President that they were "unable to

[2] In his excitement, he may have forgotten that at the end of October, midway between his scheduled hearings and the bombing of Pearl Harbor, he had assured the New Orleans Association of Commerce: ". . . The Japanese policy was just a bluff—and not too good a bluff at that. A lot of Americans like myself would like to see them bring their coal burners out for a good licking, but they won't."

approve" open hearings in August. Eliot also disclosed that
when Attorney General Biddle wrote to Dies for the evidence—
that supposedly had already been turned over to his department—of the "elaborate sabotage plot . . . uncovered by agents
of your Special Committee," the chairman merely wrote back
that his agents on the West Coast would be willing to cooperate
with Mr. Biddle's agents. "I assume," wrote Dies to Biddle,
"that with the hundreds of agents which you have you would
have no difficulty getting the facts." Pressed on these points
by Eliot in a debate early in March, Dies raised the issue of
personal privilege on the grounds that Eliot had called him
a liar, and expatiated upon Comunists in the C.I.O., upon his
record of exposing Nazis, upon the dignity of the Congress,
upon the need for patriotism in so parlous a time, and upon his
father's service in the House: "Let me say to the gentleman
that whether he serves here a long time or a short time the first
thing is to learn to love and respect the Members of this
House."

Eliot, who would be merely a short-timer but who could
hold his genealogical own with Dies by reminding the House
that *his* great-grandfather had served there ninety years before,
did not love his colleague from Texas sufficiently to halt his
attack. Much of the Japanese report, he disclosed, had been
"lifted without benefit of quotation marks." In particular, the
famous Pacific strategy map which Dies said gave "clear proof
of the intentions of the Japanese to make an assault on Pearl
Harbor" and which the Committee's agents claimed to have
obtained "under extraordinarily difficult circumstances," in
the first place did not show, as billed, "in great detail positions
of battle formations around Pearl Harbor," and in the second
place, had been published in 1935 in a large-circulation Japanese magazine named *King*, which also ran love stories and a
picture of Lou Gehrig. Another major item in the Yellow Paper
was a Japanese handbook of the U. S. Navy: "It was with great
difficulty that the agents of the Committee were able to obtain
a copy of the volume." Eliot picked up the book, published in
the early nineteen-thirties, in the Library of Congress. Marcantonio pitched in and showed that the remainder of the report

owed a great deal, none of it acknowledged, to a weekly newsletter published in Los Angeles and sold at ten cents a copy.
So scrupulous were the anonymous writers of the Committee
report in adhering to the language of the newsletter that where
the latter had "(illustration on this page)," the report had "(illustration on this page)," only, in the case of the report, there
was no accompanying illustration.

The argument about the Yellow Paper ran directly into the
annual debate over whether to continue the Committee
through 1942. No one expected anything other than a fourth
overwhelming extension, but our alliance with Russia against
the Axis combined with Dies's persistent assaults on the Administration's emergency agencies gave his opposition a record
number of votes against renewal—46 nays to 331 yeas. The
minority directed their fire mainly at the Committee's failure
to exert itself against Nazis and fascists, while the defenders
played variations on Thomas's refrain that "The Dies Committee may turn out to be the last remaining safeguard against
the dictatorship of the proletariat in America." Voorhis, fair-
minded as always but rather plaintive by now, asked once
again that the Committee function as a committee, with regular
hearings, decisions by majority, and like amenities. Not a single
meeting had been held since the previous extension. The
Committee's appropriation was not voted on until late April
owing to the unavailability of the chairman, who was at home
in Texas; it was granted $110,000 but now the opposition was
up to sixty-four members. The reason for the surprising increase
in just a few weeks was that in between the two votes Dies had
again been active.

In the closing days of March, skipping consultation with the
other members of his Committee, Dies sent an "open letter"
to Vice President Wallace, charging thirty-five officials of the
Board of Economic Warfare, which Wallace headed, with
Communist-front affiliations—again the League for Peace and
Democracy—and calling for their resignation or dismissal. The
letter, which Wallace received in his morning newspaper,
named ten of the thirty-five; mostly it had to do with an econ-

omist, Maurice Parmalee, who in 1939 had published a book with pictures called *Nudism in Modern Life,* which was ruled obscene by a district court judge. "At least," lectured the proper Dies, "there is no place in such an agency for an outstanding advocate of nudism." Wallace issued a strong rejoinder, complaining that the Congressman had not taken the trouble to bring the charges, "which might as well have come from Goebbels himself," to his attention before publicizing them, and he promised that the F.B.I. would check all of the named employees. He noted that Dies had neglected to mention that the district court's ruling on Parmalee's book had been reversed by the U.S. Court of Appeals, which, on the precedent of the *Ulysses* case, decided that "the book as a whole is not obscene" despite some questionable photographs. In the style of Marcantonio, the Vice President estimated that the letter's effect "on our morale would be less damaging if Mr. Dies were on the Hitler payroll."[3]

What, in particular, bothered Dies and other opponents of the New Deal about the B.E.W. was that in addition to having the tasks of controlling exports, stimulating imports of strategic raw materials, and engaging in economic warfare, it was supposed to be contemplating postwar economic problems. Congressmen on the right, already unhappy over the wartime restrictions on business, feared that the odd types then entrenching themselves in the emergency agencies would not readily relinquish their powers after the war. "I have reliable evidence, which I am not at liberty to disclose at the present time," Dies warned the House, "that some of those who hold key positions in our defense agencies consider themselves strategically placed for purposes of revolutionary change in our form of government and economics if and when the great crisis engulfs us." In the meantime, nudism was sufficiently naked subversion for the House, and the Congressmen had a high time with it. "I hold in my hand two of Mr. Parmalee's books," announced Repre-

[3] The most surprising people were wrapping themselves in the flag during these years. Moved by Dies's attack on the B.E.W., *The New Republic* commented: "There will presently be many American fathers and mothers of sons dead on the battlefield who may begin to ask themselves why Mr. Dies doesn't ever, not ever, do anything to help our war effort instead of hurting it."

sentative Cox, "and if I have ever seen anything that is filthy and dirty it is in these books." If a weakness for nudism were not enough, Parmalee had also written pamphlets with titles like *Farewell to Poverty* and *Bolshevism, Fascism and the Liberal-Democratic State*. The Administration was embarrassed, and in April he was dismissed, on the pretext of "reorganization."[4] Another of the ten, a specialist on Australian affairs, resigned after Voorhis accused him of Nazi sympathies because of his attacks on U.S. foreign policy in 1940. Voorhis later apologized when it became evident that the gentleman was no Nazi at all but simply a fellow-traveling pacifist during the Hitler-Stalin alliance.

All of the named officials, including the departed, were cleared by the F.B.I., and the balance of the thirty-five to whom Dies had originally referred were forgotten among the hosts of anonymous accused. But the name of one of the ten lingered, to the embarrassment of the chairman. In a speech soon after the release of the open letter, Voorhis complained about the unilateral method of operation and about the technique of listing the names of nine persons and surrounding them with "quite lurid material" having to do with a tenth, the scandalous Parmalee. Voorhis pointed out that, by definition, a Communist-front organization was composed partly of persons who were not Communists, and he directed attention in particular to the B.E.W. official named David B. Vaughn. Vaughn denied ever belonging to the A.L.P.D., and, indeed, there seemed to be a mistake somewhere. Sure enough, it turned out that the Vaughn employed by the B.E.W. was a Kentucky banker, and not the Boston University professor with whom the Committee's researchers had confused him. In May banker Vaughn sued Dies for $750,000. In July, Dies made public apology for the mistaken identification, agreed to pay Vaughn's legal fees, and hastened to submit to the House Accounts Committee a bill for $611 to cover costs in the Vaughn case and in a lesser suit that had been brought against

---

[4] The B.E.W. may have deserved its bohemian reputation. A second economist was later discharged after Dies reported that he conducted "rhythmic ritual services" in his off hours.

him for a similar reason. "There is a clear intention to sabotage
the Committee through the filing of suits," he complained, as
the House paid his court costs.

The Committee's next accusatory flurry, a mere entr'acte in
its anti-Administration marathon, came in June when, employing the Matthews manner, it attacked the Union for Democratic Action as "an organization composed chiefly of individuals
who have been a significant part of the interlocking directorate
of the Communist movement in the United States." The U.D.A.
was further charged, along with the *Daily Worker*, the *New
Masses*, and *Time* magazine, with being the spearhead of a
plot to discredit Congress and alter our form of government—
a theme that would occupy Dies more and more in his final
years. There had been no hearings on the matter; no U.D.A.
representative had been invited to present his side of the case;
and no specific accusations of Communism were made against
any individual.

The U.D.A. had in fact been formed in April 1941, before
the Nazi-Soviet rupture, for the main purpose of supporting
Administration moves to intervene in the war in Europe, and
had been assailed by the *Daily Worker* as "the fifth column of
Wall Street empire." Its first chairman was Reinhold Niebuhr
and its founders hoped to develop a strong anti-Communist
voice on the left. It had remained staunchly pro–New Deal in
this Congressional election year of 1942 and a few weeks earlier
had aroused pique on the right by collaborating with *The New
Republic* to publish a supplement entitled *A Congress to Win
the War*, which graded senators and representatives by their
agreement with Administration proposals and had no good
marks for Representative Dies or his closest political friends.
Among the Congressmen singled out as "obstructionists" were
Representatives Starnes ("Never has he voted for the domestic
legislation of the New Deal, except the T.V.A. which is so
popular in his district that he dare not oppose it"), Thomas
("has a clear record as a reactionary isolationist"), and Dies
himself ("clearly acting in the best interests of the Axis govern-

ments"). In addition, it had only hard words for such supporters of the Committee as Fish, Rankin, and Mundt.

The Committee report, gotten up in retaliation for this provocation, defined U.D.A. policy as proposing that "the sole remaining function of Congress is to ratify by unanimous vote
whatever wish is born anywhere in the whole vast structure of
the executive branch down to the last whim of any and every
Administration official." The U.D.A. did not, in truth, show any
great independence or discrimination when it came to Roosevelt's policies; still the Committee report was a campaign
document pure and simple. Voorhis, the one-man minority,
dissented from it, defending the "right of loyal American citizens to disagree politically with a majority of the Dies Committee without being branded as subversive and un-American."
There was not a single Communist in the U.D.A., he stated,
and the Committee did not stoop to pick up this gauntlet;
the demand for a hearing by U.D.A. President Frank Kingdon
went unacknowledged.

The Committee's aims had never been more clear, and the
Administration was preparing a counterblast in time for election day. In the spring of 1941, Congress had allocated $100,000
to the Department of Justice to investigate federal employees
suspected of belonging to subversive organizations. The job
was not one that Attorney General Biddle craved; it was forced
on him by a Congress goaded continuously by Dies during the
period of the German-Soviet pact. In many and diverse forums
Dies demanded that "at least one thousand government employees sympathetic with totalitarian ideology must be discharged." It took several months for him to draw up a list of
suspects for Biddle, but finally, in October, he sent along 1,121
names, accompanied by his trade mark: "The evidence which
I am submitting to you, Mr. Attorney General, indicates that
there is a new influx of subversive elements into official Washington." While Dies was complaining that subversives were
running amok through the federal bureaucracy, liberals were
complaining that charges against low-level employees were being made and acted upon without sufficient care: they were
denied hearings, the names of their accusers remained secret,

and they were sometimes dismissed without being told why, although there was reason to believe it was for nothing more sinister than working for the abolition of the poll tax or for aid to Loyalist Spain.

The attorney general's report to Congress on the uses to which he had put the $100,000 constituted a rebuttal to both sides in this dispute, but more emphatically to Chairman Dies. With the investigation largely completed, only two persons on the Dies list had been dismissed and a third had been subjected to some lesser disciplinary action. Most of the names submitted, it was evident, had simply been culled from mailing lists of fellow-traveling organizations like the National Federation of Constitutional Liberties and its capital chapter, the Washington Committee for Democratic Action, and, commented Biddle tartly, "never should have been submitted for investigation in the first place." He concluded with the observation that sweeping charges of disloyalty in the federal service were unjustified and that the results of the investigation were "utterly disproportionate to the resources expended"; he recommended that thereafter investigations of federal employees be restricted to cases where there were substantial reasons for suspecting a violation of the law. (Congress showed its appreciation by giving his department another $200,000 to proceed with the investigations Biddle strenuously opposed.)

Dies was roused to customary fury by the attorney general's report, and he used a point of personal privilege, now becoming his favorite parliamentary device, to denounce Biddle for ignoring the mandate of Congress. The Congressional directive, he pointed out, had ordered the attorney general "to investigate the employees of every department, agency and independent establishment of the federal government who are members of subversive organizations or advocate the overthrow of the federal government, and report its findings to Congress." What this meant, explained Dies, was that Biddle was supposed to supply Congress with "the names of the members of the organizations, tell who the subversive organizations are . . ." instead of presuming to make an investigation on his own, in cahoots with agency heads who were themselves on one or more tainted lists. It was the Congressman's simple desire that the Department of Justice lend its authority to publicizing the names of government employees whose affiliations may at one time have been misguided but whose loyalty to this country was not seriously in doubt. Biddle refused to turn his department into a certifying agency for the Dies Committee, and the battle went to him.[5] But the war was far from over.

A substantial part of the Committee's round-up report for 1941 and 1942 was given to complaints against Biddle, Henderson, Fly, and Wallace for not showing due fervor in pursuit of deviant federal employees. Devoted in the main to celebrating previously publicized accomplishments of the Committee—it now had 135 file cabinets containing more than a million cards —the report owed its newsworthiness to the inclusion of a dissent by Jerry Voorhis. Voorhis refused to sign for a number of reasons: Committee members had not been given a chance to discuss the report, but had had it presented to them on a "take-it-or-leave-it" basis; the charges of subversion, leveled against persons whose politics the majority found distasteful, were not adequately supported by evidence; the claim in the report that Japanese relocation was "a direct result" of the Committee's investigation of Japanese espionage was "extravagant"; in its discussion of the 1941 strikes, the report did not give sufficient credit to the over-all loyalty of American labor. Most important to Voorhis, the report contained little that might guide citizens on how to "identify, avoid and combat the propaganda activities of agents and friends of enemy nations of the United States in the current war"; he complained that the Committee had delayed for months the release of a study on Axis-front movements that he had helped to develop. Behind the delay of the Axis-front report was the Committee majority's dislike of a complimentary reference to the Administration in Voorhis's introduction. For Thomas it was "nothing more than

[5] It was in such skirmishes that Mr. Biddle earned the tribute that Professor Robert E. Cushman paid him in his study *Civil Liberties in Wartime,* published in 1943: "Congress had included in the Alien Registration Act of 1940 the most drastic law directed against sedition since the Sedition Act of 1798, and the Department of Justice might have embarked on a campaign of drastic repression, but this the Attorney General refused to do."

a whitewash of the New Deal." A report on Nazi activities was issued a few months later, without the complimentary reference, and did not make startling reading beside newspaper accounts of the government's arrest and indictment of dozens of native fascists for sedition. But by then Voorhis had resigned from the Committee.

During his four years in the company of Martin Dies, Jerry Voorhis was a disappointment to the nation's more truculent liberals as well as to those whose best friends were Communists —"wobbly as usual," commented Ickes. Although he exercised a restraining influence on the chairman's vigilante inclinations, he believed to the end that there was a place for such a committee in Congress—and not solely for the purpose of exposing oddities on the right. He believed that the Un-American Activities Committee had rendered a service to progressives by analyzing the workings of Communist fronts and to labor by exposing Communists in unions. For fellow travelers, this was a sign of lamentable weakness: in a special supplement published by *The Nation* in October 1942, the Dies Committee was attacked as "a camouflaged pill box in the fascist fight for control of our democracy." Editor Freda Kirchwey fired the troops: "It needs to be stormed and overthrown, not reformed." But Voorhis's only real weakness was that of a rational, fair-minded, and courteous man thrown into the company of men who were irrational, unfair, and discourteous and who had the power to satisfy their rudest passions. He was like a graduate student in sociology trying to talk sense to the drunkards in a skid-row bar. Again and again he asked that Committee rules be put in order to keep the chairman within bounds, and, as he conceded shortly before his resignation, he had been "one hundred per cent unsuccessful."

After each rebuff he considered quitting but, like an outmatched boxer with too many trainers in his corner, he allowed friends to persuade him to stay on and do what he could. Until, at last, when the Committee came up for a two-year extension on February 10, 1943, Voorhis cast his vote against it. It had become, he said, "more and more a political instrument of definite conservative bias, and less and less a dignified, important and effective Congressional committee." Ninety-four members, a record, voted against extension this time, but 302 voted for it. The opposition was composed largely of big-city Democrats. Other Democrats, though they might make nasty remarks about Dies in private, would not risk the disfavor of the Legionnaires and the Hearst and McCormick press with a nay, and Republicans, who had done surpassingly well in the 1942 elections, appreciated the Texan's value as an anti-Administration ally. The Committee was allotted $75,000, which included payment for David Vaughn.[6]

It was at this time, fortified by the conservative victories in the off-year voting, that Dies chose to launch his climactic attack on the Administration. This last major performance of his career gave full airing to the presumptions of the forces in Congress dedicated to resisting the executive branch. On February 1, 1943, Dies took the floor of the House for an hour and a half on another question of personal privilege. He was offended this time by the National Lawyers Guild, which had that morning placed on the desk of every representative a manifesto opposing renewal of the Special Committee: "Martin Dies and his Committee is the secret weapon with which Adolf Hitler hopes to soften up our Nation for military conquest." Dies used his ninety minutes to berate an assortment of enemies, such as *The New Republic* and Marshall Field, publisher of *PM*, to defend himself against accusations of anti-Semitism and anti-Negro sentiments, and to make patriotic periods. He was applauded at frequent intervals, which encouraged him to ever higher flights of eloquence:

> How would you like to go back to your constituents, to that father and mother who have just received word that their dearly beloved son has given his life in defense of America, how would you like to stand up there on the stump, Democrat or Republican, and attempt to defend the appointment by bureaucracy of a man

[6] Vacancies caused by the departures of the prudent Casey, the anonymous Beam, and the disheartened Voorhis were filled by Wirt Courtney of Tennessee, John M. Costello of California, and, as resident liberal, Herman R. Eberharter of Pennsylvania. A Republican, Karl E. Mundt of South Dakota, was added in acknowledgment of the election results.

who does not believe in the system these boys fought and died to preserve?

The substance of his remarks was yet another list of names—thirty-nine government employees whose ouster he demanded. Most of them worked in the recently created wartime agencies and had figured in his previous attacks on the Board of Economic Warfare, the War Production Board, and the Federal Communications Commission. Most had belonged to the League for Peace and Democracy and like groups on the left. Dies accused none of them of being C.P. members or of disloyalty to America; he attacked them as "irresponsible, unrepresentative, radical and crackpot," and issued an ultimatum to the Administration that, as the event turned out, was not mere bluster: "If you do not get rid of these people, we will refuse to appropriate money for their salaries." When he had done, Will Rogers, son of the late humorist and a new representative from California, rose to make his maiden address. He said: "I should like it to be known that I disagree with the sentiments expressed, the flamboyant manner of expression used and the use of this great forum as a means of what we in Hollywood would call personal publicity." But the critical gentleman was in a minority. The Republicans and Southern Democrats cheered Dies, and three days later Joe Hendricks of Florida rose to press the advantage.

The occasion was a billion-dollar Treasury–Post Office appropriation bill. Hendricks offered an amendment that no part of the appropriation should go to pay the salaries of any of the individuals named by Dies. Only one of these, William Pickens, a Negro economist, actually worked for the Treasury Department, but Hendricks proclaimed his intention to add his amendment to every appropriation bill that came up because, in the past, several persons on Dies's list had been ousted from one agency only to reappear in another. He was especially upset that Maurice Parmalee, the B.E.W.'s student of nudist habits, had found his way onto the Railroad Retirement Board. Hendricks was aiming at a state of things where "there will be no place else for these men to hedge hop."

There was precedent of sorts for Hendricks's proposal. In January 1942, as we have noted, during Dies's give-and-take with the F.C.C., the House deleted the salary of Goodwin Watson from the agency's appropriation, but the Senate killed the amendment. In a similar case, David Lasser, former head of the Workers Alliance, was discharged from his W.P.A. job after the House added an amendment to the 1940 Relief Appropriation Act forbidding him a salary; the provision was omitted from the 1941 appropriation bill, and Lasser turned up on Dies's 1943 list, this time as an employee of the War Production Board. Still, the idea of exempting from payment by the Treasury Department thirty-eight persons who did not work for that department, struck representatives on both sides of the aisle as far-fetched. Ludlow of Indiana called it "one of the most peculiar pieces of legislation ever presented to the House." It was natural that Voorhis would find danger in Dies's standard of whether or not an official "fell into a certain category which the gentleman categorized as 'crackpot,'" but even conservative voices like those of Dirksen of Illinois, Bender of Ohio, and Case of South Dakota—all destined for the Senate—were troubled by the wholesale blacklisting. Case said: "I am not willing to condemn thirty-eight men and women in thirty minutes on ex-parte presentation without even a specific statement on each one of the individuals concerned." The amendment was rejected by a vote of 146 to 153, whereupon Hendricks offered an amendment that barred payment to Pickens alone, and this was passed, 163 to 111.

Pickens, a Phi Beta Kappa from Yale, former teacher and dean at Negro colleges and officer of the N.A.A.C.P., was in charge of a small section of the Treasury Department's War Savings staff, his assignment to promote the purchase of war bonds by Negro organizations. Dies took exception to him because over the years he had been, among other compromising things, a vice chairman of the American League Against War and Fascism, a member of the American Committee for the Protection of the Foreign Born and the United American Spanish Aid Committee, and a contributor of articles to the *New Masses*. In a statement to Representative Ludlow, the

Treasury Department noted that it had "long been aware" of the charges concerning Pickens and was "convinced that they were without any substantial foundation . . . we are satisfied that Mr. Pickens is completely loyal to the government of the United States." The action against him by an agitated House alerted the Administration to difficulties to come with subsequent appropriation bills, and F.D.R. sought to head them off by issuing an executive order setting up an interdepartmental committee to handle complaints of subversive activity within the executive branch. It was the tactic of the school principal who invites a bunch of teenage toughs into the gym for a display of calisthenics in order to get their minds off breaking the building's windows. The haters of the New Deal were enjoying their romp too much to be so easily distracted. Clare Hoffman of Michigan, who bore to the native fascist fringe approximately the same relationship that Vito Marcantonio bore to native Communists, voiced their high spirits: ". . . last November by a majority of more than a million the American people told candidates for Congress that the waste, the extravagance, the muddling and the confusion, the crackpot plans and schemes of the starry-eyed New Deal dreamers should be brought to an end." And what surer way to do this than by eliminating the dreamers themselves?

On February 8 the House of Representatives enjoyed one of its rowdier days as the Administration, much on the defensive, attempted to do away with the Pickens amendment and substitute for it a resolution delegating to a subcommittee of the Appropriations Committee the task of investigating all charges of subversive tendencies among government employees and taking prompt action against them if the charges were sustained. The victors of the previous day were out for a kill, but passage of a billion-dollar appropriation bill was in jeopardy, and Speaker Rayburn, Majority Leader McCormack, and Minority Leader Martin conferred hurriedly at the rear of the chamber on tactics. Their great hope of success was Pickens's race. Overnight it had dawned upon the Republican leadership that many people might not understand that Pickens owed the misfortune of being singled out for execution not to any accident of birth but to the accident that he alone of Dies's thirty-nine was on the payroll of the Treasury Department at the moment when its appropriation was before the House. Hendricks assured his colleagues that he had had no idea at the time he offered his amendment that the fellow was a Negro. Hadn't he called him "*Mister* Pickens" all the previous day, when the entire world knew that "a Southerner does not refer to a colored man as 'mister'"? To guard himself against any semblance of prejudice, Hendricks never called Pickens "mister" again. The inimitable Rankin with excellent logic declared: "I voted to strike him off when I thought he was a white man, and I shall certainly not vote to put him back on because he is a Negro." But Congressmen from north of Mississippi could not afford so much logic: ". . . One poor colored man . . . ," intoned Knutson of Minnesota. "My God, that is almost lynch law." If so, it was the first time in our history that a man was saved from being lynched *because* he was a Negro.

On the next day the forces of propriety were rallied, debate was more orderly, and the nativists were indignant but not hopeful. "Somebody is playing to the Negro vote," charged Colmer of Mississippi. And Hoffman interpreted the approaching reversal as part of a conspiracy against the Dies Committee:

> Being unable to kick the Dies Committee out the front door of the Congress, the Administration and a few others, including the C.I.O. and the Communists, propose to do the job by taking over the duties of the Dies Committee and giving those duties to other committees and so get rid of the Dies Committee by kicking it out the back door.

There was truth in his argument, but even Hamilton Fish was concerned about people back home concluding that Congress had come down hard on a poor lone Negro, and the resolution to appoint a new committee was adopted by an overwhelming vote. Then, by 267 to 136, the House struck out the anti-Pickens amendment which it had inserted barely a weekend before. It also passed an amendment of Representative Dirksen, barring payment by the Treasury Department and the Post Office to any persons excluded from any other appropriation bill, a method of discouraging transfers of objectionable individuals such as David Lasser. Appointed to the new subcommittee were three Democrats and two Republicans: John H. Kerr of North Carolina as chairman, Clinton P. Anderson of New Mexico, Albert Gore of Tennessee, Frank B. Keefe of Wisconsin, and D. Lane Powers of New Jersey.[7] Dies at once promised to supply them with his complaints not merely against the thirty-nine but against the hundreds or thousands of other employees who to his mind had not been satisfactorily investigated by the attorney general.

The Kerr Committee selected for its first defendants six names from among the thirty-nine. Three of them—Goodwin B. Watson, William E. Dodd, Jr., and Frederick L. Schuman—came from the F.C.C., specifically the branch that monitored foreign broadcasts and so was the source of the report that Martin Dies was a pet of Axis commentators. The other three—Robert Morss Lovett, Jack Fahy, and Arthur Goldschmidt—were in Harold Ickes's Department of the Interior. William Pickens was left in peace. Each of the suspects was called before a closed session of the committee and questioned, on the basis of his Dies-Matthews dossier, about his undesirable associations and his opinions of Communism and capitalism. The hearings went smoothly, unimpeded by additional witnesses, counsel for the defense, observers from the accused's agencies, or any form of cross-examination. In April came the judgment. A cruel month for Watson, Dodd, and Lovett. Why the other three, including the confirmed Soviet apologist Schuman, were let off was never explained, beyond such unilluminating phrases as "not sufficient evidence to support a recommendation of unfitness." The convicted three, declared "unfit for the present to continue in government employment," were not charged with being or having been members of the Communist Party or with failing to perform their jobs satisfactorily.

[7] Investigating the executive branch was popular in the seventy-eighth Congress. Along with the Kerr Committee went the Cox Committee to investigate the F.C.C.—"the nastiest nest of rats to be found in the entire country," in Representative Cox's view—and the Smith Committee to investigate untoward behavior by the executive. Both were dominated by the Republican–Southern Democrat coalition then in its ascendance.

They were found guilty because of their association with organizations deemed subversive by the attorney general, their articles and speeches criticizing U.S. policies, capitalism and the profit system, and their support for causes, such as Loyalist Spain, which seemed suspect to the Congressmen.

Dodd, an assistant news editor at the F.C.C. with a salary of $3,200, had the lowest function and the briefest record of the three. He had been a paid employee as well as a member of the A.L.P.D.; had had the audacity to continue his membership in the Washington Bookshop after the Justice Department ruled it subversive; had spoken in behalf of such causes as Spanish relief and China relief; had written in 1938, after a trip to the U.S.S.R., that "here is a nation which carries the future of our civilization. Here there is hope, justice and progress"; and, most shocking to the tribunal, had been host at a cocktail party for the Harry Bridges Defense Fund while deportation proceedings were under way against the abominable Australian. As Representative Powers preferred to describe the occasion, he had "opened his home to Harry Bridges." (Martin Dies would not fail to note in his autobiography that years later Dodd's sister, Martha and her husband, Alfred Stern, defected to Czechoslovakia.) Dodd told the Committee that he believed in private enterprise, the capitalistic system, and the Christian religion, particularly the Baptist branch, and tried to pass some of his alleged activities off onto his late father, the former U.S. ambassador to Germany, but it availed him not.

Goodwin Watson, chief analyst for the Foreign Broadcast Information Service, had a more extensive history of rote radicalism and cooperation with leftward-leaning groups, and apologized for some of it. He had been enlightened by the Soviet-Nazi pact as to the real nature of bodies like the American Student Union. He attributed the fiery declarations of his past—including such titillating thirtyish slogans as "there is no safe compromise with capitalism"—to the depression, and explained that his views had been changed by the good works of the New Deal and his disillusionment with Soviet totalitarianism. True, he had never spoken or written as strenuously against the U.S.S.R. as he had for it, but now, he emphasized, he was a member of the *right wing* of the American Labor Party. His protestations went for nought. Representative Keefe of Oshkosh could not forgive him for sympathizing with "the Loyalist Government of Spain, which was in fact the Communist Government, was it not?"

Robert Morss Lovett was yet another case—and an extraordinary one; he challenged even the record of J. B. Matthews as a joiner. Lovett's social consciousness developed late. In 1917, when he was forty-six years old, with a long career as professor of English at the University of Chicago behind him, he became outraged by the excesses of war patriots against radicals and conscientious objectors. From then on, there was no liberal or radical cause anywhere that needed to get along without him: Sacco-Vanzetti, birth control, Mother Bloor, the abolition of capital punishment, Hull-House, Tom Mooney, industrial unions, Loyalist Spain, the Russian Revolution. "My old mother used to say to me when I was a little bit of a kid," reflected Representative Powers, faced with Dr. Lovett's record, " 'Sonny, you will always be judged by the company you keep.' " Even in his role as professor of English, Lovett could not resist finding social significance wherever he looked: "I like to read *King Lear* as having a reference to King James's proclivity for giving away the royal demesne to his favorites"—a predilection that gave him a better reputation among reformers than among literary critics. Pressure from the Illinois state legislature nearly got him thrown off the University of Chicago faculty in 1935 because he had been arrested for watching Chicago cops push around Negro girls on strike at an apron factory. The legislature was especially disturbed, as the Kerr Committee would be a decade later, at his comment to a former student that all governments, including his own, were "rotten." In 1939 the elderly fighter for good causes was appointed government secretary to the Virgin Islands, and it was of this post that the Kerr Committee decided to dispossess him.

In Lovett's defense, Harold Ickes wrote to Representative Kerr:

He has for the seventy-three years of his life found it difficult to think ill of any man, and so far as I know has never questioned the motives of anyone who sought a good objective. If the sub-committee will appreciate this essential goodness of Mr. Lovett, it will find the answer to why this man, who obviously is not a Communist, has frequently associated himself with them in one non-political enterprise or another.

The estimate was just, but the understanding of even the Sec-retary of the Interior had been taxed when in June 1941 his friend and subordinate signed his name to the call to the an-nual conference of the Communist-run League of American Writers, then still pursuing an isolationist course. Secretary Ickes was obliged to reprimand him:

> In view of the international situation and the announced and deliberate policy of the Administration, of which you are a part, to give all possible aid to the nations that are resisting Hitler and Nazism, your signature to this call represents an indiscretion of a high order and is embarrassing to this Department.

(A few days after the League denounced war against Hitler as imperialistic, Russia was invaded, and the writers reversed themselves.)

Robert Morss Lovett, like his old chum Harry F. Ward, who had led him into the paths of social service, made a career of being used by the Communists. "I am not ashamed of any action that I have ever taken in defending the Soviet Union," he told the Kerr Committee in 1943, and he told the Dies Com-mittee that he didn't recognize the term "Communist-front organization"; his alliance with the Communists was an effort to further objectives which he and they had in common: "So far as Communists are concerned, I have viewed them as human beings, capable, like the rest of us, of giving aid to humane and generous causes." In the recurrent splits on the left, he stood always, like the early J. B. Matthews, for "mini-mizing differences." Much of his interrogation was given over to his views of capitalism, socialism, and collectivism; he shocked the Congressmen by parroting all the pulse-quicken-ing propositions he had picked up in the thirties. "Mr. Lovett," interrupted Representative Keefe, the group's bully boy, "did I understand you to say that human greed is the motive of the profit system?" He stayed with the Communists through their twists and turns of 1939, 1940, and 1941—from A.L.W.F. to A.L.P.D. to both appearances of A.P.M.—but by 1948, when he wrote his autobiography, a doubt seems to have stirred in his mind.

> I still believe that liberals and Communists can work together for good in local causes, and both are deeply concerned with civil liberties in the United States, but after the League for Peace and Democracy and the League of American Writers, I am suspicious of organizations which enjoy their existence on sufferance and depend on the variable policies of a foreign power.

His suspicions were not only very late, they were also very small.

In its condemnation of Lovett, the Kerr Committee expressed the fear that he would "propagate his subversive philosophies through control of government money spent in the Virgin Islands." (One of the difficulties under which the committee labored was that it had not been supplied with a foolproof definition of the word "subversive.") No evidence whatever was produced that Lovett had done any such thing during his years there, and to judge by the nearly unanimous defense he received from the people of the Virgin Islands, this gentle and humane man seems to have been doing an exemplary job; Mr. Ickes had taken a chance on him and, despite his indiscretion in the case of the League of American Writers, he had done nothing to betray the trust. But the issues that now arose from his case, and from the cases of Watson and Dodd, had nothing to do with their professional competence and not much to do with their opinions. The three men were pawns in a political test of strength that would finally be decided by reference to the U.S. Constitution.

In May the House Appropriations Committee added an amendment to the $134 million deficiency appropriation bill which stipulated that not a penny of it or of any other supply measure was to be used to pay the salaries of Watson, Dodd, and Lovett. Debate in the House was stormy. Marcantonio delivered his standard harangue: "Hitler used the Reichstag trial, he used the Communist bogey, the same pattern that we employ here for the present restriction and subsequent destruction of democratic rights." To Representative O'Connor's question, "Whether any member of the committee, or the committee, found anything in these men's records as public servants that indicates they are not performing their duty working for the government . . . ," Representative Kerr replied, "I do not think we looked into that . . . Nobody asked us to see whether these men were conducting themselves properly." No Congressman rose at this point to remind the House that even during the September bloodletting of the French Revolution, when men were slaughtered for the cut of a coat, the judges commented, "We are not here to judge opinions, but to judge the results of them." The House supported Kerr by a vote of 318 to 62, without having been given an opportunity to read the testimony in the case, and the bill went to the Senate, which rejected it unanimously. Three times more the Senate turned back the amendment, but the House remained adamant and finally, in July, a "compromise" was reached that required the President to appoint the three men and have them confirmed by the Senate before November 15 in order for them to keep their jobs. Senator McKellar explained when he first brought the demands of the House back to the Senate: "The Senate conferees have most reluctantly felt obliged to yield to this unjust provision in order to get the appropriation bill out of Congress and enacted into law."

The deficiency measure was but one of a half dozen major appropriation bills that were being delayed by strong anti-Administration forces in Congress bent on restricting the President's expanding emergency powers. Representative Dirksen put the case candidly in his defense of the rider:

We are gradually getting to the fruition of an issue that has been growing for a long time, the issue between the bureaus that seek to branch out beyond the intent of Congress on the one hand, and the Congress on the other hand in the determination of the policies of government . . . You had better meet this issue now, because bureaucracy will grow to a point where it will lick you if you do not.

The issue was met. The Crop Insurance Program was ordered liquidated from the Department of Agriculture supply bill. The National Youth Administration was struck out of the Labor Department supply bill, and the N.L.R.B. was ordered to keep away from jurisdictional disputes. Appropriations for the Office of Price Administration and the Office of War Information were sharply cut in the war-agencies bill. Roosevelt had to bow before each of these challenges, and he had to accept the urgent-deficiency bill, too, which contained the funds for millions of dollars in overtime pay and past-due wages for thousands of federal employees. He signed the bill in July, with an angry statement that described the rider, Section 304, as unconstitutional, unwise, and discriminatory. It was, he said, an "unwarranted encroachment" on the executive branch which he would have vetoed if he could have done so without imperiling essential wartime appropriations. He added that he did not consider it binding.

Those who rejoiced in the victory over Watson, Dodd, and Lovett and the philosophies that they represented acknowledged no constitutional barriers; to them the only question was whether an employer has the right to fire an employee. Control of the purse strings, they reasoned, made Congress an employer and all federal officials were its employees, with no property rights in their jobs. Since when had the firing of a worker been construed as a judicial proceeding? Representative Hoffman stated the position in a vivid way: "We have the right to say we do not want a certain class of people or certain individuals on the payroll. It may be because their hair is red or because they are bald, or because they wear it down over their coat collars. It makes no difference at all." Representative Cannon added: "We can lop off the salary of any person as we see fit."

Their opponents argued that in depriving the three officials of their jobs, Congress had passed a bill of attainder—a legislative act inflicting punishment without a judicial trial—as well as an ex post facto law, imposing punishment for an act that was not punishable at the time it was committed. And if this were not enough, by singling out three federal employees by name, the Congress had infringed on the powers of its coequal branches of government. Secretary Ickes and the F.C.C. commissioners kept the condemned at work, without pay, beyond the November 15 deadline in order to establish grounds for a test case by the three; in fact, Lovett stayed on until the following March when Ickes had to ask for his resignation out of concern for the upcoming Interior Department appropriation. Attorney General Biddle notified Congress that it would have to find a lawyer for itself since the solicitor general was occupied in supporting the plaintiffs .

In November 1945 the U.S. Court of Claims awarded the three their back pay, which came to $2,158, on the grounds that the Congressional rider was an attempt to tie the hands of the federal disbursing officer, thus making the appropriation measure contradictory and invalid. It was a narrowly construed decision that avoided the question of the act's constitutionality: Section 304, stated Chief Justice Whaley, "constituted a mere stoppage of disbursing routine, nothing more." But the concurring opinions of three of his four colleagues were strongly critical of Congress. Judge J. Warren Madden viewed the rider's purpose as "a shocking and outrageous injustice, unique in our history." The following June the Supreme Court unanimously supported the lower court's finding and, with Frankfurter and Reed dissenting, went further. Speaking for the majority was Justice Black:

> When our Constitution and Bill of Rights were written, our ancestors had ample reason to know that legislative trials and punishment were too dangerous to liberty to exist in the nation of free men they envisioned. And so they proscribed bills of attainder. Section 304 is one.

Justice Frankfurter argued that since no offense was specified in the rider and no declaration of guilt was made, it could not be regarded as a bill of attainder. "If Congress chooses to say that men shall not be paid," he reasoned, "or even that they shall be removed from their jobs, we cannot decide that Congress also said that they are guilty of an offense." The majority, however, was more concerned with the amendment's effect than with its wording, and the effect, wrote Black, "was to inflict punishment without the safeguards of a judicial trial." Administrations to come were in this manner saved from a harassment technique of surpassing potential.

As these matters were being resolved, the Un-American Activities Committee embarked on its first public hearings in nearly two years—and the last hearings of any consequence in its status as a special committee. In June 1943 Representatives Costello, Mundt, and Eberharter began taking testimony in Los Angeles on the relocation of the West Coast Japanese-Americans who had been put into "protective custody" after Pearl Harbor. Some 112,000 people, two-thirds of them born in this country, had been compelled by an executive order, implemented by the army, to evacuate their homes in California, western Oregon and Washington, and southern Arizona. About 3,000 of them, deemed dangerous to the security of the region, were placed in internment camps; the others were divided into those who refused to take a pledge of loyalty to the United States and so found themselves in "segregation centers," and the rest, the majority, who were transported—with little in the way of lock, stock, or barrel—into desert camps, in theory until they could be placed elsewhere. The program was administered by the War Relocation Authority, a new agency which owed its creation to the resistance of Western communities to resettlement of the Japanese. Given the haste with which these thousands of families were forced to dispose of their businesses, property, and possessions; the barracks into which they were jammed—seven in a room measuring 20' by 25', without running water; the awareness on the part of the better educated among them that Japanese citizens in other parts of the country had not been put behind barbed wire and that German and Italian aliens had not been interned by the carload on the basis of nationality; given all this, it is astonishing that the troublemakers among them did not act up more violently or have a greater effect on the rest, that the army had to be called into the camps only twice to keep order.

The subcommittee event was, as usual, well heralded: DIES COMMITTEE SAYS INTERNED JAPANESE AMONG BEST-FED CIVILIANS IN THE WORLD. Chief investigator Stripling supplied the Denver *Post*, which was waging its own campaign against the W.R.A., with the fiction that Japanese trained in espionage were among those being released at the rate of 10,000 a week, while those still in the camps were being pampered. But nervousness over the threat of espionage was not the only, or the major, reason for America's exercise in mass punishment. For years the Hearst newspapers, the American Legion and its California cousins in patriotism such as the Sons and Daughters of the Golden West, and the area's farmers, businessmen and A. F. of L. unions, irritated by Japanese success in commercial ventures and by the very existence of their tightly knit, conspicuously foreign, but eminently peaceable communities, had been inveighing against the Yellow Peril. Pearl Harbor afforded these groups an opportunity to spend their passions and stock their pocketbooks by booting out their Japanese neighbors. The patriots were especially fortunate in the appointment of General John DeWitt to take charge of defense measures on the West Coast. Said the general: "I don't care what they do with the Japs, as long as they don't send them back here. A Jap is a Jap." The sentiment would not go without amen in Congress, as long as John Rankin still served there: "I am in favor of shipping them back to Japan when this war is over. The way to tell which ones ought to be shipped back to Japan is, I would take a blood test." Representative Thomas brooded over the report that the interned Japanese were enjoying excellent food and wine: "Are we to release this fat-waisted Jap while our boys on Guadalcanal are barely receiving enough food with which to keep alive?" In the Senate, meanwhile, the Military Affairs Committee was pressuring the Administration to give over control of the relocation camps to the military.

Costello, the Californian, opened his Los Angeles hearings with a procession of witnesses who could be counted on to express the most implacable sentiments toward the Japanese. They complained of the inscrutable Oriental temperament, cited instances of coddling and waste in relocation centers (where the daily food bill sometimes went as high as forty-five cents a person), mocked the teaching in the camps of Japanese pastimes such as judo and goh, instead of baseball, and warned that their fellow citizens would not be restrained from violence if the Japanese were permitted to return to their homes. They objected to the whole concept of relocation unless it meant relocating the people to someplace east of Okinawa, and they urged that the army take over from the W.R.A., which they suspected of harboring good intentions.

The mayor of Los Angeles explained that he didn't want the Japanese back because their appearance of faithfulness in their work made it so difficult to "tell who is loyal and who is not." The sheriff of California's Orange County described the perils for the Japanese in his neighborhood, as U.S. Marines returned from the South Pacific. An official of the Orange County Farm Bureau expressed dismay over the Japanese reluctance to work for white people, and noted that the state had been driven to force them to sell their property by law. An official of the Native Sons of the Golden West, which had brought suit to cancel the citizenship rights of persons of Japanese descent, called for bills that would make it mandatory that land and boats in Golden California be owned by American citizens. A representative of the Los Angeles County American Legion observed that the release of the Japanese would fill the country with "potential saboteurs and spies." The president of the Salt River Valley Water Users' Association in Arizona (where an unconstitutional law had recently been passed requiring anyone who wished to sell anything to a Japanese to give ten days' notice of his intention in a newspaper and file a declaration of intent with the governor) reported proudly that the folks in his area "have always been against them [the Japanese] coming into the community, and restrictive laws have been passed." An American Legionnaire from Phoenix wanted it plainly understood that between Arizona Japs and California Japs he played no favorites: "They are all the same. We don't want any of them." The secretary of the Los Angeles Central Labor Office said it worried him that "the Japanese all look alike," and declared that "the labor movement is positively opposed to any Japanese being allowed freedom of movement anywhere in the United States . . ." The deputy sheriff of Yuma County, Arizona, reported that the Japanese from a nearby relocation center were upsetting townspeople by monopolizing the stools at the drugstore fountain.

These spokesmen were received more warmly by Chairman Costello than the ministers and members of the Fellowship of Reconciliation who held that the great majority of Japanese were loyal to this country and ought to be released. Asked by Representative Mundt whether it was not advisable for the government to keep the Japanese out of an area where bodily harm might be done to them, a vice chairman of the Fellowship replied, "No, I would say that what we ought to do is deal with the people who would do them bodily harm." It was a stunning thought in the circumstances. Costello himself enunciated the principle behind the mass evacuation in his questioning of A. L. Wirin, the American Civil Liberties Union representative, who noted that there had been no act of sabotage on the Pacific Coast before, during, or after Pearl Harbor, and called for the immediate return of the great majority of Japanese to their homes. "Don't you think," asked Costello, "that the justification of the placing of Jews in Germany, by the Hitler regime, in concentration camps, was pretty much that the Germans did not understand the Jewish mind and therefore they thought the best thing to do was to get them out of the way?" There was no trouble understanding Costello's mind.

The hearings were carried forward in Washington, where the director of the War Relocation Authority, Dillon S. Myer, defended his wards against the previous witnesses. Myer, succeeding Milton Eisenhower in the post, was attempting to do a distasteful and difficult job (particularly difficult was the sorting out of loyal from disloyal Japanese and keeping anti-American feeling at a minimum) with a barely adequate staff drawn largely from the Indian Service, Japanese experts being busy elsewhere at the time. He made small impression on the Committee majority. Thomas saw the whole affair as another New Deal plot—"It is just a silly social experiment you are conducting." The Committee report, issued in September, though not so bluntly composed, was critical of W.R.A. practices and personnel to the point of calling for Myer's ouster. Some of the criticisms of W.R.A. methods were well taken, but the Congressmen showed no patience for the civil liberties issues that had been raised by our treatment of 85,000 citizens. This was left to Representative Eberharter, replacing Jerry Voorhis as the Committee's voice of enlightenment. In his dissent, Eberharter discussed the legal ambiguities, criticized the majority report as prejudiced and unsubstantiated, and commended the W.R.A. for doing as well as it had done, all things considered. A few months later the Committee released another report on Japanese activities in the United States; here it complimented itself on seeing to it that the Japanese were removed from the West Coast and warned against their release from relocation camps without thorough investigation. America's treatment of the Japanese among us during the war remains the darkest page in an otherwise remarkably clear civil-liberties record. It is not the fault of the majority of the Dies Committee that the page is no blacker.

Martin Dies did not play a leading part in the investigation of the relocation camps, and indeed was rarely heard from during 1943. The Detroit race riots in June brought him forward for a moment, like a beloved star making a quick duty appearance at an actors' benefit; he announced his intention to investigate. The city's mayor pleaded with him to stay away from Detroit—life was burdensome enough just then. Whereupon Dies enlarged his plans; now he proposed to make an exhaustive, nationwide study of racial hatred, which he ascribed to "a combination of un-American propaganda activities and the coddling of races by politically minded people in this country who ignore the vast differences between the protection and the coddling of a race." Having relieved himself of this diagnosis, he troubled the subject no further.

Nineteen forty-four was the last year of the Dies Committee, and the chairman used part of it to join with Clare Hoffman and other foes of F.D.R. in a slanging match against Walter Winchell. For several weeks the columnist and radio commentator was the most popular subject for argument in the House of Representatives, to such a degree that, what with the yelling of the members and the demonstrating in the galleries, Speaker McCormack was unable to keep order. Winchell had over a period of weeks been attacking anti-Administration Congressmen for hampering the war effort, charging them with hobnobbing with the fascist-minded. He did not reach for elegance: "Many of Hitler's American pals have been arrested, but too many have been renominated." He called Congress the "House of Reprehensibles" and said it included "some of the sorriest stumblebums in the nation." Winchell's support of the Dies Committee in its first years had won him the chairman's kindest feelings. "I shall always have a warm spot in my heart for you," he wrote to the columnist in December 1940. But affections cool, and now, rising on one of his points of personal privilege, Dies called Winchell a liar for linking him with rightist Joseph Kamp, hinted he might investigate his sponsor and the N.B.C. Blue Network, and threatened to pass a law of some sort if he wasn't granted equal time.

Winchell's sponsor, the Andrew Jergens Company, manufacturer of lotions, attempted to spread balm over Dies's feelings by offering him fifteen minutes immediately following one of Winchell's Sunday evening broadcasts. Dies accepted and spoke from 9:15 to 9:30 on March 26. He told Mr. and Mrs. America and All the Ships at Sea that Winchell, "a peddler of bedroom keyhole scandal to the American people," was the tool of a clique that was impugning public officials and trying "to destroy the prestige of Congress in the interest of setting up an all-powerful central executive." He promised to expose the brains and the money behind this nefarious business and begged Winchell to "remember that those who expect tolerance in others should extend tolerance to others." Winchell responded with a challenge to Dies to sue him. The two met briefly in the reception room of Station WMAL in

Washington after the broadcast. "Let's get together and tell some more lies about each other," snapped Winchell. "I'd have to go some to get even," snapped Dies. The exchange was on the level of the entire debate, and although Mr. and Mrs. America's decision of who came out on top depended on how much they liked or hated F.D.R., on one point the evidence was conclusive: the Congressman and the commentator thoroughly deserved one another. (A few years later Winchell, whose political tastes were fashioned mainly at the Stork Club, would be a cheerleader for Joe McCarthy.)

The Winchell altercation was only an interlude for Dies in this last year; his preoccupation was with the C.I.O. Political Action Committee. He had every reason to detest the P.A.C. Had it not been brought into being by what its founders called the "deplorable record of the 78th Congress"? Did it not have as its incessantly proclaimed goal the removal from Washington of those representatives who, since the Republican gains of 1942, had frustrated Administration plans regarding taxes, incomes, and price control, and had passed the Smith-Connally anti-strike bill? Did it not list among the scores of Congressmen ripe for purging seven of the eight members of the Dies Committee and all of its champions in the House, including Smith of Virginia, Cox of Georgia, and Rankin of Mississippi? Were not the dossiers of its prime movers thick with the titles of front organizations against which the Committee had done famous battle, and, indeed, did not the C.I.O. itself still harbor its twenty-one Communist unions? Was the P.A.C. not working hammer in sickle with the Administration to get a fourth term for F.D.R., and was not its chairman, Sidney Hillman of the Amalgamated Clothing Workers, so formidable a political figure that he would hold veto power in 1944 over the Democrats' choice of a candidate for the vice presidency?

Dies's campaign against the P.A.C. began in January 1944, when his Committee received its final $75,000 from the House, and lasted clear up to election day. It was accompanied by only the gesture of an investigation. Hillman turned down the Committee's demand for the P.A.C.'s financial records—which the F.B.I. had already scrutinized and which would be made available later to the Committee on Congressional Expenditures—on the grounds that the Un-American Activities Committee had no authority to investigate a political group. A subpoena was issued for him, but he was never called to testify. The charges against the P.A.C. were mighty edifices teetering on a fragment of a foundation. Dies, supervising the proceedings from his ranch in Jasper, Texas, charged that the organization had raised a slush fund of $2 million to defeat members of Congress in 1944—$250,000 to defeat him alone—in violation of the Smith-Connally law which prohibited unions from making political contributions. He charged that government officials were cooperating with the P.A.C. in violation of the Hatch Act. On a visit to Washington he notified the House that "Sidney Hillman will soon succeed Earl Browder as head of the Communists in the United States." Stripling compiled a record of telephone calls and telegrams between the P.A.C. offices and a number of high Administration officials, not omitting Mrs. Roosevelt; he concluded that the P.A.C. was "the political arm of the New Deal Administration." When Dies told him to release this report at once to any syndicated columnist he wished, he gave it to Westbrook Pegler. Dies called on the attorney general to prosecute seventy-two government officials with alleged ties to the P.A.C. If Biddle didn't act at once, then he, Dies, would demand legislation "divorcing the government from the C.I.O." J. B. Matthews pored over his lists and found that 82 of the 141 members of the National Citizens Political Action Committee, an offshoot of the C.I.O.–P.A.C., had cooperated with twenty-five Communist fronts; the P.A.C., he certified, was now the major front organization in the land, representing the Communist Party's "supreme bid for power in the twenty-five years of its history." A week before election day a three-man subcommittee—humorously composed of two Democrats, Starnes and Costello, who were still warm from defeat in their respective primaries (for which the P.A.C. took some credit), and the dependable Thomas—issued a report, an echo of the year's charges. The P.A.C. was a "rallying point for the Communist

Party and its allied groups and organizations to rise to power by taking control of a major political party." (The last official publication of the Dies Committee, acting through Costello, consisted of 2,000 pages worth of material which it had collected over the years and put hurriedly between covers at the end of 1944 lest the fruits of Matthews's labors be lost to posterity. It was, according to a staff member in 1950, "a fair cross-section of our files today." Entitled *Communist Front Organizations with Special Reference to the National Citizens Political Action Committee* and published in seven volumes, this "Appendix Nine" contained 22,000 names—some Communists, many not—and was distributed to numerous government agencies before it was ordered restricted and destroyed by the full Committee in 1945. Copies of this catch-all, which contained no hint that some of the thousands of persons listed might not be subversive, reside still in the files of our security agencies and are available to Congressmen through the Library of Congress for whatever use they may care to make of the contents.)

Once again, as so often in the Committee's essays, it was not possible to take its charges straight, yet impossible to dismiss them altogether. Its purposes were blatantly partisan, yet there was some fire within the billows of smoke. Major C.I.O. unions were still in Communist hands—though their hours were numbered—and they were influential in the P.A.C. Far from being political pariahs, in 1944 our Communists and fellow travelers in the unions and out wanted only what all liberals wanted: a fourth term for F.D.R. and the unconditional surrender of the Axis powers. Their pretensions to patriotism had never seemed more genuine, and every victory on the Eastern front added to their prestige. As for Hillman, the "Russian pantsmaker" as John L. Lewis sourly titled him, he had not somersaulted with the Communists during the Nazi-Soviet pact, but he had joined with the likes of Marcantonio, Quill, and Curran to take the New York State American Labor Party out of the hands of anti-Communist unionists. And although his eminence in Democratic politics was never what the Republican campaign cry, "Clear it with Sidney," implied, the P.A.C. did constitute a power play by left-wing union leaders ambitiously contemplating the shape of things in post-war America.

On May 12, in the middle of his battle against the P.A.C., Martin Dies announced from Texas that he would not seek reelection. He had been in ill health, with a throat ailment, for several weeks; he was wearied after fourteen years in the House; he wanted to go into private business—"I have always had a dread of becoming a professional politician, dependent upon the public for my livelihood." Moreover, as many were quick to point out cheerily, he faced a hard campaign in 1944. A few days earlier a Democratic convention in his home county, influenced now by recently organized oil refinery workers, had labeled him a demagogue. Later, he would charge that as part of its assault on him the Administration gave large contracts to industries along the Gulf Coast section of his district in order to bring in thousands of workers from other states, and that Internal Revenue agents were sent down from Baltimore in 1943 to foster innuendo in his district about his financial dealings. The steel workers, in convention at the hour of Dies's announcement of retirement, paused to celebrate what Philip Murray called "the most outstanding contribution made by Dies to our national welfare." Before the year was over, Murray and his steelworkers, Hillman and his pantsmakers, and the entire C.I.O.–P.A.C. would have a great deal more to celebrate. Not only did Roosevelt win his fourth term, but the Democrats substantially increased their majority in the House of Representatives. As sauce to the banquet for unregenerate New Dealers, the grandfather of the Dies Committee, Hamilton Fish, was retired by an independent Republican.

So there was a satisfying formal design to the career of the Dies Committee. It ended, as it began, in an election year, with an attack on C.I.O.–Communist–New Deal interlocking subversion. Having won his spurs in rides against sit-down strikers and left-wing unionists, Dies retreated before the vigor, short-lived, of the C.I.O.–P.A.C. Would his Committee be continued without him? The question did not weigh heavily in those halls where private sentiments are not always reflected by public votes. It was not quite a case of good riddance, not quite; but Dies, having said "So long, Doc" to Matthews, was gone, Mason had retired, Starnes had been defeated, and the halls of Congress were unshaken by any swell of reluctance to let their creature drift away with them into oblivion. Still, one loyal voice was raised. A day after the announcement of the chairman's intent to leave the field, one voice urged that the Un-American Activities Committee not merely be extended, but that it be made a permanent standing committee of the House: ". . . the weapon of exposure which has been so effectively used by our Committee must be maintained . . ." So, dimly intimating his own future glory, spoke J. Parnell Thomas.

Martin Dies returned to Washington in 1953 as Congressman at large from Texas and he served until 1959, bringing to twenty years his career in the House of Representatives. The Republicans were in charge in 1953, and he was received politely enough. When a Senate subcommittee was formed to suggest rules for the improvement of Congressional investigations, then in one of their more uproarious phases, the veteran investigator was invited to give expert testimony. He advised the senators: "Primarily, if you get a good chairman and a good committee you will have a good investigation. Outside of that, all you need is a few general rules to see that the witness and the public get a fair break." No one laughed openly, but his time had run out. The leaders of his party, whose memories were as long as their tenure, refused him a position on his own Committee when they took control of Congress in 1955, and he was like an aging actor returned to the stage of past triumphs only to find that other performers had won the matinee-goers' hearts. The returned's only moment came in the summer of 1954 when the Congress passed the Communist Control Act, but even that was not as punishing to the Reds as he and his odd ally in this cause, Senator Hubert Humphrey, proposed.[8]

[8] Mr. Humphrey's leadership of the Senate liberals in an attempt to add penalties against individual Communists to the 1954 bill was a transparent

It is easy for us, removed from the sound and fury of the thirties, to see that neither J. B. Matthews nor Vito Marcantonio defined the nature of the struggle that roared about the big and blustering figure of Martin Dies. It was not a struggle of Communism versus the Republic, even though some of the union chiefs and federal officials whom Dies attacked aspired to nothing grander than to function as bureaucrats in a Sovietized America. Nor was it a struggle of democracy versus fascism, even though the hearts of men like Hoffman and Rankin went out to the Christian Fronters. What Dies represented was an aching nostalgia for pre–World War I America. He stood for the small town populated by a few hundred neighborly descendants of early settlers and against the big cities with their polyglot masses. He stood for a style of life that was being shaken by industrial unions, by the Negro awakening, by revolutionary currents of every sort. He stood for fundamentalist enthusiasm against the radical enlightenment. He stood for Western insularity and against Eastern cosmopolitanism, for a strong legislature and against a strong executive, for the old verities and old slogans and against the new slogans and new demands. He stood, practically alone, he rapidly persuaded himself, for capitalism and the Constitution and God, and these were under attack from Pennsylvania Avenue and from New York City as much as from Moscow.

But Dies, unlike the Marxist ideologues, could not subsist on theories; he needed flesh, and of a certain kind. The pleasure of helping to send Earl Browder to jail was slight beside the pleasure of drawing blood from Frances Perkins, Harold Ickes, or Henry Wallace. Politics was a street brawl for him; one hit out and hoped that more blows landed on the other gang than on bystanders. Since in New Deal Washington nearly everybody belonged to the other gang the odds were in his favor. It was a severe strain for New Dealers to keep fair minds and equable tempers while being mauled—though Voorhis did re-

---

effort to erase the "soft on Communism" taint from their party in an election year and embarrass the Republican Administration, which had the good sense to oppose the measure, into a veto. The effects of Senator McCarthy's crusade have been somewhat exaggerated in the telling, but this strange legislative exhibition was one of them.

markably well—and the flamboyant chairman's windy demagogy, unflagging opportunism, and casual cruelties strained
their objectivity. He called on sinners to repent—on condition
that they repent not only the sins of Communism and those of
fellow traveling, but the multitudinous sins of liberalism as
well; he wanted them groveling or not at all.

The trouble was that Dies, having sat at the feet of Matthews, was more often than not right about the organizations
he labeled Communist fronts. He did not understand much
more about them or about what drew thousands of non-
Communists into them, and certainly he understood nothing
about the unknown individuals he condemned because he
came upon their names on a list—but on the single, crucial
point of Communist control he was right. He was right about
the American League for Peace and Democracy. He was
right about the unions he charged with Communist leadership.
He was right about the primary allegiance of the Communist
Party. And because he was right and because so many liberals
of the time found it so difficult to confess even to themselves
that a Martin Dies was closer to a central truth about Communism in America than a Harry Ward and a Robert Morss
Lovett, many resorted to foolish defenses and transparent
rationalizations that would plague them for years to come. It
was flagrantly dishonorable to throw selfless men, with whom
one had stood in worthy causes from Sacco and Vanzetti
forward, to vicious benighted inquisitors, and so liberal spokesmen found themselves arguing that Communists were pretty
much like Masons and the C.P. was like the G.O.P. The outrage
they roared at the Committee's free and easy methods would
have turned to purrs had only the methods been directed at
Father Coughlin and Gerald L. K. Smith.

Thirty years later we can see that those on both sides who
honestly believed or honestly feared that America's future
belonged to fascism or to Communism shared a great mis-
judgment; they underestimated the resilience and endurance
of our institutions. Our economic and political arrangements
were rife with inequalities; compared to other systems they
lacked theoretical underpinning and aesthetic satisfaction;

they offered little in the thirties to match the dynamism of
the fascist countries or the fervor of the U.S.S.R. But they
would confound both those who called for their overthrow
before sunset and those, like Dies, who believed they were
defending the institutions by resisting all change. Our body
politic, it turned out, was like a peculiar patient who can
survive the most extensive surgery and shed astonishingly
little blood in the process. There are no guarantees that this
will always be the case, that every operation will cost little and
end happily, but experience does allow the hope that the
radicals of the sixties, like those of the thirties, will make their
contributions within the system and not only, as they enjoy
protesting, in spite of it. It also suggests that those who wish
to crush the noisy young people today will tomorrow, when
their extravagances have become picturesque memories, live
contentedly with the changes they have goaded us into accepting.

But not Martin Dies. He went back to Texas in 1959 and in
1963 he published his autobiography. He was sixty-two years
old; the world was awry, and he uttered dry words in a dry
season. The recognition of the U.S.S.R. was "a colossal blunder." The "pink fringe around the Red core of Communism . . .
really headed America for disaster." We lost World War II
to the Communists. Newspapers had treated him unfairly and
the liberal establishment in book publishing had conspired
against him. Aliens had poured into the land. The drive for
civil rights was forwarding Communist purposes. The direct
election of U.S. Senators was a mistake. "Ultra-liberals" had
betrayed the invasion of Cuba. Why hadn't the American Civil
Liberties Union been investigated? Liberals had inflicted an
unsound fiscal policy on the country. The tax-exempt foundations were worrisome: "To realize the inherent dangers we
need only recall that Alger Hiss was president of the Carnegie
Fund." The United Nations was a "reservoir of espionage
agents." Liberals had the same goals as Communists, and responsibility for our present peril must be laid at their feet.

The memories of his battles against subversives in the government are still green for him, oases in the political desert

he sees all around. His hatreds—of F.D.R., Mrs. Roosevelt, Francis Biddle, and all the rest, most of them shades now— have grown more virulent with the decades, but that is a kind of comfort too. Because there are not many trophies left him of his important years. He cannot hope for the national eulogies which Henry Wallace and Frances Perkins and Gardner Jackson received, which all the old New Dealers have received, and will receive. America is in the hands of past antagonists, Lyndon Johnson and the Reuther boys, and Martin Dies has ended up in the same accommodating boat as Earl Browder, unhonored even by his heirs and successors.

6

★ ★ ★ ★ ★

1945-1946: Rankin's Coup

Opening Day of a new Congress is not ordinarily a productive occasion. It is short on time, long on formalities and fellowship. Such was the expectation on Wednesday, January 3, 1945, as members of the seventy-ninth Congress took their places and listened to their chaplain call on God for assistance in building "a future altogether worthy of our traditions." The future of this Congress held the end of World War II, an explosion of challenges around the globe and the resumption of unsettled political battles at home. Large matters, but one man present that day had something more homely in mind. There was a misunderstanding about John E. Rankin among those who relied for their news on the columns of *PM* or even of more objective journals. He was classed with all the other haters down South: rude, ignorant fellows not much different in nature from the farm animals which the more affluent of them owned. That he despised Negroes, Jews, aliens, and liberals was, to be sure, his foremost claim to Americanism—but along with his extensive hates and vaunted ignorance went a canny mind, an energetic temperament, and an excellent grasp of parliamentary procedure. He was not an elegant debater, but he enjoyed the sport and could be counted on to turn any sparring match into a rough and tumble and often as not to land a mean blow or two. On this Wednesday he bided his time while Minority Leader Martin introduced Speaker Rayburn and while Speaker Rayburn spoke about national unity—until Chairman Sabath of the Rules Committee made the customary proposal to adopt the rules of the previous Congress. Then Rankin arose and offered an amendment to the rules—to make the Committee on Un-American Activities a standing committee of the House, with great latitude as to what it might investigate and how it chose to go about its investigating.

The move took the House leadership by surprise, not only because it was in itself unorthodox, but because an understanding had been arrived at that any effort at reincarnating the Dies Committee would be given over to the mercies of Sabath's group. By offering his amendment now, before the Rules Committee itself had been reestablished, the forewarned gentleman from Mississippi was attempting an end run. Rankin's main argument, besides the rhetorical one that the Dies Committee had "performed a duty second to none," was that if the House did not act with dispatch, the files so assiduously collected by J. B. Matthews might be removed by unnamed persons and thrown into the Potomac River. Rankin took care to remind his colleagues that the American Legion, whose political potential loomed very large indeed as the war neared its end, had lately asked Congress to continue the Committee and make it permanent.

The leaders of the House had no inclination on this opening day to affront patriots by an insult to the memory of Martin Dies. On the other hand, they had no enthusiasm for adopting his offspring as their own unto eternity. So they entrusted their cause to Representative McCormack, who explained in his passion-quelling way that he was certainly in favor of continuance of the Special Committee, but wanted the matter taken up in proper order, via the Rules Committee. He urged a vote against "the procedure that in 150 years of Constitutional history, no Congress . . . has ever followed to establish a permanent committee of this kind." In a division on the question, Rankin's amendment was defeated by 134 to 146. Whereupon the Mississippian, with the experience of nearly a quarter of a century in the House, knew he had won. He asked for a roll call, and now the vote was 207 for the Committee and 186 against. Forty members, including the young man from Texas, Lyndon B. Johnson, voted a neutral "present." "I caught 'em flat-footed and flat-headed," Rankin rejoiced. A few minutes later, at 3:28 p.m., the House adjourned, having to its own astonishment and at some cost to its traditions, created a permanent Committee on Un-American Activities.

The majority vote of January 3, made up of 137 Republicans and 70 Democrats, 63 of them from the South, put the Administration on notice that despite F.D.R.'s success in November, the conservative coalition in Congress which had proved such a nuisance during the past two years was still very much alive. As if to still any doubts on this point, Representative Hoffman, recent victor over a strong C.I.O.–P.A.C. campaign in his Michigan district, rose on January 4 like the spirit of things past, present, and future, to carry forward Martin Dies's attack on New Dealers, parlor pinks, and left-wingers. After Hoffman had thanked God for the Un-American Activities Committee, Voorhis, who had been in the minority the day before, offered once again his outline of how to make a decent woman of her, thus prompting Rankin to declare himself against any muzzling of the new group. But Rankin added, in an unusual bow to propriety, "I do not believe, and I have never believed in smear campaigns."

Rankin's opinions were of more than ordinary interest because, as progenitor of the new Committee, he was entitled to become its chairman. This honor he let pass since he did not wish to relinquish the chairmanship of the Veterans Affairs Committee, whose future in 1945 was extremely promising, but the issue was merely nominal. The Dies Committee had in fact become the Rankin Committee. Appointed as chairman was a delegate from the Jersey City Democratic machine, Edward J. Hart, whose qualifications for the role were that he had during ten years in Congress managed to give offense neither to the C.I.O. nor to the South. He had voted against the Rankin amendment but took no part in the debate. "I am glad such a thoroughgoing American will be in charge of that

Committee," said Attorney General Biddle, with crossed fingers.[1]

Karl Mundt started the Committee on its way by sending out letters to a hundred prominent Americans, inviting them to set down their notions of what constituted "un-American activities." Walter Winchell, Eleanor Roosevelt, the Knights of Columbus, veterans' organizations, the nation's governors, Drew Pearson, Henry Wallace, Harold Ickes—all were solicited. "Unless it is held that there is no such thing as un-American activity," reasoned Mundt, "Americans should be able to agree on what it is and our Committee could then expose it." *Life* magazine called this venture "very serious and public spirited." About half of the sample replied and some weeks later the Brookings Institution, to which the replies had been turned over, submitted a monograph that was very like one of Jerry Voorhis's speeches. The Committee was reminded that its object was not to prosecute, persecute, or punish anybody— just to present the facts. The whole very serious and public-spirited study vanished at once, like a Quaker tract beneath the heels of fans pressing toward the fights.

Certainly the realistic Rankin paid it no mind. He now had his Committee; a few weeks later he had $50,000 to sustain it—"merely the beginning," he informed the House; he had a Committee counsel, Ernie Adamson, who shared his philosophy and style; and he had a chairman who could be voted down or ignored as the occasion seemed to require. (He also had the pleasure, in March, of seeing Aubrey Williams, former administrator of the National Youth Administration and a favorite target of the Dies Committee, refused confirmation by the Senate to head the Rural Electrification Administration, a victory for the spirit of Martin Dies.)

[1] The other Democrats, in addition to Rankin, were Herbert C. Bonner of North Carolina, J. Hardin Peterson of Florida, John R. Murdock of Arizona, and J. W. Robinson of Utah; though Murdock and Robinson would show displeasure at some of the Committee's doings, none of these men would play much of a part in the business of the next two years. On the Republican side, Gerald W. Landis of Indiana was named to keep company the reappointed Representatives Mundt and Thomas. And a Georgia-born lawyer, Ernie Adamson, became chief counsel.

As the spring of 1945 turned into summer, the Committee, over the objections of its chairman, embarked upon its first open hearings. At the bar once again was the Office of Price Administration. The agency, which many businessmen saw as the New Deal incarnate, was in trouble. Up for renewal in Congress, it was met with bitter attacks, and, as Hart discerned, the Committee hearings, which opened on the very day that the agency's fate was scheduled to be taken up in the House, were Rankin's contribution to the anti-O.P.A. cause. The gentleman from Mississippi made no secret of his conviction that the O.P.A.—along with the Wagner Act, the wages and hours bill, and similar novelties—was at the root of most of the nation's ills. "It is about time we got rid of the O.P.A.," he announced periodically. "I am tired of those commissars attempting to tell the American people how naked they shall go."

The hearings in June, under Adamson's direction, centered on an O.P.A. radio program, *Soldiers with Coupons*, that was being presented for fifteen minutes a week over several stations around the country. The program featured dramatic skits entitled *Black Market in Meat, Nylon Black Market*, and *Rent Control*, and the cost of the time on the New York station where it originated was borne, as a wartime public service, by Standard Brands, makers of Chase and Sanborn coffee, Fleischman's yeast, and other popular staples. The shows, written by a man of allegedly questionable political tendencies, were peopled with good guys named Tony, Sam, Nick, Irving, and Mom, who talked to landlords named Bolton or Allen or White like this: "You won't paint. You won't fix nothing. You chisel on the heat and now you want to raise the rent." The deus ex machina was always Your O.P.A.: "Sure thing, Joe, the O.P.A. was set up for little guys like you and me." These efforts did owe something to the Union Square school of dramatic literature, but to call them subversive was stretching a point. To Rankin, however, the O.P.A. was from start to finish a tool of bureaucratic subversion, and Chairman Hart was hard put to keep the hearings from straying into the policy matters then being argued over in the House. Representative Murdock helped him by persistently asking the counsel for specific evidence of wrongdoing. Thus inhibited and with no real charge against the agency except for the fact that it existed, Adamson thrashed around for three days, hinting at some sort of plot between Standard Brands and the White House, with O.P.A. Administrator Chester Bowles serving as sinister broker, to defame American business. The hearings produced nothing more spectacular than another twinge of discomfort for a severely ailing agency.

Having done what he could to advance the evisceration of the O.P.A., which represented the kind of economic order that some on the left dreamed of continuing in a peacetime America, Rankin turned West. He announced that his Committee was about to search out "one of the most dangerous plots ever instigated for the overthrow of the government . . . the greatest hotbed of subversive activities in the United States." The plot and hotbed were in Hollywood. "We're on the trail of the tarantula," said Rankin, "and we're going to follow through."

The decision to investigate the movies, long on the agenda of Martin Dies and just then under scrutiny by the Tenney Committee of the California state legislature, was made at a meeting of six of the Hart Committee's members, not including its chairman. Such a flouting of authority, not to say Congressional courtesy, would have been unthinkable during the Dies stewardship, but from the first days of Hart's appointment, it was evident that he had neither the votes nor the personality nor the heart to control his committee. One member explained to reporters how they got started on the tarantula's trail: "Mr. Rankin offered a motion to send investigators to Hollywood. We don't know what information he has but the motion was agreed to on the theory that we ought to find out whether our acting chairman is having nightmares or whether there really is something that ought to be investigated."

For Ed Hart that was the end. Two days later, he notified the Speaker that he was resigning as chairman of the Committee—"My physician has given me definite instructions to diminish substantially my activities for an indefinite time." In response to speculation that some intra-Committee dissen-

sion lay behind the withdrawal, Representative Mundt assured
the House that it was strictly a question of health; he gave
Hart A-1 clearance as a good American who "exemplified a
fearless courage and a devotion to principle which won him
the admiration of our entire Committee." Rankin, for his part,
spared no more thought for the departure of the admired chairman than he had for his presence, and replying to charges of
a witch hunt from Walter Winchell and Drew Pearson, reiterated his determination "to expose those elements that are
insidiously trying to spread subversive propaganda, poison the
minds of your children, distort the history of our country and
discredit Christianity . . ."

No sooner had John S. Wood of Georgia been named to the
Committee chairmanship than five California Democrats met
with him privately and attempted to impress upon him the
political uses to which previous investigations in their state
had been put. Rankin's reply to this piece of impertinence was
the revelation that 191 paintings, "loathsome paintings" by
contributing artists of the *New Masses,* were at that moment
hanging in the homes of film celebrities. "I am sure," he said,
"that some of them got into the home of Charles Chaplin, the
perverted subject of Great Britain who has become notorious
for his forcible seduction of white girls . . ." The source of
Rankin's animus against Hollywood—and he made no particular effort to conceal it—was the large number of Jews eminent
in the film industry. "I have no quarrel with any man about
his religion," he explained after a Committee investigator was
reported to have warned some liberal Jews to "watch their
steps" lest the fate of Germany's Jews overtake them. "Any
man who believes in the fundamental principles of Christianity
and lives up to them, whether he is Catholic or Protestant,
certainly deserves the respect and confidence of mankind."
In Rankin's mind, to call a Jew a Communist was a tautology.
His convictions led him to attribute all the horrors of the
Russian revolution to Trotsky and to see Stalin as a kind of
reformer, a seminary student who opened the churches, got
rid of the commissars, and drove the local Reds to America.
"Communism is older than Christianity," he would explain

from time to time. "It hounded and persecuted the Savior during his earthly ministry, inspired his crucifixion, derided him in his dying agony, and then gambled for his garments at the foot of the cross." In the halls of Congress he called Walter Winchell "a little slime-mongering kike" and he took glee in baiting his Jewish colleagues, particularly Sabath and Celler. One day he referred to the latter as "the Jewish gentleman from New York." When Celler protested, Rankin asked, "Does the member from New York object to being called a Jew or does he object to being called a gentleman? What is he kicking about?"[2]

The Committee went forward with its Hollywood investigation, but except for periodic hints by Rankin and Counsel Adamson of dreadful findings, "so hot" that they could not even be released, it bore no fruit. The movie industry was not fated to undergo its test of fire quite yet. Hollywood was not the only media of communication in enemy hands, however. In fact, they all were, and the Committee, under the generalship of its chief counsel, found time a few months later to cast a fleeting glance at radio, when Ernie Adamson "requested" the scripts of seven commentators in New York City, all of a leftward bent.[3] Adamson did not trouble to make nice political distinctions among them. It was sufficient that one or another had reportedly praised the Soviet army, criticized Congressmen and Chiang Kai-shek, was foreign-born or spoke English with an accent. Adamson's initiative had not been sanctioned by a Committee vote, and engendered a vigorous debate on the floor of the House, but Wood and Rankin backed him up. "Do you know the reason we called for the scripts?" asked Rankin, and replied: "Some of those scripts ought not to be drummed into the ears of the American people." Two of the broadcasters were hastily dropped by their stations, and Wood introduced a bill which would have required, among other things, that news programs be clearly distinguished from

[2] "Upon analysis," wrote Rankin's admirer Westbrook Pegler, "the worst offense charged to Rankin of Mississippi is that he has the sort of manly personal temper that most Americans respect in their friends and fellow men."
[3] They were Cecil Brown, William S. Gailmore, Hans Jacob, Johannes Steel, Raymond Gram Swing, J. Raymond Walsh, and Sidney Walton.

opinion programs and that the commentator's name, place of birth, nationality, and political affiliation be open to public inspection. "The time has come," an unidentified Committee spokesman told reporters, "to determine how far you can go with free speech." To emphasize the point, when a full-page advertisement featuring cartoons of gagged couples, headed YOU CAN'T TALK . . . IT'S UN-AMERICAN and signed by Citizens to Abolish the Wood-Rankin Committee (many of them familiar signatories from united front days), appeared in *The New York Times*, Thomas hastened to New York to question not only its sponsors but the head of the advertising agency which had placed it as well as a representative of the newspaper's advertising department.

By such efforts, the Rankin Committee after six months left no more doubt of its intentions than the Dies Committee had, and there was nothing it could do short of investigating the Daughters of the American Revolution for denying Constitution Hall to Negro performers that could placate its critics. But neither Rankin nor his talkative chief counsel Adamson were of a placating spirit; they could not open their mouths without incensing spokesmen of the various organizations, ranging from genuine civil libertarian to mere Communist, who allied themselves with a handful of Congressmen in the endless and unrewarding effort to abolish the Committee.

By the fall of 1945, when the Committee turned its attention to the Communist Party, the radical left in America was in distressed circumstances. The year began sunnily for our Communists, led by Earl Browder and nourished by the victorious alliance against the Germans. It ended under the cloud of cold war, with Browder, "the man from the heart of America," as C.P. warhorse Elizabeth Gurley Flynn liked to speak of him in better days, in disgrace and William Z. Foster carrying the proletarian banner. A few weeks after the Yalta Conference of February 1945, where it became evident that Stalin on the one hand and Roosevelt and Churchill on the other had conflicting hopes for the political future of Western Europe, Browder, personification of the wartime era of good Russian-

American feelings, promoter of the suddenly anachronistic line of "peaceful coexistence" between capitalism and socialism, was rudely cast down. The sentence was delivered in April by the French Communist chief Jacques Duclos, reprinted in May by the *Daily Worker,* and accepted by former comrades and sycophants with the customary beating of breasts. In July Browder and Browderism were denounced at a special convention, and the Communist Political Association became once again the Communist Party. It would not be very long, promised Foster at a rally in September, before the United States would be nationalizing its banks. In February 1946, Browder was expelled from the Party as a "social imperialist." The 1945 events naturally invited the attention of the Committee, and several C.P. leaders were summoned to Washington. But it was the Ham Fish experience all over again. Browder was terse and antagonistic. Foster was garrulous and antagonistic. Adamson, the interrogator, was antagonistic and inept. And an opportunity to show the extent of the American Communists' servitude to Moscow was lost as Mundt and Rankin used the hearings to exhibit their patriotic detestation of Communism and all its works.

Following tradition, the Committee moved at the end of 1945 from the Communist Party proper to groups which it was convinced were fronts: the National Council of American-Soviet Friendship, the National Federation for Constitutional Liberties and, most especially, the Joint Anti-Fascist Refugee Committee. Its attention was drawn to the last-named by a Madison Square Garden rally in September to raise money for the maintenance of some 200,000 Spanish refugees in France. The rally, whose slogan was "Break Off Relations With Franco!," was very much in the old Popular Front vein, with the acting head of the Soviet embassy, Nikolai Novikov, there to assure everyone that "Now as before the Soviet Union is the leading power in the task of protection of democracy in the whole world." Especially upsetting to numbers of people in this country was the talk by British Laborite Harold Laski, transmitted from England and broadcast to American radio listeners outside of the Garden. Laski, whom neither Rankin nor Adamson had ever heard of up to this time and whom Thomas described as the "Red fascist leader of England," shared the wishful thoughts of those who believed that Franco might actually be toppled by the displeasure of the West over his services to Hitler during the recent war. He suggested in his speech that the footdragging of America and Britain in this cause might be due to fear of hostility from the Vatican. Catholic organizations mounted a campaign of protest, and in a few weeks the Committee received thousands of postcards demanding an investigation. Rankin and Adamson, like children commanded to eat a lollypop, responded without delay.

The "Joint" in Joint Anti-Fascist Refugee Committee had reference to the fact that it was created in 1942 from a merger of three organizations, each of them qualified candidates for the Dies Committee lists: The American Committee to Save Refugees, the United American Spanish Aid Committee, and the League of American Writers. Its function was ostensibly to provide medical care and other services to Spanish refugees in France, and for this purpose it had been licensed by the President's War Relief Control Board and granted tax exemption. The Spanish refugees, for whom the world victory over fascism was a bitter irony while Franco remained in power, unquestionably needed assistance and needed it sorely, but friends of the Anti-Fascist Refugee Committee were being disingenuous when they compared the group to agencies like the Red Cross and U.N.R.R.A. Having selected its beneficiaries on political grounds, its every plea for funds constituted an attack on Franco; it could not have avoided becoming an anti-Franco propaganda source if it had wanted to, and it didn't want to. Its board of directors was sprinkled with Communists, the most prominent being Howard Fast, writer of popular novels, and the entire board was strenuously and unapologetically anti-fascist. To Rankin, Adamson, and Wood, being anti-Franco was a symptom of anti-Americanism, and they charged that the Anti-Fascist Refugee Committee was "engaged in political activity in behalf of Communists" and that it was disseminating propaganda of "a subversive character." In searching for documentation of these charges, Wood had to reach back to the

Spanish Civil War, when Dr. Edward K. Barsky, the committee's chairman, ran a hospital in Spain "organized on the model of the Soviet Republic. He [Barsky] referred to himself as the commissar and the employees of that organization were required to address each other as comrades."[4]

But the question of what the Anti-Fascist Refugee Committee had done was lost in the commotion over what it would not do. It refused to turn over the records subpoenaed by Chairman Wood "in the interest of saving time" after Adamson had asked the War Relief Control Board to revoke the group's license. Barsky claimed that he had no authority to hand over the records, since such authority was vested in the executive board. The members of the executive board, coached by their collective attorney, claimed that they had voted to give over this authority to their executive secretary, a young woman named Helen R. Bryan. Miss Bryan claimed that, "as custodian of the books and records," she had been left with "the responsibility of determining, after consultation with counsel, what action to take, within the limits of my legal rights, to protect its records from unlawful search and seizure," and she had concluded that the subpoena was invalid. It was not, she contended, pertinent to the Congressional inquiry; she doubted the constitutionality of the Un-American Activities Committee; she objected to the catch-all subpoena on the grounds that it would prevent her organization from operating; and she feared that disclosure of the records would put the families of refugees in jeopardy.

This buck-passing was designed not only to annoy Wood and Rankin and to establish a legal defense, but to feed a debate in Congress, led by Marcantonio, over the Un-American Activities Committee, and to launch a public campaign against its existence. Barsky was cited for contempt by the House at the end of March. "We are going to have a roll call on this

[4] The Committee's case against J.A.F.R.C. took up most of its report, issued June 7, 1946, which also ridiculed the Department of Justice for its sedition trial of a batch of native fascists and attacked a 1945 army pamphlet for the statement: "In the United States, native fascists have often been anti-Catholic, anti-Jewish, anti-labor, anti-foreign born." The Committee commented: "If a person is anti-white or anti-Gentile, or anti-white man, under the Army teachings, he is quite all right."

resolution," said Rankin, "and I am sure the American people will be interested in the vote." There were only four nays. And a few weeks later, after a bitter debate which pitted Rankin, Mundt, and Thomas against Celler, Marcantonio, and Helen Gahagan Douglas, the Committee set a record by obtaining contempt citations against all sixteen members of the executive board and Miss Bryan. Each of them had appeared before the Committee and, in identical language, refused to abet the investigation.

Other contempt citations were obtained that summer, on similar grounds and amid similar angry debate, against Corliss Lamont, chairman of the National Council of American-Soviet Friendship, whom the Dies Committee had, with fair accuracy, called "probably the most persistent propagandist for the Soviet Union to be found anywhere in the United States"; Richard Morford, the Council's director; and George Marshall, chairman of the National Federation for Constitutional Liberties.[5] Being tested in each of these cases was the power of the Committee to demand that documents be produced for its inspection. All of those cited, with the exception of Corliss Lamont, who had not exactly refused to produce his group's documents but had merely said they were under Morford's control, were indicted, found guilty, and rebuffed by appelate courts.

The power of Congress to punish for contempt is an old one. Since 1857 it has been a misdemeanor, carrying a sentence of from one month to one year in jail and a fine of from $100 to $1,000, to fail to appear before an arm of Congress or to answer any pertinent questions. The procedure in these cases—

[5] The citing of Marshall delayed adjournment of Congress since each time that Rankin rose to bring his Committee's resolution to the floor, Marcantonio or an ally would suggest the lack of a quorum. When a majority of the members were rounded up by the ringing of the House bell, Rankin moved to "dispense with proceedings" so that he might go ahead with his contempt citations. One of the Marcantonio group—Biemiller, Hook, and De Lacy—thereupon asked for a roll call, which showed that a quorum was no longer present, the Congressmen having left the chamber. The procedure was repeated eight times and exhausted an entire July afternoon. When Rankin protested that it constituted "a dilatory tactic," there was laughter in the House since it was he who had taught Marcantonio the trick during the debate on setting up a Fair Employment Practices Commission.

which Martin Dies, as we have seen, attempted to circumvent —is rather complicated: After a committee of either House votes to cite a witness for contempt, the case is brought before the respective House, which almost invariably accedes to the desires of the committee. The U.S. attorney is thereupon instructed to prepare a bill of indictment; a grand jury does the indicting; and the trial takes place in federal court. The Un-American Activities Committee, whose resolution grants it the broad franchise "to hold such hearings, to require the attendance of such witnesses and the production of such books, papers and documents, and to take such testimony as it deems necessary," holds the record, with no near competitor, for instituting contempt citations, and scores of witnesses have learned the truth of the lesson that District Judge Holtzoff delivered in turning down a plea by five defendants in these early cases: "A person who declines to comply with a direction of the Committee on the basis of a claim that the resolution creating it is invalid, or that the Committee is exceeding its jurisdiction, acts at his peril."

Marshall was given three months and $500; Morford, three months and $350. Five of the members of J.A.F.R.C. resigned and expressed a wish to purge themselves and so were let off with a fine of $500 and three-month suspended sentences. The others, with the exception of Chairman Barsky, were made to serve their three months, and Barsky was given six months along with a $500 fine. In turning back the appeal of Barsky *et al.*, the Court of Appeals laid down a thoroughgoing affirmation of the Committee's legitimacy and practices. Judge Edgerton wrote a blunt dissent, in words very like those the Committee's opponents had been uttering for nearly a decade and would still be uttering two decades later: "In my opinion the House Committee investigation abridges freedom of speech and inflicts punishment without trial." But he was in a two-to-one minority. Judges Clark and Prettyman strenuously affirmed the right of Congress to inquire into potential threats to the national security even if it could not be shown that these threats were clear and present. The remedy for unseemly conduct by a committee of Congress, declared the judges, lay with the Congress or the people, not with the courts. When the Supreme Court refused to review the case, Howard Fast, bound for jail, announced "the beginning of fascism in America."[6]

In his study of these events, Professor Carl Beck summarizes the points of law which were developed out of the contempt citations of the seventy-ninth Congress:

> It was held that the existence of a quorum of the Committee could only be challenged during the hearings, not upon trial; it was held that testimony taken during investigations was admissible in the trial even though it was to be used to incriminate the witness; it was held that a trial jury may be composed of government employees even though their freedom of decision may be restricted by government loyalty oaths and security programs; it was held that the Committee could subpoena documents, particularly where there existed some evidence of subversive activities; it was held that a member of the board of directors of an organization was responsible for corporate decisions; it was held that the witness cannot decide what is pertinent and not pertinent because he might well challenge all questions; it was held that freedom of speech was not unduly impinged by an investigation into political associations; and finally, it was held that the resolution establishing the Committee on Un-American Activities and the subpoenas issued by the Committee did not suffer from the vice of vagueness.

The Committee thus emerged from its encounters with Barsky, Marshall, Morford, and the rest in a stronger position than its supporters could dare have hoped.

In January 1946, while the contempt cases were in process, the Committee devoted a day to taking testimony from Gerald L. K. Smith, the country's noisiest anti-Semite, whose past associations included William Dudley Pelley, Huey Long, Francis Townsend, and Father Coughlin and whose current vehicle was the America First Party. The summons to Smith

---

[6] Meeting Fast on the street shortly before he went off to serve his time, Lillian Hellman tells us, Dashiell Hammett remarked, "It will be easier for you, Howard, if you first take off the crown of thorns."

was designed to show that, despite slanders to the contrary, the Committee was as troubled by un-Americanism on the right as on the left, and an invitation was issued to every member of Congress to come and assist in the questioning. The only response this brought was an unfriendly statement from Representatives Celler, De Lacy, Marcantonio, Patterson, and Savage, which conveyed their doubts that the Committee would give Smith the same going-over it gave Communists. The doubts were amply justified by the event. Rankin acted as Smith's advocate, Thomas as his straight man—"Would you say that [the New Deal] was more fascist or more Communist?" Chairman Wood succumbed as usual, and before the hearing was half over, Smith was being drawn out on his opinions concerning Communists in government, the armed services, unions, and the movies—"I am convinced that Frank Sinatra is not a naïve dupe." The Committee's partisans would from this time use the fact that Smith had been questioned as evidence of its impartiality in seeking out subversion, but rarely, even in the most exuberant days of Martin Dies, had it given a more open display of ideological bias.

With no perceptible plan to guide it, the Committee tended in these two years to seek inspiration in headlines, and so when a Soviet spy ring was discovered which had obtained atomic secrets with the assistance of officials in the Canadian government, it was only natural for Counsel Adamson to announce that Chairman Wood was making a secret trip which had something to do with evidence of attempts to obtain information on the atomic bomb. "We are not on a cold trail by any means," said Adamson, and when a Russian naval lieutenant was arrested by the F.B.I. in Portland, Oregon, in March, the counsel, who had no particular information about the case but was growing increasingly impressed with his own expertise in such matters, informed newspapermen that it seemed to him the fellow might be a courier. Rankin announced from time to time that there were spies in this country trying to steal the secrets of the atom bomb. Later events would support the conjecture, but neither at the time he made his charges nor ever after did he produce any evidence to back them up.

As debate over the McMahon bill, which vested control of atomic energy in a civilian board ("one of the most dangerous pieces of legislation ever to come before Congress," in the opinion of Rankin), reached its height in the House in the summer of 1946, Thomas made public a report by Adamson warning that scientists at Oak Ridge had formed societies that favored world government: "These societies are definitely opposed to Army supervision at Oak Ridge and are just waiting for the day when military administration will be thrown out." In one of the cruder Committee efforts to influence legislation which it had not studied and which was none of its authorized business, Ernie Adamson advised the country that he personally had concluded that "the Army should exercise permanent control over the manufacture of atomic energy." A version of the McMahon bill was approved despite this unsolicited advice, and some weeks later Wood reported that a year's investigation had failed to bring to light any evidence of a foreign atom-bomb spy ring at work in the United States. The atom-spy charges would remain quiescent until 1948.

In the middle of May the Committee's sponsors came before the House to ask for $75,000 more to carry out their duties. The debate took the usual form. Hatton W. Sumners of Texas, chairman of the Judiciary Committee, gave an incoherent speech on the Anglo-Saxon form of government, which the Un-American Activities Committee was laboring to preserve. Mundt read statements by J. Edgar Hoover and reminded his colleagues, "This is an election year and that roll call on the Committee appropriation should become an index which will be widely quoted in many Congressional districts . . ." Coffee criticized the Committee's coddling of Gerald L. K. Smith and its indifference to the right of free speech. Sabath asked for an investigation of the Ku Klux Klan and other rightist groups. When Marcantonio prophesied that the additional funds would go to investigate the C.I.O.'s Political Action Committee, Rankin began applauding; the Republican side of the House joined in, and the New Yorker's speech was lost in laughter.[7] Rankin ended up the debate with a denunciation of the Communist practice of raping women in Eastern Europe—"Christian women, if you please . . ." The Committee got its money, by a vote of 240 to 81, with young Lyndon B. Johnson of Texas in the minority, and spent the next several months trying to find ways to use it up.

Its random essays here and there—a power strike in Pittsburgh, the Unitarian Service Committee's assistance to Spanish refugees in France—came to naught, until the middle of October, when Thomas reached out and grasped the life buoy of Louis F. Budenz. Budenz, preeminent example of the fervent Communist turned fervent Catholic anti-Communist, was like a tourist who is drawn to the shabbiest sections of all the towns he visits. As a Communist, he was managing editor of the *Daily Worker;* as an anti-Communist since his break in 1945, he became a star performer for the passionate right. It was his inclination to melodrama that brought him to the Committee's attention in the fall of 1946. On Sunday, October 13, he delivered a radio talk in Detroit, in which he said that American Communists took their orders from a secret agent of the Kremlin. The disclosure was made in the language of *The Shadow:* "This man never shows his face. Communist leaders never see him, but they follow his orders or suggestions implicitly." On Tuesday Thomas announced that Budenz would testify before the Un-American Activities Committee. By Thursday the name of the alleged secret agent was no longer secret. A New York newspaper printed and Bundenz confirmed that it was Gerhart Eisler, also known as Hans Berger, Austrian-born Communist who had come to this country from Germany in 1941, was known to the F.B.I., and was then living with his wife in an apartment in Long Island City. The Eislers were due to leave America on Friday, on a Russian ship bound for Leipzig—"It is very strange they started to move him away as soon as I identified him," said Budenz—but the exit permit

[7] That summer, with Congressional elections approaching, Rankin, as acting chairman of the Committee, did his best to confirm Marcantonio's prophesy by ordering his investigators to begin a "thorough" inquiry into the C.I.O.–P.A.C. But nothing developed, except for a newspaper story or two.

was canceled. On being subpoened, Eisler said he was "very glad" for the chance to "defend myself against the accusation of having misused the hospitality which the great American people and its government granted me, a German anti-fascist." The *Daily Worker* wrote the whole thing off as a "provocation," a "Hitlerite Kremlin agent fable."

The questioning of Budenz was delayed until November 22 at his own request. On appearing, he reviewed his ten years in the Communist Party, apologized for his infatuation, and discussed, in an informed way, the C.P.'s subservience to Moscow and the tactical nature of the nominal disbanding of the Communist International early in the war. Rankin, Mundt, and Thomas, like handlers of a skilled but insufficiently bloodthirsty boxer, did their best during most of their three and a half hours together to free him of what inhibitions he may have had over turning the hearings into an anti-Communist rally. "I think the distinction you are trying to make, Mr. Budenz," Mundt drew him on gently, "is that what they actually have in Russia is not the Communism of Marx and Engels but a dictatorship, and Communism under which people are denied a great many things under the concepts of Communism." And Rankin, less gently—"Regarding these overrun countries, are you familiar with the rape of innocent women, the murder of innocent men, the plunder of the peasants and the robbery of the helpless people in those areas by the Communist regime?"

As for Eisler, it soon appeared that Budenz had no hard evidence of his charge that the German émigré was the representative of the Communist International in this country. That Moscow did have such a person here, however, strained credulity less than Eisler's statement at a meeting in his behalf that "there never was a Communist Party in the world that would allow anyone, even a foreign Communist, to run its business." That Eisler was Moscow's mouthpiece was quite possible; but no one could have been convicted on the basis of the speculative case made by Budenz. Eisler, in the audience, had grounds for his complaint that the Committee preferred not to question him. When he finally was called more

than two months later, after the Committee had managed
to round up additional evidence, his pleasure at the prospect
of defending himself against misuse of the national hospitality
had, as we shall see, diminished.

On November 6, about two weeks before the Budenz hearing,
the country went through its off-year Congressional elections,
and gave a great victory to the Republican Party. The G.O.P.
won most of the governorships, a narrow majority in the Senate,
and a substantial majority in the House. It was a momentous
event, a rebuff to those who had hoped to bring America out of
the war with a planned economy, and a stunning blow to the
political pretensions of the C.I.O.–P.A.C. It also bespoke a
stiffening of the nation's feelings toward our late ally, Russia.
For the Un-American Activities Committee, it meant Republican control for the first time in its history—not in itself of
overriding significance since Democratic administrations which
had endured Dies and Rankin had little worse to fear from the
blackest Republicans. But differences there would be. In
California, Jerry Voorhis, who had left the Committee in sad-
ness and disgust, lost to the unknown Richard M. Nixon, who
would leave it in triumph, for the Senate and beyond. (Joseph
R. McCarthy, meanwhile, took his seat in the Upper House.)

Less than three weeks after the election, President Truman
delegated to an interagency committee the job of testing the
loyalty of more than two million government employees. To
what extent the Truman loyalty order represented a real concern over pinkish tendencies of officials in the State Department and elsewhere, to what extent it was designed to head
off more ferocious attacks from Republican-controlled committees in the new Congress, even the men who concocted
it could not say. But insofar as the latter reasoning was involved, the Administration tactic was futile. "The Committee,"
promised Rankin, "will intensify its drive and its efforts to
remove from the federal payroll every Communist and every
other subversive individual." A day after the loyalty order was
issued, Thomas, soon to be the Committee's chairman, made it
clear that Administration purge or no Administration purge,

he took the Republican sweep as a mandate to ferret out and expose Communists and Communist sympathizers in government, unions, Hollywood, the schools, and in groups "trying to dissipate our atomic bomb knowledge for the benefit of a foreign power." During his ten years in the House and his eight years on the Un-American Activities Committee, Thomas had made it his special mission to expose the New Deal as a Communist project and New Dealers as subversive *per se*. Whatever else may be said of him, he was not secretive about his intentions toward liberal Democrats, and the Administration was amply forewarned.

In the final weeks of the seventy-ninth Congress, Rankin and Adamson gave way to the kind of frenzy that turns undergraduate beach parties into riots as the weekend ebbs. On November 14 Harlow Shapley, director of the Harvard College Observatory and officer of the Independent Committee of the Arts, Sciences and Professions—major political arm of the Russophile left—was summoned to an executive hearing for his group's audacity in trying to defeat the new Republican Speaker of the House, Joe Martin, Jr., during his campaign in Massachusetts. Rankin, the only Committee member present, cut loose. He tore a statement from Shapley's hands, ordered the police to eject his lawyer, former Congressman Thomas Eliot, yelled a good deal, and threatened contempt proceedings.

In December Rankin called on veterans' organizations to assist him in investigating "pink teachers," and Adamson, in Hollywood during a violent A.F. of L. strike against the studios, declared that it was "not open to debate" that the Communist Party was trying to gain domination of the movie industry. In the last days of the year the counsel, altogether carried away by now, released a report which he had not taken the trouble to have approved by the Committee. It told of a conspiracy to promote a Communist revolution through a general strike that would wreck the U.S. economy; of seventeen C.I.O. unions dominated by Soviet agents; of the Library of Congress being turned into "a haven for aliens and foreign-minded Americans" —at a time when "many native-born and naturalized scholars are looking for such jobs"; of improper activities by U.N.

representatives; of the danger that Communists might paralyze the Panama Canal. Adamson had managed to surpass even J. B. Matthews for sheer enterprise.

This was not the first time that Adamson had let himself go. His most curious private campaign had occurred some months before, when he took to writing letters to groups such as the Veterans Against Discrimination, in which he pointed out that their circulars in support of the F.E.P.C. bill "refer to democracy several times." He advised them that "this country was not organized as a democracy" and that the Constitution guarantees a republican form of government. Having established this much, he put the question: "Is it your purpose to conduct a propaganda campaign against the administration of the provisions of the Constitution?" When he wrote such a letter to Drew Pearson to question the closing line of the columnist's Sunday evening broadcasts, which included the offensive words "make democracy work," Pearson suggested a padded cell for the Committee counsel.

The issuance of the unauthorized conspiracy report was Adamson's last official act in behalf of a nondemocratic way of life. Rankin, the only member of the Committee to have been given an advance look at the report, found it to his taste and defended him, but Thomas announced, "Adamson will not draw one more day's pay if I become chairman of the Committee." Adamson replied that Thomas was sore because the report had not been held back for a week so that he could have put his name on it—as chairman. "Anyway," said Adamson, sounding very much like Martin Dies in his moments of self-pity, "I'm tired of the whole thing. There's lots of cussing and very little commendation attached to a job like mine." He was replaced by Robert Stripling, who had come at last, through a long apprenticeship, to his reward.

Early in January a well-expurgated version of the Adamson report was adopted and released by the Committee. All of the most colorful of the chief counsel's charges, such as the conspiracy to foment a general strike and the capture of the Library of Congress, had been dropped, and the report now contented itself with a general statement about Communists "entrenched" in government, labor, education, and "a number of" C.I.O. unions. It also recommended a batch of curbs on foreign agents and on aliens, including one to bar second-class mailing privileges to any organization distributing "un-American propaganda." It proposed further the creation of a new, independent commission in Washington with the power to discharge any government employee "whose loyalty to the United States is found to be in doubt." Not many weeks would pass before Mr. Truman acted upon such cold-war recommendations.

Measured even against the special standards established by Martin Dies, the Rankin Committee did not do very well. Even Dies's man, Stripling, was dissatisfied; referring to the detection by a staff member of a similarity between the words Kreml (the hair tonic) and Kremlin, Stripling called it an "all-time low in investigations." The antic viciousness and abiding bigotry of Rankin along with the outright silliness of Adamson were guarantees against any sort of accomplishment, but for opponents of the Committee, within the Administration and without, the replacement of Wood by Thomas was no blessing. Rankin remained, and the new chairman had backed Martin Dies for six years with unmatched consistency and glee. With Republicans in charge of the Congress, the Administration could no longer work on vestiges of party loyalty to keep the Committee subdued—not that it had had much success with its appeals to its Southern cousins anyway. In two years there would be a Presidential election, and not even the most wishful Democrat could imagine that Thomas and the G.O.P. leaders would, like ladies making believe they do not see the buffet table, delicately resist the temptations of the occasion. A long time had passed since the last G.O.P. banquet and there was hunger in the ranks. It was with such exhilarating prospects that the House Un-American Activities Committee entered what was to be the grandest period of its existence.

7

1947: The Thomas Committee

THE first business of the new Committee was old business. The five Republicans—Thomas, Mundt, McDowell of Pennsylvania, Vail of Illinois, and Nixon of California—and four Democrats—Wood, Peterson, Bonner, and Rankin—gathered on February 6 to resume hearings into the suspended Eisler affair. "Mr. Gerhart Eisler, take the stand," called Robert Stripling. "I am not going to take the stand," replied Eisler, and the relationship never improved. Eisler, who had recently been taken into custody by the Immigration authorities, refused to be sworn unless he was permitted to deliver three minutes' worth of remarks; Chairman Thomas promised him that privilege, but said that he would first have to be sworn and questioned. "That is where you are mistaken," retorted Eisler, whose soft round face and rimless glasses were incongruous with his fierce manner. "I have to do nothing. A political prisoner has to do nothing." He and Thomas yelled at one another for a quarter of an hour without getting anywhere. He was cited for contempt on the spot, and escorted back to his cell on Ellis Island while his attorney handed out to reporters his three minutes' worth of remarks, twenty legal-sized pages of them, an ideological rejoinder to Louis Budenz.

But now there was more evidence against Eisler than the surmises of Budenz. According to an F.B.I. report, Eisler had taken an extremely active role in Party work, apparently as a liaison man between the Comintern and the C.P.–U.S.A., since his arrival on these shores. His means of support were obscure, but under a false name he had been receiving a monthly check of $150 from the Joint Anti-Fascist Refugee Committee, presumably a channel for C.P. funds. A former Party member told of meeting Eisler while taking a course in conspiracy and more academic subjects at the International Lenin School in Moscow in 1931. Budenz reappeared to give further details on Eisler's role in laying down Comintern discipline to straying functionaries. And Eisler's sister, Ruth Fischer (her mother's name), who had not been on speaking terms with Gerhart since her expulsion from the German Communist Party in 1926 for anti-Stalinist sentiments, called him "the perfect terrorist type." She charged that he had helped carry out purges in China in 1930 and had had a hand in the deaths of numerous comrades, including the eminent Russian theoretician Nikolai Bukharin.

The resolution to cite Eisler for contempt was presented to the House on February 18 by Richard Nixon, making his maiden speech. The young man from California took some liberties with the facts, referring to a supposed connection of Eisler with a Canadian atom-spy ring and giving him credit for conspiratorial powers which still wanted documentation. But there was no doubt that Eisler—"the murderous little Moscow agent," as McDowell titled him—had been a hard-working Comintern emissary for years under various names, had lied his way into this country, and had traveled, in behalf of the Party, on a forged passport. Nor was there any doubt that he had been in contempt of the Committee, and the resolution to cite him was passed by the House with only one dissenting vote—Marcantonio saw the affair as "a smokescreen behind which reaction advances to trample ruthlessly over the liberties of the American people."

A few days later Leon Josephson, a former lawyer for the International Labor Defense, who, according to handwriting experts, had assisted Eisler in faking a passport application, came before the Committee. He refused to testify on the grounds that the Committee did not have authority to question him and that, anyway, the presence of Rankin, who had been elected without benefit of Negro suffrage, rendered the proceedings unlawful. Stripling charged that Josephson was "involved in an elaborate system of possible espionage in which fraudulent passports were used," and he, too, was expeditiously cited for contempt.[1]

The third contempt citation of 1947 was awarded to Eugene Dennis, general secretary of the C.P., U.S.A. Dennis, whose trim mustache and wavy hair gave him the look of the fellow who used to lose the girl in B-movies, came before the Committee of his own volition during hearings on two bills to outlaw his Party. No sooner had he taken the stand then it became evident that he and the Committee were in perfect accord; he had no intention of answering questions and they had no particular interest in asking any; he was courting a contempt citation and they were ready to oblige. He refused to give his real name—which everybody knew was Francis Xavier Waldron; when Stripling asked for it, he turned to Thomas: "Mr. Chairman, the underling, this secretary, does not dictate what I say or don't say." Voices rose, and Thomas finally ordered the guards to "Take him out!" When Stripling handed him a subpoena to return in two weeks, Dennis, playing the role to the hilt, hollered, "Who the hell do you think you are?" and cast the document to the floor. "I hold this Committee in contempt!" he roared as he was hustled away. In lieu of responding to the subpoena when the two weeks came round, he sent along a Party attorney with the message that the Committee was not a body that might lawfully subpoena witnesses to appear before it. In the House, Nixon reviewed Dennis's behavior without undue emotion—which Mundt supplied by calling the C.P. figurehead a "political Rhett Butler trying to create chaos and destroy and wreck our free civilization." Mundt demanded stiffer penalties for contempt of Congress and accused the Department of Justice of dragging its feet about prosecuting the growing numbers of the contemptuous.

Eisler, Josephson, and Dennis, all of whom would have faced more severe indictments if they had chosen to testify about

---

[1] In fact Josephson was cited twice—once for not appearing before the Committee when first summoned and once for not answering any questions when he finally did appear. The government did not press the first case.

their passport finaglings, were found guilty of contempt and given the maximum sentence—$1,000 and one year in jail. Their appeals to a higher court met sharp rejections. Dennis's attacks on the Committee's legality were dismissed by a unanimous Court of Appeals as "sheer nonsense."[2] To Josephson the Court of Appeals explained that since he had refused to answer any questions at all, he could not base a defense on the grounds that he was refusing to answer only nonpertinent questions. Justice Chase, speaking for the two-man majority, commented dryly: "The only real basis for the appellant's contention seems to be that in some way the First Amendment in protecting freedom of speech guarantees such privacy in speaking as the particular speaker may desire, and this privacy is violated by whatever disclosure occurs incidental to an investigation for legislative purposes."

Despite a strong dissent by Justice Clark of the Court of Appeals, which condemned the Committee for misusing its powers, subverting the Constitution, and jeopardizing American liberties, the Supreme Court declined to review the Josephson case. (Justices Douglas, Rutledge, and Murphy were in favor of a review.) The Court did review the Dennis conviction—but only a narrow aspect of it, the question of whether the presence of government employees on the jury deprived the defendant of his rights to a fair trial. The decision, with Black and Frankfurter dissenting, was that it did not. Eisler's case was in process of being argued before the highest court when the defendant, who had been advertising himself as "a victim of a witch-hunting hysteria in this country," fled to East Germany.

The reluctance of the judiciary in these early cases to set limits on the Committee even when the justices were plainly disconcerted by some of its procedures, derived both from respect for the investigatory powers of Congress and for that body's exclusive jurisdiction over the manners of its com-

[2] In the light of subsequent developments, "sheer nonsense" does not quite settle the charge that the election practices of the state of Mississippi were unconstitutional.

mittees. As Justice Jackson, an old adversary of the Dies Committee, wrote regarding the Eisler case:

> I should not want to be understood as approving the use that the Committee on Un-American Activities has frequently made of its powers. But I think it would be an unwarranted act of judicial usurpation to strip Congress of its investigatory power, or to assume for the courts the function of supervising Congressional committees. I should . . . leave the responsibility for the behavior of its committees squarely on the shoulders of Congress.

Thomas used these cases as yet another springboard for his unending attacks on the Administration. "Where has the Department of Justice been for the past twelve years?" he asked. "What were they doing when these comrades were traveling throughout the world on fraudulent American passports in furtherance of their foreign-directed conspiratorial activities?" For his Committee, untrammeled by the courts and secure in the support of the House, the string of successes in sending Communists and fellow travelers to jail stood as an affirmation of its powers and an invitation to proceed apace with its mission.

The anti-Communist mission was being pursued with mounting fervor in other quarters, too, in 1947. A determination to contain Russia's designs for hegemony in Europe had been growing in Washington since before the end of the war, and now it had come to a testing point in Greece and Turkey. The fortunes of the Un-American Activities Committee were always inflenced by the stars of international conflict, and not since the days of the Nazi-Soviet pact had the stars been more propitious. For veteran loathers of Communists like Thomas, the Truman Doctrine was an acknowledgment from the very bosom of softhearted liberalism of their rightness down the years. We had to be tough—internally no less than externally—and the chairman barraged the attorney general with demands for action against the Communist Party and all its accessories and accomplices. The Soviet-oriented left understood what Thomas was about and found relief in sponsoring "Free

Gerhart Eisler" rallies where our unkindness toward the
U.S.S.R. abroad and toward its devotees at home could be
whipped in tandem. At one such rally in March, Marcantonio
called for "a people's political party throughout these United
States." Gideon's Army was a-gathering.

Late that month, as the Committee was beginning its hearings into two bills to outlaw the Communist Party, the President issued a sweeping executive order designed to cleanse
Washington of suspected Communists and sympathizers.
Under its provisions an elaborate system was set up for
checking on the purity of government workers without the
nuisance of legal forms. Now not only membership in or affiliation with a group judged subversive by the attorney general
was grounds for dismissal; "sympathetic association" with a
"movement" or with a "group or combination of persons"
might do it. The files of the Un-American Activities Committee
were designated as a source of information on suspect employees. Even Rankin was moved to commend the President,
asking only that he go one step further and put an end to the
"pernicious activities" of the Anti-Defamation League. Thomas
drew attention to the fact that he had put forward a bill for
a loyalty commission that was "almost identical" with Mr.
Truman's order, and Mundt flatly took credit unto the Committee for getting the executive branch to act. Once again, an
effort by the executive to take the play away from Congress,
to put the testing of loyalty into more responsible hands than
those of the flag-waving legislators, was interpreted as a victory
for the flag-wavers. This Truman Loyalty Order had a base
in reality; with Russia and America in direct confrontation,
Communists and their hangers-on could not be trusted in
sensitive posts, a conclusion that would be heavily accented
by the revelations of 1948. Yet the postwar fears of internal
subversion would never be entirely justified by experience,
and the Administration's forced reaction to a moderate threat
would in the coming months and years help to fuel a national
mania for loyalty tests of all sorts which, with the unfailing
assistance of the Un-American Activities Committee, would
cling for a decade.

After paying their several compliments to Mr. Truman, the Congressmen turned to bills before them. This was the first time that the Committee had actually set out to grapple with legislation; unfortunately for this maiden effort, the proposed laws had no virtue except as redundant affirmation of their sponsors' hatred for Communism. One of them, the creation of Rankin, would have made it unlawful, at the risk of a $10,000 fine and ten years in jail, "in any course of instruction or teaching in any public or private school, college or university to advocate or to express or convey the impression of sympathy with or approval of, Communism or Communist ideology" or to send through the mails any publication "any part of which expresses or conveys the impression of sympathy with or approval of Communism or Communist ideology."

For five days in March, the Committee listened to an assortment of witnesses selected not for their legal acuity but for their known abhorrence of Communism. But even they proved a disappointment to Rankin. Only the representatives of veterans' groups and the Daughters of the American Revolution favored the bills. All of the most prestigious witnesses—William C. Bullitt, former ambassador to the Soviet Union and to France; William Green, president of the A. F. of L.; Eric Johnston, head of the Motion Picture Producers Association; and, of greatest consequence, J. Edgar Hoover—opposed outlawing the Party. Hoover came before the Committee like the archbishop paying a call on a group of lay brothers. He patronized them; they fussed over him. When after awing them with the proportions of the Communist threat—including the statistic that in 1917 there was only one Communist for every 2,777 persons in Russia whereas in 1947 there was one Communist for every 1,814 persons in the United States—he warned mildly against making martyrs of the Communists, that was a death knell for the legislation. The Committee voted five to three against reporting the bills, as the legislators, particularly Nixon, turned their thoughts to a law for compulsory registration of Communists.

Rankin, of course, was in the minority in this vote, and indeed his position on the Committee had deteriorated notice-

ably under the new regime. His manner was as rowdy as ever—
"Would you say that Stalin is the Genghis Khan of the twentieth century?" he asked a legionnaire. During the questioning
of Ambassador Bullitt, he gave a little talk on what the Communists had inflicted on the people of the Ukraine, "the white
people of Russia," and inquired of the ambassador whether it
was not a fact that 75 per cent of the C.P. members in this
country were Jews. But Thomas made a much tougher chairman than Wood, and the Mississippian found himself repeatedly being called back from his excursions into racism. As
Rankin's influence waned, that of the young Nixon began to
shine. Beside men like Thomas and Mundt, he was indeed a
bright spark. Though he managed to make it clear that he was
as patriotic as the next fellow, he never ranted; his questions
were lucid and to the point and he had an orderly influence
on the proceedings.

Still, he did not entirely inhibit the entertainment; the
friendly witnesses were allowed to perform pretty much as
they pleased and the hearings provided good newspaper copy.
George Earle, a former governor of Pennsylvania, announced,
"I don't think there is better than an even chance that five years
from today ten per cent of us in America will be alive." He
rambled on for a time about the perils of atomic attack from
Russia until even Thomas, no skeptic on this subject, broke in
to remark that he didn't quite understand what that had to do
with the particular bills up for discussion. The chairman himself, however, assured a commander of the V.F.W., "I am one
hundred per cent with you on the transfer of the atomic bomb
development back to the military. If we put the atomic bomb
in the hands of a group of milktoasts we can be certain that we
can just hurry the day when the bomb is going to be used
against us."

Victor A. Kravchenko, a former Soviet army captain and
official of the Soviet Purchasing Commission who had defected
in 1944 and set down his experiences in the book *I Chose Freedom,* made the front pages by declaring that "every responsible
representative of the Soviet Union in the United States may be
regarded as a possible economic, political or military spy."

There was no reason to dispute this observation, and his suggestion that the outlawing of the Communist Party would not be in accord with America's traditions of freedom was relevant to the subject at hand. But with the encouragement of Committee members, Kravchenko, who testified through an interpreter and behind an outsized pair of dark glasses that covered the entire upper half of his face, ventured the opinion that Marshall Field, publisher of the Chicago *Sun* and *PM*, was more dangerous to America than the Communists; that if you cut off the roofs of Russia one dark night, you'd discover that 75 per cent of the people were opposed to the regime; that the death of Stalin would mean no change in Soviet policies; and that Molotov would probably take over. "Horse radish is no sweeter than parsley," he reminded the Committee. This awakened the Slavic muse in Andrei A. Gromyko, then becoming well known for his *nyet*-saying as the U.S.S.R.'s representative on the U.N. Security Council. Gromyko commented: "When a dog has nothing to do, it licks its underbelly. Sometimes that attracts spectators." To which Kravchenko replied: "When the dog barks, the wind carries the dog's bark."

Walter B. Steele, still representing the American Coalition of Patriotic, Civic and Fraternal Societies, as he had when he helped to launch the Dies Committee, was permitted to read off hundreds of names, old and new, Communists and associates of Communists, fellow travelers and associates of fellow travelers, members of organizations, sponsors of meetings, writers of articles, signers of petitions—a thoroughly indigestible mass of names, names, names, for which Thomas congratulated him effusively. One cannot improve on Professor Robert K. Carr's description of this full day's testimony as possibly "the most irresponsible ever presented to the Un-American Activities Committee."

The thread of the Committee's long-standing interest in Hollywood ran through these hearings. Eric Johnston, doing his job, said that "The Communists hate and fear the American motion picture. It is their number one hate." But to Nixon's question of how many anti-Communist films Hollywood had produced in the past five years, he had to concede there hadn't been any. Nixon was also concerned about *The Grapes of Wrath* being shown in Yugoslavia. J. Edgar Hoover described *Mission to Moscow,* the film version of Ambassador Joseph E. Davies's book "explaining" the Moscow purge trials, as "a prostitution of historical fact." And Jack B. Tenney, the inquisitorial state senator from California, testified that Charles Chaplin, Fredric March, John Garfield, Edward G. Robinson, and Frank Sinatra were abetting Communism. The Committee was working up to its spectacular investigation of the movies.[3]

Although 1947 must go down in the history of the Committee as the year of Hollywood, the investigators found time and cause to expose yet once again the presence of Communists in the leadership of important unions. In February, the ten-month-long strike at the Allis-Chalmers Company drew attention to the United Auto Workers, then in the throes of a battle for control between R. J. Thomas and Walter Reuther. Former members of the Allis-Chalmers local told how the Communists were using the strike to help Thomas. In July, it was the turn of a local of the Food, Tobacco and Agricultural Workers, then striking against the Winston-Salem factories of the Reynolds Tobacco Company, and a Bridgeport, Connecticut, local of the United Electrical Workers involved in a fight against the national union's Communist leaders. No revelations were forthcoming from these hearings, but they called attention to the continued presence and latest activities of Communists within the C.I.O. and may have hastened their expulsion.

Four reports were issued in 1947, with the usual ado. Their subjects were the Communist Party, the American Youth for Democracy, the Southern Conference for Human Welfare, and the Civil Rights Congress. All were prosecutor's briefs. All contained kernels of truth; it was difficult to quarrel in 1947 with the observation that the Communist Party was an agency of

[3] It would be negligent to leave these hearings without noting that while they were going on one morning, a freshman senator entered the hearing room and was invited by Thomas to participate in the questioning. He declined, saying, "I just came over to watch the very excellent job that you gentlemen are doing. I am here merely to listen, and not to ask questions." Thus spoke Joseph R. McCarthy.

Moscow or that the Civil Rights Congress, conceived in 1946 by a merger of the International Labor Defense and the National Federation for Constitutional Liberties with such godparents as Paul Robeson, Vito Marcantonio, Lee Pressman, and the ubiquitous Harry F. Ward, was a Communist front engaged in "a campaign of vilification against the American government."[4] But all the reports were marred by an unfastidious use of evidence, sloppy organization and writing, rampant emotionalism, and wild charges. The report on the A.Y.D., one of the least effectual pieces of C.P. machinery ever created, opened with the announcement that "the specter of Communism stalks our college campuses . . ." The organizations attacked cried "Fascist!" and one was carried back to the early days of Martin Dies.

The weakest of the reports, the one on the Southern Conference for Human Welfare, was gotten together in great haste in mid-June in order that it might be released on the Sunday before a scheduled Monday evening rally at Washington's Water Gate sponsored by the Conference and featuring Henry Wallace. It was at this meeting that Wallace made it plain that there would be a third party in the 1948 elections, dedicated to the proposition that the Russians earnestly wanted peace. Thomas's announcement was timed to scare off government employees from attending the rally, which was garnished with investigators making notes.[5]

The Southern Conference for Human Welfare was formed in 1938 by united-fronters for the expressed purpose of improving the economic lot of the South in general and the Negro in particular. The Committee charged that it was "perhaps the most deviously camouflaged Communist-front operation," and

[4] In a pamphlet, entitled *America's Thought Police*, issued shortly after it had been pilloried by the Committee, the Civil Rights Congress charged, typically: "The activities of the Committee present a deadly parallel with the pattern that Hitler applied in Continental Europe."

[5] Thomas's press release was preceded by the news that he and Rankin had received death threats which they had turned over to the F.B.I. The one to Thomas was in the form of a poem:

> My little butterball
> You're due for a fall.
> Sometime in June
> There will be a boom.

showed just how well camouflaged it was by presenting a completely unconvincing batch of alleged evidence about its subversive nature. The report was a hodgepodge—heavily slanted from beginning to end, and filled with inaccuracies and irrelevancies. The major points of the indictment—that the Conference showed "unswerving loyalty" to Soviet foreign policy, that it never took issue with the policies of the C.P., that it "maintained in decisive posts persons who have the confidence of the Communist Party"—were not out and out falsehoods, but they were too broadly framed and too sketchily developed to be taken as proved. Remotely relevant items were snatched from the air and tossed into the stew. One such paragraph, a favorite ever since with the Committee's critics, indicates the lengths to which lack of hard evidence led the concocters of this report. "Entertainer at the Washington meeting [of the Conference] was Susan Reed, employed by Café Society, a night club, owned by Barney Josephson, brother of Leon Josephson, leading Communist, Soviet Secret Service operative, charged with passport frauds. Mrs. Leon Josephson also owns an interest in the enterprise. Barney Josephson has been a supporter of the New York branch of the Southern Conference."

All the tricks of the Dies days were employed: meaningless quotes from the *Daily Worker*, carefully selected extracts from resolutions, a box score of individual affiliations of sixty-two members of the Conference which could have meant anything or nothing. In a critique of the report, Professor Walter Gellhorn of the Columbia University Law School paused to explain the box-score technique:

This device involves, first, seeking to establish a tie, however tenuous, between an unpopular individual or organization and some person connected with the Southern Conference; second, ascribing to that person all the undesirable qualities of the individual or organization with whom he has been momentarily linked; and finally, attributing to the Southern Conference the qualities which have been acquired by infection, as it were, by those intermediate persons.

Unquestionably there were individuals in the leadership of the Southern Conference who attempted, with some success, to steer it along the Communist line on specific issues. In 1940 they beat down pro-allied liberals who sought support for the Administration's preparedness policy. There were others, led by Dr. Frank P. Graham, president of the University of North Carolina, who resisted. The Committee indictment, as usual, made no distinctions. Its argument that the Southern Conference's "professed interest in Southern welfare is simply an expedient for larger aims serving the Soviet Union and its subversive Communist Party in the United States" had the effect of simplifying complicated motives; though Rankin could not credit the possibility, one might be a fellow traveler and yet be sincerely distressed at the lynching of Negroes. But in 1947 the cold war was creating the same kinds of difficulties for a liberal-Communist alliance as had the Nazi-Soviet pact, and by the end of the year, the Southern Conference had faded away.

Thomas promised in June that he was arranging "an all-inclusive program of investigations and hearings on fascism" and McDowell, turned into a subcommittee for the purpose, said that he was devoting "hundreds of hours" to the matter. But by the spring of 1947 the call of Hollywood was strong, and Thomas had no intention of tying his shipmates to the mast and stuffing his ears with cotton. An investigation of the movie industry was a project dear to the heart of Martin Dies; he spoke of it as early as August 1938 and, with the aid of witness Leech, made gestures westward now and then in the ensuing years. Shortly before Pearl Harbor, when Charles Lindbergh was titillating Midwesterners with the specter of Jews propagandizing America, Senate isolationists made a pass at Hollywood for its pro-British, anti-Nazi films. But it remained for Thomas to engage the movie industry. To Rankin, Hollywood was Semitic territory. To Thomas, it was New Deal territory. To the entire Committee, it was a veritable sun around which the press worshipfully rotated. And it was also a place where real live Communists could readily be found.

A sneak preview was held in May at the Biltmore Hotel in Los Angeles, Thomas and McDowell, their quest after fascists laid to rest, presiding. The hearings were closed, but each afternoon the chairman and investigator Stripling took care to inform newspapermen of the charges issued by the witnesses whom they had chosen to hear. Robert Taylor told them that government officials had prevented him from entering the navy in 1943 until he had completed *Song of Russia* for M.G.M., a film that Thomas identified as "Communist propaganda that favored its ideologies, its institutions and its ways of life over the same things in America." Mrs. Lela Rogers, mother of Ginger, told them, according to Stripling, that Ginger had stalwartly refused to speak the line, "Share and share alike—that's democracy," in the film *Tender Comrade,* written by Dalton Trumbo, whom she classified with Clifford Odets as a Communist. Thomas said that Adolphe Menjou said that "Hollywood is one of the main centers of Communist activity in America." Speaking on his own, the chairman announced that the Screen Writers Guild was "lousy with Communists" and "the government had wielded the iron fist in order to get the companies to put on certain Communist propaganda." Committee investigators meanwhile visited Hollywood offices, warning producers to clean their houses of Communists before they were compelled to do so by Congress or public opinion.

Two weeks after their Los Angeles visit, the Thomas-McDowell subcommittee issued an indictment, based on what their fourteen friendly witnesses had told them: the N.L.R.B. was abetting the effort of Communist organizers to take control of the industry; scores of highly paid screen writers were injecting propaganda into movies; White House pressure had resulted in the production of "some of the most flagrant Communist propaganda films"; subtle techniques were used for glorifying the Communist Party, while the Communists prevented the production of films which glorified loyal American citizens; the heads of the studios had done nothing to prevent all of this. Exposure was essential; public hearings were promised. Not one of the above charges would ever be substantiated, but the publicity which these coming attractions received bespoke high success for the feature event.

The summer was given over to research, and in the early fall the case of Hanns Eisler, younger brother of the recently convicted Gerhart, was taken up by the Committee. Hanns, who wrote music for the movies, had come to America during the war, and it was the mechanics of his entry that aroused Thomas. Summoned before the Hollywood subcommittee in May, Eisler had been dismissed after an hour, with satisfaction to neither side. Thomas told reporters that the witness "sought to evade and confuse the issues." Eisler told them that he was "offended as a scholar, a scientist and a composer."

On Hanns Eisler's return in September, it became evident that Thomas was out for larger game than the pudgy and rumpled composer of *The Comintern March*. The Committee's investigators had discovered that early in 1939 when Eisler, a German refugee in this country on a temporary visa, was seeking permanent status, Eleanor Roosevelt wrote two notes bringing the case to the attention of her old friend, Undersecretary of State Sumner Welles. The First Lady's compassion for Germany's persecuted Jews was as famous as it was abundant— and it had been tapped in this instance by an acquaintance who had assured her that Eisler was no Communist. Mrs. Roosevelt was not the only one to ask the State Department for sympathetic consideration of Eisler's case in 1939 when his temporary visa was running out. Malcolm Cowley of *The New Republic*, Freda Kirchwey of *The Nation*, Russell Davenport of *Fortune*, the columnist Dorothy Thompson, and the commentator Raymond Gram Swing were among those who made representations. During the composer's stay here, a place had been found for him on the faculty of New York's New School for Social Research so that, being a titular professor, he might in time qualify as a nonquota immigrant. His supporters were moved by the plight of a homeless man of talent suffering from State Department red tape, and some of them were more moved than they might otherwise have been because of his reputation as "a progressive musician." One State Department official wrote to another at the time: "If this alien [Eisler] obtains an immigration visa and enters the United States, we are likely to hear from the anti-Communist organizations in

The Special Committee on Un-American Activities poses for its first meeting: (left to right) Joe Starnes, John Dempsey, J. Parnell Thomas, Chairman Dies, Harold Mosier, Noah Mason, Arthur Healey.

Soon they would be joined by J. B. Matthews, the man with the telephone.

Whatever their philosophical differences, the four orators pictured here shared at least one major political principle—that of the raised fist. They are (clockwise, beginning top left) Samuel Dickstein, Earl Browder, Fritz Kuhn, Martin Dies.

Mrs. Eleanor Roosevelt joined members of the American Youth Congress at their appearance before the Committee. Here she follows the testimony with (left to right): Mrs. William Hinckley, wife of the former chairman of the Youth Congress; Jack McMichael, chairman; and Mr. Hinckley.

The Committee's three least favorite personages from the labor movement during the early years were (left to right) Joe Curran, Harry Bridges, Mike Quill.

The anti-Semitic John Rankin might have been taken for an orthodox Jew after he wrapped himself in a tallis of petitions signed by Californians who supported the Committee's plan to investigate the movies.

January 11, 1939

ask 1-24-39
file

EISLER, HANNS [III]

Dear Sumner:

All these papers were brought to me, yesterday by a friend of Mr. Eisler. The man who brought them is a perfectly honest person and very much disturbed. He thinks the State Department has really told the Cuban Consul that they do not wish to admit him and he is perfectly sure that the Eislers are not communists and have no political affiliations of any kind. He is sure that they believe our form of Government is "heaven" and would be entirely agreeable without reservation to take an oath of allegiance.

I believe that the Labor Department did not examine the case carefully enough. Why not do it all over again and bring it out in the open and let the Eislers defend themselves?

Cordially,

Eleanor Roosevelt

THE WHITE HOUSE
WASHINGTON

February 7, 1939

MEMORANDUM FOR HON. SUMNER WELLES:

See Mrs. Roosevelt's note:

"Dear Sumner - This Eisler case seems a hard nut to crack. What do you suggest?

Sincerely,

E.R."

The 1947 Hollywood hearings began with an investigation of Mrs. Roosevelt's efforts to assist Hanns Eisler. They ended with ten writers, including Dalton Trumbo and John Howard Lawson, at right, being cheered off to jail.

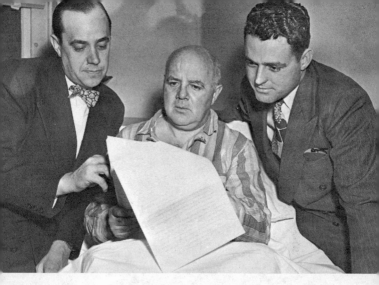

Photographers were invited into the room occupied by J. Parnell Thomas at Walter Reed Hospital, so that the Congressman, assisted by Robert Stripling (left) and Committee investigator William Wheeler, could produce an impromptu report that called Dr. Edward Condon "one of the weakest links in our atomic security."

Joining Elizabeth Bentley before the start of her momentous testimony were (left to right) Committee members John McDowell, Richard Nixon, Karl Mundt, John Rankin, F. Edward Hébert, J. Hardin Peterson, Chairman Thomas.

*Harry Dexter White made a dramatic defense against M[*]
*Bentley's charges. He died soon after this appearance, but[*]
case lived on.

this country. Of course, if he is refused an immigration visa, there will also be some repercussions among the so-called liberal elements in this country."

The Committee's case, as conveyed to the press, was that Eisler owed his final acceptance here in the fall of 1940, despite evidence of Communist activity and affiliations in his State Department folder (Stripling called him "the Karl Marx of Communism in the musical field"), to "influence and pressure exerted by certain prominent persons." That he had been at least a nominal C.P. member in Germany in the nineteen-twenties Eisler finally admitted to the Committee, amid persistent disclaimers, evasions, and parryings which soon turned comical. One of his songs, translated by the eminent American Communist, V. J. Jerome, contained the stanza:

> The Comintern calls you,
>
> Raise high Soviet banner,
> In steeled ranks to battle.
> Raise sickle and hammer;
> Our answer: Red Legions.
> We raise in our might;
> Our answer: Red Storm Troops.
> We lunge to the fight;
> Our answer: Red Storm Troops.

Confronted with this number, Eisler shrugged, "I am not responsible for literary translations."[6]

That Mrs. Roosevelt had taken an active, though by no means overbearing, interest in Eisler's plight was readily documented. That the pleas in his behalf had had some effect was evident and that Eisler did indeed succeed in gaining permanent admission to the country, despite his various services to the Red legions, was indisputable. But the course of things was not nearly so smoothly sinister as the Committee sought

[6] Representative McDowell was especially affronted by a song that Eisler wrote which ridiculed the law against abortion. This prompted Rankin to describe the body of his work as "filth," and the gentleman from Mississippi set forth credentials for this critical judgment which astounded those who had listened to him in Congress over the years: "I suppose that I am as familiar with American poetry and with English poetry generally as any member of either House."

to convey. Sumner Welles, correct and convincing in the witness chair, showed that he had replied to Mrs. Roosevelt that
there were laws on the subject of admission to this country
and even chided her a bit: "These friends of Mr. Eisler . . .
seem to think that there is some special consideration or treatment which can be given him which is not provided for in our
law or that perhaps certain liberties could be taken with the
law." He passed the First Lady's notes along to the appropriate
assistant secretary, a State Department veteran named George
Messersmith, who had been on the receiving end of the other
importunings in Eisler's behalf.

The warm feelings which Messersmith felt for any refugee
from Hitler were made warmer by the mild intervention of
Mrs. Roosevelt. Messersmith wrote to the counsel general in
Havana, the port through which Eisler hoped to enter this
country, that although the composer was "a man of very liberal
views" he [Messersmith] found it difficult to believe that he
was a Communist or ought to be excluded—"It would seem to
me that, unless there is definite and convincing proof that Mr.
Eisler does hold opinions which would exclude him, his case
can be favorably considered from that point of view." As it
turned out, Messersmith's humane indiscretion was not strikingly successful. It was nearly two years before Eisler managed
to gain permanent entry—not from the representative in Havana,
but from a consular official in a Mexican border town who,
accidentally or on purpose, failed to heed the "Stop" on the
Eisler file. No sooner had the composer crossed over to this
side of the border than the permit was withdrawn and it was
not restored until the case was heard by the Labor Department's Immigration Board, which ruled in his favor in October
1940. Although the Committee vested him with the title of
"international Communist agent," it produced no evidence that
he did anything more subversive during his years in this
country than write music for Hollywood movies.

Eisler swore at the Mexican border that he had never been
affiliated with the Communist Party and had never cooperated
with the Soviet regime: "My political belief is—I admire very
much the United States. I hate fascism in every form and I

hate Stalin in the same way as I hate Hitler." He wanted it understood that he was not a political creature. "My whole life is devoted wholly to music." He had thus not been altogether frank in entering the country, and a few days after the end of the Committee hearings, he was arrested and deportation proceedings were instituted aaginst him. He then took to repeating his brother's comparisons between the United States and Hitler Germany, and in 1948—a year in which Mr. Truman's Justice Department undertook a vigorous deportation campaign against Communist aliens as a means of demonstrating that Democrats could be just as tough on such people as Republicans—Hanns Eisler was permitted to leave the country voluntarily. Consigning Rankin, Thomas, and McDowell to the garbage heap of history, he and his pretty wife set off for Czechoslovakia.

In October 1947 the Committee had reason to be content: it had puffed up an innocuous effort to assist a victim of Hitler, albeit a Communist, into a plot against the national security, had passed off a low-budget film as a mighty extravaganza, and was ready to go to work in earnest on Hollywood.

The Hollywood hearings began on October 20 before a subcommittee of Thomas, Vail, and McDowell. It was a gala premiere. There were batteries of floodlights, microphones and cameras—one of them a TV camera, still a novelty at the time; more than a hundred newspapermen; a promised cast of dozens, featuring several of the industry's great names; and an audience of hundreds, mainly middle-aged women crushing for a glimpse of Robert Taylor, too many even for the spacious Caucus Room of the Old House Office Building.

The first witnesses, most of whom had appeared before Thomas and McDowell in the spring, were all cooperative in their fashion. Jack L. Warner, head of the studio with the most liberal reputation in Hollywood, producer of *Mission to Moscow*, extolled his own patriotism, boasted of firing a host of writers whom he deemed Communists (including several, like Clifford Odets and Irwin Shaw, who, it turned out, he had not fired at all), liberally gave the names of suspects without any accompanying evidence, pausing now and then to withdraw some names which he had given in his first appearance, and offered, on behalf of himself and his brothers, to set up a fund to ship to Russia people who didn't like the American system. Nixon, sitting in with the subcommittee, led Warner on to larger and firmer declarations of his Americanism, then put the question of how many anti-Communist films his studio had produced. Warner replied, lamely, that one was being worked on. In the businessman's testimony, defensive of himself, careless of the reputations of others, the experienced moviegoer could sense the denouement to come.

The remainder of the week was given over to even friendlier witnesses than Jack Warner, collected mostly from the membership of the Motion Picture Alliance for the Preservation of American Ideals, a conservative band which director Sam Wood had formed in 1944 to counter what he believed to be a Communist effort at a takeover of the industry. (When at the onset of their testimony, an attorney for several of the figures named as Communists by members of the Alliance rose to ask for the privilege of cross-examination, Thomas ordered him ejected from the Caucus Room.) Walt Disney, a paternal employer, told angrily of the indignities he had been made to suffer in the great studio strike of the nineteen-forties. The most plausible testimony came from writers, such as Morrie Ryskind, who had had firsthand experience with Communists in the Screen Writers Guild and gave details of their machinations for gaining power, maintaining it, and putting it at the service of causes close to the Soviet heart. (Dalton Trumbo, one of the named Communists, would later charge, with the charity for the motives of others he showed throughout the affair, that the friendly witnesses were seeking the jobs of the unfriendly ones.) The silliest testimony came, again, from Mrs. Rogers, who reported that she had saved Ginger from appearing in pictures like *None But the Lonely Heart* and *Sister Carrie* which conveyed a depressing idea of life under capitalism. She also said that she believed Clifford Odets was a Communist because she had read so in some column and had never come across a denial. The most pointless testimony came from Gary Cooper, who had been invited to Washington for show, and whose appearance (in double-breasted suit, light blue silk necktie, and white shirt) brought sighs from the spectators. Gary remembered reading some un-American stuff in scripts and rejecting them, but he couldn't call to mind the names of the scripts because he did most of his reading at night. On the issue of Communism he said, "From what I hear, I don't like it because it isn't on the level." Robert Montgomery, George Murphy, and Ronald Reagan gave calm statements of Communist activity in the Screen Actors Guild; all had been active in Guild affairs and were agreed that the Communists hadn't gotten anywhere. They declined to be drawn by Stripling into the question of whether the Communist Party should be outlawed, pointing out that they were not experts in that line. Other witnesses proved more amenable. Adolphe Menjou presented himself as a student of Marxism, Fabian Socialism, Communism, Stalinism, "and its probable effects on the American people if they ever gain power here," mentioned his friendship with Senator Taft and J. Edgar Hoover, stated unequivocally that the Communist Party should be outlawed and that universal military training should be instituted, and fully satisfied both the subcommittee and the audience, which gave him a good hand when he was done.

In their efforts to build a case against the film industry, Thomas, Vail, and Stripling spurred the first week's witnesses on to ever more fevered denunciations of Communists—in Hollywood and everywhere else. They indulged the witnesses in rumor, speculation, and surmise, allowed them to enter numerous names of alleged Communists into the record without pressing for documentation, and invited their views on matters well beyond their ken, listening soberly as the mother of Ginger Rogers declared, in response to a leading question, that the Communist Party was an agent of a foreign government and ought to be outlawed. In part, this was normal Committee treatment of friendly witnesses, but as the days drew on it became clear that Thomas needed whatever bits of support he could get to bolster a badly sagging indictment.

His original charges that Hollywood films were a trove of subversive propaganda, stocked by Washington, remained mere charges. The first five days of hearings served only to confirm what had been common knowledge in Hollywood for years: Communists were playing a significant part in the long, violent, and unsuccessful jurisdictional strike that had been troubling the film industry since 1945—an effort to form one industrial union out of the several craft unions—and C.P. members had by customary stratagems managed to turn the Screen Writers Guild to their various purposes. The Communists had been riding high during the war, and now their opponents were gleefully taking advantage of this grand opportunity to balance the accounts.

The second week was given over mainly to the accused. Most of them were writers whose names, accompanied by epithets, had recurred in the testimony of the friendly witnesses and who had reputations in Hollywood as Communists. Two of them—Emmet Lavery, president of the Screen Writers Guild, and Bertolt Brecht said that they were not members of the Party—but the others would neither deny nor confirm.[7] The confrontation between the subcommittee and the group that came to be known as the Hollywood Ten was unedifying in the extreme.[8] The ten had been advised by their attorneys, the most prominent of whom was Robert Kenny, former attorney general of California, to counter the question, "Are you now or have you ever been a member of the Communist Party?" with a rejection of the Committee's right to pose it. Moreover, they decided to be most aggressive about doing so. Thomas replied in kind; the audience applauded and booed;

[7] According to that foremost Brechtien Eric Bentley, one of the attorneys for the subpoenaed writers advised Brecht to say that he *was* a Communist on the reasoning that otherwise the Committee would forge a C.P. card in his name and charge him with perjury. Brecht, never a screen writer, was summoned because he had collaborated with Hanns Eisler on several works. His questioning by the determinedly unliterary Stripling, an exercise in aimlessness and near incoherence, is available to posterity on a record, *Bertolt Brecht Before the Committee on Un-American Activities.*

[8] Nineteen unfriendly witnesses were scheduled by the Committee: twelve writers, five directors, one producer, and one actor. The ten who took the First Amendment were: Alvah Bessie, Herbert Biberman, Lester Cole, Edward Dmytryk, Ring Lardner, Jr., John Howard Lawson, Albert Maltz, Samuel Ornitz, Adrian Scott, Dalton Trumbo.

and one after another they were dismissed, hollering, from the witness chair.

"It is the orthodox procedure of Communists," wrote Edmund Wilson after covering the Fish hearings of 1930, "to use public appearances of all kinds as pretexts for propagandist speeches . . . This practice has its value; it enables the Communist to cut out the ground from under the assumptions on which the charges against him rest, to substitute his own version of the case for the version of the society which is trying him." As if to demonstrate what Wilson meant, John Howard Lawson, Grand Old Man of Hollywood Communism and the first of the unfriendly witnesses to appear, told Thomas: "I am not on trial here, Mr. Chairman. This Committee is on trial before the American people. Let us get that straight." Thus inspired, the normally overbearing Thomas outdid himself. He turned down attorney Kenny's attack on the Committee's constitutionality, suggesting that he seek remedy in the courts, and later called Kenny back to question him about the advice he had given his clients. He gaveled down attorney Bartley Crum's demand for permission to cross-examine the first week's witnesses. He refused to allow Lawson to read a prepared statement denouncing the Committee as a fascist tool. ("Rational people don't argue with dirt," wrote Lawson and devoted most of his statement to declaiming upon his own integrity.) Thomas pounded his gavel and threatened Lawson with contempt when the writer reminded him that the friendly witnesses had been allowed to talk to their heart's content. Lawson, hamming it up, kept yelling that the Committee was trying to invade the rights of Protestants, Jews, Catholics, Democrats, and Republicans—"You are using the old technique, which was used in Hitler Germany, in order to create a scare here!" He was finally pulled away from the stand in the middle of still another proclamation of his Americanism. A few minutes later, his calm restored, he was smiling for photographers.

And so it went for four days, as the witnesses worked hard to provoke Thomas into some legal misstep which could be used in the court proceedings that lay ahead. Albert Maltz addressed Stripling as "Mr. Quisling" and complained, "Next you are going to ask me what my religious beliefs are." Thomas said he wasn't going to ask that at all, but Maltz continued with the rehearsed text: "And you are going to insist . . . that since you do not like my religious beliefs I should not work in such industry." Dalton Trumbo brought a pile of twenty scripts along with him and offered to introduce them into the record; he also offered to read a statement which compared Washington to Berlin on the eve of the Reichstag fire. "This is the beginning . . ." he yelled after being dismissed from the witness chair, ". . . of an American concentration camp." "This is typical Communist tactics," Thomas yelled back, gaveling furiously. When Edward Dmytryk, a relatively subdued witness, said he felt there was a constitutional issue involved in the Committee's question regarding his C.P. membership, Thomas thundered, "Where did you learn about the Constitution? Tell me where you learned about the Constitution?" Twice the chairman, quite beside himself, ordered a witness to leave the stand before Stripling had had an opportunity to pose the crucial question about his C.P. affiliation. A rare moment of humor in this inelegant script came when Ring Lardner, Jr., observed as Thomas, gaveling away, ordered him to depart, "I think I am leaving by force."[9]

After each uproarious interlude, a staff investigator read into the record a list of Communist credits of the reluctant witness, including the numbers of their C.P. cards. The evidence was persuasive; all had been openly active in their faith (though Lardner and Dmytryk were less noisy about it than Trumbo and Lawson), and their records were nicely in accord with their performances before the Committee. The fortunes of the dozen or two Communist writers who enlivened Hollywood's studios during the nineteen-thirties and -forties varied from Dalton Trumbo, who had come into wealth with such major screenplays as *A Bill of Divorcement, Kitty Foyle,* and *Thirty Seconds Over Tokyo,* to Alvah Bessie, who merely eked out a living, by Hollywood standards, with *Objective Burma* and

[9] Thirteen years later Lardner, the best-humored of the bunch, would concede in a *Saturday Evening Post* article that he had been a C.P. member, of an undependable sort, in 1948.

The Very Thought of You, to Samuel Ornitz, who specialized
in B-films for Republic Pictures. The only name among them
whom critics reckoned with was that of Clifford Odets. The
others were craftsmen, more or less adept at setting down
on paper the ideas in a producer's head. It was not arduous
work, except to the spirit; they were paid very well (the skilled
Trumbo earning more than $100,000 a year) and these revo-
lutionaries could mock in comfort the hands they kissed in
conference. They busied themselves with all the authorized
causes of their time—neutrality before June 1941, Russian war
relief and a second front afterward, the beginnings of the
Progressive Party. With the help of C.P. members and admirers
elsewhere in the studios, they recruited comrades to join them
in manipulating the Screen Writers Guild. They petitioned incessantly, rallied at the hint of an exploitable injustice, and
held endless cocktail parties for the raising of funds; they
ground out polemics and manifestos for the Communist press;
they cudgeled their brains over theological matters. In February 1946, Albert Maltz, one of the more talented of the cadre,
contributed an article to the *New Masses,* in which he took
mild issue with the hard cultural line of the cold war period.
The occasion for the article was an attack by the Communist
writer John Wexley on Scott and Dmytryk for cutting out of
their film *Cornered* some long propagandistic speeches which
Wexley had inserted. "I have come to believe," wrote Maltz,
"that the accepted understanding of art as a weapon is not a
useful guide, but a strait jacket." He recalled that *Watch on
the Rhine,* Lillian Hellman's anti-Nazi play, was attacked by
the *New Masses* in 1940 and praised in 1942 solely because
of political changes in Europe. He had a good word for such
unreliable writers as Steinbeck and Farrell—"Writers must be
judged by their work and not by the committees they join."
The Party hierarchy, having just expelled Earl Browder, had
no patience for such quibblings, and Maltz was smothered with
doctrinal truths. Bessie and Biberman damned him with particular fervor at a night-time meeting of their cell. In print,
Bessie, who could show not a fraction of Maltz's talent, proclaimed, "We need writers who will joyfully impose upon

themselves the discipline of understanding and acting upon working-class theory." Maltz, writer of such muscular screenplays as *The Pride of the Marines* and *Destination Tokyo,* succumbed at once. In April he recanted in the *Daily Worker,* berating himself for his "one-sided nondialectical treatment of complex issues," for his "distorted view of the facts, history and contribution of left-wing culture to American life." His article read as though it had been translated direct from the Russian, and it was evident that there was no brighter dream in Albert Maltz's constellation than to be a defendant at a Moscow trial.

For such men, a call to the Un-American Activities Committee was an opportunity to broadcast upon a national stage the stimulating messages which they had never been able to put into their movies. "The attack on the motion picture industry," Lawson told several thousand Progressive Citizens of America, "marks an entirely new phase of the drive toward thought control in the United States." Maltz told the Civil Rights Congress that if the Committee got the right to burn films "the result will be that they will get the right to burn the people who made the films." Hollywood's Communists saw themselves much as they saw Josef Stalin—honorable, tough-minded progressives beleaguered by fascistic brutes and betrayed by pansy-like liberals. How else, being writers after all and radical writers at that, could they interpret their peculiar position? How else come to terms with careers that parodied the writer's craft and a radicalism that one toasted in champagne? In charging that these men had corrupted Hollywood, Thomas had the facts of the case backwards. In Hollywood you wrote to order, and the Communists, despising what they were ordered to write, labored to maintain the illusion that, substantial salaries notwithstanding, they would always be outsiders; that whatever capitalist frivolity might emerge from their typewriters, they formed the last bastion of integrity in a corrupt trade. "Always, in Hollywood," wrote Alvah Bessie, veteran of the war in Spain and co-author of *The Very Thought of You,* "the honest writer attempts to improve on the frequently shoddy material given to him to adapt for films; he frequently succeeds—and this is sometimes called 'subversion.' "[1]

Lawson was the coach of the Hollywood team, the only one of them who had any ties of consequence with the Party chieftains in New York. "As for myself," he wrote in a left-wing magazine before his troubles came upon him, "I do not hesitate to say that it is my aim to present the Communist position and to do so in the most specific manner." A non-Communist minor writer who had been enticed into the fringes of the group told the Committee that he had heard Lawson exhort his teammates to get five minutes of Party doctrine into every film, and to place such moments in expensive scenes so that they would not be cut by the producer. Lawson was also purported to have advised sympathetic extras to behave like slobs if they were playing rich characters and to look downtrodden if they were playing poor ones.

The trouble was that despite a noble Negro here, a nasty banker there, the locker room plays never quite came off on the field. Lawson's main accomplishment was *Blockade*, his 1936 film about the Spanish Civil War; it contained not a word about Franco or fascism, and audiences might be pardoned for leaving the theatre a bit uncertain about which side they had been rooting for. The Scott-Dmytryk film *Crossfire* was a simple attack on anti-Semitism, notable only because it had taken Hollywood's Jewish producers so long to get around to the subject; it was about as subversive as the National Conference of Christians and Jews, which, to be sure, was subversive enough for John Rankin. Lester Cole put La Pasionaria's line about it being better to die on one's feet than live on one's knees into a movie about a boy's school, a fairly safe insertion since only the dedicated would recognize the source or what it *really* meant. Alvah Bessie's finest moment came when he wrote into the wartime film *Action in the North Atlantic* a scene of a Soviet plane—"its red star plainly on the fuselage"—

---

[1] In 1966 Bessie contributed to the world of letters a novel entitled *The Symbol*, based on the life of Marilyn Monroe. If there were anything to be said for a blacklist, Bessie's work would say it.

dipping a wing in salute to a U.S. merchant ship. "It's ours!" cried Dane Clark.

Thomas, who kept promising to show up Hollywood movies as a fount of Marxism, at length rested his case on three wartime films: *Mission to Moscow*, *North Star*, and *Song of Russia*. There was no doubt that all were pro-Russian—James Agee wrote that *Mission to Moscow* was "almost describable as the first Soviet production to come from a major American studio . . . a great, glad two-million-dollar bowl of canned borscht . . ."—and even more misleading about life in the U.S.S.R. than most movies were about life at home. (The Russian-born novelist, Ayn Rand, one of the Committee's expert witnesses, pointed out that *Song of Russia* showed people smiling and didn't show any bread lines.) But Thomas could not support his charge that this propaganda had been engineered by New Dealers in Washington—though they certainly did not oppose such gestures to our ally in the East. Robert Taylor apologetically took back in the fall the impression of government interference with his military life which he had left in the spring. As an M.G.M. script supervisor, a member of the Motion Picture Alliance for the Preservation of American Ideals, observed, the pro-Russian movies were "a form of intellectual lend-lease." Battles were, after all, raging on the Eastern front, and it would have been odd if among all the war films of the time there had not been one or two boosting the Soviet Union.

As the hearings proceeded, it seemed that the movie industry, which had girded for its Stalingrad, was emerging relatively unbruised from the encounter with Thomas. While former Secretary of State James F. Byrnes, still an influential figure among Southern conservatives, lent his counsel and weight in private, Paul V. McNutt, former governor of Indiana and high commissioner to the Philippines, pressed publicly and ceaselessly for Thomas's alleged list of the allegedly tainted movies. "What pictures are on such a list?" he demanded. "What lines and what scenes contain Communist propaganda?" This information Thomas, who grew indignant at such requests, never supplied, and even Representative McDowell was led to observe toward the end of the first week that he had heard no evidence of Communist propaganda, except that bankers were sometimes cast as villains.

Eric Johnston, president and spokesman for the Motion Picture Producers Association, adopted a strategy of making broad attacks on the Committee's unexpressed intentions as well as on its unconcealed techniques. He put Thomas on the defensive with warnings against censorship, and called on the leaders of Congress to overhaul the procedures of Committee investigations. The open-handed flinging about of names by the first week's witnesses, not excepting his employers, gave point to Johnston's charge: "Too often individuals and institutions have been condemned without a hearing or a chance to speak in self-defense; slandered and libeled by hostile witnesses not subject to cross-examination and immune from subsequent suit or prosecution." At the very time that this civil libertarian text was being composed, however, Johnston was suggesting to the producers that they agree not to employ "proven Communists." The producers did not, for the moment, accept this recommendation, on the technicality that such a pact might constitute a conspiracy to deprive persons of a livelihood. Instead, they put it up to Congress to rule on whether Communists were in fact agents of a foreign government.[2]

In private meetings of attorneys for the producers and the writers on the eve of the opening of the Hollywood hearings, Johnston, renowned for his winning manner, gave his personal assurances that there would be no blacklist: "Tell the boys not to worry. We're not going totalitarian to please this Committee." Even Jack Warner, who strained to bursting in his effort to please the Committee, told Thomas: "I can't, for the life of me, figure where men could get together and try in any form, shape or manner to deprive a man of a livelihood because of his political beliefs." By November he was able to figure it. At the end of the month, fifty leading motion picture

2 Stripling digressed during his questioning of Johnston to press him about a trusted assistant of his who once belonged to the Communist Party. It was the same diversion that Senator McCarthy would use, to his sorrow, against Joseph Welch in the Army-McCarthy hearings of 1954.

executives held a secret two-day meeting at the Waldorf-Astoria and emerged with the announcement that they had unanimously decided to "discharge or suspend without compensation" the unfriendly ten, whose "actions have been a disservice to their employers and have impaired their usefulness to the industry." No one would be rehired until he had purged himself of contempt or been acquitted or declared under oath that he was not a Communist. ". . . A constructive step . . ." commented Thomas.

The producers had fought back the besiegers of their town only to bend their knee to the foreign gods anyway. Sam Goldwyn, Walter Wanger, and Dore Schary were against the decision; the brothers Warner, Spyros Skouras of Twentieth Century-Fox, and Nicholas Schenck of Metro-Goldwyn-Mayer favored it. But the decisive pressure came from the New York financial interests upon which the studios relied. The brawling exhibition of the unfriendly witnesses, in addition to being an embarrassment to everyone, had apparently left some moviegoers with the idea that Hollywood was a nest of Red agitators, and it was feared that box office receipts might be affected. Even newspapers critical of the hearings were put off by the writers' performances, while the Hearst press, ever partial to the Committee, had given the proceedings lavish coverage and were clamoring for restrictive laws—"The need is for FEDERAL CENSORSHIP OF MOTION PICTURES. The Constitution PERMITS it. The law SANCTIONS it. The safety and welfare of America DEMAND it!" The dismissal of a few politically obnoxious employees seemed a cheap price for the protection of an entire industry.

A three-man delegation, led by Dore Schary, a former writer whose studio, R.K.O., had produced *Crossfire* and who had defended Scott and Dmytryk before the Committee, was sent to bear the producers' decision to a meeting of the Screen Writers Guild.[3] Schary explained to the assembled writers,

[3] Like Bertolt Brecht, Schary had been advised by an attorney for the writers to join his clients in pleading the First Amendment, with the warning that the Committee had forged a C.P. card in his name. If the attorneys for the Communists truly believed this, it may be written off as a case of hysteria.

who included six of the unfriendly ten and a number of others who faced quick dismissal, that unrepenting Communists would no longer be considered suitable for employment in the movies. "We do not expect you to condone this," he said, but added the hope that all survivors would pitch in with a new "council of unity" to help improve the industry's image. Invited shortly thereafter to accept an award for *Crossfire* by a reputable Philadelphia organization, Schary, whose studio had just fired Scott and Dmytryk over his dissent, had the grace to decline, but Eric Johnston went to Philadelphia, accepted the award, and gave a talk on the virtues of tolerance. Johnston had shown in this difficult time the qualities that had brought him to eminence with the Chamber of Commerce early in life. They were the qualities that Demosthenes showed when he wrote an oration for Apollodorus to use against Phormion and, in the same case, an oration for Phormion to use against Apollodorus —"having simply," Plutarch tells us, "furnished two adversaries out of the same shop with weapons to wound one another." It was a sorry cause indeed on which Eric Johnston could not put a noble construction.

So began the blacklist, which would torment the entertainment industry for more than a decade. Whatever the defects of Mr. Truman's Loyalty Order, it had as its justification the premise that Communists do not make trustworthy public servants. No such justification was available to the movie industry or, later, to the yet more anxiety-prone television industry. Dependent utterly on the whims of public pleasure, the moguls in Hollywood and New York, then at the height of their powers, were like those mothers who fear pneumonia in every draft. It would not have taken much courage or sacrifice to hold out against blacklisting, but they had grown flabby on a diet of public relations and collapsed before empty threats.

The particular irony of the producers' submission lay in the fact that the hearings had not gone well from Thomas's point of view. Few newspapers shared Hearst's enthusiasm for

---

If they did not believe it but were trying simply to frighten Schary and Brecht into noncooperation, that suggests that their main interest was in churning up a *cause célèbre*.

federal censorship, even of so distant a cousin as the movies. The weightiest editorial pages—*The New York Times,* the *Herald Tribune,* the Washington *Post,* the Detroit *Free Press*— roundly condemned the Committee for airing unsubstantiated charges and denying accused persons basic means of defending themselves.[4] Eminent film personalities, joined in the Committee for the First Amendment, took out full-page advertisements attacking the hearings, delivered coast-to-coast broadcasts entitled *Hollywood Fights Back,* and chartered a plane called Star of the Red Sea for a very well publicized flight to Washington, with well-publicized stopovers along the way. Thomas also took to the air—the A.B.C. network—to attack these "glamor flights" of the actors and actresses. The ogre of publicity that affrighted the producers was an old pal to the protesting stars. The newspaper reader's eye might skip over the protests of the Progressive Citizens of America, full of prophecies of the rise of fascism, but it could hardly fail to be attracted by such names, most of them untainted by Communism, as Spencer Tracy, Katharine Hepburn, Myrna Loy, Judy Garland, Gregory Peck, James Stewart, Rita Hayworth, Ava Gardner, Frank Sinatra, Humphrey Bogart, and Lauren Bacall. (After seeing the Communist writers perform, some of the actors would lose their enthusiasm for the defense.)

Attendance in the Caucus Room dropped off after the witness-stars had gone home, and a Gallup Poll taken in November indicated that as many people disapproved of the hearings as approved of them. Thomas did not have these figures at hand in the last days of October, but he sensed that his show was falling somewhat flat, and he was on the defensive. He proclaimed on October 29 that his Committee had "not been swayed, intimidated or influenced by either Hollywood glamour, pressure groups, threats, ridicule or high-pressure tactics on the part of high-paid puppets and apologists for the motion picture industry." A day later he abruptly

[4] Governor Earl Warren of California, not yet the leader of a civil libertarian Supreme Court and looking toward a possible Republican Presidential nomination in 1948, skirted the dispute. He contented himself with assuring his constituents that "for every Communist or fellow-traveler in your industry there are literally thousands of men and women who abhor Communism."

adjourned the hearings, immediately after Committee investigator Louis Russell told the interesting if scarcely relevant story of how in 1942 the Soviet vice counsel in San Francisco asked a physicist friend named George Charles Eltenton to to see what he could find out about the radiation work then under way at the University of California; Eltenton approached Haakon Chevalier, an assistant professor of romance languages and friend of the eminent physicist J. Robert Oppenheimer, who was subsequently put in charge of the Los Alamos atomic project; Chevalier put the request to Oppenheimer and was turned down flat.[5] Having thrown out this intriguing bit to the press, which had been growing sated on unresponsive witnesses, Thomas called a halt, pledging to resume his investigation in a few weeks. There were still sixty-eight Communists on his list and he was determined to expose them. Moreover, his staff, with the help of "expert analysts," was making an exhaustive study of Communist propaganda in movies, and that too would be exposed. He reiterated these intentions in the following weeks, but made no move to act upon them. The hearings, in Stripling's estimate, had taken on "the overtones of a broken record." Besides, there were ten contempt citations pending, and it was to these that Thomas now turned his energies.

The citations were brought before the Congress in November at a special session called partly for the purpose of appropriating funds to resist Communist advances in Europe, and Committee members did not let the circumstance go unnoted. McDowell read out the roster of countries that had fallen to the Communist conspiracy, starting with Russia, then informed the House that Albert Maltz, the first witness up for citing, "is a colonel in the conspiratorial, political army of Soviet Russia"—a sudden promotion for the luckless Maltz. The handful of representatives who opposed the citations—Eberharter, Holifield, Javits, Klein, Mrs. Douglas, as well as the indefatigable Marcantonio who saw the affair as another plot of

[5] Years later Dr. Oppenheimer, a favorite target of the right wing, would be stigmatized as a security risk by the Atomic Energy Commission and deprived of clearance largely because of his past association with Communists and his attempt to protect Chevalier by withholding his name from security officials when he told them of the incident in California.

monopoly capitalism—based their opposition on the way the hearings had been conducted and the motives of the Committee in conducting them. Javits granted that the Committee had ample power to allow loose charges to be made in public and then call upon the accused persons to deny them, but argued that such a procedure was nonetheless improper. In attempting to place the burden of controlling the Un-American Activities Committee on Congress itself, Javits was following the import of the Court of Appeals decision in the Barsky case, but the parent wished for no such responsibility over its child. Nixon delivered a brief, unemotional lecture to the effect that there were only two issues before the Congress: The first, a matter of fact—had the witnesses refused to answer the Committee's questions? The second, a matter of law—did the Committee have the power to ask those questions? To both Mr. Nixon answered aye, as did the Congress by a succession of overwhelming votes—347 to 17 in the case of Colonel Maltz. Where the courts had deferred to the Congress, the Congress now deferred to the courts, like two gentlemen bowing each other through a door which neither wishes to enter. The courts had ruled that they could not control unseemly conduct by Congressional committees; the Congress had showed that it would not control it. The authority of committee chairmen to pursue their own goals in their own ways was left unimpaired.[6]

The Hollywood Ten, whom Henry Wallace, beginning his campaign for the presidency, described as "most adept at carrying truth to the people," were all found guilty. Eight of them received the maximum sentence of one year in jail and $1,000; Biberman and Dmytryk were given six months and $1,000. Lawson and Trumbo, the two who had not waived trial by jury, appealed their sentences in behalf of the entire group,

---

[6] Rankin, who was annoyed that he had not been included on the Hollywood subcommittee, had a few words to contribute during this debate. He disclosed that the names of many of the signers of a petition condemning the Committee had been changed from the original—Eddie Cantor having been born Edward Iskowitz; Edward G. Robinson, Emanuel Goldenburg; Danny Kaye, David Daniel Kaminsky; Melvyn Douglas, Melvyn Hesselberg; and so forth.

which was feeling pressed for funds now,[7] on the grounds that their right of free speech included the right to remain silent and was impinged upon when they were forced under threat of punishment to disclose their political opinions and affiliations. In 1949 the U.S. Court of Appeals upheld their convictions. The unanimous decision was phrased forcefully and unambiguously, emphasizing that the Barsky, Eisler, and Dennis decisions "leave it no longer subject to the slightest doubt that the Committee was and is constitutionally created, that it functions under valid statute and resolution which have repeatedly and without exception been upheld as constitutional, that the 'question under inquiry' by the Committee was proper, that the power of inquiry includes power to require a witness before the Committee to disclose whether or not he is a Communist, and the failure or refusal of a witness so to disclose is properly punishable . . ." In a tribute to himself published soon after this decision, Trumbo wrote, "All effective communication upon any important subject . . . becomes as of June 13, 1949, the legitimate object of government regulation." The Supreme Court denied certiorari, with Justices Black and Douglas dissenting, and the Hollywood Ten went to jail, an action which Ring Lardner, Jr. told a rally of the Civil Rights Congress against America's participation in the Korean War elevated him to the company of Socrates and St. Paul.

When they got out, they were blacklisted. American Legion posts and local chambers of commerce were cooperating with newly formed and sometimes moneymaking vigilante groups in guaranteeing the purity not only of the movies but of radio and the lusty, if neurotic, infant television as well. The Committee's files and its good will were at their disposal for the infliction of misery on dissenters, and they reveled in the cowardice of show business. The blacklists flourished for years after, a blemish on the nation which has not yet been entirely removed. Hollywood turned out a number of anti-Communist

[7] The Screen Writers Guild voted against contributing to their defense and, as their incomes had tumbled precipitously, the Unfriendly Ten had to depend on outside contributions.

films such as *The Red Menace* and *The Iron Curtain* and *I Married a Communist* but found uses for the more useful of the convicted writers like Trumbo, permitting them to contribute screenplays under assumed names and for reduced wages. The less useful, such as Alvah Bessie, were simply out of luck. Having been brought West as a reward for his Party loyalties, Bessie was now exiled as punishment for them; it was poetic judgment à la Hollywood, and it secured him in his sense of righteousness. Herbert Biberman and a few other blacklisted moviemakers went to New Mexico and produced an agitprop epic called *Salt of the Earth*. The Hollywood Ten and their sympathizers pretended to believe that their dismissal from the film capital would result in a disastrous decline in the quality of American movies (not to mention the national plunge into fascism); it was a pardonable conceit, with even less substance than the industry's claim, invoked to repair Hollywood's damaged image, that Movies Are Better Than Ever. In fact, the absence of these writers mattered as little to the quality of America's movies as their presence, and when, at last, Dalton Trumbo was permitted to sign his own name again, it was attached to such extravaganzas as *Spartacus* and *The Sandpiper*. The eulogy on these men, who were never able to forgive Hollywood for what it had allowed them to become, was written by Murray Kempton:

> Their story is a failure of promise: first, of the promise in themselves, and last, of the promise of the Hollywood which was so kind to them until they became an embarrassment and then turned them out. The promise at the beginnings of most of them appears now to have been largely smoke and thunder; the promise which vanished at their end appears to have been tinsel, as Hollywood is tinsel. They were entombed, most of them, not for being true to themselves, but for sitting up too long with their own press releases.

The Hollywood hearings brought forward no heroes. The writers, puffed up with a sense of martyrdom, made a burlesque of a Jeffersonian cadre. The producers, exemplified by Warner, were like those shrewd, fawning peddlers who appeared in silent films in the days when racial stereotypes were still thought fit for public comedy. As for the Committee itself, its premise in this investigation, that movies were being subverted by a Red underground in league with New Deal bureaucrats, was asinine; its methods were gross and its intentions despicable. The philosophy that flowered under the klieg lights of 1947 would be an inspiration for much of the Committee's later work: a philosophy that held not only that Communism was a subversive doctrine, not only that Communists in sensitive positions were threats to the nation, but that the presence in this land of every individual Communist and fellow traveler and former Communist who would not purge himself was intolerable; that the just fate of every such creature was to be exposed in his community, routed from his job, and driven into exile.

8

1948: Vintage Year

NINETEEN FORTY-EIGHT stands as the most celebrated year of the Committee on Un-American Activities, a year of threat and counterthreat to which the Committee responded with enormous gusto, grasping and sometimes throttling its opportunities. It was the year of the end of democracy in Czechoslovakia and a Soviet blockade in Berlin; of domestic spy scares, security checks, deportations and harassment of Communists; of the dismal fling of the Progressive Party. It was an election year, filled with decisions that would define the limits of the cold war in Europe and the extent of our reaction to it at home. These were matters of great promise to the Committee and in pursuing that promise it showed itself at its best and at its vicious worst. It held hearings out of which, for the first time in its ten years of existence, a law would actually emerge. In its mistrust of civilian scientists and intellectuals at large, it did what it could to destroy the reputation of a government official of unimpeachable loyalty. It brought into the open smoldering antagonisms toward the Democratic Administration and forced a test of the legislature's power to probe the activities of the executive branch. It tended the spy fears of the day, producing a record number of sensational headlines as its contribution to the Republican Presidential campaign. And with its presentation of the Hiss-Chambers drama, it touched a generation of liberals to their very souls.

On February 5 a subcommittee under Richard Nixon resumed hearings into "proposed legislation to curb or control the Communist Party of the United States." The members of the subcommittee were Vail, Peterson, McDowell, and F. Edward Hébert of Louisiana, the last named replacing the invisible Bonner, who had decided to give his energies to the House Merchant Marine Committee. Two bills were up for study: one, the effort of Representative Gordon L. McDonough, would have outlawed the Communist Party; the other, from Representative Mundt, called for the Party and its front groups to be registered with the government. The Mundt bill was the serious one. Chastened by the 1947 hearings and J. Edgar Hoover's cautions regarding a total ban, the Committee majority from the outset favored the idea of registration which, so it was claimed, would subject the subversives to exposure rather than drive them underground.

Most of the witnesses during the seven days of hearings in February agreed that registration was the preferable approach. The veterans' groups and the Daughters of the American Revolution were still plumping for an outright ban, and they found allies in James Burnham and Raymond Moley. But the witnesses from bar associations, law schools, and the ranks of anti-Communist New Dealers like Morris Ernst, Louis Waldman, Donald Richberg and Adolf Berle (who would have a busy time with the Committee this year) leaned toward registration. The C.P. itself and the American Civil Liberties Union[1]

---

[1] Representing the A.C.L.U. before the Committee, Arthur Garfield Hays submitted the following measure for consideration by Congress:

A BILL to provide means to eliminate the Communist nuisance.

Whereas this was a happy land with no troubles until hordes of Communists overran us, causing high prices, strikes, conspiracies and treason; and

Whereas Communists have, since the beginning of our history, caused all the hell-raising in the United States; and

Whereas experience during the late war proved conclusively that the F.B.I., the police, the military and all of our courts and laws are incapable of doing their jobs of apprehending traitors; and

Whereas treason is hard to prove under the Constitution of the United States; and

Whereas Communists advocate deceit, confusion, and are traitors; and

Whereas one of our chief difficulties is that we cannot distinguish Communists from anyone else; and

Whereas there is a pressing need for some means of easy distinction; and opposed any more laws on the subject, while Attorney General Clark, cool toward the whole matter, granted under the questioning of Nixon that the Mundt approach seemed better to him than the McDonough approach. Ferenc Nagy, in exile from Hungary, and George M. Dimitrov, in exile from Bulgaria, were called forward to speak of the villainies which the Communists had perpetrated upon their lands, and seventy-five-year-old Admiral W. H. Standley (ret.), former ambassador to the U.S.S.R. as well as former Chief of Naval Operations, was allowed to ramble a bit on how the Communists were infiltrating our schools and inducing workers to ask for higher pay, but the general tone of the hearings, particularly when Nixon was doing the questioning, was workmanlike, several cuts above what the Committee's recent performances had given reason to expect. (Where they might have strayed without Nixon was demonstrated on February 11, when the young man slipped on an icy street and fractured his elbows. The hearings scheduled for that day thus fell into the slack hands of McDowell, which allowed Rankin, who had been kept more or less in order on his previous visits to the hearing room, to take over for an entire morning. In a surrealistic interrogation of Adolf Berle, Rankin spoke feelingly of how the white folks of Mississippi were being slandered and harassed by officials in the Justice Department who kept accusing them of unkindnesses toward their Negro neighbors.)

Out of these hearings, in April, came the Mundt-Nixon bill to "protect the United States against un-American and subversive activities." It required the registration of the Communist

---

Whereas we have all sorts of investigations, committees, commissions, but no machines to read a man's mind: Therefore be it

Enacted by the Senate and House of Representatives of the United States of America in Congress assembled:

1. That all suspected Communists or people we don't like be submitted to a mental test.

2. That we appropriate $10 billion to set up a commission to invent a mental reading machine which when applied will say "Communist" when the individual is not a loyal citizen.

3. Until such machine is fully developed, all Communists must wear boots, red shirts, fur caps (both male and female), and grow beards (both male and female).

4. This law shall be self-enacting and shall take effect immediately.

Representatives McDowell and Hébert declared themselves not amused.

Party and its front organizations; the attorney general was given the responsibility of naming the subject groups, and they were allowed an appeal and a court review. As the bill made it a crime to attempt to establish a totalitarian dictatorship under foreign domination and, further, declared that the Communist Party was trying to do exactly this, there were grounds for the belief that the C.P. would in effect be outlawed, since any Communist who registered might thereupon be jailed for his part in the ubiquitous conspiracy. The confusion on this point was dramatized in a nationally broadcast debate between the leading contenders for the Republican Presidential nomination, Governor Thomas E. Dewey of New York and Harold E. Stassen of Minnesota, as the bill was being argued over in the House. Both gentlemen appeared to favor it: Stassen favored it because it would outlaw the Communist Party; Dewey favored it because it would not.

The House debate was held soon after the issuance of another Committee report which showed, with quotations from Karl Marx, William Z. Foster and numerous Communists in between, that their Party advocated the overthrow of this republic. Nixon, handling the bill calmly through three days of acrimonious exchanges, took the position that it would outlaw solely subversive activities, whereas its opponents, notably Celler, Javits, and Holifield, insisted that it was clearly aimed at doing by indirection what could not be done directly under the Constitution—wiping out the Communist Party. As Javits interpreted the bill, if the Communists didn't register, they would be subject to prosecution for defying the law, and if they did register, they would be admitting their guilt as conspirators, by the law's definition. "If perchance it should become law," prophesied Holifield, "—and in these days of hysteria anything is possible—the Supreme Court will kill it as dead as the Alien and Sedition Laws of 1798." Nixon, for his part, kept to the substance of the case, but some of his allies let loose: "The world is dividing into two camps," announced Michigan's Dondero: "freedom versus Communism, Christian civilization versus paganism, righteousness and justice versus force and violence." To which South Carolina's Bryson called amen: "It is already later than we think. The security of this nation demands that all Communists within our borders be rendered politically and economically impotent." Mundt invoked the name of J. Edgar Hoover. Marcantonio matched him with cries of fascism. In a year when the nation was busily looking for ways to deport, dismiss, blacklist, and jail its Communists, the Mundt-Nixon bill swept through the House by a vote of 319 to 58.

Senate hearings were held at the end of May—a formality because there was small chance so late in the Congressional session of passing a highly controversial measure for which the Truman Administration had no enthusiasm. The bill was opposed by the entire left—from Americans for Democratic Action to the C.I.O., then engaged in exiling its own Communists, to the Socialist Party and, of course, the Communists—but it was the Progressive Party that made the cause its own. The Wallace campaign rested on the faith that the new party—whose sponsors suspected that they might be called upon to register as a Communist front—was the people's bulwark against plutocratic truculence abroad and totalitarian repression at home. Causes were required from which vast quantities of smoke could be stirred to conceal the fact that the fires within were very tiny indeed. So Mr. Wallace testified against the legislation, and June 1 found thousands of marchers in Washington picketing the White House, cheering Marcantonio's invective and Paul Robeson's baritone, and stalking Congressmen's offices in the interests of defeating a bill that had no chance of passing for that session. It was, spokesmen for the Progressives agreed, a splended success, one of a series of splendid successes that kept many of them in a constant state of self-delusion until November.[2]

---

[2] The near unanimous verdict after election day was that the Communists had suffered a defeat of monumental proportions, and had given a conclusive demonstration of their political incapacity. But the Committee on Un-American Activities made as much of the Wallace campaign as did the Wallaceites themselves. In a pamphlet, *Communism and Education*, published early in December 1948, as part of the series, *100 Things You Should Know About Communism*, the Committee declared: "Communism gained new recruits through the Wallace campaign, made new contacts and tapped fresh money. The largest vote cast for Communism in this country was registered in 1948 behind Wallace's name."

Chairman Thomas played no great part in his Committee's formulation of a Communist-registration bill. Legislative activity had never been of compelling interest to him, and, moreover, he was ill during the early part of the year. He was still at Walter Reed Hospital on March 1, recuperating from an attack of gastrointestinal hemorrhages, when he issued from his bedside a preliminary report to the full Committee from a subcommittee consisting of himself, Vail, and the docile Wood, on the subject of Dr. Edward U. Condon, director of the National Bureau of Standards. The technique of releasing a so-called preliminary report as a means of publicly indicting individuals and organizations without going through the rigors of formal hearings had been brought to an art by Dies and Matthews. Now Thomas employed it, against the advice even of Stripling, to call Condon "one of the weakest links in our atomic security."

If the charge had had any substance, it would have been serious. Condon, one of a handful of American physicists who had made a contribution to basic atomic energy theory, had been closely involved with the development of the A-bomb since 1939. He was only forty-six when the Committee delivered its broadside, but he had behind him a decade of work in which he had earned the trust of his employers in industry, the gratitude of government officials, and the esteem of his fellow scientists. The subcommitte report was akin to those exposés that appear each season, as books and magazine articles, where the writer's conclusions so far exceed his evidence that his sincerity is called into doubt; somebody has evidently assigned him the job and he, as a professional, has done what he could with what he has, allowing irrelevancies to creep in where useful and attempting to work up some semblance of indignation along the way. The report took care to mention that Condon's wife was of Czechoslovak descent and that he had been recommended to head the Bureau of Standards in 1945 by none other than Henry Wallace, who was Secretary of Commerce that year and whom the report identified flatly as the Communists' candidate for vice president. It placed a sinister interpretation on Condon's "associations" with East European officials, whom he could hardly have helped associating with while carrying out his own official obligations, as well as with unnamed Americans "who are members of the Communist Party." It managed to garble his membership in the American-Soviet Science Society, set up in the postwar glow as an aid in facilitating an exchange of material with the secretive Russians, to make it appear that the attorney general had put the organization on his subversive list. It was an associated group, the National Council of American-Soviet Friendship, that had made the attorney general's list, and that not until December 1947. By the time the report was issued, the scientists' group had drifted away from the National Council. "The members would be shocked beyond measure if they could read the full report in this case," said Rankin when inserting the document into the Record. How Rankin could have come to such a conclusion is a mystery since neither he nor any other member of the Committee had ever seen anything fuller or more shocking than what had been given to the press. Such is the power of reiteration, however, that a month after the report came out, Representative Vail demanded of the House: "The question is, can we entrust the very security of our nation in the hands of an individual who apparently sees nothing wrong in associating with card-holding members of the Communist Party, with associating with persons who are known to be agents of the Soviet Union and who affiliates with an organization which is in the control of Communists."

This was not the first assault by Thomas on Condon. During 1947 the Congressman had leaked three page-one articles, sprinkled with misstatements of fact, to the Washington *Times-Herald*, then owned by the McCormick interests, and had referred to the scientist unfavorably in two magazine articles. The reason for the barrage was not obscure. In attacking the probity, not to say the loyalty of Dr. Condon, whose repeated requests for an opportunity to reply went unhonored, Thomas was attempting to cast doubt on all of the scientists who had pressed, successfully, to have the Atomic Energy Commission placed under civilian control. His report concluded with the broad and unsubstantiated warning that "the situation as regards Dr. Condon is not an isolated one . . . There are other government officials in strategic positions who are playing Stalin's game . . ."

Edward Condon had been a scientific advisor to the Special Senate Committee on Atomic Energy, which reported out the McMahon bill that so angered the military community and its champions in Congress. He was known to be a liberal, and not of a noticeably anti-Communist stripe; in addition to his affiliation with the Soviet-American Friendship front, he had allowed his name to be used as a sponsor of a meeting of the Southern Conference for Human Welfare and was a friend of Harvard astronomer Harlow Shapley, the Progressive Party's leading recruit from the scientific community. Condon, like many scientists, had been irked during the war by what seemed to him extreme security restrictions on atomic research; he wrote Dr. Oppenheimer in 1943 that he found them "depressing," and he was on record as favoring a freer flow of technical information between East and West. He was not nearly as antagonistic to Russia as Thomas believed that every American scientist ought to be. Indeed, he had had the temerity in March 1946 to say that America ought to welcome Russian scientists to its laboratories, and to add, "I only mention Russia because she is right now the target of attack by those irresponsibles who think she would be a suitable adversary in the next world war." These were the opinions that invited Thomas's attention in the year in which the terms of all five members of the A.E.C. were due to expire.

Condon was not left to fight off Thomas on his own. In addition to the support of the usual array of groups opposed to anything the Committee did, he was backed by scientists throughout the country, by the Commerce Department's loyalty board, which hastened to issue him a clearance, by most newspapers and columnists, and by a number of Congressmen, notably Holifield of California. Less than a week after the release of the Condon report, the Committee came before the House with a request for an unprecedented $200,-000, twice the sum it had received the year before, to carry on its work for the balance of the year. There was no question about the House's acquiescence—the vote was 337 to 37, with Javits of New York the sole Republican in the minority—but even a few of its supporters expressed concern over the fact that in spite of repeated requests, before and after the issuance of the report, and repeated promises by Committee members ("If he's been put upon," said McDowell, "I'd rather the Committee took a shellacking than to have the public continue uncertain"), Condon had not been granted an opportunity to testify in his own behalf.

The chief defender of Condon, as it turned out, was the Truman Administration. A few days after the release of the report, the scientist was moved to the background as stage center was taken up by confrontations between Thomas and Truman, Republicans and Democrats, the Congress and the executive. A Presidential election was coming on, and the air was thick with alleged spy plots and charges of disloyalty among federal employees. Not for two decades had the Republicans been so confident. Never had the ordinarily peppy Mr. Truman been peppier. It was not in his temper to avoid a good scrap, or even to avoid reaching out for one, and in March 1948 the Thomas Committee positively forced itself upon him.

Mention was made in the Condon report of a letter sent by an unnamed former security officer in the Manhattan Project to an unnamed Congressman, who turned out to be Thomas himself. It was written in 1946, during the debate over whether control of the nation's developing atomic energy program should remain with the military or be put into civilian hands, a question to which Condon and Thomas were giving contrary answers. "May I suggest," wrote the security officer, "that you demand Dr. Condon's record of the F.B.I. It would be enlightening."

In September 1947, after Thomas had already begun his attacks on Condon, a Committee investigator was permitted by the Department of Commerce to look at the scientist's file. Included therein he found a letter from J. Edgar Hoover to Secretary of Commerce W. Averell Harriman, written in the course of a loyalty check which the department had authorized. The Committee investigator started to copy the letter, but was asked to desist before he could complete the job. The portion which he had managed to copy—with the exception of one sentence—was included in the Committee's report; it concerned mainly the association of the Condons with several individuals connected with the Polish embassy in Washington, including one man who was described by the F.B.I. as an "alleged Soviet espionage agent." The Hoover letter also noted that Condon "has been in contact as late as 1947 with an individual alleged, by a self-confessed Soviet espionage agent, to have engaged in espionage activities with the Russians in Washington, D.C., from 1941 to 1944." The self-confessed agent, it would later become known, was none other than the famous Elizabeth Bentley, and the alleged spy was Nathan Gregory Silvermaster, a government economist whom Miss Bentley had named as heading a Soviet spy group in Washington during the war. The sentence left out of the Committee report—inadvertently, according to Thomas—followed the reference to Silvermaster, and stated: "There is no evidence to show that contacts between this individual and Dr. Condon were related to this individual's espionage activities."[3]

Thomas demanded the original F.B.I. letter. Mr. Truman, who had ordered both the Commerce Department and the F.B.I. to send their copies to the White House, where they were locked away, directed the department and all departments to refer to him all requests for information relating to their loyalty programs. Thomas, still in hospital, promised that he would force the release of the letter before he was through. McDowell announced he was assigning all the Committee's investigators to the case. Nixon attacked the Commerce Department's loyalty procedures and demanded the letter. Vail told the House that Condon had associated with thirty or more persons "directly or indirectly" engaged in espionage for the U.S.S.R. Thomas, with the blessing of the House Republican leadership, offered

[3] This inadvertence was revealed by the Washington *Post*, to which the omitted sentence had apparently been leaked by the Commerce Department. The Administration made use of the *Post* in much the way the Committee made use of the *Times-Herald*.

a resolution which would order the Secretary of Commerce to surrender the report: "If President Truman, Secretary Harriman or anyone else thinks he can get away with with-holding vital information, he is very much mistaken." Republican National Chairman J. Carroll Reece, in recognition of the fact that elections were only six months away, notified 20,000 G.O.P. officials that "It is time for a showdown between those who believe in the maintenance of our representative republic and exponents of the New Deal philosophy that the people are 'too damn dumb' to understand what their government does . . ." He mentioned impeachment.

At the end of April, the House by a vote of 300 to 29 took the extraordinary step of ordering the Secretary of Commerce "forthwith" to surrender the F.B.I. letter. The issue was presented to the House as one of Congressional prerogative—"whether Congress in the due performance of its functions of legislation can require the executive branch to submit to duly authorized committees of Congress information that is necessary to properly and fully perform the duties assigned to the Congress and its committees." Even Sam Rayburn, minority leader in the House and most loyal of Democrats, voted for it, remarking, "I'm going to be swept along with the crowd today, I guess." As the Senate had not concurred in the resolution, it carried no force of law and within an hour and a half of the vote, Truman reminded his press conference of President Jackson's response on a similar occasion—"The Chief Justice has made his decision; now let him enforce it." Enforce its resolution the House could not, and in mid-May it passed a bill designed to compel executive departments, though not the President's office itself, to produce information demanded by Congress. The vote this time, 219 to 142, was divided by party, and as the Senate showed no inclination to become bogged down so late in its session in a fight over a measure that would certainly be vetoed and might prove unconstitutional, the bill was allowed to wither.

Precedent, extending back to George Washington, was with Mr. Truman on this matter; at least six previous Presidents had rejected Congressional demands for information and escaped intact. Yet the Committee kept up a drumfire of criticism. Thomas blustered about the prerogatives of the House; Nixon explained coolly that he was thinking of Condon's best interests; and Vail conducted a set of secret hearings at which employees of the Bureau of Standards were asked whether Condon had ever pressured them to join the American-Soviet Science Society. Of the several issues raised by the Condon case, none was of larger consequence in 1948 than the fate of the loyalty program itself. The Truman program, distasteful as it was to many of its supporters, had been set up in part to keep federal employees from becoming casualties of snipers in Congress. At stake in the President's refusal to release material from Condon's file was the integrity of his program, which was being run with some degree of decency, and with it the livelihoods and reputations of thousands of persons, such as Condon, who were free of any taint of disloyalty. If their records were to be given over to men with the casual interest in fairness which Thomas had shown throughout his decade with the Committee or to men like Nixon who would walk where ambition led or to the unthinking Vails and McDowells and even the Rankins in Congress or to committee staff members with pals on the Hearst and McCormick newspapers, then no employee who had ever had a kind thought for the U.S.S.R. could sleep easy. A loyalty file, rich in allegations, hints, rumors, conjecture, was as tempting to such men as a key to the local arsenal would be to delinquent teenagers, and as risky for anybody in the neighborhood.

If the Condon affair needed any further resolution, it came in July when the Atomic Energy Commission, having gone over the scientist's complete file, including F.B.I. reports of his associations, announced that "The Commission considers that his continued clearance is in the best interests of the atomic energy program." In October, Nixon proposed what had been proposed by many before him—that Congressional committees should give accused persons an opportunity to testify in their own behalf before being publicly excoriated. No semblance of an apology was forthcoming from the Committee, not with elections approaching. The following December, however,

the elections over, the case long out of the headlines, Condon
no longer in particular need of apologies, Richard Nixon allowed in a radio interview that the Committee's handling of
the Condon case had been "unfair." Condon, he said, "should
have been heard by the Committee before any statement about
him was made public." A few days later Mundt, Senator Mundt
now, said he "concurred" with Nixon. And in the following
year even Stripling, who had by then left the Committee, disclosed that he had objected to the release of the "weakest link"
report on the grounds that Condon had not been heard, but
that Thomas's impatience had prevailed. By restraining their
criticism through the rousing summer and fall of 1948 and
then voicing it as an aside in the Christmas season as the
Committee was passing into the hands of the Democrats, Nixon
and Mundt showed a nice feeling for the less demanding styles
of political honesty.

In 1951, with the security packs in full cry, Condon's
trustworthiness was again attacked by Vail, and when in
August of that year he resigned as director of the Bureau of
Standards, Vail and Harold H. Velde, the latter coming into
eminence on the Un-American Activities Committee, announced that it was a resignation "under fire." At length, in
September 1952, Condon was summoned before the Committee, mainly in order that he might be publicly questioned
about the left-wing friendships he had maintained at the
University of California Radiation Laboratory at Berkeley
from September 1943 to February 1945. His critics were irked
that he had lately invited several former colleagues who had
belonged to a C.P. group at Berkeley and took the Fifth
Amendment before the Committee in 1949 to stay with him
while in Washington. He had known them as young men
in California and refused to disown them even after their Committee appearances. He had gone so far in defense of one
physicist suspected of Communist allegiance as to chide J.
Robert Oppenheimer for his reported testimony regarding the
man in executive session before the Committee. Although it
was once again made evident that Condon's political sympathies had drawn him into the company of Communists and

Sovietphiles over the years, that he was reluctant to think ill of old friends, and that he had a constitutional antipathy to security arrangements, no one suggested any wrongdoing or even an identifiable indiscretion on his part; his worst known offense seemed to be imprudence. The purpose of putting the Committee's spotlight upon him again in 1952, when he was no longer in government employ, may be gathered from the summation of Representative Velde:

> I was an F.B.I. agent out there working at Berkeley, California, during that time. But it does appear to me, Dr. Condon, that while we do not want to cause you to be thought guilty by association with a lot of these Communists and espionage agents and so forth, it is a little peculiar that you seem to have hung around them like flies hanging around a pot of honey, and, in view of the fact that you did have at that time a very confidential assignment, I would say I am just a little bit impressed. I wonder if you could explain that for me—the fact that you had so many acquaintances, with the known Communists and espionage agents and so forth.

The unspoken assumptions and heavy innuendoes of this statement reflect the spirit of this hearing and, to an unhappy degree, of the year 1952. The Committee's annual report for that year took one final swipe at Condon, declaring him to be unqualified for any security position owing to his "propensity for associating with persons disloyal or of questionable loyalty and his contempt for necessary security arrangements." A few days later Condon was installed, amid enthusiastic applause, as president of the American Association for the Advancement of Science.[4]

Loyalty and the want of it were minor but insistent themes in the Presidential campaign of 1948. Committees in both houses of Congress issued denunciations of executive department laxity in ferreting out Reds and prosecuting spies, and

---

[4] Dr. Condon's security troubles were not yet over. In 1954, the Navy gave him a security clearance only to suspend it almost at once, causing him to resign from his position as head of research at the Corning Glass works. By October 1966, however, Condon, now a professor of physics at the University of Colorado, was considered sufficiently secure by the Air Force to be made head of its inquiry into the flying saucer phenomenon.

even Thomas Dewey, not the most demagogic of politicians, chided the Truman Administration for "Communist-coddling." Thomas, encouraged by the G.O.P. National Committee to hold open hearings during the pre-election months, sprang into action, and his Committee's contribution to the 1948 campaign, a substantial contribution, took up prime newspaper space throughout the month of September.

Having managed to obtain reports of security investigations from Manhattan Project days, the Committee focused anew on Thomas's favorite target, the scientists who had worked on developing the atom bomb. A subcommittee, under Mc-Dowell, was named to hold closed hearings into Manhattan Project espionage, and several times a week from September 2 on, reporters were informed of the witnesses summoned, the information elicited, and the great progress being made. Thomas announced that "a very important espionage case" was being studied, a case involving "one of the most important Soviet agents." It ranked, he said, as "the gravest matter" in the Committee's history. He planned to question a Russian schoolteacher who jumped out of the window of the Soviet consulate in New York to avoid being sent home, on the chance that she knew something about the grave matter. The Committee promised to reveal "a shocking chapter in Communist espionage in the atomic field." Nixon charged that Truman was preventing J. Edgar Hoover from testifying because he was "afraid of the political consequences." When one of the nominally secret witnesses took the Fifth Amendment Mc-Dowell called it "a typically Communist position," and he said that the evidence justified the indictment of three persons for wartime atomic espionage. Open hearings were ruled out because of the vital secrets that might be endangered, but a report was promised which would "shock the public" by showing that Presidents Roosevelt and Truman and Attorney General Clark had had the facts regarding a spy ring that obtained A-bomb secrets and had done nothing about them.

Truman, engaged in his remarkable one-man Presidential campaign, was not backward about meeting these attacks. He took the occasion of the opening of a meeting in Constitution

Hall of the American Association for the Advancement of Science to shake Dr. Condon's hand and give him a broad grin. He warned, as the scientists themselves were warning with a certain amount of hyperbole, that scientific work "may be made impossible by the creation of an atmosphere in which no man feels safe against the public airing of unfounded rumors, gossip and vilification." While in Oakland, California, on one of his whistle-stop trips, he remarked in the presence of those who could be counted on to print it, that the House Committee was "more un-American than the activities it is investigating." And he predicted that J. Parnell Thomas would not be sitting in the House for very much longer.

Finally, on September 28, the Committee issued its report, which it likened to the 1946 report of the Royal Commission that investigated the Canadian atom spy ring. The Committee report was far too partisan a document to bear comparison with the scrupulously prepared and dispassionate paper of the Royal Commission, but the stories it told did indeed indicate that the Russians had been trying to get atomic information during the war, and in all likelihood had picked up some.

Three separate incidents were related:

In 1943 Steve Nelson, chairman of the C.P.'s western Pennsylvania district was visited late at night by a "Scientist X" who worked at the University of California's Radiation Laboratories. (The scientist's name was withheld because he denied everything in executive session; calling him "Scientist X" was a favor to newspaper headline writers.) Soon after, Nelson met a Russian official and handed him an envelope. Later, another Russian official gave Nelson some money. (The Yugoslav-born Nelson, whose name had been dramatically Americanized from Stefab Mesarosh, refused to tell anything to the Committee, which he described as "a gathering of political pyromaniacs.")

In 1944 a Manhattan Project scientist had dinner with two Russian officials at Bernstein's Fish Grotto in San Francisco and they discussed some phases of atomic research. Whether the Russians were told anything they shouldn't have been told remained unsettled. The scientist involved conceded he may have been indiscreet, but not disloyal.

Also in 1944 a young physicist, who had been working with the Manhattan Project before he was called into the army on the recommendation of security officers who wanted him out of the way, asked another scientist whether he would like to meet one Arthur Adams, a veteran Soviet agent. The purpose of the meeting was to establish a new source of scientific information now that the first fellow was being removed from A-bomb work. The second scientist met briefly with Adams but said he got cold feet and never passed any information. The first scientist took the Fifth Amendment. Adams was not available for questioning, having fled the country when things got hot.

The Committee acknowledged that all of its information, evidently obtained from a source in army security, had been known to the government for several years, and it charged the Truman Administration with a "completely inexcusable" lack of action in these cases. The Justice Department issued a strong countercharge—that the Committee was indulging in "political activity in the field of espionage" in an election year. To the Committee's statement that "doubtless the Department of Justice has conclusive evidence" on which to base a prosecution, the department replied that "there is absolutely no competent proof here . . . of the actual or attempted communication, delivery or transmittal of information relating to the national defense to a foreign government or to one of its representatives," as required by the Espionage Act.

McDowell thereupon offered some estimates as to how many pieces of atomic information had actually been obtained by the Russians, and called for the impeachment of Attorney General Clark. When Mundt suggested early in October that the Committee cease its activities until after the election, Thomas dismissed the thought, promising to go right on exposing Communist infiltration, intrigue, and espionage wherever he found it. "As far as I am concerned," he said without a smile, "the election has nothing to do with it, nor has the election ever had anything to do with our investigations."

The report on atomic espionage presented all of the evidence at hand; the hearings had added nothing of substance to the information already known to the F.B.I. If Thomas had been in possession of additional evidence to bolster his case against the Justice Department, it would have been strikingly out of character for him to withhold it. As for the accusation that the attorney general himself was holding back evidence, that was at best speculative. The most that could fairly be said of the behavior of the Democratic Administration was that during the war, when relations with the U.S.S.R. were a matter of delicate concern, it was satisfied to stop seepages of information to our ally of the time by quiet means rather than complicate our diplomacy with spectacular arrests and trials. Whether Attorney General Clark had enough evidence to make a viable case against the accused scientists is moot—prosecutors do differ on how much evidence makes a case; but the highly inconclusive Committee report did not of itself support the charges of a "completely inexcusable" lack of action. It remained for the wartime head of the Manhattan Project, General Leslie Groves—no particular friend of the civilian scientists and certainly no enemy of the Committee—to remind everyone that "security was of course a part of the work on the atomic bomb. But at the time (the early 1940s) our major objective was to get the bomb so we could end the war and save American lives."

Leaving aside the timing of the A-bomb hearings—September of an election year—and Thomas's oft-proclaimed dissatisfaction with the atomic scientists' attitude toward military control, there remains the question of whether the revelation in 1948 of events that had taken place, under the eye of the F.B.I., in 1942–1944 was desirable. Insofar as it added to public sophistication about U.S.-Soviet relations even in the comradely war years, it no doubt had a certain value. But in order to turn the information into a political weapon, the Committee needed to make it appear that it had uncovered a nest of traitors who had done incalculable harm to America's security. On the evidence offered, it seemed that a few scientists had indeed allowed themselves to be led up the path by the Russians, but there was no evidence to support the deductions of Thomas and McDowell that any of them had actually passed along anything of any great utility. Still, the Committee had never before gotten quite so close to honest-to-goodness espionage, and it would prove loath to relinquish these cases.

We must now go back a few weeks, to July of 1948 and the beginnings of the Un-American Activities Committee's great case. Nearly twenty years have passed since Whittaker Chambers and Alger Hiss faced one another in a jammed hearing room and, like Bolingbroke and Norfolk before King Richard, hurled their accusations, denials, challenges. Their stories have been told in many books and innumerable articles, and the courts have made their judgment. Yet the drama has not staled, and the meaning of their experience is still good for an argument wherever middle-aged liberals gather.

It began with Elizabeth Bentley. Although she did not quite live up to the expectations aroused by the Beautiful Blonde Spy Queen title with which she was adorned by the New York *World Telegram* before her public appearance, her story of being a courier during World War II between Washington officials and Soviet intelligence operatives in New York was exciting enough on its own account. The "nutmeg Mata Hari," as A. J. Liebling dubbed her, had told her story to the F.B.I. in 1945. In 1948 she told it to the federal grand jury in New York which that July indicted twelve leaders of the Communist Party for violation of the 1940 Smith Act and before its term expired would indict Alger Hiss for perjury. On July 30 she told part of it in public to a subcommittee of the Senate Investigating Committee under Senator Ferguson, implicating a Commerce Department official named William Remington. The Remington-Bentley case made a companion theme to the Hiss-Chambers case. Remington, an unsinister young man who had been attracted to Communism in his teens and had the further misfortune to marry into a Communist family, admitted knowing Miss Bentley as a reporter of some sort but denied everything else. As soon as it become evident that Senator Ferguson was content to concentrate on the Remington case, as a means of pressuring the Administration to "tighten" its loyalty review procedures, Miss Bentley was summoned before the Un-American Activities Committee and encouraged, despite previous cautions regarding her testimony from the Department of Justice, to tell her entire story in public.

That Elizabeth Bentley was associated with a Communist underground in the early nineteen-forties is certain. Much less certain from her testimony was the extent of the involvement of the officials she named. Partly this was due to the nature of the operation. She knew most of her sources only through a contact and depended largely on hearsay for her opinions as to who was a thoroughgoing C.P. member, who a fellow traveler, who a hanger-on. She was not clear in many instances whether an official knew that he was involved with the Russians or believed that he was merely doing a good turn for the American Party. Her judgment of the quality and importance of the information that passed through her hands was extremely faulty.

Her testimony was further obscured by the mist in which she had lived out her strange adventure, a romantic mist composed of a plain girl's dreams of love, a lonely girl's desire for friendship, a naïve girl's idealism: "Employers, I had discovered, often fought bitterly against unionization because it meant they had to pay more wages." In her experience with Communism, she found everything she wanted most, a cause, a community, and then a lover: "Nothing mattered any more—I had found the man I loved." She was, for a few years, the heroine of all the bad novels she had ever read. The lover, a Soviet agent named Jacob Golos, she invested with the aura that certain types of teenagers save for uncles and professors of English. The political conspiracy in which he involved her became far grander in her imagination than there is any reason to believe it actually was; an official needed only to be spoken of favorably by one of the conspirators for him to become part of the conspiracy. Then in 1944 Golos died. "Goodbye, *golubchik,*" she said. "You have left me a legacy and I will not fail you." But there was no legacy, except the discovery that all the Communists who did not love her fell short of the perfection of the

one who had: "The international Communist movement, I realized, was in the hands of the wrong people."

Miss Bentley was received by the Committee with the
warmth that it customarily accorded to friendly witnesses,[5]
and she was allowed to tell her story without being pressed
for any evidence aside from her recollections. Even Rankin,
however, was taken aback by her reference to Lauchlin Currie,
who had been a White House assistant under F.D.R. for six
years. She charged that Currie, with whom she had never had
any contact, had been a source of information as well as "a
friend at court," because she had heard his name bandied about
by a man she knew to be a Communist. Rankin, annoyed that
the Committee was leaving the Remington case to the Senate,
took objection to smearing "this Scotchman in the White
House" by remote control. Miss Bentley implicated one other
important official whom she had never met—Harry Dexter
White, Assistant Secretary of the Treasury under Henry Morgenthau, who had helped design the Bretton Woods Monetary
Plan, the Morgenthau Plan for Germany, and the World Bank.
White, she said, used his influence to place C.P. members and
fellow travelers in strategic positions in government.

Miss Bentley named a score of lesser known persons as members of two rings for which she acted as a courier during the
war, and whatever doubts an observer might have been left
with regarding specific incidents or the value of the information that had been collected and passed along to the Russians,
he could hardly help concluding that U.S. security precautions
regarding Communists during the war years were less than
stringent. The central figure in the major Washington cell was
Nathan Gregory Silvermaster, an economist who had worked
in various government agencies for a period of twelve years,
from August 1935 to November 1947. His record was thick
with evidence of Communist sympathies and activities—a Civil
Service Commission report in 1942 came to the conclusion that
"Nathan Gregory Silvermaster is now and has for years been

[5] "Here," said Representative McDowell, "is an American citizen who delved
into this business and now has the courage to walk through the valley of the
shadow of publicity."

a member and a leader of the Communist Party and very probably a secret agent of the O.G.P.U."—yet he was able not only
to hold onto his jobs but to use his house as a photographic
lab and transfer point for documents. Even granting, as the
liberal press did not neglect to point out, that the Russians
were our allies during this period and the C.P., U.S.A., was a
patriotic institution, it is difficult to conceive how Silvermaster
and some of the other men named by Miss Bentley could have
hung on as long as they did without the services of some good
angel or an extraordinary lack of interest on the part of our
security services. The Committee would naturally be inclined
to put the more sinister interpretation on the facts, and the
facts seemed to bear out some of their suspicions. As a result
of the investigations set off by Miss Bentley's charges, eleven
State Department employees were abruptly dismissed from
their jobs.

In search of corroboration for Miss Bentley's recollections,
portions of which suffered from lack of outside support, Stripling turned to Whittaker Chambers. The name of this senior
editor at *Time* magazine had been whispered to him during
the spring Condon hearings by a New York newspaperman who
had learned that Chambers was to be heard by a grand jury in
New York. Committee investigators questioned Chambers and
discovered that he had been a Communist and a courier more
than a decade before, had told his story to various authorities
beginning in 1939, but knew nothing about Condon. Now, in
August, Stripling, looking to Chambers to help substantiate
Miss Bentley's recollections, issued a subpoena, naturally notifying the Hearst papers of the fact before notifying Chambers
himself.

Chambers opened his testimony with a statement composed
in the portentous style that would mark all of his writings thereafter, with none of the glibness or plays on words for which
his magazine was known. His opening speech was skillfully
put together for dramatic impact, beginning with the revelation that he had reported what he knew—though without providing any supporting evidence and leaving ambiguous the
possibilities of espionage—to authorities in Washington two

days after the Hitler-Stalin pact, and ending with a call to still-hidden ex-Communists and to Communists whose better instincts had not been altogether corroded to join him in the good struggle for which he was courageously sacrificing himself. ". . . it is better to die on the losing side," he quoted himself as saying on his departure from the Communist camp, "than to live under Communism." The substance of his testimony was that he was attached during the mid-thirties to an underground apparatus in Washington, from which two members of Elizabeth Bentley's band had apparently been recruited. He named as his Communist associates of the time eight former officials whose objective, he said, was not espionage but infiltration of the government.[6]

The period he evoked, 1934–1935, was the dawning of the New Deal when young men from good Eastern colleges were drawn to Washington by a combination of job prospects and social revolution. Business opportunities were at a low level but federal jobs were opening up at a furious pace; the capital's bureaucracy increased by 50 per cent between 1933 and 1938. The new recruits knew nothing of the tawdrier side of the Communist Party finaglings of which Chambers had had a full measure since his involvement in 1925 and throughout the Third Period, the years of the C.P.'s toughest, most uncompromising position. Whereas the poet-rebel Chambers came to the Party in despair over post–World War I civilization, from family tragedy and rootlessness and a literary man's pursuit of life's drama, the young lawyers and economists came out of Harvard and the middle classes with great expectations both for their cause and for themselves. Where he was rhetorically fatalistic, they were inexpressibly hopeful. Whereas Chambers's future, in the underground or as a C.P. functionary, was as murky as his past and as depressing, their futures were bright under an Administration which needed them and, for a time, seemed to be allowing them their heads. At once successful bureaucrats and revolutionaries of high promise, they could

[6] They were John Abt, Henry Collins, Alger Hiss, Donald Hiss, Charles Kramer, Victor Perlo, Lee Pressman, Nathan Witt. The organizer of the group and its head until his death in 1935 was Harold Ware, son of the C.P.'s Mother Bloor. Only the Hiss brothers denied Chambers's story under oath.

look forward to splendid careers as the advance cadre of a new America. Chambers, beset always by self-doubt and fear, had nothing in common with these smart young men, keen lawyers, assistants to Supreme Court justices, officials not yet turned thirty but full of credentials, coming men who knew so well how to make their way in the world which turned its back to him. Yet for a few years they were bound together in a conspiracy, sophomoric but with a terribly serious side, that would prove more treacherous to the conspirators than to the nation.

Most of the men named by Chambers and Miss Bentley—none of them, with the exception of the unfortunate Remington, in government any longer—were lavish with indignation at the charges but sparing of details about their pasts. Summoned before the Committee, they took refuge in the self-incrimination clause of the Fifth Amendment. Nathan Gregory Silvermaster, the central figure in Miss Bentley's tale, called her "a neurotic liar" but refused to say whether he ever knew the lady. He protested against "this diabolical conspiracy" but refused to say whether he was a Communist. Henry Collins, a government employee for fifteen years, then director of the American-Russian Institute, belabored the poll tax and the Committee, made known that his forebears had come to these shores in 1640 and that he had fought in the Battle of the Bulge, denied that he had violated U.S. law or knew "a man named Chambers," but would not say whether he was a Communist—or, for that matter, a member of the American Legion. Abraham George Silverman, named by Miss Bentley as the contact with Harry Dexter White, said he was deeply shocked and took the Fifth Amendment. A typical statement came from Victor Perlo, an economist named by both Miss Bentley and Chambers as a leader of a Communist group, who had gotten into the Treasury Department through the good offices of Harry White and in 1948 was working at Wallace headquarters: "It is becoming increasingly clear that despite headline spy sensations, the people resent the failure of the special session of Congress to act on the urgent problems facing the country. The people will echo Mr. Wallace's call for more red meat and less red herrings." Perlo had prepared for the record a denial of all the charges, but modified it after Nixon warned him that he might be leaving himself open to a perjury indictment.

Lee Pressman, lately separated from the powerful post of general counsel of the C.I.O. because of his commitment to the Progressive Party, attacked the hearings as an effort to take people's minds off real issues, to smear the memory of F.D.R., and to discredit Henry Wallace. For the time being, Pressman would answer no questions regarding Chambers's recollection that around 1934–1935 he was a leader of a small Communist cadre in Washington that included Alger Hiss. Two friends and associates of Pressman, John Abt and Nathan Witt, whose flagrant Communist predilections as secretary of the N.L.R.B. had resulted in his "resignation" from that post in 1941, appeared before the Committee with him. Both had been named by Chambers; both, like Pressman, were represented by an attorney who registered in their names objections to the inquiry on the grounds that it was outside the scope of Congress and that the Committee was unlawfully constituted owing to the presence thereon of John Rankin; both replied with the Fifth Amendment to all questions relating to their beliefs and associations. When McDowell sought to have them cited for contempt, they responded, "He regards as traitors those who supported Franklin Delano Roosevelt in his magnificent policy of complete unity with our wartime allies."

This set of hearings marked the first mass use before the Committee of the Fifth Amendment. Other witnesses, notably Browder and Foster in 1939, had refused to answer certain questions lest they incriminate themselves, but now the constitutional clause was being used by persons who had already testified before a grand jury and were charged with no indictable offense. There was, after all, nothing illegal about being a Communist in 1936, or even in 1944, and the three-year statute of limitations on the disclosure of confidential information had run out. In its report at the end of August, the Committee would vent its frustration by calling for laws to cope with "the new Communist tactic of evading detection and impeding the processes of legislative investigation through an unwarranted and unjustifiable misuse of the protections which the

Fifth Amendment to the Constitution rightfully provides for those unjustly accused or those decent, patriotic Americans who may at times be required to defend themselves in a court of law."

Nevertheless, the Committee did not at this point quarrel with the right to the Fifth of their presumably indecent, unpatriotic witnesses. Although Thomas was characteristically ungracious about allowing witnesses to consult with their attorneys,[7] there was satisfaction for him in hearing former New Dealers and present eminences of the Progressive Party discredit themselves in public; not only might their performances prove helpful to the Republican cause in November, but they could be taken as an affirmation of everything that he and Martin Dies had been saying for ten years about Communism and the New Deal, particularly as witnesses threw the New Deal mantle over them with such flourishes: "Because I have never attempted to conceal my strong advocacy of the rights of all New Deal principles," complained the deeply implicated Silvermaster, "I have been constantly harassed by groundless accusations of disloyalty." It would be some time before the Committee came to terms with the Fifth Amendment, but it learned quickly the publicity value of having an unfriendly witness refuse to answer a long string of Stripling's questions about his past associations. There was but a single conclusion that one could sensibly draw from the contagious reluctance to discuss the past; as Nixon spelled it out for a witness—"It is pretty clear, I think, that you are not using the defense of the Fifth Amendment because you are innocent."

Of the smaller group of men who, without availing themselves of their constitutional prerogatives, denied the Bentley-Chambers charges, three were of greatest consequence: Lauchlin Currie, the Harvard economist who served as administrative assistant to F.D.R. from 1939 to 1945 and whose name had

---

[7] During the Hiss hearings, Thomas and Stripling attempted to coerce a lawyer for one of the witnesses to give testimony regarding his advice to his client. When the lawyer refused to be sworn, Thomas lit into him. "The rights you have are the rights given you by this Committee. We will determine what rights you have and what rights you have not got before this Committee."

been dropped into a public hearing by Elizabeth Bentley; Harry Dexter White, international monetary expert and influential Assistant Secretary of the Treasury under Henry Morgenthau and first executive director of the International Monetary Fund, also mentioned by Miss Bentley and characterized by Whittaker Chambers as "a fellow traveler so far within the fold that his not being a Communist would be a mistake on both sides"; and Alger Hiss.

There was never any serious suggestion that Currie, who came to the hearing room accompanied by Dean Acheson, had been a full-fledged member of a conspiratorial group. As for Miss Bentley's description of him as "a friend at court," he had indeed exerted himself on one occasion to save Silvermaster from losing his job in government for sound reasons of security. Currie maintained that he had no inkling that his friend Silvermaster was a Communist, but "this Scotchman in the White House" evidently did have an affinity for left-wing circles in Washington, including, it would be shown in 1951, members of the Institute of Pacific Relations. He seemed to suffer from a sneaking respect for the Communists around him, an emotion that the Communists managed to make use of in his case as in others.

Harry Dexter White, who later would be named by Whittaker Chambers as one of those who had actually passed him confidential information, asked on his appearance before the Committee that he be permitted periodic rests, in deference to a heart condition. Thomas, with his ineffable bad taste, stopped the proceedings at one point to read out the request, adding, "For a person who had a severe heart condition, you certainly play a lot of sports." A few days later White died—according to that part of the nation which took the Wallace campaign seriously, martyred by the Committee. "Harry D. White," said Wallace himself, "my good friend and close associate on many New Deal committees, died Monday—a victim of the Un-American Activities Committee."

White, who had had a major hand in the Morgenthau Plan to reduce postwar Germany to a pastoral condition, made an intelligent and articulate witness, exasperating to Chairman tall and lean, of forthright demeanor, excellent diction, and agreeable comportment. (Chambers was short and round and had a tendency to mumble and slouch.) So impressive were his seemingly unequivocal denials of Chambers's story that Rankin stepped down to shake his hand. In executive session afterward, the Committee members looked at one another in silent dismay, and Hébert suggested that the case be turned over to the Justice Department: "Let's wash our hands of the whole mess." The Committee had never pretended to be an impartial court; it had, as usual, identified itself with the prosecution. "Certainly," commented Mundt during Chambers's first appearance, before Hiss had been heard, "there is no hope for world peace under the leadership of men like Alger Hiss." Elizabeth Bentley and Whittaker Chambers had become the Committee's own, and if they were proved false, the Committee would have to bear the shame. "We've been had!" lamented one of the Republicans. "We're ruined!" For a few days afterward, the Committee diverted the press with the promise of "key witnesses," efforts to partake of the publicity generated by a couple of defecting Russian schoolteachers, and announcements that uranium had been shipped to the U.S.S.R. during the war.

Only Nixon, with the support of Stripling,[9] favored pursuing the case. Nixon had already shown himself to be by far the most competent member of the Committee. He studied up on the subject at hand, paid attention to testimony, and alone of the nine Congressmen was able to lead a witness, without badgering, along an orderly line of questioning. Chambers, soon to become the youthful representative's good friend and uncritical fan, attributed Nixon's insistence on continuing with the hearings to his possession of "one of those direct minds with an inner ear for the ring of truth." But in fact what Nixon showed when reacting to Hiss's testimony, which bowled over his colleagues, was an ear for the ring of equivocation. Asked by Stripling

[9] There is a slight difference of emphasis in the recollections of Nixon and Stripling as to which of them played the more forward role at this crucial hour. Nixon writes: "I was the only member of the Committee who expressed a contrary view, and Bob Stripling backed me up strongly and effectively." Stripling writes: "But, as I pointed out, with the aid of Rep. Nixon, a *prima facie* perjury was somewhere involved."

whether he had ever seen Whittaker Chambers, Hiss had replied: "The name means absolutely nothing to me . . ." While under oath, he had avoided a categorical statement that he did not know his accuser.

Two days after Hiss's appearance, Nixon, accompanied by Hébert and McDowell, questioned Chambers secretly in a courtroom of New York's federal courthouse on Foley Square. Nixon realized that to prove that Hiss had been or still was a Communist might be impossible, but to prove that he and Chambers had known one another need not be unduly difficult if Chambers could supply details of Hiss's private life in the years 1934 to 1938. This Chambers seemed able to do in ample measure. He told of the Hiss family's nicknames, their eating and drinking habits, their furniture; he recalled that Hiss was an amateur ornithologist who had once seen a rare prothonotary warbler; he said that Hiss had turned over a 1929 Ford roadster to a C.P. member. He also mentioned what he had oddly failed to mention at his first appearance, that Hiss knew him not as Whittaker Chambers, but as "Carl."

Nine days later, during which period Nixon paid three visits to Chambers at his farm in Westminster, Maryland, and became thoroughly convinced of his truthfulness, Alger Hiss was called to an executive session in Washington. The aplomb of his previous appearance had worn off; when Hébert charged him with hedging, he expressed his indignation at the idea that the testimony of a creature such as Chambers, "a confessed former Communist and traitor to his country," should be weighed equally by the Committee with the testimony of a person such as himself. It was at this meeting that Hiss, though wary now and reluctant to say too much, unknowingly confirmed many of the details of his life which Chambers had provided. Midway through the session, Hiss, with a bit of rigmarole, gave the Committee a name, George Crosley, which he explained belonged to a magazine writer, a free-lance freeloader who had hung about him during his Nye Committee days. The name, he emphasized, had not been brought to mind by the photographs he had seen of Chambers, but by a newspaper report to the effect that Chambers had displayed considerable knowledge of the Hiss household. The Committee interpreted this to mean that Hiss now realized he could no longer get away with a flat denial.

At the conclusion of this session, on August 16, it was agreed that a confrontation between Chambers and Hiss would be arranged for August 25. But late on the night of the six-teenth, Nixon, persuaded that Hiss was lying, changed plans. Chambers and Hiss were suddenly summoned to meet in New York the very next evening. Nixon would subsequently deny charges that the change of plans was an effort to divert atten-tion from the death of Harry Dexter White on August 16. As he explained it, the date was moved up in order to deprive Hiss of "nine more days to make his story fit the facts."

The executive session in Room 1400 of the Hotel Commodore did not take long. Hiss started it off with several complaints—the suddenness of the summons, the death of Harry White, a Committee leak to the *Herald Tribune* of his disinclination to take a lie detector test. Chambers was brought into the room. After a certain amount of stage business in which Hiss in-spected his teeth, made a show of listening to his voice, and did some paltry cross-examining, the climax was reached. Hiss said: "I am perfectly prepared to identify this man as George Crosley." The session ended with Hiss advancing upon Cham-bers with clenched fists and challenging him to make his charges outside of the Committee hearing room: "I challenge you to do it, and I hope you will do it damned quickly." It is difficult to read the transcript of this encounter and not con-clude, with Whittaker Chambers, that "Alger Hiss was acting from start to finish."

By the time of the public confrontation on August 25, the nation's excitement had been whipped up by various means. There were Nixon's briefings to the press about the "George Crosley" development: "He [Hiss] went to New York with him [Chambers], stayed in a house with him, loaned him money and a car, and he didn't know he was a Communist." There were the refusals to testify of most of the men named by Chambers—with the notable exception of Donald Hiss, Alger's brother, who denied knowing Chambers under any name whatever, thereby giving Chambers the lie but also depriving his brother of a possible corroborating witness for the George Crosley story. There were newspaper reports that Mrs. Hiss and others were being questioned in private and that detective work was being done on the Ford roadster. There were Truman's continued attacks on the Committee. And there was a long and angry letter to the Committee from Hiss insisting that they get down to the question of whether he had ever been a Communist, and pay attention to Chambers's spotty past as contrasted to his own shining record: "I too have had a not insignificant role in the magnificent achievements of our nation in recent times." He referred to all the important people, senators and cabinet members and federal judges and Eleanor Roosevelt, who knew and respected him. It was, as Nixon commented, a display of "innocence by association."

The August 25 hearing, the most dramatic as well as the most crowded public event in the Committee's history, lasted for nine hours; Hiss testified for six hours, Chambers for three. Nixon, Stripling, and the others pressed Hiss hard, particularly on details relating to his disposal of the already famous Ford roadster, which investigators had traced to a man who refused to state under oath whether he was a member of the Communist Party. Hiss was extravagantly careful. He prefaced nearly two hundred answers with "to the best of my recollection," and insisted that the Committee ask Chambers, whose story was notably more direct and more plausible than his own, whether he had ever been in a mental institution. Chambers replied that he had not, "period," and played his own part for all it was worth. Asked what motives he might have for seeking to ruin Hiss, he answered: "We were close friends. But we got caught in the tragedy of history. Mr. Hiss represents the concealed enemy we are all fighting. I am testifying against him with remorse and pity. But in this moment of historic jeopardy at which this nation now stands, so help me God, I could not do otherwise."

It was to be expected that the Committee report issued two weeks after the confrontation would describe Chambers's testimony as "forthright and emphatic" while that of Hiss was "vague and evasive." But even the hopes that liberals invested in Alger Hiss were severely strained that day. Before this performance, *The Nation* wrote of the Chambers-Bentley charges, "Any neurotic exhibitionist who can claim to have been a Communist is now assured of absolution, soul-satisfying publicity, and probably more material rewards in the shape of payment for exclusive newspaper stories, lecture contracts and good jobs." But a *Nation* reporter, commenting on the August 25 meeting, had to grant that the Committee's relentless questioning of Hiss as to dates and details had "elicited answers characterized by such persistent qualifications and evasions that an objective observer might have concluded that Hiss's claim of innocence had been compromised." A few days later, Chambers accepted Hiss's challenge and stated on *Meet The Press,* where he received a rough going over from reporters for the Washington *Post* and the Chicago *Sun,* that Alger Hiss was a Communist and "may be one now." Three weeks passed before Hiss responded, and even the Washington *Post* was led to comment that "Mr. Hiss has created a situation in which he is obliged to put up or shut up. Mr. Hiss has left himself no alternative." At the end of September, Hiss sued Chambers for libel.

Alger Hiss had no alternative from the first. In his shrewd article on the case, in *Commentary,* Leslie Fiedler explained Hiss's lies by grouping him with Remington and the Rosenbergs as examples of "the Popular Front mind at bay, incapable of honesty, even when there is no hope in anything else." But there is a simpler explanation. For known Sovietphiles like Lee Pressman and Henry Collins, taking the Fifth Amendment could do only marginal damage to their already dubious reputations. For persons out of public life, taking it would in all likelihood mean a passing personal injury. But the reputation of the president of the Carnegie Endowment for International Peace had to be unshadowed. Chambers, fascinated with conspiracy in all its forms, would take Hiss's denials as evidence that the man was still a member of the Communist apparatus which, in Chambers's imagination, was omnipresent, like SMERSH or THRUSH. In 1952 Chambers would ask whether there were "people who still believe that in 1948 Alger Hiss impenitent and defiant to this hour, was still not an active Communist, working as such in close touch with some of the highest power centers in the country? Are there people who still do not see that in removing his power for evil in 1948, the secret apparatus that I had failed to smash singlehanded in 1938 was at least damaged?" But no evidence was ever adduced that Hiss had not simply drifted away from the Party in 1939 or 1940 as many young Communists did; Miss Bentley, so generous with names of wartime Washington officials, never volunteered that of Alger Hiss. In 1948 Hiss was defending a career, much too brilliant a career to survive the kind of smudge that lesser men may accept as part of life's game.

But circumstances demanded the pretense, for him as for Chambers, that there was a greater cause at stake in his fight for self-preservation. Hiss seized on the fact that Thomas, Mundt, and others on the Committee were itching to use his case as proof that the New Deal and the United Nations were tainted with subversion, and presented himself as a victim of a reactionary plot "to discredit recent great achievements of this country in which I was privileged to participate." Even after his case was decided, after he had served his time in prison, he concluded his singularly unpersuasive account of the entire affair with these words: "But nothing can take away the satisfaction of having had a part in government programs in which I strongly believed. I feel deep satisfaction that I took part in the creative efforts of the New Deal and in the formation of the United Nations. The democratic ideals which motivated me in government service continue to shape my outlook on life."

To the end, and beyond, Hiss made that plea to the liberal community, and a part of it, only too conscious of what the Committee was up to and unwilling to admit what could scarcely be denied, were caught in the snare; they made the cause of Alger Hiss their own. Their hearts went out to the personable young man who had stood at F.D.R.'s side at Yalta. They were eager to take Harry Truman's mindless sneers of "red herring" as something more substantial than the instinctive reaction of a highly political man in a difficult political situation—the Soviets acting up in Berlin, the Republicans in full cry after "Communists in government." These liberals would not concede that the Administration had done, for all practical purposes, nothing about Whittaker Chambers's story of a Washington Communist cell when he brought it to the State Department's security officer, Adolf A. Berle, a few days after the signing of the Nazi-Soviet pact. They would not, could not concede that many New Dealers, including F.D.R. himself, had been slow in taking the Communists as seriously as they deserved to be taken. Those who in 1948 associated themselves with the sad cause of Alger Hiss made an error for which the liberal cause would pay in the next half dozen years.

The maneuvers and polemics of both sides during the hearings, the Hiss trials, and afterward were generally exaggerated and at times ludicrous. Whereas Hiss claimed that he was the victim of a public hysteria whipped up by haters of Franklin Roosevelt, Chambers presented himself as the last hope of the West as it succumbed to atheistic Communism. Not only was the whole power complex of an infiltrated government and press bearing down on his head, but a conspiracy of immeasurable proportions was out to destroy him. However, as he made clear periodically, he had chosen to destroy himself for the sake of this lost and ungrateful civilization. The pudgy figure in a dark and unpressed suit wanted everyone to understand that he harbored the conscience of Raskolnikov and the mission of Jesus Christ. In the second Hiss trial, the defense would ring in a couple of psychoanalysts to explain, with appropriate phrases from their canon, that Chambers was a great liar. A better case can be made that Chambers was a truthful man, who on certain subjects could not quite separate the real from the fantastic.

For years Hiss had been the public man and Chambers the creature of the underground. Now it was Hiss who sought to conceal his past, while Chambers indulged in self-exposure worthy of Rousseau. Chambers thought of himself as a key symbol in the "crisis of the West"; he savored the allegory of himself—as time closed in on him, so history closed in on the rest of us. Despite the political notoriety he achieved, he was from first to last a literary man. He saw politics not as a battle of ideas or even of human beings, but of immense forces played out on a grand stage. What drew him to Communism in the twenties was not Marx, but Hauptmann, Ibsen, Gorky, not the plight of the working stiff but the blazing dream of revolution in which a rotten West would be annihilated. What sustained him during his years in the Party and in the underground were the heroic commitments, the sacrifices, the exhilaration of conspiracy. (On the evidence of his autobiography, *Witness,* the Communists' efforts at intrigue owed about as much to Harpo Marx as to Karl, but intrigue it undoubtedly was.) And when he fled the Party in 1938, in revulsion at the cruelty and hypocrisy of the Stalinists and their apologists in this country, he took with him two cherished possessions: a sense of ubiquitous peril and a vision of the Apocalypse. He also took God, with whom he had recently become reacquainted.

He was exasperated by those who followed the Hiss case as a kind of tennis match between two pros. For him it was the Force of History, represented by Alger Hiss in alliance with the greatest powers in the land, against one lone figure, Whittaker Chambers, who was sacrificing a fine career, a good name, and the family peace that he had belatedly found in a hopeless effort to show a blind, corrupt, ungrateful, irreligious nation how deep its infection went. He could write: "I am a man who reluctantly, grudgingly, step by step, is destroying himself that this country and the faith by which it lives may continue to exist." Chambers suffered during the Hiss case, and he wallowed in his sufferings; they were proof of what he most fervently needed to believe—that the West had been betrayed and was doomed and that he, atoning, was the unhonored messiah to the age. ". . . the world's instinctive feeling was against the little fat man who had stood up to testify for it, unasked. The world's instinctive sympathy was for the engaging man who meant to destroy it, was for Alger Hiss."

Chambers's literary bent became plain in his posthumous book, *Cold Friday,* a sandwich board proclaiming the end of the world. It reported that the critical hour for the West, after which there was no turning back, came when men transferred their faith from God to the machine. But this new faith was unsatisfying; who, after all, would give up his life for a gasoline engine? A vacuum had been created in men's souls, and into it surged the revolutionary forces of the century, proclaiming a godless faith for which men *would* be willing to die. The flabby, materialistic West could not withstand such a movement, and so for fifty years we have been afflicted by various forms of this dynamic revolutionary atheism—Russian Communism, Italian fascism, British Socialism, the American New Deal. All, in Chambers's system, had sprung from the same impulse, and were propelled toward the same authoritarian goal. The fitting end of the West would be its demolition by a product of its own technology, the hydrogen bomb. What decisively separated Whittaker Chambers from the temper of the democratic West was his belief that we urgently needed a faith for which men were willing to die, a "rallying idea . . . capable of being grasped and so overmastering millions of men . . ." He rejoiced in the robes of martyrdom. If the Hiss forces had any case at all, it was that Chambers would have been willing to destroy even an innocent Alger Hiss if, in his fiery reasoning, it served some greater purpose.

Whittaker Chambers was not, of course, the first hot American nor the last, although he gave signs of believing he was the only authentic specimen around at the time. Before we were a nation, the churches of New England were fortresses where preachers of Enthusiasm tried to stave off preachers of the Enlightenment. The Enthusiasts lost, and they have lost many other engagements during these two hundred years, but their spirit has never been entirely subdued. Its reappearance is generally accompanied by repression, brutality, and howlings in the night. It is also accompanied, often as not, by religious banners. Chambers was a peaceable, reflective, solitary man, afflicted by nightmares, some of which were real and some of which were real mainly to him. His life was dominated by a steaming imagination, which found its ultimate, incredibly satisfying, outlet in the Hiss case. Here was sufficient drama for the greediest taste, and the libel suit, which seemed at first to be an anti-climax, brought the action to new peaks of excitement.

During the pre-trial examination in November, Hiss's attorney made a routine request of Chambers to produce any letters or communications that he might have from Alger Hiss. Up until this hour, Chambers had made no public charge of espionage against anyone. Now, faced with the prospect of losing the libel suit, he went to New York and recovered from an unused dumbwaiter shaft in a Brooklyn apartment house a large envelope which he had entrusted to his wife's nephew ten years before, when he broke from the Communist apparatus. In it were sixty-five typed pages, copies or summaries of State Department documents; three memoranda in the handwriting of Alger Hiss; a long memo in the handwriting of Harry Dexter White; two strips of developed microfilm; and three cylinders of undeveloped microfilm. With the exception of the microfilm which the ever suspicious Chambers secreted in a hollowed-out pumpkin on his Maryland farm, the material was turned over to the Department of Justice. Upon learning that some new and important evidence had appeared, Nixon and Stripling, mistrustful of the attorney general and reluctant to relinquish so promising a case, paid a hurried visit to Chambers. He confirmed that he had indeed produced one "bombshell" and gave them to understand that he had another in safekeeping against the danger that the Administration might attempt to suppress the evidence in its possession. A press service dispatch published that morning provided substance for his fear: "The Justice Department's investigation of the Hiss-Chambers affair is about to die for lack of evidence, it was disclosed today. Unless something new turned up soon, officials said, there would be little use going to a grand jury with the information obtained so far." Nixon, about to embark on a vacation cruise in the Canal Zone, signed a subpoena *duces tecum* on Chambers for any and all documents he still had in his possession relating to his charges before the Committee. A few days later, with a blast of publicity, the existence of the microfilm, which had been retrieved by Committee investigators from its pumpkin, was made public. Stripling was photographed scrutinizing the film. Mundt told reporters that it contained "definite proof of one of the most extensive espionage rings in the history of the United States." Nixon was photographed hastening back from the Caribbean, and on his arrival in Washington voiced his concern over an "apparent lack of interest by the Department of Justice in getting to the crux of this case. It seems to be trying frantically to find a method which will place the blame for possession of these documents on Mr. Chambers."

An Administration which had repeatedly committed itself to a "red herring" interpretation of the Hiss case was fair game for such suspicions; it did have an interest in discrediting Whittaker Chambers. But the Committee's refusal through the month of December to let loose the evidence and forgo the spotlight it had enjoyed in August, owed something to politics as well. A triumph now would counteract the disheartening effects on the lame-duck Committee of Harry Truman's upset victory in November. Nixon's own stake in the case was tremendous; his career no less than Alger Hiss's hinged on the outcome. So the nation looked on while a committee of Congress disputed jurisdiction of a criminal case with the Justice Department.

With a federal grand jury reconvened, there was never any question about where jurisdiction belonged, but the Committee was able to exert great pressure on the attorney general's office in a variety of ways: by reporting that in the judgment of former high State Department officials Chambers's documents could have enabled the Russians to break the department's code; by calling Henry Julian Wadleigh, a former State Department employee implicated by Chambers;[1] by competing with the grand jury for witnesses; and by releasing the documents themselves piecemeal. At length, after much table-thumping and shouting and mutual recriminations, Nixon agreed to an accommodation whereby the Committee would retain possession of the microfilm but would make it available to the grand jury when it was wanted. On December 15, the

[1] Wadleigh, who took the Fifth Amendment, later confessed his part in the espionage operation, and Hiss attempted to shift onto him the guilt of purloining the compromising documents.

last day of the grand jury's life, Alger Hiss was indicted on two counts of perjury. The statute of limitations on espionage committed in 1937 and 1938 had long since run out, and the most that Hiss could be charged with was that he had lied when he said he never turned over State Department documents to Chambers and when he said he never saw Chambers after January 1, 1937. "Despite criticism from all sources from the President down," declared a victorious Nixon, "the indictment establishes beyond doubt the justification for committees of Congress investigating in this field."

Alger Hiss was convicted of perjury and given a five-year sentence at his second trial in 1950. It was the year of the outbreak of the Korean War and the onset of McCarthyism. McCarthy and his disciples relied heavily on the Hiss case to justify their ravages. They believed or pretended to believe that the Communist rings exposed by Chambers and Miss Bentley were but two of many such rings and that others, yet undiscovered, were continuing to eat away at the Republic's vitals. Partly because of Chambers's pleasure in fantasizing, partly because of Miss Bentley's eagerness to oblige, partly because of Alger Hiss's insistence on sticking to his story even after forty-four months in prison, much about the case remains dim. The Bentley and Chambers testimony taken together tended to show not that there was a widespread network of subversives in Washington during the thirties and forties, but that the Communists, at the height of their prestige, had succeeded in planting a handful of their own in government.[2]

---

[2] In his study, *The Communist Controversy in Washington*, Earl Latham writes: "Of the Communist problem in the prewar years in the federal government, the evidence supports certain summary statements. First, there does not seem to have been a planned and premeditated 'infiltration' of the federal agencies, certainly not at the start. Second, once the entry into the federal service by members of the Communist Party took place in the quick expansion of staff that began in 1933, some members of the Party formed in such groups. Third, most of the membership of the Party was pretty well scattered in ones and twos here and there, and the total—Chambers guessed about seventy-five—was not large. There were a half million federal workers in Washington alone. Fourth, there were small concentrations of members of the Party in the Department of Agriculture, certain congressional committees, and the National Labor Relations Board. Fifth, the aim of these groups seems to have been the promotion of left tendencies in the development of the public policies of the respective agencies. Sixth, the Party groups were not primarily organized for espionage. Seventh, in the three areas discussed—Department of Agriculture, congressional

Chambers maintained that Hiss was to the end a member of the Communist conspiracy, but there was no evidence that he did the Party's work after 1938—although Adolf Berle, who did not take a particularly serious view of Chambers's disclosures in 1939, recalled that toward the end of the war Hiss, then executive assistant to Assistant Secretary of State Dean Acheson (who could not believe that the Hiss boys could be *Communists*), showed a disposition to conciliate the Russians. The fact that Hiss did not come forward to confess the adventures of his youth may be marked up as readily to simple careerism as to continuing subversive intentions. It is a footnote to the affair that by becoming a liberal rallying point, Hiss proved of service to the McCarthyites. His case, in the headlines for so long, made it easy for them to exaggerate the dimensions of the internal Communist menace and to whip up a storm which did not last long but left ruins in its wake.

The last flurry of the Committee's 1948 existence was set off by the fatal fall from the sixteenth floor of a midtown New York office building on December 20 of Laurence Duggan, president of the Institute of International Education. Five hours after the body was found, Mundt, with the concurrence of Nixon, notified reporters that Duggan's name had been mentioned about two weeks earlier in a closed session of the Committee. Isaac Don Levine, the right-wing writer and editor who had taken Whittaker Chambers to see Adolf Berle in 1939, told the Congressmen that Chambers had at that time mentioned Duggan, then a State Department official, as one member of a six-man Communist apparatus which had been passing documents. Asked when he would release the other five names, Mundt quipped, "We'll name them as they jump out of windows." Apparently alerted by the Committee, the F.B.I. had questioned Duggan ten days before his death.

Duggan's superiors in the State Department, where he had

---

committees, and the National Labor Relations Board—the promotion of left tendencies was not allowed to prevail: there was a 'blow-up' in Agriculture, Senator La Follette brought the practice of hiring downtown personnel under restraint, and the bid for control of the N.L.R.B. was lost."

been a respected Latin American expert, came swiftly to his defense, and Chambers corrected Levine's recollection by explaining that he had mentioned Duggan's name only as someone he believed to be cooperating with the Communists; Chambers had had no direct contact with Duggan and had received no documents from him.[3] As protests built up after the posthumous attack, Nixon realized that he and Mundt had gone too far, carried away perhaps by their success with Alger Hiss, whose career resembled Duggan's. Hébert called the disclosure "a blunder, a breach of confidence and a violation of agreed upon precedure." Even Rankin considered it "atrocious." Mundt's defense was unspirited; his action, he explained, was meant as an aid to the New York City police, and a majority of the Committee in Washington at the moment—namely Nixon and himself—had approved it. The quicker-witted Nixon, however, saw the storm warnings and recognized that the moment had come to throw the cargo overboard; he told a television audience that as far as he was concerned Duggan was clear of charges of espionage. The protests continued, with Attorney General Clark, who was privy to the F.B.I. report on Duggan, declaring him to have been "a loyal employee of the United States government," and Mundt too decided that Duggan was "cleared," that the case was a "closed book." He and Nixon granted with the approach of Christmas Day that their hasty disclosure warranted "some honest criticism." They regretted the "misunderstandings" and "misinterpretations" which had accrued. Isaac Don Levine was not so easily put off. When Sumner Welles came to Duggan's defense, Levine countered, "Let Sumner Welles explain away Mr. Alger Hiss and how documents and microfilm were filched from the State Department when for all practical purposes Sumner Welles was Secretary of State." In this use of the Hiss case to bolster lightly

[3] Whereas Chambers remembered Laurence Duggan as someone whom he had been told would be "very sympathetic" to the Communist cause, Hede Massing, former wife of Gerhart Eisler and confessed espionage agent, went further; she said that Duggan agreed to give periodic verbal reports to a contact. She met Duggan through his close friend, Noel Field, another State Department official, who wound up in a Hungarian prison after a mysterious defection to the East. Whatever Duggan's role in the conspiracy, Levine's charges exceeded the existing evidence.

substantiated charges against a dead man, Levine displayed a mentality that would become quite popular in America in the near future.

The Committee arrived at the end of its great year balanced somewhat uncertainly between its dramatic victory in the Hiss case and the equally dramatic, if indecisive victory of its archenemy Harry Truman in the November elections. One hundred and one new Democrats were to take their places in the House in January, and according to one report, none of them had shown an interest in a seat on the Un-American Activities Committee. Harry Truman called it a dead agency, and the Committee's enemies were again dreaming of abolition. In deference to the changed circumstances, Mundt and Nixon, fresh from defaming the memory of Laurence Duggan, put forward a nine-point code, steeped in virtue and designed to make formal the rights of witnesses to counsel and other amenities, such as not having their names bandied about in public. And lest anyone had forgotten Alger Hiss, on December 30, the Committee issued its final report on the case, largely given over to details of Chambers's techniques as a courier.

Hopes for abolition of the Committee were, as always, unrealistic; the group had plenty of support around the country (where six "little" un-American Activities committees were at work in state legislatures), and not much outspoken opposition in the House. Whatever its fate in the Democratic eighty-first Congress, however, the Committee's composition would be radically changed. Mundt, who had flowered in collaboration with Richard Nixon, had been elected to the Senate. McDowell and Vail were among the less significant casualties of the Democratic sweep. Chairman Thomas had been elected for his seventh consecutive term from his safe district in New Jersey, but he had allowed his public activities to lapse shortly after being charged by the Justice Department with payroll padding, and his mission would never be resumed. Two days after the election, he came before a grand jury where, to the delight of many who had followed his career, he availed himself of the Fifth Amendment. Within the week he was indicted on charges of conspiracy to defraud the government. When these charges were first made during the election campaign, the florid, bristling sufferer from stomach ulcers called them a "dying gasp of reprisal . . . against one who has stood up against the enemies of this country and did not cower before them." But it was his career that died. While fighting subversives from January 1940 to January 1945, he billed the U.S. Treasury for salary payments to persons who did not in fact work in his office, and he pocketed the money. He was convicted, sent to the Federal Correctional Institution at Danbury, Connecticut (where he encountered Ring Lardner, Jr.), and was paroled after about nine months. Early in 1954 he attempted to return to Congress, presenting himself as "a fighter of the McCarthy type," but the Republican leadership, for whom one McCarthy at a time was proving sufficient, turned a deaf ear. A few years later he died. The poetry of the end of J. Parnell Thomas requires no gloss. It is enough to note that his talents as a public official flourished on the Un-American Activities Committee. His major appearances on the floor of Congress were in such causes as the impeachment of Frances Perkins for her failure to deport alien radicals and the denial of the benefits of the Wagner Act to unions with alien officers. Neither his record nor his personality were of a sort to awaken wide sympathy, and it was left to Martin Dies to remind us that Congressmen had been taking kickbacks since Congress began: "I hold no brief for Parnell's conduct, but what of the high crimes Administration favorites have committed with impunity?" It was a defense worthy of J. Parnell Thomas himself.

Another veteran of the Dies Committee was preparing his farewells at the end of 1948. Robert Stripling, having apprenticed at the feet of Martin Dies and come into his own at the right hand of J. Parnell Thomas, was now looking toward a career in the oil industry. He was a cold and tough investigator; the Communists were his quarry and everything else was irrelevant. Stripling was a professional, a status that he shared with Nixon; he organized his investigations for maximum impact and conducted them with a sense of order that the messianic Matthews had never been able to master. As a technician, Stripling made a significant impression on the operations of the Committee in his own time and for the future as well.

Of the Republicans, then, only Richard Nixon remained. He was, Dies wrote, "the only Congressman ever to profit by anti-Communist activity," adding sourly, "and he profited only because he backed away from it." Nixon's career was famously expedited by the Hiss case—he was Bolingbroke to Richard II, his bucket dancing in the air as Hiss's sunk down and down —but the qualities he showed on the Committee would have carried him forward in any event. He was smart, energetic, and a very fast learner of what he needed to know. He could be dogged yet agile; he had a nice instinct for when to bet high and when to cut his losses. The Committee had helped to make him, but he, more than any other member, had been responsible for giving the Committee its great year. As that year drew to a close, no one could doubt that Richard Nixon's future was exceedingly bright. As for the Committee itself, however, it would not again attain the resplendency of 1948.

9

★ ★ ★ ★ ★

1949-1950: In Contempt

AT the start of the eighty-first Congress the functioning of the Committee was delayed briefly as the Democratic leadership pondered means of taming it—since, despite the President's deepest desires, they lacked the votes for abolition. The taming process amounted to replacing Rankin and Hébert, both of whom had supported the States' Rights candidate in November, with Truman Democrats. "The word seems to have come down from Moscow to keep me off the Committee on Un-American Activities," commented Rankin when the Administration's intentions became known, and he who had led the way into the Promised Land was abruptly ejected. Renovating their rules to fit the occasion, the leaders of the House decided that no chairman of another committee could sit on the Un-American Activities Committee, thereby getting rid of Rankin, who supervised Veterans' Affairs; they decided further that every Democrat on the Committee must be a lawyer, thereby eliminating Hébert, a newspaperman. Named to join John Wood, chairman again, were Burr P. Harrison of Virginia, John McSweeney of Ohio, Morgan M. Moulder of Missouri, and the influential Francis E. Walter of Pennsylvania, who had been critical of some aspects of Committee behavior in the past. The Republicans, allowed only four members, courteously retained Thomas whose payroll padding case was in the courts,[1] and added Francis H. Case of South Dakota and

---

[1] After Thomas, convicted, resigned from Congress in January 1950, he was replaced by Bernard W. Kearney of New York, who had refused a seat on the Committee as long as Thomas remained.

Harold H. Velde, a newcomer from Illinois who had been an F.B.I. agent during the war. Richard Nixon made up the Republican complement. Frank Tavenner took over Stripling's post of chief of staff, and Louis Russell, another former F.B.I. man, became chief investigator. The Committee was granted $200,000 without debate.

It soon became evident that the changes were more than nominal. Newsreel and TV cameras were barred from the hearing room and Chairman Wood actually turned down an interview for the movies, an unheard of self-denial in Thomas's time. Wood confused the Committee's friends and foes by being a gentlemanly hunter of Communists; he was a conservative but he was not a red neck; and he was by no means a showy or particularly forceful personality. With Francis Walter instead of Rankin now lighting his way, the chairman went along at a less jarring gait than in his previous term. During the first months of the eighty-first Congress, despite persistent goading from the minority to show more zeal, there were no public hearings and no leaks from executive sessions. When in March Judith Coplon, an employee at the Department of Justice, was arrested as a Soviet spy, Nixon demanded an investigation. "This case," he announced, "shows why the department may be unfit and unqualified to carry out the responsibility of protecting the national security against Communist infiltration." But except for a short and profitless inquiry into a couple whose names had come up in the Coplon case—he an employee of the federal government, she of the U.N.—no investigation ensued. The Committee issued its reports (on atomic espionage, the Communist-run Paris Peace Conference, the need for new laws against Communists), held its closed-door meetings, and caused discontent within its own ranks. By the end of May stories began to reach the newspapers of dissatisfaction among both Republican and Democratic members. "I am disgusted," declared an unnamed Democrat, who could only have been Harrison or McSweeney. "It is hardly worth while to serve on a group that is doing so little. Some of us are getting tired of the policy of almost complete inactivity and keeping what little work we do completely secret.

It's time we began to fulfill our function of exposing Communists and un-American activities." *The New York Times* responded with an editorial commending the Committee for being vulnerable to this type of criticism. Over the next few months, the pressure to cast off the unaccustomed restraints would have some effect; for a moment that June it seemed that college textbooks might be investigated, but the impulse was quelled by a surge of protests.[2] At the end of the year such staunch opponents of the Committee as Representatives Holifield and Helen Gahagan Douglas were able to praise it for having "acted with more restraint and regard for civil liberties than ever before." The Committee, they agreed, in a nice phrase, had done "a fine job of what it had to do."

The greater part of the Committee's time in 1949 was taken up by a reprise, with embellishments, of the wartime atomic espionage cases which it had made public the year before. The F.B.I.'s evidence, though not conclusive, most seriously involved two young scientists who had been associated with the Manhattan Project. Clarence F. Hiskey, who had worked on the A-bomb at the University of Chicago, was suspected of passing information to the mysterious Soviet agent Arthur Adams. Scientist X, finally identified in October as Dr. Joseph W. Weinberg, a thirty-two-year-old assistant professor of physics at the University of Minnesota who had been with the University of California's radiation laboratory during the war, was alleged to have passed information to Steve Nelson for transmission to the Russians.

Hiskey was named a pre-war C.P. member by Paul Crouch, a long-time Party functionary lately turned informer. On his reappearance before the Committee in May, the analytic

[2] The textbook incident, which provided the Republicans with a unique opportunity to complain that the Committee was overly active, began with a petition from the Sons of the American Revolution for an investigation of the Communist infiltration of college texts. With the passive acquiescence of Chairman Wood, investigators mailed out letters to a random sampling of schools asking for a list of their textbooks. This caused such an outcry from the recipient educators that Wood was compelled to send another letter explaining that he had no intention of interfering with academic freedom. Whereupon the Republicans placed the entire blame for the abortive adventure on the Democrats.

chemist, then teaching at Brooklyn's Polytechnic Institute, denied any disloyal activities but again pleaded the Fifth Amendment, as he had the previous year, to all questions pertaining to the Communist Party, Arthur Adams, and other matters of particular interest. Weinberg, on the other hand, answered all the questions and denied all the charges. He described the accusations as a case of "mistaken identity" and was annoyed at the "Scientist X" designation that had been pinned on him. The Committee, in possession of the report of an F.B.I. agent who had audited from a nearby rooftop a meeting at Weinberg's home in August 1943, attended by Steve Nelson and four scientists with reputations as Communists, doubted Weinberg's testimony. In October it publicly accused him of lying under oath in denying that he had been a C.P. member and knew Steve Nelson or Nelson's secretary Bernadette Doyle.[3] By this time the scientists named as Weinberg's fellow cell members at the Berkeley campus of the University of California, when the Manhattan Project was under way, had pleaded the Fifth Amendment in both executive and open sessions to questions regarding their C.P. affiliations. And in a most acrimonious hearing, Steve Nelson took the Fifth on all questions having to do with his wartime activities in California.

The Committee's fascination with atom-bomb conspiracies during this period was grounded in fact, in politics, and in the general unease over the new weapon and the consequences of its development by the Soviet Union. The testimony which it heard, though vague in many particulars, was clear on one point—the Russians were most interested in the activities at the nation's radiation laboratories in the early nineteen-forties and had done what they could to tap friendly sources among the atomic scientists. In 1949 the U.S.S.R. exploded its first atomic bomb; in 1950, after sensational spy revelations in Canada and Great Britain, the Rosenbergs were arrested in this country. Together with such disquieting developments went the continuing mistrust in Congress, exemplified by the lamented Thomas, of civilian control of atomic energy—al-

[3] Weinberg was subsequently indicted for perjury, tried, and acquitted.

though all the hard cases of espionage uncovered took place while the army had custody of atom-bomb research. It was the old mistrust of the "practical" man for the brain-worker, adapted to new circumstances. As the House Committee's espionage hearings were under way in the Senate David Lilienthal, head of the Atomic Energy Commission, was being forced to defend himself against Senator Hickenlooper's discreditable charges of "incredible mismanagement."

Thwarted by the Fifth Amendment, the Committee employed against the former Berkeley scientists its most effective weapon—exposure. It was especially effective in this instance because all of the men occupied posts at major universities. One after another they came before the Committee, took the Fifth, and resigned from their jobs. (One, lately an associate professor of physics at Fisk University, was traced by a reporter to Oklahoma City where he was working as a utility company laborer at $1.20 an hour; when the reporter attempted to question him, he climbed to the top of a 110-foot water tower and refused to come down.) With the exception of Hiskey and Weinberg, the named scientists were charged only with having been Communists together during the war. For this youthful villainy, they could now be made to pay.

The justification for exposing the identities of the Berkeley scientists was that they had refused to cooperate in an investigation of substance. But the Committee, reacting to the frustration of being balked and succumbing to an underlying anti-intellectual animus, inflicted a similar penalty where it had no justification. Frank Oppenheimer testified before the Un-American Activities Committee a day after his famous brother Robert appeared at the Joint Committee on Atomic Energy in defense of David Lilienthal. Questioned first in closed session, then, suddenly and for no stated reason, in public, the younger Oppenheimer, who had resigned from the University of Minnesota's physics department before coming to Washington, conceded that he had belonged to the Communist Party from 1937 to 1941, while he was a college student, before the start of the Manhattan Project in 1942. He said that he had never turned over any information to any unauthorized persons, that he had no knowledge of anyone else doing so, and that he would have reported it had he had such knowledge. Although he conceded having met the Communist scientists at Berkeley, he was never accused of having been a member of their group or having done anything untoward during his time with the government. Where Oppenheimer balked was at questions about persons he had known during his Communist phase, in particular those who had been present at meetings with Steve Nelson: "Questions about political affiliations or sympathies or actions . . . seem to me not matters which I can talk about here, because the people whom I have known throughout my life have been decent and well-meaning people. I know of no instance where they have taught, discussed or said anything which was inimical to the purposes of the Constitution or the laws of the United States." His wife, who had been a C.P. member along with him, took an identical position. By shunning the Fifth Amendment, yet declining to answer certain questions, the Oppenheimers opened themselves to a charge of contempt. But Chairman Wood resisted bringing such a charge, explaining, "I don't know that that would do any good. I am not in favor of contempt action except in cases where a witness withholds information that is vital to Committee investigation." Why this sensible principle was not carried over to the practice of putting such witnesses on public display, Wood did not explain.

A similar instance of gratuitous publicizing came at the end of 1950 when David Hawkins, a professor of philosophy at the University of Colorado who had worked at Los Alamos as an aide to J. Robert Oppenheimer, told in executive session of his C.P. membership in the San Francisco area from 1938 to 1943. Hawkins and his wife, like the Oppenheimers, disclaimed all knowledge of espionage activities and refused to name persons they met when they were in their twenties and Communists—despite frivolous assurances from Representative Harrison that "we are not going to do anything to those people. We are not going to injure their reputations." The Hawkins's testimony, which provided some familiar reasons—such as depression and fascism—as to why students were still attracted to Communism in 1938, was promptly made public, but the subdued character of the Committee was evidenced by the fact that again Wood refrained from pressing for contempt citations. Still, given the craving, never satisfied, to turn up espionage plots, given the assumption held by several members that every Communist group was *per se* subversive and every member a likely spy, given their inability to view former Communists as individuals, and given the Committee's manner of operating, these hearings could hardly avoid injuring reputations. Nor, despite the improved procedures and the restraining influence of Wood and Walter, did all the Congressmen go out of their way to do so, particularly when the reputations in question were those of scientists or former Administration officials.

In June 1949 the Committee was reported by the Associated Press as ready "to break their first big case of industrial espionage." As it turned out, this was a case that had been broken before it had fairly been put together. Three witnesses who had worked in a Buffalo aircraft plant during the war told of how they had been solicited by one Andrei Schevchenko, a Soviet purchasing agent, to supply him with information about jet aircraft: "I am a Russian, that is true, and you are an American, but we can't let nationalities interfere with progress. Scientists must be international." The three had at once notified the F.B.I. and for three years they received $200 a week apiece for supplying Schevchenko with inconsequential and misleading data. What injected this routine incident with a certain promise for the Republicans on the Committee was the charge by one of the witnesses that former Secretary of State James F. Byrnes was responsible for letting Schevchenko get away after his efforts at espionage had been fully established. Questioned on this point, the witness explained that he had heard an F.B.I. agent complain that "Mr. Byrnes of the State Department says we can't touch him." The witness had taken as literal truth the grumble of a policeman prevented from hauling in a culprit for reasons of higher policy. The policy reasons were easy enough to grasp. It seemed more sensible during the war to keep the Russians happy with a flow of innocuous information rather than arrest one of their minor officials and bring on an intra-alliance fuss.

This case expired quickly for want of substance, but a few months later Velde, who had worked on the Scientist X affair as an F.B.I. agent during the war and was now building a reputation of sorts on the Committee, took the occasion of the Soviet announcement that they had an atom bomb to charge that the Russians had "undoubtedly gained three to five years in producing the atomic bomb" because of a soft official attitude. He declared that "there is a complete and indictable case against so-called Scientist X . . .", and that "Soviet espionage agents are still highly active in the continental United States." He called on the nation to "throw out of office those incompetents who regard their political lives as more important than our national security." Velde, along with Nixon and Case, was more than ready in December for the liveliest episode of the Committee's year, touched off by the accusations of G. Racey Jordan.

Jordan, who had been a lend-lease inspector at the Great Falls, Montana airport, a stopping-off place for planes en route to the U.S.S.R., came into prominence as a guest star on a Fulton Lewis, Jr., radio broadcast. The former Air Force major told a provocative tale of goings-on at Great Falls in 1943 and 1944—a tale in which he had tried without success to interest *Life* magazine before coming to Lewis, who until his death in 1966 was the nation's most popular radio voice of the lumpen right. Jordan maintained that several shipments of uranium and heavy water and many suitcases—some of which he had broken into, to find State Department documents with such labels as MANHATTAN ENGINEERING DISTRICT and URANIUM 92—had made their way to Russia via the Montana base. He said that in the spring of 1944 he had received instructions by telephone from the late Harry Hopkins to expedite a certain shipment and not report anything about it to his superiors. In a folder marked OAK RIDGE, he said he found a memo from Hopkins, then lend-lease administrator, to Soviet Deputy Premier Mikoyan, which read "Had a hell of a time getting these away from Groves." The Washington *Times-*

Herald printed the Lewis broadcast verbatim under the eight-column headline: HOPKINS ACCUSED OF GIVING REDS A-SECRETS.

The Joint Atomic Energy Committee as well as the Un-American Activities Committee quickly expressed interest in the story and three days after his broadcast Jordan came before the four Democratic members of the latter group, the Republicans all being out of town. Embellishing the tale outside the hearing room, Fulton Lewis told reporters that Henry Wallace had overruled General Groves in order to get the uranium shipments to Russia. Testifying two days later, Groves conceded that he had approved two relatively small shipments to the Russians in an effort to discover their sources of uranium and to avoid tipping them off to the uses to which we were putting the material; the Committee had been informed of these shipments some months before. Groves doubted that any heavy water, which he compared in value to diamonds, was shipped, and he denied ever being pressured to help out the Russians. He had never met or talked to Harry Hopkins or to anyone working for him and had had almost nothing to do with Wallace, about whose security rating he seemed to have some doubts. Walter commented afterward that in his opinion it was "highly improbable that many of the things Mr. Jordan said occurred did occur." Harrison called Jordan's account "inherently incredible."

Major Jordan would doubtless have gone into obscurity at this point had not Nixon, Case, and Velde entered a "protest in the strongest terms" at what they termed a "whitewash" accomplished in their absence. So in January the Committee took up Jordan's reminiscences again, focusing now on the only large shipment of uranium to Russia made during the war, one thousands pounds from a Canadian firm. Nixon did his best to pin responsibility on U.S. lend-lease officials, but could unearth no evidence of finagling by Hopkins or anybody else. The New York broker for the shipment, a sound business-man, stated: "No pressure from any source was used, or indeed necessary, to induce my company to fill these routine orders from the Russian Government out of readily obtainable supplies, in strict compliance with all applicable regulations, at a time when we were rushing all available supplies to our then ally." Henry Wallace came before the Committee to answer what he felt had been a slur by General Groves, and in a testy session, which Velde tried to steer onto the subject of the former Vice President's trips to China and the U.S.S.R., Wallace pointed out that his wartime Board of Economic Warfare had had no effective supervision over lend-lease.

Some weeks later a Committee staff member presented the results of his investigation of the Jordan charges. It appeared that in 1944 the Russians had shipped an astounding 1,700,000 pounds of documents via Great Falls and Jordan had complained about the quantity of stuff going through in the diplomatic pouch—but had made none of the more colorful charges he was to make under the auspices of Fulton Lewis. No White House stationery of the kind Jordan described as bearing Hopkins's signature was discovered. On a return visit to the Committee Jordan did his best to make his previous testimony conform to that of General Groves and the Committee's investigator, and added a new recollection—that among the documents he had seen bound for the U.S.S.R. were some folders marked FROM HISS and FROM SAYRE—the latter being special assistant to the Secretary of State in 1943 and Alger Hiss's superior.

The sensational elements of Jordan's story—those which suggested a conspiracy by New Deal officials to send atomic materials and secrets to Russia and had therefore aroused the interest of Nixon, Velde, and Case—were not substantiated by anything other than a diary that Jordan claimed he had kept during 1944. The diary was not subjected to scrutiny. Still, despite the understandable inclination of the liberal press to dismiss him as a fraud through and through, his experience did afford a glimpse of the sensitive and restless U.S.–Soviet lend-lease relations during the war. The Russians were continually pressing lend-lease officials for more and more supplies of all sorts, including uranium after they began their atomic researches in 1942. Many of the supplies, like the uranium, had no bearing on the war then in progress on the Eastern front, but our officials were loath to stir up a fuss which might have resulted in more complications than it was worth. The Russians were demanding and touchy; the Americans solicitous to the point of permitting them to send a mountain of intelligence matter—the bulk of it readily available material such as technical manuals and road maps—through the diplomatic pouch. A noteworthy, if unsinister, chapter in the history of the war, with a bearing on postwar relations as well. But espionage, not history, was the Committee's concern, and when despite the best efforts of the Republicans, the charges against Hopkins and Wallace fizzled, it turned to other things.

A second major area of Committee scrutiny in the eighty-first Congress, after atomic espionage, was the presence of Communists in the District of Columbia, in western Pennsylvania and Cincinnati, and in Hawaii. The District of Columbia hearings had to do with the membership of the Washington Bookshop and other front organizations and a predominantly Negro laborers' union. The Pennsylvania and Ohio hearings relied, heavily, on the lengthy testimony of Matthew Cvetic, who had worked for the F.B.I. in an undercover capacity through the nineteen-forties; the hearings touched a variety of organizations, such as the American Slav Congress, the Civil Rights Congress, and the Progressive Party, but focused particularly on Pittsburgh Local 601 of the United Electrical Workers, long known as a Communist-controlled union and expelled by the C.I.O. on that account in November 1949.[4] And the hearings in Honolulu, the Committee's first hearings outside the continental United States, had to do almost entirely with Harry Bridges's Longshoremen's Union, which was on strike in Hawaii during 1949.[5]

Although these hearings provided interesting details on the

[4] For a sense of the impact of Cvetic's testimony on the lives of some of the people he named, see Frank J. Donner's *The Un-Americans*, pp. 142–146. It was Cvetic, incidentally, who was the inspiration for that memorable film, *I Was a Communist for the F.B.I.*

[5] The Committee's investigation was used in the campaign to block Hawaiian statehood, but three of the five Committee members who went to Honolulu voted for statehood in 1950, and Representative Walter told a Senate Committee that they had found only a modest amount of Communist activity.

techniques of Communists for securing and utilizing power in labor unions and other groups, they revealed nothing that had not been known to the F.B.I. and, indeed, to many less professional observers of the embattled left-wing unions. Nonetheless, they are of significance in the Committee's history on several accounts. They were a means, in the case of the Electrical Workers, of stirring up opinion against old-line Communist leaders during their battle for survival against the C.I.O.'s newly formed International Electrical Workers Union under James B. Carey. Such intervention would prove effective in other union fights too. The hearings were good for extensive newspaper coverage in the areas concerned, and in coming years the Committee would leave Washington with greater frequency. And they brought nearer to perfection a format that would serve in many future investigations—a willing witness, either F.B.I. informer or disenchanted Communist, followed by unwilling witnesses who took the Fifth Amendment. "I don't think a Committee like this or any subcommittee has a right to go into any question of my beliefs, my associations or anything else," protested Julius Emspak, general secretary of the U.E., presaging innumerable protests to come. Along with some of the atomic scientists, these witnesses goaded the Committee to issue its critical challenge to the relevance of the Fifth Amendment in such cases.

During the questioning of the reluctant scientists, Committee members, particularly Nixon and Walter, had shown growing exasperation at the uses to which the self-incrimination clause was being put. There was little browbeating but, in repeated colloquies, the Congressmen disputed with the witnesses and their attorneys over their employment of the Fifth. Nixon told one of the scientists that he didn't "see how the witness could plead self-incrimination on whether or not another person was a member of the Communist Party." But the witness refused to answer twenty-seven questions anyway. When a lobbyist for two left-wing labor unions took the Fifth, Representative Harrison demanded of the chairman, "When are we going to start citing someone for contempt?" Now and then a member succumbed to snideness. When Clarence Hiskey, who pleaded the Fifth Amendment in preference to discussing his relations with Arthur Adams, told the Committee that he believed in the federal Constitution, Velde responded: "I know you especially believe in the Fifth Amendment to the Constitution."

Finally, the Committee resolved to bring the issue to its first test and, on two days of August 1950, the House of Representatives was called upon to approve the contempt citations of fifty-six persons.[6] The question before the House, as Representative Walter presented it, was not complicated: "Has a committee of the Congress the right and authority to issue a subpoena requiring and compelling the attendance of a witness at a hearing of a committee and to require and compel that witness to answer such questions as within the judgment of the committee are pertinent and relevant to the matter under investigation? That is the sole issue."

And so it seemed to the House. Only Marcantonio argued that the Fifth Amendment had been appropriately taken, a defensible position which he could not help leaving for a fling into demagogy. "What are you really afraid of?" he asked his colleagues, and then told them: "You fear the people and their will for peace and freedom." Marcantonio was alone that day. Even Celler, a consistent opponent of the Committee, held that the claim of immunity had no merit in cases where the witnesses were attempting to protect others and not themselves. But constitutional questions were not uppermost in his mind. He felt that the dignity of a committee of Congress, however undignified its own behavior, was at stake. Referring to Emspak, the first person up for citing, Celler said, "The witness was brash, impertinent and utterly contemptuous of Congress. I cannot allow any witness to offer affront and insult to a Congressional committee as did the witness against whom the contempt citation is brought." Emspak was cited by a vote of 373 to Marcantonio, and the other citations followed in rapid course. The following day, as the balance of the fifty-six cases came up, Representative Cox made a victory speech: "I saw them run

[6] Of these, thirty-nine had taken the Fifth Amendment in Hawaii, five were officials of the United Electrical Workers, four were scientists, and the others, including Steve Nelson, were assorted Party members and sympathizers.

yesterday, people who have been the recipients of favors of the group that the Committee on Un-American Activities are now pursuing, who have received their financial assistance and their political support. I saw them turn and like frightened children run away."

The bounty of contempt cases presented to the courts by Congress in 1950 contained an assortment of constitutional questions, the most important of which were the following: Was the plea of possible self-incrimination available to witnesses testifying before legislative committees? What type of questions did the plea protect the witness from answering? What constituted a claim of the privilege? What constituted a waiver of the privilege? Was the Committee obliged to inform the witness that his answer was unsatisfactory? "It must come from the Supreme Court," Velde told the House, "whether we can force witnesses to answer questions that will help us in our investigative work. I think it must be decided once and for all."

Velde's question and each of the others were answered by the courts to the benefit of the defendants, all but three of whom were judged not guilty—the remaining three finally winning their cases in the Supreme Court, the Warren court, in 1955. Most of the defendants relied successfully on a 1950 ruling by the Supreme Court that it was a violation of the self-incrimination clause to compel a witness to testify before a grand jury on his knowledge of Communist Party operations after he had pleaded the Fifth Amendment. Justice Black wrote: "Whether such admissions by themselves would support a conviction under a criminal statute is immaterial. Answers to the questions asked by the grand jury would have furnished a link in the chain of evidence . . ."

Further, the courts allowed the defendants considerable leeway in their manner of stating that they were pleading the Fifth Amendment; declared that questions aimed at establishing a relationship between a witness and persons who had testified against him or who were themselves accused of subversion were incriminating—and that a witness was within his rights in refusing to acknowledge that he knew certain persons; stated, in the case of Steve Nelson, that the admission of Com-

munist Party membership did not in itself constitute a waiver
of the Fifth Amendment privilege; and informed the Committee that it had the responsibility of pressing the interrogation
if it didn't like a witness's answers, and of specifically warning
a witness, when his position was unacceptable, that he might
be cited for contempt.

The meaning of these decisions, in Carl Beck's summary, was
to broaden the applicability of the Fifth Amendment plea to
any question that tended to incriminate, whether or not it, of
itself, was incriminatory, and to narrow the possibility that a
witness would lose his rights by default, entrapment, or confusion. The era of the Fifth Amendment was thus launched,
but the Court's decisions placed no substantial limitations on
the Committee's actions; it soon became apparent that the self-
incrimination plea, albeit constitutional, would subject the
pleader to public skepticism regarding his innocence. As Beck
observes: " 'I refuse to answer on the ground that it might tend
to incriminate me' has been legally sanctioned, reinforced, but
socially devalued . . ." Henceforth, in the court of public
opinion, resort to the Fifth Amendment would carry its own
penalties.

Besides its planned hearings, the Committee made a number
of sorties in 1950 prompted by events which seemed to one or
another member to warrant its attentions, thereby giving the
year's record a somewhat helter-skelter appearance.

In May came the return of William Remington, the young
Commerce Department official named by Elizabeth Bentley as
a source of information during the war. Like Alger Hiss, Remington had dared his accuser to repeat her accusations in
unprivileged surroundings. Like Whittaker Chambers, Miss
Bentley had responded on *Meet the Press*. Like Hiss, Remington had brought suit for libel—and here, for a time, the
resemblance seemed to end. Remington was cleared by a Commerce Department loyalty board in February 1949. In 1950 the
National Broadcasting Company and the program's sponsor,
General Foods, agreed to settle his suit out of court. The settlement was not at all to the liking of Miss Bentley or her attorney,

Godfrey P. Schmidt. In preparation for the suit, Schmidt had sent an investigator to Tennessee to look into Remington's associations from September 1936 to May 1937, when at the age of eighteen he had worked as a messenger for the T.V.A.; Schmidt had been "pleased" with the results. Similarly affronted by the settlement of the suit and its implication that Remington had been untruthfully accused, the Committee took testimony in executive session from the sources unearthed by Schmidt, and followed this up with a staff investigation of its own. Two of Remington's T.V.A. acquaintances, both admitted former Communists, identified him as a Party member in Tennessee; a third took the Fifth Amendment.

At his public appearance before the Committee—on the day that President Truman released the loyalty files of eighty-one State Department employees under heavy fire by Senator McCarthy—Remington granted that he had been active in union affairs during his months in Knoxville, where he had worked in an interim between his freshman and sophomore terms at Dartmouth; that he might have associated and even roomed with Communists at that time; and that they might have taken him to be one of their own. (Speaking of that period, he referred to himself as "the kid.") But he denied Party membership emphatically: "It is impossible for me ever to have been a Communist." Again he gave his version of his relationship with Elizabeth Bentley in Washington; he believed she wrote for the newspapers and he passed on no confidential information. On the following day Miss Bentley appeared and repeated her story of receiving from Remington War Production Board statistics on airplanes as well as a formula for making synthetic rubber out of garbage, which, she pointed out, Remington thought was destined merely for the American Communist Party, not the Kremlin. Now the Remington case resumed a course parallel to the Hiss case. Remington was called before a grand jury and a few weeks later was indicted for perjury for falsely denying his C.P. membership. He was tried and convicted twice, the first conviction being set aside by the Court of Appeals, and he was sent to prison where he was killed by another inmate. The Committee took full credit for reviving the Remington case and for sending that feckless young man to jail.

In August another figure from the memorable year of 1948 was summoned to Washington. The Progressive Party was falling into disarray as a result of its leadership's Communist line on the Korean War. Henry Wallace himself, belatedly discovering who was running his people's army, quit, and conspicuous among the other departures was that of Lee Pressman. "It is obvious," commented Vito Marcantonio, New York State Chairman of the American Labor Party, with the charity that true believers reserve for apostates, "that Mr. Pressman is disappointed in the amount of fees he expected to get from the Progressive movement when he left the C.I.O."

On the day before Pressman honored his summons to the Committee, New York *Herald Tribune* reporter Bert Andrews, Representative Nixon's particular friend, wrote a somewhat sensational story about the secrets that Committee members hoped to draw out of their old acquaintance, and counsel Tavenner started the hearings with the warning that he would "not be satisfied with a mere perfunctory repudiation of the Communist Party." He wanted names. But Pressman was not in a giving spirit. He conceded what he had refused to concede two years before—that he had been a member of a Communist group in Washington in 1934 and 1935—but he pointed out a number of discrepancies in Whittaker Chambers's recollections. On the single question of surpassing interest to the Committee and the nation, he replied "I have no knowledge regarding the political beliefs or affiliations of Alger Hiss"; he said that Hiss had not been a member of the Washington group during his participation, yet he managed by the fastidious phrasing of his answers to leave the impression that he knew more about Hiss than he was prepared to tell.[7] When it came to other names, he was like the girl who will not jump into bed without twenty-five minutes of urging by her suitor lest she be thought of light virtue. Pressman explained to Chairman Wood how offensive

[7] In 1952 Nathaniel Weyl told the Senate Subcommittee on Internal Security that he had been a member of the famous Communist Party cell in Washington in 1934 along with Pressman and the others, and that Alger Hiss was one of their number.

it was to him to name names and then, in a strange scene, implored the chairman to demand that he do so. Wood, as was his custom, refused to demand anything of anybody, but Nixon finally said that he was insisting on an answer and Pressman thereupon let it be known that Witt, Abt, and Kramer were Communists with him in the thirties. All three, on being recalled by the Committee, again took the Fifth Amendment, as did Abraham George Silverman; Witt, still at it, volunteered a statement about "atomic bomb diplomacy," "frightening power of monopolies," "red-baiting," and "heightened attacks on the Negro people." With his appearance in August 1950, Lee Pressman departed public life. His epitaph was delivered by Richard Nixon, who, with his sharp nose for such witnesses, concluded that Pressman was not "coming clean." Pressman was tough and smart to the end and would doubtless have made an exemplary commissar. But history had not gone his way, the expectations to which his ability entitled him had collapsed, and he made his exit, still a young man, detested by anti-Communists from Nixon to the A.F. of L., and despised by his former comrades as only one's former comrades can despise one.

A few weeks later, the Committee heard in executive session Max Lowenthal, an attorney with a long record of government service, whose main offense was that he had written a book, soon to be published, that was highly critical of the Federal Bureau of Investigation. His summons by the Committee was a frank effort to discredit the book by discrediting its author; the questioning, aimed at stigmatizing him as a devotee of left-wing causes and persons, was as unfriendly as it was insubstantial. The Lowenthal hearings were made public in November, two days before the publication of his book. There is nothing to add to Professor Carr's summation of this incident: "That the Committee had any legitimate basis for questioning Lowenthal even in executive session is doubtful, in view of the questions actually put to him; that it had any justification for making public his testimony, beyond a desire to tar him as a person who had been investigated by the Un-American Activities Committee, is in no way apparent."

Carr also criticizes the appendix to the Remington, Pressman, Lowenthal hearings, composed of the names of selected persons referred to in the course of testimony, accompanied by selected associations, all presented as being information from the Committee's files regarding their "Communist record and activities." However obnoxious these associations, such as the National Lawyers Guild and the Anti-Fascist Refugee Committee, seemed to the Committee staff, to cite them as parts of an individual's "Communist record" was a leap, with malice aforethought, into hyperbole.

The possible consequences of this sort of uninhibited listing were illuminated a week after the Lowenthal hearing, when Hazel Scott, the Negro pianist (then married to Representative Adam Clayton Powell), came voluntarily before the Committee to protest that she had been smeared in *Red Channels*, a publication devoted to blacklisting people in show business, which was then being studied with utmost piety by radio and television executives. In a forceful statement against the newly prosperous blacklisters, Miss Scott contended that most of the affiliations credited to her by *Red Channels* were inaccurate. Her statement was received apathetically by the members present, except for Harrison, whom it aroused to a curious defense. He pointed out that *Red Channels* merely reprinted material from official publications, like those of the Un-American Activities Committee; hence, was it not unjust to blame entrepreneurs for simply giving wider distribution to reports from such reputable auspices? Miss Scott's suggestion that the publishers of *Red Channels* might check their facts before distributing to employers accusations against their employees made no impression on Harrison; the Committee had no quarrel with the logic that led from irresponsible listings to unconscionable pressures.

Among the other celebrities who came before the Committee during the eighty-first Congress were Edward G. Robinson and Jackie Robinson, the former to reply in executive session to an attack on him by *Red Channels* for his association with front groups over the years, the latter to point out, with other prominent Negroes in open session, that Paul Robeson's statement

that American Negroes would not fight in a war against the
U.S.S.R. "sounds very silly to me." Jackie Robinson's statement
was forthright and sensible—"The fact," he observed, "that it is
a Communist who denounces injustice in the courts, police
brutality and lynching when it happens doesn't change the
truth of his charges"—yet there was something troubling about
citizens feeling compelled to come before an investigatory body
to declare their allegiance to the flag. It was particularly troubling that persons whose livelihood was imperiled, as Hazel
Scott's was, could find no better forum from which to reply.
The choice before those attacked was not inviting. Once the
charges had been circulated in public, it was impossible to
ignore them and damnably hard to answer them with dignity.

The Committee's triumphant hour of the 1949–1950 Congressional session came not from any of these asides but, at
last, from the passage of a law. In the spring of 1950 the Congressmen returned to the Mundt-Nixon bill of 1948. Eleven
days of hearings were given over mainly to opponents of the
measure, comprising the entire American left: liberals and
socialists, Communists, Communist sympathizers and haters of
Communists, each of them being asked at the outset whether
he was at present or had at any time been a member of the
Communist Party. With variations of style and emphasis, the
witnesses opposed the idea of registering Communists and their
hangers-on as discouraging to political freedom, but their
words fell on ears filled with other noises.

In the year of the Korean War and the perjury conviction of
Alger Hiss, the Congressional mood for anti-Communist legislation found expression in Senator McCarran's Internal Security
Act, which incorporated the registration provisions first proposed in 1948. Both "Communist-action" and "Communist-
front" organizations would have to register with the attorney
general. In recognition of the fact that the Voorhis act of 1940,
also aimed at getting the C.P. to register, had not managed to
do so, the 1950 measure required further that officers of a subversive organization must register if the organization itself did
not. In a bow to the Constitution, the new bill stated that be-

longing to such an organization was not of itself a crime, and that registration was not to be used as evidence against an individual in any prosecution. Did this mean that a registrant could be certain that he would not be ensnared by the Smith Act? No one could provide that assurance.

Mr. Truman tried to ward off the McCarran bill by sending a special message to Congress on August 8, 1950 (the day that Henry Wallace bade farewell to the Progressive Party), asking only that existing sabotage and espionage laws be strengthened. The burden of his message was given over to the warning that the pending legislation was "so broad and vague in its terms as to endanger the freedoms of speech, press and assembly protected by the First Amendment. Some of the proposed measures would, in effect, impose severe penalties for normal political activities on the part of certain groups, including Communists and Communist Party-line followers. This kind of legislation is unnecessary, ineffective and dangerous." He was ignored. Three weeks later, the bill was passed in House and Senate by crushing votes[8] and a strongly worded veto was overridden easily in both Houses.

For the next decade and a half, the registration requirement, like a lighted fire cracker in a Three Stooges' routine, would be tossed about among the Communist Party, the executive branch, and the courts without, however, going off. The juggling started in April 1953 when the five-man Subversive Activities Control Board, appointed by the President and con-

[8] The debate in the House, efficiently and fairly managed by Nixon, was enhanced by contributions from every member of the Committee and John Rankin, who after reading off a list of names that included the Rosenbergs, Harry Gold, David Greenglass, and Morton Sobell, called the attention of the House to the fact that "There is not a single Christian or a single white gentile among those Communists which I have just named . . ." McSweeney, after confessing that "I cannot understand a Communist," delivered himself of the following poem:

> If you don't like your Uncle Sammy
> Then go back to your home o'er the sea;
> To the land from which you came—whatever be its name
> But don't be ungrateful to me.
>
> If you don't like the stars and Old Glory,
> If you don't like the red, white and blue,
> Then don't act like the cur in the story:
> Don't bite the hand that is feeding you.

firmed by the Senate, concluded that the Communist Party was a Communist-action organization and hence had to register with the attorney general. The Party, whose spokesmen had said flatly from the beginning that they had no intention of registering, appealed; the Court of Appeals upheld the statute; the Supreme Court returned the case to the board so that it might study challenges raised against the credibility of three of the attorney general's witnesses; the board reaffirmed its decision; the Court of Appeals sent the case back again so that the defendants might be given an opportunity to examine F.B.I. reports, in accord with a rule laid down by the Supreme Court in the 1957 Jencks case; the board again declared that the Communist Party must register; the Court of Appeals affirmed this ruling; and the Supreme Court agreed to review the case.

In June 1961, by a vote of five to four, the Supreme Court upheld the constitutionality of the registration requirement; in October the board's order became final; in December the Communist Party was indicted for its failure to register; it was found guilty in district court and was fined $120,000. In December 1963, a three-judge panel of the Court of Appeals for the District of Columbia reversed the conviction on the grounds that the government had not proved there was anyone alive willing to run the risk of incriminating himself by registering as an officer or member of a party that had been labeled "a criminal conspiracy," and in June 1964, the Supreme Court declined to review this decision. The Justice Department tried again, this time producing two F.B.I. informants who had been Party members and said that they would be happy to register the Party and submit a list of its members to the attorney general. On their testimony the Party was convicted in 1965. In March 1967, this conviction, too, was overthrown by the Court of Appeals, which pointed out that by subjecting the Communist Party "to the combined sanction of compelled disclosure and criminal punishment," the McCarran Act was "hopelessly at odds" with the constitutional privilege against self-incrimination. At this the Justice Department gave up. "The case is dead," said a spokesman.

Meanwhile, in May 1962, the attorney general had brought

action against ten C.P. members under the provision of the law that required individual members to register if the organization failed to do so, as was patently the situation. In November 1965, a unanimous Supreme Court ruled that the Justice Department could not require registration of individual members because even though they could not be prosecuted for their admission of membership, it might yet be used as evidence or as an investigatory lead that would subject them to prosecution under other federal laws "in an area permeated with criminal statutes." Thus, during more than a decade and a half of litigation, not one person, not one group ever registered under the 1950 law.

The Committee performed rites of resuscitation over the corpse of the Subversive Activities Control Board in August 1967. Mourners came forward to support a bill introduced by Committee Chairman Edwin E. Willis and others which would have the board determine who the Communists are and then have the attorney general enter their names in a public register. This would relieve Communists of the duty of incriminating themselves and, more to the point, give the vestigial S.A.C.B. something to do. (Shortly before these hearings, President Johnson demonstrated his opinion of the S.A.C.B. by appointing to it, as a $26,000-a-year wedding gift, the new husband of a former White House secretary.) In December 1967 a makeshift bill of this sort found its way through the ninetieth Congress, but its fate in the courts remains problematical.

The Internal Security Act remains to this day the outstanding legislative accomplishment of Richard Nixon, Karl Mundt, and the House Committee on Un-American Activities. Deformed, unfinished, sent before its time into this breathing world scarce half made up, its cruel fate, unlike that of King Richard, was to survive. Dragged along through the courts into a time when the internal Communist menace can barely be taken seriously even by Congressmen, its main accomplishment has been to confirm the solid virtues of judicial delay. This law designed to expose Communists has exposed itself and its makers, slight men who built careers upon the distracted times.

In June 1949, two days after the Committee had taken its pleasure of Frank Oppenheimer, Harry Truman held a lengthy press conference in which he suggested that the spy hunts and loyalty oaths then becoming popular were symptoms of the sort of hysteria that had come upon the nation after World War I, and that they would in time subside. But Truman was not destined to look upon that happy hour from the White House. In the early nineteen-fifties the nation's puzzlement and anxiety over the peculiar turns of the postwar world would find channels of expression in suspicion and vengeance. Soon Truman's own Secretary of the Navy would be plumping for preventive war. Senator McCarthy gave instruction by example on how the frustrations aroused by tension in Berlin, war in Korea, and a great Communist victory in China might be relieved if the guilt were only laid on Professor Owen Lattimore and pinkoes in the State Department. The arrest and trial of the Rosenbergs gave substance to the general unease and afforded the satisfaction of having flesh-and-blood people to punish for the disturbing realization that our enemies too possessed an atom bomb.

The Un-American Activities Committee would be nudged into the shadows as Senator McCarthy bestrode the land, but it contributed during this period to the public cultivation of a taste for quick, easy vengeance. Its repeated exhumation and glamorization of rather pallid espionage cases, its insistence on ever harsher laws, its continuing assaults on individuals—these showed the way. In December 1950, the Senate, envious of this pioneering role, created the Internal Security Subcommittee of the Senate Judiciary Committee, which, guided by Senators McCarran, Eastland, and Ferguson, would keep things churning during 1951 and 1952 with an investigation designed to bill the State Department and the Institute of Pacific Relations with the loss of China.

As long as the Truman Administration held office, a liberal White House facing a conservative Congress, the politics of Communist-hounding had irresistible allure. When the first Hiss jury was dismissed, Nixon and Velde immediately charged the judge with bias and threatened to call before the Committee the witnesses he had barred at the trial. In one of the more amusing public utterances of a career that has not been marked by wit, young Mr. Nixon said: "A handful of Administration apologists, who find themselves unable to defend Judge Kaufman's conduct in the Hiss case on the facts, are attempting to turn the case into a political issue which it is not."

The Congressional elections of 1950 went badly for Truman and very well for the Un-American Activities Committee. In the California senatorial race, Richard Nixon, campaigning almost entirely on the Communist issue and with more vigor than scruples, defeated Helen Gahagan Douglas, who had been one of the Committee's most persistent critics in the House. The *most* persistent critic, Vito Marcantonio, was beaten by an alliance of Democrats and Republicans in the East Harlem district which he had represented for eight terms. The Democrats lost twenty-eight seats in the House and five in the Senate, including that of the Majority Leader Scott Lucas. They retained a narrow numerical lead in both houses, but for practical purposes a coalition of conservatives would control the eighty-second Congress. The lesson that the victors took from the election was expressed by Republican National Chairman Leonard Hall, who attributed his party's gains to "resentment against the Administration's coddling of Communists at home and appeasement of Russia and Communist China abroad." This partisan sermon would be preached and acted upon most diligently until, in 1954, the trap that had been set for White House Democrats was found to be a hazard to White House Republicans as well.

10

★ ★ ★ ★ ★

1951-1952: Many Are Called

With Marcantonio gone, the only chiding that the Committee had to endure as it received $200,000 in the eighty-second Congress came from well-wishers. "Many people believe that there was a little slowdown in the Committee last year," noted the Republican Minority Leader Joe Martin, and Rankin did one of his turns: "While our boys are being killed or freezing to death in Korea, these Reds ought not to be permitted to undermine their country." Representative Walter found himself in the unusual position of defending the Committee against Representative Brown of Ohio for not publishing the testimony of an F.B.I. informer who had turned out to be an ex-convict and a mental case as well as a liar. It was Clare Hoffman of Michigan who brought his colleagues back to solid ground. "I do not know what the discussion is all about," he remarked, "but from past experience, I realize the Committee is going to get all the money it asks for and when it asks for it." The demands for increased activity would not go unheard. The message of the off-year election, the spurrings of Republican members[1] who knew themselves to be in the ascendance, the exhilarating examples of loyalty investigations in the Senate and around the country, the national suspicions, fears and cravings to strike back raised to a new pitch by the war in

---

[1] Joining Velde and Kearney were Donald L. Jackson of California, who replaced Senator Richard Nixon, and Charles E. Potter of Michigan, a severely disabled veteran himself soon destined for the Senate. Three Democrats—Wood, Walter, and Moulder—remained and their company was filled out by Clyde Doyle of California and James B. Frazier, Jr., of Tennessee.

Korea—these elements taken together would produce a most active two years. In 1951 and 1952 the Committee would hold more than a hundred days of public hearings at which more than three hundred persons would testify.

Again Hollywood called. Nowhere could the Committee find targets who were so celebrated and so vulnerable; publicity had created them, publicity could, and in a number of cases would, destroy them. In February Jackson and Potter gave out that they were dissatisfied with the "implied clearance" that had been issued to Edward G. Robinson after his voluntary appearance and soon the press was carrying the names of the well-known actors and lesser known, yet glamour-tinged writers and directors who had been subpoenaed. The lengthy list was made up of one-time C.P. members who had been scheduled for questioning before the abrupt cessation of the 1947 hearings, of Party-cause contributors whose names had been contributed by Paul Crouch and of others who were mentioned after the curtain went up.

One group of actors and writers, heirs to the spirit, the politics, and the attorneys of the Hollywood Ten, took the Fifth Amendment on the grounds that they would run the danger of self-incrimination if they answered any questions regarding their association with any organizations or persons who had been linked with subversive intentions. Had they been called in 1947, they would doubtless have taken the First Amendment and ended up in jail. Now there was no question of jail. The Committee was being roundly chastized for its wholesale contempt citations, and although Velde would have liked to go on with this losing game, the Democrats did no more now than dispute in an academic way a particular interpretation of the self-incrimination clause and point out to a witness the unfortunate impression he was leaving. As Wood put it to one man, "If you say [the question of whether you are a member of the Communist Party] would incriminate you, it leaves one conclusion in my mind and in the mind of every other fair-minded person within sound of your voice. Now, if in fact you are not a member of it, then your statement that it would tend to incriminate you isn't a true statement." The chairman raised this

argument repeatedly, to no avail, and his colleagues were sometimes moved to more forceful language. Moulder, far from the
most zealous inquisitor, told a writers' agent who had been one
of the prime movers within the Communist clique, ". . . your
refusal to testify so consistently leaves a strong impression that
you are still an ardent follower of the Communist Party and its
purpose." Moulder had no legal right to this impression, but
in the instance common sense could admit no other. Despite
frequent displays of skepticism, the Committee carried out its
interrogations without the emotion that had sputtered around
J. Parnell Thomas. Jackson, Potter, and Velde tended to be
argumentative and Doyle was long-winded, but Wood, bol-
stered by Walter, managed most of the time to keep things in
a reasonably low key; the resistant witnesses were by and large
not overly provocative.

At the other end of the witness range were those—notably
the writers Richard Collins and Martin Berkeley and the actor
Sterling Hayden—who had left the Party and now testified
fully and willingly about their former activities and associates.
Names were the food of the second Hollywood investigation—
not quite the delectable names of 1947 like Gary Cooper and
the mother of Ginger Rogers—but many more of them, writers,
directors, character actors, and here and there a star. The
hunger for names was a practical matter; if counsel Tavenner
had not been able to press witnesses for names and more names,
his interrogation would have amounted to very little. Despite
an occasional outburst by Velde about the Communist propaganda that was slithering through the movies, this proved to
be as profitless a line in 1951 as in 1947 and, deprived of the
target of the screen itself, the investigators naturally took aim
at individuals. On hand to whet the inquisitorial appetite was
Representative Jackson who was given to observations like
". . . it seems to me that the time has come to be an American
or not an American." When the writer-producer Carl Foreman
expressed a reluctance to name-drop, Jackson delivered a talk
about the casualties in Korea and concluded, ". . . the ultimate
test of the credibility of a witness before the Committee, as
far as I am concerned, is the extent to which he is willing to

cooperate with the Committee in giving full details as to not only the place of activities, but also the names of those who participated with him in the activities of the Communist Party . . ."

The heads of the motion picture industry took the Congressmen's concentration on names rather than on films as a sign of grace, and bowed joyfully to it. Their behavior in 1951 made 1947 seem an age of heroes. Having been assured that the Committee did not intend this time round to impose on the industry's higher movers, the Association of Motion Picture Producers publicly disassociated themselves from the witnesses, promised to invoke the 1947 Waldorf "interdict" against employees who took the Fifth Amendment, hailed the Committee for its endeavors, and spurred it on to root out Communists in government, in schools, on newspapers, in radio and television and in defense plants—anywhere, in fact, particularly if it wasn't Hollywood.

The main support that the first, hard-line takers of the Fifth Amendment received was from the Hollywood branch of the Council of the Arts, Sciences and Professions, a tainted relic of the Progressive Party. The unions washed their hands and turned away. As the Screen Actors Guild, Ronald Reagan presiding, informed Gale Sondergaard, wife of the Hollywood Ten's Herbert Biberman, on the day she took the Fifth, the Guild would fight against any secret blacklist, but "On the other hand, if any actor by his own actions outside of union activities has so offended public opinion that he has made himself unsaleable at the box office, the Guild cannot and would not want to force any employers to hire him." Not long after, Actors Equity made it clear that politically undesirable members would have to look elsewhere for solace: "This Council believes that all participants in the international Communist Party conspiracy against our nation should be exposed for what they are—enemies of our country and our form of government."

Hollywood was in a shaky position in the early nineteen-fifties. The moguls had felt the impact of television but had not yet regrouped their forces and accommodated themselves to the new prince of entertainment. Neighborhood movie theaters were shutting down by the dozens, and the government had recently forced the studios to divest themselves of theater chains in deference to the anti-trust laws. Under such blows of circumstance, the frail spirits of moviedom could hardly be expected to rise to the defense of Communists. The producers, the guilds, the craft unions formed themselves into the Motion Picture Industry Council, under the guidance of the anti-Communist A. F. of L. leader Roy N. Brewer, whose solitary purpose was to give the Un-American Activities Committee a franchise to investigate to its heart's content. In a statement to the Committee which was distributed by newsreel to the country's 18,000 movie houses, the Council declared:

> This country is engaged in a war with Communism. Eighty-seven thousand American casualties leave little room for witnesses to stand on the First and Fifth Amendments; and for those who do we have no sympathy . . . In time of crisis, we believe that the demands of American patriotism make necessary that witnesses respond to the call of their country, as represented by your Committee, and give you all the information necessary to the success of your objective.

The Hollywood Ten had all been members of the Communist Party. Now the Committee moved in on ex-Communists and on fellow travelers, and these found themselves in a difficult position. If they took the Fifth Amendment, their Hollywood careers would, for the foreseeable future, be ended. But to testify about their friends was for some a repugnant as well as an uncertain means of salvation. The first witness to struggle with the dilemma was Larry Parks, a young actor whose major film accomplishment had been his imitation of Al Jolson's mannerisms as he mouthed the words to *Mammy* in *The Jolson Story*. In his appearance, on the day that Alger Hiss went to jail, Parks became the first Hollywood personality to admit to having been a Communist; he had belonged to a small cell during the war. But he pleaded with the Committee not to make him name names. In his case, as in others to follow, Wood and Walter showed an inclination to defer to the witness' obvious sincerity. Why, Walter asked the unmoved Tavenner, was it essential to force Parks to give names "when we already know them"? The Committee never made up its collective mind on this subject; Parks was let off on condition that he testify fully in executive session. This he did, and the next day Velde, carried away with gratitude, extolled him on the floor of the House for being not only "a loyal and true American" but "a great actor." Encomiums notwithstanding, Parks was left with his career in limbo, the film he was scheduled to do for Columbia studios having been canceled when he received his subpoena.

Larry Parks's experience was not reassuring to the witnesses who followed. Whatever Chairman Wood's inclinations, he was in no political position to make deals with former Communists as to what they might testify about and what they could keep back; at the first hint of such leniency, Jackson and Velde would have gone to the nation with cries of Communist-coddling. Witnesses who belonged neither among the hard-core resisters ("If I have to choose between crawling in the mud with Larry Parks or going to jail like my courageous friends of the Hollywood Ten," announced the writer Paul Jarrico, "I shall certainly choose the latter") nor among the informers (screenwriter Martin Berkeley gave the Committee a gross of names) did not have many paths open to them. One was that taken by the director Edward Dmytryk, lately of the Hollywood Ten, who had been making $2,500 a week before the 1947 investigation and had not been employed since his release from prison. Dmytryk had been a C.P. member for only a few months during the U.S.-Soviet wartime alliance and, with his friend Adrian Scott, had left the Party around the time of the humbling of Albert Maltz. When Scott and Dmytryk were called before the Committee in 1947, their attorney, Bartley Crum, advised them to testify, but he had been beaten back by the hard-nose faction led by Lawson, who wanted a united front and a rousing issue. Sympathy for deserving causes such as the condition of the Negro rather than political discernment had brought Dmytryk into the ambiance of the Party. He was exploited more painfully than most fringe members, at last finding himself jailed and blacklisted for a faith that was barely his. In his 1951 appearance he gave only a few names of persons he had known as Communists, all of whom were known to the Committee too, but having gone through the forms, he was left to resume his career.

A year later this incident was repeated. Now it was Elia Kazan, famed director of stage and screen, who changed his mind. In executive session Kazan admitted to having been a Party member for less than two years in the nineteen-thirties when he was connected with the Group Theatre in New York, but refused to talk about his fellow members. Some weeks later, having experienced a dramatic change of heart, he informed the Committee: "I have come to the conclusion that I did wrong to withhold these names before, because secrecy serves the Communists and is exactly what they want. The American people need the facts and all the facts about all aspects of Communism in order to deal with it wisely and effectively. It is my obligation as a citizen to tell everything that I know." He did not, in fact, know a great deal; he produced a handful of stale names such as those of Clifford Odets, who was long out of the Party, Morris Carnovsky, who had already taken the Fifth Amendment, and J. Edward Bromberg, who had died some months earlier, soon after his forced appearance before the Committee. The new Kazan also published an advertisement which told of his being inveigled into the Party during the depression, emphasized his hatred of Communists and urged all liberals to "speak out." Kazan's rhetoric outstripped the substance of his part, and some critics—particularly those on the left who could credit only uncooperative witnesses with principles—connected his self-imposed mission with the requirements of his career, an idea that may have been suggested by the conclusion of his public statement: "The main pictures I have made and the plays I have chosen to direct represent my convictions. I expect to continue to make the same kind of pictures and to direct the same kind of plays." Had he not testified, his expectations as regards pictures would surely have been disappointed.

The Committee had its most fun with big-name personalities who had never been Party members but had given of their money and their fame over the years to many causes sponsored by Communists. They were peculiarly vulnerable; they could not resist the Committee without ruining their careers but they could not cooperate without making themselves out to have been perfect fools. The most famous of them chose the latter course. Like José Ferrer, who in order to win an Academy Award for his portrayal of Cyrano de Bergerac despite opposition from the Motion Picture Alliance for the Preservation of American Ideals, had had to take out paid advertisements assuring Hollywood that he was no Communist. Ferrer, whose attorney for his appearance was Abe Fortas, tried to oblige the Committee in every way. He asked that Congress or the Justice Department set up a warning service to keep people like him out of trouble and assured the members that notwithstanding any petitions he may have lent his name to in the past, he was now opposed to the Committee's abolition. "When did you change your mind on that score?" asked Representative Kearney. "Well," Ferrer replied, "today, among other things." But even this did not save him from the reprimand of Velde for not voting in national elections.

John Garfield, too, did his best to make himself appear a simpleton, marvelously naïve about politics, who had helped support a variety of Communist fronts despite his firm hatred of Communism. Yet his performance was not quite silly enough to allay all suspicions. Tavenner wondered about him siding with China in its war against Japan, and when Garfield mentioned that he had once been given an unfavorable review by the *Daily Worker*, Velde, the former F.B.I. agent, quickly asked where he had gotten hold of a copy of that newspaper. Edward G. Robinson, whose estimable career had ground to a near halt since his credit in *Red Channels*, came once again before the Committee humble past the point of embarrassment: ". . . I feel that this is the only tribunal where an American citizen can come and ask for relief from smears, false accusations and innuendoes." He now realized that he had been imposed on by the Communists, and he was glad the Committee had exposed them and he wanted nothing more than for Representative Jackson to say publicly that he (Jackson) believed that he (Robinson) was not a member of the Communist Party.

It was difficult for persons whose professional lives were at stake to come out from their Committee encounters with much style. Among the witnesses who granted that they had been Communists but were so no longer and would be willing to discuss their own adventures without, however, answering questions about anybody else, the most eloquent statement came from Lillian Hellman. In a letter preceding her appearance, she wrote that she had been warned by her attorney, Joseph Rauh, that if she answered questions about herself she would have to answer questions about others or risk being held in contempt. She offered to waive the Fifth Amendment if the Committee would refrain from asking her about other people:

> I am not willing, now or in the future, to bring bad trouble to people who, in my past associations with them, were completely innocent of any talk or any action that was disloyal or subversive. I do not like subversion or disloyalty in any form and if I had ever seen any I would have considered it my duty to have reported it to the proper authorities. But to hurt innocent people whom I knew many years ago in order to save myself is, to me, inhuman and indecent and dishonorable. I cannot and will not cut my conscience to fit this year's fashions, even though I long ago came to the conclusion that I was not a political person and could have no comfortable place in any political group.

Chairman Wood had no choice but to reply that "the Committee cannot permit witnesses to set forth the terms under which they will testify." Had Miss Hellman and others who adopted her position—such as the talented writer, director and former Communist Robert Rossen—taken their chances instead of taking the Fifth, they might have been agreeably surprised. Despite the insistence of Jackson and Velde on names, Walter, as acting chairman, had on occasion allowed an earnest witness to speak of his past without repeating yet once again for Counsel Tavenner names which the Committee had in its possession many times over. With the contempt citations of 1949–1950 being shot down by the courts, Wood and Walter were not eager to trouble the Congress again so soon, and although they were not at all consistent about it, they more than once expressed their doubts as to the value of pressing a witness for redundant information.

It seemed for a time that the issue might come to a head in the case of a prominent Hollywood writer and producer named Sidney Buchman, who admitted that he had been in the Communist Party from 1938 to 1945, but refused to answer questions about persons who "never, to my knowledge, planned or committed or suggested an illegal act." Buchman did not take the Fifth, and at Tavenner's urging, Walter directed him to answer the questions. He still declined, his foresighted attorney taking pains to point out to Walter that a quorum of the Committee was not present, as Jackson had left the hearing room. Buchman was again subpoenaed, but now instead of appearing, he sought delays on suspect grounds of ill health while he brought a fruitless action in district court to test the validity of the subpoena. Buchman was cited for contempt —for refusing to obey a summons of the Committee. In contempt he indubitably was, and the House approved the citation by a vote of 316-0. He was found guilty and given a one-year suspended sentence and a fine of $150. The Committee had gotten its man, but the really interesting question, on the naming of names, remained unsettled.

Some of the testimony in the 1951–52 motion picture hearings was enlightening as regards the sociology of Hollywood. The Communist Party used its friends among the actors and writers mainly as big names for and big contributors to its innumerable causes. (The actors and writers, for their part, seemed to be attracted to the Party mainly out of a desire to *do* something—although one of them, an actor from New York noted for his tough-guy roles, recalled that he had been lured into a Marxist study group with the promise, "Get to know this stuff, and you will make out more with the dames.") A writer named George Beck told of being at a party for the *New Masses* with his agent, an important figure among the Hollywood Communists. When the time came round for fund raising the agent said, "Beck offers fifty. Is anybody going to match it?" It was matched whereupon the agent, without consulting the writer, called out, "Now Beck tops that with a hundred." And when that sum was met, he yelled, "Beck offers one hundred and fifty." Beck concluded the tale: "That is the contribution I made to the *New Masses*." Another client charged that after he left the Party, the same agent sabotaged his career by turning down assignments for him.

Budd Schulberg, who had belonged to the Party in the late thirties, provided a good case history of the clumsiness of commissars in dealing with independently inclined writers. When, while still a Party member, Schulberg was working on *What Makes Sammy Run?* John Howard Lawson insisted on seeing the manuscript. The young man refused to show it and was passed upward to the C.P.'s cultural chieftain V. J. Jerome[2] who harangued him about his incorrect attitude. When the book was published in the spring of 1941, a *Daily Worker* critic, insufficiently briefed by his superiors, wrote ". . . I've a feeling that all critics, no matter their carping standards, will have to admit they've found the Hollywood novel in *What Makes Sammy Run?*" Two and a half weeks later the critic, better instructed now, took back everything: "The first error I made was in calling the book the Hollywood novel."

The friendly witnesses were nearly unanimous regarding the inability of the Communists to influence the course of American films. The co-authors of *Song of Russia*,[3] that tribute to Soviet heroism, good works, and clean living, had been compelled to remove from their script words like "community" and to cloud the fact that much of the action took place on a collective farm. Nor were they permitted to have the Russian

---

[2] Jerome was the perfect Stalinist critic. When Hollywood finally got around to producing films about Negroes, such as *Home of the Brave, Pinky, Lost Boundaries,* and *Intruder in the Dust,* Jerome dismissed them not because of any aesthetic deficiencies but because they were designed "to strengthen the basic strategy of the white ruling class which seeks to conceal the imperialist source of Negro oppression and to blunt any kind of struggle against capitalism and war."

[3] The collaborators on this film, Richard Collins and Paul Jarrico, had been among the most active of Hollywood's Communists. In 1951 they broke up when Collins testified fully before the Committee and Jarrico took the Fifth Amendment. It was but one of many friendships that were shattered in the course of these hearings.

girl teach the American musician—born in Iowa—how to drive a tractor. An illuminating anecdote on the Communists' illusions regarding their influence on the minds of men had to do with the character actor who rushed into a friend's house one day yelling, "By golly, I got away with it!" What had he gotten away with? "Well, I was shooting this picture, and I had to wait for the elevator, so I pressed the button and there is a pause and the director said, 'Whistle something and fill in.' So I whistled four bars of *The Internationale!*" With such evidence, only the F.B.I.-trained Velde could continue to suspect that the Party had been cunningly sneaking propaganda into the movies. In its annual report for 1952 the Committee, while commending itself for blocking off Hollywood as a source of C.P. funds, backed away from its earlier charges that the movies had been corrupted, stating only: "Had these Communist efforts gone unexposed, it is almost inevitable that the content of motion pictures would have been influenced and slanted and become a medium for Communist propaganda." The investigation that had been billed as the cure for an epidemic now turned out to be an exercise in prophylaxis.

The 1951–52 assault on Hollywood quickly took its place among the most successful engagements in the history of the Committee. The idea that it was interested in persecuting anyone, declared Doyle early in the proceedings, was "damnably false," but there was nothing much else for it to be interested in. No espionage, no promise of legislation, no exposure of propaganda, and not much information except in the way of marginal sociology. It was a punitive expedition pure and simple, a purging of the undesirables. "If we could eliminate from the entertainment world people who decline to answer if they are members of the Communist Party, it would make me very happy," said Chairman Wood, and no spokesman from the cowering film industry—executive, guild leader, or union official—could bring himself to suggest that this was an odd undertaking for a committee of Congress. When in its annual report for 1951 the Committee criticized the studios for not getting rid of their Communists fast enough, the Motion Picture Industry Council's defense was that Hollywood had pioneered in firing Communists as far back as 1947 and was restrained now only by court rulings that unpopular political opinions were not sufficient grounds for breaking contracts. A few weeks later the studio executives and Eric Johnston made peace with the American Legion by agreeing to investigate more than two hundred employees listed in the Legion's bad books. The accused individuals were asked to refute, in writing, allegations concerning their loyalty. Other studios, meanwhile, were hiring their own "investigators," whose main job was to keep right-wing pressure groups pacified.

Bright names went, some temporarily, some forever, into eclipse; old friendships were demolished; men who had left the Communists in disgust learned that democracy can produce despotisms too. If the hearings revealed something about Communism in Hollywood, they revealed more about Hollywood itself, a soft place where giving in and selling out were so much a part of things that any effort to stand fast against the odds of the early nineteen-fifties was unthinkable. "The air has been cleared," said a studio executive in the fall of 1951, like a householder assuring the burglars that they have gotten everything of value and ought to try next door now. But it would be years before producers dared openly to defy the blacklist, before Hollywood's air would begin to be cleared of the eructations of this time.

The times, the propitious times, determined the extent and direction of the Committee's enterprise through the eighty-second Congress. So propitious were the times that the Committee's oldest, most reliable acreage, the loyalty of government officials, had attracted the attentions of others. Originally staked out by Martin Dies himself, it had now fallen to Senator McCarthy, making a name for himself with his onslaughts on the State Department, and by Senator Pat McCarran of Nevada, whose Subcommittee on Internal Security was engaged in reasonably informative, seemingly endless hearings designed to show how a group of Communist sympathizers in policy positions had betrayed Chiang Kai-shek. Succumbing to the building pressures, in April 1951 the President stiffened the test of loyalty for federal employees. Under his first executive order, a man could be fired if "reasonable grounds existed for belief that the person involved is disloyal to the government of the United States." Now all that was required was "reasonable doubt as to the loyalty of the person involved." Hundreds of cases were reopened.

Through the insistence of Velde, the Committee called into public hearing Oliver Edmund Clubb, a suspended State Department official soon to resign under the cloud of having sold out China to Owen Lattimore and the Institute of Pacific Relations. Clubb, a China specialist, had been named by Whittaker Chambers as having paid a visit to the offices of the *New Masses* in 1932. He had indeed done so, on a brief trip to New York, carrying a letter of introduction from a left-wing American journalist in China named Agnes Smedley. He described Chambers in his diary as "a shifty-eyed unkempt creature . . ." The Committee could not believe that a young Foreign Service officer could be interested, in 1932, in meeting and talking to intellectuals on the far left without some conspiratorial intent. Upon learning that Clubb had studied the Chinese revolutionaries in the early thirties, counsel Tavenner, an interrogator not ordinarily given to archness, asked, "As a result of your definitive study, did you arrive at the conclusion Chinese Communists were all agrarians?" The name of the deceased Miss Smedley came up again in the testimony of Major General Charles Willoughby, who had served as General MacArthur's intelligence chief. In his rambling testimony, Willoughby connected her with a Russian spy ring in the Far East before and during World War II. The general, who had already been heard by Senator McCarran's group and was being lionized by Washington votaries of General MacArthur (recently and abruptly relieved of his duties by the President), entertained the Congressmen with a statement on the "sinister background of world conspiracy," which took the Committee somewhat afield from its customary areas of concern.

Though the fall of China was a most promising subject now

that American troops were confronting Chinese troops in Korea, the Committee could not compete with McCarran and McCarthy, and except for a chance excursion such as those with General Willoughby and the unlucky Clubb, it tended domestic soil. As the Hollywood hearings demonstrated, even those who a few years before had protested against Communist-hunting expeditions now granted that the pursuit of Communists, wherever they might be found, was a natural right of Congress. In fact, it seemed to be a right of whoever cared to pursue them. From around the country came inspiriting reports of Communists being exposed, suspended, fired, evicted, tried, deported, boycotted, blacklisted, and physically set upon. The public temper invited, and the Committee joined in the sport.

When in June 1951, the Supreme Court affirmed the conviction of eleven Communist Party leaders on charges of advocating the overthrow of the government, Walter expressed the thought that the Committee might be "decisioned" out of a job. But in fact the decision had the opposite effect; it strengthened the use of the Fifth Amendment and, in a perverse way, made the Committee's work easier than ever. It did not really matter in most of the hearings of these years that most witnesses took the Fifth, for no information was being sought. The typical hearing opened with an F.B.I. informer or disaffected Communist who delivered himself of several score names of Party members he had encountered. The overriding purpose of the hearing was to spread on the public record names already known to official agencies. When those named appeared and took the Fifth Amendment, it was as satisfactory as a confession.

Although several witnesses comported themselves indecorously, the Wood Committee brought only two more contempt citations—which were approved by the Congress without a negative vote. One was against a Detroit Negro, Arthur McPhaul, who refused to give over the records of the Civil Rights Congress; the other against one Saul Grossman for failing to produce the records of the Michigan Committee for the Protection of the Foreign Born, as well as for refusing to answer questions relating to the records. In these citations, the Committee relied for precedent on the recently decided case of Rogers *v.* U.S. where the Supreme Court had ruled that since Mrs. Rogers had voluntarily testified that she was treasurer of the Denver Communist Party, she would not be further incriminated by handing over the Party's records. Both men were found guilty—Grossman on the single count of refusing to answer the question of whether or not he would produce the records and not on the production of the records themselves. On appeal, Grossman's conviction was reversed because he had not been specifically directed to answer the question for which he was held in contempt. (Called before the Committee again in 1956, he surrendered the records under protest.) McPhaul's conviction—he was sentenced to nine months and a fine of $500—was upheld by a five-to-four decision of the Supreme Court. The dissenters—Black, Douglas, Brennan, and Warren—maintained that although Congress did have the right to obtain the records in question, the Committee had not proved that McPhaul in fact had custody of them; hence, by holding him in contempt without demanding such proof, the courts had denied him the presumption of innocence to which every accused is entitled. But the rule of the majority was that the Fifth Amendment did not protect a witness from the requirement that he supply records kept in a representative rather than a personal capacity even though their production might tend to incriminate him. By 1960, when this case was decided, a five-to-four split was a common outcome in Supreme Court cases involving the Un-American Activities Committee.

Like super-heroes of the comic strips, members of the Committee swooped down on Los Angeles, Boston, Philadelphia, Chicago, and Detroit, confounded resident malefactors and flew off again. The ostensible purpose of most of the 1951–52 hearings was to look into Communist activities in important defense industries, a purpose general enough to take the Committee wherever it wanted to go and spacious enough to encompass anybody who lived in a city that could boast of some factories. The Los Angeles hearings, however, did not have even this excuse. In the course of the Hollywood investigation, mention had been made of Communist cells of doctors and lawyers in California. Former Communists were called and gave modest amounts of information along with a sizable list of names, most of which were connected with two organizations that had been in the fore of opposition to the Committee for years—the National Lawyers Guild and the Council of the Arts, Sciences and Professions. Both bore all the earmarks of Communist influence.

More than two dozen of the named lawyers came before the Committee on September 30 and October 1, 1952, and most of them behaved according to form. They were exceedingly talkative, highly argumentative, abusive of the witnesses who had named them, and disdainful of the Committee; formally counseled by Robert Kenny and his associates, they took the Fifth Amendment and other amendments with patriotic embellishments. Among those summoned were Ben Margolis and Charles J. Katz, advisors to the Hollywood Ten, who had developed the strategy of the First Amendment. They had been mentioned repeatedly in the testimony of former Communists as the Party's prime movers in Los Angeles, recruiters of bright young lawyers and proselytizers of not-so-bright actors. Margolis made a particularly trying witness. Hardly had he taken his place than he was delivering speeches—"I was born in New York City on April 23, 1910, and almost from the first day that I can remember I have hated tyranny and that is why I feel the way I do about this Committee . . . I have nothing but contempt for this Committee, and I will show it as long as I am up here." He was faithful to his word, unable even to resist arguing with Representative Jackson over which of them was more patriotic. Katz, an older man, was more subdued. He cautioned the Committee not to draw unwonted inferences from witnesses taking the Fifth Amendment "at a time such as this, in circumstances such as these"; he reminded the Congressmen that "it is the law that when one invokes the privilege of the Fifth Amendment, he admits no guilt, that the privilege exists for the innocent . . ." In coming months and years, the generous helpings of the Fifth Amendment being taken at Congressional

hearings would come in for a great deal of analysis, cooler and
more sophisticated analysis than that offered either by the
witnesses who pleaded self-incrimination or by the Congressmen who received the plea with ill grace.

The most serious charge raised against the Committee's
round-up of the Communist lawyers of Los Angeles was that
it constituted an effort to discourage attorneys from taking
on unpopular causes. Whether this was in fact in back of one
or more of the Congressmen's minds, the effect could hardly
be otherwise in a period when a public stand against the trial
of the C.P. leaders or against the operations of the Committee
was taken as evidence of Communist affinity. In a sense, the
lawyers who had striven with some success to turn every good
cause into a Communist cause were only getting their deserts
when their own cause, however good, came to seem tainted.
But such a set of hearings, when Communist lawyers were
being threatened with disbarment and non-Communist lawyers
were uneasy about taking on the defense of Party members,
could only add to that political prudence which sapped the
nation of its dissenting spirit in the early nineteen-fifties.

A few of the Committee's friendly witnesses became celebrities as a result of their appearances.[4] Twenty-nine-year-old
Mrs. Mary Markward, who had served the F.B.I. from within
the Communist Party of Washington, D.C., and Maryland for
six years, received long applause from spectators after she

---

[4] The Committee took brief looks into Communist activities among veterans,
peace groups, and farm organizations during this period, and in February 1952,
it introduced the nation to Harvey M. Matusow, a twenty-six-year-old former
C.P. member and professed authority on Communist youth groups, who put
more than a hundred names into the record, including the members of the
folk-singing group, The Weavers, who thereupon had their current engage-
ment cut short owing to public protest. Matusow told of five-year-olds being
taught such rhymes as:

> Jack Sprat could eat no fat.
> His wife could eat no lean.
> Because their Congress had done them in
> And picked their pockets clean.

After three busy years as friendly witness for the Senate Internal Security Subcommittee, the Permanent Investigating Subcommittee, the Subversive Activities
Control Board, and the Justice Department and a campaigner for the Republicans in 1952, Matusow repented of being an ex-Communist, became an ex-
ex-Communist, and zestfully took to exposing himself and those who had
egged him on. He wrote a book, *False Witness*, and went to jail for perjury.

read out a batch of names already known to the Justice Department. The more interesting part of her testimony had to do with the Party's difficulties in getting reliable workers, a situation that made it easy for her, given her special incentive, to advance rapidly to the post of district treasurer. Tavenner, as always, was content to settle for names, but some of the Congressmen could not resist troubling the rather simple young woman with weightier matters. "Am I to understand," asked Doyle, who hated to let a witness go without some thoughtful exchange, ". . . that the Communist Party of the United States was definitely backing the projection of Soviet Communism in the nations of Europe right after the war . . . ?" More than thirty persons named by Mrs. Markward—left-wing union officers, ladies involved in the synthetic peace movement which the Communists had put together to oppose the U.S. role in Korea, Progressive Party boosters—took the Fifth Amendment.

Boston was covered by Herbert Philbrick, an advertising man who had cast off his Communist disguise in 1949 as a surprise witness at the trial of the C.P. leaders in New York. He had served the F.B.I. for nine years (a career that would soon become the basis, in a way, of a TV series) and he was able to provide the Committee with some fifty names, the most prominent being that of Dirk Jung Struik, professor of mathematics at the Massachusetts Institute of Technology. Professor Struik's political sympathies were well known: he was executive director of the Massachusetts Council of American-Soviet Friendship, a member of the Progressive Party, and a lecturer at Communist schools. Off the stand he called Philbrick a liar and explained that though he was a Marxist he had never joined the Party. On the stand he courteously pleaded the Fifth Amendment to a hundred questions. A few weeks later Struik was indicted, under the Massachusetts Smith Act, for conspiring to overthrow the government of the United States and the Commonwealth of Massachusetts. The indictment was dismissed in 1956 when the Supreme Court handed down its ruling against state sedition laws; Struik was censured by the

M.I.T. faculty for his want of candor but was retained in his teaching post.

Many of the names delivered by Philbrick belonged to organizers for the Electrical Workers (U.E.), which had been thrown out of the C.I.O. and was now fighting to keep its members from deserting for James Carey's International Union of Electrical Workers (I.U.E.–C.I.O.). The U.E., which had recently affiliated with the comradely Farm Equipment Workers Union, was the main subject of the Committee's 1952 hearings in Chicago and Philadelphia too. In Chicago pickets singing *Solidarity Forever* rushed into the Federal Building and pounded so loudly on the door of the hearing room that they drowned out the testimony. U.E. leaders charged that the Committee had come to Chicago to break its 26,000-man strike against International Harvester, a charge hotly denied by Chairman Wood. But three important union negotiators were compelled to appear before the Committee. They asked to be excused because they were busy with the strike and excused they were—but not before they took the Fifth Amendment.

In these hearings, the Committee relied, not on F.B.I. informants, but on union men who had broken with the Party. They drew a convincing picture of the way in which a disciplined cadre of Communists could control a large union and turn it to parochial uses. Policies and candidates determined on beforehand at meetings of the cadre, sometimes supervised by a C.P. functionary who did not even belong to the union, became the union's policies and the union's officers. Party membership became a requirement for the ambitious organizer, and he had to be prepared to oppose the Marshall Plan in the name of his local's electricians if the ruling came down. The issue of whether to strike or not to strike was tied in with the world strategy of the U.S.S.R. The hearing also recalled, however, the remarkable part that rank-and-file Communists of the thirties had played in building America's labor movement, the firings, jailings, beatings they had endured in the union's cause. They were a tough bunch, but not nearly as tough as the manipulators in New York, and many of them found themselves trapped by their own early commitment. There was nothing particularly lovable about the men who took the Fifth Amendment, but it was saddening all the same to be shown how unsightly were the ashes from the fires of the thirties.

The most noteworthy of the Committee's field trips was the one it made to Detroit, that "arsenal of democracy," as Wood identified it, in February and March of 1952. Announcements of this journey were issued by Michigan's Representative Potter, who was looking toward a Senate seat that fall. With this in mind and impressed with the impact of television coverage, as lately demonstrated by Senator Kefauver's crime investigations, Speaker Rayburn barred TV cameras from all committee hearing rooms. The Republicans cried foul, but the order stood. The Detroit hearings focused on Local 600, the United Auto Workers' largest local, representing more than 50,000 Ford Workers. Despite the victory of the Reuther forces in the U.A.W., Local 600 had never been entirely cleansed of Communists, and witness after witness took the Fifth Amendment, several of them most truculently. Potter played a prominent part in the questioning; when a particularly antagonistic Negro organizer got onto the subject of the hanging and bombing of Negroes in the South, Potter came back with the number of American casualties in Korea.

In airing the Communist records of Local 600's organizers and officers, the Committee provided Walter Reuther with an opportunity for a housecleaning. After the hearings, the U.A.W. took over the local, citing as cause the "overwhelming evidence" of Communist manipulation. Under the provision of the union constitution barring Communists, several lesser officials long known to be C.P. members were ousted, and the non-Communist position within the union was strengthened. It was easy to make an argument for the desirability of removing from union leadership persons who had demonstrated their subservience to the Communist Party; their tendency to turn the union into an ideological instrument had been amply documented. But there were other repercussions of the Detroit hearings that were harder to justify. Witnesses were

fired from their jobs and hustled out of factories by fellow
employees; a violinist was suspended by the Detroit Federation
of Musicians; a student was expelled by Wayne University;
two men were ordered evicted from a Detroit public housing
project. Here, in this spontaneous collaboration of individuals
and organizations of all sorts, lay the Committee's future. It
could expose a man and leave his punishment to others. Those
few years that comprise the McCarthy era were marked by a
readiness to punish as well as by a propensity to accuse. The
Committee, which had no direct means of getting at witnesses
who took the Fifth, could now let them go, in confidence that
some at least would be made to suffer for their sins. The Reds
could not be hung, but with luck they might be fired by their
bosses, abused by their neighbors, and harassed by local
officials.

To a period steaming with suspicions, accusations, and investigations, the Committee contributed a report entitled *The
Shameful Years*—a review of Soviet espionage from 1919 on-
ward—which gained considerable popularity. Wood and his
colleagues asked Congress for a law that would provide capital
punishment or a life sentence for peacetime espionage. They
asked for the admission of wiretap evidence in espionage cases,
stricter passport requirements, and the revocation of military
commissions held by persons who took the Fifth Amendment.
They reached out repeatedly after newsworthy tidbits, which
yielded no broth but kept the pot boiling. When, at the end
of September, General Walter Bedell Smith, director of the
Central Intelligence Agency, remarked while testifying in a
$2 million libel suit brought by Senator McCarthy against
Senator Benton, that "I believe there are Communists in my
organization," he was hastily summoned by the Committee
to explain himself. It turned out that there wasn't anything to
explain; obviously if the general had known of any Communists in the C.I.A. he would have fired them. He had meant
merely that, like all officials in highly sensitive agencies, he had
to operate on the assumption that Communists had infiltrated
his staff. General Smith used his appearance to give a strong

commendation to Harry Truman for his support of the nation's
security arms.

Chairman Wood, having decided to retire from Congress,
was left with time on his hands during the fall of 1952, and
while most committees remained idle after the summer adjournment, he busied himself with investigations, none of which
was designed to benefit Adlai Stevenson's Presidential campaign. Stevenson was running against a powerful tide that
reached from coast to coast. On the day in October that the
Committee spent questioning doctors in Los Angeles, three
New York City professors were suspended for declining to say
whether they were Communists, and General Eisenhower,
campaigning in Wisconsin, called for the reelection of Senator
McCarthy in a speech from which a defense of General George
C. Marshall against McCarthy's slurs had been cut out. Richard
Nixon, who owed his nomination for the vice presidency at
the age of thirty-nine to the Hiss case, made loyalty the princi-
pal weapon of his campaign, going so far as to argue that
Stevenson was not fit to be President because he had submitted
a deposition on behalf of Alger Hiss in his first trial for perjury.

In later years, when his behavior in the campaigns of 1950
and 1952 would come to seem somewhat careless, Nixon would
appear before the nation a changed man, like the newly
crowned Henry V matured past the riots of youth, putting
Falstaff on notice, "Presume not that I am the thing I was."
In later years, too, this period to which McCarthy lent his
name would be remembered by some as a time of black repression, when the police state was upon us. That, of course, is
a trick of memory. Even during his few years of cruelly
used power, McCarthy was never free of attack. Richard
Rovere reminds us that on most college campuses it was safer
to be anti-McCarthy than pro-McCarthy. Yet many people
were hurt; many more were frightened; caution was in the
air. Liberals were stalled and on the defensive. Like the
whiskey in *The Iceman Cometh*, liberalism had lost its kick
and a kind of numbness had set in. The ideological certainties
of the thirties had been cut away; the Stalinists, who with all
their crudities and connivings had lent spirit to innumerable

good causes, were consigned to limbo. Political innovation in America had entered a deep freeze that would last out the decade.

The Committee's work in 1952 ended with the Eisenhower landslide. The Republicans won a narrow majority in the House and for the first time in its history (and, as of this writing, the last), the Committee would be run by Republicans during a Republican Administration. This situation created a tension between the Easterners in the White House and the Midwesterners in Congress, between Establishment etiquette and Populist passions that would explode in the Army-McCarthy hearings of 1954. As 1952 came to a close, however, Harold Velde, chairman designate of the Committee on Un-American Activities, liberated from the bonds imposed by Wood and Walter, saw only opportunities ahead.

11

★ ★ ★ ★ ★

1953-1954: The Velde Capers

HAROLD H. VELDE's main claim to election to Congress at the age of thirty-eight was that he had been an F.B.I. agent. "Get the Reds out of Washington and Washington out of the Red" was the slogan with which he captured the 1948 Republican primary. His credentials were appropriate to the season, and during his four terms in the House, Velde would find frequent occasion to recall them to his colleagues, to Committee witnesses, and to newspaper reporters. His record as a Congressman, as might have been foreseen, had more of an investigative than a legislative cast. Velde in no way resembled the gorgeous Everett McKinley Dirksen, whom he had replaced in the House. He had no stage presence at all, mellifluity was not one of his gifts, and his essays at lawmaking reached a high point with a bill that would have required the Librarian of Congress to list the books in the Library's collection that might be regarded as subversive. He also proposed instituting a loyalty oath as a requirement for participating in national elections. He voted with the Taft wing of his party—against foreign aid, for 90 per cent farm parity, for an end to rent control. In his opposition to public housing he was more Taft-wing than Taft himself.

For some observers chairman-presumptive Velde evoked the shade of Martin Dies, who had just been returned to Congress in the flesh with, he claimed, "about a hundred thousand names of persons engaged in subversive activities," and was more than agreeable to taking a place on the Committee he had sired.

Velde was agreeable, too, but the unforgiving Democratic leadership would have none of it. "I'm not especially wedded to this Committee," announced Representative Walter in a refreshing comment on a fellow Democrat, "but if it were necessary for no other reason than to keep from giving Dies a seat, I would remain a member. I don't think he has any constructive contribution to make to the Committee's work." Martin Dies did not get his seat.[1]

Under the chairmanship of the peaceable Wood, Velde and Jackson had acted as constant goads; they wanted more investigations and tougher investigations. Now the Committee was theirs; their Republican colleagues, with the sometime exception of Kearney, were of a like mind with them on most matters, a markedly conservative mind, and the Democrats, out of party loyalty and milder temperaments, took on a restraining role. They were not very effective. In the eighty-third Congress the Committee established a remarkable record of 178 days of taking testimony from more than 650 witnesses, most of whom answered questions with the Fifth Amendment.

The record was set with the help of subcommittees which Velde deployed through the country like a feudal monarch giving work to lesser lords. The spring weeks of 1954, when the Army-McCarthy hearings were occupying the capital's press corps and when Congressmen were beginning to look toward their constituencies with anticipation, proved an especially busy time. In Albany, a subcommittee led by Kearney, the upstate New Yorker, was exposing yet other officials of the United Electrical Workers as well as several state employees who resigned from their jobs rather than answer questions; a subcommittee led by the Californian Jackson was in San Diego exposing a mixed bag of Communists; a subcommittee in Detroit and environs led by Michigan's Kit Clardy was exposing, with the aid of an F.B.I. informant identified only as Witness X, college-educated "colonizers" from New York who had taken unskilled jobs in the auto industry—at the behest,

[1] The only change in the Democratic complement, which was reduced from five to four by the election, was the departure of Chairman Wood. To the three holdover Republicans were added Kit Clardy of Michigan and Gordon H. Scherer of Ohio.

one might reasonably infer, of C.P. headquarters; a subcommittee led by Velde of Illinois was exposing more left-wing union organizers in Chicago. There were also visits to Seattle where a woman, a Communist of some twenty years' standing who had been convicted and sent to the penitentiary for violation of the Smith Act, gave the names of hundreds of her former comrades from various walks of life; to San Francisco where I.L.W.U. officials were exposed; as well as to Philadelphia, Baltimore, and Dayton, Ohio, where, in September of the election year, Representative Scherer got his chance to be a subcommittee chairman in the vicinity of his constituency.[2]

The Hollywood and New York entertainment worlds were invaded yet again—with TV cameras in use now—as Velde, like a frugal housewife, squeezed out a last few names to fatten the industry blacklist. (By now the A. F. of L.'s American Federation of TV and Radio Artists had voted to expel or otherwise discipline any member who declined to answer questions about his Communist connections, past or present.) The main novelty in the Los Angeles hearings was that the undercover F.B.I. agent turned out to be a sixty-eight-year-old grandmother, who delivered herself of 120 names, mostly obscure. Another F.B.I. source reported that Communists were upset by radio soap operas because they didn't show woman's role in the revolutionary struggle, and Party theoreticians objected to stars lending their prestige to the capitalist system by reading commercials. In New York City, Artie Shaw wept with remorse over having been duped by the Communists; Lionel Stander whipped up a furious storm in the course of taking the Fifth Amendment; Jerome Robbins named a few Broadway names; and Robert Rossen repented of his 1951 refusal to speak, because he had decided that in the ongoing world crisis no one "can ever indulge himself in the luxury of individual morality" against the needs of national security. Rossen testified that he had been a Communist from 1937 to 1947 and had contributed about $40,000 to Party causes; he gave fifty-seven

[2] It was in these Ohio hearings that former Rep. Hugh DeLacy of Washington, a prominent opponent of the Committee during his years in Congress, took the Fifth Amendment.

names, most all of them well worn by now from Committee handling.

But to review all the campaigns of these two years is to court redundancy. They were neither more nor less justified than similar explorations under Wood—though they were run a shade, sometimes several shades, less pleasantly in accord with the chairman's inclinations. Clardy, a right-wing lawyer from Lansing, whom an excitable writer for *The Nation* dubbed a "junior McCarthy," took the honors for choler, with Scherer a hard breath behind. (During the Michigan visit, the two worked in tandem. Scherer charged a witness with perjury and, when the man tried to reply, Clardy shut him up.) The main purpose of the hearings—more often than not their only purpose —was to publicize the names of persons identified as having Communist affiliations and sympathies, past or present, and so submit them to the passions of the hour.[3] These years of the zealot gave a brutal twist to a precept of Epicurus, that least zealous of philosophers, who advised, "Let nothing be done in your life which will cause you fear if it becomes known to your neighbor."

What distinguished the Committee under the chairmanship of Velde was not so much the quantity of its investigations or their quality, as the direction they took. Never had the country experienced such an epidemic of investigations as it did in 1953 and 1954. With Senator Jenner directing the Internal Security Subcommittee and Senator McCarthy banging away at the State Department until the Voice of America cried uncle, then entering into his fatal battle with the army, investigations came to be the main business of a Congress that had no taste for innovative legislation—unless it was on the order of the Communist Control Act which was aimed at strengthening the security legislation of 1950 and applying it to "Communist-infiltrated organizations," but had the effect only of further muddying already muddy waters. The Administration, inclined

---

[3] Walter Reuther greeted the Committee with a sensible statement that urged witnesses to avoid taking the Fifth Amendment if possible, but emphasized that the United Auto Workers would resist the discharge or disciplining of any member on the sole ground that he had claimed the privilege against self-incrimination.

toward a generalized passivity on domestic affairs and having taken office with the promise of patching up Democratic security loopholes, could not actively discourage the new investigations, yet could not wholeheartedly encourage them either since no one could tell where they might lead. Four months after taking office, President Eisenhower mollified Congressmen by shifting the Truman test of suitability for federal employment from the question of loyalty to the broader one of security. Henceforth, the question would be "whether the employment and retention in employment of any civilian officer or employee . . . is clearly consistent with the interests of the national security." As 1953 began, there seemed to be no off-limits signs for the hunters of Communists, and the Velde Committee soon found itself entangled in two of the most sensitive areas of our national life—education and religion.

America's schools and colleges offered the investigators an inviting prospect on several counts. There were undoubtedly Communists, former and current, to be found there, men and women who had received their own schooling in the thirties and had imbibed the popular ideals of the period. Educated beyond the ability of the society to use or reward them, many entered the middle class at its bottom rungs, taking teaching jobs which offered low pay and uncertain status; they made up a classic body of disaffected intellectuals. Most had broken with Communism or drifted away years before, but some were still caught up in the dream. The Party offered them what the society withheld, a sense of mission and of consequence, and as long as that was true, nothing that had happened in Russia since their early commitment could shake their faith. They had paraded their beliefs in the thirties and forties, working for a multitude of Party-approved causes (most of which happened to be quite deserving in their own right), and now, in the fifties of the cold war, their livelihoods were at the mercy of whatever winds shook their local school boards or college administrations.

For mentalities like those of Velde, Jackson, Scherer, and Clardy, the groves of Academe were choked with the weeds of subversion. J. Edgar Hoover spoke for them when, in a talk on the spirit of free inquiry, he said, "Some professors have aided the Communist cause by tearing down respect for agencies of government, belittling tradition and moral custom and by creating doubts in the validity of the American way of life." Through its entire career, the Committee on Un-American Activities had had to put up with attacks from university professors, singly and in concert. Most of the scientists named in the Committee's investigation of wartime atomic espionage were holding down good posts at prominent universities when they were called to testify. It was intolerable to Velde to think that there should be a privileged sanctuary for the opponents of his Americanism, and for weeks before he assumed the chairmanship of the Committee he was promising to rout out Communists from the educational scene. The fact that Senator McCarran had set himself a similar task in the eighty-second Congress and that Senator Jenner intended to carry on the work in the eighty-third was no deterrent; it was the time of the investigator in the land and there were enough schools to go around.

Velde's announced intentions naturally aroused educators. In a talk to the annual convention of the American Association of School Administrators in February 1953, Mrs. Agnes Meyer, wife of the owner of the Washington *Post* and a diligent worker for better education, delivered an all-out denunciation of Jenner, McCarthy, and Velde, and in particular questioned the I.Q. of the last named. Velde responded as members of his Committee had responded to criticism for years, by associating Mrs. Meyer with "pinks and others following the Communist Party line" and by releasing her dossier, in which she was credited with writing a letter in 1947 to a pro-Russian magazine in praise of the Russians and being lauded for it by *Pravda*. This turned out to be a clerical error; the letter had in fact been written by a Mrs. Mayer, not Meyer, and she lived in Port Clements, B.C., not Washington, D.C. On having this pointed out to him, Velde fired a staff member whom he said was to blame.

This beginning did nothing to reassure educators about what

lay before them, and liberal journals made much of the incident. (Representative Franklin D. Roosevelt, Jr., went through the motions of offering a resolution to remove Velde from his chairmanship, whereupon the House yawned and by a vote of 315 to 2 gave the Committee $300,000.) But the question of whether members of the Communist Party had a place on any American faculty was one over which civil libertarians differed. Whereas Albert Einstein urged intellectuals not to testify, Norman Thomas, who bore the scars of attacks from both left and right, held simply that "The right of the Communist to teach should be denied because he has given away his freedom in the quest for truth." Thomas despised men like Jenner and Velde and was under no illusion regarding their intentions, but he defended their right to investigate Communists in positions of trust and sensitivity. In his view, teachers who had been Communists some time in their past deserved forgiveness—"But he who today persists in Communist allegiance is either too foolish or too disloyal to democratic ideals to be allowed to teach in our schools."

Many college administrators found themselves between two sets of pressures: one from faculty members who took the position that the only proper criteria for judging a teacher were his acts and intentions, not his ideology or associations; the other from trustees and state legislators who tended to be more concerned about the reputation of their institutions than the careers of an odd Communist or two. No working consensus was ever reached, but the administrators, while insisting on fair investigative procedures and extolling academic freedom, tended to side with the trustees. Whereas the American Association of University Professors adopted a resolution to the effect that membership in a legal organization was not in itself a disqualification for teaching and opposed the automatic dismissal of teachers who took the Fifth Amendment, the Association of American Universities resolved that present Communist Party membership "extinguishes the right to a university position." The latter group, which spoke for the heads of thirty-seven major institutions, maintained further that a teacher who took the

Fifth must bear the burden of proof of his fitness to continue teaching.

The conflict came to a head at Rutgers when two professors who had taken the Fifth Amendment before the Senate Internal Security Subcommittee were fired despite the backing of a faculty review committee. The president of the university, Webster Jones, argued that professional competence was irrelevant to this issue. He granted that the freedom of a witness to remain silent was his civil right, but emphasized that a university was a public trust, that "academic freedom entails the obligation to render an explanation as clearly and rationally as possible, whenever such an explanation is called for by duly constituted governmental bodies acting within the limits of their authority." He took as given the fact that C.P. membership was not compatible with freedom of inquiry. "It is no invasion of privacy but a necessary measure of protection of the freedom of all of us to seek to determine whether teachers and others in public positions of trust are committed to the discipline and program of the Communist Party."[4]

By this reasoning, the Communist teachers had no choice; they would be fired if they refused to speak and they would be fired if they spoke. Seen as conspirators, that was no more than they deserved, and to judge by the Party's own directives, one could only believe—as Norman Thomas and Sidney Hook believed—that Party members would hew to the Party line in whatever subject they happened to be teaching and so indoctrinate their students. But this belief involved a simplification both of what takes place in a college classroom and of what Party membership meant to the individual teachers. They made up a diverse bunch, intellectually and emotionally. There were few "conspirators" among them, and many good honest teachers. It was with this in mind that one group of educators, under Buell Gallagher, who had just been named head of the City College of New York, asked that the "kind and degree of involve-

---

[4] In 1956 Rutgers was one of six universities censured by the American Association of University Professors for, among other offenses, dismissing a faculty member who took the Fifth Amendment before a Congressional committee. The others were the University of California, Ohio State, Temple, Jefferson Medical College, and the University of Oklahoma.

ment" with the Communist Party be established before a man was dismissed.

Another notable dissent from the automatic dismissal rule came from a faculty group at Columbia University, led by Lionel Trilling. The Columbia professors criticized the school investigation as unnecessary because the number of teachers ever committed to Communism was negligible, and harmful because it was creating "an atmosphere of apprehension and distrust that is jeopardizing the cause of free inquiry and threatening the right to dissent." Regarding the Fifth Amendment, the Trilling group observed that its protection did not extend beyond the committee room and that its use entailed the drawing of inferences, bad or good, but that "it cannot be made a condition of membership in the teaching profession that a person surrender rights which are guaranteed by the law of the land." As for C.P. membership, the professors conceded that it "almost certainly implies a submission to an intellectual control which is entirely at variance with the principles of academic competence," yet concluded, with a bow to life instead of to logic (or to the president of their university, who took the opposite view), that "in the present state of affairs" wisdom suggested that there be no academic test of fitness other than an individual's demonstrated competence and personal integrity.[5]

For Chairman Velde the debate was academic. Turning about an article of faith frequently cited by civil libertarians, he said, "It's a lot better to wrongly accuse one person of being a Communist than to allow so many to get away with such Communist acts as those that have brought us to the brink of World War Three." The Administration, which was devoting 1953 to the placating of Senator McCarthy, looked on benevolently. As the House Committee's hearings approached, the recent president of Columbia University explained, in a manner

---

[5] In January 1967, a decade after the issue had gone the way of most issues, the Supreme Court came out on the side of the Trilling group. In voiding New York State's complex of loyalty laws for teachers, Justice Brennan, speaking for the five-man majority, declared invalid the provision that mere C.P. membership without "any showing of specific intent to further the unlawful aims of the Communist Party" is sufficient cause for dismissal.

that was becoming famous, that he would be the last one to curtail Congressional investigations but he was opposed to prejudging anyone's guilt, that he was all for academic integrity but "would have none of traitors." The Republican leadership, like a mother who doesn't mind what her children do as long as they don't maul one another while doing it, made a lazy effort to keep the Jenner group and the Velde group from colliding as they snatched at star witnesses. General Wilton B. Persons, the President's liaison with Congress, met with McCarthy, Jenner, Velde, and a man from the F.B.I. to work out some sort of combined program, and Velde explained that whereas Jenner would be searching for organized Communist activity and dealing with institutions, he would be concentrating on individual members of the Communist Party. This Velde saw as "coordination" rather than competition. As their investigations proceeded, however, all through 1953 and well into 1954, the main discernible differences were that the Jenner Committee was more efficiently run and got fuller newspaper coverage.[6]

Velde started off late in February with several witnesses of distinction who had belonged briefly to the Party during their days at Harvard in the thirties. Robert Gorham Davis, professor of English at Smith, Daniel Boorstin, associate professor of history at the University of Chicago, and Granville Hicks, who had made no secret of his sympathies either during his Party days or after he broke away as a result of the Hitler-Stalin pact, were all treated courteously. The most insinuating question put to them was why they had not spoken out after their break, in the manner of Louis Budenz. Scherer, Clardy, and Jackson pressed them, somewhat defensively, for testimonials as to the fair treatment they were meeting at the Committee's hands. "Do you feel," Scherer asked Davis, "that

[6] Now and then Senator McCarthy took time out from his other work to interject himself into the area of education—by inveighing against the "smelly mess" at Harvard after that university declined to fire an ex-Communist teacher who pleaded the Fifth Amendment, or by threatening legislation to take away the tax exemption from foundations that gave money to any college with Fifth Amendment people on its faculty. "Touch their pocketbooks and they get religion," said Joe—but, for the most part, he left America's teachers to Jenner and Velde.

your experience today has interfered in any way with your academic freedom or the academic freedom of any professor at Smith College?" Walter, who was establishing himself as the Committee's voice of reason, held a calm conversation with Hicks, in the course of which he made the near-heretical statement, "I am sure that the Communist Party membership has been reduced considerably—certainly the eggheads have all gotten out of it . . . and I think the situation is exaggerated now." Clardy made up for this by notifying Hicks that Americans for Democratic Action was a Communist front. Both Boorstin, who believed that a Party member should not be permitted to teach in the public schools or in the social science departments of colleges, and Hicks, who thought it was better to let a stray Communist teach than strain the fabric of academic freedom, were allowed to have their reasonable says.

But the amiable tone did not last out even the second day of hearings. Soon witnesses, beginning with Wendell Furry, the Harvard physicist, and Barrows Dunham, the head of Temple's philosophy department, were taking the Fifth (Dunham refused to speak at all, beyond begrudgingly giving his name, address, and birthday), and Committee members were arguing with them about their rights to the self-incrimination clause and their views in general. When Furry said he didn't believe that the U.S.S.R. started the Korean War, Jackson countered: "Do you make a distinction in your mind as between one who seeks the overthrow of the government by force and violence in this country and one in the lines of North Korea who seeks the overthrow of the United States of America by force and violence in Korea?" (When, however, Tavenner got started on the remote case of Furry's wife's sister's husband, who had been involved in the 1946 Canadian spy trials, Kearney pulled him up short.) For months thereafter, subcommittees went about the country and exposed some teachers wherever they alighted. Like socialites who throw their little shooting parties when the society reporters are all occupied with more impressive events, the subcommittees lost out to the Jenner group in the competition for national publicity. But local newspapers did nicely by them, and though the game was small it was abundant. They were cheered on by J. Edgar Hoover himself who, delivering his periodic warning to the House Appropriations Committee that the Communist threat was bigger than ever, declared that "Every Communist uprooted from our educational system is one more assurance that it will not degenerate into a medium of propaganda for Marxism." Before the Jenner and Velde committees and the state and local groups they inspired to action were done with their season's shooting, hundreds of teachers, having taken the Fifth Amendment, would be removed from the nation's schools and colleges by resignation, dismissal, and suspension.

To those who interpreted this record as a diminution of academic freedom, the Committee majority usually explained that they were in no wise concerning themselves with what anyone taught; they were merely out to get Communists, in schools as elsewhere. But if some of the objections to the hearings were overwrought, the defense was rather too cool; it drew too nice a line between pursuing individual Communists and influencing entire faculties. Although the investigators stayed clear of matters of curricula and brought up the subject of classroom indoctrination only in a general way, their campaign could have but one effect. It was an incitement to the dimmest right-wingers around the country, whose hatred of Communism took in everything that went under the head of progressive education. Along with the more potent McCarthy and Jenner investigations, it acted as an inhibitor of classroom controversy. And it undoubtedly contributed to that much-lamented phenomenon of the fifties known to magazine readers as the Silent Generation.

The Committee's encounter with the churches began in an offhand manner on March 9, 1953, when Velde, being interviewed on the Mutual Network program, *Reporters' Roundup*, allowed as how it was "entirely possible" that he might get into the "church field." It was not an entirely original idea, the Committee, in a 1951 report, having "observed with dismay the inordinately large proportion of clerics among the persons who are aiding or supporting the Communist 'peace'

campaign in this country," and Velde made it explicit that he
was interested in individuals, not in the churches themselves.
"We would not be investigating the churches any more than
we are now engaged in investigating the colleges and universities." Not a day passed before other members of the Committee were disassociating themselves from the notion of such
an investigation. Kearney was "absolutely opposed." Even
Jackson said it was "unwarranted." Everybody wanted it
understood that Velde was speaking strictly for himself, and
the Republican House leadership lectured the chairman on
the subject. In an unaccustomedly strong statement, President
Eisenhower told his press conference that he could see no
possible good being accomplished by questioning the loyalty
of America's churches—which, to be just, Velde had certainly
not done. Walter's demand for a Committee resolution forbidding the chairman to announce an investigation not approved by the full Committee was acceded to without dissent.

But the matter was not to be laid so easily to rest. The Committee's opponents—including quite a number not known for
their piety who were nonetheless willing to become champions
of religion if that was what was needed to knock Velde flat—
did not have it all their own way. From evangelical enclaves
within the Protestant fold support began to build up for an
investigation. Fundamentalists had long fumed over the kind
of Protestantism preached and practiced by the National Council of the Churches of Christ in the U.S.A., which represented the
country's largest, wealthiest, most respectable Protestant communities. Flickering here were vestiges of the long fight between Enlightenment and Enthusiasm in America's churches,
as well as the familiar political tensions between big cities and
rural areas, between the outward-looking Eastern seaboard and
the provincial Midwest. Soon the American Council of Christian Churches, fourteen Protestant denominations that had
banded together in 1941 "to offset the modernist, socialist influence of the National Council of Churches," was circulating
a petition among clergymen asking for an investigation. "The
searchlight on religious leaders has long been needed," an-

nounced the Council's general secretary. Mail favoring an investigation began arriving at Committee offices.

This support for Velde had an immediate effect. On March 17 Representative Jackson ("I am a Congregationalist by birth and breeding. The little white church across the street from my birthplace in South Dakota holds a special place in my affections") delivered a long speech in the House, in which he took back his initial, "hasty" reaction to Velde's radio statements. Now, he declared, he was "happy and proud" to associate himself with them. And he singled out as his particular target the foremost critic of the Committee among high Protestant officials, G. Bromley Oxnam, Methodist Bishop of Washington and one of the presidents of the World Council of Churches. "Having served God on Sunday and the Communist front for the balance of the week over such a long period of time," said Jackson, "it is no wonder that the bishop sees an investigating committee in every vestry." Jackson received an ovation for his speech.

Now the fire that seemed to have expired at the lighting flared again, and it would stay alive for many months. Bishop Oxnam, in the center of the flame for most of that time, was no prayerful martyr; he gave as good as he got. After Velde counseled a group of churchmen in Chicago to ponder the new "sin" of subversion when they were inclined to criticize proposals to search for Communists among the clergy, Oxnam told a group in Philadelphia that "There are some who insist that the hallelujahs of religion shall always support the hurrahs of the state." He challenged the Congressmen "to name one clergyman who holds a position of large responsibility in any Protestant church who is a member of the Communist Party." The bishop himself had never been charged with being a Communist, but he was much inclined to the social gospel and from time to time, in response to an attack by him on its methods, the Committee would release from its files an item connecting him with some Communist front. The *ad hominem* method of replying to criticism, ever popular with the Committee, aroused Oxnam to demand a full and open hearing. This he received— but not before another drama concerning Communists among the clergy and starring J. B. Matthews had been performed on another stage of the Capitol.

Matthews had come into his own during the cold war. Among the "consultants on Communism" who had formed themselves into a profession of sorts, serving state legislators, American Legion posts, the public relations departments of large and nervous companies, and the banquet chairmen of patriotic organizations, J. B. Matthews occupied a position roughly equivalent to that occupied by Joe McCarthy among the nation's investigators. As part of his educational works, Matthews contributed articles on aspects of the internal Communist peril to the *American Mercury*—once the playground of H. L. Mencken, now a backyard lot where right-wingers threw empty bottles into the air so that they might watch them crash— and it was only natural that the subject of Communist clergymen having been raised by Velde and seconded by Jackson, Matthews would have something to say in behalf of their position. (The May issue of the magazine had carried his article on *Communism and the Colleges*.)

Reds and Our Churches was published in the July 1953 issue of the *Mercury* and was inserted into the Congressional Record by Representative Clardy, who commended it to all members. Designed as a defense of Velde against the burst of criticism that followed his mild remarks on radio, the article led off with this sentence: "The largest single group supporting the Communist apparatus in the United States today is composed of Protestant clergymen." Matthews went on to report that in the previous seventeen years the Communist Party had enlisted the support of at least 7,000 clergymen (compared to barely 3,000 college professors)—"Party-members, fellow travellers, espionage agents, Party-line adherents and unwitting dupes." The way Matthews had arrived at this imposing figure was by adding up the names of clergymen he had found signed to petitions, resolutions, advertisements, and whatever in support of causes favored and promoted by Communists—notably the Stockholm Peace Appeal during the Korean War and pleas for clemency for the Rosenbergs. The reference to espionage agents was hyperbole, and the article named no card-carrying cleric.

As Matthews's clippings and calculations demonstrated, Communist causes had over the years held a continuing attraction for a segment of the Protestant clergy, and if Matthews's interests had run along a different path, he might have begun a worthwhile discussion as to why this should have happened. Was it that in addition to being more open to pleas for peace and mercy than their brethren among the fundamentalists, who still preached the religion militant, or among the Catholic priesthood, which was by and large willing to leave social justice to another place, Protestant clergymen were suffering from some ambiguity of role? They and their congregations were very much in this world, but what in heaven's name was their job? Well, one job they might reasonably take as their own was to bring the teachings of Jesus to bear on war or on capital punishment or even on the inequities of capitalism, and though harboring no particular affection for Stalin, they might have been imprudent enough to lend their signatures to petitions framed precisely to catch men of excess good will and scant political sophistication. It was scarcely a sin, after all, to believe that the execution of the Rosenbergs was an act of cruelty. These were matters that might have borne speculation, but they were no part of J. B. Matthews's trade.

About a week before his article's appearance Matthews had been named executive director of Senator McCarthy's Permanent Subcommittee on Investigations. The Democrats on the committee—Senators McClellan, Symington, and Jackson—had been showing increasing pain over McCarthy's stunts during these high-flying days, and the Matthews article presented them with an opportunity for a burst of ground fire. They denounced it as "a shocking and unwarranted attack against the American clergy," and with the support of Senator Potter called for Matthews's removal. (Even old Senator Byrd criticized Matthews and worked behind the scenes for his dispatch, but Senators Dirksen and Mundt, the senior Republicans on McCarthy's committee, held their peace.) McCarthy resisted for a day, but gave in after Nixon had a private chat over lunch with Mundt, and President Eisenhower spoke up, delivering his first direct shot at McCarthy, who had been having a rollicking time lately creating havoc in United States libraries abroad with no visible sign of displeasure from the White House. Upon receipt of a telegram from the co-chairmen of the Commission on Religious Organizations of the National Council of Christians and Jews, which labeled Matthews's article "unjustifiable and deplorable," the President replied that he shared their convictions. It had all the earmarks of a preconceived maneuver, and McCarthy "very reluctantly" accepted Matthews's resignation.

The Democrats did not let the matter rest there; when the subcommittee voted a Republican four to a Democratic three to give Chairman McCarthy authority to hire and fire staff members, they walked out of the committee and stayed out for several months. "If they don't want to take part in uncovering the graft and corruption of the Truman-Acheson Administration," commented McCarthy, "they are, of course, entitled to refuse." The remaining Republicans, however, did not accede to McCarthy's wish to call Matthews before them to give his evidence; they suggested that he go to the House—and the Un-American Activities Committee agreed to hear him.

But that hearing would never be held. In April of the following year, after experiencing some investigational vicissitudes, the Committee reversed itself. For one thing, Matthews did not exude an odor of success after his removal from his briefly held job; in fact he did not smell at all good. For another, the prospect of reawakening the Communist clergy dispute had become less enticing than ever after Bishop Oxnam's appearance. The Oxnam hearing, which filled the Old House Caucus Room, began at 2:30 p.m. on July 21 and, with a break for dinner, ran until 12:30 that night. The bishop's title, his record, and his firm but unprovocative manner made him a very different sort of witness from those to whom the Congressmen had lately been subjected, and the encounter offered an unusually clear view of the nature of the Committee and its dominant members and staff.

Although material from the Committee's files had been used

against him by the fundamentalists, not even a former F.B.I.
agent could call Oxnam a Communist and not even a Communist could call him a reliable fellow traveler. His associations with Communist fronts had been few and fleeting and
his entire history, actions as well as words, left no doubt that
he was opposed to the Party, to its ideology, and to its vassals
in this country. He was not much of a theologian, but he was
too smart a man of affairs to play the dupe for very long—he
never signed the Stockholm Peace Appeal. The worst he had
done was to allow the use of his name by a few organizations
to whose activities he did not pay sufficient attention. He had
also lent his efforts to a host of liberal causes, been against
Franco, and, along with everybody from Mike Quill to Leverett
Saltonstall, had belonged to the National Council of American-
Soviet Friendship during the war. And, finally, he was a critic
of the Committee on Un-American Activities. "It seems singularly peculiar," said Clardy before the hearing, "that every time
he's taken a stand he's taken that stand against the Committee
and not on our side." The case against him was scantily fleshed,
but Clardy, Jackson, and the newly hired counsel, Robert L.
Kunzig, tried to make a meal of the bare bones.

Kunzig conducted most of the questioning, and it is not easy
to say how much of his performance should be laid to simple
ineptitude, how much to a shrewd assessment of the need to
jazz up an exceedingly weak set of charges. He made a hash
of chronology, jumping about over the decades and landing as
far back as 1923; glossed over all events of the previous thirty
years, including the ups and downs of America's relations with
Russia; and made absolutely no distinctions regarding the nature of involvement with a front. Even where Oxnam reasonably explained or flatly denied an alleged association with a
given person or group, Kunzig proceeded to fill the record with
previously taken testimony and citations relating to that person
or group, thereby leaving the impression with the inattentive
listener that he was saying something about the witness at
hand.

Since Oxnam had been an active member of the American
Civil Liberties Union since 1946, Kunzig quoted a Fish Com-

mittee report from 1931 that held that the A.C.L.U. (which divested itself of its Communists in 1940) was closely allied to the Communist Party. When Oxnam testified that he had accepted an invitation in 1943 to become chairman of the executive committee of the Massachusetts Council of American-Soviet Friendship from Dirk Struik—the M.I.T. mathematics professor who had recently taken the Fifth before the Committee—Walter remarked, with no justification, "The fact of the matter is, this professor was a Russian spy, was he not?" When Oxnam admitted that he had belonged to the Committee on Militarism in Education in 1935, when it was opposing compulsory R.O.T.C. in the colleges, Kunzig recalled that ten years before that the group had been given $10,000 by the Garland Fund, which was subsequently cited as Communist by the Dies Committee. Oxnam admitted being "editorial advisor" of a magazine called the *Protestant Digest* from 1940 to 1942, not giving much time to the job and quitting when informed by Roger Baldwin that Communists were running it. Whereupon Kunzig noted that the publication had made the attorney general's list in 1947, tagging on this interesting legal point—"I might add the lists are retroactive." Kunzig also quoted Louis Budenz as saying the *Protestant Digest* was anti-Catholic; when Oxnam sought to defend himself against the implication that *he* was anti-Catholic, Velde delivered the punch line, "I regret very much that you brought the subject of anti-Catholicism up at all."

Although certainly not disposed in Oxnam's favor, Velde made a polite chairman. He occasionally admonished the audience, which was distinctly pro-Oxnam, to restrain itself, but allowed the bishop to reply fully and more often than not quite effectively to Kunzig's questions and innuendoes. When Oxnam complained about the Committee's habit of releasing inaccurate information about his activities which had been clipped from the *Daily Worker*, Velde chided him kindly: "In response to a question a while ago you indicated that you didn't know about your being listed on letterheads of certain organizations until you learned through our files that you were listed. I feel that you, as a good American citizen, should appreciate the fact that our Committee made this knowledge about you available." There is no reason to assume he was joking; Velde rarely joked.

Walter's position through the long day was never quite certain. He agreed with Oxnam that raw information of the sort that had been distributed about him should be confined strictly to the Committee, not given out, but he was peeved at the bishop for joining with those who opposed the McCarran-Walter immigration law, a matter that Walter brought up abruptly and the relevance of which no one questioned. There was never any doubt about where Jackson and Clardy stood; they were undeviating anti-Oxnamites. After Oxnam told of breaking off relations with Harry F. Ward, his teacher years before at the Boston School of Theology, because of Ward's Communist sympathies, Jackson made much of a tribute that Oxnam had paid in 1939 to Ward's accomplishments, and Clardy wanted to know why Oxnam hadn't turned his old professor in to the F.B.I. The only outspoken friend Oxnam had on the Committee was Doyle, whom Velde did his best to quash. It was Doyle who objected to Kunzig's producing documents from the year 1923 without advance notice and to the counsel's practice of listing citations of organizations to which Oxnam denied belonging. And it was Doyle who, at the end of the session after midnight, moved "that the record show in these hearings that this Committee had no record of any Communist Party affiliation or membership by Bishop Oxnam." To the astonishment of Oxnam and everyone else, the motion was immediately seconded by Jackson. But the Congressman relented no further. He objected to a second motion by Doyle asking that a note to the effect that Oxnam had denied membership in an organization be affixed wherever Kunzig had inserted the citations for such an organization—and the motion was defeated.

A photograph taken afterwards showed a smiling Velde shaking Oxnam's hand—but had the bishop in fact been cleared? Not according to Walter, who, thinking perhaps of the hard words which his immigration law was still suffering from the liberal community, said: "I don't know why anyone would say he was cleared because no one ever charged him with anything. I think the hearing demonstrated very clearly that the Communists are using well known and highly placed persons as dupes and the bigger the name the better for their cause. I place Bishop Oxnam as being in this category." That the Communists had used the bishop's name was certain, but his record by no means bore out Walter's conclusion. What the hearing showed was how narrowly men like Jackson and Clardy construed anti-Communism—one had to turn in old friends to the F.B.I. and be a supporter of the Committee on Un-American Activities. It showed how little men like Velde and Kunzig cared for orderly investigation. And it showed how entrenched the Committee was in the mechanically vindictive method of establishing individual guilt pioneered by J. B. Matthews. Bishop Oxnam deserved a much more generous apology from the Committee than he could ever have hoped to receive.

But if, despite the Committee's best efforts, Bishop Oxnam could not be remade to fit the image of a model fellow traveler, there were a few such among the Protestant clergy. Like Harry Ward, their identities were no secret. Five of them had been named by J. B. Matthews in his famous article[7]—but only after years of having contributed their names to Communist causes of impressive diversity and number. As Reinhold Niebuhr wrote, they had long been "protected by anti-Stalinist 'liberals' in the church who foolishly thought that the 'prophetic' spirits in the church were bound to be accused of disloyalty and therefore that the charge of Communist sympathies was a validation of the 'prophetic spirit.'"

The most energetic of this small but busy group was Jack R. McMichael. In 1939, still a seminarian, the lanky and loquacious young man from Georgia had appeared before the Dies Committee in his capacity of chairman of the American Youth Congress. He was subsequently ordained, and since the

[7] The five clergymen described by Matthews as "top pro-Soviet propagandists" were: Harry F. Ward, professor emeritus of the Union Theological Seminary; Kenneth Ripley Forbes, executive secretary of the Episcopal League for Social Action; Jack R. McMichael, executive secretary of the Methodist Federation for Social Action; Willard Uphaus, coordinator of the American Peace Crusade; and Joseph F. Fletcher, professor of Christian Social Ethics at the Episcopal Theological School in Cambridge.

end of World War II had been executive secretary of the Methodist Federation for Social Action, a loosely affiliated church organization concerned entirely with the affairs of this world, which the Committee had attacked in a 1952 report and from which McMichael's political proclivities had caused Bishop Oxnam to resign. In June 1953, with the heat on, McMichael gave up his post and took a small congregation in northern California. In July, a few days after Bishop Oxnam's appearance, he was called to Washington and placed in the witness chair.

McMichael had been identified as a member of the Young Communist League and the Communist Party in closed hearings of the Committee by two professional ex-Communists whose fortune it was rarely to be subjected to cross-examination, Manning Johnson and Leonard Patterson, and by a husband-and-wife team of undercover F.B.I. informants. McMichael denied their charges; indeed, he denied even knowing any of them, and had a fine time turning his appearance into a vaudeville routine with overtones of a revivalist session. He talked on and on in a Georgia drawl, made long speeches and little jokes, referred with mock officiousness to a set of diaries he had brought with him, and carried off a performance that threw the Committee into a worse tizzy than usual, as he notified it that he had to answer to Almighty God and not to it or to the attorney general. McMichael prefaced his denial of Party membership with a reference to "my six-year-old girl and my eight and ten-year-old boys" who had heard the charge over the radio. He told Velde, ". . . we are fellow Methodists and we understand each other . . ." While denying membership in a list of organizations mentioned by one of the informants, McMichael observed, "He refers to the Federal Bureau of Investigation. I have never been a member of that." When counsel Kunzig, driven desperate, shouted at him, McMichael replied, "I used to sell boiled peanuts as a little boy. I can speak as loudly as you." His tactics were particularly effective against Clardy, who began to behave like a slugger being jabbed maddeningly by an opponent with much faster footwork. When Clardy pressed him for an answer to a question about his student activities, McMichael said, "Thirteen years ago, brother —whatever your name is—that's quite a long while." He talked tirelessly without rancor, and when Clardy, steaming, hollered at him, "Be still!" he replied amicably, "I am not moving very far." At length the unhumorous Velde, who had been pounding his gavel for silence with as much effect as if he were commanding the sun not to rise, caught the spirit of the occasion: "The chair," he announced to McMichael who had been calling for an opportunity to deliver another short speech, "will allow you two minutes to make any derogatory statements you may want concerning this Committee." The event ended in inconclusive exhaustion as Velde, relieved of getting rid of the young man, handed a transcript of the proceedings over to the Justice Department for a possible perjury indictment. But although the Committee's informants had excellent reason to assume that McMichael had been a Communist in the nineteen-thirties and early forties, assumptions were not the stuff of which successful indictments are made.[8]

After this ordeal, Velde called no more clergymen. The Committee had come up with only one minister—a Los Angeles Unitarian—whom it had dead to rights and who had already taken the Fifth in 1951. But the bulk of the testimony from informants concerned ministers who had worked for Communist-directed causes but could not be pinned down as Party members. So Velde did what the Committee had periodically been criticized for doing before and had periodically vowed not to do again—he made public accusations that had been elicited in closed session from the old ex-Communist Benjamin Gitlow and the young ex-F.B.I. man Herbert Philbrick against several clergymen, who immediately denied being Communists but were not invited to testify. Philbrick, who had recently con-

---

[8] McMichael was accompanied at his hearing by Frank J. Donner, an attorney just beginning his encounters with the Committee. In 1961 Donner published a book, described as "the first fully documented account of the notorious House Committee on Un-American Activities," in which he gave this summary of McMichael's appearance: "In the 1953 hearing of the Rev. Jack R. McMichael, the Committee left no stone unturned in its brutal drive to ruin him. It refused to permit him to explain his answers, put words in his mouth and used highly questionable evidence against him." None of this is entirely untrue, but like so many of the attacks on the Committee, it conveys neither the flavor of the hearing nor the character of the witness.

tributed to the *Christian Herald* an articled entitled *The Communists Are After Your Church,* had been induced to gives names of suspect ministers by Clardy and Kunzig against his own sounder instincts. "Mr. Philbrick," urged Kunzig, "seeing as we are here in executive session and this testimony being confidential, do you feel you could tell the Committee the names of these ministers in the Boston area whom you, as you said, have a pretty good idea were the ones that you feel were members of the Communist Party?" Philbrick allowed himself to be thus inveigled, and three months later his confidential testimony was made public. Embarrassed in October at being quoted as the author of charges which he could not prove in July (his testimony being of this sort, "He is one of the individuals who, I am sure of in my own mind, is operating under Communist Party discipline"), Philbrick criticized the Committee for releasing his testimony "prematurely," before "all facts had been assembled and the probe completed . . ."

Public indignation, however, was directed mainly at Gitlow. Whereas a majority of the Protestant ministers named had been named before by Matthews, Gitlow added in passing two rabbis who, he said, had "carried out the instructions of the Communist Party or collaborated with it" more than thirty years before. They were Stephen S. Wise and Judah L. Magnes, both deceased, both men of outstanding reputations. (Gitlow also put John Haynes Holmes of New York's Community Church in this company.) He could not have selected more eminent rabbis if he had tried, and whatever one thought of their political tendencies in 1920, labeling them Communist functionaries was too much. Although Gitlow's testimony was based entirely on his memory of Party life at a time when associating with Communists was a much different proposition than it was in 1953, there was no way to refute him except to recall the good works which the two had done. These were widely recalled, and the Committee came in for another lambasting from press and pulpit. Velde had attempted a cheap coup and had been caught at it.

The cries of the Committee's opponents that it was engaged in an attack on religious freedom and was violating the line between church and state were hardly justified by anything Velde or Jackson actually did. Still there was no question that their investigations had been fueled by the un-Christian feelings of the evangelical sects toward their upper-strata brethren. Fundamentalist enthusiasm, however, could not carry one very far in national politics, and for want of any real news, the investigation soon petered out. In January 1954 Velde held a makeup meeting with a small unrepresentative but respectable Protestant-Catholic-Jewish group, and in its annual report for 1953, the Committee observed in the section devoted to religion that "only a very small number of clergymen in the United States have been consistent fellow travelers with the Communist Party," and even offered some excuses for those who had been misguided. What had begun with a bang ended in a mumble.

Although the Committee was well financed during the eighty-third Congress, receiving $575,000, more than any House investigating committee had ever received, and although it did a prodigious amount of testimony taking, it operated always under the shadow of others. The pursuit of individual Communists in schools around the country was minor league sport compared to the exhibitions that Joe McCarthy was putting on at the expense of the State Department and the military. So it was only natural that when an opportunity seemed to present itself to play in the majors, Velde would rise to it eagerly. The apparent opportunity came in November 1953, when Attorney General Brownell reopened the case of Harry Dexter White. In a speech to the Executive Club of Chicago, Brownell charged that in January 1946, President Truman had nominated White, then Assistant Secretary of the Treasury, to be executive director for the United States in the International Monetary Fund, despite an F.B.I. report delivered a month before which had reviewed White's activities as a Soviet spy. Another F.B.I. report, said Brownell, was delivered to Pennsylvania Avenue before White's Senate confirmation in February. Truman replied to Brownell, in words he would have to take back, that he knew nothing about any F.B.I. report: "As soon as we found White was disloyal we fired him." White's resignation in April 1947, after the Justice Department had failed to get a grand jury indictment against him, was accepted by Truman with "sincere regret and considerable reluctance."

There was not much question that the attorney general had the facts of the case straight, but no one could miss the political instigation behind his charge, whose phrasing conjured up black doings at the White House: "Harry Dexter White was known to be a spy by the very people who appointed him to the most sensitive and important position he ever held in government service." The speech had been cleared with Sherman Adams, Eisenhower's chief of staff, with Press Secretary James Hagerty, and, in a vague way, with Eisenhower himself. Brownell's resort to F.B.I. files was a particularly sensitive point. If Congressional committees to which such material had been barred under Truman could now get hold of it or if the Republicans were planning to strew about selected items in preparation for the 1954 elections, the country was in for a bitter political harvest. Senator Jenner immediately announced that his committee planned to reopen the White case, and his first announced witness would be Truman's former military aide and crony, Major General Harry H. Vaughan, to whom the F.B.I. reports had assertedly been handed. Thereupon, the Un-American Activities Committee also subpoenaed Vaughan, and there was speculation that a joint meeting might be held.

Now Velde made a spectacular move, his try for the big leagues. Taking the position that his Committee had a parent's prerogative on anything having to do with Elizabeth Bentley and Harry Dexter White, irked by Jenner's effort to lay first hands on the child ("We should get in the act," Velde's man Kunzig told the other Committee members), the chairman, on his own authority, sent forth subpoenas to James F. Byrnes, governor of South Carolina, who was Secretary of State in 1946 and remembered the F.B.I. warnings about White; to Supreme Court Justice Tom Clark, who was attorney general in 1946; and to Harry S. Truman. Sending a subpoena to a former President was a novel idea, untested in law, but Velde's intent was clear as day. The first attacks came from the Democrats on his Committee. Walter, to whom Velde was careful to defer during hearings, called the enterprise, "the most incredible, insulting, un-American thing that I've encountered in my twenty-one years in Congress." He charged that, in a race for headlines with Jenner, Velde had violated the Committee rule—adopted after the chairman's off-the-cuff remarks about an investigation of the clergy the previous spring—that required approval of a Committee majority for any major investigation. Doyle, in California, wired his strenuous opposition. Kearney, the Committee's only Eastern Republican, added his displeasure.

That was but the beginning. Had Harold Velde been a more notable figure, what came upon him now might be compared to those late scenes in *Richard III* when the king's allies presumptive decline to do combat or go over to the enemy. Velde's subpoenas were politely rejected by all parties. President Eisenhower, defending his predecessor's patriotism, said that he (the President) would not have subpoenaed him (the former President). The House Republican leadership sent a forceful emissary to the Committee's Republicans to get them to leave the field to Jenner. Jenner shrugged off Velde's ambitions for a joint hearing of Vaughan, giving the Congressman a front-row seat to the Senate hearing as ironic consolation. When Velde announced that he intended to question the foreman of the grand jury that had heard the evidence in the White case, the Justice Department stepped in and forbade the man from testifying, grand jury proceedings being secret. The chairman was left with no witnesses, no audience and few supporters. Newspapers that had backed Eisenhower in 1952 and were critical of Truman's handling of the White case were yet more critical of Velde's presumption. Brownell, following the President's lead, said that he had not meant to impugn Truman's loyalty, merely to suggest that "laxity" on matters of security had prevailed in the White case. And after being invited to appear before the House Committee, the attorney general chose to appear before the Senate Committee instead and did so, together with J. Edgar Hoover, before the biggest audience of the investigating season, not counting radio and television.[9] Richard, in his difficult hour, called for a horse; Harold Velde was left promising the readers of *U.S. News* that he would not give up the field.

The Harry Dexter White affair was a victory for the Republicans—but a dangerous one. Truman, in a television talk, reversed himself, conceding that he had discussed the White case with members of his Cabinet; White had been allowed to take a post with the International Monetary Fund, he explained, so that the F.B.I. might carry on its investigations with a view toward getting an indictment. But the next day J. Edgar Hoover told the Jenner Committee that the F.B.I. had not been a party to any such arrangement, that his opinion had not been solicited, and that had it been up to him, he would have had White fired. Brownell's original statement of the facts of the case had been substantially correct; Truman's had been untrue. But Velde's initiative showed how easily such public charges could get out of hand, or, more precisely, get into irresponsible hands. By the end of 1953, the Administration had plenty of reason to be cautious about encouraging aspiring McCarthys.[1]

The Truman subpoena was not the only source of discontent within the Committee as 1954 began. The Agnes Meyer gaffe, the arousal of the clergy, the discharge of numerous staff members whose places were taken by persons more compatible to the new chairman (Robert Kunzig quite upstaged his associate counsel, Frank Tavenner)—these rankled Democratic members and gave special pause to the independently inclined Kearney, who charged publicly that the staff was wasting money and "jockeying for advantage over one another, trying to get raises which are undeserved and engaging in backbiting." Staff dissension reached such a pass that Velde appointed a subcom-

---

[9] Sherman Adams tells us in his memoirs that Brownell hoped his accusation "would take away some of the glamour of the McCarthy stage play."

[1] Through the fall and winter of 1953 and into 1954, the Committee made halfhearted efforts to get the Civil Service Commission to release its records of an employee of the Mediation and Conciliation Service who had been cleared for his job four times despite a record of cooperating with Communists in an A.F. of L. union. But the Administration abided by Truman's 1948 directive denying such papers to Congressional committees.

mittee of himself, Walter, and Kearney to look into it. While they were looking, in January 1954, Velde generated an uproar by firing Louis J. Russell, an F.B.I. alumnus who had been named chief investigator by Chairman Wood in 1949. When Velde explained that Russell had acted in ways that had embarrassed the Committee, Walter—against whom Velde already held a grudge for backing Truman's story about why he hadn't fired Harry Dexter White—commented sarcastically that Russell "didn't call for an investigation of religion." In fact, said Walter, "Whatever constructive work has been done by the Committee was done by him." But though Kearney shared his feeling that Russell was being made the goat for Committee blunders, the chief investigator was past defense. He had showed the poor judgment to borrow $300 from Edward G. Robinson, a former witness; the loan may have been innocent on both sides, but Russell was cooked.[2] The issue, however, remained alive. In March, ex-General Kearney returned to the attack, declaring the staff situation to be "rotten" and "intolerable" and threatening to quit if it was not cleared up. He said that one of Velde's appointees, who was supposed to have been fired in January for inefficiency, was still at work, and he was particularly irritated at the news that Velde had taken a staff man back to Illinois to assist him in a primary fight. Velde's response was that Kearney had unfortunately "fallen for the sucker pitch" of "left-wing editorialists and extremists."

Although Velde won in the primary, his taste for adventure was quelled by the cuffings he had received in 1953. He was, politically speaking, a frivolous man, but he had never shown the joy in his work that Martin Dies exuded. The second half of his term as chairman, coinciding with Joe McCarthy's time of troubles, offered fewer incentives to his chastened spirits and he played it safe. More than eighty days of hearings were held in 1954, but they were of a routine sort, subcommittees settling in various cities, calling up resident Communists, asking the

---

[2] Courtney E. Owens, who had been with the Committee for six years, was named to succeed Russell.

customary questions, and getting the customary refusal to testify on grounds of the Fifth Amendment. When a number of witnesses were cited for contempt, the courts, as if parties to the teasing of Harold Velde, returned fewer indictments than he sought and very few convictions indeed.

12

★ ★ ★ ★ ★

The Fifth Amendment

THE Committee, its spokesmen somewhat apologetic about troubling the House yet again, pressed twenty-nine contempt citations against witnesses who appeared before it in 1953 and 1954. The citations fell into two categories, the larger having to do with persons who had pleaded the Fifth Amendment on questions regarding residence, schooling, and employment, which Committee members felt could not possibly incriminate them. The others involved witnesses who challenged the pertinency of inquiries into their political activities and associations but did not stand on the Fifth Amendment.

The former batch of citations brought the Committee unmitigated disappointment. A Detroit grand jury refused even to indict six persons who had declined to answer questions during a disorderly set of hearings conducted by Clardy, whose technique of dealing with obstreperous witnesses was to match their abuse with his own. In other cities, where indictments were issued, district courts acquitted the defendants—including Barrows Dunham, the first to be cited. Where district courts convicted, a court of appeals reversed the conviction. And the four cases in which convictions were upheld at the appeals level—on the grounds that an answer to the question, "Where do you live?" would not have been incriminatory—were reversed by the Supreme Court. Even answers to such innocuous questions, held the Court, might be dangerous. All but one of the eighteen persons cited for misuse of the Fifth Amendment went free, and that one would certainly have gotten off too

had he carried forward his appeal, as his offense was no different from the others.

The decisions in these contempt cases carried to its utmost
limit the principle laid down by the court in 1950 when it ruled
in favor of a man who had refused to tell a grand jury about
his knowledge of the workings of the Communist Party. As we
noted earlier, Justice Black stated on that occasion, "Whether
such admissions by themselves would support a conviction
under a criminal statute is immaterial." The crucial point was
that the witness' answers to the grand jury questions "would
have furnished a link in the chain of evidence needed in a
prosecution . . . for violation of (or conspiracy to violate) the
Smith Act." Now, in the mid-fifties, it was established that
virtually any question, no matter how seemingly trivial or remote from criminal activities, fell under this cover.

Legally, then, the question was settled, but the repercussions
of taking the Fifth Amendment were by no means exclusively
legal,[1] and they led to an emotional debate among respectable
persons as to what inferences one might reasonably draw when
a witness would not say whether he or she was a Communist
on the grounds that "no person . . . shall be compelled in any
criminal case to be a witness against himself." Prominent liberals took the position that no inferences whatever should be
drawn, since an individual might in his past have done something altogether innocent which could now get him into trouble
with the law. The most important statement of this position,
widely distributed by the Fund for the Republic and widely
quoted by liberal press and jurists, was set down by Dean
Erwin N. Griswold of the Harvard Law School. It was a largehearted argument by a man who had allowed his distress at
the way legislative inquiries were being conducted to fog his
thinking. In order to defend the no-inference rule, Griswold
offered the hypothetical case of a professor who joined the
Communist Party in the nineteen-thirties or -forties, limited

---

[1] At the height of the "Fifth Amendment–Communist" vendetta, the New
York State senate unanimously passed a bill authorizing employers to fire any
employee who pleaded self-incrimination, and in Washington, D.C., a secondhand piano dealer who took the Fifth before the Committee was denied the
renewal of his license to buy and sell secondhand merchandise.

his activities solely to study groups, and quit in disillusionment at the outbreak of the Korean War. On being haled before a Congressional committee some years later, Griswold went on, such a man would be justified in taking the Fifth Amendment on the grounds that "Persons have been prosecuted under the Smith Act for membership in the Communist Party plus something else." Even though our hypothetical professor had no inkling of what the "something else" might be, what other evidence might be adduced against him, he had a right to take the Fifth, and any inference that he was therefore guilty of anything would be unwarranted. Griswold also invented the case of a non-Communist who feared that if he testified, his innocent membership in front groups in the past might be construed as evidence of Communist affiliation and so land him in trouble.

Dean Griswold's examples and the even more fanciful hypothetical cases thought up by others of the no-inference persuasion were deficient in one major regard: they had little to do with the reality of Congressional investigations. Witnesses who in fact told the Committee about their past membership in the Communist Party or front groups, far from being charged with anything, were fulsomely thanked and commended for their patriotism. No study-group Communists were ever prosecuted; the big Communist trials involved long-time C.P. leaders and functionaries. As for men like Hiss and Remington, it was their perjury, not their Party activities, that sent them to prison. Moreover, as Sidney Hook showed in a devastating retort to Griswold, the no-inference principle ran squarely against common sense. One might cherish the Fifth Amendment, agree with the dean that it represented "one of the great landmarks in man's struggle to make himself civilized,"[2] and defend sturdily the right of every man to take it and the duty of every court to respect it, yet not be able to blink away the presump-

---

[2] Griswold's light argument fairly blew away in its own rhetoric: "I believe the Fifth Amendment is and has been through this period of crisis, an expression of the moral striving of the community . . . a reflection of our common conscience, a symbol of the America which stirs our hearts . . . very nearly a lone sure rock in a time of storm . . . a symbol of the ultimate moral sense of the community . . ."

tion that a man who chooses to be silent rather than to speak has something to hide; even Dr. Griswold's hypothetical professor, though guiltless of any crime, *had* been a member of the Communist Party. The question was, in Hook's words, "Not knowing whether a person is innocent or guilty, what can reasonably or naturally be inferred from a refusal to answer a pertinent question, put by someone authorized to ask the question, on the ground that a truthful answer would tend to be incriminating?"[3]

The liberal community had not always been enamored of witnesses who would not speak up. It showed small sympathy for the discomfiture of businessmen in the Congressional hearings of the nineteen-twenties and -thirties and did not strain to invent hypothetical circumstances to prove that Frank Costello was pure in spirit because he preferred not to answer Senator Kefauver's questions in 1951. In 1936, then Senator Hugo Black, in his much-quoted *Harper's* article on Congressional investigations, evidenced great annoyance with unresponsive witnesses; he started his article with Woodrow Wilson's line, "If there is nothing to conceal, then why conceal it?"[4] The change of heart was of course due to the change in feeling on the left toward Congressional investigations since the campaigns of Martin Dies. There was concern over the investigators' tendency to pry into witnesses' ideas as well as their activities; there was distaste for the constant efforts to get witnesses to inform on old friends; there was sympathy for those whose careers were jeopardized by a subpoena; and there was an unmistakable indulgence toward the Communist

[3] There was a period when witnesses, advised that an answer to *any* question regarding past activities might jeopardize their right to the Fifth Amendment on the question of Communist Party membership, simply took the Fifth down the line. In these instances, the Committee's counsel and members frequently asked about espionage activities of which there was no evidence as well as about far-fetched and inconsequential matters designed to show up the witness as uncooperative or build up his refusal-to-answer score for the benefit of the press or simply for the sake of amusement. In regard to the rote Fifth Amendment response to such questions, no inference was warranted except that the Committee was taking advantage of the witness' situation.

[4] Conservatives have not failed to remind liberals of their earlier tolerance for the browbeating of witnesses. John J. McCloy said in 1953: "If the liberals had been more expressive when the so-called Congressional investigations of the thirties were studiously violating personal rights and when business was the target, there would have been less likelihood of excesses in this day and age."

witnesses that neither racketeers nor businessmen aroused. However much one objected to the Committee's motives and methods, a study of the hearings over the years left little doubt that the overwhelming majority of witnesses called before it had been correctly marked down as members or former members of the Communist Party; in 1953, 280 persons were heard, there being sworn testimony of their Communist affiliation in each case, and in every case but one—the Rev. Jack McMichael—the witnesses either admitted membership or pleaded the Fifth Amendment.

It was easy to sympathize with those—by no means a majority—who would have agreed to tell about their pasts if only the Committee then refrained from pressing them for information about former associates. But even under the generous limits allowed by the courts, the protection of third parties was not a valid reason for taking the Fifth Amendment. One might find the Committee and all its works obnoxious, but that was not a valid reason either. Giving witnesses an extensive benefit of the doubt and assuming that their reliance on the Constitution was founded on some reason other than a disinclination to testify against themselves, they were committing perjury. Telford Taylor, after building up an historical case for the no-inference position, was constrained to point out that most witnesses had no "solid legal and practical necessity" for taking the privilege and were "playing into the hands of those extremists who are trying to make the Fifth Amendment synonymous with guilt and subversion." It required a thorough suspension of disbelief on the part of a spectator to hear a man take the Fifth and draw no inferences from it—other than to conclude, as some did, that the fellow was a martyr. In a cogent essay on the subject, C. Dickerman Williams wrote ". . . The self-incrimination privilege benefits society through the compulsion which it exerts on enforcement officers to prove their cases by external evidence rather than by confessions extracted from suspects. But it does not mean that a given individual found in a compromising situation shows his innocence by failing to make a full disclosure." His shaft was aimed at those who overlooked the positive duty of citizens to testify before legally constituted bodies and who refused to concede that witnesses who did speak out about their past Communist associations were by no means all vile informers and witch hunters. As a matter of fact, as Alan Westin emphasized, they were carrying out a responsibility to the democratic community which the silent witnesses had relinquished.

Taking the Fifth Amendment was an act not of heresy but merely of self-protection. Used promiscuously, in response to questions about one's birth or education, as Carl Beck wrote, it "makes a mockery of a constitutional privilege established for the protection of the individual from the arbitrary exercise of power. By subverting this privilege, these witnesses eroded its efficacy and thereby contributed to the rejection by the public of the worthwhileness of the self-incrimination plea." It is presumptuous to ask anyone to be a martyr—but then a man who hides should not expect to be presented with a martyr's crown. Yet, in reaction against McCarthy's yawps about "Fifth-Amendment Communists" and against the invidious notion that once a man took refuge in the Fifth he thereby lost all claim to the ordinary needs of life, such as a job, some well-meaning persons surrendered their wits altogether and took to defending a prudent reliance on the self-incrimination clause not only as a sign of innocence but of positive nobility. It was, and remains, an example of the befuddling sentimentality that is a bane of liberal opinion.

As for the investigators and prosecutors who found themselves frustrated by the courts' comprehensive definition of self-incrimination under the Fifth Amendment, they were, in a way, to blame for their own fix. They had for years been demanding ever more stringent laws against Communists; the existence of such laws now constituted the rationale for the taking of the Fifth. Casting about for a corrective, the investigators hit upon the idea of offering witnesses immunity from prosecution, which had been tried in other circumstances over the years. A grant of immunity, it was argued, would enable a court or committee to overleap the constitutional bar against compelling someone to testify against himself. Such a law, the product of Attorney General Brownell, with investigators in both Houses of Congress serving as godfathers, was passed in August 1954. The Compulsory Testimony Act provided that in any case involving a danger to the national security, a United States attorney might, with the approval of the attorney general, ask the court to instruct a witness that he would not be excused from giving evidence on the ground that it might incriminate him; once instructed, no such witness could thereafter be prosecuted on the matter in question and so he could not claim the Fifth Amendment. A Congressional committee could ask the district court to grant immunity if two-thirds of the committee approved. Critics of the immunity law pointed out that it might not protect a witness against prosecution in a state court and would certainly not protect him from such side effects as losing his job. Some accustomed defenders of the underdog opposed the bill for the unexpected reason that it would provide an escape hatch for the guilty. The new law was quickly tested and upheld by the Supreme Court. Justice Frankfurter, speaking for the majority, took pains to praise the virtues of the Fifth Amendment, even quoting Dean Griswold, but the immunity law was nevertheless constitutional, he explained, because "once the reason for the privilege ceases, the privilege ceases." Justice Douglas, in the minority with Justice Black, quoted Dean Griswold more extensively than Justice Frankfurter. Douglas argued, as he would on other occasions, that the framers of the clause against self-incrimination meant much more than their bare words conveyed. In his view, the clause was designed in part "to prevent any Congress, any court and any prosecutor from prying open the lips of an accused to make incriminating statements against his will."

Not long after the new law took effect, Representative Walter, its major advocate in the brief House debate, suggested that it be used against a man from Flint, Michigan, whom Clardy, acting chairman of the Detroit subcommittee, called "one of the most contemptuous witnesses that it has been my experience to hear." The witness countered, "You have been one of the most contemptuous persons I have ever faced," and Clardy directed Tavenner to take appropriate steps. But despite the fact that there was good reason to believe that the witness had been sent to Flint as an auto union "colonizer" by the Communist Party, the immunity law was not invoked. Commenting on the failure to compel witnesses to testify after being granted a weapon with which to do so, Carl Beck wrote:

> The fact that the Committee has not exercised this power would seem to indicate either that it realizes that its investigations are not of enough importance to warrant granting immunity or that full testimony by racalcitrant witnesses would point up the weaknesses of the Committee, and perhaps raise the legal question of the pertinency of certain information to the legislative purpose and function of a Congressional investigation.

For all the commotion of the hearings and the anger of the Congressmen at being defied and often scolded by witnesses, it had been apparent for some time that the Fifth Amendment was sufficient for the Committee's purposes. The main object of virtually every public appearance lay in the appearance itself. This observation played a part in two Supreme Court decisions which determined the fates of those witnesses who were cited for withholding their cooperation from the Velde Committee—and, later, the Walter Committee—on grounds other than the Fifth Amendment. These decisions still stand as the court's major statements on the scope of the Committee on Un-American Activities.

The first decision concerned John T. Watkins, a vice president of the Farm Equipment Workers Union, who admitted in the Chicago hearings in April 1954 that although he had never been a card-carrying Communist, he had cooperated with the Party "to such a degree" between 1942 and 1947 "that some members may honestly believe that I was a member of the Party." Having conceded so much, Watkins then delivered a principled statement, framed by his attorney Joseph Rauh, in which, in contrast to those who wrapped themselves in the spacious folds of the Fifth Amendment, he bared his breast and invited the Committee to do its worst:

I would like to get one thing perfectly clear, Mr. Chairman. I am not going to plead the Fifth Amendment, but I refuse to answer certain questions that I believe are outside the proper scope of your Committee's activities. I will answer any questions which this Committee puts to me about myself. I will also answer questions about those persons whom I knew to be members of the Communist Party and whom I believe still are. I will not, however, answer any questions with respect to others with whom I associated in the past. I do not believe that any law in this country requires me to testify about persons who may in the past have been Communist Party members or otherwise engaged in Communist Party activity, but who to my best knowledge and belief have long since removed themselves from the Communist movement. I do not believe that such questions are relevant to the work of this Committee—nor do I believe that this Committee has the right to undertake the public exposure of persons because of their past activities. I may be wrong and the Committee may have this power, but until and unless a court of law so holds and directs me to answer, I must firmly refuse to discuss the political activities of my past associates."

Having singled out the most sensitive aspect of the Committee's way of life, Watkins stuck to his resolve. As names were put to him by Kunzig, he replied regarding persons he believed still belonged to the Party and refused to talk about the others, despite directives from the chairman. He was cited for contempt, indicted, found guilty in district court, and given a twelve-month suspended sentence and a fine of $500. A divided Court of Appeals ruled against his contention that the Committee had exceeded its authority with him, holding that the questions put were pertinent and that the exposure of names was incidental to its legislative purpose. The case went to the Supreme Court, which in 1957 reversed this decision.

Opponents of the Committee rejoiced over the court's ruling.[5]

[5] The court handed down three other decisions along with that on Watkins that satisfied civil libertarians. In one five California Communists convicted under the Smith Act were freed and a new trial was ordered for nine others. In a second a professor at the University of New Hampshire was upheld in his refusal to tell the state attorney general about his lectures at the university or his efforts in behalf of the Progressive Party. In the third the court ruled unanimously that Dean Acheson had violated his own regulations in 1951

The Washington *Post* viewed the decision as "a landmark in the long struggle to keep Americans free from oppressive and arbitrary governmental power," and Alan Barth told readers of *The New Republic* that "civil liberties have come back into fashion." After reviewing what he took to be the rules newly laid down for Congressional investigating committees by the court, Barth concluded: "The Un-American Activities Committee, as presently conceived, cannot possibly operate under those strictures." The applauders were misled by a combination of their desires and the Chief Justice's prose. Writing for the majority, Warren declared that "there is no Congressional power to expose for the sake of exposure," that "no inquiry is an end in itself; it must be related to, and in furtherance of, a legitimate task of the Congress." He referred to the "confusing breadth" of the Committee's "excessively broad charter." He spoke of the First, Fourth, and Fifth Amendments and described the post–World War II investigations by Congress as involving "a broad-scale intrusion into the lives and affairs of private citizens." These were all points that the Committee's critics had been making for two decades, but though his remarks would sustain the critics for years to come, the Chief Justice was merely indulging himself. Hosannas were unwarranted.

The issue decided in the Watkins case was, in fact, a narrow one; it centered on the Committee's obligation to inform a witness as to why specific questions were pertinent. In this, said the majority, Justice Clark dissenting, the Committee had clearly failed. Its authorizing resolution, the remarks of the chairman and Committee members to Watkins, and the nature of the proceedings all suffered from the "vice of vagueness." The hearing presumably had to do with legislation to deny the services of the National Labor Relations Board to Communist-controlled unions, but of the thirty names put to Watkins, seven were not connected with any union—one person operated a beauty parlor and one was a watchmaker. When Watkins

when he dismissed John Stewart Service, a career Foreign Service officer who came under attack during the *Amerasia* affair, for his alleged sympathy to the Chinese Communists.

questioned their pertinency, Velde replied with a reference to the Committee's franchise to look into "subversion and subversive propaganda"—a "woefully inadequate" reply, according to the court. Watkins was acquitted, then, not because of any inherent defect in the Committee, but because his right to due process had been violated when he was not adequately informed as to why the questions put to him were pertinent. In a concurring opinion, Justice Frankfurter stated the crux of the matter without Warrenesque embellishment:

> Prosecuting for contempt of Congress presupposes an adequate opportunity for the defendant to have awareness of the pertinency of the information that he has denied to Congress . . . Accordingly the actual scope of the inquiry that the Committee was authorized to conduct and the relevance of the questions to that inquiry must be shown to have been luminous at the time when asked and not left, at best, in cloudiness.

Although Representative Jackson charged that the court had rendered his Committee and the Senate Subcommittee on Internal Security "innocuous as two kittens in a cageful of rabid dogs" and David Lawrence devoted a three-page editorial in *U. S. News* to the theme that "Treason has won its biggest victory," the Watkins decision was merely procedural. The Committee would thereafter take more care in setting forth the purposes of its hearings and the pertinency of its questions, but neither the acclamations of its enemies nor the forebodings of its friends were justified.

How little justified they were was made evident in 1959, when the court handed down its ruling in the case of Lloyd Barenblatt. Barenblatt, a young psychology instructor who had taught for a term at Vassar, came before the Committee in June 1954, during one of its hearings on "Communist Methods of Infiltration (Education)," after being named as a C.P. member during his student days at the University of Michigan. In a lengthy brief, which Velde would not permit him to read but did allow into the record, Barenblatt explained that he would refuse to answer questions about his association with the Communist Party or with the Michigan Council of the Arts, Sciences and Professions on the grounds that they intruded upon his personal life and the Committee did not have the authority to ask them. He took care to state, "I do not invoke the Fifth Amendment in declining to answer," and he did not raise the question of relevance, as Watkins had two months before. His conviction of contempt in district court was affirmed by the Court of Appeals and then reaffirmed in the light of the Watkins decision. In December 1958 the case came before the Supreme Court, where the fires of hope sparked in liberal hearts by the Watkins decision were ground out. The court's decision, written by Justice Harlan—joined by Frankfurter, Clark, Whittaker, and Stewart—examined one after another the main judicial arguments that had been leveled against the Committee and dismissed them all.

Was the authorizing resolution vague? Yes, but it had been defined by the "persuasive gloss of legislative history."

Was the Committee authorized to investigate Communists in education? A teacher had no immunity from being questioned merely because he was a teacher—"an educational institution is not a constitutional sanctuary."

Were the witness's rights to freedom of speech and association under the First Amendment abridged by the investigation? Perhaps, but these rights had to be balanced against the need of the government to preserve its existence.

Was the witness adequately apprised of the subject of the investigation and the pertinency of the questions? Incontestably.

Would the fact that the Committee had no motive other than to expose Barenblatt as a Communist invalidate his conviction? Although "there is no Congressional power to expose for the sake of exposure," the motives of the Committee were not sufficient to vitiate an investigation if a legislative purpose was being served, as was the case here.[6]

Justice Black—with the concurrence of Warren and Douglas and partial concurrence of Brennan—delivered a ringing dissent

[6] Beck notes that although the majority used the Committee's history to add precision to its vague mandate, it declined to use that same history as a guide to its motives.

that still lifts spirits wherever the Committee's opponents gather (sometimes lifting them so high that they overlook the fact that they lost the case). The authorizing resolution, argued Black, was too vague to support any conviction for a refusal to testify. He objected to the notion of a balancing test of national security against the rights guaranteed by the First Amendment. He charged—and here Brennan joined him—that it was clear as day that "exposure and punishment is the aim of this Committee and the reason for its existence." The record in the Barenblatt case showed that there was no purpose to the investigation except "exposure purely for the sake of exposure," and Barenblatt's rights were impaired by the Committee's ability to inflict "humiliation and public shame."

So were the liberal hopes raised by the Watkins decision cast down. Whatever the Commitee's intentions and whatever its effects, it was constitutional. The majority of the court showed itself as reluctant as ever to impose standards of conduct on an arm of the Congress, and it showed itself responsive to the exigencies, vital or merely fashionable, of national security. Still, it was a near thing for the Committee. The rebuff of the Watkins case, the close decision on Barenblatt, the powerful dissent, the criticism implicit in the Harlan ruling—these had a chastening effect, at least to the extent of bringing more order into its proceedings during the late fifties and into the present decade.

But we have run ahead of our story. It was inherent in the work of the Committee—partly because of its broad mandate, partly because of the type of Congressman attracted to a career of Communist-tracking, and partly because of the strategies and manners of many witnesses—that its tone and direction were determined largely by bad tempers. (What could be expected of Clardy or Scherer when a witness took to yelling at them, as one did in Seattle, that they were "phony Congressmen" who "ought to be investigated by psychiatrists"?) During the eighty-third Congress, the Committee formalized its rules of procedure with eight unexceptionable provisions designed to prevent unilateral decisions on the part of the

chairman and rash actions on the part of the staff and to
protect the reputations and rights of witnesses, particularly
by inviting persons named as Communists to appear, yet the
hollering and the mutual recriminations did not abate. As for
the Committee's habit of exposing for no other purpose than
exposing, it was clear by now that there was no alternative
to this but to go out of business. At the end of its term, the
Velde Committee issued a report on "Neo-Fascist and Hate
Groups," but its trade was frankly in Communists and there
was nothing to be done with Communists except to expose
them.

And then, as always, there were political requirements and
temptations. Led by the indefatigable Richard Nixon, the
Republicans made Communists-in-government the great issue
of the 1954 elections. Senator McCarthy having received his
censure in the Senate, the Communist issue was in the hands
of more respectable forces, civic-minded pyromaniacs. During
his thirty-three-state campaign for Republican candidates,
Nixon bore down hard on Truman for losing six hundred
million people to the Communists in seven years. He made
much of the fact that the Communist Party and Americans
for Democratic Action agreed on the desirability of recognizing
Red China and on the undesirability of the Eisenhower security
program and of "the Committee which brought out the evidence which convicted Alger Hiss." Three weeks before the
election the Civil Service Commission, egged on by Nixon,
announced that 6,926 federal employees had been dismissed
or had resigned under the new security program, leaving the
impression that these were all subversives appointed by Truman; a year later it was disclosed that more than 40 per cent
of them had been hired after the Republican Administration
took office, and most of those dismissed had not been charged
with disloyalty.

The Democrats recaptured control of both chambers that
November, but their margins were slim—twenty-nine seats in
the House, one in the Senate—and, for most purposes, the
Republican-Southern coalition remained in effective charge.
For the Committee, however, it meant a seemingly more con-

sequential change. Clardy, the ill-tempered lawyer whose affectation it had been to address people as "Witness" rather than by name, had been defeated in Michigan and was replaced on the Committee by an affable Democrat from Louisiana, Edwin E. Willis. And, of course, Harold Velde had to give over his gavel of office to Francis E. Walter. Liberal hearts leaped when a day after the election the chairman presumptive proposed nothing less than the abolition of the Un-American Activities Committee and the transfer of its functions to a subcommittee of the House Judiciary Committee which, it was understood, he would head. But the House Minority Leader Joe Martin let it be known that he would oppose such a move and the scheme was prudently dropped. "I don't propose," said Walter, "to take any step that would lend color to the phony Communist issue raised so frequently by the Republicans in the last campaign. This is not a political issue."

As 1954 came to a close, the Committee's opponents, an optimistic lot, had new grounds for optimism. Whereas every previous chairman had been a Congressional nonentity until the Committee shed its lustre upon him, Walter, who had come to the House in the year of Franklin Roosevelt's first election, was a power in his own right—chairman of the House Democratic Patronage Committee and ranking Democrat on the Judiciary Committee. He had voted against making the Un-American Activities Committee permanent, and had been named to it by loyal Democrats in an effort to protect the Administration from excessive abuse. His behavior was not altogether predictable, but he did object to several of Velde's adventures, and he was not given to joining Clardy, Jackson, and Scherer in the harassment of witnesses. Liberals held his sponsorship of the restrictive McCarran-Walter immigration law against him (on a 1952 campaign stop in Walter's district, with the Congressman on the platform, Adlai Stevenson refrained from asking for his reelection), yet they might, in time, have warmed toward a man who said out loud that he did not like Martin Dies or Joe McCarthy; who opposed the setting up of a committee to investigate tax-exempt foundations; who rebuked Velde for reporting out the Communist Control Act without taking a word of testimony on the measure—"the most flagrant attempt to jam legislation down the throat of the Committee . . . that I have ever seen"; and who declared, in reference to Velde's hiring of a new investigator a day after he resigned from the Air Force because he had passed a secret document to the Committee, that "surreptitious methods of pilfering files will not be tolerated by the Committee."[7] Perhaps a new day, more or less, was dawning.

[7] The captain referred to did not stay long with the Committee. Hired in November 1954, he was retired in January 1955, and the following August was arrested for having filched the secret document. It was a report from the Air Force's Office of Special Investigations on Jay Lovestone, the A. F. of L.'s anti-Communist specialist, who had been expelled by the Communist Party in 1929. He was of interest to the Committee because he had been named in executive testimony in 1953 by a dismissed Labor Department official as the "kingpin" who placed Communists in government. The allegation was wild, but not too wild for Clardy to use as the basis of a charge as he was separated from national life that there was "a gigantic world-wide network of Communists, previously unidentified, even now in the State, Labor and other departments."

13

★ ★ ★ ★ ★

1955-1956: The Walter Committee

THE HEARINGS of the Committee for the years 1955 through 1960 reflect changes of consequence that took place in that half decade. In 1955 the loyalty-security mania had reached its crest and was already abating. The war in Korea was over; Stalin was dead; the Hiss and Remington and Rosenberg affairs were fading into history and so was the terrible McCarthy. The Republican in the White House was scarcely vulnerable to charges of being soft on Communism and the Democrats in Congress were not of a mind to press such charges. Just as the country, uplifted upon the rhetoric of John Foster Dulles, would be slow to recognize what was happening—at least until the 1956 events in Hungary scotched the brave talk of "liberation"—so the Committee, caught in its own music, seemed to be going about its business as usual . . . but in fact business was off. In the eighty-fourth Congress, the Committee's index tells us, there were 121 days of public hearings, a large number but well below Velde's record of 178 days. The backlog was being used up, and raw materials were not so abundant. The number of hearings in the following four years added together would not reach the 1955–1956 figure.

The annual report of the Committee for 1954 asked, as usual, for more severe punishments of Communists, including an amendment to the Smith Act to make proof of C.P. membership *prima facie* evidence that an individual was conspiring to teach and advocate the overthrow of the U.S. government; it also commended the Detroit school system for removing

[367]

teachers who took the Fifth Amendment because "the delivery of a student into the tutelage of a member of the Communist Party has been responsible for the destruction of thousands of American homes." But otherwise the Committee's first weeks brought a strangely bright promise to its opponents. Chairman Walter again rebuffed an effort by Congressman Martin Dies, supported by Senator Joseph McCarthy, to come back to his old neighborhood.[1] Walter then announced that the Committee was overstaffed and overpaid, and soon counsel Kunzig and other Republican appointees "resigned." (Mrs. Harold Velde, the Committee's "official reporter," resigned along with them.) Walter asked Congress for $50,000 less for the year than the $275,000 that the group had gotten in 1954, a remarkable gesture on the part of a committee chairman. One of his economy measures was to do away with the leather-bound Committee identification cards ordered by Velde, the former F.B.I. man. Reports that the Congressmen had held a two-and-a-half-hour meeting devoted mainly to the subject of fair play for witnesses, like the promises that the Senate Investigations Subcommittee and the various loyalty boards were going to pay more attention to individual rights, were greeted by liberals with hopeful hearts. BACK TO THE AMERICAN WAY, called *The New York Times*.

The overture was unfamiliar. Not so the production. Walter never promised to leash up the Committee; what he promised was to "go after Communists as Communists," instead of as members of trades, professions, or avocations, and public hearings opened on the last day of February with a familiar bang. The third scheduled witness, John T. Gojack, vice president of the United Electrical, Radio and Machine Workers of America, that favorite Committee target, had barely taken his seat before he was denouncing the hearings as a "union busting venture." Gojack, a salty Midwestern organizer, was in fine fettle. He called the rival I.U.E.–C.I.O. "the only McCarthyite union in America," and wrote off the witnessess who

[1] McCarthy devoted part of a speech to Dies: "The leadership of the Democratic Party said, 'We won't put you on that Committee,' because they knew that Martin Dies wouldn't trifle with Communists. It was part of the continued effort to break Martin Dies."

had testified against him as two paid liars and one paid lunatic, but he declined to speak of the non-Communist affidavits he had signed and which were required of union officials by the Taft-Hartley Act. After lambasting the Committee for most of a morning, he complained to Representative Scherer, "You have been extremely provocative toward me. You have tried to provoke me into arguments here."

Gojack's only unorthodox act was to take the First Amendment rather than the Fifth when asked if he was a Communist at the moment in 1949 when the U.E. was expelled by the C.I.O., on the grounds that the Committee did not have the right to put such questions to him. He was cited for contempt without delay, but it would be more than eleven years before his case would be settled by the courts. His first conviction for contempt was thrown out by the Supreme Court in 1962 because his indictment had failed to specify the subject under inquiry by the Committee. A few months later he was reindicted for refusing to answer six questions, the first of which was, "Are you a member of the Communist Party?" He was found guilty and sentenced to three months' imprisonment and a fine of $200. The Court of Appeals upheld the conviction, but in June 1966 a unanimous Supreme Court voided it.

The American Civil Liberties Union, which filed a petition with the court in the case, hoped that the justices would take the opportunity to review the question of the Committee's constitutionality, and reverse its 1959 Barenblatt decision. The A.C.L.U. argued that since the world conditions which had led the court to choose national security over individual rights in 1959 had changed, the justification for invading the First Amendment rights of witnesses no longer existed. Justice Black agreed with the A.C.L.U., but the majority of the court, in a reprise of the Watkins decision, made their ruling on narrower grounds. The "question under inquiry," wrote Justice Fortas, was neither properly authorized nor specifically stated, and its purpose was not clearly understood even by members of the subcommittee, whose jurisdiction, moreover, had not been properly defined. Once again the high court cuffed the Committee but resisted knocking it flat.

A few weeks after the Gojack hearings there occurred a political sensation which, though not strictly Committee business, belongs in this history for what it tells about Francis Walter and his altered course in the last decade of his career from a responsible and generally respected legislator to a man obsessed.

The undisguised intent of the McCarran-Walter Immigration Law of 1952, based as it was on a system of national origins quotas for admitting immigrants, was to keep Eastern and Southern Europeans and Asians of all sorts out of the country. Thus, the law, passed over Mr. Truman's veto when security was the national bugbear, constituted a considerable political handicap in large cities filled with Italians, Poles and Slavs, whose kinsmen in the suffering Old World were being frankly discriminated against; and during the 1952 election both presidential candidates promised to do something about it. Mr. Eisenhower redeemed this promise with the Refugee Relief Act of 1953, which was supposed to admit more than 200,000 non-quota immigrants by the end of 1956. It was a grudging piece of legislation, bound in with requirements that each refugee prove that a job and home awaited him here, and capped with the provision that the good work be administered by the director of the State Department's Bureau of Security and Consular Affairs, a former F.B.I. man named R. W. Scott McLeod, whose first impulse upon seeing huddled masses was to search them. McLeod, in debt to Senator McCarthy for his job, participated in the demoralization of the State Department in the fifties. So restrictive was the legislation and so fastidious was the administrator that by the end of 1954 only a minute percentage of the designated number of refugees had been granted entry, and of these the overwhelming majority, fortunately for them, had relatives in this country.

Pressed by liberal and minority groups, as well as by G.O.P. politicos in the big cities, to show more enthusiasm for carrying out the Administration's own law, the State Department in January 1956 hired Edward Corsi to be special advisor to the Secretary of State on refugee and immigration matters. It was an appointment that pleased both those who were worried about votes and those who were worried about people. Corsi was a prominent New York Republican who had been Commissioner of Immigration under both Hoover and Roosevelt. An immigrant himself, having been brought here at the age of ten, he was full of ideas for letting non-Anglo-Saxons onto these shores. The State Department, more enamored of Corsi's image than of anything he might actually recommend, sent him off on a trip to Europe (accompanied by a former Texas ranger who filed confidential reports with McLeod) and trusted he would enjoy himself and not prove troublesome. But they reckoned neither on Corsi's humanitarian passions nor on the paternal feelings of Francis Walter for his immigration bill. Corsi had been publicly critical of the McCarran-Walter law before coming to Washington and in Walter's view that was sufficient cause not only to declare him unfit for his new post but also to question his loyalty. Relying on the Committee's files, Walter attacked Corsi for having belonged to a few Communist-front organizations in the nineteen-thirties, affiliations which Corsi denied and which Walter did not attempt to substantiate. Instead, in the middle of March, he sent a confidential letter to Secretary of State Dulles which took Corsi to task for "having expressed contumacious disdain and contempt" for the laws he was supposed to be administering and again referred to "Mr. Corsi's association with highly objectionable groups and organizations branded as subversive by the attorney general and his neglect to resign from such organizations after their true nature had become a matter of common knowledge . . ." These charges were flimsy, but Dulles could not lightly disregard a complaint from the chairman of the House Judiciary Subcommittee on Immigration Laws. Corsi had known Dulles and Attorney General Brownell, both New York Republicans, for years, but, as he later complained, "after Walter made his unfounded charges, nobody spoke out. Nobody was around. I've never felt so much a stranger."

In April, Corsi, who had recently rented a house in Arlington for six months, was belatedly informed that his appointment had been a temporary one; now that his ninety days were almost up, he was presented with the opportunity of "making a survey with reference to the possibilities of land settlement in Latin America and other areas." A variety of reasons were advanced for exiling Corsi to exotic places—the same Dulles who had welcomed him in January as "the best qualified" man in the country to break the immigration logjam now found him unqualified because he was not a good administrator—but the credit belonged entirely to Francis Walter. If J. Parnell Thomas or Harold Velde had done this kind of job on Corsi, there would have been no cause for surprise, but Walter's career had been of a distinctly different sort. Up until his sponsorship of the immigration bill, he been no darling of the right wing, but he had invested so much of himself in that bill and been so hurt and angered by the outcry against him within the party he had served for so many years that after 1952 anyone who criticized his law was marked in his mind as a probable subversive and could be fought on that premise. The conduct of the Un-American Activities Committee under his chairmanship becomes less mystifying if we allow that the same man who disdained Dies and McCarthy could for the last ten years of his life nourish and exercise a powerful grudge against the whole liberal community.

Despite the attentions of the Messrs. Scherer and Jackson,[2] the Committee's record in the eighty-fourth Congress was distinguished by unusual courtesy and coherence. The stuff of the proceedings, however, was much the same as it had been for the past few years. Like a TV format come to weary middle age, the operations settled into the established informant–Fifth Amendment pattern. A policewoman from Brook-

[2] Both Congressmen continued to be irritated by the use to which the Fifth Amendment was being put, and could be counted on to dispute a witness' right to the Fifth, to press subcommittee chairmen to demand answers to their questions, and to threaten contempt proceedings. During hearings in Los Angeles Jackson asked a former Communist whether she knew anyone named Francik Mizokljyk, "a Pole, I imagine." When the witness pleaded the Fifth, as she had been doing all along, Jackson announced that the name was totally fictitious; he had made it up to demonstrate that the self-incrimination clause was being used in response to questions that could not possibly incriminate anyone. He made his point, but only at the cost of revealing a frivolous attitude toward entrapping a witness before a Congressional committee. Scherer performed the same trick on a Newark paperhanger in September 1958; he used the name Joseph Stepovich, but refrained from identifying him as a Pole.

lyn gave several hundred names of Party members she had known in Flatbush in the nineteen-forties. The Committee to Secure Justice for the Rosenbergs, peace organizations in several cities, and a half dozen New York State summer camps were shown to be weighted with Communists. Two days were given over to "Attempts at Subversion and Espionage by Diplomatic Personnel"—which had to do with the peculiar activities of a man from the Soviet Embassy named Mikheev in openly approaching three government employees for information that was not classified. Hə was either an honest researcher or a delightfully inept spy. In either case, the Committee's script did not measure up to its title. And, in another hearing, former Representative Jerry J. O'Connell, a Montana Democrat who had been mentioned in friendly testimony as an accomplice of the Communists, conceded to the Committee that he had participated in quite an array of front organizations. In speaking of his own political philosophy, O'Connell, a hard-working fellow traveler, showed how much he owed to the pat phrases of the thirties: "I can be a non-Communist, and yet not anti-Communist, just like I can be a Democrat and yet not an anti-Republican."

Not all of the hearings were amiable. More than a thousand U.E. members demonstrated in front of the Newark hotel where Representatives Scherer and Doyle, described by the picketers as "a bunch of rats," were staying when they opened another investigation of Communist control of a big U.E. local. Events inside the hearing room, too, were stormy. The union organizers and business agents named as Communists by an unidentified F.B.I. source, as well as by former colleagues, were loud and insulting, given to expostulating on the subject of stool pigeons and union busters and fascists, but shy about their own activities. "Mr. Chairman, I say again that if you prefer to believe the word of stool pigeons and paid informers and other assorted finks, that is okay with me, except I will stand on the privilege of the Fifth Amendment." It was an ungallant display which left a clear impression that the stool pigeons, informers and finks were telling the truth about the U.E. officials. Three Newark teachers who took the Fifth were fired and turned to the courts for redress, and, as a result of the Committee's visit, the Newark City Council unanimously adopted a loyalty oath for all city employees.

Hearings in Los Angeles aimed at a rebellious Musicians Union local were timed to assist the national union beat down the rebels. Left-wing union officials were also called up in Seattle and Denver, and Communist influence in the Young Progressives of America, the Civil Rights Congress, and the Labor Youth League were aired in Milwaukee, where it was disclosed that two undercover F.B.I. informants had been conscientiously including one another in their reports to the home office. As the number of C.P. members declined, the proportions of delegates from the F.B.I. naturally increased, and in North Carolina, too, a pair of informants dutifully exposed one another for the Congressmen's benefit.

The Committee's files, which John Rankin had gone to such lengths to preserve from the Potomac River, were put to notable, if not novel, use during the eighty-fourth Congress. They were employed by Southerners against the civil-rights movement, which had gained great momentum with the Supreme Court school integration decision of 1954. In February 1956, States' Rights activists in Louisiana publicized the alleged Communist-front associations of Hulan Jack, Manhattan borough president and a Negro, when he visited New Orleans to participate in a Catholic interracial program. The information had been released by the Committee's staff director to Senator James O. Eastland of Mississippi, who courteously passed it on to his neighbors in Louisiana.

A few weeks later, as a prelude to a large civil rights march on Washington, Representative E. C. Gathings of Arkansas read into the Congressional Record the Committee's citations for leaders of the National Association for the Advancement of Colored People. Those listed included Roy Wilkins, A. Philip Randolph, Ralph Bunche, Robert Weaver, Morris Ernst, John Haynes Holmes—quite a distinguished roll. Each name was preceded by a disclaimer:

The public record, files and publications of this Committee contain the following information concerning the subject individual.

> This report should not be construed as representing the results of an investigation by or findings of this Committee. It should be noted that the individual is not necessarily a Communist, a Communist sympathizer or a fellow-traveller unless otherwise indicated.

Anyone who had followed the careers of most of the persons listed knew that although their battles in the Negro's cause brought them into alliance with Communists now and then, they were neither Party members nor facsimiles. By presenting the citations straight, without a critical gloss, and by notifying the Congress that 44.1 per cent of the N.A.A.C.P. leaders had been cited by the Un-American Activities Committee (a calculation that included Eric Johnston who had two "citations" to his name—both involving his position with the Motion Picture Producers Association at the time of the 1947 Hollywood hearings), Gathings sought to stigmatize the entire civil rights movement.[3] He was congratulated for his presentation by several Southern colleagues.

Succumbing again to the allure of show business, the staff of the Velde Committee had rounded up the names of another batch of Broadway people whom it was left to the Walter Committee to herd into the public corral. In July 1955 the news got out that about two dozen persons—most of them actors, with a scattering of other occupations—had been subpoenaed for August hearings at the U.S. Court House on Foley Square. Walter, who had begun his tenure as chairman with a vow not to investigate specific trades or professions, now promised to cover the "broad field" of entertainment in New York City. Pressed to explain the purpose of the investigation, he referred vaguely to Communist infiltration of the entertainment unions and to the filling of Communist coffers with Broadway salary checks, but neither line was pursued. Most of the witnesses were several steps below star rank and whatever their inclinations they could hardly have done much to keep the

[3] This was not the last time that Gathings would deliver this recital. After he read the citations into the Congressional Record again in 1963 during the debate on civil rights legislation, the Committee's staff director, Francis J. McNamara, told me, "We can't control what Congressmen do with the material."

Communist Party afloat. As for the unions, they had some time since shaken off the remnants of Communist influence, and a few days before the start of hearings, the American Federation of Television and Radio Artists authorized its local units to take disciplinary measures against any member who failed to answer questions before a Congressional committee. A recalcitrant performer might be fined, censured, suspended, or expelled on the charge of conduct prejudicial to the welfare of the union. A.F.T.R.A. had previously condemned the black-listing organization which called itself AWARE for circulating lists of entertainment figures named in reports of the Un-American Activities Committee, but by this vote the union put itself on the side of those who held that resort to the Fifth Amendment was sufficient reason to deprive a man or woman of even the most innocent livelihood.

But for the cloud of the blacklist, the subcommittee's few August days in New York would have been merely frivolous. The blacklisters, however, went all out to turn it into an occasion. Representatives Walter, Willis, and Scherer were welcomed to New York by a statement signed by such anti-Communist warriors as George Sokolsky, Eugene Lyons, Victor Lasky, Manning Johnson, and Vincent Hartnett, who was then making a living as a compiler of dossiers on show business personalities. He called himself a "talent consultant" and charged $5 a head for short reports, $20 for long reports. On the evening of the first day of hearings Walter was guest of honor at a rally, put on by a group called Alliance, Inc., Archibald B. Roosevelt presiding. "Is Joe McCarthy out of business?" asked Archibald Roosevelt, and the audience yelled back, "No!" There Walter, not entirely comfortable in the McCarthy mantle, said that he hoped theatrical employers would be "traditionally American and withhold judgment until they know what all the facts are." (The American Civil Liberties Union made its own contribution to the art of the pro forma statement when it called on the Committee to confine its questioning "strictly to conspiratorial acts.")

In its four days at the courthouse, which were honored by visits from Bernard Baruch and Hamilton Fish and during which the hiring of Elizabeth Bentley as Committee consultant was announced, the Committee heard twenty-three witnesses, most of whom had previously been mentioned by Martin Berkeley, Elia Kazan, Lee J. Cobb, or Jerome Robbins or who were in AWARE's bad books. One young man, briefly exposed to the C.P.'s Broadway branch in the forties, cooperated with the Committee and was assured by Walter that in the cold war his contribution might be equal to that of a division of infantry. The other witnesses declined to answer the critical questions; eighteen of them took the Fifth Amendment; one took the First Amendment; three took no amendments. A few were obnoxious in the hard-line style; their main objection to the blacklist seemed to be that it was not directed against people they didn't like, such as Kazan and Cobb. (Before the anti-Communists found it in their power to blacklist Communists, the Communists did what they could to keep anti-Communists from working. But they were not nearly so effective at it.) "Is this the Kazan that signed the contract for $500,000 on the day after he gave names to this Committee?" asked a producer who had been dropped by C.B.S. in 1951 upon being mentioned as a candidate for a Committee subpoena. "Would you sell your brothers for $500,000?" But for the most part the hearings were placid. The most serious offense revealed in the professional lives of the accused had to do with a skit presented at a New York State summer camp by Elliot Sullivan, an actor who had been featured in some eighty movies and seventy-five radio shows before being set down in the blacklister's bible, *Red Channels*. The skit had to do with two sneaky-looking fellows selling the Bill of Rights to each other; after the sales were completed, they both revealed themselves as F.B.I. agents and arrested one another. The Congressmen felt that this was a insult to the Bill of Rights since the sale price was only one dollar.

Sullivan, who two weeks earlier had taken the Fifth Amendment before the Committee, now stood on the First Amendment and was duly cited for contempt along with an actor named George Tyne, who questioned the pertinency of his alleged Communist connections to the Committee's work, and the folk singer Pete Seeger, bard of the Wallace movement and a popular figure in Communist-front festivities. Seeger put on a folksy manner in the witness chair, presenting himself as a "banjo-picker" who knew nothing of Communists, but just went around the world making the common people happy with his songs. But when the usual questions were put to him, he dropped the stage business and objected calmly and succinctly to the intrusion on his privacy: "I am not going to answer any questions as to my associations, my philosophical or religious beliefs, or how I voted in any elections or any of these private affairs. I think they are very improper questions for any American to be asked, especially under such compulsion as this."[4]

Tyne and Sullivan were acquitted of contempt in 1961, when the district court found their indictments "fatally defective" because the government had not submitted the Committee's resolution ordering the hearing. Seeger was sentenced to a year in prison—after a trial in which Chairman Walter was put on the stand—but in 1962 the Court of Appeals unanimously reversed the conviction on the grounds that *his* indictment was defective too, for much the same reason. Seeger's indictment had included the Committee's authorization to its clerk to undertake the entertainment investigation, but had omitted specific authorization for the subcommittee hearings. The judges, responding to the government's contention that this omisison was a "hypertechnical" point, took a high road:

> A defendant, faced with possible loss of liberty, should not at the commencement of the prosecution, be made to guess whether the inquiring body has power to exact his testimony . . . We are not inclined to dismiss lightly claims of constitutional stature because they are asserted by one who may appear to be unworthy of sympathy. Once we embark upon shortcuts by creating a category of the "obviously guilty" whose rights are denied, we run the risk that the circle of the unprotected will grow.

[4] Despite the surge of popularity of folk singing in the late nineteen-fifties and early sixties, the talented Seeger was not seen on network television between 1950 and 1967. In September 1967, the producers of the Smothers Brothers Comedy Hour and executives at C.B.S. judged that the weather had cleared sufficiently to hire him. So, finally, he appeared, but was not permitted to sing a song critical of President Johnson.

Nevertheless, for all the fine language, the Committee had unquestionably authorized the Seeger hearings, and the court's decision did indeed rest on a technicality that saved the judges from confronting Seeger's claim that his constitutional rights had been violated.

Although there was not much in the way of an immediate future for the subpoenaed entertainers in the movies, television, or radio, most of them would continue to find theater work. (Zero Mostel, the outstanding talent among those called up in August, could not make it in from California owing to professional commitments and so did not take his Fifth Amendment until October.) Broadway, relatively free of political censorship and dependent on a small, liberal, big-city clientele, was not susceptible to the pressures that could put a local movie house out of business or give a TV sponsor the shakes, and off-Broadway liked nothing better than to have its little-noticed productions picketed. Still, the employment opportunities of entertainers who had been marked down as Communists were diminished and there were protests, demonstrations, and exposés on the left against the existence of a show-business blacklist watched over by kindred spirits of Joe McCarthy. The Committee's majority, including the chairman, took these flurries personally and, in the spring of 1956, with the publication of a report on blacklisting by the Fund for the Republic, found a means of replying to them.

The Fund for the Republic, run by the erstwhile head of the University of Chicago, Robert M. Hutchins, had been set up by the Ford Foundation in 1951 to support activities "directed toward the elimination of restrictions on freedom of thought, inquiry and expression in the United States." Since 1953, when it was turned loose and became, in Hutchins's phrase, "a wholly disavowed subsidiary of the Ford Foundation," with fifteen million dollars to keep it going, it had directed its energies against everything that the Committee on Un-American Activities considered American. Its very first act was to give $25,000 to the American Bar Association for a study of Congressional investigating committees. It distributed works by critics of the investigations such as Telford Taylor, Alan Barth, and Dean

Griswold[5] and films of the impressive Ed Murrow–J. Robert
Oppenheimer TV interview; it financed studies of the effects
on individual rights of the federal security program; it gave
$150,000 to the American Friends Service Committee for use
in legal cases "to strengthen the right to freedom of conscience,"
$240,000 to the Southern Regional Council for "education in
intergroup relations in twelve states," and $5,000 to a Quaker
group in Pennsylvania for hiring a librarian who had invoked
the Fifth Amendment. In 1955 it produced a *Bibliography of
the Communist Program in the United States* which at once
had to be revised because of charges from scholars of "inexcusable sloppiness," "distortion by omission," and a tendency
to discriminate against sophisticated anti-Communist writers
like Arthur Koestler, Dwight Macdonald, Max Eastman, and
Bertram Wolfe, while including trivial material from the Party
press. Hutchins, who had a reputation as a baiter of boobs
to maintain, said in public, "I wouldn't hesitate to hire a
Communist for a job he was qualified to do provided I was
in a position to see that he did it"—and, indeed, the Fund
had hired a newspaperman after he took the Fifth before a
Senate committee.

This record was sufficient to bring down attacks from the
American Legion, whose national commander charged that
the Fund was trying to "persuade Americans that Communism
is not and never has been a serious threat to the United States,"
from senators like John Bricker and representatives like B.
Carroll Reece, and from Fulton Lewis, Jr., who called it "an
extensive ideological political propaganda organization, promoting the doctrines of the Americans for Democratic Action
and all points to the left of that, fighting the security programs
by which the federal government tries to protect itself against
every infiltration, fighting also the Congressional investigators
who seek to expose Communists and the methods the Communists have used in the past to infiltrate our government up
to the very highest level." In June of 1956 Francis Walter,

[5] The Fund made no pretense of objectivity in these matters. It put out
35,000 copies of the Griswold book, *The Fifth Amendment Today,* and only
1,000 copies of an effective rebuttal by C. Dickerman Williams.

who suspected the Fund's directors of lobbying for repeal of his immigration law, announced that he intended to investigate the body, with a view to answering the question, "Is this foundation, with its vast reservoir of funds and power a friend or foe in the nation's death struggle against the Communist conspiracy?" Two weeks later Walter said the investigation was being postponed, but in July it suddenly came to life again.

The largest grant allotted by the Fund in its first years was $300,000 for "an account of Communist influence in major segments of U. S. society," and one of the studies undertaken was of "Blacklisting in Private Industry." In context, "industry" meant the entertainment industry, and the end of June 1956 saw the publication of a two-volume *Report on Blacklisting* written by John Cogley, former executive editor of *Commonweal*. It charged that blacklisting had become an institution in movies, radio, and television, that hundreds of persons were being denied employment because of their Communist associations, and that industry leaders had given over responsibility for judging accused individuals to the very people who had promoted the blacklist in the first place. Executives in Hollywood deferred to the American Legion, while the producers, advertising agencies, and sponsors of radio and TV shows were guided by *Red Channels*—a list of alleged Communists in entertainment put out by three former F.B.I. operatives in 1950—and AWARE, formed in 1953 to "combat the Communist conspiracy in entertainment communications," whose main function was to issue bulletins on the backgrounds of performers. The Cogley report also told how several Communist-hunters, led by the columnist George Sokolsky and the former Hollywood A. F. of L. leader Roy Brewer, were engaged in a "rehabilitation" campaign for those unjustly accused or truly repentant—a mission which some of their allies frowned upon as soft on sinners. *Report on Blacklisting* was not a model of sound journalism. It made extensive use of anonymous informants—fearful members of a frightened industry;[6] printed

---

[6] Cogley later complained that those in the industry who had protested bitterly to him of blacklisting when assured of anonymity did not step forward to say a word in support of his report when it came under attack.

charges of vigilante activities without in all cases taking pains to check with the alleged vigilantes; and relied heavily on tales of individual injustice—mistaken identity and the like—instead of coming to grips with the central issue of whether it was justifiable to keep even a thrice-proven Communist out of a job that had nothing to do with the national security. Yet with these defects, this was by far the best report done up to that time on a subject that few knowing people in Hollywood or New York cared to talk about for publication. A blacklist there indubitably was, and industry leaders, true to their careers, had given it into the charge of zealots and con men; the masters of the mass media had entangled themselves in loyalty oaths, security checks, and clearance procedures that were debasing to the accused and sources of temptation to their accusers.

Protests against Cogley's work were raised as soon as it was published. The Committee was on excellent terms with the American Legion and with AWARE, and Walter did not have to read the report to know that he disagreed with it on two counts. First, he denied there was any such thing as a blacklist and second, he wanted all Communists driven out of films, theater, radio, television, and, if feasible, out of the country. On July 10 he opened his "Investigation of So-Called 'Blacklisting' in Entertainment Industry—Report of the Fund for the Republic, Inc." The first witness was John Cogley, in 1953 a "personal assistant" to Robert Hutchins at the Fund for the Republic. He had been subpoenaed to appear instead of merely being invited, and from the outset it was evident that Walter had no great interest in the subject of blacklisting, but a driving desire to blacken Cogley's report and, through that, the Fund and all its works. The interrogation was conducted by Richard Arens, formerly with the Senate Internal Security Subcommittee, who had taken over as Committee staff director in May. Spurning the forms of objectivity, he attacked at once, beginning with a quotation from the conservative Catholic publication, *The Tablet*, to the effect that the liberal Catholic publication, *Commonweal*, was not Catholic at all. He brought two major charges against Cogley's report: first, that it had been assembled by persons of suspect background and second, that it did not give the Communist affiliations of the "sad cases" which it reported—"Did you at any place in your treatise list the Communist-front record of Larry Adler and of Paul Draper, which is as long as two arms?" In a sense, Cogley had brought this kind of attack on himself for basing his argument on cases of mistaken identity rather than granting at once that most of the blacklistees were or had been Communists (or had done their darndest to pass as such), and arguing against the blacklist even in their desperate cases. As to the first charge, Arens was particularly unfortunate in the persons he picked out as Communist sympathizers. One was Dr. Maria Jahoda, a social scientist who had belonged to the Socialist Democratic Party in Austria before coming to this country in 1945 ("only in 1945," was the way Arens put it and he wanted to know whether Cogley had checked with the F.B.I. before hiring her); she had contributed an interesting paper on the difficulties encountered by *anti*-Communists in radio and television. Another was Paul Jacobs, who had belonged to the Young Communist League twenty years before and had taken part in the wars against Stalinists in labor unions and elsewhere ever since. And a third was Michael Harrington, a proudly confessed socialist. "You, of course, are aware of the fact," said Arens to Cogley, "that Lenin, the key philosopher of Communism, had said socialism is only one transition toward Communism." Doyle and Moulder showed some signs of sympathy for Cogley during his interrogation, but were even less effectual than usual.

The next day Arnold Forster, counsel of B'nai Brith's Anti-Defamation League and a major source of Cogley's information, told how he had prevailed upon influential right-wingers to help "rehabilitate" some unfortunates. Then came an honor guard of the country's preeminent blacklisters. James F. O'Neil of the American Legion said that blacklisting was reprehensible but that persons identified with the Communist apparatus should not be employed in the entertainment industry. Vincent W. Hartnett, the "talent consultant," and Paul R. Milton, a founder of AWARE, Inc., and Godfrey P. Schmidt, AWARE's president, and Roy M. Brewer, who had by now moved from union leader to industry executive, and Francis J. McNamara —formerly with the anti-Communist organ, *Counterattack*, at the time of his appearance director of the American Sovereignty Campaign of the Veterans of Foreign Wars, and today director of the Committee on Un-American Activities—agreed with O'Neil. McNamara said he liked to think of his work as similar to that of Dun & Bradstreet—handing out credit ratings on people—and nobody called Dun & Bradstreet a blacklisting outfit. These witnesses were treated with surpassing deference; they were permitted to say whatever they wished at their own length, and after listening to them Walter announced what he might have announced before the hearings began, that in his view "the Fund for the Republic report is a partisan, biased attack on all persons and organizations who are sincerely and patriotically concerned in ridding the movie industry and radio and television of Communists and Communist sympathizers."

Walter had promised that some of the allegedly blacklisted performers would be called to testify, and two—Gale Sondergaard and Jack Gilford—were subpoenaed. The careers of both had been buffeted by winds from the right, but instead of questioning them about their experiences, Arens put them, once again, through the Fifth Amendment ritual. He used them not for information about the blacklist but to drive home the point that those who complained of being blacklisted were in fact Communists. That, in the minds of Walter, Arens, Jackson, Scherer, and their friends among the veterans, was sufficient cause for denial of employment not only in entertainment but virtually anywhere—and it was the central point at issue in the Committee's sudden foray, a week after Cogley's appearance, into the Fund for the Republic's award of $5,000 to the Plymouth Monthly Meeting, whose library committee had hired a former Communist. "The Committee wishes to know," said Walter at the outset, "more about the factors which prompted the Fund for the Republic to consider the retention of a Communist a defense of 'democratic principles' worth $5,000 of its tax-exempt money."

This one-day hearing opened with the researcher who had looked into the case for the Fund. Arens directed his questions at showing that she had interviewed in the main persons favorable to the retention of Mrs. Mary Knowles, who had been having trouble finding a job since being named as a former Communist by Herbert Philbrick and taking the Fifth Amendment. The library committee of the Quaker Meeting hired her upon her assurance that she had not been a member of a subversive organization since 1947, and Arens brought forward four prominent residents who wanted Mrs. Knowles removed. The last witness, received more coolly than the four, was a member of the library committee who had voted to hire her. Such was the dissension among the Friends, whipped up by a band called Americans Alerted,[7] that the $5,000 gift was still being held in escrow, and several major benefactors of the library had withdrawn their support. Arens established the point that the Fund's award had fed controversy in Plymouth. But it was a small accomplishment for the director since the gift had been frankly designed to bolster resistance to the sentiment, assiduously promoted by his Committee, against giving aid, comfort, or sustenance to politically abhorrent persons.

Chairman Walter's justification for troubling himself over the case of a small-town librarian and a report on blacklisting was that the Fund for the Republic, being a tax-exempt operation, could not lightly spend its money on causes which he did not deem to be in the soundest interests of the United States. Although foundations were the province of another Congressional committee, the rationale was not absurd; liberal groups have often complained of the uses to which rightwingers like H. L. Hunt have put their tax-exempt money, the nub of the argument being that one man's education is another man's propaganda. But despite repeated requests for a full hearing from the Fund's prestigious directors—Paul G. Hoffman, John Lord O'Brien, Elmo Roper, and James D. Zellerbach

[7] Americans Alerted sent out flyers of this sort: "Did you also know that Mrs. Knowles is by no means the only Security Risk working or living in this immediate neighborhood? That Plymouth-Whitemarsh has been and still is being infiltrated?"

among others—and promises by Walter that there would be such a hearing for "this multi-million dollar propaganda machine which enjoys tax exemption," the Committee never picked up the challenge of an open confrontation. It chose instead the tactic of hit-and-run assault and verdict by press release.

A better ordered, more solidly fleshed set of hearings began in December 1955, when Herbert Fuchs, a former attorney for the National Labor Relations Board, told the Committee in public session what he had previously told it in executive session—that during most of his years with the government, from 1937 to 1948, he had been a participant in Communist cells made up of N.L.R.B. lawyers and other federal employees. Fuchs came to public attention in September 1955, midway between his executive testimony and his open hearing, when it was announced that he was being dropped from the law faculty of American University, in Washington, D. C., where he had been teaching since 1949. At his first meeting with the Committee in June, Fuchs refused to testify about others, whereupon the president of the university assured him of support. In July he changed his mind, named names, and was given a choice by the president of suspension or a leave of absence, both preliminary to the non-renewal of his contract. Representative Willis took note of the fact that American University was a Methodist institution in whose policies Bishop Oxnam had a substantial hand, and implied that the bishop was seeking to penalize Fuchs for cooperating with the Committee. The university, in an indefensible position, did not trouble to defend itself. When the ultimatum became known, Fuchs found himself championed by a peculiar alliance of Communist-hunters and civil libertarians, which included Representative Walter and Reinhold Niebuhr, Representative Scherer and the American Civil Liberties Union, the American Committee for Cultural Freedom and the *Saturday Evening Post*. Virtually the only groups that did not wear Fuchs's colors were those that had been loudest in their complaints over the firings of teachers who had refused to cooperate with Congressional committees.

During the hearings on federally employed Communists that followed Fuchs's testimony, the Emergency Civil Liberties Committee, several of whose more eminent supporters were themselves in process of taking the Fifth Amendment, sent a petition to the House of Representatives calling the investigation "illegal, invalid and contrary to the Committee's enabling resolution." The phrasing was standard but hardly compelling since the Committee, for a change, was actually looking into the activities of Communists in government agencies, a job that was historically within its compass if anything was.

Fuchs made a careful and believable witness. Among the former government employees he named were seventeen attorneys who, he said, had been in his Communist group at the N.L.R.B.—a fair number out of a legal review staff that rarely went above 115 and was sometimes as low as twenty-five. As the hearings proceeded, two of the persons named corroborated Fuchs's testimony and a third said he had socialized with the group but had never belonged to the Party; only one of the lawyers, a woman, denied the accusations. The others called up all took the Fifth Amendment.[8] Not among these named by Fuchs but also taking the Fifth were two familiar faces, Edwin S. Smith, member of the N.L.R.B. until 1941, and Nathan Witt, the board's secretary for most of Smith's tenure and an intimate of Lee Pressman's before the Korean War came between them. By 1956 Edwin Smith, who had been indignant when charged with leftist leanings by Martin Dies, was a registered agent of the Soviet Union, in the trade of selling photographs of the U.S.S.R. and the People's Democracies to United States publications; he had already pleaded self-incrimination before a Senate committee.

[8] Most of those who pleaded the Fifth were associated with the National Lawyers Guild. Walter, who wanted to bar lawyers from representing witnesses before the Committee unless they swore they were neither Communists nor former Communists, had to endure hearing attorneys David Rein and Frank Donner take the Fifth and then having them reappear alongside clients in the hearing room. When some weeks later Leonard Boudin, an outstanding counsel for unfriendly witnesses, was called up and angrily denied ever having been a Party member, Walter's small supply of patience gave out and he demanded that the attorney be investigated for perjury—though there was no evidence against Boudin except his legal specialty. In 1960 Boudin was still representing witnesses and Walter was still calling him a Communist.

The N.L.R.B. hearings followed accusations by Senator McCarthy that the agency was "literally honeycombed" with promoters of Communist movements; the board, now with a Republican majority, responded by putting three hundred more jobs into the "sensitive" category, which required F.B.I. clearance. Arens attempted in his questioning to draw a picture of Nathan Witt bringing his Communist protégés into the N.L.R.B. for the purpose of subverting the American labor movement. He demanded to know whether any "Communist organization masquarading as a labor union" was denied bargaining rights by the N.L.R.B. in the thirties, and had to be reminded that there was nothing in the Wagner Act damning Communist unions. The N.L.R.B. had previously been looked into by a special committee under Representative Howard Smith in 1940 and by a saner Senate committee in 1953, where evidence was adduced that Witt and Smith went out of their way to be of service to Lee Pressman and Harry Bridges. They were severely criticized by their N.L.R.B. colleagues and knowledgeable persons in the labor movement. But the picture was not so simple as Arens would have liked.

As Fuchs did his best to explain, Communists in the thirties were heart and soul in favor of the Wagner Act and it required no dissimulation on their part to carry out its provisions with zeal: ". . . we told ourselves and were told that to be good Communists at the National Labor Relations Board the better job we did for the board and for the government, that was it." When asked whether decisions had been loaded in favor of Communist unions, Fuchs referred Arens to the records of twenty years past—a laborious pursuit which counsel did not undertake—and avowed, to Arens's incredulity, that the Communists in the N.L.R.B. were not faking their official duties. The point that Fuchs tried to get across was one the Committee always had difficulty in crediting: that in the nineteen-thirties, Alger Hiss notwithstanding, there was no question of divided loyalties for the majority of Communists in government. They were mainly talkers, not couriers, and they needed no directives from Moscow on how to conduct their professional duties. They were young, idealistic, ambitious, and they believed in the New Deal. Earl Latham points out what single-minded hunters of conspiracy invariably overlooked—"that there was a motion and life in the government service that was quite independent of any contrivance, responding to the restlessness of people interested in promotions, increases within grade, new opportunities, more challenging responsibilities, more interesting jobs; and responding also to the continuous creation of new agencies, and therefore of new chances of interesting and financially rewarding employment." Which is no more than to say what by the mid-fifties it was difficult to remember— that the Communists in government in the thirties were subject to all the minor vices common to ambitious young bureaucrats, and also partook of their virtues.

In the spring of 1956, the Committee turned to a subject close to the chairman's troubled heart. Complementing his anxiety over undesirable foreigners coming to this country was an annoyance that undesirable Americans should be able to leave it from time to time. He had been offended lately by a Court of Appeals decision that took from the State Department's Passport Office some of the arbitrary powers (such as denying passports without a hearing) it had exercised upon Americans wishing to travel abroad, and he had introduced a bill to restore to the Secretary of State power to prohibit passports to Communists and their sympathizers and to deny rejected applicants access to evidence against them that might compromise investigative sources. Meanwhile, he called upon Mr. Dulles simply to refuse passports to any persons against whom there was "adverse security information"—which would have meant defying the courts. Passport legislation was, strictly speaking, in the purview of the House Judiciary Committee, but Walter sought to aid his cause by producing before the Committee on Un-American Activities a number of persons who, he said, had participated in a "skillfully organized Communist passport conspiracy by which Party members and fellow travelers are enlisted to travel abroad in the service of Soviet propaganda and subversion." The reference was to voyagers who, defying government injunctions to shun Com-

munist lands, wound up at youth conferences and peace conferences in Warsaw and Peking, visited Prague and Moscow,
and took part in anti-American spectacles wherever they went.
One of them had, in the cause of peace and world amity,
delivered a broadcast from Peking in 1952 to the effect that
United States troops in Korea had packed three hundred
children into a building, set it afire, and then machine-gunned
the mothers who tried to rescue the children. Their host countries obliged them by stamping their visas on separate pieces
of paper rather than in their passports to make their return
to this country less troublesome.

The Committee had its facts in order, and most of the witnesses called up took the Fifth Amendment. One of the more
prominent, the Communist apologist and divine Willard Uphaus, who had lent his name to Communist charges that
America used germ warfare in Korea, was in an orotund mood.
He waved a Bible and reminded the Committee that "Jesus
stood before Pilate and He didn't answer a single question
when asked." To which Arens responded, "Well, He wasn't
asked whether He was hooked up with Communist conspiracy."
Where Uphaus took as his sermon Peace Through Brotherhood
("We are all human beings, sir," he observed when Walter
chided him for speaking of Republicans and Communists in
the same breath. "We are all children of God. They too are
beloved, just as well as other people."), Paul Robeson blew
the trumpets of proletarian war. His appearance was all hollering and thumping and gaveling and speechifying: ". . . I am
not being tried for whether I am a Communist, I am being
tried for fighting for the rights of my people who are still
second class citizens . . ." and ". . . in Russia [in 1934] I felt
for the first time like a full human being, and no colored
prejudice like in Mississippi and no colored prejudice like in
Washington . . ." On being asked whether he had made a
speech in Moscow praising Stalin, he threw back an indictment
that would be heard a decade later from James Baldwin and
LeRoi Jones and Black Nationalists: "You are responsible and
your forebears for sixty million to one hundred million black
people dying in the slave ships and on the plantations, and

don't you ask me about anybody, please." Robeson's great
talent had raised him far above the run of American Communists, but his rhetoric did not rise with him, and one could
sympathize with Walter when he muttered, "I have endured
all of this that I can," and abruptly adjourned the hearing.

Robeson was threatened with contempt for his performance,
but although he was inordinately contemptuous and although
he was having passport troubles at the time, the Committee
thought better than to give him yet another stage for his
resonant defiance. Contempt citations were, however, brought
against two other eminent witnesses who had been having
difficulty prying their passports loose from the State Department: Otto Nathan, professor of economics at New York University and the executor of Albert Einstein's estate, and the
playwright Arthur Miller. Neither could claim Robeson's
degree of loyalty to the Kremlin, but both had been involved
with the Party and its fronts and both, without taking advantage of the Fifth Amendment, refused to answer Arens's
questions regarding their past associations. Their manners,
however, were dissimilar, a reflection not only of their differing
temperaments but the differing approaches of their attorneys.
Nathan, accompanied by Leonard Boudin, whose own recent
Committee appearance had been full of angry exchanges,
assumed a righteous air. When asked whether he was a Party
member, he referred Arens to a non-Communist affidavit he
had signed in 1953 and when asked whether the affidavit was
truthful, he took the question as an insult: "Mr. Chairman, I
resent the implication that I have made a statement under
oath which shouldn't be correct. I refuse to answer. I think
there is a limit beyond which counsel may not be permitted
to go." Nathan also refused, understandably, to hand over
to the Committee the passport he had finally been granted by
the State Department after a two-and-a-half-year delay. In
declining to give answers to Arens, Nathan questioned the
jurisdiction of the Committee and the purpose of the hearing
and took the First, Fourth, and Ninth Amendments, but not
the Fifth.

Whereas the Nathan hearing caused Arens to shout and

pound, Arthur Miller's appearance was notable for its air of
sober amiability. Miller—accompanied by Joseph Rauh, who
was identified with Americans for Democratic Action rather
than with the National Lawyers Guild—readily conceded that
he had run with the Communists during the nineteen-forties,
though he didn't recall ever signing a C.P. application form.
But he had learned his lesson: "I would not now support a
cause or movement dominated by Communists." This declaration did not prevent the Committee's director from leading him
through a review of his career[9] as a signer of statements put
out by the Civil Rights Congress against anti-Communist
legislation and the Un-American Activities Committee and in
behalf of Gerhart Eisler and Howard Fast. Despite a certain
fuzziness on a number of points, Miller made a credible witness.
He was responsive, collected, and only moderately sententious.
He was decently annoyed at the uses to which the Communists
had put his play about witch hunting in Salem, *The Crucible*
(Howard Fast interpreted it as a statement on the Rosenberg
case), and graciously evasive about the rupture of his friendship with Elia Kazan since the latter's testimony. So reasonable
was Miller in the witness chair that his prolonged attachment
to and exploitation by Communists became difficult to understand. Where the playwright balked, toward the end of
his appearance, was at the point where John Watkins—who
had also enjoyed Rauh's counsel—had balked. Asked to give
the names of C.P. members who had been at meetings he
attended in 1947, he replied, in words similar to those Lillian
Hellman wrote in 1952: "I could not use the name of another
person and bring trouble on him. These were writers, poets,
as far as I could see, and the life of a writer, despite what it
sometimes seems, is pretty tough. I wouldn't make it any
tougher for anybody. I ask you not to ask me that question."

[9] In his researches, Arens came across a one-act play that Miller wrote with
Norman Rosten in 1938, on a Federal Writers project. Entitled *Listen, My
Children*, it had to do with a Congressional investigating committee and opened
upon the following scene: "In the center of the room, in a rocker, sits a man.
He is securely tied to a chair, with a gag in his mouth and a bandage tied
over his mouth. Water, coming from a pipe near ceiling, trickles on his head.
Nearby is a charcoal stove holding branding irons. Two bloodhounds are tied
in the corner of room."

The request went to no avail. Jackson and Scherer, the members most adamant about compelling witnesses to tell all, observed that if every witness were permitted to let his conscience be his guide as to which questions he would and would not answer, the Committee would be hard put to get any information from anybody. The only alternative they would grudgingly allow to full disclosure was the stigma of the Fifth Amendment.

Eight contempt citations were dispatched by the House on July 25, 1956, at the behest of the Committee on Un-American Activities—against Arthur Miller, Otto Nathan, Pete Seeger, Elliot Sullivan, George Tyne, and three witnesses who had withheld their cooperation at hearings in St. Louis in June —John W. Simpson, William E. Davis, and Anne Yasgur Kling. Only the citation against Miller was debated, a distinction he owed at least as much to his prominence as a writer as to the circumstances of his refusal to answer questions. Three New York Democrats took up his defense. Celler noted that he had been responsive and respectful and warned that citing so eminent a figure would do America no good abroad. Klein put into the record a study which Joseph Rauh had submitted to Chairman Walter of other witnesses who had refused to give names to a committee of Congress, yet escaped citation. And Multer asked Jackson: "Will the gentleman tell the House please what legislation has been interfered with because you do not know the names of certain persons associated with this man?" Jackson did not need to reply; Miller was cited by a vote of 373 to 9.

None of the July 1956 citations was upheld by the courts. The Seeger, Sullivan, and Tyne cases we have already reviewed. Of the St. Louis witnesses, Simpson and Davis—who had histories of affiliation with Communist-run unions—took the Fifth Amendment beginning with the question of where they were born and owed their acquittal to the courts' ruling that even such routine inquiries might somehow prove incriminating. Mrs. Kling, who had worked in C.P. offices in 1945–1946 and quit the Party in 1947, took her place beside John Watkins and Arthur Miller. "Mr. Tavenner," she said, "I will

tell you anything that you want to know about myself and my
activities, anything you want to know. I have nothing to conceal. I engaged in no criminal or illegal activity. But I am not
a tattletale, and I don't want to snitch on anybody." Her
lawyer relied on the Watkins case, which was then under consideration by the Supreme Court, and his client, who had
testified politely and fully about her own activities, was acquitted in district court because she had not been informed
by the Committee of the pertinence of the questions regarding
individuals she had known. Nathan was acquitted for the same
reason after the Watkins decision. Miller had to carry his case
to the Court of Appeals,[1] which found in September 1958 that
he had not been adequately apprised that he risked contempt
if he refused to answer questions on grounds of conscience.
Since Walter had agreed to defer pressing Miller for names
until counsel Rauh submitted a brief, the witness "had a right
to leave the hearing room thinking that the direction to answer
was still suspended, if not abandoned." Thus the court managed, without becoming involved with substantive issues, to
escape the embarrassment of sending an international celebrity
to jail.

Walter brought 1956 to an end with hearings in a half dozen
cities "to examine the widespread counterattacks which the
Communists have launched in order to subvert the legislative and executive programs designed to thwart them." Specifically, the chairman was impatient with the continuing attacks
on his immigration law. The leadership of both parties, not
excepting the President, had gone on record during the 1956
campaign in favor of liberalizing the law, and Walter's purpose
in the November and December hearings was to promote the
belief that the liberalization campaign was Communist-direct-

[1] As Miller brought his appeal, the Committee released a reproduction of a
card, dated 1943, in which "A. Miller," a "writer" of 18 Schermerhorn Street,
Brooklyn—a former address of the playwright—applied for membership in the
Communist Party. The card was not signed by Miller, who described it as
"either a forgery or . . . done unknown to me." In the place set aside for the
name of the person proposing the new member was the signature of "Sue
Warren," a one-time acquaintance of Miller's, who had declined to answer any
of the Committee's questions. Miller called the release of the ambiguous card
"a transparent attempt to influence the course of my appeal," and so it was.

ed, aimed, in the words of his first witness, Archibald Roosevelt, at "bleeding-heart" Americans and "well-meaning people who have been brainwashed." Roosevelt said he didn't want the country turned into a "polyglot boardinghouse." The strategy of the hearings was transparent. In Washington, Youngstown, Chicago, Los Angeles, San Francisco, and Seattle, officials of the American Committee for the Protection of the Foreign Born, a Communist Party front of long standing, were called up and identified as Party members. One after another the witnesses, several of whom had been before the Committee on other occasions, took the Fifth Amendment. Walter sought by this display to show up the opposition to his law as merely Red. In this he was inadvertently allied to the Communist Party, which always enjoyed being accounted a leader of popular causes onto which it tagged as they went roaring past. As the A.C.L.U. of Northern California observed, "We don't need public hearings to discover that a handful of Communists has seized upon our harsh and discriminatory immigration laws as a means of making political hay."

These hearings were the most disorderly of the year. Having exhausted his deferentiality on Archibald Roosevelt, Arens, who had helped draft the McCarran-Walter law, gave way to this kind of question: ". . . when our boys were fighting and dying with their hands tied behind their backs, being mowed down by the Communist traitors over there, being shot down by North Koreans, which side were you on?" The more truculent witnesses met him on his own level. The secretary treasurer of the International Longshoremen's and Warehousemen's Union, who chose not to deny that he had written Communist tracts under another name, notified Arens, "You are a little two-bit publicity hound," and was shortly thereafter removed from the hearing room. When Arens called on a witness who had just been identified as a Party member by a former F.B.I. operative, to "look him in the face so that there will be no faceless informers here . . ." the gentleman replied, "You wouldn't care for me to puke over the table by looking him in the face." The unfriendly witnesses had harsh remarks for seeming comrades who had been serving the Party in behalf of the F.B.I.,

setting them down as paid informers and unworthy of belief—
but not a single accused Communist took the opportunity to
deny the allegation under oath. Several of the lawyers, too,
were argumentative. In Los Angeles, A. L. Wirin and John W.
Porter, accompanying Mrs. Rose Chernin Kusnitz, executive
secretary of the Los Angeles Committee for the Protection of
the Foreign Born (who had been convicted under the Smith
Act and would, in a few months, be freed by the Supreme
Court), kept inserting themselves into the questioning despite
repeated warnings to be quiet. Arens, who enjoyed noting that
some of the lawyers attending on witnesses had themselves
been identified as Communists, took to asking Porter's clients
whether they knew a Communist by the name of John W.
Porter. He ragged the attorney further by calling him "Comrade Porter." Scherer, suffering from the barbs of Wirin,
charged that Mrs. Kusnitz was lying when she said she had
personally prepared a carefully phrased document stating her
reasons for not testifying. Wirin seemed determined to force
the Committee's hand, or at least drive Scherer to distraction,
and the Congressman's comment gave him an opportunity to
protest: "Do I have to sit and hear someone call my client a
liar in this hearing? This is a disgrace." Scherer and Velde insisted that Wirin be ordered out of the room; Doyle, the acting
chairman, acceded. No sooner was Wirin led away by a marshal, than co-counsel Porter withdrew because his client was
no longer adequately represented, whereupon the questioning
had to be put over to the next day. Ever afterward the Committee's opponents used this event and the ouster of attorney
Daniel G. Marshall after a similar run-in with the sensitive
Scherer as case studies in undue process.[2] Arens's aspersions
and incitements during the Los Angeles hearings prompted the
board of governors of the California State Bar to censure the
Committee for its "grossly offensive" treatment of lawyers.

[2] Other evictions came early in the Los Angeles hearings, when a retired
brigadier general noted for his activities as vegetarian and prohibitionist was
led from the Federal building after attempting to denounce the Committee and
Doyle. A few minutes later, a lawyer was ordered out because he guffawed at
the chairman's observation that the hearings were aimed at helping Congress
to legislate efficiently.

In this series of hearings, Francis Walter had his most direct confrontation with his enemies and the enemies of his law, the people who had been calling him a bigot up and down the land. After the November 1956 elections, Walter said that only one consideration was preventing him from giving up the chairmanship—his resignation would be interpreted as a victory "by my enemies." The campaign against the McCarran-Walter law was, in his mind, directed against him personally and as an embodiment of the national security; it impugned his integrity and threatened the republic. Moreover, it stood for all of the other movements that had been gaining force during his first term as Committee chairman, toward easing security restrictions in this country and reducing cold war tensions abroad. His immigration bill was a product of the cold war, and every sign of warmer relations with Russia brought nearer an immigration thaw as well. The Committee's reports and declarations during this period had one overriding message: "the menace of Communism remains unabated." In the spring of 1956 after Khrushchev's attack on Stalin, Walter brought together thirty-nine persons whom he described as "authorities" on Communism—a group tilted heavily to the right by such publicists as James Burnham, Clarence Manion, William Randolph Hearst, Jr., Whittaker Chambers, Louis Budenz, Francis McNamara, and the national commander of the American Legion—and they came through with a report entitled *The Great Pretense*. The fruit of their thought was distilled in Walter's preface: ". . . anti-Stalinism is but a political artifice, fraudulent and more dangerous than any other produced by the Kremlin thus far." J. Edgar Hoover contributed a summation.

For the men who had obliged Walter by proclaiming this news, as for the Un-American Activities Committee itself, there could be no change in U.S.–Soviet affairs, barring defeat for one party and victory for the other. Their careers were built on the immutable menace of Communism. The anti-Communism which, for most of them, had begun in honest disillusion and justified outrage had hardened into unquestioning faith; having given themselves to one truth, they could tolerate no other, and now nothing that happened in the real world could shake their belief in the less complicated world whose gates they guarded. As for Francis Walter, concern for national security, pride of authorship, and personal sensibilities merged into a force that would compel him to stand until the end of his life like the pathetic king of legend against the inexorable tides.

14

*****

1957-1960: Operation Abolition

THE rioting that took place in San Francisco's City Hall in
May 1960 as a result of a visit by three members of the
Committee on Un-American Activities has properly been celebrated as marking a critical stage in the Committee's history.
It was startling in its violence, but the powder for the explosion
had been scattered over many months. In the closing years of
the decade,[1] as the nation tired of security checks, loyalty
oaths, and unending investigations, and as relations between
Russia and America warmed somewhat, the Committee gave
itself to incantations directed at resuscitating the drooping
spirits of vigilanteism. The voice was usually the voice of
Chairman Walter, but the hands were the hands of Arens and
Scherer and J. Edgar Hoover, of Legionnaires and blacklisters,
informers and defectors, of aging ex-Communists trapped by
the experience of the thirties and young careerists loath to give
up the power of the fifties. Committee hearings were less frequent but the number of reports and "consultations," with consultants chosen for dependability, rose; month after month the

---

1 Walter remained chairman throughout these years, and there were only
minor changes in the Committee membership. Robert J. McIntosh, a freshman
Republican from Michigan, took the place of Velde, who did not run for reelection in 1956, and when McIntosh was defeated in the Democratic sweep
of 1958, he was replaced by another Michigan Republican, August E. Johansen.
In January 1958, Frazier went off to the Ways and Means Committee and was
replaced by William M. Tuck, a former governor of Virginia. General Kearney
did not run in 1958; his Committee seat went to another upstate New Yorker,
William E. Miller. In the fall of 1960, Frank S. Tavenner, Jr., took over as
staff director from Arens, who went to his rewards as a commissioner in the
Court of Claims, and Alfred M. Nittle became Committee counsel.

Committee turned out old warnings in old packages. Walter and Arens showed more respect for the cause of Marxism-Leninism than the globe's bewildered Communists, as powerful nationalist impulses broke out in Eastern Europe, as the dispute between Russia and China flared, as Communist unity strained and shattered with the shattering of Stalinism. The world looked on in amazement—but the Committee's message was that nothing had changed, nothing could change except for the worse, Communism was Communism, revolution was perpetual. To prove which they quoted Marx, Lenin, and Hoover. They were the last, truest believers.

When the minuscule C.P. U.S.A. fragmented itself to near invisibility after the Soviets crushed the Hungarian rebellion in 1956, the Committee warned that numbers did not count, the Party was a greater menace than ever since it had now gone underground. Like so many Romeos coming upon the corpse of their beloved, the Congressmen cried to the heavens, "The Communist Party of the United States is not out of business; it is not dead; it is not even dormant." Once the Committee had worried that the Party was attracting more and more adherents. Now it worried over the decline in membership. Representative Tuck warned, "A conspiratorial force may actually weaken itself when it increases in size." After Nikita Khrushchev shook the underpinnings of the Communist world with his speech on the crimes of Stalin, the Committee warned that it was but part of a sinister hoax to get us to drop our guard. As modest talks began with the new Soviet rulers, the Committee warned that negotiation with the U.S.S.R. was sheer folly, that all trade was at our peril, that Soviet visitors to this country would only reinforce their preconceived notions of capitalism. In celebration of Khrushchev's trip to America in September 1959, the Committee put out a series of reports on *The Crimes of Khrushchev*. When Sputnik was launched, the Committee attributed the accomplishment to the theft by Communist conspirators of America's scientific secrets, and warned that espionage was still rife. When our U-2 plane was shot down over the Soviet Union, Walter cautioned the world not to be distracted by a mischance of U.S. espionage from the subject of Communist subversion. In the spring of 1959, as a U.S. exhibition was opening in Moscow, the Committee created a minor furor over the fact that works of left-wing artists were included, and had Ben Shahn and Philip Evergood in to take the Fifth Amendment to prove it. By suggesting that peaceful coexistence between the United States and the U.S.S.R. was a real possibility, witness Joseph Starobin, former foreign editor of the *Daily Worker* who had dropped out of the Party in 1953, set himself against both his late comrades and his present inquisitors. In a foreword to a Committee report on the history of Communist machinations issued in 1958, when talk of a summit conference and an agreement on nuclear testing were in the air, Walter lamented over "the sorry spectacle of otherwise intelligent American leaders willing to negotiate with Communism's masters at international conference tables as if there were a real foundation of sincerity and good faith."

In all of this, one could hardly miss the flowering of an obsession. Where sane men the world over breathed a bit more easily at every reduction in the long, dangerous international tension, Walter saw only new threats. To his fear of undesirable foreigners polluting these shores was added a fear of undesirable Americans catching or spreading infection abroad. He discerned a menace of vast proportions in the propaganda —incredible stuff—which Communist countries shipped to this country and even in the languishing foreign-language sheets that elderly men still managed to put out in New York and Chicago, and under his direction the Committee became a counter-propaganda agency. He was a Platonist in the sense that Russia's rulers were Platonists, seeing a danger to the state wherever one's citizens encountered unorthodox ideas. The Russians sealed their borders to protect their Marxist "science" from reality, yet Walter paid their discredited ideology the tribute of fear. His whole effort in these years when men began to reach out toward one another, tentatively, suspiciously, but hopefully withal, was toward closing up, clamping down, as if only so could he still his inner trembling.

These were desperate years for Francis Walter. In succumbing to zenophobic passions and committing himself utterly to

the ways of the Committee he had once criticized, he had for-
feited his hope of succeeding Sam Rayburn as Speaker of the
House. He remained loyal to his party and retained influence
in the House, but he had become set in the dated style of
suspicion and repression just at a time when fresh fashions were
stirring the land. Not all the letters of support from American
Legion posts or testimonial dinners by the right-wing guard
could save him; he was embattled by reality and there were
moments in these indescribably frustrating years when he
could barely make out friend from foe. In June 1958 the Supreme Court, that unmistakable foe, ruled that the State Department had no authority to deny passports to applicants
because of their "beliefs and associations." The five-to-four
decision was handed down on June 17 to take effect on July
11. Since the government did not intend to ask for a rehearing,
the State Department instructed the director of the Passport
Office, Miss Frances G. Knight, to start issuing the passports
that had been held up. She began to do so on June 24, delivering passports to several dozen known and suspected Communists, including such old Committee antagonists as Paul
Robeson and Harry Bridges. Walter was well aware that Miss
Knight was no advocate of free travel for political undesirables
—she had cooperated with him in drawing up a bill to tighten
passport requirements and was in the bad book of liberals—
yet such was his grief and rage that he lashed out even at her,
charging in a letter to Secretary Dulles that while corrective
legislation was pending she was "going out of her way to issue
passports to these Communist agents . . ." But everyone knew
there was no hope for such legislation in that session of Congress; the lady had merely been doing what for her must have
been a distasteful job—only to have an ally compound her
distress. Such were the distractions of the time.

Of the reduced hearings between 1957 and 1960, some were
frivolous, in that mode of cruel frivolity which had become a
Committee specialty. In the spring of 1957 a subcommittee
under Moulder ("Now, of course, we are not worried about
communizing Beethoven and Bach, and we do not feel that

the performance of a concerto by a Communist is in itself subversive") visited New York City for the purpose of routing out some three dozen musicians associated with the Metropolitan Music School, the Symphony of the Air, and Local 802 of the Musicians Union who had been identified as Communists and duly took the Fifth Amendment. Arens, who often told witnesses he was not concerned with their beliefs, only with their actions, took full advantage of them. "What is your position on Communism?" he asked one musician. "Are you for it or against it?" The best known of the witnesses was Earl Robinson (whom Arens called "Mr. Robeson"), composer of *Ballad for Americans, Lonesome Road, The House I Live In,* and other synthetic and edifying folk songs. "I hope my music will always be used in the fight against fascism," declared Robinson to the delight of Arens who was trying to prove that the Party could employ friendly musicians for political purposes. Arens exhibited a notice printed in the *Daily Worker* in 1938 that a lecturer at the music school had spoken on "the bourgeois music culture in the period of monopoly capitalism," while another man, a guitar instructor, was responsible for a people's song called "Gol-dern Red."[2]

Having done what they could to damage the livelihoods of these detested persons, the Congressmen went back to Washington. But they returned to New York a year later to call up a dozen show business people—a conductor, a publicist, a director, as well as a few actors—who had somehow been missed on previous visits. Joseph Papp, a stage manager for C.B.S. and the guiding force behind the New York Shakespeare Festival which was putting on free plays in Central Park, was the biggest name the Committee could find this time around—and he indicated that he had left the Party several years before. The

[2] I went up to my boss one day to ask him for a raise.
    He wept and said he didn't have the dough.
Well I knew for all his crying that the plutocrat was lying,
    And *that's* just what I told the so and so.
        And what d'ya think he said?
    "Why you're nothing but a gol-dern Red (straight from Russia)
    You're nothing but a gol-dern Red.
Yes: and if the truth be told, you're receiving Moscow gold.
    Yes, you're nothing but a gol-dern Red. . . ."

show business mine was about worked out. Even Hollywood
was recovering from the blackest days of the blacklist, and
the Committee had to be satisfied with getting one man fired
by N.B.C. and another canceled from the Ed Sullivan show.
(Five distinguished trustees of the Stratford, Connecticut,
American Shakespeare Festival, bankers all, resigned to protest
the retaining of a stage manager who took the Fifth.)

The July 1959 hearing on the American National Exhibition
in Moscow which, according to Walter, included the works of
twenty-two artists with "significant" records of affiliation with
Communist fronts and causes, was taken up mainly by one
Wheeler Williams, president of the American Artists Professional League and the sculptor responsible for the statue of
Senator Robert A. Taft at the Taft Memorial in Washington.
The judges for the exhibition, he complained, had slighted
traditional artists in favor of social protest paintings and
"meaningless doodles," which failed to give a true image of
America, as they contained "next to nothing to show the wondrous natural beauty with which God has endowed our beloved
land, to portray its glorious history, its heroes or its valiant
people of varied races, and nothing to picture the wondrous
architecture of our cities or charm and beauty of our villages
and towns." If there remained any question of the kind of art
Mr. Wheeler liked, he resolved it by telling how impressed he
was with the paintings of tractor drivers and milkmaids that
the Soviets had sent to tour America.[3]

There were other hearings, not so ludicrous as the flight into
art, but still gratuitous, as Walter and Arens, like marginal oil
operators setting up their derricks adjacent to a rich strike,
tried to draw off some of the publicity of sensational incidents
as it gushed forth. Thus, the Committee owed its first big newspaper story of 1957 to the extravagant Boris Morros, Russian-
born Hollywood composer and double agent whose testimony

[3] Asked to comment on this controversy, President Eisenhower said: "Now
I think I might have something to say, if we have another exhibition anywhere,
to the responsible officials of the methods they produce, or get the juries, and
possibly there ought to be one or two people like that, like most of us here
say, we are not too certain exactly what art is but we know what we like and
what America likes—whatever America likes is after all some of the things that
ought to be shown."

before a grand jury had lately resulted in several indictments of Americans on charges of spying for the U.S.S.R. and the flight to Czechoslovakia of Mr. and Mrs. Alfred Stern, he a millionaire investment broker, she the daughter of the late William E. Dodd, former U.S. ambassador to Germany. (". . . we are visiting this peace-loving country," Stern told reporters, "and enjoying an interesting and restful trip.") The Senate Internal Security Subcommittee had set a hearing for Morros, but Walter got to him first, took testimony in executive session, and had the triumph of being the one to bring Mrs. Stern's name into the story. Morros's tale of his twelve years as a counterspy made exciting copy, but he did not require the services of the Un-American Activities Committee to tell it. He told it over and over, with flourishes, in press conferences, on TV shows, in articles, and finally in a book. The Committee merely provided him with one more stage, and his appearance gave Walter a chance to announce, "The facts now in the possession of the Committee indicate that a number of American citizens have been and may still be involved in Soviet espionage." The facts he referred to have yet to be produced. In October he called a number of former federal employees who had known or worked with one of the implicated persons during their time with such government agencies as the O.P.A. and the B.E.W. All had already been questioned by the F.B.I.; all declined to testify regarding their own Communist affiliations. The Committee had no evidence against any of them and expected no cooperation, but went through the motions of a hearing which it then published under the title *Investigation of Soviet Espionage*.

Walter and Jackson charged onto page one again in February 1960, after the Pentagon repudiated an Air Force training manual briefly in use at the Lackland Air Force Base in Texas which instructed student reservists that Communists had infiltrated United States churches and that thirty of the ninety-five persons who had worked on a Revised Standard Version of the Bible for the National Council of the Churches of Christ were affiliated with subversive organizations. It was the Bishop Oxnam affair all over again. Right-wing fundamentalists, im-

passioned as ever against the liberal disposition and ecumenical
inclinations of the National Council, had managed to plant the
charges, taken mainly from the writings of J. B. Matthews and
the Un-American Activities Committee's files, in the manual.
One evangelist tract listed in the appendix was entitled, *The
National Council of Churches Indicts Itself on Fifty Counts of
Treason to God and Country*. Hardly had the recently appointed Secretary of the Air Force Dudley C. Sharp withdrawn
the manual,[4] with the apologies of the Secretary of Defense,
than he found himself summoned before Walter's Committee
in closed session. Whereas other Congressmen were threatening to investigate the inclusion of the charges, Walter intended
to investigate their withdrawal. The poor Secretary, under
simultaneous attack from the right and the center, made himself as agreeable as he could, giving "this fine Committee" to
understand that he had no quarrel with its work, but merely
did not feel it was appropriate for the Air Force to get involved
in the issue of whether there were Communists among the
clergy. Pressed hard by Arens and eight of the Committee's
members to say that he did not mean to repudiate the material
in its files, he conceded, "I would say that I certainly agree
with the assumption that the Communist Party would obviously in its activities attempt to infiltrate the churches . . ."
On the basis of such observations, Walter told reporters afterward that Sharp had said "admittedly everything in the manual was true." Before leaving the witness chair, the Secretary
had to endure a threat by Jackson that "some sort of hell [the
word was changed to 'ruckus' in the record of the hearing] will
break loose on the floor of the House" if the author of the tract
were punished. When a group of Protestant ministers asked
Walter for an apology, he invited them to testify about the
material that the Committee had collected over the years. They
wisely declined to be diverted from the issue, as they saw it,

[4] The Air Force was suffering a certain embarrassment over its instructional
materials at this time. Other manuals had recently been found which taught
the airmen how to wash the dogs and polish the shoes of officers, how to encourage drinking in open messes run for profit, and how to use dining utensils:
"The fork is used to lift, turn or move large or small pieces of food in a sani-
tary and practical manner."

of the propriety of the Air Force "indoctrinating reservists on religious questions." For weeks after, Fulton Lewis, Jr., devoted a portion of his daily broadcast to attacks on the liberal clergy, and Jackson capped the incident by accusing the National Council of promoting obscene books by Communist sympathizers.

In August of 1960, Walter partook of yet another juicy news story when Speaker McCormack invited him to inquire into the case of Bernon F. Mitchell and William H. Martin, young bachelor friends who had suddenly left their jobs as cryptographers at the National Security Agency and gone off, presumably behind the Iron Curtain. McCormack expressed dissatisfaction with the Pentagon's assurances that the men had no information which could be "prejudicial to the security of United States communications," and it may have crossed his mind that a bit of publicity about a security slip under a Republican Administration could do no harm to the fortunes that November of John F. Kennedy. Unable to get other committee chairmen to take an interest in the event, he turned to the one committee where he could count on action. Walter immediately introduced a resolution in the House calling for a complete study of the personnel practices of all U.S. Intelligence agencies. It was too late in the session for anything to come of this, but the Russians kept his cause alive by putting on a news conference in Moscow at which Martin and Mitchell announced they had defected out of a fear that U.S. intelligence methods, particularly reconnaissance flights like that of the ill-fated U-2, would lead to war. Now the case could not be ignored. President Eisenhower told a news conference that he saw a need for a review of hiring procedures in sensitive agencies, and the House Armed Services Committee appointed a three-man subcommittee to study the matter—an effort to take the play away from the Un-American Activities Committee. When Walter asked the President to order various government agencies to make available to him the names of persons who had regained federal employment after being dropped as security risks—long a sore point with the Committee—the President replied as his predecessors had replied in similar instances, negatively, citing the separation of powers.

Both House committees held closed hearings into the case. Walter issued periodic charges, the testimony of N.S.A. officials to the contrary notwithstanding, that at least one of the defectors was a homosexual. The Defense Department refused to let him have the personnel files on the two, but he was given a defector named Artamonov, a former Soviet naval captain, whom he put on the stand in public hearing, to tell about Soviet intelligence machinations. Despite Walter's efforts, the Mitchell-Martin case made little impact; the main lesson to be drawn from it was simply that security cannot be foolproof, or defector-proof. Neither of the men was listed in the Committee's files, and although N.S.A. dutifully went through the motions of tightening its personnel procedures, nothing less than constant surveillance could have prevented their astonishing flight. What was significant about the response to the affair was that with elections only a few weeks away Democrats showed so little desire to make political capital of it. Walter's passions came out of pathology, not politics, but his colleagues seemed to recognize that the time of the security champion had waned. There was no disposition to reopen old wounds or to take fresh vengeance for them. They had had enough of charges of "softness" and so, it appeared, had the country. Reflecting on what Nixon would have made of an N.S.A. defection in 1952, one could only admire the Democratic leadership and give thanks for the altered temper of the country.[5]

Public hearings in the eighty-fifth and eighty-sixth Congresses, generally well covered in local papers, took subcommittees to thirteen cities, as well as to Puerto Rico, where

---

[5] Walter pursued the case into 1961, with unexpected results. The agency's head of personnel and its security chief were both compelled to resign: the former because he had once claimed on an employment application that he had been awarded a law degree by Harvard, when in fact he had spent only a year in Cambridge and had gotten his degree from a less prestigious establishment, and then compounded this offense by substituting a correct form for the boastful one; the latter because he had accepted an undisclosed favor from some party that did business with the government. The case also resulted in a tightening up of N.S.A. regulations, several other dismissals, and, as we shall note a few pages hence, a new piece of security legislation.

twelve witnesses were cited for contempt only to have their indictments dismissed in 1962, when a district court upheld their contention that in authorizing the Un-American Activities Committee to conduct hearings within the continental United States, the Congress had not meant to include Puerto Rico. The informant–Fifth Amendment pattern was followed in the majority of the hearings—John Lautner and Armando Penha being the most productive informants of the period. The emphasis was on the ritual exposure of Communists, numbers of whom had been exposed before, but some light was thrown on Party activities in these difficult years. It was shown that the Jefferson School of Social Science in New York, which had dissolved itself in 1955 shortly after being adjudged a Communist front by the Subversive Activities Control Board, had set up shop again at a different address as the Faculty of Social Science. This prompted Walter to introduce another of his security bills—this one to insure that an S.A.C.B. order against an organization would apply to any successor organization. Chicago hearings into the left-wing United Packinghouse Workers indicated that several union leaders had resigned their C.P. memberships not out of disillusionment with the Party but merely to abide by the technical provisions of the Taft-Hartley Act. Officers and members of the American Communications Association—which had been expelled by the C.I.O. in 1950 and was being investigated by the Senate Internal Security Subcommittee when the Un-American Activities Committee set sights on it—were shown to be working around installations that would be regarded as sensitive in case of emergency, and seamen with records of Communist activity were shown to be sailing American merchant ships. Hearings in Gary, Indiana, disclosed that college graduates from New York had concealed their educational attainments to take jobs in heavy industry, presumably at the behest of Communist headquarters.

These hearings were not as difficult to justify under the Committee's mandate as the others held between 1957 and 1960, which had no discernible purpose other than to publicize the names of alleged Communists and cause them as much trouble as possible with their neighbors and employers. But even here the information obtained was not compelling. By now, the Committee was like a tiresome uncle who insists on telling his old ghost stories in broad daylight to nephews with other things on their minds. All of the reluctant witnesses were known to the F.B.I., and none had ever been charged with any act of disloyalty to this country. The Faculty of Social Science made no effort at camouflage. The A.C.A. members had worked at their jobs for many years, and although there was no way of refuting the *possibility* that in case of war with Russia a pro-Communist teletype operator *might* blow up an R.C.A. installation or take home Defense Department messages, the Committee's conclusion that "Communists' penetration of sensitive communications facilities constitutes a direct danger to American security" was a highly colored summary of what the hearings had actually disclosed. As for the Communist "colonizers" in the steel industry, only a determined demonologist could find much menace in their conspiratorial pretensions; even John Lautner, usually amenable to the Committee's needs, made the point that the purpose of the "colonizers" was to re-establish a Communist foothold in heavy industry—a difficult enough task—not to blow up any steel plants. But the investigators were nothing if not determined to find concealed perils. Upon locating an identified Communist in New Haven who held an executive post with the Children's Services of Connecticut, Willis and Kearney took care to point out, "In this capacity she made the decisions as to what home should receive the children and what was the best plan for the child."

The careful statement of legislative purpose with which the chairman began each inquiry and the explanations of pertinence which Arens delivered to balky witnesses became part of the ceremony after the Watkins decision, but the hearings themselves bore little resemblance to those of committees that seriously weighed pending bills. At most, as in the passport-security hearings of 1959, which were aimed at discrediting the Supreme Court's 1958 passport ruling, an official in favor of security legislation would be invited to testify; the only opponents of such legislation called as witnesses were persons like Harry Bridges[6] or the general manager of the *Daily Worker,* who were asked not about their opinions of the bills but about their Communist associations, and were held up as frightful examples when they took the Fifth Amendment. There was never much pretense of considering more than one side of the case regarding a proposed law. Walter opened the passport hearings with a reference to the Supreme Court decision, and at once passed judgment on what had yet to be considered: "Today, now the bars are down. Communist agents, propagandists and Communist sympathizers have a blanket invitation to come and go as they will . . . this situation is of direct benefit to the international Communist movement, and of direct detriment to security interests of our nation."

Walter promised after the Watkins decision that Congress would "pass the type of legislation that even the Supreme Court will understand." But although he and Scherer proposed numerous measures designed to redo what the Supreme Court was in process of undoing in the whole field of security, it was a rare piece of legislation that was put in their charge. Scherer vented his annoyance that they were not even entrusted with his own bill that authorized the federal government to take measures to guard defense facilities against individuals believed disposed to acts of subversion. In its first twenty years of life, the Un-American Activities Committee produced one law—the Internal Security Act of 1950. As though exhausted by that uncertain accomplishment, in the ensuing ten years it held not a single hearing on a specific piece of legislation. (The Committee's champions sometimes take credit for the Communist Control Act of 1954, that mysterious measure which announced that the Communist Party "should" be outlawed, then did not quite outlaw it, but in fact the major provisions of the bill originated in the Senate and Velde reported it out over the vigorous objections of Walter, Doyle, and Frazier without troubling to hold any hearings.) In 1954 and again in

---

[6] Shipping out of West Coast ports had gone smoothly during the Korean War despite Bridges's adherence to the Communist line. Yet in 1959, as one of the few left-wing union leaders of the thirties still alive and kicking, he was exhibited as a prime threat by the Committee because he said he would advocate a boycott if Chiang Kai-shek tried to retake the Chinese mainland.

1962, the Committee reported two amendments of no great consequence to its Internal Security Act—the first calling for the listing of all printing equipment in the possession of Communist-action and Communist-front organizations, the other relieving the Defense Department of the requirement that it publish a list of strategic defense facilities from which Communist Party members were barred. (By requiring such a listing in the first place, the Internal Security Act had inadvertently abetted enemy spies.) In 1963 the Committee completed its record of legislative accomplishment when it produced another amendment to the Internal Security Act, giving the Secretary of Defense power to dismiss summarily any employee of the National Security Agency, "an example, just one more example," commented the *National Review* with no humorous intent, "of the continuing legislative usefulness of the House Committee on Un-American Activities . . ." This bill, which owed its life to the Mitchell-Martin defection, was signed into law in 1964, and is now being reviewed by the Supreme Court.

Straining to provide the exhibitions in various cities with some legislative aura, Walter pressed into service one Irving Fishman, a New York Customs official. Jurisdiction over ". . . the diffusion within the United States of subversive and un-American propaganda . . ." was explicit in the Committee's mandate, and Fishman leavened the parades of local left-wingers with data on the number of pieces of Soviet propaganda entering the country through New York or New Orleans or Boston. What Mr. Fishman had to say could have made a thin pamphlet, but between June 1956 and May 1960 he was called on to perform a dozen times—in Washington, Philadelphia, San Francisco, New Orleans, Buffalo, Boston, Atlanta, and Newark. The highlight of his appearance usually came when he reached into the mail sack he carried with him and produced a genuine piece of Communist propaganda.

The Committee's legislative record, or want of record, was used gleefully by critics to demonstrate that despite its large annual allocation and staff ($654,000 and fifty-six members in the eighty-sixth Congress), the Committee on Un-American Activities produced remarkably few laws, and this became a tender point during Walter's chairmanship. Whereas neither Thomas nor Velde had had any great legislative aspirations, Walter considered himself a lawmaker, and not a season passed without a stream of proposals issuing from his office. At the outset of the eighty-sixth Congress, he made known that he wanted jurisdiction over immigration and passport legislation. As chairman of the Judiciary Committee's subcommittee on immigration, he had to work under Emanuel Celler, the committee's liberal chairman, and the change would have relieved him of that frustrating connection. It would also have given him the power base to which he felt entitled after a quarter century in the House and would have given his Committee a true legislative function at last. But Speaker Rayburn, at the first news conference of the eighty-sixth Congress, said, "We're not going to do that," and that was that. So Walter, who had once been among the inner group of policymakers in the House, now had to content himself with calling for the passage of bills that were not in his committee's jurisdiction. His annual favorite became the Omnibus Security Bill, a hodgepodge of measures designed to reverse numerous Supreme Court decisions, prohibit Communist lawyers from practicing before executive departments and Congressional committees, tighten passport controls and regulations regarding aliens, and so forth. Some of these measures were adopted as parts of other laws handled by other committees, whereupon the Un-American Activities Committee and its defenders could claim them as the Committee's accomplishments. Indeed, hardly a piece of repressive legislation went through that, by this easy criterion, the Committee might not claim as its own, yet of the 12,000 bills filed in the House of Representatives in the eighty-sixth Congress, only eleven were referred to the Un-American Activities Committee—and not one of these was passed. Insofar as the Committee deserved credit for various executive orders on security and laws such as those which broadened the scope of the Foreign Agents Registration Act, the Espionage Act, and the Smith Act, it was in the role of publicist, not legislator.

In its single-minded drive after names, the Committee swept by certain observations of witnesses that might have given it profitable pause. Howard Fast, having at last broken with the Party upon discovering that Jews had been among those slaughtered by Stalin, was questioned in closed session and commented afterward that the Committee, with its implacable demands for names, had made it virtually impossible for a man to leave the Party and retain any dignity. Dignity was not the word that sprang to mind regarding Fast, but his point was well taken. The self-righteousness of the Committee's members and staff obstructed it in the performance of its avowed informational function. Faced with an ex-Communist, Arens required repentance, abasement, and conversion. His questions were designed to be asked, not answered. He demanded of a witness in Buffalo: "Are you now thoroughly disgusted with the fact that you have been associated with the Communist ideology, which is atheistic, which is the very antithesis of Christian morality as we know it in this country?" The less polemical, less ambitious Tavenner was better at drawing out information. In several sets of hearings, he encouraged men who had quit the Party after the Soviet intervention in Hungary to tell of their feelings and experiences despite the fact that they took the Fifth on naming former friends. Granted this much permissiveness, the witnesses spoke intelligently and with evident honesty about the crises of conscience that had been stirred in Party ranks by the events of 1956, and one of them observed, much as Howard Fast had, that the Committee's habit of asking every dissenter to become an informer was hindering open debate within the Party. (The Committee was inconsistent about pressing for contempt citations against witnesses who were willing to testify about themselves but balked at naming others without relying on the Fifth Amendment; their fates seemed to hang on the composition and temper of the day's subcommittee, and on whether Arens or Tavenner was handling the interrogation. At times Tavenner was truly startling. When a Los Angeles witness took the Fifth, the counsel said: "It is quite apparent, Mr. Chairman, there is no use asking him questions if he refuses to answer regarding his membership." Had this principle been strictly followed, the Committee could have conserved a great deal of energy.)

In another area, too, the Congressmen and counsel Arens, like tourists who have eyes for nothing but what is in their guide books, went hastily by a sight that deserved pondering. In March 1959 and again in May witnesses who had been publicly identified as Communists while they were in fact working within the Party for the F.B.I. told of the harrassment they had suffered from anti-Communist neighbors and fellow workers. A packinghouse worker in Chicago said that ". . . my family and myself have been discriminated very badly and hurt, cut up to pieces because people pointed and thrown bricks and slapped me in the face and done everything imaginable because the neighborhood I lived in, there are no Communists and they can't stand a Communist." The Congressmen were sympathetic but did not pursue the matter. The experiences of the F.B.I. informants merely confirmed the charges delivered from the Supreme Court bench, the floor of Congress, and lesser platforms that in its accustomed role of exposing Communists, the Un-American Activities Committee was in fact inciting to punishment. Subcommittee members had no sympathy to spare for what happened to non-F.B.I. witnesses after they left the hearing room and allowed no testimony on that subject. "The hearings are public," said Moulder blandly to a witness who feared for his job if his place of work were made known, "and what may result from your testimony in the form of publicity can't be controlled by this Committee." But the attentive listener could find echoes in informants' ordeals of the ordeals of hundreds of other people who were guilty of no known crime.

By Walter's time, the F.B.I. informant had become a major actor in the Committee's ceremonies. These men and women were not proper F.B.I. agents, but Communist Party members, nominal or disillusioned, who for reasons of patriotism or more obscure motives reported regularly on their activities and the people they met. While the Committee's research staff occupied itself with clipping names and associations from the *National Guardian* and feeding them into its endlessly growing files, it was the informants who supplied most of the matter required for hearings. As the Communist Party fell apart, they were

permitted to break cover and testify. By and large, they had
little news to impart once they had delivered up their lists of
names, but they could be counted on to reply affirmatively
when Arens or one of the Congressmen asked whether in their
opinion the Communist Party was more of a menace now
than ever before.

In its public pronouncements on the subject, the Committee
always indicated that its cooperation with the F.B.I. consisted
mainly of giving the Bureau access to its remarkable files. But
it became evident during the chairmanship of former F.B.I.
operative Velde that the relationship was not so one-sided.
The Committee could usually boast of having one or more
former F.B.I. men on its staff—as indeed could many of the
vigilante operations that flourished in the nineteen-fifties.
Friendly cooperation outside of channels presented no particular problem given an understanding between the F.B.I.'s
director and the Committee's chairman or staff director, and
it was clear that, through unofficial means, the Committee was
getting at least as much help from the F.B.I. as it was giving.
The cooperation reached a dramatic peak in 1959. Previously
the Committee had used informants who had already broken
with the Party, but in Pittsburgh in March and in Chicago in
May and again in Washington in June 1960 the Congressmen
had the satisfaction of unveiling F.B.I. agents who had been
C.P. members in good standing "up to the present minute."
What they had to say was of marginal interest—the Communists, reported the Chicago man, were "nothing but a bunch
of rattle snakes"—but their debut under Committee sponsorship
made for good newspaper copy. It was a performance that
would have been impossible without the cooperation, or at least
acquiescence, of J. Edgar Hoover.

Early in the life of the Un-American Activities Committee,
Hoover had had reason to be annoyed at some of Martin Dies's
adventures, but under Walter's chairmanship a close and mutu-
ally rewarding relationship bloomed between Committee and
Bureau. The F.B.I. used the Committee to turn what Chairman
Dies had early called "the light of pitiless publicity" on persons
against whom it could take no other action—and in so doing

reaped a fair amount of publicity for itself. The Committee used the prestige of the F.B.I. and its enduring director to bolster its own apocalyptic philosophy. When Hoover announced in 1958 that the Communist Party was "well on its way to achieving its current objective, which is to make you believe that it is shattered, ineffective and dying," the Committee hastened to incorporate his remarks in its record. "When it has fully achieved this first objective," the director of the F.B.I. went on, in words that have remained comfortably the same over the decades, like the old slippers that go with mindless evenings at home, "it will then proceed inflexibly toward its final goal." The two groups were under attack from much the same quarters and their spokesmen came quickly and warmly to one another's defense when a slur was cast. "Where in God's name would our nation be," asked Doyle of a disrespectful New York musician, "if the F.B.I. wasn't able to get patriotic American citizens to go into these organizations in which Communists, crooks, cheats and traitors infiltrate?" Not receiving a satisfactory response, he added, "You ought to be ashamed of yourself for attacking the F.B.I." At times the Congressmen's adoration verged on the blasphemous. "If you cannot trust the F.B.I.," Willis once asked, "whom are you going to trust?" Hoover reciprocated this worshipful regard by writing a letter to Walter when the Committee came under attack from the Emergency Civil Liberties Committee, to say that "real Americans" wouldn't be fooled by the campaign. The Committee and the Bureau behaved during these years like a pair of mischievously indiscreet lovers. They were not officially affianced and so had to maintain a certain distance in public, yet so fond were the glances they exchanged, so endearing the sentiments, that observers could hardly help speculating over what they did together when the lights were out.

The worshipful feelings that Walter, Arens, and Scherer held for the F.B.I. impelled them into one of the great Committee follies of the period. In May 1958 Cyrus S. Eaton of Cleveland, known as a bearer of odd opinions for a man who had made several fortunes in coal, iron, and steel (he wanted closer relations with the U.S.S.R. and recognition of Communist China), was interviewed on a television series designed by the Fund for the Republic. The seventy-four-old Eaton had recently taken to sponsoring an annual international meeting of scientists at his birthplace in Pugwash, Nova Scotia, and he used the TV interview to voice his disdain for the "scores of agencies" engaged "in investigating, in snooping, in informing, in creeping up on people." He said that they made "no contribution to the upbuilding of this country and its respect abroad," and added that there were no Communists to speak of in the United States, "except in the mind of those on the payroll of the F.B.I." Eaton spoiled his performance by announcing that "Hitler in his prime, through the Gestapo, never had any such spy organization as we have in this country today"—still it was certainly one of the more refreshing shows of the TV season. No one could recall that the F.B.I. had ever been criticized on a national network before, and assuredly not by a chairman of the board of the Chesapeake and Ohio Railroad.

For the right wing, it was heresy. Three days after the broadcast, a thousand New Yorkers gathered at Hunter College, under the auspices of AWARE and eighteen other anti-Communist organizations to listen to Roy Cohn, William Buckley, and Gordon Scherer—in the city with a subcommittee investigating entertainers—defend the Un-American Activities Committee, the Internal Security Subcommittee, and the F.B.I. Eaton, declared Scherer, had "made a tremendous contribution to the Soviet cause." Walter demanded equal time from the American Broadcasting Company and sent forth Arens to uphold the honor of the Federal Bureau of Investigation. While doing so, Arens made public the fact that Walter had signed a subpoena for the millionaire to come before the Committee and explain himself. Upon this incitement, the Committee's critics entered the fray. The A.C.L.U. called the subpoena action a "clear-cut demonstration of the Committee's power to coerce American citizens and penalize them for expressing their opinions on controversial issues." *The New York Times*, which a few months before had complimented the eighty-fifth Congress on the "total absence of irresponsible and merely punitive Congressional investigatory action," now denounced the Committee for "a preposterous and dangerous arrogation of unconstitutional power." Senators Humphrey and Douglas issued a gentle rebuke to the Committee on the floor of the Senate—Douglas called the action "perhaps impetuous" and "ill-considered." The subpoena was never served. After an angry confrontation in Scherer's office which ended with Walter walking out—"My stomach could not take it"—and Eaton charging he had been bullied and pushed around, the chairman blew a faltering retreat: "It is believed that no useful purpose can be served by permitting Mr. Eaton to repeat the groundless accusations that Iron Curtain countries have used for propaganda purposes." Insofar as there is a last word in this sort of argument, Eaton seems to have had it. A few weeks after the aborted meeting a Cleveland engineering magazine carried an article by the industrialist which observed that some members of the Committee were "not noted for their intellectual depth or high ethical standards."

The Eaton incident passed, but the sentiments that the eccentric industrialist expressed with such gusto were shared by members of the Establishment. Cold-war security innovations were being rejected wholesale by the Warren court,[7] and aggrieved feelings on the Committee, where each new decision was received like a death in the family, were worsened by the justices' treatment of the twenty-eight contempt citations that issued from the hearings of 1957–1960. (The Committee had by now laid permanent claim to the cup for contempt citations, having in its two decades instituted more of them than all the other committees of the Congress put together.)

The results of the earliest tests were not displeasing to the Congressmen, and left them unprepared for the rain of blows that followed. The first cases involved two witnesses who had the bad luck to be called up in July 1958, midway between the Watkins decision and the Barenblatt decision. The hearings,

[7] In 1956 the court curbed state sedition laws and put restraints on federal security risk dismissals. In 1957 it limited the application of the Smith Act. In 1958 it ruled that the Secretary of State did not have the power to deny passports on the grounds of an applicant's beliefs or associations. In 1959 it voided the use of secret informers in the industrial security program.

held in Atlanta, concerned Communist activity in the South. Willis, as acting chairman, and counsel Arens took pains to spell out the authority of the Atlanta subcommittee and the legislative purpose of the hearing: the possible amending of the Communist Control Act and the Foreign Agents Registration Act. (These ceremonious speeches constituted the sole changes in the Committee's manners as a result of the Watkins decision over which liberals had prematurely rejoiced.) The reluctant witnesses, both identified as Party members, were Carl Braden, field secretary of the Southern Conference Educational Fund, which, according to Arens, was "for all practical purpose" a successor organization to the Southern Conference for Human Welfare, and Frank Wilkinson of the Emergency Civil Liberties Committee, which had been set up with the clear purpose of combating the Un-American Activities Committee. Both men refused their cooperation: Braden charged that the Committee was in Atlanta to discredit integrationists and Wilkinson gave only his name, adding, "As a matter of conscience and personal responsibility, I refuse to answer any questions of this Committee." Neither took the Fifth Amendment. Having sought sanctuary among the dicta of Watkins, they were undone by the thrust of Barenblatt. The high court decided their cases in February 1961. Speaking for the same five justices who had formed the majority in the Barenblatt case, Justice Stewart observed that it was not the intention of Congress to immunize from interrogation by the Committee all those who were opposed to its existence. To the minority's plausible charge that Braden and Wilkinson had been called as witnesses *because* they opposed the Committee (Wilkinson was not subpoenaed until he arrived in Atlanta to stir up protests against the hearings, and Braden had been instrumental in drawing up a letter from two hundred Southern Negroes asking that the Committee stay out of the South), Stewart countered that it was not the function of the court to speculate on the motives of Congressmen.[8]

---

[8] In his dissent, Justice Black deserted the judicial Muse for the Muse of the horror tale. The result of the Wilkinson decision, he wrote, was that "from now on anyone who takes a public position contrary to that being urged by

The Braden-Wilkinson decision remains the Committee's last major victory in the Supreme Court. In June 1961 the Court overturned the conviction of Bernhard Deutch, a young nuclear physicist and a recipient of one of the batch of contempt citations issued in 1954. Deutch had admitted to being a Party member between the ages of eighteen and twenty-one, but refused to answer any questions about individuals he had known in those years. The five-to-four decision, written by Potter Stewart, held that the government had not proved that the questions asked of Deutch, a student at Cornell at the time, were pertinent to the Committee's topic of inquiry, which was ostensibly Communist Party activities within the Albany area, with special reference to unions. In joining with Warren, Douglas, Black, and Brennan, whose aversion to the Committee had been repeatedly demonstrated, Stewart shifted the court's balance. In 1962 the same five-man majority rejected a group of six contempt-of-Congress convictions, two of which—Norton Anthony Russell and John Gojack—derived from the Un-American Activities Committee, because their indictments had not identified the specific subject under inquiry at the time of the defendants' alleged default. (Clark and Harlan dissented, while the ailing Frankfurter and the recently arrived White did not participate.) Moreover, in overturning convictions in a pair of cases—Frank Grumman and Bernard Silber—that arose out of the Committee's 1957 investigation into the communications industry, the court decided that it itself might take note of a faulty indictment even though the defendant made no mention of it in his appeal, thereby casting a shadow of uncertainty over nearly every contempt case then pending.

A still more ominous decision was handed down in 1963, in the case of Edward Yellin, who had refused to answer questions

the House Un-American Activities Committee should realize that he runs the risk of being subpoenaed to appear at a hearing in some far-off place, of being questioned with regard to every minute detail of his past life, of being asked to report all the gossip he may have heard about any of his friends and acquaintances, of being accused by the Committee of membership in the Communist Party, of being held up to the public as a subversive and a traitor, of being jailed for contempt if he refuses to cooperate with the Committee in its probe of his mind and associations, and of being branded by his neighbors, employer and erstwhile friends as a menace to society *regardless of the outcome of that hearing.*"

on grounds of the First Amendment in the 1958 hearings in Gary, Indiana. Here the court ruled for the defendant on the ingenious grounds that the Committee had failed to comply with its own Rule IV-A, which called for an executive hearing if, among other reasons, the majority of a subcommittee believed that a public hearing might unjustly injure a witness's reputation. Arens had turned down a request by Yellin's attorney for an executive hearing without giving the subcommittee an opportunity to consider the question. It would be an easy matter for the Committee thereafter to arrange its rules without disturbing in the slightest its accustomed methods of operation. The omen lay in the fact that this decision was the first on a Committee contempt case written since Felix Frankfurter had been replaced on the high bench by Arthur Goldberg. Now, even with Stewart joining Clark, Harlan, and White in dissent, the five-to-four majority which had given the Committee victory in the Barenblatt case and the Braden-Wilkinson case had conclusively swung the other way.

The cannon of the Supreme Court and Cyrus Eaton's six-shooter were not the only armament leveled against the temples of security in the late fifties, and the Un-American Activities Committee made a prime target. Anti-Committee protests there had always been, outside the hearing room and inside, from Communists, friends of Communists, and authentic civil libertarians, but now there were more protests and more vigorous ones. Some witnesses, particularly the hard-line C.P. members, raised cain as a matter of tactics. Some were incited by the snideness of Arens or the bullying of Scherer. Since no court ever held a witness in contempt of committee because he had behaved contemptuously, the only option available to the Congressmen when their patience was tried was to order troublesome persons from their sight, a penalty that was generally accepted like a medal.

The unfriendly witnesses followed as strict a pattern as the investigators, and charges of racism became popular accompaniments to the Fifth Amendment as the civil rights movement built up national momentum. In 1960 Paul Robeson, Jr., the Negro C.P. pillar Benjamin Davis, and Jesse Gray, the Harlem agitator, told off a subcommittee that was in New York to ask questions about the Vienna Youth Festival, where middle-aged officials of the Party from middle Europe had put their young American comrades through the usual anti-American exercises. In September 1958 a Negro witness in Los Angeles demanded of the Committee why it wasn't investigating the efforts being made in Little Rock, Arkansas, to nullify the Supreme Court's ruling on school integration, and across the country in Newark that month another Negro witness, on being asked where he was born, replied, "Mr. Arens, I was born in the state where yesterday the Reverend Martin Luther King was arrested by the courthouse at Montgomery, Alabama." The Newark hearings, the rowdiest of the 1958 season, had to be recessed on opening day owing to the noise. The following day a U.S. marshal took matters into his own hands and ejected the aforementioned Negro because the man called him Wyatt Earp. When the witness's lawyer objected, the marshal, incensed by suggestions from the audience that he belonged in Little Rock, warned, "I will throw you out too." Willis, chairman of the Newark subcommittee, afterward commended the peace officer for his "astute law enforcement and decorous conduct." As for demonstrations outside the building, such as those that greeted the 1959 subcommittee in San Juan, the unvarying response of the Congressmen was to credit them to the Emergency Civil Liberties Committee, formed in 1951 as a kind of benevolent and protective association for Communists in trouble, and they took to summoning activist opponents, like Frank Wilkinson and Carl Braden, who had tainted political records. In Chicago in 1959, two leaders of the Chicago Committee to Defend Democratic Rights, which had been organized to demonstrate against the investigation of the meat packers, were subpoenaed and charged with C.P. affiliations. By their behavior in the Committee room, such witnesses did nothing to refute the Committee charge that Communists were behind the opposition.

Rousing though a number of the hearings were between

1957 and 1960, they only served as curtain raisers to the great anti-Committee outburst of the period, the May 1960 demonstrations in San Francisco. California first worked its appeal on the Committee in Martin Dies's time, and it never flagged. No year passed between 1951 and 1960 that did not find a subcommittee in Los Angeles or San Francisco calling forth alleged Communists in entertainment, in education, in the professions, or merely at large. These visits were generally met by an angry opposition that featured but was by no means limited to familiar Communist apologists, and four days of hearings in San Francisco in June 1957, which opened a day after the Watkins decision had been delivered, did a great deal to broaden the base of protest. As a grim overture to these hearings, whose subject was the "extent, character and objectives of Communist Party activities within the professions," a young cancer researcher named William K. Sherwood committed suicide. He left a note expressing his anxiety over the publicity that was about to rain upon him: "My life and my livelihood are now threatened by the House Committee . . . I will be in two days assassinated by publicity . . . I would love to spend the next few years in laboratories but I would hate to spend them in jail." To settle the blame for a man's suicide on any exterior cause is a dubious enterprise, but the Committee's critics seized the opportunity. They exploited a statement that the biochemist had prepared—"The Committee's trail is strewn with blasted lives and the wreckage of youthful careers"—and a charge which his widow attempted without success to have put in the record: "You have helped to kill my husband and make my four children fatherless . . ." Whatever the justice of this accusation, it could not fail to impress upon the public what the Chief Justice had had in mind when in his opinion in the Watkins case he chastened the Committee for exposing for the sake of exposure. The suicide also drew attention to the fact that the San Francisco subcommittee, headed by Walter, was allowing the hearings to be televised in defiance of the no-TV rule laid down by Speaker Rayburn before the 1952 Detroit hearings and again when the Democrats recaptured Congress in 1955. (The televising of hearings in New

Orleans and in Baltimore earlier in the year had escaped notice.) Although Rayburn told reporters that his ban still held—"There will not be any more committee or subcommittee hearings in Washington or anywhere else televised or broadcast by radio. Period."—Walter permitted the TV cameras to continue operating, and it required a private meeting of the two men, who had once been close but had drifted apart as Walter went the way of the subversive hunter, to get the matter settled; there would be no television, period.

None of the people called to testify in June 1957—teachers, lawyers, doctors, actors, an architect, a radio broadcaster—were charged with having done anything remotely subversive, and if not for the suicide and the ensuing dispute over TV coverage, these hearings would not have been long remembered. But many Californians had not yet been able to forget them when the Committee, with great fanfare, again turned its attentions westward in 1959. Its actions in that year and the next seemed designed to test whether the temper of the country had really changed since Harold Velde roamed, and the answer was soon forthcoming. Early in June, Walter announced that 110 California teachers, seventy in Los Angeles and forty in the San Francisco area, had been subpoenaed for hearings later that month. They were a vulnerable group, for under a 1950 state law a loyalty oath was a prerequisite for obtaining teaching credentials. The Committee denied leaking their names, but a good number found their way into northern California newspapers. Protests followed; a spokesman for the northern California branch of the American Civil Liberties Union called the procedure "needless, sadistic harassment that cannot possibly be helpful for legislative purposes."

The harassment had only begun. Earlier in the year a Los Angeles subcommittee under Walter had taken two days of testimony in executive session from persons whom unidentified informants had named as having attended C.P. meetings. All took the Fifth, and the Committee released the transcripts a few weeks later without giving the source of its information or holding the anticipated public hearings. It was a case of run and hit. Now, in June, hearings of the subpoenaed teachers were postponed to September because, according to Walter, the ramifications of the situation were "so extensive and malignant" that further investigation was required. His action gave observers grounds for suspecting that there were too few ramifications rather than too many—indeed, that there was hardly any situation at all. The California Teachers Association, complaining that the leaking of names and the delay had put the subpoenaed teachers in the position of standing accused for an entire summer with no opportunity to reply, made the mistake of suggesting that the Committee pass along its information to local school boards, which could then hear the accused teachers in private. To everyone's amazement and his own evident relief, Walter accepted that proposal. He agreed to give the names to local boards so that they might interrogate the teachers and send the transcripts to the Committee. When the A.C.L.U. sought to enjoin the Committee from passing on its files—which, once again, were compilations of uninvestigated charges from unidentified sources—the material was hastily delivered to state authorities. The state's attorney general promised that he would keep the names secret, whereupon investigator William A. Wheeler, the Committee's California specialist, sent the names directly to county officials.

As a result of these maneuverings, several teachers lost their jobs. The price of this accomplishment to the Committee was high, however. It had taken the role of an adjunct police agency, supplying raw data to authorities with the power to punish. The role was not entirely untried, but it had not in recent years been played so nakedly. Unable to conceive that the California performance could find offense in the eyes of any but traitors and their dupes, the members of the Committee searched for Communist and fellow-traveling instigators of the ensuing protests. But if the protests—from newspapers, unions, and Episcopal, Methodist, and Quaker groups, among others—did not represent quite the groundswell of indignation that publicists on the left liked to pretend, they were not so mysteriously motivated that one had to go rooting about for Communists. How large a part this opposition played in turning back the Committee is a matter for speculation, but certainly the retreat heartened opponents for the battle soon to come.

Appropriately, it was a representative from California, James Roosevelt, who in these years raised aloft the standard in Congress against the Un-American Activities Committee. The flag had little starch to it. While individual Congressmen were willing to criticize the Committee for its random adventures, such as that involving the Air Force manual, even the most liberal of them had no spirit for an open confrontation. Through the nineteen-fifties, the Committee's annual appropriation rose steadily and passed the House with no semblance of debate. When it was given $305,000 in 1958, objection was uttered by a single legislator, Roy W. Wier, a Minnesota Democrat. (New York's Adam Clayton Powell said afterward that he was against the appropriation too because the Committee had not investigated the Ku Klux Klan.) A year later, with the appropriation up to $327,000, Wier was joined by Roosevelt, after the latter's proposal to turn the Committee's functions over to the Judiciary Committee had been allowed to perish in the Rules Committee. This proposal was unanimously rejected by the House Republican Conference, which took the unusual step of singling it out for rebuke, and Speaker Rayburn, concerned as ever for the Democratic Party's image, would not permit it to come to the floor; nevertheless, it was well publicized and had the effect of stirring up fresh waves of discontent with the Committee's practices. In April 1959 Harry Truman provided the discontented with a valuable quotation when he called the Committee the "most un-American thing in the country today." A week later, at the prodding of his friend and fellow Missourian Morgan Moulder, Truman added that he had had in mind the excesses of Martin Dies and Harold Velde, but the Committee's critics, who were in no mood for nice distinctions between one chairman and another, continued to make capital of the original, unqualified remark.

On April 25, 1960, Roosevelt rose again in the House to ask flatly that the Committee be abolished. His speech, "The Dragon Slayers," based mainly on the 1959–1960 record, was a good-humored, reasoned argument against the Committee's

justification for existing. Referring to its constant warnings
of possible espionage by Communists wherever unearthed, he
granted that left-wing meat workers might conceivably poison
the nation's meat supply, but made it plain that he was not
considering becoming a vegetarian on that account. He said
that he could see no end to the Committee's anxieties "except
to say that such heretics cannot be permitted gainful employment, and then I suppose we should put them to death to avoid
watching them starve." Roosevelt pointed out that whatever
one thought of the Air Force training manual's remarks about
the clergy, they were no business of the Un-American Activities
Committee; Air Force manuals fell within the jurisdiction of
the House Armed Services Committee. He noted that the
$327,000 allocated to the Committee on Un-American Activities
in 1960 was substantially more than the sums given most House
committees, including such consequential bodies as the Ways
and Means Committee and the Judiciary Committee, which
actually handled legislation. The Un-American Activities Committee, in Roosevelt's summation, was expensive, useless, redundant, "sanctimoniously cruel," "an agency for the destruction of human dignity and Constitutional rights." Scherer's
response ten days later was to say that such criticism was just
the sort of thing that came from Communists.

The greater part of Roosevelt's speech in April 1960 was given
over to the previous year's subpoenaing of teachers, and that
clumsy affair was still green when, a few weeks later, Willis,
Scherer, and Johansen presented themselves in San Francisco
with the intention of questioning several dozen witnesses about
"current operations" of the Communist Party of northern
California. These were not, it turned out, the promised, delayed, suspended hearings of the California teachers; only six
teachers took the Fifth Amendment on this visit. Most of the
three days in San Francisco's City Hall were divided between
two informants—Karl Prussion, who had left the Communist
Party nine months earlier after more than twenty years in it
on behalf of the F.B.I., and Barbara Hartle, a redeemed Communist who had made her peace with the Committee in 1956—
and a handful of local C.P. lights. (Irving Fishman, the customs

Alger Hiss claimed that the newspaper photograph above, published before his public confrontation with Whittaker Chambers, below, was what gave Chambers the idea of telling the Committee that the Hiss he knew years before was deaf in one ear. In the scene below, Hiss is third from left at the second table, for some reason smiling.

Posed around Robert Stripling as if they were studying the microfilm found in Whittaker Chambers's pumpkin were (left to right) Committee investigators Louis Russell, William Wheeler, Robert Gaston, Donald Appell, C. E. McKillips.

The appearance of the microfilm caused Richard Nixon to interrupt a Caribbean cruise and, with the assistance of the Coast Guard, hasten photogenically back to Washington.

In the aftermath of their remarkable case, Chambers sought out the quiet of his Maryland farm and Hiss was taken to the penitentiary.

Did Chairman Velde's smiling handshake at the conclusion of Bishop G. Bromley Oxnam's ten hours of testimony mean that all was forgiven? Not exactly.

The gentleman pointing something out to Representative Francis Walter was Matthew Cvetic, one of the early Committee informants.

During the periodically renewed hearings on show business during the nineteen-fifties, (clockwise) the actor John Garfield apologized for his past enthusiasms; the choreographer Jerome Robbins gave the names of a few Communist associates; the bandleader Artie Shaw wept; and the playwright Arthur Miller announced that he was planning to marry Marilyn Monroe.

When fire hoses did not extinguish the anti-Committee demonstration in the San Francisco City Hall, the police took to dragging demonstrators down the marble staircase.

Flowers, applause, and a cute baby greeted Mrs. Dagmar Wilson, a leader of Women Strike for Peace, as she approached the Committee's witness chair.

Robert Shelton, the Ku Klux Klan head, shown here getting decked out for a rally and cross-burning in South Carolina, was more sedately received when his turn to testify arrived.

The high point of the hearings of opponents of the war in Vietnam came as attorney Arthur Kinoy was vigorously assisted from the room. Representative Joe Pool, who had ordered Kinoy out, explained the Committee's decision to dismiss remaining witnesses identified as representing anti-Vietnam war groups.

official whose appearance at Committee functions had become a custom, was also on hand, with his mail sack.)

The informants were superlatively obliging. In addition to supplying names, Prussion told the Congressmen that 10,000 Communists were enough to carry out an insurrection and Mrs. Hartle, who had been convicted under the Smith Act, replied in the affirmative when Arens asked, "You have found your way back to God and patriotism, is that correct?" Peaceful coexistence with the Soviets, she reported, was a snare and a delusion. The professional Communists, too, outdid themselves. They were extraordinarily obstreperous. They played to the TV cameras—in use again despite the events of 1957—and presented themselves alternately as champions of democracy and martyrs to the inquisition. They baited Congressmen and counsel with relish; one man addressed his long speech on the reasons why he was taking the Fifth Amendment to "Honorable beaters of children and sadists . . ." Another told Arens that he sounded "halfway like a nut." (Arens was in form, too. Questioning a witness who had visited the Far East some years before, he asked: "While you were there, did you make inquiries respecting the emasculation, the crucifixion of the Christian missionaries who had been teaching in Red China?") During a recess on the first day several witnesses, accompanied by a few members of the audience, made use of an available microphone to attack the Committee and sing *The Star Spangled Banner*. The Congressmen let this act, recorded by the TV cameras, proceed for a while, then called the riot squad to lead the singing group away. The master of ceremonies, Archie Brown, a Communist longshoreman, was removed twice that Thursday and so was not available when he was called to the witness chair. On Friday he was summoned again, but this time he couldn't make it because of the commotion taking place just beyond the doors of the hearing room. He finally did appear on Saturday, attempted to make a motion to "disqualify the Committee," and was ejected for the third time, thereby setting a record that still stands.

The great events of the May hearing occurred outside the hearing room. The days leading up to the Committee's visit

were full of warnings. Students from the Berkeley campus of
the University of California and San Francisco State College
joined in demonstrations against the long-delayed execution
of Caryl Chessman; hundreds of residents of the Bay Area
attended a lively meeting of the Berkeley board of education
at which two probationary teachers who had been subpoenaed
the year before were given a hearing; student newspapers ran
attacks on the Committee by faculty members and other groups
that recalled the events of 1959; the one University of California student who had been subpoenaed—because he was a
delegate to the 1959 national C.P. convention—did some
agitating around campus; anti-Committee groups of various
political shadings welcomed the investigators to San Francisco
with protest meetings and statements. Emotions were building
up, and as the Congressmen set to work on May 12, one thousand people, mostly students, demonstrated against them in
Union Square, while several hundred others marched around
City Hall and lined up before the doors of the hearing room.

On the second day of the hearings, Friday, the number of
demonstrators had grown substantially. A fair degree of order
was maintained outside City Hall, where loudspeakers were
set up to relay the hearings. Inside the building, however,
some two hundred students seeking admission to the hearing
room grew incensed upon observing that most of the seats
were set aside for friends of the Committee. Investigator
Wheeler had issued passes, he explained on opening day, "to
keep the Communists from stacking the meeting. We wanted
some decent people in here." Wheeler feared that if spectators
were admitted first-come-first-served, the hearings would get
out of hand; the students were prepared to guffaw at appropriate moments and the hostile witnesses were prepared to
play up to them. But by packing the hearing room, he provided
the protestors with a real cause and an effective rallying cry. On
the first day, before breaking into *The Star Spangled Banner*,,
the subpoenaed witnesses, led by Archie Brown, kept yelling
for the Committee to "Open the doors! Open the doors!" On
Friday morning the students gathered peacefully, but became
restive as the hours passed and only a handful of their number

were admitted. They were noisy enough to disturb a judge attempting to carry on his duties in another room of the building. The precise cause of the event that has entered the annals of the Un-American Activities Committee as "the Communist-led riots" remains shadowed in controversy. The police, backed by the Committee and J. Edgar Hoover, maintained afterward that a student leaped the barricade, assaulted a policeman with his own billy, and led a surge of students toward the hearing room. But the young man charged with this aggression was found not guilty. The students and their defenders maintain that at 1:15 p.m., with no particular warning and for no particular cause, the police turned high-pressure fire hoses on them. For the next half hour, they were washed out of the rotunda of the building and dragged bumping down City Hall's marble stairs, with an occasional assist from a policeman's club. "People should be able to differ without being disagreeable," commented Mr. Willis. Upwards of five dozen demonstrators, two of whom were alleged to be Communists, were hauled off to jail, the charges against all but one—the young man accused of jumping the policeman—being dismissed by a sensible judge two weeks later.

Giving way to their uncontrollable tic, the Congressmen on the scene at once blamed what Willis called "probably the worst incident in the history of the Committee" on the Communists. Scherer told the House that the riots were "clearly planned at the highest Communist levels" and J. Edgar Hoover accommodated the Committee with a report entitled *Communist Target—Youth; Communist Infiltration and Agitation Tactics,* which used self-congratulatory statements of Communist leaders to prove that "such a Communist coup has not occurred in the San Francisco area for twenty-five years." The Committee's most elaborate exposition of its view of the affair was presented in the form of a forty-five-minute movie, put together by a commercial firm in Washington out of subpoenaed TV newsreel films, and narrated by Fulton Lewis III. A tricky piece of work, replete with distortions and irrelevancies, gossip and surmise, it became a *cause célèbre* in itself, exciting protests and counterprotests wherever it was shown.

Events were presented out of sequence in order to strengthen the connection between Communists and students; a shot of Harry Bridges, who had nothing to do with the demonstrations, was inserted for flavor; as the film showed students being thumped down the stairs, Fulton Lewis III spoke feelingly of the trials of the police. (An amended version had to be produced to repair the more blatant distortions in the original.) *Operation Abolition*—the film's title was taken from a 1957 report on the Emergency Civil Liberties Committee—became an official document of the Committee and hundreds of prints were soon circulated to private groups and TV stations around the country, and seen by millions of people, to the profit of the Washington company. An excellent antidote, *Operation Correction*, produced by the Civil Liberties Union of northern California, used the same film strips with a different narration to expose the misleading techniques of the Committee's hired hands, but it never managed to catch up with the original. Nor did *Autopsy on Operation Abolition*, a pro-con documentary put out by the Catechetical Guild of St. Paul, a large publisher of Catholic educational aids.

Since the days of the Paris Commune, Marxists have taken to themselves credit for events in which they played but a passing part, and they have been supported in their pretensions by their heartiest foes. Something of what the Committee's spokesmen saw in the San Francisco disturbances, as set forth by Scherer in an astonishing harangue at the conclusion of the hearings, was visible even to objective eyes. Communists and their sympathizers in campus groups and the Emergency Civil Liberties Committee (Frank Wilkinson was on hand and so won a featured role in *Operation Abolition*) were prominent in the efforts to build up resentment against the Committee before its visit. At the hearings, the subpoenaed Communists did their utmost to incite a riot. And there was no doubt that the Party was delighted with the results. But that was all that Scherer, Hoover, and the others saw, all that they had ever seen in protests against the Committee; this time the explanation was not necessary, it was not sufficient. By calling the 5,000 students who demonstrated outside City Hall on the last day of hearings "victims of this despicable propaganda plot," Scherer displayed his own incapacity to sense the impulses at work among the young people at Berkeley and elsewhere around the country. The Committee's subpoenas and cancellations and the final growling withdrawal in California in 1959 had prepared the ground for the May 1960 demonstrations; Wilkinson and his cohorts had tended it, as did many non-Communists and anti-Communists; and the police had assisted in their inimitable way. But a demonstration of such proportions and such vehemence required something more than this. For the students, the upsurge in San Francisco proclaimed the end of a decade of cold-war hibernation; college campuses were becoming centers of national discontent over larger issues than the Un-American Activities Committee.

"Looking at the riots and chaos Communists have created in other countries, many Americans point to the strength of our nation and say, 'It can't happen here,'" wrote J. Edgar Hoover. "The Communist success in San Francisco in May, 1960, proves it can happen here." But the policeman Hoover had no inkling of what was really happening. In 1960 students had already been moved to action by the civil rights struggle; in a few years they would be holding teach-ins on Vietnam. Their protests would take diverse and sometimes puzzling forms—Caesar is supposed to have remarked on first hearing Brutus speak in public, "I know not what this young man intends, but whatever he intends, he intends vehemently"—but no Party line could accommodate them. Though the radicals of the thirties might march along with the radicals of the sixties when conditions seemed suitable, their dreams were not the same. The new activists spared no particular affection for the Soviet paradise; nor were their emotions locked up with the Moscow trials or the war in Spain. Their discontent was formless and pervasive. They saw after eight years of Dwight Eisenhower what the young have often seen, their destinies in the hands of old, cautious, unimaginative, unfeeling men, and they needed to break out. The campus at Berkeley became a testing place of this remarkably non-ideological, even anti-ideological movement, and the arrival of the Un-American Activities Committee, which had been engaged in the harassment of teachers, students, and political non-conformists for twenty years, was galvanic. "Nobody incited us, nobody misguided us," declared fifty-eight of the arrested students after the charges against them were dismissed. "We were led by our own convictions, and we still stand firmly by them."

To those who converged on City Hall, the Committee, represented by men made nervous and angry by any show of unorthodox opinion, stood as a symbol and tool of the Establishment, a deadening hand extended from Washington to quash the impulses of dissent wherever they might spring up. How could these young men and women, in their teens and early twenties, be expected to know that the Committee itself had been doing battle with the Establishment since its earliest days and that never had it been farther from the center of America's political life than in the year of the election of John F. Kennedy?

15

★ ★ ★ ★ ★

1961-1966: The Lean Years

IN 1961 and 1962, Francis Walter served the new Administration as a Congressional lieutenant. His long tenure and
forceful personality, his strong position among the Democratic
representatives, his reputation as a conservative, albeit aber-
rated, and a party regular, albeit temperamental, combined to
make him a valuable contact for the White House in a Congress that was not enthusiastic over New Frontiers. But while
he was concluding his career amid the expressed esteem of
those who needed his services (at a dinner in his honor in
1961 Speaker Rayburn, letting bygones be gone, praised
Walter for having "dug out more dens of disloyalty than any
man who has ever lived in the United States"), his Committee,
already a shadow, was fading, fading.[1] There were but forty-
four days of published hearings in the two years of the eighty-
seventh Congress, several closed to the public, few newsworthy.

Most of the organizations selected for the Committee's table
made meager fare. They had a handful of members, little
money, short lives, and no influence. There was the Fund for
Social Analysis, set up early in 1958 as, frankly, "an informal
organization of individuals interested in aiding Marxist research," whose function was to give modest grants-in-aid "for
studies of problems posed by Marxist theory and its applica-

---

[1] Joining Walter on the Committee in the eighty-seventh Congress were four
Democrats—Moulder, Doyle, Willis, and Tuck—and four Republicans—Scherer,
Johansen, Donald G. Bruce, a freshman from Indiana, and Henry C. Schade-
berg, a freshman from Wisconsin. Tavenner was director, Alfred M. Nittle,
counsel, and John C. Walsh, co-counsel.

tion." The Fund's bent was evident from the names of grantors and grantees—Barrows Dunham, Russell Nixon, Herbert Aptheker—and though these scholars were not above making a bit of propaganda for their side, their pursuits were harmless as well as predictable. There was the National Assembly for Democratic Rights, organized at a Giant Freedom Rally in September 1961 as a response to the June decision of the Supreme Court upholding (temporarily) the McCarran Act. It was the creature of groups threatened by the law with forced registration. With W. E. B. Du Bois, John Abt, Rockwell Kent, Willard Uphaus, Carl Marzani, and Benjamin Davis among its sponsors and well-wishers, the exposure of this group as being "under concealed control of the Communist Party" was an exercise in the self-evident. There were the Medical Aid to Cuba Committee and Friends of British Guiana run, respectively, by admirers of Fidel Castro and Cheddi Jagan. To judge by the Committee's information, these groups had done nothing more than they were avowedly in existence to do: send medical supplies to Cuba and a printing press to the People's Progressive Party of then British Guiana. This set of hearings, which opened two weeks after the October 1962 Cuban missile crisis, was not the first or the last demonstration of Committee interest in Castro's supporters in this country. The Fair Play for Cuba Committee, the major pro-Castro group, had already been claimed by the Senate Internal Security Subcommittee, but on a trip to the West in April, Doyle and Tavenner had studied "Communist and Trotskyist Activity Within the Greater Los Angeles Chapter of the Fair Play for Cuba Committee" and found "a significant increase in the power and influence" of southern California's Trotskyists. (The Los Angeles visit was the first to that part of the country by a subcommittee since the demonstrations in San Francisco. Hundreds of pickets were at hand on opening day, but their interest fell off when it became apparent that whatever was being done was being done in closed session, with a minimum of publicity.)

A few certifiable C.P. functionaries who had quit or been ousted for "revisionism" or "ultra-leftist dogmatism" or other sins during the Party's late ideological turmoils were summoned but refused redemption at the Committee's hands. The Committee thereupon concluded, on the basis of a presentation by Francis McNamara, its staff authority, that the Communist Party was not a democratic institution. There were also hearings on the communications union, on Soviet propaganda outlets, on the World Youth Festival in Helsinki, on the oppressive conditions in Russia and China, and on Communist activities in Cleveland, in the course of which, once again, a man identified as a Party member by an F.B.I. informant turned out to be an F.B.I. informant himself. Taken in all, the Committee's record for the greater part of 1961 and 1962 was like summer television, heavily dependent on cheap packages and reruns.

The feature event of the eighty-seventh Congress came in December 1962 when a subcommittee under Doyle held hearings in Washington on Women Strike for Peace. As emperors once claimed descent from the heavens, so activist groups of every sort attribute their existence to a spontaneous urge of that contemporary divinity, the Ordinary American. In the case of W.S.P., it was the Ordinary American Housewife, and there was more substance to the claim than usual. The perils of radioactive fallout, particularly to young children, had been dramatically publicized during the last years of the Eisenhower Administration, and even the least political mother reading her copy of *Redbook* or watching television must have felt uncomfortable at the insistent connecting of her baby's bones to nuclear tests. The more political took quickly to the suggestion in September 1961 of a Washington, D.C., illustrator of children's books, Mrs. Dagmar Wilson, that women get together and work for a test ban, an avowed Kennedy goal that was meeting resistance in Congress, the Pentagon, and the Atomic Energy Commission, as well as in the Kremlin, which had a few weeks before broken a two-year moratorium and ordered a resumption of testing. The issue in the fall and winter of 1961–1962 was whether the United States would resume its own tests, and the major efforts of the rapidly and loosely organized W.S.P. were directed at discouraging such a response. In November 1961 tens of thousands of women in dozens of cities demonstrated for a test ban. In January 1962 some 1,700 women converged on Washington to picket the White House and buttonhole Congressmen. In February there was picketing at the United Nations. In April, shortly before the President ordered a new round of U.S. tests, fifty-one of the women made a well-publicized flight to Geneva to lend encouragement to the disarmament negotiators.

The Committee, which had preached in years of reports, consultations, and friendly testimony that anything less than a call for holy war against the Soviets was suspect, could only take a sour view of the ladies' activities, and the December hearings were arranged by the staff to make the best connection they could between Communists and the peace movement. The hearings were designed to show, as an obliging writer in the *National Review* commented afterward, that the women's activities "are—if not controlled by the Communists—at least of immense help to the Communist peace offensive." The staff began its demonstration, rather oddly, with a young New Yorker who, under F.B.I. instructions, had accepted $3,000 from a pair of Russian U.N. employees to finance his campaign for a seat in the state assembly. He was in no way connected with Women Strike for Peace or any other peace group. But Counsel Nittle managed to extract from his testimony the nugget that the Russians wanted him to emphasize in his campaign speeches such subjects as peace, disarmament, nuclear testing, and trade with the Communist bloc. As the hearings progressed, Nittle called a few leaders of peace groups other than W.S.P. who had substantial records as Communists or fellow travelers. Their relationship to W.S.P. was remote but sufficient for the Committee's purpose; despite the assurance of Chairman Doyle, aged seventy-five and vaguer than ever, that being for peace did not automatically make one a Communist, the hearings were arranged to cast the darkest shadow possible on the entire peace movement.

Among those attracted to Women Strike for Peace were numbers of veterans of leftist battles of the thirties and forties, some of them Party members. The nuclear test ban was much more than a Communist cause, but it was a cause in which apologists for the U.S.S.R. had an interest, particularly in the months when President Kennedy was pondering the resumption of U.S. tests. Having been through many previous wars, the old-timers moved into the organizational jobs that most of the W.S.P. supporters, young mothers and busy ones, were content to leave to others. The older women were experienced, they were enthusiastic, and they had no infants at home in need of diapering. It was a handful of such peace workers from the New York area on whom the Committee turned a jaundiced eye in December.

The witnesses and the scores of women, a few with babies, most with hats, who made up the greater part of the audience found more fun in the hearings than their interrogators. They rose and sat as one, laughed and applauded on cue. "This movement was inspired and motivated by mothers' love for their children," said the first woman to take the Fifth Amendment, an elderly resident of Scarsdale who, according to Nittle, had been a C.P. member when she taught in the New York public schools a decade or more before. "When they were putting their breakfast on the table they saw not only Wheaties and milk, but they also saw strontium 90 and iodine 131." Applause. (On the first day, too, a man who had worked for the F.B.I. for eleven months before quitting and writing a harsh article about J. Edgar Hoover was ejected when he yelled out an unfavorable opinion of the proceedings.)

On the second day there were bouquets for each witness. "It is nice to get the flowers while you can smell them, isn't it?" observed Doyle, who would be dead in three months. Nittle, attempting to demonstrate, with the help of a chart of organization, that the W.S.P. women were being manipulated by a clique of New York Reds, got into some baffling exchanges with witnesses who insisted that their operations were highly flexible, that jobs went to whoever would do them and the movement ran, somewhat haphazardly, by itself. "This appears to be a most elusive organization . . ." said Nittle as desperation set in. There was a touch of feigned ingenuousness in the testimony, but had Nittle ever watched the workings of his local P.T.A., he would have found it easier to believe or, at any rate, understand the ladies. Matters soon got quite beyond Doyle, who kept insisting that the last thing he intended was to discredit the peace movement; on the second day he had to apologize for having said on the first day, "So far as we know, she is a Communist now because there is no evidence that she is not. If she is not, here is an opportunity for her to clear it up."

Most of the witnesses took the Fifth Amendment, but three —a woman charged with being a member of the American Student Union and the Young Communist League at Vassar in the thirties, who burst into tears on leaving the stand; another, who testified that she had not been a C.P. member for at least five years; and a man who had been adjudged a Communist by the Subversive Activities Control Board in 1956— refused to discuss their past activities or present associations on grounds of the First Amendment. Reeling before adverse court decisions, the Committee made no effort to press contempt charges against any of them. Yet another witness put on display was Elizabeth Moos, mother-in-law of the unfortunate William Remington and a vintage worker in Communist causes; she had nothing special to do with Women Strike for Peace, having given her energies mainly to the Stockholm Peace Appeal and similar causes instigated from abroad. That the Committee summoned her at all was evidence of its intentions toward the W.S.P.

The final witness was Mrs. Dagmar Wilson, the Washington lady generally credited with having gotten the idea for Women Strike for Peace. Nittle made it explicit that he had no evidence of Communist sympathies on Mrs. Wilson's part, and embarked again on a line of questioning designed to show that W.S.P.'s Communists or former Communists were running things, perhaps under supervision of the Kremlin. Mrs. Wilson, affecting a certain giddiness, answered most of Nittle's questions, thereby adding to his confusion. The only question of consequence that Nittle put to her, the question that the Committee had been working up to for three days, was this: "I would like to ask whether you would knowingly permit or encourage a Communist Party member to occupy a leadership position in

Women Strike for Peace." Mrs. Wilson replied: "Well, my dear sir, I have absolutely no way of controlling, do not desire to control, who wishes to join in the demonstrations and the efforts that the women strikers have made for peace. In fact I would also like to go even further. I would like to say that unless everybody in the whole world joins us in this fight, then God help us." When Nittle pressed her on whether she planned to take any action to prevent Communists from assuming places of leadership or to eliminate those who had already attained such places, she answered, "Certainly not."

This answer, though understandable in the circumstances and refreshing after a decade in which it was rarely allowed in public that Communists were also human beings, was nonetheless glib. The precedent for these hearings was a 1960 investigation, by the Senate Internal Security Subcommittee under Thomas J. Dodd, of the National Committee for a Sane Nuclear Policy. As a result of Senator Dodd's initiative and amid heartfelt anguish, reluctant expulsions, and sad resignations, the leaders of SANE decided that they could not in the future abide the presence of Communists. In part, this was a merely prudential move; at stake was the future of a growing and effective organization whose goals would be jeopardized by any suspicion of Communist direction. But in the light of the entire history of American Communism, it was also sound policy on a higher level; as the SANE statement noted, members of the Communist Party are "not free . . . to apply to the misconduct of the Soviet or Chinese government the same standards by which they challenge others."

For Mrs. Wilson to take a similar stand publicly at the instance of the Un-American Activities Committee was unthinkable; it would have been interpreted as an admission of guilt and a note of retreat. Moreover, since W.S.P. was not so tightly controlled as SANE, even had she been so inclined, she would have had no ready way to remove the Communists, no charters to revoke or staff to be fired. W.S.P. was given mainly to the spectacular gesture—picketing the White House, a flight to Geneva. By the time of the hearings, the women had already experienced their greatest moments; the enthusiasm that had been so quickly generated would quickly wane. (The hearings before the Committee may actually have stimulated W.S.P. for a time. Upon leaving the Caucus Room, seventy women walked twenty blocks to the White House, bearing signs on the order of END THE ARMS RACE, NOT THE HUMAN RACE and PEACE IS AMERICAN.) The Senate's ratification of the test-ban treaty in September 1962 was a victory that would turn W.S.P., briefly a notable phenomenon, into just another peace group of mostly well-meaning women. As for the Communists among them, the worst they could do within such an organization was to add their inimitable anti-American touches to the signs they had printed up.

There was something excessive in handing out bouquets to witnesses who preferred not to incriminate themselves, and Mrs. Wilson's explanation of her position regarding Communists was not a model of clear thinking—"The solid support of the women for those who took the Fifth is an indication that we are simply not concerned with personal points of view" —but the ladies of W.S.P., like more objective observers, could not fail to discern the Committee's purpose in bringing on these hearings and they were in no mood to capitulate. It was an obvious and awkward attack on the supporters of a nuclear test ban and it left the well-meaning Doyle and the ill-prepared Nittle floundering in confusion, bathed in ridicule. It would be some time before the Committee again engaged itself with peace organizations, and then it would choose its subjects with more care.

On May 31, 1963, Francis Walter, ill since the beginning of the year, died of leukemia. He had brought to the chairmanship of the Committee a greater distinction, competence, and sense of legislative purpose than it had ever known. But like the respectable burgher turned loose in a brothel, he gave way to his surroundings and exhibited the more perverse side of his nature. It was as though he caught infection from the shades of men he knew to be inferior to him: Martin Dies, J. Parnell Thomas, Harold Velde. Many of the symptoms he despised in them reappeared during his chairmanship: malice, vindictiveness, irresponsibility, inanity—all flourished in the Committee hothouse, fertilized and tended by Arens and his staff. Whatever its psychological cost, sublimation is often a virtue in politics; in giving Walter an opportunity to act out, the Committee distorted a notable career. At the end, after serving in the House for more than fifteen terms, he was anathema on the left yet, except for certain ceremonial occasions, no hero of the right. In 1962 the Conservative Society of America gave his Committee its highest rating of all standing committees of Congress, but gave him a rating of zero on his voting record. "That means," explained Edith Kermit Roosevelt in her newsletter of the distant right, "Rep. Walter is listed by the hard-core conservative group as voting liberal-socialist 100 percent of the time." The Democratic leadership valued him, yet was periodically exasperated by his more manic moods. So complicated a figure was he that on his passing, the liberal Washington *Post* found for him respectful words which it had had no occasion to print while he lived. The Committee, like a bartender whose grief over a customer's passing depends on how much he drank, wrote in its memorial tribute, ". . . his many contributions in the field of national security will be an everlasting monument to his memory and will serve as a living inspiration to all those who serve after him." But it was those heady liquors of international security that betrayed the man.

The torch was handed on to Edwin E. Willis of Louisiana, who, his party's leaders could feel confident, would not use it to burn down the House. Willis, aged fifty-nine, had been in Congress for fourteen years without starting any fires. There were several other changes on the Committee in 1963. Scherer, the alleged Birchite, and Moulder, the putative liberal, retired, and Doyle, who had never wearied of his role of kindly Uncle Clyde though he wearied everyone else, died,[2] and was

[2] These departures left three Democratic vacancies, which were filled by Joe R. Pool of Texas, Richard H. Ichord of Missouri, and George F. Senner, Jr., of Arizona. The single Republican vacancy was taken by John M. Ashbrook of Ohio. Some months before these changes there was a major staff change: Francis J. McNamara became Committee director, with Tavenner staying on as general counsel and Nittle as counsel.

commemorated by the Committee in lines which he had himself composed:

> Four things you must do
> If you would make your record true;
> To think without confusion clearly,
> To love your fellow men sincerely,
> To act from honest motives purely,
> To trust in God in Heaven securely.

Under Willis, but through no fault of that gentleman, un-enterprising though he was, the Committee now settled into the role of the aging rake, living in comfort, tended still by loyal retainers, rocking in his chair and musing idly upon the high times of a lusty youth. Then, without notice, roaring up from the rocking chair, pulling on his trousers, and tearing into town where, likely as not, a bunch of streetcorner trouble-makers would be waiting for him, winking and elbowing one another at the sport in store. The question one now began to ask as the Committee charged forth on its infrequent adventures was not, as in the old days, what it was going to inflict on others, but what unpleasantness the others had planned for the Congressmen this time.

On September 12 and 13, 1963, for example, the Committee's Washington hearings of a group of young leftists who had paid a summer visit to Cuba erupted into the noisiest, most violent scenes since San Francisco. After repeatedly, and to no avail, warning his audience to desist from hurrahing every time a witness delivered himself of a rouser against the "racists that are sitting up here in front of me right now," Willis told the police, "Okay, throw them out," and with kicks, screams, and yells of "Fascist!" and "Police brutality!" and "It's like Nazi Germany!" thrown out they were.

The pandemonium in September was part of a series of hearings that occupied the Committee for much of 1963 and into 1964. (The 1964 hearings were quiet, except when a member of the American Nazi Party dashed down the aisle, vaulted a railing, and, hollering, "Down with Castro!", tried to slug a witness.) The Congressmen were bothered by the fact that known and suspected Communists seemed to be going to Cuba at their pleasure despite a State Department ban on such trips. The offenders were in the main members of the Progressive Labor Movement, the creation of two upstate New York men who had been expelled from the Communist Party in 1961 for their Chinese-Albanian tendencies. The P.L.M. youths led sizable groups of students, not all Communists, on visits to Cuba in the summers of 1963 and 1964—expenses paid by the Cuban government, with spending money thrown in. There they were feted by the Cuban Institute for Friendship Among the Peoples, and played ping-pong and baseball with their host Fidel. The P.L.M. leaders missed no opportunity to speak ill of the leaders and institutions of their own country, and they returned home with tales of the glories being wrought in the people's democracy to the south. (One young man, who went along in behalf of the F.B.I. brought home other tales; he became a friendly witness before the Committee.)

The Committee went after these pilgrims on two grounds: first, that they had violated the State Department regulation forbidding travel to Cuba, a charge being studied by a grand jury as well; and second, that they had acted as propagandists for a foreign regime while abroad and after their return. Although counsel Nittle tried to make something of a detective story out of the mechanics by which the group leaders had purchased their tickets and traveled to Cuba via Paris and Prague, the witnesses were anything but secretive about their journeys. They took the Fifth Amendment in response to questions about their fellows ("Certainly to know the names of individuals can be in no way of help to the Congress in framing legislation," said one. "It may be of help in framing individuals but not to frame legislation"), but they were voluble regarding the trip itself, the virtues of Castroism, the defects of the United States, their distaste for the Committee, and their faith in Marxism. The hearings thus became a series of high-school cafeteria debates, with victory on points going easily to the witnesses. For one thing, there was substantial doubt whether the State Department could in fact enforce the ban it had promulgated. Moreover, the witnesses were more practiced debaters, quicker-witted for the most part than any of the Congressmen who took them on and much sharper than counsel Nittle, who was subject to fits of confusion. The outburst on the second day was brought on as much by the incapacity of Chairman Willis to handle the argument of his witness, Phillip Abbott Luce, a young employee of the Emergency Civil Liberties Committee who had acted as press relations man for the touring students, as by the readiness of the P.L.M. partisans to demonstrate:

CHAIRMAN: Did you have knowledge of the State Department rulings that this trip or any other trip without validation of passport constituted a violation of the law and regulation I just quoted a while ago, whether you agreed with them or not? Did you have knowledge of that ruling by the State Department?

LUCE: I would be very lax in my homework if I did not, sir; but again, it is no law. It is Public Notice 179.

CHAIRMAN: You disagree with the ruling of the State Department?

LUCE: I not only disagree with it; it is absolutely and totally unconstitutional.

CHAIRMAN: Are you an attorney?

LUCE: I am not an attorney, but obviously I have as much knowledge of this as you since you cannot find what the law is.

CHAIRMAN: I quoted it to you.

LUCE: You did not quote it to me. You quoted a public notice. Public notices do not have the effect of law. And don't come on to me about that 1185 (b), because that is the Walter-McCarran Act . . .

. . . .

CHAIRMAN: And you don't agree with the law?

LUCE: It is not a law. It is a public notice. I do not agree with the public notice because I consider it unconstitutional. I would also like to say this to you, sir . . .

CHAIRMAN: Now we are getting down to it. In other words you take the position that this law and this regulation are unconstitutional?

LUCE: Sir, it is not a law. It is a public notice. Even if there was a law, however, even if there was a law, which there is not, I believe along with Thoreau, Emerson and other people throughout American history that certain rules and regulations must be broken. Now, we did not break a law. We broke a public notice. I want to make that very clear.

CHAIRMAN: But if in your opinion there was a law, you would say . . .

LUCE: I would consider it my duty to break that law as much as the Negro voters in the state of Louisiana and Danville, Virginia, Mr. Tuck, consider the breaking of the state laws when they try to vote.

(*Demonstration in hearing room.*)

CHAIRMAN: Get them out.

LUCE: "Get them out." Throwing them out for clapping. This may be something you can get away with in Louisiana or Virginia, but I can't understand it here.

The general quality of the debates may be appreciated in an exchange from the 1964 hearings, between Representative Senner of Arizona, not the blackest reactionary on the Committee, and a twenty-four-year-old P.L.M. enthusiast named Yvonne Marie Bond:

MISS BOND: This country has monopolies rather than the free enterprise that it is so highly touted to be. I pondered on the solution for these problems for a long time and I was cynical because I thought it had to do with the nature of man that things should always be thus. Then I discovered socialism and found that things don't always have to be.

SENNER: When you use the word "socialism," are you talking about communism? Are you not talking about communism when you say socialism? There is a difference, and you know it.

MISS BOND: Socialism is that stage of economic development before communism.

. . . . .

MISS BOND: I found out about socialism and the fact that man is able to change his environment and his economic and social structure. I started reading about countries which were socialist, such as Cuba, the Soviet Union and China and other socialist countries. Cuba especially impressed me because it was such a small place and because they seemed to have made such rapid development in alleviating malnutrition and poverty in such a short time. In recalling all the poor people and the

Negro people and the highly taxed workers and even middle-
class people . . .

SENNER: Miss Bond, I think this eighty-eighth Congress has done
more for education, civil rights and everything else to move this
country in the direction of equal opportunities for all. If you
will study history correctly, you will find that more millionaires
have been made since World War II in this country than ever
before in its history.

MISS BOND: While others remain poor. That is just a cure for
the symptoms, not the disease.

SENNER: I want to ask you this question: What would happen to
you if you would oppose Fidel Castro in the manner that you
are opposing the United States government now? What would
happen to you?

MISS BOND: That is a silly question because I would not oppose
Fidel Castro simply to oppose him. It is not a matter of opposi-
sition for opposition's sake; it pertains to reality, to concrete
things.

The troopers of the Progressive Labor Movement would,
willy nilly, be lumped in with the new left, that catch-all for
youthful discontents in the nineteen-sixties, but except in their
willingness to flaunt their Marxist faith before the Congressmen, they were barely distinguishable from the old left. It
was Cuba now instead of the U.S.S.R. that captured them, and
Castro instead of Stalin, but their slogans, their pretensions,
their simplifications were the stuff on which the radicals of the
thirties had built their towers too. They could in one breath
damn Representatives Willis and Tuck for coming from districts where Negroes were deprived of the vote, and acclaim
the absence of elections in Cuba: "The Cuban people don't
want an election. They honestly do not care to have an
election at the national level at this time." Their debut under
the Committee's auspices was sufficient to put off even so tried
a friend of the left, old and new, as the journalist I. F. Stone
who withdrew as moderator of a Town Hall panel discussion
on travel to Cuba after the September 1963 hearings with the
observation that the students' views "seem to me a mixture
of naïveté, Negro nationalist distortions (understandable
enough in the light of the Negro's anguish, but still distortions),

and out-of-this-world leftism." The Town Hall meeting, presided over by the dependable Corliss Lamont, began with a search by a P.L.M. security band of suspicious-looking characters as they entered and by the forcible ejection of anti-Castroites. It ended on a heavy note of irony when the young radicals requested a police guard to lead them safely to the subway past a mean-looking crowd.

The Committee did not accomplish its announced purposes with these hearings. The students had the better of the legal argument over the State Department[3] ban as well as of the larger controversy over the freedom of Americans to travel wheresoever they would. "Why shouldn't they go?" Robert Kennedy is reported to have said of the first group when he was attorney general. "If I were twenty-one years old, that's what I would like to do this summer." The proposition, suggested by more than one Congressman, that the youths be compelled to register as foreign agents because of their affinity for Castro was silly and invidious. In putting the tiny P.L.M. group on public display, the Committee was in fact aiming beyond the issue of travel in Cuba. These students had all been active in more important protest movements on which the Committee, weighted with conservative Republicans and Democrats from the South, cast a baleful eye; they could be found in all the demonstrations for Negro rights and against the war in Vietnam, shouting the most fiery slogans, waving the wildest banners. "Mr. Maher," asked Representative Senner of a rich young man from Texas who had made the Cuba trip in 1964, "have you contributed any money to any groups to carry on street riots after the passage of the Civil Rights Act of 1964?" The Committee was assiduous in its search for discreditable people who could be blamed for disagreeable occurrences and was expert at finding them. "In any corner of the civilized world," observed Carlyle, "a tub can be inverted and an articulate speaking biped mount thereon." In a demon-

---

[3] In 1967 the Supreme Court upheld the action of a district court in dismissing the indictments against fifty-eight travelers to Cuba. The statute under which the government had attempted to prosecute them, the court observed, was inapplicable since the youths held valid passports at the time of their unauthorized journey.

stration of tens of thousands a couple of dozen P.L.M. extro-
verts never had any trouble attracting attention. What they
lacked in good sense, they made up in audacity, and their
exploits in the coming months and years would continue to be
grist for the Committee's ever grinding mills.

On the first day of the turbulent September 1963 hearings
five leaders of the Cuban pilgrimage were summoned to an
executive session of the Committee and were asked to testify
behind closed doors since, as Chairman Willis explained, a
grand jury was inquiring into "matters relating to the subject
of this hearing." The witnesses were not impressed, suspecting
perhaps that Willis was losing heart for what promised to be
a public ordeal, and the five insisted on their right to be
exposed for exposure's sake. Willis conceded, and all lent their
voices to the ensuing commotion.

In December 1964 a similar incident occurred, with different
results. The Committee's preference for public hearings through
the years was famous, in some circles notorious. Where closed
hearings were allowed, it usually indicated that the Committee
had not yet accumulated sufficient evidence to proceed openly
or that public proceedings threatened to result in unfavorable
public relations. There is dispute over which reason prevailed
in December when a subcommittee under Joe Pool of Texas
started an inquiry into the visit to this country in 1963 of
Kaoru Yasui, dean of the law school at Hoesi University in
Japan, a visit that had reportedly caused controversy between
permissive and restrictive elements within the State Department. Yasui, director in his country of the Council Against
Atomic and Hydrogen Bombs and a recipient of the Lenin
Peace Prize, had come to the United States for a lecture tour
arranged by the left-wing *National Guardian* and sponsored
by prominent members of the peace movement. The Committee's staff, ever alert to such activity by such individuals
under such auspices, sought information from the State Department on the events leading up to the visit, and then summoned
for executive questioning three persons who had interceded
in Yasui's behalf: Russell Nixon, general manager of the

National Guardian; and Dagmar Wilson and Donna Allen, leaders of Women Strike for Peace. Nixon, formerly Washington representative for the United Electrical Workers, presented no unusual problems. He had been identified as a Communist before the Committee on several occasions and had taken the Fifth in 1956. But the memory of the 1962 run-in with Women Strike for Peace was still fresh, and the Congressmen, who had nothing on the ladies, could not have wished for a repeat performance.

As a reminder of the earlier festivities, the witnesses received twenty large vases of flowers from W.S.P. chapters around the country at their appearance in Washington on December 7, 1964. There they, together with Nixon, refused to testify in secret. They pointed out that their formal representation to the State Department was part of the public record, and they saw no advantage to giving testimony in private which the Committee might later release, when and as it saw fit. Their testimony, they maintained, would neither endanger the national security nor defame innocent persons—the two official reasons for conducting hearings *in camera*. But Representative Pool, trying out for the role of Committee bully boy vacated by Clardy and Scherer, was not about to give the ladies another chance to make their interrogators look silly. He refused to open up the hearings, as was his prerogative under the Committee's rules, and the three witnesses were cited for contempt.

Since the House was not in session, Speaker McCormack transmitted the contempt citation to the U.S. attorney for the District of Columbia, upon being advised by the House parliamentarian that such a transmittal was mandatory. The three were indicted, tried, convicted, and given a suspended sentence of four to twelve months and fined $100 apiece. In August 1966 the Court of Appeals overturned their convictions. Once again, the judiciary based its ruling not on a substantive issue—the defendants claimed that a closed session would have violated their freedom of speech by depriving them of an opportunity publicly to deny any involvement in subversive activities—but on a close technical point. In a two-to-one decision, the court held that Speaker McCormack had erred in assuming he had no choice but to pass along the case to the U.S. attorney. In the absence of the Congress, according to the court, the speaker was required to subject the contempt citation to his independent scrutiny. The decision, which kept intact the Committee's five-year losing record in the courts, presaged nothing; had the House been in session, the citations would without doubt have been overwhelmingly approved. Yet the incident held significance for the future; once again the Committee had demonstrated a fascination with the peace movement and once again it had found a means of publicizing the part being played in it by people with records like Russell Nixon's.

Occupying most of the Committee's attentions in 1964 were three sets of hearings of passing note. Between February and May seven days were given to a batch of bills providing for the creation of a Freedom Commission and a Freedom Academy. These institutions, the idea for which had aroused enthusiasm on the political right for several years,[4] were hailed by its champions as the free world's reply to the Lenin School in Moscow. The Freedom Academy would, in the words of a chief sponsor, A. Sydney Herlong, Jr., of Florida,

> prepare not only government foreign affairs personnel, but also private citizens and foreign students, to understand Communist political warfare and subversion and to give them the capacity to organize all of the methods and means which free men can properly employ to defeat Communist subversion and political warfare, while seeking to build and preserve independent countries.

The Committee's hearings consisted almost entirely of testimony from ardent supporters: conservative Congressmen, a former Chief of Naval Operations, American Legion officials, professors from Catholic universities who had served the Committee as consultants, Herbert Philbrick, representatives of Radio Free Europe and the National Captive Nations Com-

---

[4] A bill authorizing a Freedom Academy passed the Senate by a voice vote in 1960, but met the resistance in the House of Francis Walter, who reportedly opposed the Academy out of fear that it would be infiltrated by Communists.

mittee, and similarly disposed experts. Only two witnesses—W. Averell Harriman, speaking for the Department of State, and Adolf A. Berle—restrained their rapture. The State Department preferred to set up a National Academy of Foreign Affairs, exclusively for government officials. Berle was in favor of a Freedom Academy with apologetically rendered reservations: "Let me say something here that I hope will not shock the Committee unduly. If a country, of its own accord and minding its own business, decides to build a situation not based on private property and not unfriendly to the United States, I do not think the United States would have any real right to object, nor perhaps should it object." In the circumstances, this diffident support for the self-determination of nations came as something radical. The other witnesses did not trouble Chairman Willis with reservations.

It was not often that the Committee devoted itself to a real bill, but the hearings, which continued into 1965, were so arranged that they became not so much legislative occasions as opportunities for the Committee's friends and clients to parade their patriotism, lament the national deficiency of anti-Communist zeal, and advance the view—so often advanced in the Committee's publications—that Communist successes in various parts of the world were all of a piece and were due to treachery on the part of the Reds and ineffectuality or worse on our part. They wanted stronger anti-Communist medicine than the State Department was willing to concoct, and they saw the proposed Freedom Academy as a combination training camp for commandos and Jesuit retreat where men would be presented with the Truth so that they might then go and set others free. The Committee recommended passage of a Freedom Academy bill in 1966, and little has been heard of it since.

In the continuing pursuit of Communists during the spring and early summer of 1964, subcommittees settled upon Buffalo and Minneapolis. The Buffalo event, picketed by a couple of hundred students, had its moments. The first unfriendly witness, an instructor at the State University, started off with a request to tape record his interrogation and when this was denied, carried out an inspection of the witness table to make sure it was not bugged. Another witness, who had taken the Fifth during the Committee's 1957 visit to the city, was joined in dissent by his wife, seated in the rear of the courtroom:

WOLKENSTEIN: Let me have my say. What is this? The United States or is this the Hitler Germany regime?

POOL: The witness will be seated. You are going to be held in contempt.

MRS. WOLKENSTEIN: Don't tell him that. You insulted our whole family.

POOL: Remove that lady.

WOLKENSTEIN: You will not remove that lady.

MRS. WOLKENSTEIN: I will not leave.

WOLKENSTEIN: You leave her alone.

MRS. WOLKENSTEIN: I will slap you if you touch me; that's my husband.

The lady was removed, swinging at the marshals as she went.

Despite such interruptions, the Buffalo and Minneapolis hearings proceeded in their ordered course. The F.B.I. informants gave names. The persons named took the Fifth. (Except for a man in Minneapolis, a lawyer, who willingly told the Committee that he had not been a member of the Communist Party since September 1950, but refused to answer questions about the years before that on the novel grounds that the Committee's resolution was limited to appraising the workings of the Internal Security Act and the Subversive Activities Control Act, both passed in September 1950; he did not invoke the self-incrimination clause, and the Committee did not press contempt charges.[5]) In both cities the chairman opened and closed the proceedings with a few remarks on the importance of his visit. In Minneapolis Willis took as his theme a statement by

---

[5] In 1966 the Supreme Court threw out the contempt conviction of a New Hampshire man, a former Communist, who had refused to answer questions put by his state's attorney general concerning his Party activities before the year 1957, when the New Hampshire Subversion Act became effective. Upholding his claim to the First Amendment, Justice Douglas wrote that "the staleness of both the basis for the investigation and its subject matter makes indefensible such exposure of one's associations and political past—exposure which is objectionable and damaging in the extreme to one whose associations and political views do not command majority approval."

Gus Hall, secretary general of the C.P., U.S.A.: "For the good of Minnesota, I would pledge that we do everything we can to build the Communist movement within the state." Willis went on from there:

> Has the Communist Party lived up to the pledge made to the Communists of this district by Gus Hall? Is it pouring more money into this area, more literature, more speakers? Just what are the commissars of the Communist Party doing to build the Communist movement in this state? What have they done in the past? How have they done it or tried to do it? Who are their agents? What are they now doing to subvert the democratic process in this district? These are some, though by no means all, of the questions to which the Committee hopes to obtain answers.

But the Congressmen knew the answers they would get before they started. They were like celebrants at a ritual who have long lost the meaning of their ceremonies and go faithfully, dumbly through the forms. Fourteen witnesses identified as Communists were called in Buffalo and eleven in Minneapolis. Of these, several had been named in previous proceedings or had made no great secret of their affiliation. Others had broken with the Party during one of its recurrent traumas. The Committee found grave menace in the remaining handful of Party stalwarts and a few neo-Trotskyites.

Had the Congressmen actually listened to the tales of their informants—simple folk who strove to be obliging in generalities about ever-growing menaces but seemed to stay close to the facts regarding particulars—they might have been comforted. For what the informants had encountered during their years in the service of the F.B.I. (a Buffalo man reported to the F.B.I. on his Party activities from 1942 until 1962, probably a record) bore little resemblance to the apparatus of conspiracy that one encountered in the Committee's reports. What they found were a few aging men, stranded by events and seeking to return to the wide road they believed they once traveled. The Party was in sorry shape, low on members and on cash, torn by the dissension endemic to movements that have lost their base in reality. Its fading leaders reached out desperately for recruits and found themselves harboring spies; they tried to play the old game, to take over an N.A.A.C.P. chapter, a local P.T.A., a labor union, and were rebuffed or ignored. They found comfort in Marxist study groups where, with a few fellow addicts, they could smoke the pipes of revolutions past and dream on miracles to come. Only the peace movement and the civil rights movement were spacious enough to let them in and allow them the illusion that they were still at the hot center of American radicalism. This illusion the Un-American Activities Committee reinforced, like a physician who shares his patient's taste for opium. The Congressmen saw the Party not as the ailing thing it had become but as the mighty adversary it never quite was. In continuing to stage such public exhibitions around the country, the Committee's staff and membership were only responding to the ache of their own infatuation.

The next set of big-city hearings took place in Chicago, amid clamorous protests, at the end of May 1965.[6] Hundreds of youthful pickets walked, yelled, and sang in front of the old U.S. Court of Appeals building on Lake Shore Drive, while the F.B.I. took moving pictures from a strategic window, and dozens of demonstrators were arrested for lying under paddy wagons and crashing through barricades. The more significant protest, however, occurred within the hearing chamber, and it came not from the few teenagers who had to be carted away for joining in a chorus of *My Country 'Tis of Thee*, but from three subpoenaed adults who walked out on the Committee after objecting to its inimitable ways. Chairman Willis was unmoved by their objections and a district court judge in Chicago dismissed their petition for an injunction a day before the hearings were due to open, but the issues raised by the three may yet be put to a proper test.

To begin with, on May 13, twelve days before the start of the hearings, the names of most of the persons subpoenaed were

---

[6] Lyndon Johnson's resounding victory over Barry Goldwater in 1964 had its repercussions on the makeup of the Committee. The Democrats gained an extra place, which was filled by a young Atlanta moderate, Charles L. Weltner. Among the Republicans, only Ashbrook of Ohio survived into the eighty-ninth Congress, and he was joined on the Committee by John H. Buchanan, Jr., of Alabama and Del Clawson of California. On the death of Frank S. Tavenner, Jr., in 1964, William Hitz was named general counsel.

published in a Chicago newspaper. The leaking of names, contrary to the Committee's own Rule XVI,[7] was not unusual. Where it happened, Chairman Willis expressed mystification: "Now how those things leak out, I don't know." He insisted that the rule had never been violated, which caused some laughter in the hearing room in Chicago. In Minneapolis he promised to fire any staff member whom reporters identified as having given out names, and implied that enemies of the Committee were doing the leaking "in order to make us the scapegoat." In Chicago he put the blame on Richard Criley, an alleged Communist and head of the Chicago Committee to Defend the Bill of Rights. Criley, noting that the subpoenas had been entrusted for delivery to the police department's "Red Squad" and that the names were first printed in the Chicago *American,* a Hearst paper, said he was not at all mystified.

The most prominent of the published names was that of Dr. Jeremiah Stamler, director of the Division of Adult Health and Aging and the Heart Disease Control Program of the Chicago Board of Health, associate professor at Northwestern University Medical School, member of professional societies, recipient of research grants, winner of awards. Two days after his name had been publicized, Dr. Stamler signed an oath drawn up by the president of the Board of Health, to the effect that he had neither engaged in subversive activities nor consorted with subversive groups or persons during his association with the Board of Health. This declaration which, as Willis took care to point out, did not mention the word Communist, saved his job for a time, but the Congressmen were not to be put off so lightly. It was on behalf of Dr. Stamler and of an assistant of his, a research nutritionist named Yolanda F. Hall, that a wide-ranging challenge was brought against the Committee.

The first request by the attorneys for Stamler and Mrs. Hall was that all testimony relating to them be taken in executive session and that they themselves be questioned in private rather

---

[7] "No member of the Committee or staff shall make public the name of any witness subpoenaed before the Committee or subcommittee prior to the date of his appearance."

than in open hearing, in accord with House Rule XI, 26(m).[8]
Chairman Willis turned down both requests, arguing that the
witnesses who were likely to give defamatory evidence—two
F.B.I. informants—had already been heard in executive session,
and everyone mentioned by them as a member of the Communist Party had been sent a letter with the offer of an opportunity to appear voluntarily in a closed hearing. In this way,
said the chairman, the Committee had complied with its rule,
and he added that his invitations had all gone unacknowledged.
He did not add that any witness who had accepted his offer
would in all likelihood have been summoned to return in public
anyway. (In June, a woman who had been ill during the Committee's visit to Chicago was heard in executive session in
Washington. She declared she was not a Communist, that she
believed Communists to be "a deceitful and disruptive force"
and that "for a considerable period I have had no association
or activity that could remotely be deemed Communist." But
she pleaded the Fifth Amendment on questions relating to her
past activities, and after a half hour Chairman Willis opened
the hearings to the public. All of her testimony, public and
executive, was included in the transcript of the Chicago hearings.) If a witness volunteered testimony in private, it could
be released at the discretion of the Committee, and in no case
would he be given an opportunity to cross-examine his accusers.

Ordinarily, demands to be allowed to cross-examine have
been uttered in the secure knowledge that they would not be
granted; whatever one's feelings about the police informer as
a species, a reading of the record over the years gives little
reason to doubt that the informers' charges before the Committee have, with some regrettable exceptions, been substantially accurate. But the evidence brought against Dr. Stamler
and Mrs. Hall was not of the usual sort. It was irregular even
by the Committee's standards, and the cross-examination requested by their attorney might have been enlightening.

Two informants gave testimony in Chicago, Negroes who

---

[8] Rule 26(m) provides "if the Committee determines that evidence or testimony at an investigative hearing may tend to defame, degrade or incriminate
any person it shall—(1) receive such evidence or testimony in executive session . . ."

had served the F.B.I. as C.P. members during the nineteen-fifties and up until 1963, and counsel Nittle's questioning played hard on Communist participation in civil rights and peace organizations. Each identified several persons as Communists, their lists duplicating one another as there were evidently no longer enough prominent Party members extant in Chicago to keep two informants occupied without some overlap. But in their presentations, which took up the first day and a half of the Chicago meeting, neither informant mentioned the name of either Jeremiah Stamler or Yolanda Hall.

On the afternoon of the second day, after the informants had been excused, Nittle was questioning a man with a record of C.P. activity going back to the nineteen-thirties; in 1950 he was state education director of the Communist Party of Illinois. This witness had taken the Fifth Amendment more than forty times, when Nittle put this question: "While you were an instructor at the Chicago Workers School, did you also know Yolanda Hall?" Mrs. Hall's attorney objected strenuously to having his client's name slipped into the hearing in such a manner; the witness continued to take the Fifth Amendment; and Nittle proceeded with his line of questioning: "Did you then know Yolanda Hall to be a member of the Communist Party?" As a matter of fact, everyone knew that Mrs. Hall once belonged to the Party. In July 1949, testifying in behalf of the C.P. leaders being tried under the Smith Act, she had admitted as much. In 1949, too, she had taught political economy at the South Side branch of the Party's Chicago Workers School. That was the freshest evidence that was produced regarding Mrs. Hall, and opponents of the Committee charged that her subpoenaing was stimulated by property owners in her Chicago neighborhood who were incensed by her efforts in behalf of open housing for Negroes. By injecting her name into the hearings in the form of questions about events of fifteen years before which he knew would not be answered, Nittle lent credence to this charge.

Whereas the evidence against Mrs. Hall was stale, evidence against her superior, Dr. Stamler, was missing altogether. His name was not mentioned in testimony until the last day of hearings when Nittle made up for the oversight, again with questions to witnesses who, it was clear, had determined to give no answers to anything: "The Committee's investigation discloses that the person who served as the Illinois youth coordinator of the American Youth Crusade was Dr. Jeremiah Stamler. Do you know Dr. Stamler?" None of Nittle's questions had a more definite base: "The Committee is also informed . . ." "The Committee also possesses information, which it believes reliable . . ." Soon Nittle was saying: "Exhibits previously introduced indicate that you were a leader of the Communist-organized and -controlled American Peace Crusade at the same time Dr. Jeremiah Stamler was the coordinator of its youth branch in this state"—although in fact no exhibits were introduced that even mentioned Dr. Stamler. To another witness who had been taking the Fifth by rote, Nittle said: ". . . the Committee is in possession of information which it believes to be completely reliable, that in the years 1956 and 1957 you attended meetings of the Communist Party at the residence of Dr. Jeremiah Stamler. Is this true?" A moment later, he asked whether Dr. Stamler's wife, who had never been referred to up until that moment, had not acted as chairman of the alleged C.P. meetings.

The Committee had been pained over the years at the charge that "faceles informers" were used against its witnesses, and in fact there had been little basis to it since the time of Harold Velde. The informants' faces were not always of the highest type, but it was usually known whence the accusations came. In Dr. Stamler's case, however, they could be traced no further than the Committee counsel himself, who claimed no firsthand acquaintance with his subject. In an effort to give a semblance of substance to the wispy charges against Stamler, Nittle called back to the stand one of the informants and asked him a few questions about a meeting held in his home in 1959 and attended by Claude Lightfoot, a prominent C.P. official:

NITTLE: Was Dr. Stamler's name mentioned in the course of that meeting?
ARMSTRONG: (the F.B.I. informant): Yes.
JENNER (Stamler's attorney): Mr. Chairman, does the . . .

ARMSTRONG: I want to say here that Dr. Stamler's name was mentioned, but I myself did not even know Dr. Stamler at that time. But he was mentioned.

NITTLE: Now will you tell the Committee please . . .

ARMSTRONG: He was discussed, not mentioned.

. . . . .

NITTLE: Now will you tell us what was said by Claude Lightfoot, if anything?

ARMSTRONG: Well, in discussing Dr. Stamler, he just said that we have a noted heart specialist, a very renowned heart specialist.

JENNER: Mr. Chairman, you as a noted law teacher—I object on the ground that this is obvious hearsay.

CHAIRMAN: Your client will have an opportunity to face what you have been referring to as accuser and confront him and under oath to deny all this. Proceed.

JENNER: I request that opportunity.

CHAIRMAN: Proceed.

NITTLE: Will you proceed, Mr. Armstrong, to relate that.

ARMSTRONG: Well, he said that there was a noted heart specialist by the name of Jeremiah Stamler and he was a loyal Party member doing good work among the professional people. He did not discuss in detail and that is about the gist of it. Dr. Stamler. If you want to know more in other ways, maybe I can tell you.

NITTLE: That is all, Mr. Chairman.

That, indeed, was all. Nittle's questions to unresponsive witnesses were phrased to invite the inference that there was weighty support behind them: "The Committee is informed that at the time you were contacted by Dr. Stamler, you were advised by him that you were one of several persons chosen to give up their identity and to move to new areas to carry on in case Communist Party leaders were put away. Did he tell you that?" But the nature of the support was never disclosed. When asking the House for contempt citations against Stamler and Mrs. Hall in October 1966, Willis and Ichord quoted executive testimony by Staff Director McNamara to the effect that both subjects had been engaged in C.P. activities in recent years. The only source of information credited by McNamara was a newsletter put out by an arm of the radical right called the American Security Council. The Committee's staff director has always exercised considerable autonomy, and such was the Congressmen's faith in McNamara that it never occurred to them to check his evidence before making his charges public.

Stamler and Mrs. Hall were represented at the hearings by Albert E. Jenner, Jr., of the Chicago law firm of Raymond, Mayer, Jenner, and Block. Former president of the Illinois State Bar Association, senior counsel for the Warren Commission, member of the Federal Loyalty Review Board in the early nineteen-fifties, and a Republican, Jenner was not the prototypical counsel for witnesses before the Committee, and Chairman Willis allowed him extraordinary latitude, which he used to the full[9] in stating his objections. Jenner demanded an investigation of who had leaked the names of the subpoenaed witnesses. He objected to the Committee's refusal to hear his clients and all testimony regarding them in executive session and to allow him to examine all evidence and cross-examine the informants. He objected to the manner in which unattributed charges were placed in the record and asked permission to examine counsel Nittle. His protests that the investigation had no legislative purpose and was in violation of his clients' rights to due process had been made by many attorneys at many other hearings, but the events in Chicago gave them special force.

Jenner, a trial lawyer for many years, argued:

It is clear from what had occurred in these hearings on May 25 and 26 and to this point today—one, that public hearings are not needed and were not needed, because you have already heard Lola Belle Holmes and Lucius Armstrong [the F.B.I. informants] and others apparently in executive session and the repetition in these public hearings has served, as it could only serve, particularly under the type of examination of the distinguished counsel

[9] Jenner did not appear until the final day of the Chicago hearings. On the first two days he was represented by an associate, Thomas P. Sullivan, who had the misfortune to be faced not with Willis, out ill, but with Joe Pool. When Sullivan attempted to object to the first injection of Yolanda Hall's name by counsel Nittle, Pool interrupted him continuously and had the marshals push him back into his chair.

for the Committee, to injure persons whom they charged and counsel has charged without being under oath to be or to have been members of the Communist Party; and, two, the questioning of my clients will be of a defamatory and prejudicial nature and be harmful to their good reputations, which they cherish.

He emphasized that Dr. Stamler and Mrs. Hall were not invoking the privilege against self-incrimination—"They have committed no crime and have been loyal to our country"—but were refusing to testify on other constitutional grounds. A few minutes later, by Jenner's direction, both witnesses walked out of the hearing room. (A third witness, Milton Cohen, also walked out defiantly, to the cheers of the spectators, and joined Mrs. Hall and Stamler in their suit. Unlike them, he had been identified as a C.P. member by the two informants. Although the ten other subpoenaed witnesses and their attorneys registered protests in much the same language as Jenner, they covered themselves by taking the Fifth Amendment, which had the effect of making their other arguments academic.)

In April 1966 the Stamler-Hall-Cohen suit against the members of the Committee was dismissed in district court on the grounds that the plaintiffs had no standing to sue. In November the Court of Appeals returned the case to the lower court for a hearing on the constitutional issues raised. In a two-to-one decision the judges maintained that although the constitutionality of the Committee had been sustained in the Barenblatt decision, the allegations in the present case—that the Committee was bent on exposing witnesses to public scorn, obloquy, harassment, and intimidation with no legislative purpose, but to deter them and others in the exercise of their rights under the First Amendment—warranted a hearing. (As of this writing, their case has not yet been reconsidered by the lower court.)

A few weeks before the Court of Appeals' decision, the Committee brought to the House its contempt citations against Yolanda Hall, Jeremiah Stamler, and Milton Cohen. Debate was hot. Pressed hard by Fraser of Minnesota for a reason why the request for an executive hearing was not granted, the unadept Ichord found himself arguing in *favor* of executive hearings: ". . . the hearings are in progress and you have all of these pickets outside and beatniks walking around and people trying to create disorder and you have a ruckus and disorder." Pressed by Yates of Illinois for the reason why Yolanda Hall had been called to testify, Willis replied: "Mr. Speaker, if I could answer that question in open forum, I should be glad to do so but some of these days I shall be happy to tell the gentleman from Illinois the reason therefore." Asked by Yates for the origin of the derogatory information about Stamler and Mrs. Hall that director McNamara had passed on to the Committee, Ichord conceded that he was in the dark. He did not know whether the information was true or not: ". . . this was a summary of what was in the files, of what the investigators and the F.B.I. had reported to the House Committee on Un-American Activities." Pressed by Hays of Ohio on whether friendly witnesses were paid by the Committee, Willis said that he was "getting sick and tired of all these dog-goned intimations about dishonesty." Hays had discovered that the Committee was paying some of its friendly witnesses when, as a member of the House Administration Committee, he was asked to approve their contracts. On raising the issue in the House he was met with indignation from members of the Committee: "My goodness," said Willis, "that has never been indulged in." Before the day was done, the indignation had turned to a reluctant admission that Hays was correct; some witnesses had been paid . . . but *honi soit*.

The members of the Committee could bear up under the slings of debate because they knew that they would be vindicated on the final vote. A motion to recommit to a select committee the first contempt resolution debated, the one against Milton Cohen, lost by 90 votes to 181. That was the best the opposition could manage. In fact, it established a new record. The citation against Jeremiah Stamler was put through by a vote of 174 to 37.[1]

The resolutions passed in October marked the second time in 1966 that the House was asked to vote on contempt citations

[1] In July 1967 the three were indicted by a federal grand jury in Chicago on the contempt-of-Congress charges, whereupon Dr. Stamler and his assistant were placed on "inactive status" by the Chicago Board of Health.

issuing from the Committee on Un-American Activities. On February 2 Willis asked for proceedings against seven officials of various Ku Klux Klan groups who had refused, during public hearings in Washington in October 1965, to turn over their records to the Committee. All took the Fifth Amendment, but Willis argued that, by the Supreme Court's 1960 decision in the McPhaul case, the plea of self-incrimination did not protect a witness against a request for documents held in an official capacity.[2] Objections to the citations on constitutional grounds as well as on grounds of simple distaste for the Committee were voiced by Representatives Ryan, Burton, Edwards, and others whose antipathy to the Ku Klux Klan was more pronounced than that of most of the Committee's members, but the contempt resolutions were voted rapidly one after the other. In October 1966 Robert M. Shelton, Imperial Wizard of the United Klans of America, received a maximum sentence of one year in prison and a $1,000 fine in district court. Three other Klansmen subsequently pleaded guilty, and their cases, along with the remaining three, who have pleaded not guilty, await the disposition of Shelton's appeal.

The proposal in 1965 for an investigation of the Klan originated with Charles L. Weltner, a natty young representative from Georgia, who owed his victory in the Democratic primary to Atlanta's many registered Negroes and its higher-income whites. During his first term in the House, 1963–1964, Weltner became the lone Congressman from the states of the Old Confederacy to vote for final passage of the Civil Rights Act of 1964. (At the end of his second term, in 1966, he withdrew from his campaign for reelection rather than run on the same ticket with Lester Maddox, the segregationist gubernatorial candidate.) Weltner sought and obtained a place on the Un-American Activities Committee in 1965 with the purpose of starting up an investigation of the Klan, which had resumed its abominable ways in resistance to the civil rights movement. On February 1 the young man from Georgia attacked the

[2] Arthur McPhaul, refusing to submit the records of the Civil Rights Congress in 1952, said: "I wonder if the Kluxers of Georgia have ever been asked to produce their records."

"invisible empire" on the floor of the House: "I believe I speak for the vast majority of Southerners in calling for action. For in doing nothing, we will inaugurate a second century for the Ku Klux Klan."

The novelty of having a Southerner and a member of the Un-American Activities Committee ask for such an investigation stirred considerable comment. The Committee had won the hearts of Klansmen at birth. A K.K.K. pamphlet of 1942 stated: "The vicious fight on the Klan sprang from the same source which has fought the Dies Committee from the day of its inception." An Imperial Wizard once paid Martin Dies the compliment of acknowledging that his program "so closely parallels the program of the Klan that there is no distinguishable difference between them." In those early years critics like Samuel Dickstein protested that the Committee was not doing enough to harass un-Americans on the right, and in truth there was small enthusiasm among its members for such adventures then or later. Francis Walter, forgetting the origins of his Committee, took the position that its investigative mandate covered Communists exclusively. As for the Committee staff, it was composed of professional Communist-hunters, set in their ways and not readily diverted; the K.K.K., after all, had never been put on anyone's subversive list. By 1965 the Committee's critics, though admiring of Weltner's initiative, took the position that the Committee should not be investigating anything, right or left, not even the universally despised Ku Klux Klan. They wanted federal legislation against the Klan, but they wanted it to originate in the Judiciary Committee.

Skepticism abounded in the Capitol that the K.K.K. investigation would get beyond what Chairman Willis called a "look-see," a "peek." (Also being peeked at were the Minutemen, the Black Muslims, and the American Nazi Party.) But on the evening of March 25, 1965, a Detroit woman, Mrs. Viola Gregg Liuzzo, who had been shuttling Negro civil rights workers back to Selma, Alabama, after the march to Montgomery, was shot and killed in her car. Four Klansmen—one of them later identified as an F.B.I. informant—were arrested, and before anyone had been brought to trial, President Johnson made a dramatic appearance on television, accompanied by Attorney General Katzenbach and J. Edgar Hoover himself. The President blamed the Klan for the murder—one of a series of murders of civil rights workers in the South that were resulting in the indictments but not the convictions of K.K.K. members—and suggested that Congress might wish to conduct an investigation.

The commission could have gone to the Judiciary Committee, but the Un-American Activities Committee won out because of its unrivaled immunity to charges of bias in behalf of Negro rights. In April the House voted the Committee an additional $50,000 for the investigation, over the objections of forty-three members, mostly liberals joined for the moment with a couple of arch-segregationists. (Where Ryan of New York feared that the investigation would be "the opening wedge of a witchhunt into civil-rights organizations," Walker of Mississippi wanted it to be extended to S.N.C.C., C.O.R.E., and S.C.L.C.) Of the six Negroes in the House, four voted against the appropriation and two did not vote. Civil rights leaders, wary of where the Committee might turn next, were unanimously opposed; they asked that the K.K.K. be studied by a special commission appointed for the purpose.

The Ku Klux Klan became the main business of the Committee in the latter half of 1965 and into 1966. A subcommittee of four Southerners—Willis, Pool, Weltner, and Buchanan—and one Northerner, Ashbrook of Ohio—the only Congressman from his state to vote against the 1964 Civil Rights Act—opened hearings in Washington on October 19; before they came to an end the following February, they had consumed thirty-seven days. The opening weeks ran simultaneously with the trial in Hayneville, Alabama, of Klansman Collie Leroy Wilkins for the murder of Mrs. Liuzzo. While an all-white jury in Hayneville was engaged in acquitting Wilkins, the Washington hearings were disappointing both those who had predicted a whitewash and those who had been hoping for a spectacle.

Robert M. Shelton, the ravaged-looking Imperial Wizard, had been expected to answer questions, but at the last minute he announced that he was taking the Fifth Amendment lest otherwise he forfeit his dignity as a free American and be eternally damned: "I am a God-fearing man." (For a Kluxer to take the Fifth like an ordinary Commie was poetry; for him to take the Fourteenth, as Shelton and his brothers in the faith repeatedly did, was epic.) Counseled by a soft-voiced, permanently apologetic attorney from Raleigh, North Carolina, the eminent Klansmen called on in the first days of the hearings all resorted to their rights under the Constitution. They racked up quite a record of Fifths, but it was not like the Chicago hearings of the previous spring. The Klansmen uttered their respectful declinations in quiet voices; there were no disturbances in the House Caucus Room, and the dozen or more uniformed police and plainclothesmen had nothing to do. After the first crowded day, the number of spectators fell off sharply.

Set beside the Klan's reputation and the grim event that had led to these hearings, the charges put in the record by the Committee's staff were trivial—yet the show had its moments. For those who had always known that the Klan was composed of clowns and clods, it was satisfying to learn that they thought of themselves as kligrapps (secretaries), klokards (lecturers), and kludds (chaplains). Donald T. Appell, the staff member in charge of the investigation, produced evidence that Wizard Shelton had been channeling his blood brothers' contributions into a Tuscaloosa account belonging to an invention of his called the Alabama Rescue Service and then taking the money out to buy himself a Cadillac and lesser staples at his nearby Piggly-Wiggly supermarket. He was alleged to have shaken down an engineering firm in trouble with the state, and had evidently been kicked out of the Alabama Knights of the K.K.K. for withholding dues from the reigning Wizard. The Grand Dragons of Virginia and North Carolina (where Klan checks were made out to one's local "improvement association" or "sportsmen's club"—"Your donation will be used to help make our community a better place to live") were impecunious drifters before their elevation in Shelton's Klandom, whereupon overnight they became affluent models for poor white lads all over the South. Dragon Jones of North Carolina even made a profit on the sale of sheets; the material cost him about $3.20

and the finished article, with peaked hat, went for $15. It was also disclosed that a lot of crosses had been burned and that the White Knights of the Ku Klux Klan of Mississippi had passed around a memorandum on permissible techniques of good-humored harassment; these included the use of itching powder, tear gas, snakes and lizards and mad dogs.

The hearings were broken off in November after the attorney general took exception to the Committee's calling two Klansmen indicted and freed in the murder of Lemuel Penn, a Negro reserve officer who was shot and killed in 1964 as he was driving home to Washington, D.C. from a training base in the South. The case, explained the attorney general, was before the Supreme Court. When the inquiry resumed in the new year, it turned from the account books toward more colorful matters. A Georgia Kluxer conceded that he was financing a movement against kosher food. A Grand Empress of the Klan, a lady in Cincinnati who had allegedly worked up schemes for killing the President, the Vice President, Martin Luther King, and others, was put on the stand. A former Klansman told of taking part in nightrider bombings of the homes of Negroes in McComb, Mississippi. A Louisiana man admitted that he had helped out in a flogging.

The hearings throughout were conducted in much the same manner as the hearings into Communist activities. The main differences were in the subdued responses of the witnesses who, off the stand, blamed not the Committee but Lyndon Johnson and Martin Luther King for their discomfiture. The Committee staff was able to produce some evidence of wrongdoing, mostly petty finaglings, rarely available in the case of Communists. Although there was no question that a majority of the Committee would have embarked on an investigation of the civil rights movement with pleasure, the fear of some liberals that the K.K.K. hearings would be turned into such a party was misconceived. It did justice neither to the political sense of the Congressmen nor to their personal attitudes. Far from wishing to defend the Ku Klux Klan, the Southerners were out to show that the Klansmen were crooks and freaks (Buchanan, in a burst of wit, called Shelton the Imperial Lizard) and had nothing in common with decent citizens of the South, like the members of White Citizens Councils who sit on juries.

The impact of these drawn-out hearings on the fortunes of the Klan is difficult to estimate. They may, oddly, have been a heavier blow than any a more respectable body could have delivered. The Committee's habit of asking questions that it knew would not be answered, its interest in matters that belonged to night court, its reliance on publicity to do the job of punishment, its infatuation with Fifth Amendment records—these might well have worked on the level where the K.K.K. operates most successfully. The North Carolina used-car dealer who startled the Committee while in the witness chair by resigning as treasurer of his Klavern (the White County Improvement Association) and turning over a batch of canceled checks, explained that he was disillusioned by the Klan leaders' refusal to testify. "Anyone who takes the Fifth Amendment," he told reporters, "either has something to hide or is a Communist." Men who could abide a little crowding of a pushy Negro might yet be offended by the idea of a Grand Dragon gouging lesser knights on the price of a sheet, or using the 50-cents-a-month Imperial Tax to buy molasses not for the gas tanks of civil rights workers but for his own table. What the Rev. Roy Woodle, former Grand Kludd of North Carolina, didn't like about his chiefs was that they wore diamond rings, traveled first class, and employed shills at rallies. He was annoyed that they weren't working harder to preserve segregation in the South.

The President had asked for laws against the Klan, which gave the Committee an opportunity to display its legislative incompetence. To produce a workable federal law that could cover what the bill put forward by Chairman Willis called "the reprehensible, terroristic activities of the Klan movement" required a certain finesse. Whatever qualities the Willis bill had, finesse was lacking; it was written in the go-get-'em style that typified the Committee's work. It provided severe penalties, up to life imprisonment, for any agent of a "clandestine organization" who would commit or "conspire to commit" a crime of violence. In hearings held in July 1966, a spokesman for the American Civil Liberties Union observed that the bill's definition of a "clandestine organization" was broad enough to cover college fraternities. Attorney General Katzenbach told the Committee he was concerned over the section of the bill that made it a crime to "willfully teach, advise or advocate" the use of violence, since the Supreme Court had questioned the Smith Act's prohibitions against teaching and advocating the overthrow of the government. The attorney general was also doubtful about a provision of the Willis bill, devised by Representative Weltner, that would have authorized the Justice Department to seek injunctions against acts of violence in the planning stage. Katzenbach, like officials of the civil rights organizations, preferred to rely on Title V of the Civil Rights Bill of 1966, which broadened federal criminal laws against harming or intimidating persons exercising their legal rights.

The majority of the Un-American Activities Committee did not support the Administration's civil-rights program (only two of the Committee's nine members, Weltner and Senner, voted for the ill-fated 1966 bill) and if one were of a suspicious mind, one might suspect that the crudely drawn Willis measure, which even Ichord found "unenforceable and unconstitutional," was designed with an eye less to confounding the Ku Klux Klan than to confusing the civil rights debate. In any case, the Committee approved its K.K.K. bill only at the close of the Congressional session, and it subsided without a murmur in the last days' business.

At about the same time that the K.K.K. bill was going under, another Committee product was actually passed by the House of Representatives. Conceived by Joe Pool, it made it a federal crime to give assistance to forces engaged in "undeclared war" with this country or to interfere with the movement of military personnel or supplies. That this hapless measure reached the floor of the House on October 12, 1966, was due to Representative Colmer of Mississippi, who exercised his privilege as a member of the Rules Committee to call up a resolution setting the terms of debate on the bill. That it passed, despite a notably inept presentation by Pool, Ashbrook, and Ichord, was due to the nearness of the November elections and the assurance that it would not get through the Senate where leaders of both parties had only scorn for it. As Representative Edwards, the Committee's foremost opponent and a candid man, observed during the debate in the House: "Indeed, I presume that this body has in mind a quick passage while holding its nose, secure in the knowledge that our indiscretion will be cured by quiet death in the other body; thus reemphasizing the wisdom of our founders in providing a bicameral Congress."

The Pool bill, one of several of a like nature put forward in 1966, came to the floor patched with amendments that could not cover its constitutional and logical holes. It was, as the attorney general explained in testimony before the Committee in August, flatly unnecessary. The Trading with the Enemy Act and other statutes made it unlawful to transfer funds to blocked countries, yet did not infringe on free speech or obstruct the work of the International Red Cross as the Pool measure would probably have done, and a variety of laws were already at hand to prosecute people for getting in the way of military traffic. Moreover, the offenses that had excited the Committee's legislative genius were hardly worthy of a second look. A handful of Vietcong rooters had raised a lot of hell and a little money ($1,500 evidently made its way to Czechoslovakia and from there, presumably, to the National Liberation Front) and collected some blood (which, so far as was known, never got close to Vietnam). Ramsey Clark, making his first appearance before the Committee as attorney general, offended the Congressmen by suggesting that pro-Vietcong elements in America did not constitute a threat to the land, that their noisy carryings-on near military bases amounted mainly to headline seeking:

> I would say that the people who stand in front of a troop train with the realization that they have no potential of stopping it, particularly when the train never slows down, continues ten miles an hour, and before it reaches them they scatter off the track, that is seeking publicity rather than an effort to stop a train that they know they cannot stop.

The Committee, which had recently decided that the American Nazi Party and the Minutemen and even the Black Muslims did not warrant their full attention, could not bring the same cool judgment to bear on the bearded youths and long-haired girls who waved the Vietcong flag in public.[3] The visceral revulsion of staff director McNamara and subcommittee chairman Pool and ranking Republican Ashbrook against these unkempt types combined with the opportunity to attack opponents of the war in Vietnam on their most bizarre flank, led to the Committee's hearings of August 1966. It was all of a piece with the carelessly drawn bill. The conduct of these hearings brought a new barrage of criticism upon the Committee and turned Joe Pool of Texas into something of a national figure.

The American Civil Liberties Union sought to block the August hearings and at the same time to start an action challenging the constitutionality of the Committee by going into district court for an injunction.[4] The A.C.L.U. argued that the Committee's mandate to investigate "propaganda" ran counter to the First Amendment. To everyone's surprise, a ten-day restraining order was granted, a day before the scheduled opening of the hearings, by U.S. District Judge Howard F. Corcoran, brother of the New Deal's Tommy Corcoran, who had been appointed to the bench by President Johnson in 1965. Never before had a committee of Congress suffered enjoinment, and Pool, with the approval of Speaker McCormack, announced

[3] Reporting to the House the decision not to pursue the American Nazi Party of George Lincoln Rockwell, Willis explained: "He wants to see front-page headlines about his organization. He would like to see his picture featured on nation-wide TV newscasts and spread over the pages of newspapers in all parts of the country. It would give him the publicity he not only wants, but desperately needs, at this point. I do not believe the Committee should accommodate him on this matter." Willis might have applied the same reasoning to the Progressive Labor Movement.

[4] The A.C.L.U.'s strategy of seeking injunctive relief followed from a 1965 Supreme Court decision extending relief to officers of the Southern Conference Educational Fund who had been harassed by Louisiana officials and threatened with criminal prosecution under the state's Subversive Activities and Communist Control Law. Concerned over the "chilling effect on free expression of prosecutions initiated and threatened in this case," the majority urged the lower courts to give the appellants declaratory relief that would enable them to test the provisions of the law, which was so vaguely worded as to be of doubtful constitutionality, before they were prosecuted under it.

that hearings would begin at 10 a.m. on August 16 as planned, injunction or no injunction. There were calls in the House for the impeachment of Judge Corcoran. A hastily summoned three-judge panel of the Court of Appeals dissolved the restraining order shortly before 10 a.m., and as the A.C.L.U. set forth on the long road of judicial review to attempt again to test the Committee's constitutionality, the hearings opened. Whatever the legal shortcomings of the brief-lived injunction, it was an omen which, had it been heeded, would have spared the Committee a disagreeable few days and considerable chagrin.

As the witnesses summoned for the Vietnam hearings[5] were of the same generation—mostly under thirty—and ideological bent—Progressive Labor—as those who had caused such a commotion at the 1963 Cuba-travel hearings, the Committee had every reason to look forward to a rousing time. An extraordinary force of federal marshals and Capitol police was laid on, and the officers were kept busy during the first four days of hearings carrying out witnesses and spectators, some fifty of whom were booked for disorderly conduct before things quieted down. But it was not the hissing, booing, cheering, hollering, screaming, kicking, and calls to "Get out of Vietnam!" that caused the Committee its greatest distress in August of 1966. All of this was, in a way, welcome, as showing up the bad manners of the Chinese-Albanian left. There were other developments, unforeseen, that were far from welcome.

The first witness was Phillip Abbott Luce, who had gone on the Cuba trip in the summer of 1963, had been a member of the Progressive Labor Movement for about six months of 1964, and had baited the Committee with particular skill on his last appearance. Luce, an articulate young man, began his 1963 testimony with an attack on a previous witness who had traveled to Cuba for the F.B.I., calling him "this creep, this fink." Now, in 1966, it was his turn to be called a fink and take

---

[5] The Committee preceded these hearings by subpoenaing membership lists of anti-war organizations from the University of California at Berkeley and the University of Michigan. Their compliance brought about a statement in July 1967 by the American Council on Education urging colleges and universities to resist all such future demands.

his seat amid a storm of catcalls. Having changed his mind about the P.L.M., he now regaled the Committee with its revolutionary program and the names of its leaders. Since the main objective of the P.L.M. was to draw attention to itself by staging picturesque incidents and since it had no life of any consequence outside of its rather frenetic public life, little that Luce said was news. Still, the Committee, which he had characterized in 1963 as "the scum of Congress," was appreciative, and his reformation was something to behold. Whereas in 1963 he had criticized Willis for ejecting demonstrators—"This may be something you can get away with in Louisiana or Virginia, but I can't understand it here"—in 1966 he criticized the demonstrators. Two months later, during the debate in the House over the contempt citations resulting from the Chicago hearings, Representative Hays named Luce as having received $1,000 from the Committee for services rendered. The contract had been quietly arranged by director McNamara. One of those unaware of it was general counsel William Hitz. After being fired by McNamara in October 1966, purportedly for not earning his $25,000 a year salary,[6] Hitz circulated to each member of the Committee a memorandum which disclosed that Luce had been offered the contract as a "consultant" more than a month before he testified.[7] Young Luce thereby became the first man in history to go from the employ of the Emergency Civil Liberties Committee to the employ of the Un-American Activities Committee. McNamara, Luce's patron and instigator of the Vietnam hearings, laid the failure to inform his colleagues of the contract to inadvertence.

The second day of those rowdy August hearings achieved a climax with the eviction from the Caucus Room of an attorney. Beginning with its efforts to obtain a restraining order, the American Civil Liberties Union had determined to make the Vietnam hearings an all-out test of the Committee's constitu-

[6] Chester D. Smith, a Defense Department intelligence specialist, was named in December to replace Hitz as general counsel.

[7] No one thought to remind Representative Ichord of his statement during the debate on the Stamler-Hall contempt citations: "There is nothing wrong with the Committee hiring a witness who might have testified before the Committee in regard to Communist activities at an earlier date, because that would be after the fact."

tionality, and an unusually forceful complement of lawyers, including the A.C.L.U.'s executive director, John de J. Pemberton, was present,[8] with an extensive list of objections to the proceedings. As Representative Pool had demonstrated during his few hours in the chair at the Chicago hearings, he had little patience for defense attorneys. "Mr. marshal, set this man down" was his natural response when a lawyer rose to make an objection. Pool, elected in 1963 to the Congressman-at-large seat once held by Martin Dies (after the leading candidate was opportunely indicted for income tax evasion), was distinguished in the House mainly for his shape; he stood about five foot six and weighed well over two hundred pounds. He was affable enough, but not versed in the parliamentary graces. Still, if he did not always grasp what the Eastern lawyers were complaining about, he knew they meant him no good. Unable to cope when they became argumentative, he tended to rely on a heavy gavel and on commands that they be quiet and sit down or else.

The incident that culminated in the ousting of counsel Arthur Kinoy, who had been on the defendants' side in the Chicago hearings too, began when a friendly witness, a writer for the *National Review*, mentioned the name of one of the subpoenaed witnesses. Kinoy objected, as attorneys had previously objected, to having his client named in open session and to being denied the right of cross-examination. Joined by his partner, William Kunstler, Kinoy persisted in his objections after they had been overruled. Voices became loud, and before Pool knew it, he was banging his gavel and ordering the lawyer taken away. The next day's papers showed the peppery little man, shorter even than Joe Pool and about a hundred pounds lighter, being hustled out of the hearing room by three or four marshals who seemed huge beside him. One had an armlock on his neck. By the time Pool, embattled by protesting lawyers and possibly troubled by second thoughts over the scene, agreed to allow Kinoy back into the hearing room, the

---

[8] Attorneys cooperating with the A.C.L.U. included William M. Kunstler, Arthur Kinoy, Jeremiah S. Gutman, Beverly Axelrod, and Frank J. Donner. In addition, Joseph Forer and Ira Gollobin were present and heard from.

lawyer had been taken off to the police station. (He was later convicted of disturbing the peace and is appealing.)

It was at this point that the hearings began to deteriorate into farce, with Joe Pool playing the fool of fate. First the lawyers, all of them, one after another, delivered formal statements of withdrawal, and two subpoenaed witnesses—the director of the new, small, and determinedly radical Free School of New York, where he taught "Marxism and American Decadence," and the founder of the U.S. Committee to Aid the National Liberation Front—simply walked out on the Congressmen.[9] The other witnesses, formally without attorneys now, were excused until next day, and the Committee turned with relief to an assistant district attorney from Alameda County, whose jurisdiction took in the campus at Berkeley. He told of the demonstrations around troop trains, military bases, and induction centers staged by a far-out, far-left group called the Vietnam Day Committee. (One of their pamphlets, *Brief Notes on the Ways and Means of "Beating" and Defeating the Draft*, advised: "Be an undesirable. Go for a couple of weeks without a shower. Really look dirty. Stink. Long hair helps. Go in barefoot with your sandals tied around your neck.") When a witness whose name was mentioned in the course of the friendly testimony rose to object, Pool had to be restrained by Ashbrook from ordering him thrown out of the room.

As the unfriendly witnesses reappeared, still without counsel, it became clear that the subcommittee was prepared to let them depart in peace. "I would suggest, Mr. Chairman, that you proceed as quickly as you can to conclude this part of the investigative hearing," advised Representative Ichord after the walkout of the lawyers. The Congressmen had already questioned two of the young leftists in the first days of the hearings and they had proved compulsively responsive about their opinions, joyfully abusive of the Committee, and exceedingly taxing.

[9] The A.C.L.U. brought a suit against the Committee in behalf of these two witnesses, Dr. Allen M. Krebs and Walter D. Teague, 3d. In September 1967, a three-member panel of federal judges ruled that they did not have jurisdiction to decide on the constitutionality of the Committee since it had been formed not by an act of Congress but by a resolution of the House of Representatives. The ruling is being appealed.

One managed to put the entire preamble of the constitution of the Progressive Labor Party into the record. When Pool asked the other whether he believed he "ought to help the Viet Cong, the North Vietnamese, so they can go back into battle and kill our boys," the witness retorted: "You are sending them there to die. And Johnson is sending them there to die, and they all, all this government and the big business are sending them there to die and bleed, and then you try to assume that I am against them."[1] As in the Cuba travel hearings, the new leftists enjoyed this sort of exchange more than the Congressmen, and Pool presently gave up the debate and contented himself with coaxing his witnesses to take the Fifth Amendment.

After the Kinoy arrest, the subpoenaed youths were offered an opportunity to have their testimony postponed for three months, a euphemistic way of getting rid of them, but most refused, preferring the opportunity to have a go at the Congressmen on the spot. The first of these, a student at Stanford, gave the Nazi salute as Pool was swearing him in. He responded willingly to questions about his part in collecting money for the North Vietnamese Red Cross, but refused to talk about those who had worked with him, spurning the repeated invitations of the Congressmen to avail himself of the Fifth Amendment: "I will not answer this question on the grounds that it nauseates me and I am liable to vomit all over this table." Three others did take the Fifth, among their numerous and vociferously presented objections to the Committee, but made no effort to conceal their sympathies, affiliations, or activities. They were voluble, sophomoric (while being sworn in, one

---

[1] Counsel Nittle, too, fell into exchanges with this young man from which he had trouble extricating himself.

GORDON: The blood of American G.I.s is on the hands of Johnson and on the hands of all those abetting and aiding him.

NITTLE: It isn't on the hands of President Johnson. The responsibility, you well know, rests in Peking and in Moscow.

GORDON: . . . Where is the Peking troops in South Vietnam? It is American troops that have gone in, forced to go there. Why are you covering this up?

NITTLE: Now will you tell us, please . . .

GORDON: You talk about blood, you talk about aid. What about if your aid in Vietnam is American bombs? They are killing our people there.

NITTLE: Will you tell us, please . . .

POOL: Let's have order.

held up a fist, with the middle finger erect, and a couple of them had to be dragged away from the witness chair), and splendidly vituperative. "I will proceed alone," said a West Coast organizer for the P.L.M., "to confront and take on this racist committee of cowardly, yellow-bellied reactionaries as representatives of the U.S. government, not of the people, that is conducting a genocidal war in Vietnam that is against the best interests of the American and Vietnamese people."

The last two witnesses uttered statements which were rare in the Committee's history—". . . yes, I am a Communist and I am proud to say that I am a member of the Progressive Labor Movement," and ". . . I am a P.L.P. member and proud to say that, proud to say I am a Marxist-Leninist, a revolutionary Communist." Most of this latter young man's testimony was given over to attacks on the Committee, the Johnson Administration, bosses, union stooges, racists, and other undesirables, and after he was carried off yelling, "The blood of the Vietnamese is on the American government!", the Committee had had enough. Chairman Pool concluded abruptly and lamely: "We have the information we set out to obtain. The need for enactment of the bill is clear. We see no need to continue the investigative phase of this hearing. All witnesses against whom subpoenas are still outstanding are hereby excused from their subpoenas." A young man in the uniform of the American Revolution, who had been waiting for three days to be called so that he could distribute parchment reprints of the Declaration of Independence, objected with such vehemence that he had to be hustled out of the room and off to the police station.

Joe Pool of Texas, modestly endowed in everything but flesh, desiring nothing more than the kind of satisfaction that had come so readily to other chairmen of other subcommittees, might be forgiven for wondering why this cross had been laid on him. Even Everett Dirksen commented after the hearings were cut short: "This spectacle can do the Congress no good." For years the Committee had trusted unwaveringly in the premise that the Communist Party was a secret conspiratorial organization whose members were dedicated to subverting the land and so had to be exposed. For years it had interpreted the

Fifth Amendment as a form of confession. For years witnesses whose livelihoods were in jeopardy had been baited for failing to speak up. Now none of this applied. Aesopianism was passé. The witnesses in August 1966 admitted they were Communists, advertised their anti-war protests, defied the Committee, and were not cited for contempt. The Committee was browbeaten in its very citadel.

Yet despite the embarrassment they suffered, the abuse they took, and the ineffectuality they displayed in dealing with this new species of radical, the members of the Committee could conclude the hearings with a certain satisfaction. It was not the familiar satisfaction of making middle-aged ex-C.P. members cower behind the Fifth Amendment; the students had too little to lose to let the Congressmen take their pleasure of them without screams and kicks. But the main purpose of the hearings had been noisily served. The nation had been shown that the peace movement was infested by a rude bunch of America-haters; to those who subscribed to the reasoning of the Committee, protests against the war in Vietnam could henceforth be written off.

As for the exuberant young members of the Progressive Labor Movement, for them the August appearance was like a second shot on the Ed Sullivan show. One must resort to show business for a comparable case of so much being made of so little. To accept the estimate of Phillip Abbott Luce, there are a thousand card-carrying P.L.M. members in the entire country, and their ideology owes at least as much to good old American exhibitionism as to the writings of Chairman Mao. In their disgust with their own country and disdain for liberals and everybody else over the age of thirty, they cannot acknowledge how much of the defiance they showed in the hearing room was subsidized by that part of square America which brought down McCarthy and is reflected in the Warren Court. Arrogant, short-tempered, long-winded, they were peculiarly effective against the Un-American Activities Committee; when Joe Pool was in the chair, the House Caucus Room was no place for philosophers or gentlemen.

These last vaudeville-like hearings of 1966 were great fun, but it was the kind of fun that leaves a bad aftertaste. What we were witnessing was a confrontation between the benighted and the loud-mouthed, a monster film in which the worst of the stand-patters met the worst of the dissenters, and each fed on the other. It was an indecent display, but fans of both sides claimed a victory. "Those of us who sat listening to the spirited answers of the subpoenaed witnesses," wrote a leader of Women Strike for Peace, "derived a vicarious satisfaction from the experience." She saw emerging from the brawl "the beginning of a new unity among peace, civil liberties and civil rights advocates" —a return to the united front. And a few days after it was all over the Veterans of Foreign Wars gave Representative Pool a gold medal, three cheers, a parade, a standing ovation, and a chorus of *For he's a jolly good fellow*. Pool was touched. He said: "The House Committee on Un-American Activities is now in its greatest hour."

16

★ ★ ★ ★ ★

1967 . . . : Un-American?

As the House Committee on Un-American Activities rounds out the third decade of its existence,[1] it appears to be succumbing to the allure of the two great protest movements of our time. The attraction, to be sure, is perverse—there is something about the spectacle of people picketing for peace in Vietnam or marching for votes for Negroes that sets teeth on edge around the Committee's offices—but its recent gestures are at one with the spirit that has brought the Committee the special place that it occupies in the Congress and in the country. Foreign perils and domestic turbulence have provided the stuff of its labors since Martin Dies set about exposing the Detroit sit-down strikes as part of a Moscow-directed insurrection, and now the clouds of war and civil discontent are full of promise. In truth, the Committee cannot prosper without threats abroad and fears at home; it owes its most resplendent hours to the postwar confrontation in Berlin, the Communist victory in China, espionage cases in New York and Washington, war in Korea—and lacking in such fertilizing events, the early nineteen-sixties brought a series of dry seasons. Hearings have been rowdy, inconsequential, humiliating. The Committee

[1] Edwin E. Willis of Louisiana remains chairman in the ninetieth Congress. The Democrats on the Committee are William M. Tuck of Virginia; Joe R. Pool of Texas; Richard H. Ichord of Missouri; and John C. Culver of Iowa—a newcomer who has dissented from all of the Committee's 1967 legislative proposals. The Republicans: John M. Ashbrook of Ohio; Del Clawson of California; Richard L. Roudebush of Indiana; and Albert W. Watson of South Carolina. Francis J. McNamara remains staff director; Chester D. Smith is general counsel; Alfred M. Nittle is counsel.

has suffered rebuff upon rebuff from the courts. It has encountered increasing opposition in Congress and out. Once its tales of Soviet espionage made the front pages, but hearings in April 1967 into even that colorful subject went unattended. A parched decade.

But now it may be that those lowering clouds, seeded by the frustrations of Vietnam and the fears in our simmering cities, are about to open again. Did not the President use the occasion of presenting the Medal of Honor to a marine's widow to contrast her husband's sacrifice with the "hostile placards and debating points" of the war's critics "thousands of miles away from the battlefield on which he fell"? Has not the Secretary of State reported that "the Communist apparatus" is hard at work on peace demonstrations? Has not our former ambassador in Saigon warned that "disunity in America prolongs the war" in Vietnam? Has not our most celebrated general concurred? And did not the House of Representatives pass a bill, by a vote of 386 to 16, to make public mutilation of the flag a federal crime? This is Committee weather. Representative Pool, whose conduct of the raucous 1966 hearings into the Progressive Labor Movement was unedifying to the point of burlesque, has become a prophet. "The voice of Congress this year," a Northern liberal was quoted as saying in June 1967, "is old Joe Pool."

The Committee's main contribution to the anti-dissent chorus of 1967 came in the form of a report released on March 31, two weeks before the Saturday set for major peace demonstrations in New York and San Francisco. The report was a typical Committee document in its casual association between the evidence adduced and the judgment rendered. It reviewed the busy part that Communists—particularly students urged on by Bettina Aptheker, daughter of Herbert—had played in the planning for the event, and from this trampoline leaped to the assertion: "Such success as the instigators and organizers of Vietnam Week may have in staging anti-U.S. demonstrations April 8–15, and in turning out large numbers of people for the New York and San Francisco demonstrations may be attributed primarily to the Communists." The motives behind the report do not bear much scrutiny; it was gotten together and issued to discredit the protests in advance and to discourage participation. (In a revealing foreword, Chairman Willis explains that he is not opposed to "honest and responsible dissent from American policy by patriotic Americans" which will add to the public's "appreciation of the basic correctness of the policy our Government is pursuing.") On the day the demonstrations were held and scores of thousands marched on both coasts, the President let it be known that the F.B.I. was keeping its eye on anti-war activity, and Joe Pool demanded that Governor Rockefeller call out troops and tanks to safeguard property.[2]

Civil rights presents trickier terrain. Chairman Willis cannot but be sensitive to the fact that today more than ever his Committee is dominated by Southerners and conservative Republicans, with not a single Eastern or Western liberal among them. Should he undertake a direct assault on a prominent civil rights group, as his predecessors once assaulted the N.A.A.C.P., he would be vulnerable on that account and would have to be prepared for a powerful show of resistance. While diehard Southerners may continue to use the Committee's files to discredit Negro and white activists, it is not likely that Mr. Watson of South Carolina will have his way, that the cautious Willis will plunge directly into the whirlpool of civil rights. Yet the attraction is surely there, has been there since Martin Dies rebuked left-wingers for giving the poor Negro the idea that he ought to have a measure of equality. "I deplore the fact," said Dies in 1942, "that throughout the South today subversive elements are attempting to convince the Negro that he should be placed on social equality with white people, that now is the time for him to assert his rights."

Just as one may get at the Vietnam dissenters via the youths who cause commotions at military bases, so one may find an access route into the civil-rights movement. In October 1966 Chairman Willis announced that his Committee was under-

[2] Two former stalwarts of the Committee, ex-Representatives Donald C. Bruce of Indianapolis and Fulton Lewis III, who helped put out *Operation Abolition*, have produced a film about anti-war demonstrations, entitled *While Brave Men Die*, which they are showing with reported success to the Daughters of the American Revolution and similar audiences.

taking "a preliminary inquiry" to determine the extent to which "subversive elements" were involved in "organized rioting, burning, looting and other tragic acts of violence . . ." (This announcement came a few weeks after Joe Pool had placed in the Congressional Record an article by the ever reliable J. Edgar Hoover on the theme "Communist influence is being injected into civil disobedience.") By the mid-nineteen-sixties the remarkable surge of support for the Negro's claims had ebbed; the backlash was being felt. In the fall of 1966, Republicans used "law and order" as a dominant campaign theme, with evident effect. The perennial riots in Negro ghettoes, terrifying in themselves and in what they reveal of the rage that festers in our cities, were taken by a number of legislators as an invitation for a reprisal against the civil-rights movement. As the Un-American Activities Committee prepared its part in the counterattack, dozens of "anti-riot" bills were pending before the House Judiciary Committee.

When a group of civil-rights leaders expressed concern over the Committee's 1966 initiative and petitioned the House to block it, Willis declared: "We have no intention of investigating the civil-rights movement or the opinions or positions of any individual or organization on the civil-rights issue. Those things are none of our business . . . The Committee on Un-American Activities . . . has no jurisdiction in such matters and it has no intention of trying to inject itself into them." Roy Wilkins could not have said it more succinctly—but Willis could not let the subject go at that. He added: "If we should learn in the course of our investigation that a certain organization is actually controlled and dominated by the Communists carrying out the work of the Communist Party, we would not hesitate to investigate their operations." The preliminary inquiry was entrusted to Representative Tuck of Virginia, one of the members who had been urging an investigation of Communist infiltration of civil-rights groups, and the staff—which for practical purposes *is* the Committee—went scouting for what it manages to find wherever it looks.

So far a direct encounter between the Committee and the civil-rights movement remains only a promise. There is pressure for it, but there is strong pressure against it from powers in the House who have no taste for a repetition of the rowdy hearings of the recent past. Willis does not usually flout the wishes of his party's leadership, but the subject is alive and kicking for all it is worth. In the summer of 1967, a few days after the Newark, New Jersey, ghetto erupted, a bill making it a federal crime to cross state lines to incite a riot swept through the House of Representatives by a vote of 347 to 70. Edwin Willis served as floor manager. After the Detroit outbreak, the worst yet, he let it be known that the evidence of "subversive influence" gathered by Committee investigators "will justify public hearings." Hardly had the fires of Detroit burned themselves out when a Presidential commission and two Senate groups were inquiring into the subject of riots in the cities, but the Un-American Activities Committee was not to be denied. In August the gist of a "secret" staff study was leaked to newspapers; to no one's surprise, it drew attention to the role of militant Negro groups and Communists in whipping up hatred of authority among Negroes. The promised hearings opened in October 1967 and as this is written are ambling unprovocatively along under Governor Tuck, while the Senate Permanent Subcommittee on Investigations, covering much the same subject, is getting most of the newspaper space.

The Committee's present interests represent no break with tradition, and its knack for attaching itself to popular passions is again creating tactical difficulties for its opponents.[3] The young men who court notoriety by waving the Vietcong flag and burning the American flag are prime exhibits for Edwin Willis, who characterizes Vietnam dissenters as "Communists, fellow travelers and a motley collection of unkempt hippies and beatniks, cowardly draft card burners and treasonous flag burners and the ilk that will unite with them." And riots in the cities are invitations for repressive action to men who have

---

[3] In writing of the opponents of the Committee in this chapter, I mean those who sometimes act as defenders of individual Communists but are not the Party's collaborators or apologists—that is, persons more likely to contribute to the American Civil Liberties Union than to the Emergency Civil Liberties Committee and more responsive to the pronouncements of Americans for Democratic Action than to those of the National Lawyers Guild.

fought every effort to ease the conditions of ghetto life. (A day after it passed the anti-riot bill, the House turned down a measure to fight rats in the nation's slums. Only two members of the Committee, Willis and Culver, voted for this bill.) An understandably frightened public is understandably receptive to calls for tougher laws, more police, harsher penalties.

To add to the liberal burden, those, like the staff of the Committee, who set themselves the task of finding Communists and fellow travelers in the peace and civil-rights movements will find them without having to look very hard. When *The New Republic* ran an editorial mocking the Committee's report on Vietnam Week, Bettina Aptheker, that chip off old Herbert, chided the editors for not giving the Communists sufficient credit for their role in the April 15 marches. Moderate peace organizations like SANE gave them credit enough to abstain from official participation that day. Just what attitude to adopt toward self-advertising Communists, old style and new, Moscow-oriented and Peking-oriented, has been a cause of fresh soul-searching among liberal intellectuals in the nineteen-sixties. The old resentments have cooled, and most liberals seem ready to grant that it is silly in 1968 to go on rating ex-Communists by the day and month in 1939 or 1945 or 1956 that they quit the Party, rather like the French émigré nobles in Coblenz who divided the imagined spoils of the restoration according to the date that one fled France. Nor are liberals eager to abet the hunters of Reds by giving our Communist remnants more attention than their condition warrants. Yet the issues that seemed to have been battled out in the nineteen-thirties will not lie quiet in the post-Stalin era. Is it becoming for men who champion freedom in its full variety to make common cause, even in the noblest pursuits, with the champions of totalitarianism? Is it moral? Is it practical? Can such collaboration benefit the liberals' high purposes or will it in fact work against them?

Whereas the non-Communist left is divided over these questions, the Communists and the scourges of Communists are, as usual, allied. The Communists have often followed, with regard to their lay organizations, the model of gamblers who put hirelings without criminal records in nominal charge of their enterprises in Las Vegas; just as the syndicate makes sure to get its regular cut, so the Party has made sure to take a substantial share of credit for all benefits proceeding from the worthy groups. The investigators of the Committee on Un-American Activities, suspicious of all leftward-leaning organizations and all their works, have for thirty years delightedly given the Communists their claimed share of credit, and more. Issues of great moment—from the New Deal to industrial unionism to a nuclear-test ban—have enjoyed the Committee's attentions. In most cases there has been substance to the charges of Communist machinations just as there has been substance to the countercharges of red herring. Sorting out the charges and countercharges has fallen to mere liberals, who have sometimes pretended that the Communists were social democrats at heart and have sometimes responded to the Committee's incursions by looking the other way. But there have always been voices among them that were at once sophisticated about the Communists and unfearing of the Committee, and these have been heard to better effect in recent years.

Liberal opposition peaks regularly in odd-numbered years, when the new House of Representatives meets and goes through the formality of adopting the rules of the previous Congress, including all of its standing committees. This occasion brings forth editorials and petitions and calls for abolition from Congressmen like Edwards of California and Ryan of New York. But abolition has never been a realistic goal. As Representative Edwards sadly remarked in 1965, "A standing committee once established is immensely difficult to get rid of, even though its mandate is probably unconstitutional and its behavior embarrassing and belittling to the Congress."

The Committee's opponents in the House have therefore directed their attacks toward its appropriation, which must be approved annually. In the eighty-ninth Congress, it received $848,000, over and above its basic staff budget of about $162,000; this was the fourth highest appropriation among the twenty standing committees of the House, substantially more than the sums given to such productive arms of the Congress as the Committee on Interstate and Foreign Commerce, the Committee on Banking and Currency, or the Committee on the Judiciary. So it came as a notable victory for the opposition when in April 1967 the $400,000 requested by the Committee for its year's work was cut to $350,000 by the House Administration subcommittee entrusted with reviewing such appropriations. Then the opponents rounded up ninety-two votes for a motion which would have compelled the Committee to justify its budget at open hearings. There were 304 votes against this motion, but not since the Committee's establishment as a permanent body in 1945 had the liberals in Congress managed to rally such an expression of dissatisfaction with its behavior.

Yet even on this day of victory, only forty-three representatives voted against the actual appropriation, an improvement over 1961 when there were only six opposing votes, but far from the smell of success. The liberals owed their modest achievement of April 1967 to the display put on by the egregious Joe Pool at his Vietnam hearings of the previous summer and, barring some even more flagrant episode, there is no reason to suppose that they will do much better in the future. The Committee can continue to rely on a staunch body of supporters in the House as well as on the disinclination of Congressmen to register an unfriendly vote which will have to be explained to American Legion posts back home.

A more likely source of an effective blow to the Committee is the judiciary, which has already delivered it so many slaps for bad manners and has quite undone its preeminent legislative accomplishment, the Internal Security Act of 1950. The Committee's four doughty foes—Warren, Black, Douglas, and Brennan—remain on the bench, and they have been joined by two juniors from whom Willis, Pool, *et al.* have no reason to look for indulgence. The dossier of Thurgood Marshall has periodically been plucked from the Committee's files and waved about by arch-segregationists. And it was Abe Fortas who wrote in gloomy 1953 that "the [Congressional] hearing has become a weapon of persecution, a useful tool to the demagogue, a device for the glory of the prosecutor and of shame for the accused."

If the Stamler-Hall-Cohen case that originated in the Chicago hearings of 1965 or the Krebs-Teague case that came out of the 1966 Vietnam hearings should find its way up to the high tribunal while this six-justice group is intact, the Committee stands to receive a sharper rebuff than it received in the prematurely acclaimed 1957 Watkins decision. At any rate, such is the liberal hope. No court can do away with the Committee, but if the witnesses who walked out in Chicago and Washington are upheld in their major arguments against the Committee's status and procedures, unfriendly witnesses of the future will have been provided with a sturdy shield for defiance. They will not be able to prevent any Congressman from making any accusations he wishes, but they may be relieved of the obligation to participate in their own pillory.

The points scored annually by liberals in Congress against the Committee's existence are barely contestable—and for all practical purposes Committee members gave up contesting them some time ago, relying instead on evocations of the Communist menace and their own patriotism. The Committee's annual expenditure and the size of its staff, so much larger than most committees of the House, represent an exorbitant cost for so meager a legislative record.[4] Its files of names and affiliations, which Chairman Willis cites often as being of inestimable help to federal investigators of all sorts, arouse special disquiet among liberals; not only do they presume that they are listed therein, but they question the propriety of a committee of Congress keeping political dossiers on citizens. And, of course, liberals continue to be put off by the Committee's uncivil methods of carrying out its uncertain mandate. But valid as the reiterated criticisms are, they do not quite explain the vehemence with which liberals, along with virtually the entire intellectual community,[5] have rallied against the Committee.

[4] Responding in 1965 to criticisms that the normal Committee complement of between fifty and sixty staff members seemed excessive, Representative Ashbrook, the Committee's ranking Republican, explained: "Without sufficient staff we might well have a fishing expedition here and there and stray into paths which lead to irresponsibility."

[5] In 1961 a professor of classics at the University of Illinois named Revilo P. Oliver (destined to become an adornment of the Birch establishment) who

There are few causes in our history that have kept liberal passions at the boil for so long. "Frankly," Chairman Willis has said, "while I do not question their sincerity, I just do not understand these people."

They are not so difficult to understand. For thirty years the most cherished ideals of liberalism and many of its heroes have been among the Committee's main targets. Liberals have had their motives impugned and their patriotism questioned. They have seen associates and acquaintances harried by investigators and have read of the ordeals of witnesses with whom they could easily identify. Their responses to the recurrent assaults have not always been intelligent or entirely honest. There were periods, before the outbreak of World War II and in the early postwar years, when many liberals, bemused by the dream of the Popular Front or having tolerated it to their later chagrin, fought back by denying the undeniable and defending the indefensible. On finding themselves vulnerable to the Committee's charges, some have cried like hurt children at their tormentors, "You're one too!," accusing the Committee itself of being un-American. Such has been the liberal contribution to the debasement of political discourse.

Had Martin Dies and J. B. Matthews and their successors contented themselves with arguing that the Communist Party or the German-American Bund was un-American because it conducted its affairs by the grace of a foreign state, one would have been hard put to challenge them. But the Communists were never sufficiently satisfying game; Dies was out to get the New Deal, and as he and Thomas and Velde moved on to fellow travelers and others, the Committee's rationale became increasingly tenuous. Soon the Congressmen were taking logically impermissible shortcuts; it was no longer a man's loyalty to the U.S.S.R. that made him a likely subversive but his adherence to causes favored by those who were loyal to the

---

wished to show that not all intellectuals despise the Committee made public a statement in its defense signed by 139 college administrators and teachers from seventeen schools. To fill out his company, Professor Oliver had to mine institutions like Catawba College, the Chicago Lutheran Theological Seminary, and Roberts Wesleyan College, thereby confirming what had been apparent for years—that the country's intellectuals despise the Committee.

U.S.S.R. So the famous files were built up, wherein support of Loyalist Spain, antagonism to the Smith Act, and, of course, any expressed hope for the disappearance of the Committee all became black marks in one's dossier. It was guilt by extension. The Communist Party, that band of social climbers, always loved to brag of its roots in American radicalism. The claim was humorous coming from the Soviet fan club, but the causes to which the Communists gave their considerable energies, such as industrial unionism and Negro rights, did have authentic roots and, like an army company straying beyond reach of its supply station, the farther the Committee moved from paid functionaries of the Party, the weaker became its lines of support.

No critic of the Committee will take exception to these unoriginal observations, but they bear on the liberal side of the debate too. Just as there is nothing historically un-American about wanting to do away with A.T.&T. or the Catholic Church, so there is nothing un-American about union-busting or anti-Semitism or the Ku Klux Klan, and unless one is prepared to blank out large and significant patches of our history, there is nothing un-American about the Un-American Activities Committee. An organization, as J. B. Matthews taught, may be known by the company it attracts, and none of the men who have led the Committee in its endless campaigns represents anything unique in our national political life. The swaggering demagogy of Martin Dies was run-of-the-mill stuff back in Texas. The unstinting bigotry of John Rankin showed him to be the true representative of the voters in his home district, scarcely an alien or the son of an alien among them. And what is un-American about the brutality of J. Parnell Thomas, the cunning of Richard Nixon, the mindless opportunism of Harold Velde, the xenophobia of Francis Walter, the stupidity of Joe Pool? The fact that such are the men who have found a home with the Committee is revealing, but not on account of any want of "Americanism."

The Committee's Americanism runs deep. It can trace its ancestry to colonial times, when we hounded religious eccentrics, and to the Revolution, when we tyrannized Tories. The fear of Jacobinism that brought us the Alien and Sedition Laws in the eighteenth century was not unlike the fear of Bolshevism that brought us the Internal Security Act in the twentieth century. In World War I we imprisoned socialists, pacifists, and German sympathizers, and in World War II, with the Committee's blessing, we forced thousands of people to leave their homes and gather in camps because they were of Japanese descent. For three decades the Committee has labored in behalf of America's nativists, preserving the verities of the small town against adulteration by the big city, shoring up pietist truths against erosion by the social gospel, defending the flag from soilage by aliens, intellectuals, crackpots. It is precisely the Committee's Americanism that is so troubling, in its reminder that this is not the land exclusively of Lincoln and Jefferson.

In a time like the present, when our repressive instincts are under reasonable control, the Committee exists to keep us from smugness, from forgetting how suddenly an external or internal threat or imagined threat can bring a relapse into that delirium where common sense mingles with common superstition, intelligence rides with ignorance, and honest men find themselves in league with charlatans, self-aggrandizers, and maniacs. The Committee, like the distemper itself, has raged and subsided, has invigorated the political body and ravaged it, has compelled us to confront real weaknesses at the very moment that it was sapping our fundamental strengths. At times the fever has been efficacious, a stimulant to an apathetic constitution, but more often it has been all pains and rashes which left the body debilitated, even disfigured. Invariably the nation has recovered, but not without casualties. Lacking these casualties, the people whose reputations and livelihoods have been blithely hazarded, the Committee's career would lack meaning. They are its achievement. It has established a record not of laws but of Fifth Amendment pleas and contempt citations and disrupted lives. The proudest exhibit of the Committee's thirty years is its spacious files filled with the names, associations, activities, and public utterances of thousands of Americans.

From the start the Committee has been egged on by the

nation's entire lumpen right. Whatever foray it rode out upon, it wore, and still wears, the colors of Legionnaires, policemen, and ladies of the D.A.R., fundamentalist congregations in the South and Midwest and McCarthyite Catholics in Boston and New York and vigilantes everywhere. Trapped by a terrible nostalgia, these truculent cheerleaders of repression are fighting against the sense that their economic, social, and political positions have deteriorated, that control of their country's destiny, and their own, is slipping inexorably away. Their neighborhoods are changing; the country is changing. They are not, most of them, readers of poetry or, indeed, much else, but they might find words for their feelings in Yeats: "Things fall apart; the centre cannot hold; Mere anarchy is loosed upon the world." Alas, they can look for no Second Coming. Their passions cry for outlet, and since they cannot declare war on all America, or even concede that it is some genius of America itself that is doing them in, they set out after Reds, pinks, blacks, foreigners, beatniks—conspirators all. The Un-American Activities Committee is the engine of their vengeance, and for thirty years it has run on flesh and blood.

The endless harassment of individuals for disagreeable opinions and activities has created the greatest anxiety, revulsion, indignation, outrage among liberals. In protesting against the Committee's bloodlettings, liberals are only affirming their position in the war between the enthusiasts and the men of the Enlightenment which already raged when our country began. Between the Committee and the liberal spirit no reconciliation is possible, for the Committee embodies the drive to ban, censor, forbid, jail that has cursed the land for two hundred years. Whether or not the emotions stirred by the war in Vietnam and by the ghetto riots will reinvigorate the Committee, whether or not the Congress will limit its appropriation or the courts narrow its range, the division between freedom and security, between the pardoners and the punishers will not be healed. It is wider and deeper than the division between right and left in America, where the left has its doctrinaires and the right its libertarians. The awareness that even if the Committee were abolished tomorrow the gulf would remain, dangerous as ever, will deter no one from carrying a placard for abolition. Nor can it solace those who have been hurt during the years of rampage. But let us hope that the thought that the Committee on Un-American Activities can inflict on the nation only what the nation in its paranoiac seizures is willing to endure, may provide some small comfort for the unquiet shade of Sam Dickstein.

Appendix I

Chairmen of the House Committee
on Un-American Activities

1938–1944:   Martin Dies, Jr. (D., Texas)
1945:   Edward J. Hart (D., N.J.)
1945–1946:   John S. Wood (D., Ga.)
1947–1948:   J. Parnell Thomas (R., N.J.)
1949–1952:   John S. Wood (D., Ga.)
1953–1954:   Harold H. Velde (R., Ill.)
1955–1963:   Francis E. Walter (D., Pa.)
1963–   :   Edwin E. Willis (D., La.)

Appendix II

Hearings and Reports of the
House Committee on Un-American Activities

SPECIAL COMMITTEE: 1938–1944

Public Hearings

Vol. 1: Aug. 12, 13, 15–20, 22, 23, 1938; Washington, D.C.
Vol. 2: Sept. 15–17, 1938; New York. Sept. 28–30, Oct. 4–6, 1938; Washington, D.C. Oct. 11–13, 1938; Detroit. Oct. 17–22, 1938; Washington, D.C.
Vol. 3: Oct. 24–27, Nov. 4–6, 14–17, 19, 21, 1938; Washington, D.C.
Vol. 4: Nov. 19, 22, 23, 28, Dec. 1, 5–9, 14, 1938; Washington, D.C. (supplement) Dec. 15, 1938; Washington, D.C.
Vol. 5: May 18, 22–24, 31, June 1, 1939; Washington, D.C.
Vol. 6: Aug. 16–18, 21–24, 28, 29, 1939; Washington, D.C.
Vol. 7: Sept. 5–9, 11–13, 1939; Washington, D.C.
Vol. 8: Sept. 18–20, 22, 23, 25, 27, 1939; Washington, D.C.
Vol. 9: Sept. 28–30, Oct. 5–7, 9, 11, 13, 14, 1939; Washington, D.C.
Vol. 10: Oct. 16–21, 23–25, 28, 1939; Washington, D.C.
Vol. 11: Oct. 28, 30, 31, Nov. 1–3, 27, 29, 30, Dec. 1–3, 1939; Washington, D.C.
Vol. 12: Feb. 7, 8, 10, March 25, 28, 29, April 2–4, 1940; Washington, D.C.
Vol. 13: April 11, 12, 19, 23–25, May 6, 8, 9, 21, 1940; Washington, D.C.
Vol. 14: Aug. 29, 1940; Washington, D.C. Oct. 1, 2, 4, 1940; Newark. May 21, 22, 26, 27, 29, June 10, 12, Aug. 11, 1941; Washington, D.C.

Vol. 15: June 8–12, 15–18, 1943; Los Angeles. June 18, 1943; Parker, Arizona. July 1–3, 6, 7, 1943; Washington, D.C.

Vol. 16: Nov. 29, 30, Dec. 1, 6–9, 20, 1943; Washington, D.C.

Vol. 17: Sept. 27–29, Oct. 3–5, 1944; Washington, D.C.

Executive Hearings Made Public

Vol. 1: Sept. 20, Oct. 6, 9, 11, 12, 14, 1939; Washington, D.C. Nov. 9, 10, 1939; New Orleans. Nov. 17, 18, 1939; Chicago. Nov. 20, 1939; Detroit.

Vol. 2: March 9, 11, 1940; Miami Beach. March 21, June 3, 1940; Washington, D.C. July 8, 1940; New York. July 8–11, 1940; Austin. July 16, 17, 1940; Beaumont, Texas.

Vol. 3: July 17, 1940; Chattanooga. July 18, 1940; Houston. July 19, 22, Aug. 5, 1940; Beaumont, Texas. July 26, 1940; Washington, D.C. Aug. 6, 1940; Orange, Texas. Aug. 16, 17, 1940; Los Angeles. Aug. 19, 20, 1940; San Francisco.

Vol. 4: Oct. 2, 3, 1939; Chicago. Aug. 23, 24, 1940; Kansas City, Mo. Aug. 26, 27, 1940; New York. Oct. 1, 2, 1940; Newark. Oct. 17, Nov. 6, 8, 1940; Los Angeles.

Vol. 5: Nov. 2, 1940; St. Louis. Nov. 18, 1940; Chicago. Dec. 11, 20–22, 1940; March 4, Aug. 5, 7, 8, Dec. 18, 19, 1941; Washington, D.C.

Vol. 6: Oct. 30, 1941; Jan. 15, 16, 19–22, 26, March 26, April 17, 1942; Washington, D.C.

Vol. 7: March 23, 29–31, April 1, 2, 5–9, 16, 1943; Washington, D.C. April 19, 1943; New York.

Reports

House Report No. 2. Annual Report. Jan. 3, 1939.

House Report No. 1476. Annual Report. Jan. 3, 1940.

House Report No. 1. Annual Report. Jan. 3, 1941.

House Report No. 2277. Annual Report, Part 1. June 25, 1942. Part 2 (minority views on annual report). July 7, 1942.

House Report No. 2748. Annual Report. Jan. 2, 1943.

House Report No. 717. Japanese in the United States (including minority views on war relocation centers). Sept. 30, 1943.

House Report No. 1161. The Peace Now Movement. Feb. 17, 1944.

House Report No. 1311. C.I.O. Political Action Committee. March 29, 1944.

Report of a Special Subcommittee on the Tule Lake Riot. 1944.

Minority Views on Tule Lake Segregation Center. 1944.

Index to Hearings, Volumes 1–14, Reports, 1939–44; Appendixes I-V. 1942.

Appendixes

Appendix I. A compilation of original sources used as exhibits to show the nature and aims of the Communist Party, its connections with the U.S.S.R. and its advocacy of force and violence. 1940.

Appendix II. A preliminary digest and report on the un-American activities of various Nazi organizations and individuals in the United States, including diplomatic and consular agents of the German government. 1940.

Appendix III. Preliminary report on totalitarian propaganda in the United States. 1941.

Appendix IV. German-American Bund. 1941.

Appendix V. Transport Workers Union. 1941.

Appendix VI. Report on Japanese activities. 1942.

Appendix VII. Report on the Axis front movement in the United States—Nazi activities. 1943.

Appendix VIII. Report on the Axis front movement in the United States—Japanese activities. 1943.

STANDING COMMITTEE: 1945–1967

79th Congress

Hearings on Office of Price Administration. June 20, 21, 27, 1945.

Hearings on Communist Party. Sept. 26, 27, Oct. 17–19, 1945.

Hearings on Gerald L. K. Smith. Jan. 30, 1946.

Hearings on Joint Anti-Fascist Refugee Committee. April 4, 1946.

Hearings on Louis F. Budenz. Nov. 22, 1946.

House Report No. 1996. Sources of financial aid for subversive and un-American propaganda. May 10, 1946.

House Report No. 2233. Annual Report. June 7, 1946.

House Report No. 2742. Annual Report. Jan. 2, 1947.

80th Congress

Hearings on Gerhart Eisler. Feb. 6, 1947.

Hearings regarding Communism in labor unions in the United States. Feb. 27, July 23–25, 1947.

Hearings regarding Leon Josephson and Samuel Liptzen. March 5, 21, 1947.

Hearings on H.R. 1884 and H.R. 2122, bills to curb or outlaw the Communist Party of the United States. March 24–28, 1947.

    Testimony of William C. Bullitt. March 24, 1947.

    Testimony of J. Edgar Hoover. March 26, 1947.

    Testimony of Eugene Dennis. April 9, 1947.

    Testimony of Walter S. Steele. July 21, 1947.

    Testimony of Victor Kravchenko. July 22, 1947.

Hearings regarding Hanns Eisler, Sept. 24–26, 1947.

Hearings regarding Communist infiltration of the motion-picture industry. Oct. 20–24, 27–30, 1947.

Hearings on H.R. 4422 and H.R. 4581, proposed legislation to curb or control the Communist Party of the United States. Feb. 5, 6, 9–11, 19, 20, 1948.

Hearings regarding Communist espionage in the United States Government (including interim report on hearings, Aug. 28, 1948). July 31, Aug. 3–5, 7, 9–13, 16–18, 20, 24–27, 30, Sept. 8, 9, 1948.

Excerpts from hearings regarding investigation of Communist activities in connection with the atom bomb. Sept. 9, 14, 16, 1948.

Hearings regarding Communist espionage in the United States Government, Part II. Dec. 7–10, 14, 1948.

House Report No. 209. Communist Party of the United States as an agent of a foreign power. April 1, 1947.

House Report No. 271. American Youth for Democracy. April 17, 1947.

House Report No. 592. Southern Conference for Human Welfare. June 16, 1947.

House Report No. 1115. Civil Rights Congress. Nov. 17, 1947.

Report on Dr. Edward U. Condon. March 18, 1948.

Report on proposed legislation to control subversive Communist activities in the United States. April 10, 1948.

House Report No. 1844. Protecting the United States against un-American and subversive activities. April 30, 1948.

House Report No. 1920. The Communist Party of the United States as an advocate of overthrow of government by force and violence. May 11, 1948.

Report on Soviet espionage activities in connection with the atom bomb. Sept. 28, 1948.

Second report, Soviet espionage within the United States Government. Dec. 31, 1948.

Annual Report. Dec. 31, 1948.

81st Congress

Documentary testimony of Gen. Izyador Modelski. March 31, April 1, 1949.

Hearings on Soviet espionage activities in connection with jet propulsion and aircraft. June 6, 1949.

Hearings regarding Steve Nelson. June 8, 1949.

Hearings regarding Toma Babin. May 27, July 6, 1949.

Testimony of Paul Crouch. May 6, 1949.

Testimony of Philip O. Keeney and Mary Jane Keeney and statement regarding their background. May 24, 25, June 9, 1949.

Hearings regarding Communist infiltration of radiation laboratory and atomic bomb project at the University of California, Berkeley, Calif. (vol. I). April 22, 26, May 25, June 10, 14, 1949.

Hearings regarding Clarence Hiskey (including testimony of Paul Crouch). May 24, 1949.

Hearings regarding Communist infiltration of minority groups (part I). July 13, 14, 18, 1949.

Hearings regarding Communist infiltration of minority groups (part II) (testimony of Manning Johnson). July 14, 1949.

Hearings regarding Communist infiltration of labor unions (part I). Aug. 9–11, 1949.

Hearings regarding Communism in the District of Columbia (part I). June 28, 29, July 6, 12, 28, 1949.

Hearings regarding Communist infiltration of radiation laboratory and atomic bomb project at the University of California, Berkeley, Calif. (vol. II) (identification of Scientist X). Aug. 26, 1949; July 1, Sept. 10, 1948; Aug. 14, Sept. 14, 27, 1949.

Hearings regarding Communist infiltration of labor unions (part II) (security measures relating to officials of the UERMWA-CIO). Dec. 5, 6, 1949.

Testimony of James Sterling Murray and Edward Tiers Manning (regarding Clarence Hiskey and Arthur Adams). Aug. 14, Oct. 5, 1949.

Hearings regarding shipment of atomic material to the Soviet Union during World War II. Dec. 5, 7, 1949; Jan. 23–26, March 2, 3, 7, 1950.

Exposé of the Communist Party of western Pennsylvania (part I) (based upon testimony of Matthew Cvetic, undercover agent). Feb. 21–23, March 13, 14, 24, 1950.

Hearings regarding Communist activities in the Territory of Hawaii (part I). April 10–12, 1950.

Hearings regarding Communist activities in the Territory of Hawaii (part II). April 13–15, 1950.

Hearings regarding Communism in the United States Government (part I). April 20, 21, 25, 29, May 4–6, 1950; July 30, Aug. 7, 1948; June 8, 1950.

Hearings regarding Communist activities in the Territory of Hawaii (part III). April 17–19, 1950.

Hearings on H.R. 3903 and H.R. 7595 (legislation to outlaw certain un-American and subversive activities). March 21–23, 28–30, April 4, May 2–4, 1950.

Exposé of the Communist Party of western Pennsylvania (part II) (based upon testimony of Matthew Cvetic). March 24, 25, 1950.

Testimony of Philip A. Bart (general manager of Freedom of the Press, publishers of the *Daily Worker,* organ of the Communist Party) and Marcel Scherer (coordinator, New York Labor Conference for Peace and formerly district representative of District 4, UERMWA-CIO). June 21, 1950.

Hearings regarding Communist activities in the Cincinnati, Ohio, area (part I). July 12–15, Aug. 8, 1950.

Hearings regarding Communist infiltration of minority groups (part III) (testimony of Josh White). Sept. 1, 1950.

Hearings regarding Communism in the United States Government (part II). Aug. 28, 31, Sept. 1, 15, 1950.

Exposé of the Communist Party of western Pennsylvania (based upon testimony of Matthew Cvetic and documents of C.P. of western Pennsylvania) (part III). June 22, Sept. 28, Oct. 13, 21, 1950.

Hearings regarding Communism in the District of Columbia (part II). Dec. 6, 11–13, 1950.

Testimony of Edward G. Robinson. Oct. 27, Dec. 21, 1950.

American aspects of the assassination of Leon Trotsky. July 26, Aug. 30, Oct. 18, 19, Dec. 4, 1950.

Hearings regarding Communist infiltration of radiation laboratory and atomic bomb project at the University of California, Berkeley, Calif. (vol. III). Dec. 20–22, 1950.

Hearings regarding Communist infiltration of labor unions (part III). Aug. 29, 30, 1950.

Hearings regarding Communist espionage. Nov. 8, Dec. 2, 1949; Feb. 27, March 1, 1950.

Testimony of Hazel Scott Powell. Sept. 22, 1950.

House Report No. 1954. Review of the Scientific and Cultural Conference for World Peace. April 26, 1950.

House Report No. 1951. American Slav Congress. April 26, 1950.

House Report No. 1952. Report on atomic espionage (Nelson-Weinberg and Hiskey-Adams cases). April 26, 1950.

House Report No. 1953. Congress of American Women. April 26, 1950.

House Report No. 1950. Annual Report for 1949. April 26, 1950.

House Report No. 2986. Hawaii Civil Liberties Committee—a Communist front. Aug. 24, 1950.

The Communist "peace petition" campaign (interim statement). July 13, 1950.

House Report No. 3123. National Lawyers Guild. Sept. 21, 1950.

Report on the *Honolulu Record*. Oct. 1, 1950.

House Report No. 3248. The National Committee to Defeat the Mundt Bill—a Communist Lobby. Jan. 2, 1951.

House Report No. 3249. Annual Report for 1950. Jan. 2, 1951.

82d Congress

Hearings regarding Communist activities in the Territory of Hawaii (part IV). July 6, 1951.

Communist infiltration of Hollywood motion-picture industry (part I). March 8, 21, April 10–13, 1951.

Communist infiltration of Hollywood motion-picture industry (part II). April 17, 23–25, May 16–18, 1951.

Communist infiltration of Hollywood motion-picture industry (part III). May 22–25, June 25, 26, 1951.

Hearings relating to Communist activities in the defense area of Baltimore (part I) (based on testimony of Mary Stalcup Markward). June 19–21, 26–28, July 11, 13, 1951.

Hearings relating to Communist activities in the defense area of Baltimore (part II) (Maryland Committee for Peace and Baltimore County Committee for Peace). June 28, July 10, 12, 1951.

Hearings relating to Communist activities in the defense area of Baltimore (part III). June 19, 20, 26–28, July 10, 12, 13, 1951.

Hearings on American aspects of the Richard Sorge spy case. Aug. 9, 22, 23, 1951.

Exposé of Communist activities in the state of Massachusetts (based on the testimony of Herbert A. Philbrick). July 23, 24, Oct. 10, 11, 1951.

Communist infiltration of Hollywood motion-picture industry (part IV). Sept. 17–19, 1951.

Communist infiltration of Hollywood motion-picture industry (part V). Sept. 20, 21, 24, 25, 1951.

Hearings regarding Communist activities among farm groups. Feb. 28, March 9, 1951.

Communist tactics among veterans' groups. July 13, 1951.

Testimony of Oliver Edmund Clubb. March 14, Aug. 20, 23, 1951.

Communist infiltration of Hollywood motion-picture industry (part VI). May 10, Sept. 10–12, 1951.

The role of the Communist press in the Communist conspiracy. Jan. 9, 10, 15–17, 1952.

Communist infiltration of Hollywood motion-picture industry (part VII). Jan. 24, 28, Feb. 5, March 20, April 10, 30, 1952.

Communist activities among professional groups in the Los Angeles area (part I). Jan. 21–26, April 9, 1952.

Communism in the Detroit area (part I). Feb. 25–29, 1952.

Communism in the Detroit area (part II). March 10–12, April 29, 30, 1952.

Communist activities among youth groups (based on testimony of Harvey M. Matusow) (part I). Feb. 6, 7, 1952.

Methods of Communist infiltration in the United States Government. May 6, June 10, 23, 1952.

Communist infiltration of Hollywood motion-picture industry (part VIII). May 19–21, 1952.

Communist activities among professional groups in the Los Angeles area (part II). May 22, July 8, 1952.

Testimony of Lynne L. Prout. Feb. 14, 1952.

Communist activities in the Chicago area (part I). Sept. 2, 3, 1952.

Communist activities in the Chicago area (part II). Sept. 4, 5, 1952.

Testimony of Dr. Edward U. Condon. Sept. 5, 1952.

Communist activities among professional groups in the Los Angeles area (part III). Sept. 30, Oct. 1, 2, 1952.

Communist activities among professional groups in the Los Angeles area (part IV). Oct. 3, 6, 7, 1952.

Communist infiltration of Hollywood motion-picture industry (part IX). Aug. 19, Sept. 29, 1952.

Testimony of Gen. Walter Bedell Smith. Oct. 13, 1952.

Communist activities in the Philadelphia area. Oct. 13–16, 1952.

Communist infiltration of Hollywood motion-picture industry (part X). Nov. 12, 13, 1952.

The March of Treason. Feb. 19, 1951.

House Report No. 378. The Communist "Peace" Offensive. April 25, 1951.

House Document No. 137. Guide to Subversive Organizations and Publications. May 14, 1951.

House Document No. 136. 100 Things You Should Know About Communism. May 14, 1951.

House Report No. 1229. The Shameful Years. Jan. 8, 1952.

House Report No. 2431. Annual Report for 1951. July 2, 1952.

House Report No. 1661. Review of the Methodist Federation for Social Action. March 27, 1952.

House Report No. 2516. Annual Report for 1952. Jan. 3, 1953.

83d Congress

Communist methods of infiltration (education). Feb. 25–27, 1953.

Communist methods of infiltration (education) (part II). March 12, 13, 17, 18, April 14, 16, 1953.

Investigation of Communist activities in the Los Angeles area (part I). March 23–25, 1953.

Investigation of Communist activities in the Los Angeles area (part II). March 26–28, 1953.

Investigation of Communist activities in the Los Angeles area (part III). March 30, 31, 1953.

Investigation of Communist activities in the Los Angeles area (part IV). April 7, 8, 1953.

Investigation of Communist activities in the Los Angeles area (part V). Dec. 2, 1952; Feb. 17, March 12, 27, April 7, 13, 1953.

Communist methods of infiltration (education) (part III). April 21, 22, 1953.

Communist methods of infiltration (education) (part IV). April 23, 27, 1953.

Investigation of Communist activities in the New York City area (part I). May 4, 1953.

Investigation of Communist activities in the New York City area (part II). May 5, 1953.

Investigation of Communist activities in the New York City area (part III). May 6, 1953.

Investigation of Communist activities in the New York City area (part IV). May 7, 1953.

Communist methods of infiltration (education) (part V). April 29, May 19, 26–28, 1953.

Communist methods of infiltration (government-labor) (part I). April 17, May 14, June 9, 1953.

Francisek Jarecki, flight to freedom. July 1, 1953.

Soviet schedule for war, 1955. May 13, 14, 1953.

Investigation of Communist activities in the Columbus, Ohio, area. June 17, 18, 1953.

Communist methods of infiltration (education) (part VI). June 22, 24, 29, July 1, 1953.

Testimony of Stephen H. Fritchman. Sept. 12, 1951.

Communist methods of infiltration (government-labor) (part II). July 20, 1953.

Investigation of Communist activities in the New York City area (part V). July 6, 1953.

Investigation of Communist activities in the New York City area (part VI). July 7, 1953.

Investigation of Communist activities in the New York City area (part VII) (based on the testimony of Manning Johnson). July 8, 1953.

Investigation of Communist activities in the New York City area (part VIII) (based on the testimony of Manning Johnson). July 13, 14, 1953.

Investigation of Communist activities in the Los Angeles area (part VI). March 21, 1951; June 2, 1953.

Investigation of Communist activities in the Albany, N.Y. area (part I). July 13, 14, 1953.

Investigation of Communist activities in the Albany, N.Y. area (part II). July 15, 16, 1953.

Investigation of Communist activities in the Los Angeles area (part VII). Sept. 4, 1953.

Testimony of Dr. Marek Stanislaw Korowicz. Sept. 24, 1953.

Hearings regarding Jack R. McMichael. July 30, 31, 1953.

Investigation of Communist activities in the Philadelphia area (part I). Nov. 16, 1953.

Investigation of Communist activities in the Philadelphia area (part II). Nov. 17, 18, 1953.

Communist methods of infiltration (government-labor) (part III) (based on testimony of James McNamara). Sept. 15, 1953.

Investigation of Communist activities in the San Francisco area (part I). Dec. 1, 1953.

Investigation of Communist activities in the San Francisco area (part II). Dec. 2, 1953.

Investigation of Communist activities in the San Francisco area (part III). Dec. 3, 1953.

Investigation of Communist activities in the San Francisco area (part IV). Dec. 4, 1953.

Investigation of Communist activities in the San Francisco area (part V). Dec. 5, 1953.

Investigation of Communist activities in the Los Angeles area (part VIII). Nov. 23, 1953.

Communist methods of infiltration (education) (part VII). May 15, 1953.

Testimony of Bishop G. Bromley Oxnam. July 21, 1953.

Communist methods of infiltration (entertainment) (part I). Jan. 13, 1954.

Investigation of Communist activities in the Philadelphia area (parts III, IV). Feb. 16, 17, 1954.

Communist methods of infiltration (education) (part VIII). April 21, June 8, 1953; April 12, 1954.

Investigation of Communist activities in the Baltimore area (parts I-III). May 18, March 25, 26, 1954.

Investigation of Communist activities in the Chicago area (parts I-III). March 15, 16, April 29, 1954.

Investigation of Communist activities in the Albany, N.Y. area (parts III–VI). April 7–9, 1954.

Communism in the District of Columbia-Maryland area (testimony of Mary Stalcup Markward). June 11, 1951.

Investigation of Communist activities in the State of California parts I–X). Feb. 1, 24, March 1, April 12, 19–22, 1954. Sept. 11, 1953.

Investigation of Communist activities in the state of Michigan (parts I–V) (Detroit). April 28–30, May 3–5, 7, 1954.

Investigation of Communist activities in the state of Michigan (parts VI, VII) (Lansing). May 10, 11, 1954; June 8, 1953.

Investigation of Communist activities in the state of Michigan (parts VIII–X) (Flint). April 30, May 12–14, 1954.

Communist methods of infiltration (education) (part IX). June 28, 29, 1954.

Communist activities among youth groups (based on testimony of Harvey M. Matusow) (part II). July 12, 1954.

Investigation of Communist influence in the field of publications (*March of Labor*). July 8, 15, 1954.

Hearings regarding Communism in the District of Columbia (part III). July 14, 15, 1954.

Investigation of Communist activities in the Pacific Northwest area (part I). Oct. 3, 1952; March 16, May 28, June 2, 9, 1954.

Investigation of Communist activities in the Pacific Northwest area (parts II, III) (Seattle-Hartle). June 14, 15, 18, 1954.

Investigation of Communist activities in the Pacific Northwest area (parts IV–VIII) (Seattle). June 14–19, 1954.

Investigation of Communist activities in the Pacific Northwest area (parts IX, X) (Portland). June 18, 19, 1954.

Investigation of Communist activities in the Pacific Northwest area (part XI) (Appendix). June 14–19, 1954.

Investigation of Communist activities in the Philadelphia area (part V). July 30, 1954.

Investigation of Communist activities in the Dayton, Ohio, area (parts I–III). Sept. 13–15, 1954.

Investigation of Communist activities in the state of California (part XI). Sept. 17, 1954.

Investigation of Communist activities in the Dayton, Ohio, area (part IV). Nov. 17–19, 1954.

Investigation of Communist activities in the state of Michigan (parts XI–XII). Nov. 17–19, 1954.

Communist methods of infiltration (entertainment) (part II). Dec. 14, 1954.

Communist methods of infiltration (government-labor) (part IV). Jan. 13, Dec. 15, 1954.

Investigation of Communist activities in the state of Florida (parts I, II). Nov. 29, 30, Dec. 1, 1954.

House Report No. 1694. Organized Communism in the United States. May 28, 1954.

House Report No. 1192. Annual Report for 1953. Feb. 8, 1954.

Colonization of America's Basic Industries by the Communist Party of the U.S.A. Sept. 3, 1954.

Preliminary Report on Neo-Fascist and Hate Groups. Dec. 17, 1954.

The American Negro in the Communist Party. Dec. 22, 1954.

Report on the *March of Labor*. Dec. 22, 1954.

House Report No. 57. Annual Report for 1954. Feb. 16, 1955.

84th Congress

Investigation of Communist activities, New York area (part I) (testimony of Jean Muir). June 15, 1953.

Investigation of Communist activities in the Fort Wayne, Ind. area. Feb. 28, March 1, April 25, 1955.

Investigation of Communist activities, New York area (part II) (youth organizations). March 16, 1955.

Investigation of Communist activities in the Seattle, Wash. area (parts I, II). March 17–19, June 1, 2, 1955.

Investigation of Communist activities in the Milwaukee, Wis. area (parts I, II). March 28–30, May 3, 1955.

Investigation of Communist activities, New York area (parts III, IV). May 3–6, 1955.

Investigation of Communist activities in the Newark, N.J., area parts I, II). May 16–19, July 13, 1955.

Investigation of Communist activities, New York area (part V) (summer camps). July 25, 28, 29, Aug. 1, 1955.

Investigation of Communist activities in the Ohio area (testimony of Keve Bray). July 13, 1955.

Investigation of Communist activities in the Los Angeles, Calif. area (parts I–IV). June 27–30, July 1, 2, 1955.

Investigation of Communist activities in the San Diego, Calif. area. July 5, 6, 1955.

Investigation of Communist activities (The Committee to Secure Justice in the Rosenberg Case and affiliates) (parts I, II). Aug. 2–5, 1955.

Investigation of Communist activities, New York area (parts VI–VIII) (entertainment). Aug. 15–18, Oct. 14, 1955.

Investigation of Communist activities in the Los Angeles, Calif. area (part V). Oct. 13, 1955. (*Note:* Part VI of the Los Angeles hearings, held April 18–21, 25–29, 1955, were executive and have not been released).

Investigation of Communist infiltration of government (parts I, II). Dec. 13–15, 1955.

Investigation of Communist infiltration of government (parts III–V). Feb. 14–16, 21, 23, 24, 28, 29, March 1, 1956.

Investigation of Communist activities in the North Carolina area. March 12–14, 1956.

Investigation of Communist activities in the Los Angeles, Calif. area (part VII). April 16, 1956.

Investigation of Communist activities in the Los Angeles, Calif. area (part VIII) (testimony of Nikolai Khokhlov—thought control in Soviet art and literature; discontent of the Soviet people with Communist leadership). April 17, 1956.

Investigation of Communist activities in the Los Angeles, Calif. area (parts IX, X). April 19–21, 1956.

Investigation of Communist activities in the Rocky Mountain area (parts I, II). May 15–18, 1956.

Investigation of the unauthorized use of U.S. passports (parts I–IV). May 23–25, June 12–14, 21, 1956.

Investigation of Communist propaganda in the United States (part I) (foreign propaganda—entry and dissemination). June 13, 1956.

Investigation of Communist activities in the St. Louis, Mo. area (parts I–IV). June 2, 4–6, 8, 1956.

Investigation of Communist propaganda among prisoners of war in Korea (Save Our Sons Committee). June 18, 19, 1956.

Investigation of Communist infiltration of government (part VI). June 20, 28, 1956.

Investigation of so-called blacklisting in entertainment industry (report of the Fund for the Republic, Inc.) (parts I–III). July 10–13, 17, 18, 1956.

Investigation of Communist propaganda in the United States (part II) (foreign propaganda—entry and dissemination in Philadelphia, Pa., area). July 17, 1956.

Investigation of the award by the Fund for the Republic, Inc. (Plymouth Meeting, Pa.). July 18, 1956.

International Communism (testimony of Ernst Tillich). Sept. 10, 11, 1956.

Investigation of Communist activities in the New Haven, Conn., area (parts I, II). Sept. 24–26, 1956.

Investigation of Communist activities in the Los Angeles, Calif., area (part XI). Dec. 16, 1953; June 6, July 5, 1956.

Hearings on attempts at subversion and espionage by diplomatic personnel. May 10, 11, 1956.

Investigation of Communist activities in the Youngstown and northern Ohio areas. Nov. 26, 27, 1956.

Investigation of Communist propaganda in the United States (part III) (foreign propaganda—entry and dissemination in the San Francisco, Calif., area). Dec. 10, 11, 1956.

Communist political subversion (part I). Nov. 12–14, 28, Dec. 11, 13, 14, 1956.

Communist political subversion (part II) (appendix). Nov. 12–14, 28, Dec. 2–8, 11, 13, 14, 1956.

House Report No. 1648. Annual Report for 1955. Jan. 17, 1956.

House Report No. 2189. The Great Pretense—a symposium on anti-Stalinism and the 20th Congress of the Soviet Communist Party. May 21, 1956.

House Document No. 206. Trial by Treason—The National Committee to Secure Justice for the Rosenbergs and Morton Sobell. July 17, 1957.

House Document No. 226. Guide to Subversive Organizations and Publications (revised). Aug. 5, 1957.

House Report No. 53. Annual Report for 1956. Feb. 11, 1957.

International Communism (part I—revolt in the Satellites) (consultation). Oct. 29, 30, Nov. 1, 17, 20, 1956.

85th Congress

International Communist propaganda activities. Jan. 30, 1957.

International Communism—Red China and the Far East (testimony of Chiu-Yuan Hu). Feb. 1, 1957.

Investigation of Communist propaganda in the United States (part IV) (foreign propaganda—entry and dissemination in the New Orleans, La., area). Feb. 14, 1957.

Investigation of Communist activities in the New Orleans, La., area. Feb. 15, 1957.

Investigation of Communist activities in the New Haven, Conn., area (part III). Feb. 26, 27, 1957.

Investigation of Communist Propaganda in the United States (part V) (New York City area). March 12, 13, 1957.

Investigation of Communist propaganda in the United States (part VI) (New York area). March 14, 15, 1957.

Investigation of Communist propaganda in the United States (part VII) (Chicago, Ill., area). March 26, 27, 1957.

Investigation of Communism in the Metropolitan Music School, Inc., and related fields (part I). April 9, 10, 1957.

Investigation of Communism in the Metropolitan Music School, Inc., and related fields (part II). Feb. 7, 8, April 11, 12, 1957.

Investigation of Communist activities in the Baltimore, Md., area (part I). May 7, 8, 1957.

Investigation of Communist activities in the Baltimore, Md., area (part II). May 9, 1957.

Hearings held in San Francisco, Calif. (part I). June 18, 19, 1957.

Hearings held in San Francisco, Calif. (part II). June 20, 21, 1957.

Investigation of the unauthorized use of U.S. passports (part V). July 26, 1957.

Investigation of Communist activities in the Newark, N.J., area (supplemental). July 24, 1957.

Investigation of Communist penetration of communications facilities (part I). July 17–19, Aug. 2, 9, 1957.

Investigation of Communist propaganda in the United States (part VIII) (Buffalo, N.Y., area). Oct. 1, 1957.

Investigation of Communist activities in the Buffalo, N.Y., area (part I). Oct. 2, 1957.

Investigation of Communist activities in the Buffalo, N.Y., area (part II). Oct. 3, 4, 1957.

Investigation of Communist penetration of communications facilities (part II). Oct. 9, 1957.

Investigation of Soviet espionage. Oct. 7–9, Nov. 20, 1957.

Investigation of Soviet espionage (part II). Feb. 28, 1956; Feb. 25, 1958.

Investigation of Communist infiltration and propaganda activities in basic industry (Gary, Ind., area). Feb. 10, 11, 1958.

Investigation of Communist activities in the New England area part I). March 18, 1958.

Investigation of Communist activities in the New England area (part II). March 19, 1958.

Investigation of Communist activities in the New England area (part III). March 14, 20, 21, 1958.

Investigation of Communist propaganda in the United States (part IX) (student groups, distributors, and propagandists). June 11, 12, 1958.

Communism in the New York area (entertainment). June 18, 19, 1958, May 8, 1958; April 1, 1957.

Communist infiltration and activities in the South. July 29–31, 1958.

Communist infiltration and activities in Newark, N.J. Sept. 3–5, 1958.

International Communism (part II—revolt in the Satellites) (Horvath, Kiss). March 20, 1957.

International Communism (Communist control of Estonia) (August Rei). March 10, 1957.

International Communism (The Communist mind) (Frederick Charles Schwarz). May 29, 1957.

International Communism (Communist penetration of Malaya and Singapore) (Kuo-Shuen Chang). May 29, 1957.

Who Are They? (part I—Khrushchev and Bulganin). July 12, 1957.

Who Are They? (part II—Mao Tse-tung and Chou En-lai). Aug. 23, 1957.

Who Are They? (part III—Zhukov and Konev). Aug. 30, 1957.

Who Are They? (part IV—Ulbricht and Kadar). Sept., 1957.

Who Are They? (part V—Tito and Gomulka). Oct. 11, 1957.

Who Are They? (part VI—Kim Il Sung and Ho Chi Minh). Oct. 25, 1957.

Who Are They? (part VII—Thorez and Togliatti). Nov. 22, 1957.

Who Are They? (part VIII—Lombardo Toledano and Prestes). Feb. 21, 1958.

Who Are They? (part IX—Hoxha and Gheorghiu-Dej). Aug. 5, 1958.

House Report No. 1182. Communist Political Subversion (the campaign to destroy the security programs of the U.S. Government). Aug. 16, 1957.

International Communism (the Communist trade offensive) (Marcus, Emmet, De Rochefort). June 26, 1957.

The Ideological Fallacies of Communism (Fineberg, Sheen, Polling). Sept. 4, 25, Oct. 18, 1957.

Operation Abolition. Nov. 8, 1957.

International Communism (the present posture of the free world) (Constantine Brown). Oct. 21, 1957.

International Communism (espionage) (excerpts of consultation with counterspy Boris Morros). Aug. 16, 1957.

International Communism (Communist designs on Indonesia and the Pacific frontier) (Gen. Charles A. Willoughby). Dec. 16, 1957.

House Report No. 1360. Annual Report for 1957. Feb. 19, 1958.

The Erica Wallach Story. March 21, 1958.

The Communist Program for World Conquest (Gen. Albert C. Wedemeyer). Jan. 21, 1958.

Communist Psychological Warfare (brainwashing) (Edward Hunter). March 13, 1958.

Chronicle of Treason (reprint of series of articles by Rep. Francis E. Walter, appearing in the *Philadelphia Inquirer,* Sept. 29–Oct. 3, 1957). March 3–9, 1958.

House Report No. 1724. Organized Communism in the United States (revised). May 14, 1958.

International Communism (Communist propaganda activities in Canada) (Milan Jakubec). April 3, 1958.

Communist Psychological Warfare (thought control) (Constantin W. Boldyreff). April 7, 1958.

International Communism (Communist encroachment in the Far East) (Maj. Gen. Claire Lee Chennault). April 23, 1958.

What Is Behind the Soviet Proposal for a Summit Conference? (Dallin, Bouscaren, Atkinson, McNamara). April 30, 1958.

The Ideology of Freedom Versus the Ideology of Communism (Dr. Charles W. Lowry). June 5, 1958.

Communist Strategy of Protracted Conflict. (Strausz-Hupé, Cottrell, Dougherty). May 20, 1958.

The Irrationality of Communism (Dr. Gerhart Niemeyer). Aug. 8, 1958.

International Communism in Yugoslavia (the myth of "Titoism") (Dr. Alex N. Dragnich). Sept. 15, 1958.

House Document No. 119. Patterns of Communist Espionage. April 20, 1959.

House Document No. 187. Annual Report for 1958. March 9, 1959.

86th Congress

The Kremlin's espionage and terror organizations (testimony of Petr S. Deriabin). Released, March 17, 1959.

Southern California district of the Communist Party—structure, objectives, leadership (part I). Sept. 2, 3, 1958.

Southern California district of the Communist Party—structure, objectives, leadership (part II). Sept. 4, 5, 1958.

Southern California district of the Communist Party—structure, objectives, leadership (part III). Feb. 24, 25, 1959.

Current strategy and tactics of Communists in the United States (greater Pittsburgh area) (part I). March 10, 1959.

Problems of Security in industrial establishments holding defense contracts (greater Pittsburgh area) (part II). March 11, 1959.

Problems arising in cases of denaturalization and deportation of Communists (greater Pittsburgh area) (part III). March 12, 1959.

Communist infiltration of vital industries and current Communist techniques in the Chicago, Ill., area. May 5–7, 1959.

Passport security (part I) (testimony of Harry R. Bridges). April 21, 1959.

Passport security (part II). April 22–24, June 5, 1959.

The American National Exhibition, Moscow, July 1959. July 1, 1959.

Communist training operations (part I). July 21–22, 1959.

Testimony of Clinton Edward Jencks. July 22, 1959.

Testimony of Arnold Johnson, Legislative Director of the Communist Party, U.S.A. Sept. 22, 1959.

Western section of the southern California district of the Communist Party (part I). Oct. 20, 1959.

Western section of the southern California district of the Communist Party (part II). Oct. 21, 1959.

Western section of the southern California district of the Communist Party (part III). Oct. 22, 1959.

Issues presented by Air Reserve Center Training Manual. Feb. 25, 1960.

Communist training operations (Communist activities and propaganda among youth groups) (part II). Feb. 2, 3, 1960.

Communist training operations (Communist activities and propaganda among youth groups) (part III). Feb. 4, 5, March 2, 1960.

Communist activities among Puerto Ricans in New York City and Puerto Rico (New York City) (part I). Nov. 16, 17, 1959.

Communist activities among Puerto Ricans in New York City and Puerto Rico (San Juan) (part II). Nov. 18–20, 1959.

Communist espionage in the United States (testimony of Frantisek
   Tisler). Released, May 10, 1960.

Testimony of Anthony Krchmarek and Charles Musil. May 26, 1960.

Communist activities among seamen and on waterfront facilities
   (part I). June 6–8, 23, 1960.

Communist penetration of radio facilities (CONELRAD–Communications) (part I). Aug. 23, 24, 1960.

Testimony of Capt. Nikolai Fedorovich Artamonov (former Soviet
   naval officer). Sept. 14, 1960.

Northern California district of the Communist Party—structure, objectives, leadership (part I). May 12, 1960.

Northern California district of the Communist Party—structure, objectives, leadership (part II). May 13, 1960.

Northern California district of the Communist Party—structure, objectives, leadership (part III). May 14, June 10, 1960.

Northern California district of the Communist Party—structure, objectives, leadership (part IV) (appendix). May 12–14, June 10,
   1960.

House Report No. 41. Communist Legal Subversion (the role of the
   Communist lawyer). Feb. 23, 1959.

House Report No. 259. Report on the southern California district
   of the Communist Party—Structure, Objectives, Leadership,
   April 3, 1959.

Language as a Communist Weapon (Dr. Stefan T. Possony). March
   2, 1959.

Communist Persecution of Churches in Red China and Northern
   Korea. March 26, 1959.

Control of the Arts in the Communist Empire (Ivan P. Bahriany).
   June 3, 1959.

Who Are They? (part X—Karl Marx). Aug. 28, 1959.

Communist Lobbying Activities in the Nation's Capital. Sept. 3,
   1959.

The Communist Parcel Operation. Sept. 3, 1959.

Crimes of Khrushchev (part I). Sept. 4, 1959.

Crimes of Khrushchev (part II). Sept. 9–11, 1959.

Crimes of Khrushchev (part III). Sept. 10, 1959.

Crimes of Khrushchev (part IV). Sept. 21, 1959.

Crimes of Khrushchev (part V). Dec. 17, 1959.

Crimes of Khrushchev (part VI). Dec. 17, 1959.

Crimes of Khrushchev (part VII). Jan. 8, 1960.

House Document No. 336. Facts on Communism, Vol. I (The Communist Ideology). Feb. 9, 1960.

House Report No. 1251. Annual Report for 1959. Feb. 8, 1960.

Lest We Forget! A pictorial summary of Communism in action (Dr. Klaus Samuli Gunnar Romppanen). Jan. 13, 1960.

Communist Economic Warfare (Dr. Robert Loring Allen). April 6, 1960.

Communist Target—Youth: Communist infiltration and agitation tactics (J. Edgar Hoover). July, 1960.

Soviet "Justice": "showplace" prisoners versus real slave labor camps (Adam Joseph Galinski). April 4, 1960.

How the Chinese Reds Hoodwink Visiting Foreigners (Robert Loh). April 21, 1960.

House Report No. 2228. The Communist-Led Riots Against the House Committee on Un-American Activities in San Francisco, Calif., May 12–14, 1980. Oct. 7, 1960.

House Document No. 139. Facts on Communism, Vol. II (The Soviet Union, from Lenin to Khrushchev). April 13, 1961.

House Report No. 2237. Annual Report for 1960. Jan. 2, 1961.

87th Congress

Hearings related to H.R. 4700, to amend Section 11 of the Subversive Activities Control Act of 1950, as amended (The Fund for Social Analysis). May 31, June 7, Aug. 16, 1961.

Hearings relating to revision of H.R. 9120 and H.R. 5751, to amend the Subversive Activities Control Act of 1950. Sept. 13, 1961.

Manipulation of public opinion by organizations under concealed control of the Communist Party. (National Assembly for Democratic Rights and Citizens Committee for Constitutional Liberties) (parts I, II). Oct. 2, 3, 1961.

Communist penetration of radio facilities (CONELRAD—communications) (part II). Oct. 26, 27, Nov. 29, 1961.

Hearings on structure and organization of the Communist Party of the United States. Nov. 20–22, 1961.

Hearings relating to H.R. 9753, to amend section 3(7) and 5 (b) of the Internal Security Act of 1950, as amended, relating to employment of members of Communist organizations in certain defense facilities. Feb. 7, 1962.

Hearings relating to H.R. 10175, to accompany H.R. 11363, amending the Internal Security Act of 1950. March 15, 1962.

Testimony by and concerning Paul Corbin. Sept. 6, 13, Nov. 13, 27, 28, 1961; March 15, July 2, 1962.

Communist propaganda—and the truth about conditions in Soviet Russia (testimony of David P. Johnson). May 22, 1962.

"Intellectual freedom"—Red China style (testimony of Chi-chou Huang). May 24, 25, 1962.

Communist activities in the Cleveland, Ohio, area (parts I, II). June 4–7, 1962.

Communist outlets for the distribution of Soviet propaganda in the United States (parts I, II). May 9, 10, 17, July 11, 12, 1962.

Communist youth activities (Eighth World Youth Festival, Helsinki, Finland, 1962). April 25, 27, Oct. 4, 1962.

U.S. Communist Party assistance to foreign Communist governments (Medical Aid to Cuba Committee and Friends of British Guiana). Nov. 14, 15, 1961.

Communist activities in the peace movement (Women Strike for Peace and certain other groups). Dec. 11–13, 1962.

Rules of Procedure, Committee on Un-American Activities. Revised 1961.

House Report No. 25. U.S. Merchant Vessel and Waterfront Security Act of 1960. Feb. 23, 1961.

House Report No. 309. Amending the Subversive Activities Control Act of 1950 (parts I, II) (to accompany House Report No. 5751). April 26, Sept. 14, 1961.

House Report No. 309. Dissemination of Communist Propaganda in the United States (part II) (to accompany House Report No. 5751). Sept. 14, 1961.

Supplement to Cumulative Index to Publications of the Committee on Un-American Activities, 1950 through 1960. June, 1961.

House Report No. 1278. The Truth about the Film *Operation Abolition* (part I). Oct. 5, 1961.

House Report No. 1282. Manipulation of Public Opinion by Organizations Under Concealed Control of the Communist Party (National Assembly for Democratic Rights and Citizens Committee for Constitutional Liberties) (parts I, II). Nov. 30, 1961.

Guide to Subversive Organizations and Publications (and appendixes). Dec. 1, 1961.

House Report No. 1283. Communist Penetration of Radio Facilities (CONELRAD—communications). Dec. 5, 1961.

House Report No. 1278. The Truth about the Film *Operation Abolition* (part II). Dec. 27, 1961.

The New Role of National Legislative Bodies in the Communist Conspiracy. Dec. 30, 1961.

House Report No. 2559. Annual Report for 1961. Nov. 5, 1962.

House Report No. 1362. Publication in Federal Register of Lists of Defense Facilities. Feb. 19, 1962.

House Report No. 1665. Protection of Classified Information Released to U.S. Industry and Defense Contractors. June 28, 1962.

House Report No. 2120. Amending the Internal Security Act of 1950 to Provide for Maximum Personnel Security in the National Security Agency. Aug. 2, 1962.

Security Practices in the National Security Agency (defection of Bernon F. Mitchell and William H. Martin). Aug. 13, 1962.

The Communist Party's Cold War Against Congressional Investigation of Subversion. Oct. 10, 1962.

Communist and Trotskyist Activity Within the Greater Los Angeles Chapter of the Fair Play for Cuba Committee. Nov. 2, 1962.

House Report No. 176. Annual Report for 1962. Jan. 2, 1963.

88th Congress

U.S. Communist Party assistance to foreign Communist governments (testimony of Maud Russell). March 6, 1963.

"United front" technique of the southern California district of the Communist Party. April 24–27, 1962.

Violations of State Department travel regulations and pro-Castro propaganda activities in the United States (part I). May 6, 7, 23, 1963.

Violations of State Department travel regulations and pro-Castro propaganda activities in the United States (part II). July 1, 2, Aug. 5, 1963.

U.S. Communist Party assistance to foreign Communist parties (Veterans of the Abraham Lincoln Brigade). July 29, 1963.

Violations of State Department travel regulations and pro-Castro propaganda activities in the United States (part III). Sept. 12, 13, 1963.

Defection of a Russian seaman (testimony of Vladislaw Stepanovich Tarasov). Sept. 19, 1963.

Violations of State Department travel regulations and pro-Castro
propaganda activities in the United States (part IV). Oct. 16,
Nov. 18, 1963.

Hearings on bills providing for creation of a Freedom Commission
and Freedom Academy (part I). Feb. 18, 19, 1964.

Hearings on bills providing for creation of a Freedom Commission
and Freedom Academy (part II). Feb. 20, April 7, 8, May 19,
20, 1964.

Communist activities in the Buffalo, N.Y., area. April 29, 30, 1964.

Communist activities in the Minneapolis, Minn., area. June 24–26,
1964.

Testimony of the Rev. James H. Robinson. May 5, 1964.

Violations of State Department travel regulations and pro-Castro
propaganda activities in the United States (part V). Sept. 3, 4,
28, 1964.

House Report No. 631. "United Front" Technique of the southern
California district of the Communist Party. July 31, 1963.

House Report No. 108. Amending the Internal Security Act of 1950
to Provide for Maximum Personnel Security in the National
Security Agency. March 13, 1963.

World Communist Movement: Selective Chronology, 1818–1957;
Vol. II, 1946–1950.

House Report No. 1739. Annual Report for 1963. Aug. 10, 1964.

A Communist in a "Workers' Paradise" (John Santo's own story).
March 1, 4, 5, 1963.

World Communist Movement: Selective Chronology, 1818–1957;
Vol. III, 1951–1953.

House Report No. 971. Annual Report for 1964. Sept. 9, 1965.

89th Congress

Hearings on bills providing for creation of a Freedom Commission
and Freedom Academy. March 31, April 1, 28, May 7, 14, 1965.

Communist activities in the Chicago, Illinois, area (parts I, II).
May 25–27, June 22, 1965.

Testimony of Juanita Castro Ruz. June 11, 1965.

Testimony of Wladyslaw Tykocinski. April 6, 1966.

Hearings on bills to make punishable assistance to enemies of the
U.S. in time of undeclared war (part I). Aug. 16–19, 1966.

Hearings on bills to make punishable assistance to enemies of the

U.S. in time of undeclared war (part II). Aug. 19, 22, 23, 1966.

Hearings on bills to curb terrorist organizations. July 20–22, 1966.

Activities of Ku Klux Klan organizations in the United States (part I). Oct. 19–22, 25, 1965.

Activities of Ku Klux Klan organizations in the United States (part II). Oct. 26–28, Nov. 1–4, 9, 1965.

Hearings regarding bills to curb terrorist organizations, July 20–22, 1966.

World Communist Movement: Selective Chronology, 1818–1957; Vol. IV, 1954–1955.

House Report No. 629. Freedom Commission and Freedom Academy. July 20, 1965.

Rules of Procedure, Revised. Sept. 14, 1965.

House Report No. 1928. Annual Report for 1965. Aug. 31, 1966.

House Report No. 1908. Obstruction of the Armed Forces. Aug. 29, 1966.

House Report No. 2335. Organizational Conspiracies Act of 1966. Oct. 21, 1966.

House Report No. 460. Annual Report for 1966. June 28, 1967.

90th Congress

Communist Origin and Manipulation of Vietnam Week (April 8–15, 1967). March 31, 1967.

House Report No. 326. Obstruction of the Armed Forces. May 31, 1967.

House Report No. 648. Organizational Conspiracies Act of 1967. Sept. 19, 1967.

House Report No. 733. Internal Security Act of 1950—Amendments. Oct. 4, 1967.

Notes

H refers to hearings before the Committee on Un-American Activities
R refers to reports of the Committee
C.R. refers to the Congressional Record

CHAPTER ONE

PAGE

4 ff. See Telford Taylor's *Grand Inquest* (New York, 1955) for a critical history of Congressional investigations, with particular reference to the Committee on Un-American Activities.

5 Frankfurter on investigations: *New Republic*, May 21, 1924, p. 329.

5 1919 investigation: U. S. Sen., 65th Cong., 3d sess. *Bolshevik Propaganda*—Hearings before a Subcommittee of the Judiciary. U. S. Sen., 66th Cong., 1st sess. *Brewing and Liquor Interests and German and Bolshevik Propaganda*—Report of the Subcommittee of the Judiciary.

6 ff. 1930 investigation: Debate—*C.R.*, May 22, 1930, pp. 9390 ff. Hearings—U. S. Cong., House, 71st Cong., 2d sess. Special Committee to Investigate Communism in the United States. Report—U. S. Cong., House, 71st Cong., 3d sess. Special Committee on Communist Activities in the United States—*Investigation of Communist Propaganda*.

7 (fn) Wilson on depression: *New Republic*, Jan. 14, 1931, p. 234.

7 Wilson on Fish: *New Republic*, Dec. 24, 1930, p. 58.

8 (fn) Foster on Comintern: Quoted in Howe and Coser: *The American Communist Party* (New York, 1962), p. 154.

10 ff. 1934 investigation: Debate—*C.R.*, March 20, 1934, pp. 4938 ff. Hearings—U. S. Cong., House, 73d Cong., 2d sess. Special Committee on Un-American Activities—*Investigation of Nazi Propaganda*. Report—U. S. Cong., House, 74th Cong., 1st sess. Special Committee on Un-American Activities—*Investigation of Nazi and Other Propaganda*. See also Howard M. Kline: *Some Practices of Congressional Investigating Committees*, p. 340 (Unpublished doctoral thesis, School of Citizenship and Public Affairs, Syracuse University, 1937).

11 Dickstein on camp: *N. Y. Times*, Aug. 24, 1934, p. 6.

12 Schlesinger on 1935: *The Politics of Upheaval* (Boston, 1939), p. 69.

12 Wilson on "informing function": *Congressional Government* (New York, 1900), p. 203.

13 Lippmann on "good precedents": *Forum*, Sept. 1930, p. 129.

13 Frankfurter on safeguards: *New Republic*, May 21, 1924, p. 329.

13 ff. Dickstein on Committee: *C.R.*, Jan. 21, 1937, p. 6106.

14 ff. Dickstein on Bundists: *C.R.*, April 27, 1938, p. 5881; *N. Y. Times*, May 23, 1938, p. 5.

18 ff. Dickstein–Cochran–Maverick debate: *C.R.*, Dec. 21, 1937, pp. 2031 ff.

20 Shannon on "foreign-born citizen": *Congressional Digest*, Nov. 1939, p. 282.

21 ff. Dies resolution debate: *C.R.*, May 26, 1938, pp. 7568 ff.

CHAPTER TWO

PAGE

24 ff. See August Raymond Ogden's *The Dies Committee* (Washington, D. C., 1945) for a dispassionate survey of the Committee's activities from 1938 to 1944.

25 La Follette on Communists: *Collier's*, Feb. 8, 1947, p. 22.

25 ff. Thomas on Federal Theatre: *N. Y. Times*, July 27, 1938, p. 19.

26 Viereck subpoena: *N. Y. Times*, Aug. 4, 1938, p. 1.

26 Dies on radio: *N. Y. Times*, Aug. 10, 1938, p. 6.

26 ff. Dies before hearing: *H.*, Aug. 12, 1938, p. 2.

28 Metcalf hearing: *H.*, Aug. 12, 1938, pp. 3 ff.

28 Frey headlines: *N. Y. Times*, Aug. 14, 1938, p. 1.

28 ff. Historian on Frey hearings (Jerold S. Auerbach): *Journal of American History*, Dec. 1964, p. 435.

29 (fn) *New Republic* editorial: Nov. 13, 1939, p. 301.

29 Frey hearings: *H.*, Aug. 13, 15, 16, 1938, pp. 91 ff.

29 Sullivan report: *N. Y. Times*, Aug. 15, 1938, p. 1.

29 ff. Steele hearings: *H.*, Aug. 6, 17, 1938, pp. 277 ff.

30 ff. Poll: *N. Y. Daily News*, Oct. 31, 1938, p. 4.

31 Dobrzynski hearing: *H.*, Nov. 15, 1938, pp. 2207 ff.

32 Frey on industrial workers: Quoted in Howe and Coser: *American Communist Party*, p. 239.

32 T.W.U. witness: *H.*, Sept. 16, 1938, p. 1039.

32 *P. O. Quarterly*: April 1939, p. 235.

32 Thomas question: *P. O. Quarterly*, April 1939, p. 237.

33 Dies on Sullivan report: Ogden: *Dies Committee*, p. 58.

33 Frey on Brophy: *H.*, Aug. 16, 1938, p. 268.

34 Woll on Dewey: *H.*, Nov. 22, 1938, p. 2437.

34 J. Roosevelt church contributions: *H.*, Dec. 6, 1938, p. 2836.

35 Jemison hearing: *H.*, Nov. 22, 1938, p. 2435.

35 Ickes on Jemison: *The Secret Diary of Harold Ickes* (New York, 1954), Vol. 2, p. 506.

35 Dies on smears: *N. Y. Times*, Feb. 12, 1939, IV, p. 12.

35 ff. Dies autobiography: *Martin Dies Story* (New York, 1963), p. 67.

36 Howlers: See *N. Y. Times*, Nov. 6, 1938, IV, p. 10.

36 Starnes on Marlowe: *H.*, Dec. 6, 1938, p. 2857.

36 ff. For Matthews's apologia, see *Odyssey of a Fellow Traveller* (New York, 1938), published by John Cecil Rovere, head of the National Immigration Board, whose mission it was to keep refugees from Nazism out of this country because they were all Reds.

38 (fn) Madison Square Garden meeting: See Howe and Coser: *American Communist Party*, pp. 299 ff.

38 Matthews on big business: See J. B. Matthews and R. E. Shallcross: *Partners in Plunder* (New York, 1935).

40 Shirley Temple: *H.*, Aug. 22, 1938, p. 918.

40 (fn) Ickes and Perkins: *N. Y. Times*, Aug. 31, 1938, p. 1.

40 Kempton on fronts: *Part of Our Time* (New York, 1955), p. 154.

41 Consumers Research quotes: *Consumers Digest*, Feb. 1938. Quoted in George Seldes: *Witch Hunt* (New York, 1940), p. 136.

42 Matthews quotes: *Odyssey*, pp. 183, 267, 34.; *N. Y. Times*, Aug. 22, 1938, p. 2.; Kempton: *Part of Our Time*, p. 175.

43 Thomas on Federal Theatre: *N. Y. Times*, Aug. 10, 1938, p. 6.

43 (fn) Workers Alliance: *H.*, Sept. 15, 1938, p. 1007.

44 Federal Theatre hearings: *H.*, Aug. 19, 20, 22, 1938, pp. 775 ff.

44 Woodward–Flanagan hearings: *H.*, Dec. 5, 6, 1938, pp. 2729 ff. For Mrs. Flanagan's story of Federal Theatre, see *Arena* (New York, 1940).

PAGE

44 (fn) Woodward on "capitalistic press": *H.*, Dec. 5, 1938, p. 2807.
45 Rovere on Communist culture: Quoted in Kempton: *Part of Our Time*, p. 197.
45 Critic on Federal Theatre: *Commonweal*, July 14, 1939, p. 300.
45 (fn) Dirksen on Federal Theatre: *C.R.*, June 16, 1939, p. 7373.
46 Lavery on Federal Theatre: *Commonweal*, Aug. 4, 1939, p. 351.
47 Strecker case: 307 U.S. 22 (1940).
48 Bridges case: 326 U.S. 135 (1945).
48 Knowles hearings: *H.*, Oct. 24–26, 1938, pp. 1717 ff.
49 Minnesota hearings: *H.*, Oct. 17, 18, 1938, pp. 1359 ff.
49 Dies on "expedience": *N. Y. Times*, Oct. 18, 1939, p. 11.
49 Gadola–Barringer hearings: *H.*, Oct 21, 22, 1938, pp. 1674 ff.
50 Murphy defense: *N. Y. Times*, Oct 22, 1938, p. 1.
50 Dies on Murphy: *Martin Dies Story*, p. 124.
50 ff. F.D.R. on Murphy: *N. Y. Times*, Oct. 26, 1938, p. 1.
51 Dies pledge: *N. Y. Times*, p. 13.
52 Krock on election: *N. Y. Times*, Nov. 10, 1938, p. 15.
52 Dies on F.D.R.: *Martin Dies Story*, p. 138.
52 Ickes on Dies: *Secret Diary*, Vol. 2, p. 570.
52 ff. "Supreme Shouter": *N. Y. Times*, June 27, 1937, p. 20.
53 *Collier's*: Jan. 14, 1939, p. 50.
54 Ickes v. Dies: *Secret Diary*, Vol. 2, p. 504. *N. Y. Times*, Nov. 14, 1938, p. 12; Nov. 21, 1938, p. 1.
54 (fn) Ickes: *Autobiography of a Curmudgeon*, (New York, 1943), p. 298.
54 "Loaded Dies": *Secret Diary*, Vol. 2, p. 546; *N. Y. Times*, Jan. 17, 1939, p. 1.
55 First report: *R.*, Jan. 3, 1939.
55 Thomas on Perkins: *C.R.*, Jan. 24, 1939, pp. 702 ff.
55 Dies allocation: *C.R.*, Feb 3, 1939, p. 1128.
55 Ickes on Democrats: *Autobiography*, p. 573.
55 Rayburn on Dies: Quoted in *American*, May 1940, p. 22.
56 ff. *New Republic:* June 15, 1938, p. 144; Aug. 2, 1938, p. 50.
57 *Nation:* Aug. 27, 1938, p. 198.
57 Lawyers petition: *The Dies Committee—A Review of Its Proceedings.* Memo and Petition by Members of the American Bar to the Members of the House of Representatives, 1939.
57 Hook–Kirchwey: *Nation*, May 27, 1939, p. 603.
58 *New Republic:* June 15, 1938, p. 144.

CHAPTER THREE

59 Dies on fascists: N.B.C., Aug. 8, 1938; printed in *Vital Speeches*, Sept. 15, 1938, p. 731.
59 ff. Moseley case: *N. Y. Times*, May 19, 1939, p. 1.
60 For a round-up of the headlines, see *Nation*, June 3, 1939, p. 61.
61 ff. Moseley hearings: *H.*, May 22–24, 31, June 1, 1939, pp. 3285 ff.
61 Moseley call: *N. Y. Times*, May 21, 1939, p. 28.
62 Moseley speech: *H.*, May 31, 1939, p. 28.
63 ff. First Kuhn hearing: *H.*, Aug. 16, 1939, pp. 3705 ff.
64 Bundist testimony: *H.*, Aug. 18, 1939, pp. 3891 ff.
64 Second Kuhn hearing: *H.*, Oct. 19, 1939, pp. 6043 ff.
64 Ogden on pact: *Dies Committee*, p. 129.
64 ff. Browder on Nazi–Soviet agreement: Earl Browder: *Fighting for Peace* (New York, 1939); quoted in Howe and Coser: *Am. Communist Party*, p. 387.

PAGE

65 ff. Browder hearing: *H.*, Sept. 5, 1939, pp. 4275 ff.

66   Hardman on C.P.: *New Republic*, Sept 17, 1930, pp. 122 ff.

67   Kazin on pact: *Starting Out in the Thirties* (Boston, 1965), p. 141.

67   Gitlow hearing: *H.*, Sept. 7–9, 1939, pp. 4529 ff.; Oct. 17, 1939, pp. 5981 ff.

67 ff. Krivitsky hearing: *H.*, Oct. 11, 1939, pp. 5719 ff.

68   Foster hearing: *H.*, Sept. 29, 1939, pp. 5323 ff.

69   Hicks resignation: *New Republic*, Oct. 4, 1939, p. 244.

69   Cameron on pact: *The Listener*, Oct. 21, 1965, p. 213.

70 ff. Ward hearing: *H.*, Oct 23, 1939, pp. 6213 ff.

70   Coffee on Ward: *C.R.*, Oct. 25, 1939, p. 879.

71   A.L.P.D. list: *N. Y. Times*, Oct 26, 1939, p. 1.

72   A.L.P.D. statement: *N. Y. Times*, Oct. 29, 1939, p. 27.

72   (fn) *Daily Worker*, Nov. 5, 1956; cited in Howe and Coser: *Am. Communist Party*, p. 496.

72   Baldwin on Communists: *New Republic*, March 18, 1940, p. 372.

72   (fn) A.L.P.D. Christmas card: *N. Y. Times*, Dec. 10, 1939, p. 1. For the debate in Congress on release of the A.L.P.D. list, see *C.R.*, Oct. 25, 1939, p. 485.

73   *Nation* on A.L.P.D.: Nov. 4, 1939, p. 485.

74   A.L.P.D. statement: *N. Y. Times*, Oct. 26, 1939, p. 14.

74   *New Republic* on Communists: Aug. 31, 1938, p. 90.

75   Dies v. Administration: "sordid procedure"—*N. Y. Times*, Oct. 28, 1939, p. 1; "grieved and pained"—*N. Y. Times*, Oct. 29, 1939, p. 22; 2,850 "known Communists"—*N. Y. Times*, Sept. 27, 1939, p. 1; F.D.R. on Dies —*N. Y. Times*, Sept. 30, 1939, p. 8; Thomas on Murphy—*N. Y. Times*, Oct. 23, 1939, p. 1; "most inappropriate"—*N. Y. Times*, Oct. 24, 1939, p. 12; Ickes on Murphy—*Secret Diary*, Vol. 3, p. 54.

76 ff. Curran hearings: *H.*, Oct. 28, 30, Nov. 2, 3, 1939, pp. 6457 ff.

77   Kempton on Curran: *Part of Our Time*, p. 86.

77 ff. Youth hearings: *H.*, Nov. 27, 29, 30, Dec. 1, 2, 1939, pp. 6829 ff.

78   Howe and Coser on A.Y.C.: *Am. Communist Party*, p. 359. A more favorable, more ingenuous picture of the A.Y.C. may be found in *American Youth Today* by Leslie A. Gould (New York, 1940), to which Mrs. Roosevelt contributed a strained foreword.

79   Mrs. Roosevelt on youths: *N. Y. Times*, Dec. 5, 1939, p. 8.

80 ff. Lash hearing, 1939: *H.*, Dec. 1, 1939, pp. 7062 ff.

80   *My Day* on Lash hearing: Quoted in *N. Y. Times*, Dec. 3, 1939, p. 34.

81 ff. A.S.U. meeting: *N. Y. Times*, Dec. 31, 1939, p. 11.

82   Lash hearing, 1942: *H.*, Jan. 21, 1942, pp. 2787 ff.

82   Dies on Lash on army: *N. Y. Times*, Jan. 24, 1942, p. 19.

82 ff. Dies on Lash: *U. S. News*, August 20, 1954, p. 56; Aug. 27, 1954, p. 95.

83   Dies on Trotsky and Rivera: *N. Y. Times*, Dec. 7, 1939, p. 22. On deportations: *N. Y. Times*, Dec. 25, 1939, p. 10.

83   Lovestone hearing: *H.*, Dec. 2, 1939, pp. 7096 ff.

84   Matthews on C.U.: *N. Y. Herald Tribune*, Dec. 11, 1939, p. 1.

84   Voorhis on Matthews: *N. Y. Times*, Dec. 12, 1939, p. 1.

85   *Business Week* on consumer movement: Dec. 10, 1939, p. 17.

85   For background on the C.U. report, see *C.R.*, Jan. 23, 1940, p. 601, and *N. Y. Times*, Dec. 12, 1939, p. 22.

85   (fn) Matthews on *Good Housekeeping: Partners in Plunder*, p. 50.

85 ff. Annual report, background: *Nation*, Jan. 13, 1940, pp. 36 ff.

86   Annual report: *R.*, Jan. 3, 1940.

86   (fn) Carey on U.E.: *C.R.*, Jan. 23, 1940, p. 583.

86   *N. Y. Times* editorial: Jan. 5, 1940, p. 18.

87 ff. House debate: *C.R.*, Jan. 23, 1940, pp. 572 ff.

PAGE

87 Gallup poll: *N. Y. Times,* Dec. 15, 1939, p. 21.
87 Dies speech: *N. Y. Times,* Jan. 7, 1940, p. 13.
88 Appropriation: *C.R.,* Jan. 25, 1940, p. 688.

CHAPTER FOUR

89 *Nation* on Christian Fronters: Jan. 27, 1940, pp. 89 ff.
89 ff. Pegler on Coughlin: *N. Y. World Telegram,* Jan. 23, 1940, p. 17.
90 Dies at rally: *Vital Speeches,* Dec. 15, 1939, pp. 152 ff. Delivered at "Mass Meeting for America" in Madison Square Garden, Nov. 29, 1939.
90 ff. Rules Committee: *N. Y. Times,* Jan. 23, 1940, p. 1.
91 *Nation* exposé: Jan. 27, 1940, p. 1.
91 Pelley booklet: *The Suppressed Speech of Maj. Gen. Moseley,* North Carolina, 1939.
92 Harold Weisberg: He has lately reappeared as the author of several books attacking the credibility of the Warren Report. See *Whitewash* (New York, 1965).
92 Pelley on "sucker": *N. Y. Sun,* Feb. 3, 1940, p. 17.
92 Stripling on forgery: *The Red Plot Against America* (Drexel Hill, Pa., 1949), p. 33.
92 ff. Hook on forgery: *N. Y. Times,* Feb. 1, 1940, p. 10; Feb. 4, 1940, p. 15; Feb. 7, 1940, p. 1. *C.R.,* Feb. 13, 1941, p. A637.
93 *Nation* on scoop: Feb. 10, 1940, p. 147; Feb. 17, 1940, p. 240.
93 (fn) Dies on conspiracy: *Martin Dies Story,* p. 115.
94 Stripling on Pelley: *Red Plot,* p. 34.
94 Pelley hearing: *H.,* Feb. 7, 1940, pp. 7201 ff.
94 Pelley on Dies: *N. Y. Sun,* Feb. 6, 1940, p. 3.
95 Dies on Communists: *N. Y. Times,* March 27, 1940, p. 13.
95 ff. Dies on C.P. raid: *U. S. News,* Aug. 20, 1954, p. 67.
96 C.P. raid decision: 33 F. Supp. 619.
96 Dies on decision: *N. Y. Times,* May 4, 1940, p. 6; April 6, 1940, p. 4.
96 ff. C.P. officials hearings: *H.,* March 25, 28, 29, April 3, 4, 1940, pp. 7335 ff.
97 Contempt cases: For a review of the Committee's contempt cases from these early ones up to the mid-1950's, see Carl Beck's *Contempt of Congress* (New Orleans, 1957).
98 Ogden on publicity: *Dies Committee,* p. 201.
98 ff. Celler on "dose of salts": *C.R.,* June 22, 1940, p. 9036.
99 (fn) Marcantonio on Smith Act: *C.R.,* June 22, 1940, p. 9034. See also Howe and Coser: *Am. Communist Party,* p. 418.
99 Abraham Lincoln Brigade hearings: *H.,* April 23, 24, May 8, 1940, pp. 7727 ff.
99 ff. Union hearings: *H.,* April 23, 24, May 8, 1940, pp. 7892 ff. Quill quotes —pp. 8093, 8106, 8111.
101 Leech hearing: *H.:.* July 16, 1940, pp. 927 ff.
102 Actors' testimony: See *Executive Hearings,* Aug. 16, 17, 20, 26, 27, 1940.
102 Rankin on actors: *C.R.,* March 6, 1946, p. A1150.
102 (fn) Havenner case: San Francisco *Chronicle,* Oct. 30, 1944, p. 7. For Havenner's recital of the facts, see *C.R.,* Jan. 11, 1945, p. 206.
102 ff. Dorothy Parker speech: *Directions,* April 1940, p. 4.
103 ff. Patman—Byoir hearings: *H.,* Aug. 29, 1940, pp. 8164 ff.; Aug. 11, 1941, pp. 8829 ff.
104 ff. Dies speech: *C.R.,* May 17, 1940, p. 6295.

PAGE

105 ff. Quotes on saboteurs: Dies—*N. Y. Times,* Oct. 19, 1940, p. 4; chemist—*H.,* Oct. 1, 1940, pp. 8232 ff.; Starnes: *N. Y. Times,* Oct. 3, 1940, p. 1; Dies on lists—*N. Y. Times,* Oct. 22, 1940, p. 13; Hercules plant—*N. Y. Times,* Sept. 18, 1940, p. 25.
105   Willkie on Committee: *New Republic,* March 18, 1940, pp. 370 ff.
105 ff. Dies on Willkie and F.D.R.: *N. Y. Times,* Aug. 28, 1940, p. 21; on sabotage—*N. Y. Times,* Nov. 13, 1940, pp. 1, 4.
107 ff. Sumners on foreigners: *C.R.,* Nov. 25, 1940, p. 13738.
108   Voorhis on "totalitarian state of mind": *C.R.,* Nov. 25, 1940, p. 13736.
109 ff. White Book—including Zapp quotes: *Appendix II,* 1940.
109   *N. Y. Times* editorial: Nov. 23, 1940, p. 8.
110   Jackson charge: *N. Y. Times,* Nov. 24, 1940, p. 1.
110   Dickstein on Fassbender: *C.R.,* Jan. 21, 1941, p. 214.
110 ff. Dies on Jackson: *N. Y. Times,* Nov. 24, 1940, p. 32.
111   Dies on strikes: *N. Y. Times,* Nov. 27, 1940, p. 12.
111 ff. Dies—F.D.R. exchange: *N. Y. Times,* Nov. 26, 1940, p. 14. *C.R.,* Feb. 11, 1941, p. 895; Nov. 18, 1941, p. 9203. *Newsweek,* Dec. 9, 1940, p. 15. *U. S. News,* Aug. 20, 1954, p. 58. *Martin Dies Story,* p. 143.
113   Dies on million dollars: *N. Y. Times,* Nov. 30, 1940, p. 9. On "personal relief"—*N. Y. Times,* Dec. 3, 1940, p. 1.
113   Gallup poll: *N. Y. Times,* Dec. 4, 1940, p. 19.
113 ff. Dies—F.B.I. exchange: *New York Times,* Dec. 1, 1940, p. 47; Dec. 11, 1940, p. 17; Dec. 17, 1940, p. 1.
114 ff. Bund report: *Appendix IV,* 1941
115   Kunze hearing: *H.,* Oct. 1, 1940, pp. 8251 ff.
115   (fn) K.K.K. hearing: *H.,* Oct. 2, 1940, p. 8313.
115   Axis report: *Appendix III,* 1941.
115 ff. Annual report: *R.,* 1941.
117   Committee extension: *C.R.,* Feb. 11, 1941, pp. 886 ff.

CHAPTER FIVE

118   Ogden on Committee: *Dies Committee,* p. 249.
118   Filene and I.P.A.: Edward L. Bernays: *Biography of an Idea* (New York, 1965).
119   I.P.A. retort: *N. Y. Times,* Feb. 23, 1941, p. 116.
119   *Mr. Dies Goes to Town: Propaganda Analysis,* Jan. 14, 1940, pp. 43 ff.
120 ff. S.W.O.C.—Dies v. Murray: *C.R.,* March 24, 1941, pp. A1352 ff.; March 26, 1941, pp. A1423 ff. and 2574 ff.; March 31, 1941, pp. A1509 ff.
122   Dies on campaign: *Martin Dies Story,* pp. 78 ff.; *N. Y. Times,* July 11, 1941, p. 8.
123   A.P.M. Hearings: *H.,* May 21, 22, 1941, pp. 8391 ff.
124   Dies on Hitler and Stalin: *N. Y. Times,* June 24, 1941, p. 3; Oct. 20, 1941, p. 1.
125   O.P.A.—Dies v. Henderson: *C.R.,* Aug. 8, 1941, pp. 6926 ff.; *N. Y. Times,* Sept. 8, 1941, p. 1. *C.R.,* Nov. 28, 1941, pp. 9201 ff.
126   Brady on socialism: Quoted in *C.R.,* Nov. 25, 1941, pp. 9211 ff.
127   Dies—Watson: *C.R.,* Nov. 28, 1941, pp. 9201 ff. *N. Y. Times,* Nov. 27, 1941, p. 22.
127   F.C.C. on Dies: *Newsweek,* Jan. 5, 1942, p. 7; *C.R.,* Feb. 12, 1942, p. A505.
127 ff. Dies on Cowley: *C.R.,* Jan. 15, 1942, pp. 407 ff.
128   Dies on O.C.D.: *N. Y. Times,* Feb. 9, 1942, p. 9.
129   (fn) Dies on Japan: Quoted in *C.R.,* March 11, 1942, p. 2296.
129   Yellow paper: *Appendix VI,* 1942.

129   Voorhis on Yellow Paper: *C.R.*, Feb. 24, 1942, p. A726.

129 ff. Eliot–Dies–Marcantonio: *C.R.*, March 4, 1942, pp. 1921 ff.; March 6, 1942, pp. 2030 ff.; March 7, 1942, pp. 2055 ff. and A880 ff.

131   Debates on Committee: *C.R.*, March 11, 1942, pp. 2282 ff.; March 30, 1942, pp. 3216 ff.; Vote—April 28, 1942, p. 3754.

131 ff. Dies–Wallace: *N. Y. Times*, March 30, 1942, p. 1.

132   (fn) *New Republic:* April 6, 1942, p. 445.

132   Dies on defense agencies: *C.R.*, Jan. 15, 1942, p. 409.

132 ff. Cox on Parmalee: *C.R.*, March 30, 1942, p. 3204.

133 ff. Vaughn case: *C.R.*, March 30, 1942, pp. 3213 ff.; July 9, 1942, p. A2876. *N. Y. Times*, July 19, 1942, p. 24. *C.R.*, Feb. 18, 1943, p. 1110.

134   U.D.A. report: R. #2277, *Special Report on Subversive Activities Aimed at Destroying Our Representative Form of Government*, 1942.

134 ff. *New Republic* supplement: May 18, 1942.

135   Dies on subversives: *N. Y. Times*, June 24, 1941, p. 3; Oct. 20, 1941, p. 1.

136   Attorney General's report: U. S. Cong., House, 77th Cong., 2d sess. Document No. 833—*Report of the Federal Bureau of Investigation*, Sept. 3, 1943.

136 ff. Dies reply: *C.R.*, Sept. 24, 1942, pp. 7441 ff.

137   (fn) Cushman: *American Political Science Review*, Feb. 1943, p. 47.

137   Annual report: Part One, June 25, 1942. Part Two (dissent), July 7, 1942.

137 ff. Thomas on whitewash: *C.R.*, Jan. 8, 1943, p. 60.

138   Axis report: *Appendix VII*, 1943.

138   Ickes on Voorhis: *Secret Diary*, Vol. 3, p. 379.

138   *Nation* supplement: Oct. 3, 1942.

138 ff. Voorhis on rules: *C.R.*, Feb. 8, 1943, p. 724; Feb. 10, 1943, p. 807.

139 ff. Dies–Rogers: *C.R.*, Feb 1, 1943, pp. 474 ff.

140   Hendricks amendment: *C.R.*, Feb. 5, 1943, pp. 645 ff.

142   Treasury Dept. on Pickens: *N. Y. Times*, Feb. 7, 1943, p. 20.

142 ff. Pickens debates (including Hoffman quote): *C.R.*, Feb. 8, 1943, pp. 697 ff.; Feb. 9, 1943, pp. 732 ff.

144 ff. Kerr Committee: U. S. Cong., 78th Cong., 1st sess. Special Subcommittee of the Committee on Appropriations: *Hearings on the Fitness for Continuation in Federal Employment of G. B. Watson and W. E. Dodd, Employees of the F.C.C., and Robert Morss Lovett, an Employee of the Department of the Interior.*

145   Dies on Dodd: *Martin Dies Story*, p. 168.

146 ff. Lovett: See his autobiography, *All Our Years* (New York, 1948), written, incidentally, in the Ridgefield, Connecticut, home of Martha Dodd Stern.

147   Ickes on Lovett: *All Our Years*, pp. 346 and 291.

147 ff. Lovett quotes: *H.*, April 16, 1943, p. 3522. *All Our Years*, pp. 302 and 291.

148 ff. Watson–Dodd–Lovett debate: *C.R.*, May 18, 1943, pp. 4581 ff.

149   McKellar on "unjust provision": *C.R.*, May 26, 1943, p. 6407.

149 ff. Dirksen on bureaucracy: *C.R.*, May 17, 1943, p. 4552.

150   F.D.R. on "unwarranted encroachment": *N. Y. Times*, July 14, 1943, p. 1, and *C.R.*, Sept. 14, 1943, p. 7521.

150   Courtney–Hoffman: *C.R.*, Feb. 8, 1943, p. 698.

150 ff. Watson–Dodd–Lovett case: For a partisan, yet illuminating analysis of the constitutional issues, see "participant-observer" Frederick L. Schuman's article in *American Political Science Review*, Oct. 1943, pp. 819 ff.

151 ff. Court decisions: 66 F. Supp. 142 (1945). 328 U.S. 303 (1946).

152 ff. Relocation: For a concise report on the relocation problem, see *Fortune*, April 1944, pp. 8 ff. It is more extensively treated in Morton Grodzins's *Americans Betrayed* (Chicago, 1949).

153   Denver *Post* report: June 4, 1943. Cited in Ogden: *Dies Committee*, p. 279, as "a positive misstatement."

153   Dewitt on "Japs": Quoted in *Fortune*, April 1944.

153   Rankin on "blood test": *C.R.*, June 28, 1943, p. 6684.

153   Thomas on food: Statement made May 19, 1943, cited in *H.*, July 6, 1943, p. 9650.

153 ff. Relocation hearings: Los Angeles—*H.*, June 8–12, 15, 16, 17, 1943, pp. 8833 ff.; Washington—July 1, 3, 6, 7, 1943, pp. 9391 ff.; Dillon Meyer—July 6, 1943, pp. 9599 ff.

156   Relocation reports: *R.*, Sept. 30, 1943. *Appendix VIII*, 1943.

156   Dies on race hatred: *N. Y. Times*, June 27, 1943, p. 13.

157 ff. Winchell–Dies: *C.R.*, March 27, 1944, pp. 3128 and A1523; March 9, 1944, pp. 2434 ff. *N. Y. Times*, March 27, 1944, p. 9.

159 ff. C.I.O.–P.A.C. report: *R.*, March 29, 1944.

159 ff. P.A.C. attacks: *C.R.*, March 9, 1944, p. 2434. *N. Y. Times*, July 29, 1944, p. 26; Aug. 3, 1944, p. 16; Oct. 4, 1944, p. 17; Oct. 30, 1944, p. 9.

161   Dies retirement: *N. Y. Times*, May 13, 1944, p. 1. *Martin Dies Story*, p. 82.

162   Thomas on exposure: *N. Y. Times*, May 14, 1944, p. 28.

162   Dies return: *N. Y. Times*, July 15, 1954, p. 10.

CHAPTER SIX

167 ff. The first six years of the Standing Committee's existence are the subject of Professor Robert K. Carr's estimable *The House Committee on Un-American Activities, 1945–1950* (Ithaca, N.Y., 1952).

168   Rankin motion: *C.R.*, Jan. 3, 1945, pp. 6 ff.

169   "Flat-footed": Stripling: *The Red Plot Against America*, p. 50.

169   Hoffman–Voorhis–Rankin: *C.R.*, Jan. 4, 1945, pp. 46 ff.

169 ff. Biddle on Hart: *N. Y. Times*, Jan. 14, 1945, p. 4.

170   Mundt survey: *N. Y. Times*, Jan. 23, 1945. *Life*, March 26, 1945, p. 30. *Liberty*, Sept. 22, 1945, pp. 11 ff. Brookings Institution—*Suggested Standards for Determining Un-American Activities*, Washington, D.C., 1945.

170   Rankin on $50,000: *C.R.*, March 7, 1945, p. 1856.

171   Rankin on O.P.A.: *C.R.*, Nov. 21, 1945, p. 10885.

171 ff. O.P.A. hearings: *H.*, June 20, 21, 27, 1945.

172   Rankin on Hollywood: *N. Y. Times*, July 1, 1945, p. 20.

172 ff. Hart resignation: *C.R.*, July 2, 1945, p. 7142. Mundt statement—*C.R.*, July 3, 1945, p. 7186.

173   Rankin on subversives: *C.R.*, July 9, 1945, p. 7377.

173   Rankin on Chaplin: *C.R.*, July 19, 1945, p. 7738.

173 ff. Rankin on Jews: *C.R.*, Feb. 19, 1946, p. A872; Feb. 27, 1946, p. 1727; July 18, 1945, p. 7739; Feb. 11, 1946, p. 1225; Oct. 24, 1945, p. 1032.

174   (fn) Pegler on Rankin: *C.R.*, April 30, 1945, p. A2369.

174 ff. Radio commentators: Adamson—*N. Y. Times*, Oct. 19, 1945, p. 21. Report—*R.*, June 7, 1946. Rankin—*C.R.*, Oct. 24, 1945, p. 1032. Wood bill—*N. Y. Times*, Nov. 22, 1945, p. 24. Spokesman—*Ibid.*, Nov. 7, 1945, p. 25. Advertisement—*Ibid.*, March 14, 1945, p. 18.

176   Duclos on Browder: *Daily Worker*, May 27, 1945, p. 1.

176   Browder hearings: *H.*, Sept. 26, 27, Oct. 17, 19, Nov. 8, 1945.

176   J.A.F.R.C. rally: *N. Y. Times*, Sept. 25, 1945, p. 1.

PAGE

177   Thomas on Laski: *C.R.*, March 28, 1946, p. 2746.

177 ff. J.A.F.R.C. charges: *N. Y. Times*, Jan. 2, 1946, p. 15. *C.R.*, March 28, 1946, p. 2745. (fn) Report: *R.*, June 7, 1946.

178   J.A.F.R.C. hearings: *H.*, April 4, 1946.

179   Contempt citations: J.A.F.R.C.–*C.R.*, March 28, 1946, pp. 2744 ff.; April 16, 1946, pp. 2761 ff. Lamont–*C.R.*, June 26, 1946, pp. 7589 ff. Morford–*C.R.*, Aug. 2, 1946, pp. 10748 ff. Marshall–*C.R.*, July 31, 1946, pp. 10592 ff. (fn) Marcantonio delay–*C.R.*, July 29, 1946, pp. 10406 ff. See Beck: *Contempt of Congress*, and Carr: *House Committee*, Chapter XI.

180 ff. Court decisions: Holtzoff–72 F. Supp. 58 (1947). Barsky *et al.*–167 F. 2d 241 (1948).

181   Fast on fascism: *N. Y. Times*, June 18, 1948, p. 10. (fn) See Lillian Hellman's introduction to Dashiell Hammett's *The Big Knockdown* (New York, 1960).

181   Beck summary: *Contempt*, p. 35.

181 ff. Smith hearing: *H.*, Jan. 30, 1946.

182 ff. Atom spies: Adamson–*N. Y. Times*, March 8, 1946, p. 3; March 27, 1946, p. 1. Rankin–*N. Y. Times*, June 27, 1946, p. 4. Rankin on McMahon bill–*C.R.*, July 19, 1946, p. 9448. Adamson on army–*N. Y. Times*, July 12, 1946, p. 5. Wood–*N. Y. Times*, Oct. 24, 1946, p. 6.

183 ff. Debate on Committee: *C.R.*, May 17, 1946, pp. 5209 ff.

184 ff. Budenz–Eisler: *N. Y. Times*, Oct. 14, 1946, p. 12; Oct. 16, 1946, p. 6. N. Y. *World Telegram*, Oct. 17, 1946, p. 1. *N. Y. Times*, Oct. 18, 1946, p. 1. Eisler on "provocation"–*N. Y. Times*, Dec. 23, 1946, p. 15.

185   Budenz hearings: *H.*, Nov. 22, 1946.

185   Eisler on C.P.: *N. Y. Times*, Dec. 12, 1946, p. 9.

185 ff. Eisler hearing: *H.*, Feb. 6, 1947.

186   Rankin on federal payroll: *N. Y. Times*, Dec. 26, 1946, p. 11.

187   Thomas on atom bomb: *N. Y. Times*, Nov. 27, 1946, p. 4.

187   Shapley hearing: *N. Y. Times*, Nov. 15, 1946, p. 14.

187 ff. Rankin–Adamson on investigations: *N. Y. Times*, Dec. 4, 1946, p. 44; Dec. 27, 1946, p. 1.

188   Adamson on democracy: See *C.R.*, Feb. 5, 1946, p. A508. Pearson–*C.R.*, Feb. 1, 1946, p. 1230.

188   Thomas–Adamson break: *N. Y. Times*, Dec. 28, 1946, p. 3; Jan. 1, 1947, p. 2.

188 ff. Annual report: *R.*, Jan. 2, 1947.

189   Kreml: Stripling, *Red Plot*, p. 57.

CHAPTER SEVEN

190 ff. G. Eisler hearing: *H.*, Feb. 6, 1947.

191   Contempt citation: *C.R.*, Feb. 18, 1947, pp. 1127 ff.

191 ff. Josephson hearing: *H.*, March 5, 1947.

192   Dennis hearings: *H.*, March 26, April 9, 1947.

192   Contempt citations: *C.R.*, April 22, 1947, pp. 3813 ff.

193   Dennis case: 171 F. 2d 986 (1948); 339 U.S. 162 (1950).

193   Josephson case: 165 F. 2d 82 (1947).

193   Eisler case: 338 U.S. 189 (1949).

194   Thomas on passports: *C.R.*, April 22, 1947, p. 3804.

195   Truman loyalty order: Executive Order #9835 (1947). 12 Fed. Reg. 1935.

196 ff. Anti-Communist hearings: *H.*, March 24–28, 1947. Bullitt–March 24; Green–March 25; Johnston–March 27; Hoover–March 25; Earle–

PAGE

March 28; V.F.W.—March 27; Tenney—March 26; (fn) McCarthy—March 28.

197 ff. Kravchenko hearing: *H.*, July 22, 1947.

198 Kravchenko-Gromyko: *N. Y. Times*, July 24, 1947, p. 4.

198 Steele hearing: *H.*, July 21, 1947.

198 Carr on Steele: *House Committee*, p. 53.

199 Allis-Chalmers hearing: *H.*, Feb. 27, 1947.

199 Union hearings: *H.*, July 23–25, 1947.

199 ff. Reports: Communist Party—*R.*, April 1, 1947. American Youth for Democracy—*R.*, April 17, 1947. Southern Conference—*R.*, June 16, 1947. Civil Rights Congress—*R.*, Sept. 2, 1947.

200 (fn) Civil Rights Congress: *America's Thought Police* (New York, 1947).

200 (fn) Thomas poem: *N. Y. Times*, June 13, 1947, p. 8.

201 Gellhorn on Southern Conference: *Harvard Law Review*, Oct. 1947, p. 1197. See also *American Scholar*, Spring 1948, pp. 139 ff.

202 Thomas—McDowell on fascism: *N. Y. Times*, June 13, 1947, p. 8. *C.R.*, June 13, 1947, p. A2831.

202 ff. L.A. hearings: *N.Y. Times*, May 15, 1947, p. 1; May 16, 1947, p. 1; May 17, 1947, p. 8. *C.R.*, June 6, 1947, p. A2687.

204 Thomas-Eisler exchange: *N. Y. Times*, May 13, 1947, p. 19.

204 ff. H. Eisler hearings: *H.*, Sept. 24–26, 1947. State Dept. official—Sept. 26, p. 156; Stripling quotes—*H.*, Sept. 24 and *N. Y. Times*, Sept. 27, 1947, p. 1. Eisler song—*H.*, Sept. 24, p. 156; (fn) Rankin—Sept. 24, p. 60; Welles—Sept. 24; Messersmith—Sept. 25.

207 ff. Hollywood hearings, first week: *H.*, Oct. 20–24, 1947. Warner—Oct. 20; attorney ejected—Oct. 20, p. 118; Disney—Oct. 24; Ryskind, Oct. 22. Trumbo on unfriendly witnesses—*The Time of the Toad* (Hollywood, Calif., 1949). Mrs. Rogers—Oct. 24; Cooper—Oct. 23; Montgomery, Murphy, Reagan—Oct. 23; Menjou, Oct. 21.

210 ff. Hollywood hearings, second week: *H.*, Oct. 27–30, 1947. Lavery—Oct. 29; Brecht—Oct. 30, and (fn) *Bertolt Brecht Before the Committee on Un-American Activities*—Folkway Records, FD 5531. Wilson on Communists—*New Republic*, Dec. 24, 1930, p. 158. Lawson—*H.*, Oct. 27; Kenny—Oct. 28; Maltz—Oct. 28; Trumbo—Oct. 28; Dmytryk—Oct. 29; Lardner—Oct. 30, and (fn) *Saturday Evening Post*, Oct. 14, 1961, p. 38.

213 ff. Maltz incident: *New Masses*, Feb. 12, 1946, p. 19, and Oct 12, 1946, pp. 24–25. See Daniel Aaron's *Writers on the Left* (New York, 1961), p. 386.

214 ff. Lawson-Maltz-Bessie quotes: *N. Y. Times*, Nov. 17, 1947, p. 14, and Nov. 3, 1947, p. 19. Alvah Bessie's *Inquisition in Eden* (New York, 1965), p. 99, and (fn) *The Un-Americans* (New York, 1957). *H.*, Oct. 27, 1947, p. 296.

215 ff. Hollywood Ten's films: For a content analysis, see Dorothy B. Jones's *Communism and the Movies: A Study of Film Content*, in John Cogley's *Report on Blacklisting* (New York, 1956), Vol. 1.

216 Agee on *Mission to Moscow*: *Nation*, May 22, 1943, p. 749.

216 October hearings: *H.* Oct. 20–24, 27–30, 1947. Rand—Oct. 20; Taylor—Oct. 22; M.G.M. script supervisor—Oct. 22.

216 McNutt–Johnston: *N. Y. Times*, Oct. 27, 1947, p. 26, and Oct. 26, 1947, p. 54.

217 (fn) Stripling–Johnston: *H.*, Oct. 27, 1947, pp. 314 ff.

217 Johnston to writers: Quoted in Gordon Kahn's *Hollywood on Trial* (New York, 1948), p. 5.

217 Warner on livelihoods: *H.*, Oct. 20, 1947, p. 53.

218 Waldorf decision: *N. Y. Times*, Nov. 26, 1947, p. 1.

218 Hearst editorial: Quoted in Kahn: *Hollywood on Trial*, p. 139.

PAGE

220   (fn) Warren: *N. Y. Times*, Dec. 7, 1947, p. 66.
220   Thomas quotes: *C.R.*, Nov. 20, 1947, p. A4211. *H.*, Oct. 29, 1947, p. 401.
221   Russell on Oppenheimer: *H.*, Oct. 30, 1947.
221   Stripling on "broken record": *Red Plot*, p. 75.
221 ff. Contempt citations: *C.R.*, Nov. 24, 1947, pp. 10769 ff.
222   Wallace on Ten: *N. Y. Times*, Jan. 29, 1947, pp. 10769 ff.
223   Contempt case: 176 F. 2d 49 (1949).
223   Trumbo on government regulation: *Time of the Toad*, p. 17.
224   Bessie career: See *Inquisition in Eden*.
224   Biberman career: See his *Salt of the Earth* (Boston, 1965).
224   Kempton on Ten: *Part of Our Time*, p. 182.

CHAPTER EIGHT

227 ff. Communist control hearings: *H.*, Feb. 5, 6, 9–11, 19, 20, 1948. Burnham —Feb. 19; Moley—Feb. 11; Ernst—Feb. 11; Waldman—Feb. 6; Richberg —Feb. 6; Berle—Feb. 11; Clark—Feb. 5; Nagy—Feb. 6; Dimitrov—Feb. 19; Standley—Feb. 9; (fn) Hays—Feb. 10, p. 208.
229   Communist control report: *R.*, May 11, 1948.
229 ff. House debate: *C.R.*, May 17–19, 1948. Javits—May 18, p. 5860; Holifield—p. 5873; Dondero—p. 6020; Bryson—p. 6022.
230   (fn) Communism report: *R.*, Dec. 4, 1948.
231 ff. Condon report: *Report to the Full Committee of the Special Subcommittee on National Security*, March 1, 1948. For a critical analysis of the report and of Thomas's campaign against Condon, see the pseudonymous Louis Welborn's *The Ordeal of Dr. Condon*, in *Harper's*, January 1950, pp. 46 ff. Also, Representative Holifield's presentations to the House—*C.R.*, July 22, 1947, pp. 9770 ff. and March 9, 1948, pp. 2435 ff.
232   Rankin-Vail on report: *C.R.*, March 2, 1948, p. A1306, and April 1, 1948, p. 4001.
232 ff. Thomas on Condon: Washington *Times-Herald*, March 23, 1947, p. 1; March 25, 1947, p. 1; July 17, 1947, p. 1. *American* magazine, June 1947, p. 16. *Liberty* magazine, June 26, 1947.
233   Condon on Russia: Quoted in *C.R.*, March 9, 1948, p. 2443.
234   McDowell on Condon: *N. Y. Times*, March 7, 1948, p. 1.
234 ff. Hoover letter: Condon report, *Report to the Full Committee . . .* , p. 4. Washington *Post*, March 4, 1948, p. 1.
236   Thomas on Truman: *N. Y. Times*, April 8, 1948, p. 1.
236   Reece letter: *N. Y. Times*, May 2, 1948, p. 32.
236   House order: *C.R.*, April 22, 1948, pp. 4777 ff.
236   Truman reply: *N. Y. Times*, April 23, 1948, p. 1.
237   A.E.C. clearance: *N. Y. Times*, July 16, 1948, p. 1.
238   Nixon on Condon: *N. Y. Times*, Dec. 20, 1948.
238   Mundt on Condon: *N. Y. Times*, Dec. 23, 1948, p. 8.
238   Stripling on Condon: *Red Plot*, p. 86.
238   Vail attack: *C.R.*, April 23, 1951, pp. 4214 ff.
238   Velde on resignation: *N. Y. Times*, Aug. 11, 1951, p. 7.
238 ff. Condon hearing: *H.*, Sept. 5, 1952.
239   Condon in report: *R.*, Dec. 28, 1952, pp. 73 ff.
240   Atomic espionage hearings: *H.*, Sept. 9, 14, 16, 1948.
240   Committee members' quotes: Thomas—*N. Y. Times*, Sept. 14, 1948, p. 1, and Sept. 18, 1948, p. 1; Nixon—*N. Y. Times*, Sept. 25, 1948, p. 1; McDowell—*N. Y. Times*, Sept. 22, 1948, p. 8, and Sept. 26, p. 1.

PAGE

241   Truman on investigation: *N. Y. Times*, Sept. 14, 1948, p. 1, and Sept. 23, p. 1.
241 ff. Atomic espionage report: *R.*, Sept. 28, 1948.
242 ff. Justice Dept. dispute: Justice Dept.–*N. Y. Times*, Sept. 30, 1948, p. 1; McDowell–*N. Y. Times*, Oct. 1, 1948, p. 1; Thomas–*N. Y. Times*, Oct. 5, 1948, p. 1; Groves–*N. Y. Times*, Sept. 11, 1948, p. 1.
244   Books by principals in the Hiss–Chambers case include: Whittaker Chambers's *Witness* (New York, 1952); Alger Hiss's *In the Court of Public Opinion* (New York, 1957); Elizabeth Bentley's *Out of Bondage* (New York, 1951); Richard Nixon's *Six Crises* (New York, 1962), pp. 1–71; Robert Stripling's *Red Plot*. Other books include Ralph de Toledano and Victor Lasky's *Seeds of Treason* (New York, 1950); Alistair Cook's *A Generation on Trial* (New York, 1952); Fred Cook's *The Unfinished Story of Alger Hiss* (New York, 1958); Lord Jowitt's *The Strange Case of Alger Hiss* (New York, 1953); Meyer A. Zeligs's *Friendship and Fratricide* (New York, 1967).
244   "Blonde Spy Queen": *N. Y. World Telegram*, July 21–23, 1948, p. 1.
245 ff. Bentley hearing. *H.*, July 31, 1948. Miss Bentley's quotes on Golos are taken from her book, *Out of Bondage*.
246   Bentley on Currie: *H.*, July 31, 1948, p. 553. Rankin on Currie–*H.*, p. 557.
246 ff. Civil Service on Silvermaster: *H.*, Aug. 3, 1948, p. 613.
247 ff. First Chambers hearing: *H.*, Aug. 3, 1948.
249 ff. Hearings of the accused: Silvermaster–*H.*, Aug. 4, 1948; Collins–Aug. 11; Silverman–Aug. 12; Perlo–Aug. 9; Pressman–Aug. 20; Witt–Aug. 20; Abt–Aug. 20.
250   Witt–Abt statement: *N. Y. Times*, Oct. 1, 1948, p. 12.
250 ff. Committee report: *R.*, Aug. 28, 1948.
251   (fn) Thomas to lawyer: *H.*, Sept. 8, 1948, p. 1310.
251   Silvermaster on disloyalty: *H.*, Aug. 4, 1948, p. 590.
251   Nixon on Fifth: *H.*, Aug. 12, 1948, p. 837.
252   Chambers on White: *H.*, Aug. 13, 1948, p. 906.
252   Currie hearing: *H.*, Aug. 13, 1948.
252 ff. White hearing: *H.*, Aug. 13, 1948; Thomas to White–p. 881.
252   Wallace on White: *N. Y. Times*, Aug. 18, 1948, p. 5.
253   White "Creed": *H.*, Aug. 13, 1948, p. 878.
253   Chambers on White: *Witness*, p. 29.
253   Bentley on White: *Bondage*, p. 164.
253   White on Silvermaster: *H.*, Aug. 13, 1948, p. 898.
253   (fn) Rebecca West on White: London *Sunday Times*, March 22, 1953, quoted in *C.R.*, May 26, 1953, p. A2963.
254   For the A.A.A. story, see Arthur M. Schlesinger, Jr.'s *The Coming of the New Deal* (Boston, 1958), pp. 77–80.
254   Chambers on Hiss: *Witness*, p. 338.
254   Peters hearing: *H.*, Aug. 30, 1948.
254   Truman on "red herring": *N. Y. Times*, Aug. 6, 1948, p. 1.
254 ff. First Hiss hearing: *H.*, Aug. 5, 1948.
255   Hébert suggestion: *Six Crises*, p. 10.
255   Mundt on Hiss: *H.*, Aug. 3, 1948, p. 579.
255   Republican's lament: *Six Crises*, p. 10.
255   (fn) Nixon–Stripling: *Six Crises*, p. 10, and *Red Plot*, p. 116.
255   Chambers on Nixon: *Witness*, p. 355.
256   Hiss on Chambers: *H.*, Aug. 5, 1948, p. 647.
256   Second Chambers hearing: *H.*, Aug. 7, 1948.
256 ff. Second Hiss hearing: *H.*, Aug. 16, 1948.
257   Nixon explanation: *Six Crises*, p. 30.

PAGE

257   First Hiss–Chambers confrontation: *H.*, Aug. 17, 1948. Hiss on Crosley —p. 975; Hiss challenge—p. 988.

257   Chambers on Hiss "acting": *Witness*, p. 605.

257   Nixon's briefings: *N. Y. Times*, Aug. 22, 1948, p. 13.

257 ff.   Donald Hiss hearing: *H.*, Aug. 13, 1948.

258   Hiss letter: *N. Y. Times*, Aug. 25, 1948, p. 1.

258   Nixon comment: *Six Crises*, p. 43.

258 ff.   Hiss–Chambers public confrontation: *H.*, Aug. 25, 1948.

258   Disposal of Ford: *H.*, Aug. 26, 1948.

258   Chambers's quotes: *H.*, Aug. 25, 1948, pp. 1176, 1191.

258 ff.   Report on Hiss case: *R.*, Aug. 28, 1948.

259   *Nation* articles: Aug. 14, 1948, p. 173; Sept. 4, 1948, p. 251.

259   *Meet the Press* interview: *N. Y. Times*, Aug. 28, 1948, p. 251.

259   Washington *Post* editorial: Cited in *Six Crises*, p. 45.

259   Fiedler on case: *Commentary*, Aug. 1951, p. 110.

259 ff.   Chambers on Hiss: *Witness*, p. 445.

260   Hiss defense: *In Court*, pp. 102, 419.

261   Psychiatrists: For an elaborate psychoanalytic exegesis on Chambers, see Zeligs: *Friendship and Fratricide*.

261 ff.   Chambers on himself: *Witness*, pp. 715, 769; *Cold Friday* (New York, 1964), pp. 67, 12.

264   Justice Dept.: *N. Y. Times*, Dec. 2, 1948, p. 3.

265   Mundt–Nixon on microfilm: *N. Y. Times*, Dec. 4, 1948, p. 1, and Dec. 7, p. 1.

265   Officials on code: *H.*, Dec. 7, 1948.

265   Wadleigh hearing: *H.*, Dec. 9, 1948. For Wadleigh's story, see *N. Y. Post*, July 11–24, 1949.

266   Nixon on indictment: *N. Y. Times*, Dec. 16, 1948, p. 1.

266   (fn) Latham on thirties: *The Communist Controversy in Washington* (Cambridge, Mass., 1966), p. 149.

267   Berle on Hiss: *H.*, Aug. 30, 1948, p. 1296.

267 ff.   Duggan case: Nixon—*N. Y. Times*, Dec. 1, 1948, p. 1. Mundt—*N. Y. Times*, Dec. 25, 1948, p. 1. (fn) Hede Massing: *This Deception* (New York, 1951). Criticisms and retractions: *N. Y. Times*, Dec. 3, 1948, p. 1, and Dec. 25, p. 1. Levine on Welles: *N. Y. Times*, Dec. 23, 1948, p. 1.

269   Truman on "dead agency": *N. Y. Times*, Dec. 10, 1948, p. 1.

269   Mundt–Nixon code: *N. Y. Times*, Dec. 28, 1948, p. 1.

269   Hiss case report: *R.*, Dec. 31, 1948.

269 ff.   Thomas jailed: *N. Y. Times*, Nov. 9, 1948, p. 1.

270   Thomas released: *N. Y. Times*, Feb. 8, 1954, p. 11.

270   Dies on Thomas: *Martin Dies Story*, p. 84.

271   Dies on Nixon: *Martin Dies Story*, p. 179.

CHAPTER NINE

272   Rankin on Moscow: *N. Y. Times*, Jan. 16, 1949, p. 1.

273   Nixon on Coplon: *N. Y. Times*, March 6, 1949, p. 2.

273   Short hearing: *H.*, May 24, 1949.

273   Democrat on "inactivity": *N. Y. Times*, May 29, 1949, p. 10.

274   Editorial: *N. Y. Times*, May 31, 1949, p. 22.

274   Holifield–Douglas: *N. Y. Times*, Dec. 26, 1949, p. 13.

274   Crouch hearing: *H.*, May 6, 1949.

274 ff.   Hiskey hearing: *H.*, May 24, 1949.

275   Weinberg hearing: *H.*, April 21, 1949.

275   Accusation: *R.*, Sept. 29, 1949.

PAGE

275   Scientists hearings: *H.,* April 26, 1949; May 25, 1949; June 10, 1949; Sept. 27, 1949.
275   Nelson hearing: *H.,* June 8, 1949.
276 ff. Oppenheimers hearing: *H.,* June 14, 1949; Oppenheimer quote—p. 358.
277   Wood on contempt: *N. Y. Times,* June 15, 1949, p. 1.
277 ff. Hawkins hearing: *H.,* Dec. 20, 1950.
278   A.P. on "espionage": *N. Y. Times,* June 5, 1949, p. 3.
278   Espionage hearing: *H.,* June 6, 1949.
279   Velde on espionage: *N. Y. Times,* Sept. 26, 1949.
279   Jordan broadcast: Washington *Times-Herald,* Dec. 3, 1949, p. 1.
280   First Jordan hearing: *H.,* Dec. 5, 1949.
280   Lewis embellishment: *N. Y. Times,* Dec. 6, 1949, p. 1.
280   Groves hearing: *H.,* Dec. 7, 1949.
280   Walter–Harrison: *N. Y. Times,* Dec. 8, 1949, p. 1.
280   Republican protest: *N. Y. Times,* Dec. 9, 1949, p. 1.
280 ff. Second Jordan hearings: *H.,* Jan. 23, 24, 1949; broker quote—Jan. 24, p. 1039.
281   Wallace hearing: *H.,* Jan. 26, 1949.
281   Staff investigator hearing: *H.,* March 2, 1950.
281   Third Jordan hearing: *H.,* March 3, 1950.
282   D.C. hearings: *H.,* June 28, 29, July 6, 12, 28, 1949; Dec. 6, 11–13, 1950.
282   Pennsylvania–Ohio hearings: *H.,* Feb. 21–23, March 13, 14, 24, 25, June 22, July 12–15, Aug. 8, Sept. 28, Oct. 13, 21, 1950.
282   Honolulu hearings: *H.,* April 10–15, 17–19, 1950.
283   Emspak hearing: *H.,* Dec. 5, 1949; quote—p. 839.
283   Nixon on Fifth: *H.,* April 26, 1949, p. 302.
283   Harrison demand: *N. Y. Times,* July 13, 1949, p. 19.
284   Velde to Hiskey: *H.,* May 24, 1949, p. 397.
284 ff. Contempt citations: *C.R.,* Aug. 10, 1950, pp. 12234 ff., and Aug. 11, 1950, pp. 12284 ff.
285 ff. Constitutional questions: For this summary of the questions raised by the contempt cases, as for much else in this chapter, I am indebted to Professor Beck.
285 ff. Court decisions: Supreme Court on Fifth Amendment—340 U.S. 59 (1950); leeway for defendants—96 F. Supp. 491 (1951); incriminating relationship—349 U.S. 1950 (1955); Nelson case—103 F. Supp. 215 (1952); C.P. membership no waiver—349 U.S. 155 (1955); Committee's responsibility—349 U.S. 219 (1955).
286   Beck summary: *Contempt,* p. 86.
286 ff. Remington hearings: *H.,* April 20, 21, 29, May 4, 5, 1950; Remington quote—May 4, p. 1817; Bentley testimony—May 6.
288   Marcantonio on Pressman: *N. Y. Times,* Aug. 12, 1950, p. 30.
288   Andrews's story: *N. Y. Herald Tribune,* Aug. 7, 1950, p. 1.
288 ff. Pressman hearing: *H.,* Aug. 28, 1950; Pressman quote—p. 2845.
289   Witt–Abt–Kramer hearing: *H.,* Sept. 1, 1950.
289   Silverman hearing: *H.,* Aug. 31, 1950.
289   Nixon on Pressman: *N. Y. Times,* Aug. 29, 1950, p. 1.
289   Lowenthal hearing: *H.,* Sept. 15, 1950.
289   Lowenthal book: *The Federal Bureau of Investigation* (New York, 1950).
289   Carr quote: *House Committee,* p. 203.
290   Appendix to hearings: *Hearings Regarding Communism in U. S. Government,* Part II, pp. 2960–61.
290   Scott hearing: *H.,* Sept. 22, 1950.
290   E. G. Robinson hearings: *H.,* Oct. 27, Dec. 21, 1950.
290 ff. J. Robinson hearing: *H.,* July 18, 1949; quote—p. 479.

PAGE

291 Mundt–Nixon bill hearings: *H.*, March 21–24, 28–30, April 4, May 2–4, 1950.

292 Truman messages: *C.R.*, Aug. 8, 1950, pp. 12018 ff. Veto—*C.R.*, Sept. 22, 1950, pp. 15629 ff.

292 Internal Security Act: Public Law 31, 81st Cong., U.S. Code Title 50; Sections 781 and 811.

292 (fn) House debate: *C.R.*, Aug. 29, 1950; Rankin–p. 13725; McSweeney –p. 13733.

293 Jencks case: 77 S.C. 1007 (1957).

293 Constitutionality upheld: 81 S.C. 1357 (1961).

293 1963 reversal: 11 U.S. App. D.C. (1963).

293 1967 reversal: Citation not available at this writing.

294 1965 ruling: 86 S. Ct. 194 (1965).

294 1967 hearings: Transcript not available at this writing. See *R.*, Oct. 4, 1967, the Committee's report on H.R. 12601, the Willis bill, with a dissent by Culver. For House passage, see *C.R.*, Nov. 28, 1967.

295 Truman press conference: *N. Y. Times,* June 17, 1949, p. 1.

295 I.P.R. investigation: For an illuminating review of these hearings, which many on the left refused to take seriously, while some on the right made too much of them, see Latham: *Communist Controversy,* pp. 296 ff.

295 ff. Nixon on Hiss case: *N. Y. Times,* July 13, 1949, p. 19.

296 Hall on Communist-coddling: *N. Y. Times,* Nov. 19, 1950, p. 20.

CHAPTER TEN

297 Allocation: *C.R.*, Feb. 8, 1951, pp. 1151 ff.

298 Jackson–Potter on Robinson: *N. Y. Times,* Feb. 10, 1951, p. 6, and Feb. 23, 1951, p. 24.

298 ff. Hollywood hearings: *H.*, March 8, 21, April 10–13, 17, 23–25, May 10, 16–18, 22–25, June 25, 26, Sept. 10–12, 17–21, 24, 1951; Jan. 24, 28, Feb. 5, March 20, April 10, 30, May 19–21, Aug. 19, Sept. 29, Nov. 12, 13, 1952.

298 Wood on Fifth: *H.*, Sept. 21, 1951, p. 1703.

299 Moulder on Fifth: *H.*, April 24, 1951, p. 385.

299 Collins hearing: *H.*, April 11, 1951.

299 Berkeley hearing: *H.*, Sept. 19, 1951.

299 Hayden hearing: *H.*, April 10, 1951.

299 Jackson to witness: *H.*, Sept. 19, 1951, p. 1627.

299 ff. Jackson to Foreman: *H.*, Sept. 24, 1951, p. 1753.

300 Actors Guild to Sondergaard: *N. Y. Times,* March 21, 1951, p. 41.

300 Actors Equity on exposure: *N. Y. Times,* April 20, 1951, p. 25.

301 M.P.I.C. statement: *H.*, Sept. 17, 1951, p. 1416.

301 ff. Parks hearing: *H.*, March 21, 1951.

302 Velde on Parks: *C.R.*, March 22, 1951, p. 2890.

302 Jarrico on Parks: *N. Y. Times,* March 24, 1951, p. 9.

302 Dmytryk hearing: *H.*, April 23, 1951.

303 Kazan hearing: *H.*, April 10, 1952; quote–p. 2407.

303 Kazan advertisement: *N. Y. Times,* April 12, 1952, p. 7.

304 Ferrer hearing: *H.*, May 22, 1951.

304 Garfield hearing: *H.*, April 23, 1951.

304 ff. Robinson hearing: *H.*, April 30, 1952.

305 Hellman hearing: *H.*, May 21, 1951; letter–p. 3541; Wood to Hellman –p. 3546.

305 Rossen hearing: *H.*, June 25, 1951.

306 Buchman hearing: *H.*, Sept. 25, 1951.

PAGE

306 Buchman contempt citation: *C.R.*, Feb. 5, 1952, pp. 826 ff.
306 Actor on dames: *H.*, April 23, 1951, p. 4364.
306 ff. Beck's donation: *H.*, Sept. 25, 1951, p. 1817.
307 Client's complaint: *H.*, Sept. 19, 1951, p. 1525.
307 Schulberg hearing: *H.*, May 23, 1951.
307 (fn) Jerome: *N. Y. Times*, May 20, 1951, II, p. 5.
308 Actor on *Internationale*: *H.*, Sept. 19, 1951, p. 1602.
308 1952 report: *R.*, Jan. 3, 1953.
308 Doyle on persecution: *H.*, April 11, 1951, p. 215.
308 Wood on elimination: *N. Y. Times*, Sept. 22, 1951, p. 8.
308 1951 report: *R.*, Feb. 17, 1952.
309 Executive on cleared air: *N. Y. Times*, Sept. 30, 1951, II, p. 5. See Cogley's *Report on Blacklisting*.
310 1951 loyalty order: #10241 (1951) 16 Fed. Reg. 3690.
310 Clubb hearings: *H.*, March 14, Aug. 20, 23, 1951.
310 Willoughby hearings: *H.*, Aug. 9, 23, 1951.
311 Supreme Court on C.P. leaders: 341 U.S. 494 (1950).
311 ff. McPhaul, Grossman contempt citations: *C.R.*, June 20, 1952, pp. 8625 ff.
312 Rogers v. U.S.: 340 U.S. 367 (1951).
312 Grossman appeal: 229 F. 2d 775 (1956).
312 McPhaul appeal: 81 S. Ct. 138 (1960).
312 ff. Los Angeles hearings: *H.*, Jan. 21–26, April 9, May 22, July 8, Sept. 30, Oct. 1–3, 6, 7, 1952. Margolis—Sept. 30; Katz—Oct. 1.
314 (fn) Matusow: *H.*, Feb. 6, 7, 1952. *False Witness* (New York, 1955).
315 Doyle on C.P.: *H.*, July 11, 1951, p. 739.
315 Philbrick testimony: *H.*, July 25, 1951.
316 U.E. negotiators hearing: *H.*, Sept. 3, 1952.
317 Detroit hearings: *H.*, Feb. 25–29, March 10–12, April 29, 30, 1952.
318 *The Shameful Years*: *R.*, Jan. 8, 1952.
318 ff. Smith hearing: *H.*, Oct. 13, 1952.
319 Rovere on McCarthy era: *N. Y. Times Magazine*, April 30, 1967, pp. 23 ff.

CHAPTER ELEVEN

321 Dies on subversives: *N. Y. Times*, Nov. 25, 1952, p. 18.
322 Walter on Dies: *N. Y. Times*, Nov. 24, 1952, p. 12.
322 ff. Spring 1954 hearings: Kearney in Albany—*H.*, April 7–9; Jackson in San Diego—April 12, 19–22; Clardy in Detroit—April 28–30, May 3–5, 7, 10–14; Witness X—April 30; Velde in Chicago—March 15, 16, April 29.
323 Other hearings: *H.*, Seattle—June 14, 19, 1954; San Francisco—Dec. 1–5, 1953; Philadelphia—July 30, 1954; Baltimore—May 18, March 25, 26, 1954; Dayton—Sept. 13–15, 1954; (fn) DeLacy—Sept. 14, 1954.
323 Agents in L.A.: *H.*, March 28, 31, 1953.
323 Shaw hearing: *H.*, May 4, 1953.
323 Stander hearing: *H.*, May 6, 1953.
323 Robbins hearing: *H.*, May 5, 1953.
323 ff. Rossen hearing: *H.*, May 7, 1953.
324 *Nation* on Clardy: Feb. 13, 1953, p. 132.
324 Scherer–Clardy in Michigan: *H.*, April 30, 1954, p. 5207.
324 (fn) Reuther: Quoted in Taylor: *Grand Inquest*, p. 213.
325 Eisenhower executive order: #10450 (1953), 18 Fed. Reg. 2489.
326 Hoover on professors: *N. Y. Times*, Nov. 14, 1954, p. 75.

326   Agnes Meyer talk: *N. Y. Times,* Feb. 18, 1953, p. 1.
326   Velde on Meyer: *N. Y. Times,* Feb. 18, 1953, p. 1.
327   Thomas on teachers: *N. Y. Times Sunday Magazine,* Feb. 8, 1953, p. 8.
327   A.A.U.P. resolution: *N. Y. Times,* March 29, 1953, p. 20.
327 ff. A.A.U. resolution: *N. Y. Times,* March 31, 1953, p. 1.
328   Jones on Fifth: Quoted in *C.R.,* March 17, 1953, p. 2021.
328 ff. Gallagher position: *N. Y. Times,* March 7, 1953, p. 10.
329   Trilling position: *N. Y. Times,* Nov. 8, 1953, p. 28, and Nov. 26, 1953, p. 30.
329   (fn) Supreme Court: 87 S. Ct. 675 (1967).
329   Velde on Communists: *N. Y. Times,* Feb. 9, 1953, p. 28.
329 ff. Eisenhower on investigations: *N. Y. Times,* Feb. 26, 1953, p. 16, and Jan. 17, 1953, p. 6.
330   (fn) McCarthy: *N. Y. Times,* Jan. 6, 1954, p. 13.
330 ff. Education hearings: Davis—*H.,* Feb. 25, 1953; Boorstin—Feb. 26, 1953; Hicks—Feb. 26, 1953. See also Hicks's *Part of the Truth* (New York, 1965), pp. 266–269. Furry—Feb. 26, 1953; Dunham—Feb. 27, 1953.
332   Hoover warning: *N. Y. Times,* April 5, 1953, p. 32.
332   Velde on churches: *N. Y. Times,* March 10, 1953, p. 1.
332   1951 report: *R.,* April 25, 1951.
333   Opposition to investigation: *N. Y. Times,* March 11, 1953, p. 12.
333   Eisenhower on churches: *N. Y. Times,* March 20, 1953, p. 1.
333 ff. American Council on investigation: *N. Y. Times,* March 11, 1953, p. 12.
334   Jackson on investigation: *C.R.,* March 17, 1953, pp. 2017 ff.
334   Velde to churchmen: *N. Y. Times,* May 17, 1953, p. 32.
334   Oxnam retort: *N. Y. Times,* June 27, 1953, p. 18.
335   Matthews article: *American Mercury,* July 1953; reprinted in *C.R.,* June 27, 1953, pp. A3904 ff.
337   Eisenhower on article: *N. Y. Times,* July 10, 1953, p. 1.
337   McCarthy on Democrats: *N. Y. Times,* July 11, 1953, p. 1.
337 ff. Oxnam hearing: *H.,* July 21, 1953. See also Oxnam's *I Protest* (New York, 1954).
338   Clardy on Oxnam: *N. Y. Times,* April 23, 1953, p. 17.
340 ff. Walter on Oxnam: *N. Y. Times,* July 23, 1953, p. 7.
341   Matthews article: *American Mercury,* July 1953.
341   Niebuhr on "prophetic spirits": *Christian Century,* Aug. 19, 1953, p. 936.
341 ff. McMichael hearings: *H.,* July 20, 21, 1953.
343   (fn) Donner: *The Un-Americans* (New York, 1961), p. 102.
343   L.A. Unitarian hearing: *H.,* Sept. 12, 1951.
343 ff. Gitlow hearing: *H.,* July 7, 1953.
343 ff. Philbrick testimony: *H.,* July 6, 1953.
344   Philbrick criticism: *N. Y. Times,* Oct. 2, 1953, p. 8.
345   1953 report: *R.,* Feb. 8, 1954.
345 ff. Brownell on White: *N. Y. Times,* Nov. 7, 1953, p. 1.
346   Kunzig quote: *N. Y. Times,* Nov. 11, 1953, p. 1.
347   Walter on subpoena: *N. Y. Times,* Nov. 11, 1953, p. 1.
348   (fn) Adams: *First-Hand Report* (New York, 1961), p. 140.
348   Velde in *U. S. News:* Nov. 29, 1953, pp. 65 ff.
348   Truman talk: *N. Y. Times,* Nov. 17, 1953, p. 1.
348   Hoover testimony: *N. Y. Times,* Nov. 18, 1953, p. 1.
348   Kearney charge: *N. Y. Times,* March 23, 1954, p. 1.
349   Walter quotes: *N. Y. Times,* Jan. 17, 1954, p. 29, and Jan. 16, 1954, p. 7.
349   Kearney–Velde: *N. Y. Times,* March 23, 1954, p. 1, and March 26, 1954, p. 8.

CHAPTER TWELVE

PAGE

351 ff. Once again I am indebted to Carl Beck's *Contempt of Congress* for the review of the Fifth Amendment cases.

351 ff. Contempt citations: *C.R.*, May 11, 1954, pp. 6375 ff.; July 23, 1954, pp. 11598 ff.; Jan. 5, 1955, pp. 11 ff.

351 ff. The following took the Fifth Amendment: Ole Fagerhaugh; Barrows Dunham; Bolza Baxter; George Tony Starkovich; Thomas G. Moore; John Rogers MacKenzie; Donald M. Wollam; Herbert Simpson; Mrs. Millie Markison; Benjamin F. Kocel; Paul Ross Baker; Curtis Davis; Evelyn Gladstone; Marvin Engel; Martin Trachtenberg; Carl Harvey Jackins.

The following took the First Amendment or objected to questions on grounds of pertinency, or both: Bernhard Deutch; John T. Watkins; Mrs. Goldie E. Watson; Lawrence Baker Arguimbau; Marcus Singer; Horace Chandler Davis; Lloyd Barenblatt; Lee Lorch, Robert M. Metcalf; Norton A. Russell.

The following purged themselves of contempt, and proceedings were dropped: Wilbur Lee Mahaney, Jr.; Francis X. T. Crowley; Richard E. Adams.

352   Court reversals: They were based on 341 U.S. 479 (1951). 1950 precedent: 340 U.S. 159 (1950).

352 ff. Griswold: *The Fifth Amendment Today* (Cambridge, Mass., 1955). For a more garbled essay taking Dean Griswold's position, see "Does Silence Mean Guilt?" by Laurent B. Frantz and Norman Redlich, *Nation*, June 6, 1953, pp. 471 ff.

353 ff. Hook: *Common Sense and the Fifth Amendment* (New York, 1957), p. 33.

354   Black on witnesses: *Harper's*, February 1936, p. 275.

354   (fn) McCloy on liberals: May 2, 1953 address, quoted in Taylor: *Grand Inquest*, p. 82.

355   Taylor: *Annals of the American Academy*, July 1955, pp. 114 ff.

355   Williams: *Fordham Law Review*, Vol. 24, 1955–56, p. 19.

356   Westin: *Commentary*, June 1953, pp. 537 ff.

356   Beck on Fifth: *Contempt*, p. 112.

356 ff. Immunity law: 64 Stat. 745.

357   Critics of law: See Leonard Boudin's *The Fifth Amendment, Freedom's Bastion, Nation,* Sept. 29, 1951, p. 258.

357   Frankfurter decision: 350 U.S. 422 (1955).

357   Walter suggestion: *H.*, Nov. 17, 1954, pp. 7116 ff.

358   Beck on immunity: *Contempt*, p. 121.

358 ff. Watkins hearing: *H.*, April 29, 1944.

359   Appeals Court: 233 F. 2d 681 (1956).

359 ff. Supreme Court: 354 U.S. 178 (1957).

359   (fn) Other decisions: 354 U.S. 298 (1957); 354 U.S. 234 (1957); 354 U.S. 363 (1957).

360 ff. Reactions to Watkins decision: Washington *Post*—June 19, 1957, p. 6; *New Republic*—July 1, 1957, pp. 9 ff.; Jackson—*C.R.*, June 27, 1957, p. 10534; Lawrence—*U. S. News*, June 28, 1957, pp. 152 ff.

361 ff. Barenblatt hearing: *H.*, June 28, 1954.

362   Appeals Court: 252 F. 2d 129 (1958).

362 ff. Supreme Court: 79 S. Ct. 1081 (1959).

363   Seattle hearing: *H.*, June 14, 1954.

364   Neo-fascist report: *R.*, Dec. 17, 1954.

365 ff. Walter quotes: on Communist issue—*N. Y. Times*, Nov. 17, 1954, p. 6; on Dies, McCarthy—*C.R.*, Aug. 4, 1954, pp. 13324 ff.; on Communist

PAGE

Control Act—*C.R.*, Aug. 16, 1954, p. 14642; on employee—*N. Y. Times,* Dec. 22, 1954, p. 15.

366   (fn) Clardy: *N. Y. Times,* Dec. 16, 1954, p. 20.

CHAPTER THIRTEEN

367   Number of hearings: See *Supplement to Cumulative Index to Publications of the Committee on Un-American Activities, 1955–1960,* Washington, D.C., June 1961.

367   Annual report: *R.,* Feb. 16, 1955.

368   (fn) McCarthy: *N. Y. Times,* Jan. 15, 1955, p. 7.

368   *Times* editorial: Jan. 23, 1955, p. 12.

368   Walter promise: *N. Y. Times,* Jan. 21, 1955, p. 7.

368 ff.   Gojack hearings: *H.,* Feb. 28, March 1, 1955.

369   First Supreme Court decision: 369 U.S. 759 (1962).

369   Second Supreme Court decision: 86 S. Ct. 1689 (1966).

371 ff.   Corsi case: Walter on Corsi—*N. Y. Times,* April 16, 1955, p. 1; Corsi on charges—*N. Y. Times,* April 10, 1955, p. 1; State Dept. on Corsi—*N. Y. Times,* April 9, 1955, p. 1.

372   (fn) Jackson: *H.,* June 28, 1955, p. 1535.

372   (fn) Scherer: *H.,* Sept. 3, 1958, p. 2787.

372 ff.   Various hearings: Brooklyn policewoman—*H.,* May 3, 1955; peace groups—Aug. 2–5, 1955; summer camps—July 25, 28, 29, Aug. 1, 1955; diplomatic personnel—May 10, 11, 1956; O'Connell—June 1, 2, 1955 (quote) p. 594.

373 ff.   Various hearings: Newark—*H.,* May 16–19, 1955; Los Angeles—April 16, 1956; Seattle—March 17–19, June 1, 2, 1956; Denver—April 15–18, 1956; Milwaukee—March 28–30, May 3, 1955; North Carolina—March 12–14, 1956.

374 ff.   Gathings: *C.R.,* Feb. 23, 1956, p. 3215, and July 29, 1963, pp. 1359 ff.

375   Walter on entertainers: *N. Y. Times,* July 20, 1955, p. 1.

376   AWARE–A.F.T.R.A.: See John Henry Faulk's *Fear on Trial* (New York, 1964); also Louis Nizer's *The Jury Returns* (New York, 1966), Chapter 4.

376   A. Roosevelt on McCarthy: *N. Y. Times,* Aug. 16, 1955, p. 1.

376   A.C.L.U. on Committee: *N. Y. Times,* Aug. 15, 1955, p. 5.

376 ff.   Entertainment hearings: *H.,* Aug. 15–18, 1955. Quote on Kazan—Aug. 18, p. 2440; Sullivan—Aug. 16 (also Aug. 1, 1955); Tyne—Aug. 15; Seeger—Aug. 18 (quote) p. 2449.

378   Appeals Court on Seeger: 203 F. 2d 478 (1962).

379   Mostel hearing: *H.,* Oct. 14, 1955.

380   Communist bibliography: Arthur Sutherland and others: *Bibliography of the Communist Program in the United States* (New York, 1955).

380   Criticisms of bibliography: See *N. Y. Times,* Oct. 29, 1955, p. 1.

380   Hutchins on Communist: *N. Y. Times,* Nov. 8, 1955, p. 34.

380   Legionnaire on Fund: *N. Y. Times,* June 11, 1956, p. 1.

380   Lewis on Fund: Quoted in *New Republic,* Sept. 26, 1955, p. 4.

381   Walter on Fund: *N. Y. Times,* June 11, 1956, p. 1.

381   Blacklisting report: Cogley: *Report on Blacklisting.*

381   (fn) Cogley: *N. Y. Times,* Aug. 15, 1956, p. 28.

382 ff.   Blacklist hearings: *H.,* July 10–13, 17, 18, 1956. Cogley—July 10; Forster—July 11; O'Neil—July 11; Hartnett—July 12; Milton—July 13; Schmidt—July 13; Brewer—July 12; McNamara—July 13; Walter on Fund—July 13; Sondergaard—July 13; Gilford—July 18.

385   Knowles hearing: *H.,* July 18, 1956. Walter quote—p. 5457.

385   (fn) Americans Alerted: Quoted in *New Republic,* Aug. 27, 1956, p. 13.

PAGE

386   Walter on tax exemption: *N. Y. Times,* Aug. 30, 1956, p. 12.
386 ff. N.L.R.B. hearings: *H.,* Dec. 13–15, 1955. Fuchs–Dec. 13.
386   *Saturday Evening Post* editorial: Dec. 10, 1955, p. 12.
387   E.C.L.C. petition: *N. Y. Times,* Feb. 15, 1956, p. 9.
387   Additional N.L.R.B. hearings: *H.,* Feb. 14–16, 21, 23, 24, 28, 29, March
      1, June 20, 28, 1956. Smith–March 1; Witt–March 1; (fn) Rein–Feb.
      21; (fn) Donner–June 28; (fn) Boudin–June 12; on lawyers, see *R.,*
      Feb. 23, 1959, and Walter's reiterated charge against Boudin–*H.,* Aug.
      23, 1960, p. 1879.
387   McCarthy accusation: *N. Y. Times,* Nov. 16, 1955, p. 15.
389   Latham on employees: *Communist Controversy,* p. 129.
389   Walter on travel: *N. Y. Times,* May 23, 1956, p. 21.
389 ff. Passport hearings: *H.,* May 23–25, June 12–14, 1956. Uphaus–May 23
      (quote), p. 4372; Robeson–June 12 (quotes), pp. 4499, 4506; Nathan–
      June 12 (quote), p. 4552; Miller–June 21 (quotes), pp. 14522, 14529.
      (fn) *Listen My Children*–C.R., July 25, 1956, p. 14528.
393 ff. Contempt citations: *C.R.,* July 25, 1956, pp. 14491 ff. Simpson hearings
      –*H.,* June 4, 5, 1956; Davis hearing–*H.,* June 6, 1956; Kling hearing–
      H., June 6, 1956 (quote), p. 4923. Multer to Jackson–*C.R.,* July 25,
      1956, p. 14535.
394   Miller appeal: 259 F. 2d 187 (1958).
394   (fn) C.P. card: *H.,* July 26, 1951, pp. 1345 ff.; Miller quote–*N. Y.
      Times,* Aug. 25, 1957, p. 20.
394   Walter on "counterattacks": *N. Y. Times,* Nov. 12, 1956, p. 15.
395   Roosevelt hearing: *H.,* Nov. 12, 1956.
395 ff. Various hearings: Washington–*H.,* Nov. 12–14, 1956; Youngstown–
      Nov. 26, 28, 1956; Chicago–Dec. 3, 4, 1956; Los Angeles–Dec. 5–8,
      1956; San Francisco–Dec. 11, 1956; Seattle–Dec. 13, 14, 1956.
395   A.C.L.U. on hearings: *N. Y. Times,* Dec. 10, 1956, p. 55.
395   Arens on Korea: *H.,* Dec. 5, 1956, p. 6712.
395   I.L.W.U. secretary-treasurer: *H.,* Dec. 11, 1956, p. 6681.
395   Party member on informer: *H.,* Dec. 3, 1956, p. 6491.
396   Wirin–Porter: *H.,* Dec. 7, 1956.
396   Marshall ouster: *H.,* Dec. 8, 1956.
396   (fn) Lawyer ouster–*H.,* Dec. 6, 1956.
396   California state bar: *N. Y. Times,* March 28, 1957, p. 24.
397   Walter on chairmanship: *N. Y. Times,* Nov. 21, 1956, p. 8.
397   Committee quote: *R.,* Jan. 17, 1956.
397   *The Great Pretense: R.,* May 21, 1956.

CHAPTER FOURTEEN

400   Committee on C.P.: *H.,* Sept. 5, 1958, p. 2902.
400   Tuck on C.P.: *H.,* Nov. 18, 1959, p. 1615.
400   *Crimes of Khrushchev: R.,* Jan. 8, 1960.
401   Shahn–Evergood hearings: *H.,* July 1, 1959.
401   Starobin hearing: *H.,* March 15, 1957.
401   1958 report: *R.,* May 20, 1958.
402   Supreme Court on State Dept.: 78 S. Ct. 1113 (1958).
402   Walter letter: *N. Y. Times,* June 23, 1958, p. 15.
402 ff. Musicians hearings: *H.,* Feb. 7, 8, April 9–12, 1957. Moulder quote–
      April 9, p. 612; Arens quote–April 10, p. 747; Earl Robinson–April 11
      (quote), p. 72; (fn) *Gol-Dern Red*–April 9, p. 661.
403 ff. Show-business hearings: *H.,* May 8, June 18, 19, 1958.
404   American exhibition hearing: *H.,* July 1, 1959. Wheeler quote–p. 918.
404   (fn) Eisenhower comment: *N. Y. Times,* July 2, 1959, p. 3.

PAGE

404 ff. Morros story: *N. Y. Times*, Aug. 18, 1957, p. 1.

405   Stern on trip: *N. Y. Times*, Aug. 21, 1957, p. 1.

405   Morros book: *My Ten Years as a Counterspy*, with Charles Samuels (New York, 1959).

405   Walter on espionage: *N. Y. Times*, Aug. 22, 1957, p. 3.

405   Espionage hearings: *H.*, Oct. 7–9, 1957.

406   Sharp hearing: *H.*, Feb. 25, 1960. Sharp quote–p. 1301; Jackson to Sharp–p. 1316.

406   Walter on Sharp: *N. Y. Times*, Feb. 26, 1960, p. 6.

407   Jackson on N.C.C.C.: *C.R.*, April 20, 1960, pp. 8430 ff.

408   Artamonov hearing: *H.*, Sept. 14, 1960.

409   Faculty of Soc. Sci. hearing: *H.*, July 21, 22, 1959.

409   Chicago hearings: *H.*, May 6, 7, 1959.

409   A.C.A. hearings: *H.*, July 17–19, Aug. 2, 9, Oct. 9, 1957; Aug. 23, 24, 1960.

409   Seamen hearings: *H.*, July 7–8, 23, 1960.

409   Gary hearings: *H.*, Feb. 10, 11, 1958.

410   New Haven hearings: *H.*, Feb. 26, 27, 1957; quote–p. 179.

410 ff. Passport security hearings: *H.*, April 21–24, June 5, 1959.

411   Walter on Watkins decision: *N. Y. Times*, June 20, 1957, p. 12.

411   Scherer annoyance: *H.*, March 11, 1956, p. 408.

411   Communist Control Act: P.L. 83-637.

412   Printing equipment: P.L. 83-557.

412   Defense facilities: P.L. 87-474.

412   N.S.A.: P.L. 88-290.

412   *National Review*: Oct. 9, 1962, p. 255.

413   Omnibus Security Bill: See *Annual Report* for 1957, Feb. 19, 1958, p. 4.

413   Critics and defenders: See Frank Donner's *The Un-Americans* and William Buckley's *The Committee and Its Critics* (New York, 1962).

414   Fast on Committee: *N. Y. Times*, Feb. 22, 1957, p. 2.

414   Arens demand: *H.*, Oct. 2, 1957, p. 1651.

414   Tavenner technique: See *H.*, Oct. 22, 1959, p. 1229.

414   Witness's observation: *H.*, Sept. 3, 1958, p. 118.

414   Tavenner question: *H.*, Oct. 22, 1959, p. 1264.

415   March hearing (Pittsburgh): *H.*, March 10, 1959.

415   Chicago hearing: *H.*, May 7, 1959, p. 637. Packinghouse-worker quote –p. 637.

415   Moulder on publicity: *H.*, Oct. 22, 1959, p. 1256.

416   Pittsburgh and Chicago hearings: *H.*, Oct. 22, 1959, p. 1256.

416   Washington hearings: June 7, 1960.

417   Hoover on C.P.: *H.*, Sept. 5, 1958, p. 2903.

417   Doyle on Hoover: *H.*, April 9, 1957, p. 678.

417   Willis on Hoover: *H.*, May 9, 1957, p. 1069.

417   Hoover letter: *N. Y. Times*, Nov. 14, 1957, p. 39.

418   Eaton interview: *N. Y. Times*, May 5, 1958, p. 1.

418   Scherer on Eaton: *N. Y. Times*, May 8, 1958, p. 29.

418   Arens on subpoena: *N. Y. Times*, May 20, 1958, p. 40.

418   A.C.L.U.: *N. Y. Times*, May 21, 1958, p. 28.

418 ff. *Times* compliment: Sept. 1, 1957, IV, p. 8.

419   *Times* criticism: Sept. 24, 1958, p. 20.

419   Douglas–Humphrey: *C.R.*, May 29, 1958, p. 9830 ff.

419   Walter retreat: *N. Y. Times*, July 1, 1958, p. 36.

419   Eaton last word: *N. Y. Times*, July 11, 1958, p. 17.

419 ff. Braden–Wilkinson hearing: *H.*, July 30, 1958; Wilkinson quote–p. 2681.

420   Court decisions: Wilkinson–81 S. Ct. 567 (1961); Braden–81 S. Ct. 584 (1961).

PAGE

421 ff. Other decisions: Deutch—81 S. Ct. 1587 (1961); six contempt convictions—82 S. Ct. 1038 (1962); Silber—82 S. Ct. 1287 (1962); Grumman —81 S. Ct. 1560 (1962); Yellin—347 U.S. 109 (1963); Hartman (note) —82 S. Ct. 1574 (1962); Turoff (note)—291 F. 2d 864 (1961); Shelton (note)—327 F. 2d 601 (1963).

421 ff. Here, in summary, are the outcomes of the contempt cases that arose between 1957 and 1960. Frank Wilkinson and Carl Braden were convicted and sentenced to twelve months in jail for refusing to answer questions in the 1958 Atlanta hearings without taking the Fifth Amendment. Paul Rosenkrantz was given three months for doing the same thing in the 1958 Boston hearings. Donald C. Wheeldin got thirty days and a fine of $100 for failing to respond to a subpoena in Los Angeles in 1958. No true bill was delivered against Edwin A. Alexander, who testified extensively in Chicago in May 1959 about his disillusioning experiences with the Communist Party but refused to give names on grounds of conscience. The indictment against Sidney Herbert Ingerman, who took a similar position in Buffalo in 1957, was dismissed. The Supreme Court's 1962 decision in the case of Norton Anthony Russell that his indictment had been insufficient was applied to the benefit of Louis Earl Hartman, who had relied on the newly delivered Watkins decision in San Francisco in June 1957, and to Martin Popper, an attorney who had declined to talk about his alleged C.P. membership in the Washington passport hearings of April 1959. (Russell was reindicted and acquitted in March 1964 because it had not been shown that he was aware of the subject under inquiry at his hearing in 1955—another effort by the judiciary to tighten up Committee procedures.) The Supreme Court's decision regarding executive hearings, handed down in the case of Edward Yellin, an alleged "colonizer" who was uncooperative in Gary, Indiana, in February 1958, benefited three other witnesses cited in Gary—Robert Lehrer, Alfred James Samter, and Victor Malis. Also benefiting from the Yellin decision were Frank Grumman and Bernard Silber, in their retrial after their first conviction had been overturned for a faulty indictment, and Sidney Turoff, who had defied the Committee in Buffalo in October 1957. (Turoff's first conviction was reversed by the Court of Appeals, which found the admission in his trial of detailed testimony of his C.P. activities to be highly prejudicial.) The indictment against Harvey O'Connor, head of the Emergency Civil Liberties Committee, who threw his subpoena to the floor when it was served on him at a rally in Newark in September 1958, was dismissed following a ruling by the Court of Appeals in a related case that a subpoena must be authorized by the full committee and is invalid if authorized by the chairman alone. And, as already noted, twelve contempt citations growing out of the visit to San Juan were dismissed upon the district court's decision that the Committee had no jurisdiction beyond the limits of the continental United States.

423   Robeson–Davis–Gray hearings: H., Feb. 2–5, 1960.
423   Los Angeles Negro: H., Sept. 3, 1958.
423   Newark Negro: H., Sept. 4, 1958; quote–p. 2837.
423   Newark hearings: H., Sept. 3–5, 1958 (recess), p. 2902.
423   San Juan hearings: H., Nov. 18–20, 1959.
423   Chicago hearing: H., May 5, 1959.
424   San Francisco, 1957: H., June 18–21, 1957.
424   Suicide note: N. Y. Times, June 18, 1957, p. 23.
424   Widow's charge: N. Y. Times, June 19, 1957, p. 18.
425   Rayburn on TV: N. Y. Times, June 21, 1957, p. 12.
425   A.C.L.U.: San Francisco Chronicle, June 6, 1959, p. 1.

PAGE

425   Los Angeles hearings: *H.*, Feb. 24, 25, 1959.
426   Walter on postponement: *S. F. Chronicle*, June 12, 1959, p. 7.
427   Truman on Committee: *N. Y. Times*, April 30, 1959, p. 17.
427 ff. J. Roosevelt speech: *C.R.*, April 25, 1960, pp. 864 ff.
428   Scherer response: *C.R.*, May 5, 1960, p. 9649.
428 ff. San Francisco, 1960 hearings: *H.*, May 12–14, 1960. Prussion—May 13; Hartle—May 12 (quote), p. 1957; Fishman—May 12; "Honorable beaters. . . ."—May 13, p. 2065; "halfway like a nut"—May 13, p. 2013; Arens on emasculation—May 14, p. 2135; Brown appearance—May 14.
430   Wheeler on "decent people": *S.F. Chronicle*, May 13, 1960, p. 1.
431   *Communist-Led Riots: R.*, Oct. 7, 1960.
431   Willis on disagreeable people and "worst incident": *S.F. Chronicle*, May 14, 1960, p. 1.
431   Scherer on riots: *C.R.*, June 2, 1960, pp. 11760 ff.
431   *Communist Target—Youth: R.*, July 1960.
431   Views of riots: For contrasting views, see Donner: *The Un-Americans*, pp. 190 ff. and Buckley: *The Committee*, pp. 176 ff.
432   *Operation Abolition R.*, Nov. 8, 1957.
432   Scherer harangue: *H.*, May 14, 1960, pp. 2170 ff.
433   Hoover on riots: *Communist Target—Youth*.
434   Students' statement: *N. Y. Times*, June 2, 1960, p. 3.

CHAPTER FIFTEEN

435   Rayburn on Walter: *N. Y. Times*, June 26, 1961, p. 18.
435 ff. Fund for Social Analysis hearings: *H.*, May 31, June 7, Aug. 10, 1961.
436   National Assembly for Democratic Rights hearings: *H.*, Oct. 2, 3, 1961.
436   Cuba–British Guiana groups hearings: *H.*, Nov. 14, 15, 1962.
436   Fair Play for Cuba Committee: *R.*, Nov. 2, 1962. *H.*, Nov. 20–22, 1961.
437   Communications union hearings: *H.*, Oct. 26, 27, Nov. 29, 1961.
437   Soviet propaganda hearings: *H.*, May 9, 10, 17, July 11, 12, 1962.
437   Youth festival hearings: *H.*, April 25, 27, Oct. 4, 1962.
437   Russia–China hearings: *H.*, May 22, 24, 25, 1962.
437   Cleveland hearings: *H.*, June 4–7, 1962.
437 ff. W.S.P. hearings: *H.*, Dec. 11–13, 1962.
438   *National Review* on W.S.P.: Jan. 15, 1963, p. 24.
438 ff. W.S.P. hearings: New Yorker—*H.*, Dec. 11; Scarsdale lady—Dec. 11, p. 2074; Doyle on flowers—Dec. 12, p. 2126; Nittle on elusiveness—Dec. 12, p. 2139; Doyle apology—Dec. 12, p. 2126; Vassar lady—Dec. 12; former C.P. lady—Dec. 11; alleged Communist—Dec. 13; Mrs. Moos—Dec. 12; Dagmar Wilson—Dec. 13 (quote), p. 2200.
441   SANE statement: Quoted in *Nation*, March 11, 1961, p. 201. See Dodd's speech, *C.R.* May 25, 1960, pp. 11632 ff.
442   Wilson on Fifth: *N. Y. Times*, Dec. 14, 1962, p. 1.
443   E. K. Roosevelt on Walker: *Between the Lines*, April 8, 1962.
443   Tribute to Walter: *R.*, Aug. 10, 1964, p. 157.
444   Tribute to Doyle: *R.*, Aug. 10, 1964, p. 158.
444 ff. Cuba hearings: *H.*, May 6, 7, 23, July 1, 2, Aug. 5, Sept. 12, 13, Oct. 16, Nov. 18, 1963; Sept. 3, 4, 28, 1964. Friendly witnesses—Sept. 12, 1963; witness on "framing"—Sept. 4, 1964, p. 2080; (fn) Supreme Court on travel—87 S. Ct. 574 (1967); Luce—Sept. 12, 1963, pp. 756–7; Bond —Sept. 3, 1964, pp. 2040–1.
445   For details of the Cuba trip, see Phillip Abbott Luce's *The New Left* (New York, 1960), pp. 61 ff. For an account of the formation and character of the P.L.M., see Jack Newfield's *A Prophetic Minority* (New York, 1966), pp. 149 ff. Also Luce, pp. 81 ff.

PAGE

448   Cuba elections quote: *H.*, Sept. 28, 1964, p. 2185.

448 ff.   Stone on leftists: *N. Y. Times*, Sept. 14, 1963, p. 1.

449   Kennedy on Cuban travel: See Arthur Schlesinger, Jr.'s *A Thousand Days* (Cambridge, Mass., 1965), p. 700.

449   Senner question: *H.*, Sept. 4, 1964, p. 2150.

451   Nixon–Wilson–Allen case: 369 F. 2d 198 (1966).

452 ff.   Freedom Academy hearings: *H.*, Feb. 18–20, April 7, 8, May 15, 20, 1964. Herlong–Feb. 20, p. 939; Harriman–Feb. 20; Berle–May 20 (quote), p. 1467; 1965 hearings–*H.*, March 31, April 1, 28, May 7, 14, 1965.

453 ff.   Buffalo hearings: *H.*, April 29, 30, 1964. Minneapolis hearings: *H.*, June 24–26, 1964. Instructor–April 29; Wolkenstein–April 29, pp. 1608–9; Minneapolis lawyer–June 25, 1964; (fn) Court decision–86 S. Ct. 1148 (1966); Willis-Hall quotes–June 24, p. 1687.

456 ff.   Chicago hearings: *H.*, May 25–27, 1965.

457   Names published: Chicago *American*, May 13, 1965, p. 1.

457   Willis on leaks: *H.*, May 25, 1965, p. 344.

457   Willis in Minneapolis: *H.*, June 25, 1964, p. 1834.

457   Willis–Criley exchange: Chicago *Daily News*, May 19, 1965, p. 1.

457   Stamler–Board of Health: *N. Y. Times*, June 3, 1965, p. 17.

458   Executive session made public: *H.*, June 22, 1965, pp. 557 ff.

459 ff.   Chicago hearings: Nittle questions regarding Hall–*H.*, May 26, pp. 429, 436; Nittle questions regarding Stamler–May 27, pp. 508, 511, 524; Nittle–Armstrong exchange–May 27, p. 549.

461 ff.   McNamara on source: *C.R.*, Oct. 18, 1965, pp. 26444, 26458.

462 ff.   Jenner objections: *H.*, May 27, 1965, pp. 537 ff., 544, 547.

463   Appeals Court decision: 371 F. 2d 413 (1966).

463 ff.   Contempt citations: *C.R.*, Oct. 18, 1966, pp. 26384 ff. Ichord on executive hearings–p. 26450; Willis on Hall–p. 26412; Ichord on information –p. 26458; Willis on paid witnesses–pp. 26459, 26393.

465   K.K.K. citations: *C.R.*, Feb. 2, 1966, pp. 1657 ff.

465   McPhaul case: 81 S. Ct. 138 (1966). (fn) McPhaul on Kluxers: *C.R.*, June 30, 1952, p. 8626.

465   Weltner on K.K.K.: *C.R.*, Feb. 1, 1965, p. 1592.

466   K.K.K. pamphlet: Quoted in *Nation*, Oct. 3, 1942, p. 309.

466 ff.   Johnson on TV: *N. Y. Times*, March 27, 1965, p. 1.

467     $50,000 appropriation: *C.R.*, April 14, 1965, pp. 7740 ff.

467 ff.   K.K.K. hearings: *H.*, Oct. 19–22, 25–29, Nov. 1–4, 1965. (Transcript of the 1966 hearings not available at this writing.) Shelton–Oct. 20; used-car dealer–Oct. 22 (quote) Washington *Post*, Oct. 23, 1965, p. 1; Woodle–Oct. 22.

470   Willis bill: (H.R. 15678) *C.R.*, June 14, 1966, pp. 12503 ff.

470 ff.   Hearings on Willis bill: *H.*, July 20–22, 1966.

471   A.C.L.U. on Willis bill: *H.*, July 21, 1966.

471   Katzenbach on bill: *H.*, July 20, 1966.

471   Ichord on bill: *C.R.*, April 5, 1967, p. 3531. See also *R.*, Sept. 19, 1967, where Culver joins Ichord in opposition.

471   Pool bill: (H.R. 12047) *C.R.*, Oct. 12, 1966, pp. 2517 ff. Edwards on passage–p. 25183.

472   Hearings on Pool bill: *H.*, Aug. 19, 22, 23, 1966. Attorney General– Aug. 23, p. 1337. See also *R.*, May 31, 1967, which contains Culver's dissent.

473   (fn) Willis on Nazi Party: *N. Y. Times*, Feb. 10, 1966, p. 2.

473 ff.   Vietnam hearings: *H.*, Aug. 16–19, 22, 23, 1966.

473   (fn) Court decision: 85 S. Ct. 1116 (1965).

474   (fn) American Council on Education: *N. Y. Times*, July 15, 1967, p. 27.

PAGE

474 ff. Luce testimony: *H.*, Aug. 16, 1966. Prior appearance—*H.*, Sept. 13, 1963. See *The New Left*.
475   Luce payment: *C.R.*, Oct. 20, 1966, p. A5454.
475   (fn) Ichord: *H.*, Aug. 18, 1966, p. 2649.
476 ff. Vietnam hearings: Kinoy ouster—*H.*, Aug. 17, pp. 1026–27; asst. D.A.—Aug. 17 (pamphlet quote) p. 1078; Ichord quote—Aug. 17, p. 1070; preamble to P.L.M. constitution—Aug. 17, p. 1023; witness to Pool—Aug. 16, p. 986; (fn) Nittle–Gordon exchange—Aug. 14, p. 984; Stanford student—Aug. 18, p. 1169; West Coast organizer—Aug. 19, p. 1203; "yes, I am a Communist"—Aug. 19, p. 1195; "I am a P.L.P. member"—Aug. 19, p. 1205; Pool conclusion—Aug. 19, p. 1212.
479   Dirksen on hearings: *N. Y. Times*, Aug. 21, 1966, p. 2.
481   W.S.P. leader: Donna Allen in *Liberation*, Oct. 1966, p. 7.
481   Pool to V.F.W.: *N. Y. Times*, Aug. 27, 1966, p. 15.

CHAPTER SIXTEEN

483   Espionage hearings: Transcript not available at this writing.
483   President's statement: *N. Y. Times*, May 3, 1967, p. 5.
483   Rusk statement: *N. Y. Times*, April 17, 1967, p. 9.
483   Lodge statement: *N. Y. Times*, April 27, 1967, p. 10.
483   Flag-burning bill: (H.R. 10480) *C.R.*, June 20, 1967, pp. H.7488 ff.
483   Liberal on Pool: *N. Y. Times*, June 19, 1967, p. 28.
483   Report on peace demonstrations: *R.*, March 31, 1967. Willis foreword—pp. 1–2.
484   Dies on social equality: Quoted in Gellerman's *Martin Dies* (New York, 1944), p. 245.
484 ff. Willis on "preliminary inquiry": See *C.R.*, Jan. 30, 1967, pp. 720 ff.
485   Hoover article: *C.R.*, Aug. 29, 1966, pp. 2007 ff.
485   Willis to civil rights leaders: *C.R.*, Jan. 30, 1967.
486   Anti-riot bill: (H.R. 421) *C.R.* July 19, 1967, pp. H.8924 ff. See *N. Y. Times*, July 27, 1967, p. 1, for Willis on riots.
486   "Secret" staff study: *N. Y. Times*, Aug. 3, 1967, p. 16.
486   Fall 1967 hearings: No transcript available at this writing.
486   Willis on dissenters: *C.R.*, May 8, 1967, p. A5178.
487 ff. *New Republic* editorial: April 29, 1967, pp. 3–4.
487   Bettina Aptheker: *New Republic*, June 10, 1967, pp. 34–35
488   Edwards on Committee: *C.R.*, Feb. 25, 1965, p. 3647.
489   Fortas on hearings: *Atlantic*, Aug. 1953, pp. 42 ff.
490   (fn) Ashbrook: *C.R.*, Feb. 25, 1965, p. 3658.
490   (fn) Oliver: *N. Y. Times*, Jan. 29, 1961, p. 43.
491   Willis on liberals: *C.R.*, Feb. 25, 1965, p. 3667.

Selected Bibliography

Association of the Bar of the City of New York. *The Federal Loyalty-Security Program.* New York, 1956.

Barth, Alan. *The Loyalty of Free Men.* New York, 1952.

———. *Government by Investigation.* New York, 1955.

Beck, Carl. *Contempt of Congress.* New Orleans, 1957.

Bentley, Elizabeth. *Out of Bondage.* New York, 1951.

Bessie, Alvah. *Inquisition in Eden.* New York, 1965.

Biddle, Francis. *The Fear of Freedom.* New York, 1951.

Buckley, William F., and the editors of the *National Review.*

———. *The Committee and Its Critics.* New York, 1962.

Carr, Robert K. *The House Committee on Un-American Activities, 1945–1950.* Ithaca, N.Y., 1952.

Chambers, Whittaker. *Witness.* New York, 1952.

———. *Cold Friday* (edited by Duncan Norton-Taylor). New York, 1964.

Cogley, John. *Report on Blacklisting* (two volumes). New York, 1956.

Dies, Martin. *The Trojan Horse in America.* New York, 1940.

———. *The Martin Dies Story.* New York, 1963.

Donner, Frank. *The Un-Americans.* New York, 1961.

Gellerman, William. *Martin Dies.* New York, 1944.

Griswold, Erwin N. *The Fifth Amendment Today.* Cambridge, Mass., 1955.

Hiss, Alger. *In the Court of Public Opinion.* New York, 1957.

Hook, Sidney. *Heresy, Yes—Conspiracy, No!* New York, 1953.

———. *Common Sense and the Fifth Amendment.* New York, 1957.

Howe, Irving and Lewis Coser. *The American Communist Party.* New York, 1962.

Kahn, Gordon. *Hollywood on Trial.* New York, 1948.

Kempton, Murray, *Part of Our Time.* New York, 1955.

Latham, Earl. *The Communist Controversy in Washington.* Cambridge, Mass., 1966.

Lovett, Robert Morss. *All Our Years*. New York, 1948.

Matthews, Joseph B. *Odyssey of a Fellow Traveler*. New York, 1938.

Nixon, Richard. *Six Crises*. New York, 1962.

Ogden, August Raymond. *The Dies Committee*. Washington, D.C., 1945.

Oxnam, G. Bromley. *I Protest*. New York, 1954.

Seldes, George. *Witch Hunt*. New York, 1940.

Stripling, Robert E. *The Red Plot Against America* (Edited by Bob Considine). Drexel Hill, Pa., 1949.

Taylor, Telford. *Grand Inquest*. New York, 1955.

Trumbo, Dalton. *The Time of the Toad*. Hollywood, Calif., 1949.

Warren, Frank A., III. *Liberals and Communism*. Bloomington, Ind., 1966.

Index

Some other books published by Penguins and Pelicans are described on the following pages

TOWARD A DEMOCRATIC LEFT

Michael Harrington

In an intense and highly readable book, the author of *THE OTHER AMERICAN* and *THE ACCIDENTAL CENTURY* examines the political, social, and economic problems of our times and poses the urgent need for new political alliances in the United States that will cause the government to take constructive action on the many domestic and international crises that face us. Mr. Harrington holds that liberalism as it has been known for three decades cannot respond to the problems of America today unless it moves sharply to the democratic left. By "left" he means "a program and movement which socialists and radicals can support, but which appeals to the most traditional American aspirations for reform as well." He proposes formation of a political party built by the new Leftists, labor unions, white collar workers, youth groups, and black power advocates, which would work to change government policies through democratic means. This new Pelican edition contains a new Afterword, written in November 1968 and entitled "The Road to 1972."

THE ACCIDENTAL CENTURY

Michael Harrington

Michael Harrington, whose *The Other America* stirred the nation to action against poverty, turns, in his new book, to the cultural and intellectual crisis confronting the United States and the rest of the Western world in the 20th century. The crisis has been brought about by the "accidental revolution," in which an unplanned social and creative technology has haphazardly reshaped our lives and put in doubt all our ideologies and beliefs. The resulting decadence threatens to destroy Western civilization and with it the Western concept of man. The technological and social revolution of the 20th century will continue; but, says Mr. Harrington, it must cease to be accidental. It must become conscious, planned, and democratic through the political intervention of man. An exciting and provocative book by one of the most brilliant social critics of our time.

THE MOST PROBABLE WORLD

Stuart Chase

One of America's foremost social critics and economists charts the great trends and forces of our time to draw a realistic profile of the world we are shaping for the twenty-first century. Stuart Chase examines the achievements and hazards created by science and technology and sets forth the social, political, and scientific problems which we must solve if the most probable world is to be peaceful and secure.

Overpopulation, pollution, and new weapons could make a wilderness of the world. Yet the same imagination and skill of which these evils are by-products could free man from drudgery, sickness, famine, and armed conflict. Today the dangers and the potentialities are dovetailing with unprecedented speed.

Using the most up-to-date information, Mr. Chase discusses the arms race, environmental pollution, urban problems, human psychology, the uses of atomic power, the UN, automation, East-West economic differences, the influence of the automobile, and a promising new program of education which can prepare the leaders of future generations for coping with the complexities of a dynamically changing society.

This arresting study is not science fiction but an expert's hard look at the world of the future—a world near enough to be a challenge for our time.